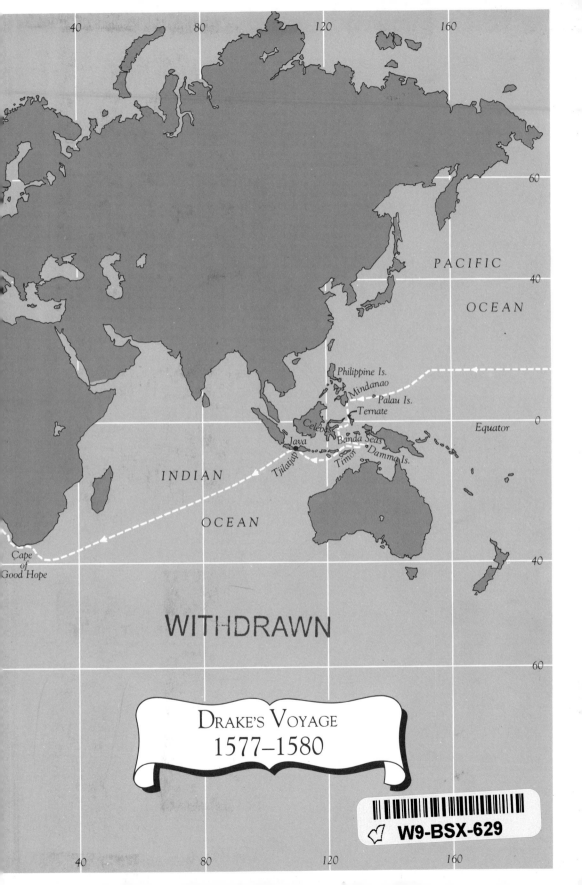

PACIFIC

OCEAN

60

40

Philippine Is.
Mindanao
Palau Is.
Ternate
Celebes
Java
Banda Seas
Tjilatjap
Timor
Damma Is.

Equator

0

INDIAN

OCEAN

40

Cape
of
Good Hope

WITHDRAWN

40

60

DRAKE'S VOYAGE
1577–1580

W9-BSX-629

40    80    120    160

# SIR FRANCIS DRAKE

## JOHN SUGDEN

A John Macrae Book
HENRY HOLT AND COMPANY
New York

*This book is for*
*Terri,*
*as I promised*

Library of Congress Cataloging-in-Publication Data

Sugden, John.
Sir Francis Drake / by John Sugden. — 1st American ed.
p.      cm.
Includes bibliographical references and index.
1. Drake, Francis, Sir, 1540?–1596.      2. Explorers—America—
Biography.      3. Explorers—Great Britain—Biography.      4. Admirals—
Great Britain—Biography.      5. Great Britain—History, Naval—
Tudors, 1485–1603.      I. Title.
E129.D7S84    1990
942.05'5'092—dc20
[B]    90-25571
CIP

ISBN 0-8050-1489-6

FIRST AMERICAN EDITION

Printed in the United States of America
Recognizing the importance of preserving the written word,
Henry Holt and Company, Inc., by policy, prints all of its first
editions on acid-free paper.

1   3   5   7   9   10   8   6   4   2

# CONTENTS

# LIST OF ILLUSTRATIONS

# PREFACE

Few have enjoyed as great or as durable a reputation as Sir Francis Drake. In his own day he was the most celebrated of Englishmen, as famous in Europe and America, said a contemporary chronicler, as Tamburlaine was in Africa and Asia. There was a lively trade in portraits and ephemera, and dispatches across Europe, from London, Paris, Antwerp, Madrid, Rome and Venice, were full of his name. Even enemies were stirred to admiration. 'Just look at Drake!' cried Pope Sixtus V. 'Who is he? What forces has he? And yet he burned twenty-five of the King's ships at Gibraltar, and as many again at Lisbon. He has robbed the flotilla, and sacked San Domingo. His reputation is so great that his countrymen flock to him to share his booty. We are sorry to say it, but we have a poor opinion of this Spanish Armada, and fear some disaster.' Indeed, so remarkable did Drake's successes seem that the superstitious attributed them to his mastery of the black arts and supernatural forces. Even the defeated mariners and soldiers of the Armada returned to Spain in 1588 protesting that 'Sir Francis Drake . . . was a devil, and no man.'

Four hundred years later Drake's name is still a household word, although there is less agreement about his significance. A German statue raised in the nineteenth century in Offenburg credited him with introducing the potato to Europe. To some he was the founder of the naval and maritime tradition that ultimately gave Britain the empire of the seas, and to others merely the quintessential boy's story-book hero. J. B. Black regarded him as the most brilliant of the Elizabethans, and A. L. Rowse as 'all in all . . . the greatest sailor in the history of the world', but others cast Drake as a greedy filibuster whose raids distracted England from the pursuit of more peaceful and profitable overseas endeavour. A recent correspondent of *The Mariner's Mirror* considered him too irresponsible and impetuous to warrant a general command and fit for nothing more than hit-and-run privateering adventures. To Margaret Thatcher, lately addressing the Congress of the United States, he was a symbol of resolution in the face of adversity.

Two cities, half the world apart and gazing upon different oceans over which Drake's *Golden Hind* left its wake, remember him with more than a common reverence: Plymouth, for long Drake's home town, still guarding the western approaches to England, and San Francisco in California, currently the fourth city of the United States. The nomenclature of both places commemorates the great sailor, most notably in San Francisco's Drake-Wiltshire and Sir Francis Drake hotels and the Sir Francis Drake Boulevard, and Plymouth's Drake Circus and statue on the Hoe. The cities have led the quadri-centennial celebrations of the events of Drake's career: in 1949 California saw the establishment of the Drake Navigators' Guild, of which Chester Nimitz was once chairman, and between 1973 and 1980 a state-appointed Sir Francis Drake commission pondered the evidence attached to Drake's historic visit to the area in 1579, when he claimed Nova Albion for England. The American pageants and exhibitions that marked the quadri-centennial of the visit itself were soon repeated at Plymouth as it celebrated 'Armada 400'. In a microcosm of the good relationship between two great English-speaking nations, Plymouth and San Francisco have acknowledged their shared heritage. In 1979 the Lord Mayor of Plymouth unveiled one plaque to Drake by the Golden Gate Bridge, while the following year the American ambassador to Britain unveiled another in Plymouth. A replica of the *Golden Hind*, built at Appledore in Devon, was sailed to San Francisco, where she was fittingly exhibited in 1975.

Surprisingly, a biography of Drake is long overdue. Since Sir Julian Corbett's classic *Drake and the Tudor Navy*, published in 1898, a tremendous amount of research has been done, some of it published in monographs, and much in the articles and notes of academic journals, where it has been relatively inaccessible to the general public. More than that, the publication of the documents for Drake's career has steadily advanced throughout this century, principally on account of the efforts of the Hakluyt and Navy Records Societies, and some twenty volumes of primary materials bearing heavily upon Drake's career, as well as many others of more marginal interest, are now available. With the recent appearance of collections by Kenneth R. Andrews, *The Last Voyage of Drake and Hawkins* (1972), Mary F. Keeler, *Sir Francis Drake's West Indian Voyage, 1585-86* (1981), and Richard B. Wernham, *The Expedition of Sir John Norris and Sir Francis Drake to Spain and Portugal, 1589* (1988), the English, and for the most part the Spanish, sources for all of Drake's major voyages are in print for the first time. It is a work of synthesis, drawing together both these materials and the disparate researches of the scholars, that is required.

Then, too, it is unfortunate that the earlier biographies of Drake, with the exception of Corbett's, have been little more than brief, loosely connected accounts of his voyages, and have presented an excessively one-dimensional figure. The man himself has often been lost in his deeds, and the other, non-maritime, aspects of his career, which would have offered a broader perspective, have been almost totally ignored. To some extent this was inevitable, for Drake remains an elusive person. Relatively few of his letters survive, and most of those deal solely with official matters. The man's private world, his relationships, ideas, values, attitudes and aspirations, must continue to be, therefore, largely irrecoverable and fuel for guesswork. But Drake's biographers, unlike their subject, have also been generally content to trace well-blazed paths, and most of them produced mere extrapolations from earlier lives and better-known histories. They took their cues from Corbett, who was largely interested in Drake's contribution to naval development, and from historians of Elizabethan maritime expansion, who, excellent within their remit, were in no sense biographers of Drake. In the present book I have tried to redress the balance, and to portray Drake as one of the many-sided personalities in which the Elizabethan period was so rich. Here I have written not only of the great seaman, but also of the vigorous social climber, the businessman and property magnate, the town Mayor, civic leader and parliamentarian, and the magistrate, and have attempted, as far as the sources allow, a fuller understanding of the man.

It is hoped that even those familiar with the existing biographies of Drake will find something fresh in this account, which seeks not only to provide an up-to-date and respectably comprehensive life of Drake, but also to shed further light on aspects that have been overlooked. His family and career in England, his first voyages to the West Indies and his services in Ireland, and his plans to support the Portuguese pretender, Dom Antonio, in a voyage to Terceira in 1581 are examples of areas that have hitherto been little explored.

Since the book is intended for the general reader rather than the specialist, I have not encumbered the text with exhaustive footnotes. However, some notes are indispensable in a work of this kind, and readers may or may not refer to them, according to their individual purposes. I have employed the notes as guides to the principal sources, to identify quotations and the more disparate sources of information, and to clarify some of the arguments in the narratives. Full details of materials referred to in the notes can be found in the bibliography, which additionally attempts to collect the most valuable and notable items of Drakeana. A glossary deals with some of the more unusual terms undefined in the text. In quoting from primary sources I have modernized spelling and punctuation to facilitate reading, but the integrity of the passages has been preserved. Throughout, dates are given Old Style, since that was the calendar used by the England of Drake's day.

My thanks go above all to my brother, Philip, who not only urged me to undertake this project, reviewed the chapters and brought to the deciphering of original manuscripts a remarkable facility in translating Elizabethan script, but also handled part of the research while I was abroad. Without his assistance and encouragement the book would not have been finished. I am also indebted to the Public Record Office (London); the Record Offices of Somerset (Taunton), West Devon (Plymouth) and Devon (Exeter); the departments of manuscripts and printed books of the British Library, London; the university libraries of Warwick, London and Cambridge; the West Country Studies Library, Exeter; the Newberry Library, Chicago; the Central Public Libraries of Plymouth and Kingston-upon-Hull; Terri Egginton, who took me to some of Drake's West Country haunts; and to my publishers, Barrie and Jenkins, for their encouragement and advice. A book, like a ship, requires many willing hands, and without all their enthusiasm and cooperation, I fear this one would never have left the stocks.

John Sugden
Hull, England, 1989

Who seeks by worthy deeds to gain renown for hire,
Whose heart, whose hand, whose purse is pressed to purchase his desire,
If any such there be, that thirsteth after fame,
Lo! Hear a means to win himself an everlasting name.
Who seeks by gain and wealth to advance his house and blood,
Whose care is great, whose toil no less, whose hope is all for good;
If any one there be that covets such a trade,
Lo! Hear the plan for commonwealth, and private gain is made.
He that for virtue's sake will venture far and near,
Whose zeal is strong, whose practice true, whose faith is void of fear;
If any such there be, inflamed with holy care,
Here may he find a ready means his purpose to declare;
So that for each degree this treatise doth unfold
The path to fame, the proof of zeal, and way to purchase gold.

Sir Francis Drake, 1583

# CHAPTER ONE

# 'BY GOD'S FAITH!'

Drake, conquering Drake . . .
In strength of men he putteth not his trust,
But to his God and cause which still is just.
He learned hath that God is our chieftain,
Who brings him forth and safely back again.

Henry Roberts, *The Trumpet of Fame*, 1595

FROM THE DESOLATE GRANITE UPLANDS OF DARTMOOR – THEN AS NOW A WILD EX-
panse of rock, heather and swamp – the River Tavy ran south-westerly until it
emptied into the estuary of the Tamar north of Plymouth. Where the river abandoned the moor it enriched the lowlands and encouraged the development of agri-
culture on substantial estates that were once owned by the Benedictine monks of
Tavistock Abbey, in its day the largest monastic house in Devonshire and for hundreds of years the nucleus of settlement in the beautiful and varied valley of the
Tavy. From this country came Francis Drake. At the time of his birth the abbey
and its lands no longer belonged to the Church, for they had suffered the fate of
other religious houses during the tempestuous and reforming reign of Henry VIII.
They had been confiscated and in 1539 had passed into the hands of the powerful
Russell family.

The town of Tavistock continued to thrive, sitting on the north bank of the
Tavy. Its locals farmed lands once leased from the abbey, scratched a living from
tin workings on the south-western edge of Dartmoor, produced the coarse woollen
cloths known as 'straits', fished for salmon in the river or provided an assortment
of local crafts and services. Their goods might be sent down-river to Plymouth for
export, or carried overland on pack-horses or carts. Not a few men of Tavistock
eventually found themselves a trade at sea, either fishing for pilchards and herrings
from Plymouth, Exeter or Dartmouth, or plying between south-west France and
England with cloth, tin and wine.

The Drakes had lived at Tavistock for a century or more.[1] Before the dissolution of the monasteries, Francis Drake's grandparents, John and Margery
Drake, held a lease from the abbot providing them with the buildings and lands of
the part of Crowndale, a mile below Tavistock, that was within the parish of

---

[1] Original sources for Drake's childhood are the outlines in Camden, *Annals*, and in Edmund Howes's
continuation of John Stow's *Chronicles*. Eliott-Drake, *Family and Heirs of Sir Francis Drake*, is the standard
work on the family. The first important biography of Drake was Barrow's *Life, Voyages and Exploits of
Admiral Sir Francis Drake*, but the author found difficulty in gaining access to important manuscript
materials. Julian Corbett's masterly *Drake and the Tudor Navy* was not only the foundation for modern
scholarship in the subject but remains the only comprehensive biography. It is in great need of revision,
but still repays study. Of scholarly outlines of Drake's career published since, Andrews, *Drake's Voyages*, is
outstanding. There have been many popular biographies, of which the best as well as the most readable is
Mason, *Life of Francis Drake*.

Tavistock – a farm on the west bank of the Tavy known simply as Crowndale. The lease was good for the lives of John and Margery and their eldest son, John. Such leases were not uncommon in sixteenth-century Devon, and marked the Drakes as members of the class of yeoman farmers, those more substantial and secure small farmers who were becoming the mainstay of rural communities and supplying the incumbents of parish posts from churchwardens to constables. Some have said that the origins of Francis Drake were mean, but they were not of the meanest kind. John and Margery Drake held about 180 acres. Typical copyholders, from whose ranks the Drakes had undoubtedly sprung, farmed rather less, and their title depended upon customary right only, and was not, like that of the Drakes, fully defensible in law. About three-quarters of manorial tenants in the sixteenth century were copyholders, and in Devon there was also a swelling number of wage-earners with little or no land whatever who sought work where it could be found. They knew hardship and insecurity of a kind that John and Margery Drake would not have experienced.

When John, Lord Russell (later the first Earl of Bedford) and his wife, Anne, obtained the wealthy lands of Tavistock Abbey they renewed the lease to the Drakes in 1546. The tenants agreed to maintain the hedges and ditches on their land and to keep the buildings in good repair. They paid an immediate sum of £6 13s 4d and a yearly rent of £4 6s 8d, and upon Margery or John junior succeeding to the property they would have to give up their 'best beast' as heriot.[1] Here, in the valley of the Tavy, the Drakes raised their family. A second son, Edmund, was born to John and Margery, as well as two other sons and two or three daughters, one of them named Anna. It was Edmund who was to be the father of Francis Drake.

Edmund had not the security of his eldest brother, who would inherit the Crowndale farm, but he was allocated some land by his father. Thus, the Lay Subsidy rolls of 1544 rate the holdings of John and Margery at £20; those of the heir, John, at £5; and some belonging to Edmund at £4. Occasional contemporary comment, both English and Spanish, referred to Francis Drake's father as a sailor, but the Lay Subsidy rolls and a legal document of 1548 suggest that he derived a living from the land, and in the latter he was expressly described as a shearman.

The year of Francis Drake's birth is not known. Edmund married one of the Mylwaye family, as we may infer from his will, and he had by her twelve sons in all, of whom the eldest was Francis and the youngest surviving Thomas. A portrait which Nicholas Hilliard painted of Sir Francis in 1581 declared the admiral then to be forty-two years of age, an estimate the artist presumably obtained from his subject. It would place Drake's birth about 1538 or 1539. However, in 1586 a Spaniard wrote that Drake 'admits he is 46 years old', which suggests his birthdate was 1540.[2] Other, circumstantial, evidence points to a later date. Drake's nephew implied that his uncle was not born earlier than 1542, and Edmund Howes, who knew the admiral, tells us that Drake was twenty at the time of his first voyage to

---

[1] Leases of Crowndale to John and Margery Drake, and to their son John, 8 September, 1519, and 8 October, 1546, Drake Papers, Devon County Record Office, 346M/F599-600, T973-974; Eliott-Drake, 1: 4-6.

[2] Diego Hidalgo Montemayon in Wright, ed., *Further English Voyages to Spanish America*, 129.

the Guinea coast in 1566. Distressing as it may be, we must frankly admit that none of this establishes the year of Drake's nativity.

What is certain is that the Drakes stood in good stead with the Russells, their landlords, sufficiently so for Lord Russell's son, the youth Francis Russell, to stand as godfather to Edmund's eldest son and to provide him with his Christian name. Edmund understood the importance of patronage, for in Tudor England a man's prospects depended much upon the claims he held upon the attention and favour of the mighty. In this instance many years would pass before this scant connection with the Russells yielded dividends, but that may be because tenant Edmund Drake took his family from Devon while his eldest son was only a boy.

The flight of Edmund Drake to Kent has been misinterpreted by previous biographers. They have accepted the story that Edmund passed to his sons and they to others – Francis to William Camden and Thomas to his own son – that Edmund fled from Devon because of religious persecution. 'His father,' Camden wrote of the admiral, 'embracing the Protestants' doctrine . . . fled his country and withdrew himself into Kent.'[1] Repeating the family tradition, Sir Francis's nephew spoke of Edmund suffering for his faith and 'being forced to fly from his house near South Tavistock in Devon, into Kent.'[2] There is no doubt that, like Russell, Edmund Drake became a good Protestant, but that this version was less than the truth, and that the increasingly pious Edmund Drake harboured a dark secret even from his sons seems evident from the following entry in the patent rolls for 1548:

> December 21, 1548. Whereas Edmund Drake, shearman, and John Hawkyng, alias Harte, tailor, late of Tavistock, Devon, are indicted of having on 25 April 2 Edward VI, at Tavistock, stolen a horse worth £3, of one John Harte; and whereas William Master, cordyner, and Edmund Drake, shearman, late of Tavistock, are indicted of having on 16 April 2 Edward VI, at Peter Tavy, Devon, in the king's highway (via regia) called 'le Crose Lane' assaulted Roger Langisforde and stolen 21s 7d which he had in his purse.
> Pardon to the said Drake, Hawkynge and Master of all felonies before 20 Oct. last. By p.s. (II. 893. Westm. 18 Dec.).[3]

From this we learn that in 1548 Edmund was indicted for two offences of robbery – stealing a horse and beating Roger Langisforde and rifling his purse on the highway, petty and sordid sixteenth-century crimes. He was described as being 'late of Tavistock' before the end of the year, which suggests that although he was pardoned he had already bolted. It is also worth noting here Edmund Drake's association with one 'Hawkyng' or 'Hawkynge'. This may be a reference to the famous seafaring family whose destiny was to be so entwined with Drake's, for the grandfather of John Hawkins, the great seaman, was a John Hawkins of Tavistock. He was not, apparently, the alleged horse-thief, but probably a relation. There was a family connexion between the Drake and the Hawkins lineages, and this document is the first that brings the two celebrated names together.

[1] Camden, Annals, 2: 110-11.
[2] Sir Francis Drake Revived (1626), reprinted in Wright, ed., Documents Concerning English Voyages to the Spanish Main, 251.
[3] I discussed this document in Sugden, 'Edmund Drake of Tavistock', 436.

But before we hastily conclude that Edmund's story of religious persecution was a total fiction designed to mask a more ignoble flight, it should be emphasized that there were religious disturbances in 1549 and they evidently drove the Drake family, if not Edmund himself, from Tavistock. While this unrest does not explain Edmund's flight, it provided him with his excuse and may have warned him against any precipitate return to his native county.

It is difficult now for many people to understand the intense religious ferment of Reformation England. To do so one must be aware of the part played by religion in the sixteenth-century world, and the many functions it served. Religion explained the mysteries of life and creation, underpinned the social order, protected people from the powers of evil, and comforted the distressed and bereaved. Ultimately it dispensed justice in the hereafter. Relatively unchallenged by the rudimentary sciences of the day, it was not something about which men could be complacent, for it governed life upon earth and the prospects for the soul beyond death.

The early sixteenth century had witnessed strong criticism of the Roman Church and an exaggerated anti-clericalism that depicted the clergy as greedy, corrupt, sinful and hypocritical. The Drakes must have heard of many of the charges that were brought against priests: of exorbitant fees, rents and tithes; of clergy securing several benefices when they could occupy but one; of the vindictiveness of the ecclesiastical courts; and of all manner of immoralities taking place behind the monastery doors. In harness with this popular anti-clericalism there was growing intellectual criticism of Catholicism itself. A more personal religion was advocated which devalued the role of the priest as an intermediary between God and man and condemned the excessive ceremonialism of the Roman religion. These criticisms took several forms, but one of the most influential was Lutheranism. It asserted that only through faith in Christ did people win salvation, and that attempts to solicit divine favour by other means – by venerating images, saints and shrines; by performing penances or receiving blessings; by enjoining the prayers of others; even by carrying out good works – were superfluous. Protestant teachers denied the concept of purgatory, and sought to replace Latin services and scriptures with vernacular versions that might be more accessible to the people. And they attacked Catholic doctrine and ritual, denied transubstantiation, reduced the sacraments, and endeavoured to abolish papal taxation. All this struck at the heart of the Catholic Church.

Henry VIII gave an important impetus to the Reformation in England when, unable to obtain a male heir from his wife, Katherine of Aragon, he tried to induce the Church to annul his marriage so that he could take Anne Boleyn as a new bride. The Pope resisted, and a series of acts of Parliament in the 1530s and 1540s detached England's Church from the obedience of Rome and invested the right to define doctrine and forms of religion with the English Crown. Once the control of Rome had been severed, it was easier for the reformers slowly to recast England's religion in a Protestant character.[1]

Probably it was the king's attacks on the property of the Church that brought the Reformation home to the people of Devon. In 1536 small priories like those at Barn-

[1] For the English background to Drake's career, see Elton, *England Under the Tudors*; Youings, *Sixteenth Century England*; Mackie, *The Earlier Tudors*; and Black, *The Reign of Elizabeth*.

staple, Exeter and Totnes were confiscated by the Crown, and three years later so were the larger religious houses, including Tavistock Abbey. After Henry's death, Protector Somerset confiscated the chantries, chapels endowed to enable priests to pray for the souls of the departed founders. He promoted the Reformation more vigorously still, inveighing against the use of images and reducing the number of holy days. In 1549 he imposed a new Prayer Book and replaced the Latin service by one in English.

Staunch Catholics inevitably reacted, and it was a rebellion in 1549 against the Act of Uniformity that drove the Drakes from Tavistock. Even before the flight of Edmund the family had heard the rumbling discontent. In 1548 conservatives in Cornwall had resisted the government's injunctions to remove images from churches and chapels, only to be speedily suppressed. Young Francis Drake may have seen the warning to rebels exhibited in the town of Tavistock, one of the withered limbs of an executed insurgent brought from Plymouth for the purpose, after the fashion of the day. In the summer of 1549, a few months after Edmund Drake's pardon, the greater rebellion occurred, one that was short-lived but bloody. Members of the Cornish peasantry, encouraged by a few gentry, rejected the new Prayer Book and, gathering arms, marched into Devon. On the way they captured Trematon Castle, across the Tamar estuary from Plymouth, and it was said that

> they seized on the castle, and exercised the uttermost of their barbarous cruelty (death excepted) on the surprised prisoners. The seely gentlewomen, without regard of sex or shame, were stripped from their apparel to their very smocks, and some of their fingers broken, to pluck away their rings. [1]

Fear spread before the rebel force, and some of the locals in its path sought refuge in Plymouth Castle or on the island of St Nicholas in Plymouth Sound. Some of the rebels remained at Plymouth, but others marched north-east, by way of Tavistock, and then struck out across the wilds of Dartmoor to join a force of Devonshire rebels from Sampford Courtenay at Crediton. The Drakes, it may be presumed, fled, for the family disappears from the Lay Subsidy rolls of Tavistock after 1549. Unable to capture Exeter, the insurgents were soon suppressed by an army of Italian mercenaries commanded by none other than the Drakes' landlord, Lord Russell. He had an additional satisfaction in putting down the revolt, because among the demands of the rebels had been the restitution to the Church of Tavistock Abbey.

How did the rising affect Edmund Drake and his son? We cannot be sure, because there is no information about their whereabouts in 1549. It seems likely that Edmund had not returned to Tavistock after leaving the parish under a cloud the previous year. However, one point is certain. Years later Sir Francis spoke of the western rebellion, and blamed it for his father's flight to Kent. He must have heard stories of the rising from many people, perhaps from his father and other members of his family. Drake's grandfather, John, lived until 1566, and his grandmother until 1571. The boy's oldest uncle died in the 1560s. Another uncle, Robert, married Anna Luxmore, and their son, another John, served under Francis Drake in some of his voyages. The admiral's youngest uncle, also John, outlived most of his nephews and died in the early years of the seventeenth century. These Drakes remained in Devon, and after Francis returned

---

[1] Rose-Troup, *The Western Rebellion of 1549*, 129. See also Cornwall, *Revolt of the Peasantry, 1549*.

to the county as a young man he must have met them again, and he may have learned more fully from them of the Drakes' flight from Tavistock in the heady days of the Edwardian Reformation.

When Edmund Drake quitted Devon he made his way to Kent, and set up home in the hull of a ship, probably a hulk, moored or beached in the River Medway. Here Edmund's younger sons were born, and here he found employment. Somerset's government had begun to use the Medway as a place to lay up and repair the ships of the new Royal Navy, and vessels were being transferred from various ports to Gillingham Reach, where the high tides and extensive mud flats made it convenient for grounding. With the ships came sailors, and Edmund found a precarious living at Gillingham, reading prayers to the seamen of the king's navy. A literate man, he was able to live down his shady past and emerge a preacher of the new faith.

In Kent, more so than in Devon, young Francis absorbed the sights and sounds of the sea. He saw the king's ships, large and small – the sailing ships of the battlefleet, the small pinnaces and the oared barges. He watched tiny merchantmen of 20 to 80 tons, two- and three-masters, shipping provisions to London or picking their way along the coasts or across the Channel to France, Picardy and the Low Countries. He became familiar with the thriving fishing vessels.

Here, too, Drake passed from childhood to youth against the background of religious unrest that continued to trouble the nation. Throughout Europe the middle ground between Catholic and Protestant, between Rome and Geneva, was beginning to fall away, and extremists burned with the desire to impress their faith upon others, believing that religious uniformity was essential to both salvation and a stable society and that it was better to brutalize one's fellows than to suffer them to die in an erroneous faith. In 1553 Mary, the daughter of Henry VIII and Katherine of Aragon, succeeded to the throne after the short reign of her weak half-brother. Staunchly Catholic, she was determined to restore her realm's links with Rome and to set aside the Reformation, and she repealed the Act of Uniformity and Prayer Book of 1552, the twin peaks of Edwardian reform. Worse still, Mary proposed to marry Philip of Spain, the son of and heir to Charles V, King of Castile and Holy Roman Emperor. To fears for the Reformation and of the restitution of church property were now added traditional English suspicions of the foreigner, and religion and xenophobia combined to produce Wyatt's rebellion.

It germinated in Kent, and drew most of its leaders from the Medway valley and its close hinterland. Some of the rebels believed that the Spanish marriage would bring to England a coterie of foreign favourites who would supplant the likes of themselves in offices of honour and profit. Others had religious motives. It is believed that there were hopes that Mary could be unseated and replaced by her sister, the young Princess Elizabeth. Although simultaneous risings were planned in Devon, Hertfordshire and Leicestershire, it was in Kent that Sir Thomas Wyatt raised his standard in January of 1554 and gathered the only forces that constituted much of a threat. Some of them were from Gillingham, where the Drakes lived. It was a weak enough force, a mere few thousand men, but Wyatt led them to London where he was defeated without much difficulty in February.

Francis Drake would have heard of Wyatt's rebellion, and probably of the execution of some of the rebels in Kent. Whether or not he made much of it, Mary's reign cannot have left him untroubled. The queen did indeed marry Philip, and presided over the persecution of heretics. Some Protestants fled abroad, to Frankfurt, Zurich and Geneva. Others, like Edmund Drake, remained, living as quietly as they could, no easy matter for the man who read prayers for a living. The least fortunate were seized and burned, perhaps three hundred in all, fifty-four of them in Kent. As a youth Drake saw the work of the twin forces that he eventually dedicated himself to overthrow: Rome and Spain. Exactly how they affected him must remain a matter of speculation, but in his maturity one of his favourite books, and one of the few he took with him around the world, was John Foxe's *Acts and Monuments*, published in 1563, a history of the Protestant martyrs of the reign of Queen Mary.

Throughout his life, Drake's profound faith was arguably his most salient characteristic, and it provided the mainspring of his tempestuous career. There would be other motivations – patriotism, profit and personal grievances against the Spaniards – but none was greater than his Protestantism. Those who have portrayed him purely as an avaricious freebooter have underestimated both the religious climate of the day and Drake's own intense piety. It was his confidence in God's protection and the belief that God worked through him that gave him the courage to brave the greatest dangers. His favourite oaths were 'By God's Faith!' or 'If God Wills'. In his prime he spent several hours a day in worship, and his surviving letters are replete with references to his God. His common dispatches were frequently prayers. In one typical example he addressed Francis Walsingham, one of Queen Elizabeth's greatest ministers, in 1588:

> Let us all, with one consent, both high and low, magnify and praise our most gracious and merciful God for his infinite and unspeakable goodness towards us; which I protest . . . that my belief is that our most gracious Sovereign, her poor subjects, and the church of God hath opened the heavens in divers places, and pierced the ears of our most merciful Father, unto whom, in Christ Jesu, be all honour and glory. So be it, Amen, Amen.[1]

Drake was never a penman, but from such tortuous passages emerges something of the homage he paid to his Lord. Indeed, at the height of his career, when he stood as the most famous of Englishmen, he troubled to write to the same John Foxe whose book had so inspired him, reminding him that 'our enemies are many but our Protector commandeth the whole world' and exhorting all to 'pray continually, and our Lord Jesus will hear us in good time mercifully.'[2]

The earliest evidence, from the 1560s, shows that Drake's religious convictions were not only deep but extreme and uncompromising. In time he would find himself a spiritual home among the Elizabethan Puritans, for to Drake the Roman Church was not merely corrupted by the excrescences of the centuries and in need of reform; it was a false church, administered, as he said, by Antichrist, and fit only to be eschewed and condemned. The foundations of such extremism were laid in Kent by Edmund Drake at the time of the Marian counter-Reformation.

In 1558 Elizabeth became Queen of England, and at once, but with tact and moderation, busied herself in establishing the Church of England, for all its spirit of compromise still a Protestant church independent of Rome. The change boded well for

---

[1] Drake to Walsingham, 10 August, 1588, Laughton, ed., *Defeat of the Spanish Armada*, 2: 97-100.
[2] Drake to Foxe, 27 April, 1587, Harleian MS 7002, f. 8, British Library.

Edmund, and he was ordained a deacon and made Vicar of Upchurch in Kent on 25 January, 1561, a position he held until his death. Upchurch was a quiet parish lying south of the Medway estuary, situated on the salt marshes that pass along Kent's northern coast. It had some of the wildness of Devon, although it was different in character, with wide grassy flats broken by creeks and inlets that teemed with birdlife. The post promised some security for Edmund, but little for his substantial brood. True, there was a small income to be had from tithes, and Edmund would have possessed a piece of church land – the 'glebe' – to farm himself or lease out. But the land was not very productive, and unlike many yeoman farmers of his native Devon Edmund Drake had only a life tenure; upon his death his house and land would pass to the succeeding incumbent. There would be little to bequeath to his sons.

Providing for the latter must indeed have been a considerable difficulty for the needy preacher. Although some of the twelve sons probably died in infancy, sufficient remained to tax a man of such modest means, and Edmund's burden was increased by the early death of his wife.[1] Most of the boys were sent to sea; one, Edward, died at Upchurch, and the youngest, Thomas, was placed with a Mr Thomas Baker of London. By the time of his death Edmund had them off his hands, and willed most of his possessions to his youngest son, bequeathing nothing to the others.

Something of the atmosphere of the old man's household can be glimpsed from his will, made on 26 December, 1566, shortly before his death. Like a true Protestant he committed his spirit to God, and omitted the once customary references to the saints. A chair and a cushion passed to Richard Mylwaye, a relative of his wife, and all un-mentioned property to the nurse who had tended him in his last illness. His son, Thomas, received a feather bed and two pillows; a basin; platters; pewter dishes and pots; pen and ink; candlesticks; kettles; a mortar and pestle; five shirts; and something more important than all of them:

> I give unto the same Thomas, my son, two chests with all my books, which, my son, I would he should make of them above all other goods. But remember my wish to be new set in the beginnings of the Romans and so trim the book and keep in bosom and feed upon; make much of the Bible that I do here send thee with all the rest of the goodly books.[2]

Francis Drake had been taught to read and write by his father, but he was then put to schooling of a different kind, in the tides and shoals of the Medway and the choppy waters of the North Sea and the English Channel. Sometime in the 1550s Edmund had found his eldest son a position with the owner and master of a small coasting bark which carried freight about the region, occasionally sailed to France and the Low Countries, and helped to pilot ships in and out of ports. Although our source does not specifically say so, it is probable that the young Drake was apprenticed to the skipper,

---

[1] Drake's mother seems to have died before 1558. The youngest son, Thomas, was born about 1556. In his will Edmund Drake, then Vicar of Upchurch, made no provision for his wife, who must have been dead. He also asked that he be buried in his churchyard beside his son, Edward, which suggests that his wife had not died at Upchurch. Edmund probably moved to Upchurch from Gillingham in 1561, but the parish registers for Gillingham, which survive from 1558 and are deposited at the Kent Record Office at Maidstone, contain no references to the Drakes during this period.

[2] Eliott-Drake, 1: 18-19; Drake Papers, 346M/F589.

that is, Edmund would have paid him a sum of money in return for a formal indenture of his son upon stipulated terms. Such apprentices were often taken as young as eleven years of age, and might serve from seven to twelve years more, but they enjoyed security of employment and could not, like other hands, be dismissed when a voyage ended.

In the next few years the boy proved himself an apt enough pupil, and he won the affection and respect of the bark's owner, an old man who had no wife or family of his own and who seems to have regarded Francis as his son. There was much to learn about tides and currents, shoals and landfalls and the prevailing winds. Francis found out how to box the compass, sound for depth, and make use of the sun and stars, and he learned to handle a bark in all weathers. He must also have endured the hardships of life at sea, the uncomfortable and crowded accommodation, the cold food and wet clothing when storms prevented fires from being lit, the stale beer and victuals, and the seven-day week.

For all that, Drake's prospects were not negligible; like the Church that was Edmund's calling, the sea did not debar those humbly born from achieving some status. Rank and wealth were important, surely, but wind and wave favoured no man above another, while a sailor of small account, if he was able, conscientious and lucky, might become a master, an officer responsible for the handling or, in smaller vessels, the command of a ship. Masters earned higher pay than ordinary seamen as well as the privilege of drawing additional allowances, and not a few of them, among whom was probably Drake's captain, eventually owned ships of their own. And between master and common mariner intermediary posts were to be had, like that of boatswain or master's mate. Drake was to be particularly fortunate, because the old man with whom he served his apprenticeship died and, having no other to receive his possessions, willed his bark to the boy he had trained.[1]

Alone now, Drake determined to return to his native county, and perhaps to call to account some family connections. He sold the bark but retained a few of the men, whom he brought to Plymouth, and here he evidently contacted his kinsmen, the prosperous shipowning brothers William and John Hawkins. It was probably for them that he served as a purser on a trading voyage to north-eastern Spain in about 1564. The purser represented those owners who did not accompany their ships and safeguarded their interests, superintending the financial aspects of a voyage, paying crews, discharging customs duties and accounting for cargoes. Drake, as a man of education and experience, and through his relationship to the Hawkins brothers, would have been a natural choice for such a position. When the trip was over he was recruited for another adventure under the auspices of the brothers, but this one took him further than he had been before, to territories claimed exclusively by the greatest of nations, imperial Spain.

[1] Valuable explorations of Elizabethan seafaring are Scammell, 'Manning the English Merchant Service in the Sixteenth Century', and Andrews, 'The Elizabethan Seaman'.

CHAPTER TWO

# BEYOND THE LINE

Good Eolus be friendly now, and send a happy gale,
That Captain Drake and all his men on seas may safely sail;
And God that guides the heavens above, so prosper thee mayhap,
That all the world have cause to say, thou liest in Fortune's lap.

Henry Roberts, *A Most Friendly Farewell*, 1585

EVEN AS DRAKE'S LITTLE BARK WAS SHUFFLING BACK AND FORTH ACROSS THE Channel, the troubles that had afflicted England were tearing the nations of Europe apart. Among the literate and influential classes within reach of the Calvinist propaganda that flooded from Geneva a new faith grew apace. The winds of Protestantism were sweeping the breadth of the Continent, and one by one the kingdoms fell before them. Elizabeth established a Protestant church in 1559. Beyond the North Sea Sweden did likewise. In Germany the reformers gained the upper hand. France was plunged into a civil war in 1562, and while the monarchy became a brickbat between the hostile factions the Calvinist churches threw their influence behind the Prince of Condi and against the Catholic Guises. The Netherlands, which were then ruled by Catholic Spain, saw the maturation of another alliance, this time between Protestantism and aggrieved Dutch nobles who complained that their former liberties were being curtailed. Divided among themselves the Protestant churches may have been, but to the orthodox this tide was fearful indeed. 'In many countries,' sighed a Venetian, 'obedience to the Pope has almost ceased, and matters are becoming so critical that if God does not interfere they will soon be desperate.'[1]

From Orthodoxy's inevitable response to this gigantic crisis grew what later centuries called the Counter-Reformation. Catholicism strove to dam back the tide threatening to engulf it, both by raising its own performance and by resisting heresy by force. In lengthy debate the Catholic bishops at last clarified their own faith and put it upon a more defensible and efficient footing, but their counter-stroke looked beyond a mere reform of the Catholic Church towards a battle in which power and arms would be decisive, a battle in which one man above all others would stand as the mainstay of the papacy and orthodox religion – the mightiest monarch in Christendom, Philip II of Spain.

Philip was a little under thirty years of age when he succeeded his father to become King of Spain and its wide dominions in 1556. His inheritance was vast: principally, Spain itself, the Netherlands, part of Italy, and most of the new territories of South and Central America. In some respects Philip was not unlike the man Francis Drake was becoming. He, too, wove the interests of God and country into one, and believed himself an instrument of both. Drake was to emerge as a Protestant hero for the new England Elizabeth was forging; Philip no less earnestly

[1] Green, *Renaissance and Reformation*, 177.

10

promoted the Catholic faith, hoping to protect his people from the fate that ultimately met all heretics and to advance the country's imperial ambitions at the
same time. But apart from the undoubted energy and religious zeal that propelled
both men, there were few other parallels between the mean Devonshire seaman
and the powerful king. Where Drake grew bold, confident and decisive, Philip was
tortured with indecision and self-doubt, agonizing over each move he made.
Where Drake was bluff and charismatic, Philip felt secure only among his books
and papers. He was awkward and uneasy in company, an aloof, almost reclusive
figure, whose secretive manner, impassive countenance and whispering voice dis-
concerted rather than engaged those with whom he worked. While Drake swag-
gered his decks, gregarious and assertive and full of cheer, lonely Philip toiled
night and day at his desk, filling the margins of the countless papers that passed
before him with a wandering scrawl that testified that few details escaped the
king's attention. In his solitude, too, he dwelt upon the private tragedy of his life.
By 1570 he had been thrice married (once to the English queen, Mary Tudor) and
thrice widowed, and his only heir had been Don Carlos, so vindictive, so idiotic
and irresponsible an heir that he was imprisoned by the order of his own father.
When Don Carlos died in custody malicious tongues accused the king of his
murder.

Whatever his personal life may have been, Philip was a dutiful king with an
astonishing capacity for work. He attempted to deal as justly with his people as he
knew, and strove for the imperial and national integrity of his country. Partly
because of it, his relations with the papacy were turbulent. The popes relied upon
Philip, but they seldom trusted him, fearing that religion was for him a convenient
mask for secular, and, as they saw it, baser ambitions. Nevertheless, both parties
needed the other. Without the strength of Philip, the Counter-Reformation
lacked teeth. For his part, Philip was a devout Catholic, determined to unite his
dominions beneath one faith, and he relied heavily upon the enormous subsidies
the papacy awarded him as well as the authority with which the Pope's support invested Spain's undertakings.

Although Spain's traditional European rival, France, was in eclipse, the
advance of heresy in the north posed an additional unwanted burden upon Philip.
He was already championing Christendom against the Turks in the Mediterranean, and the Moors in the south of his own country were not crushed until
1570. After the loss of forty-two vessels in an attack upon the island of Djerba in
1560, it took Philip four years to rebuild his Mediterranean galley fleet. Gradually
he restored Christian supremacy, but only in 1571 did his naval victory at Lepanto
succeed in deflecting the Turks eastwards to easier conquests away from Europe.
No, to commit himself to a war against Protestantism at a time when the forces of
the Ottoman Porte remained unchecked on the other side of the continent was
not the easiest decision for a monarch as diffident as Philip.

Yet Philip was convinced that political unity within his territories depended
upon religious unity. Not for him was the path of toleration. He rooted out
embryonic Protestantism in Spain and censored its literature, and he supported
the Inquisition's terrifying purge of heretics. In 1567 he ordered an army under the
Duke of Alba into the Netherlands to restore it to order, and declared, 'I have pre-

ferred to expose myself to the hazards of war . . . rather than allow the slightest derogation from the Catholic faith and the authority of the Holy See.' But to effect his purpose he needed money.[1] Spain possessed the finest troops in Europe, the dreaded Spanish *tercios*, but these were the minority of the soldiers Philip required for his formidable undertaking. For the rest he must rely upon mercenaries – Italians, Walloons and Germans – whose fidelity depended upon the reliability of the paymaster. And Spain had been bankrupt as recently as 1557. Although the Crown drew no less than four-fifths of its revenue from Castilian taxes and papal subsidies, Philip's offensive in the Netherlands rested substantially upon another source of income, the silver that was ponderously shipped across the Atlantic from the Americas.

Spain's discoveries in the New World had been the remarkable fruits of the quest for the riches of Eastern trade, which Columbus had hoped to tap by sailing west, and were developed by men hungry for minerals and treasure, for glory and adventure, for prestige and the souls of the pagans. By virtue of Columbus's discovery of the West Indies in 1492 Spain claimed a monopoly on the exploitation of the Americas, just as her imperial rival, Portugal, set up similar pretensions upon the Indian Ocean after her voyagers had sailed around the Cape of Good Hope. In an effort to mark the boundaries of the two empires, in 1493 Pope Alexander VI issued papal bulls dividing the new territories and conferring on Spain the right to the Americas. And by the Treaty of Tordesillas the following year Spain and Portugal recognized their respective monopolies, the former's in the west and the latter's to the east.

The pace and character of Spanish expansion were the stuff of heroic legend. It soon became obvious that the new lands in the west represented not part of the East Indies but a continental land-mass between Europe and Asia. In the first decades of the sixteenth century Spanish expeditions had conquered and pillaged the native civilizations of Mexico and Peru and circumnavigated the globe. From the West Indies Spanish settlement filtered into mainland South and Central America, and a colonial administration was established under the jurisdiction of two viceroys, one in New Spain (Mexico) and the other at Lima in Peru. Important if rudimentary towns developed, Santo Domingo on the island of Hispaniola, Havana on Cuba, San Juan on Puerto Rico, Panama and Nombre de Dios on the isthmus of Panama, and Cartagena on the Caribbean coast of South America, the legendary Spanish Main itself. A ranching, planting and mining economy produced hides, sugar, ginger and – above all – treasure.

Europe was tantalized not so much by the feat of discovery and colonization itself as by the fabulous wealth upon which the Spaniards stumbled. In 1545 rich silver deposits were located at Potosi in what is now Bolivia and three years later more at Zacatecas in Mexico. By the 1560s, when Drake first saw the Caribbean, the mines were producing upon a large and regular scale, and a transatlantic trade between Seville and the New World had emerged. Spain sent two fleets, or *flotas*, a year to America, perhaps as many as seventy vessels in convoy, carrying goods

[1] Elliott, *Europe Divided*, 166. For Spain in the sixteenth century see Elliott, *Imperial Spain*, and Lynch, *Spain Under the Habsburgs*.

the colonies needed – food, clothing, wine, oil and equipment. The annual Mexican *flota* left Seville in the spring, bound for Vera Cruz. A few months later the Panama *flota* followed, but it headed for Nombre de Dios on the isthmus of Panama, unloading its exports before wintering in the sheltered harbour of Cartagena on the mainland. In the following spring it returned to Nombre de Dios to collect silver which had been brought from Peru, and at Havana united with the homeward-bound Mexican *flota* for the return, under escort, to Seville.

Between 1556 and 1570, 40 million ducats of silver were brought into Spain. The arrival of the annual treasure fleets was always an occasion of great importance, not only for Spain but for Europe in general. Some of the silver paid merchants for the goods they had exported to the Americas, but about two-fifths of it went to the Spanish Crown, forming upwards of 11 per cent of the king's total revenue. It was essential to Spain if she was to meet her gigantic commitments in Europe, for it redeemed the country's debts to the German and Genoese bankers whose credit kept Philip's army of mercenaries in the field.

Such a lucrative system symbolized as well as maintained Spain's prestige, and inevitably aroused the envious attention of foreign nations. The Spaniards acknowledged that their colonial trade could not entirely exclude the foreigners, and granted licence to Portuguese merchants to enable them to participate in it upon the payment of appropriate taxes. Despite the provision, however, an unregistered contraband trade soon flourished, and slaving became one of the worst features of it. The new American economy was labour intensive, and Portuguese slavers found a ready demand for the unfortunate blacks they shipped from Africa, an area within the monopoly claimed by Portugal. From the 1520s French corsairs also appeared in the Caribbean, extending the warfare between France and Spain to the New World, and their boldness increased. In the 1550s they captured Havana and Cartagena.

By the time Drake appeared in the West Indies, the Spaniards had already confronted two waves of interlopers: the illicit traders, usually Portuguese or French, and the French freebooters. Efforts had been made to strengthen defences, but they had been only marginally successful. One problem lay in the lack of an effective central control able to co-ordinate and support local defences. The West Indian islands, Florida, and part of the Spanish Main were administered by the *Audiencia* of Santo Domingo; that part of the Main east of the isthmus of Panama as far as Rio de la Hacha fell within the jurisdiction of the *Audiencia* of New Granada at Santa Fé de Bogotá; Panama had its own *Audiencia*, but while it was ultimately accountable to the Viceroy of Peru areas to the north-west effectively fell beneath the control of the Viceroy of New Spain in Mexico. Confronted with highly mobile adversaries flitting about the coasts in swift, small-oared ships, it is not surprising that the Spanish colonies met the attacks with difficulty.

The towns of the Caribbean also remained woefully vulnerable, their scant fortifications ill equipped with artillery and soldiers. For their defence they relied primarily upon a feeble, badly trained and under-armed militia. Before 1560 only Santo Domingo could muster more than two hundred white militia, and excessive reliance had to be placed upon blacks and American Indians whose fidelity to

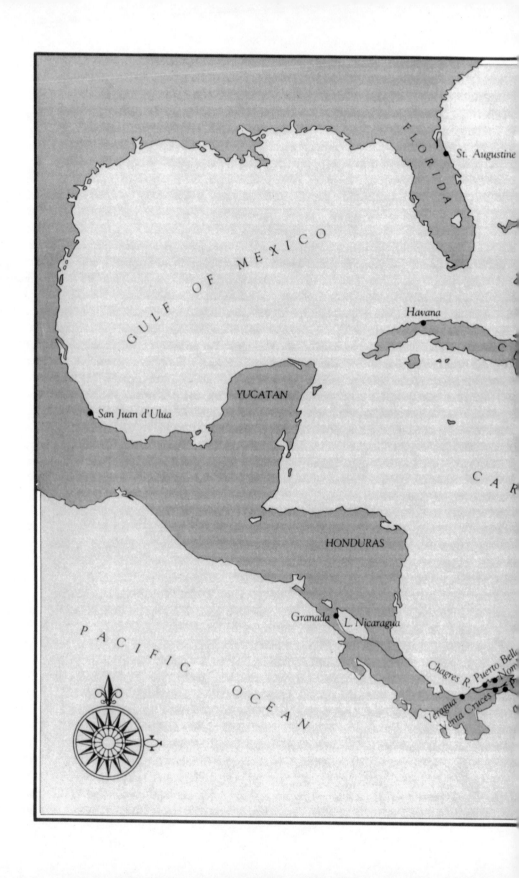

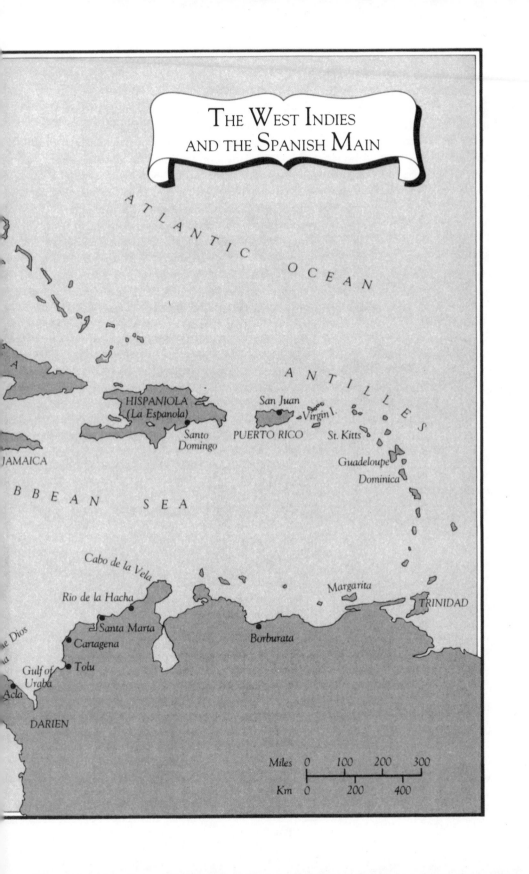

# THE WEST INDIES
## AND THE SPANISH MAIN

ATLANTIC OCEAN

ANTILLES

HISPANIOLA
(La Espanola)

San Juan

Virgin I.

PUERTO RICO

St. Kitts

Santo
Domingo

Guadeloupe

Dominica

JAMAICA

BBEAN    SEA

Cabo de la Vela

Margarita

TRINIDAD

Rio de la Hacha

Santa Marta

Borburata

de Dios

Cartagena

Gulf of    Tolu
Uraba

Acla

DARIEN

| Miles | 0 | 100 | 200 | 300 |
| --- | --- | --- | --- | --- |

| Km | 0 | | 200 | | 400 |
| --- | --- | --- | --- | --- | --- |

Spain was very understandably in doubt. Few of the defenders possessed long-range weaponry such as matchlocks or crossbows, and most were armed only with pikes or swords. At sea Spain made an earnest attempt to respond to the threats to the Caribbean by appointing as commander of a new Indies fleet of twelve galleons Pedro Menéndez de Avilés, who had just driven a presumptive French colony from Florida; his orders were to suppress the corsairs, but his boast 'that no corsair shall come to these parts without being lost, nor any ship trading without licence' was scarcely fulfilled.[1] His ships were built in the winter of 1567-8, but three were lost before they reached the Americas and the balance, when they were not being withdrawn for convoy duty with the *flotas*, proved incapable of catching the light-draught privateers employed by the French. In 1570 Menéndez was ordering eight small frigates for service with his squadron, so dissatisfied was he with the force at his disposal.

Too often defence remained local in character, dependent upon the resources of private individuals, and lacking the direction the Crown might have given it. Nor did the peace of Cateau-Cambrésis, which ended hostilities between France and Spain in Europe in 1559, bring peace to the Caribbean. The corsairs adhered to the view that, west of the line established at the Treaty of Tordesillas, an imaginary boundary 370 leagues west of the Azores and the Cape Verde Islands, the regulations governing European relations were not applicable. In the words of a phrase which has continued to engage historians, there was to be 'No Peace Beyond the Line'.

After his invasion of the Netherlands in 1567 Philip II was only too painfully aware of the importance of his American silver, for it dazzled all Europe and guaranteed his credit, but he believed that the precious treasure fleets would be adequately protected by the convoy system he had established even if a more general defence of the West Indies remained difficult. His richly laden silver ships continued to plod relentlessly across the Atlantic. However, a new and potentially more dangerous adversary had recently crossed the line – an English squadron this time, under the command of that Plymouth shipowner, Master John Hawkins.

Although a race of islanders, the English were late contenders for world-wide empire. They were a maritime nation, it was true, but throughout the early sixteenth century they had been content to watch their export trade in woollen cloth expand in Europe and leave bolder overseas adventures to others. John Cabot, it was also true, had left Bristol in 1497 and discovered Newfoundland or Nova Scotia for England, but nothing had grown from it except periodic fishing off the Canadian banks. Similarly, although Henry VIII had been sensible of the importance of controlling the English Channel and had created a powerful navy, servicing his ships in royal dockyards at Portsmouth, Woolwich and Deptford, that force had not invariably been kept up to strength. When Drake was but a child the number of ships of 400 tons or more in England's navy had fallen from twelve to

---

[1] Andrews, *Spanish Caribbean*, 95. Spain's defence of the West Indies is dealt with by Hoffman, *The Spanish Crown and the Defense of the Caribbean*. For the *flotas*, see Chaunu, *Séville et l'Atlantique*, vol. 3. The great age of discovery generally is examined in Parry, *Age of Reconnaissance*.

three. But in the 1550s the pace of the country's overseas activity sharpened. Her cloth trade, funnelled through Antwerp, was faltering, and the London merchants wondered whether they had depended too heavily upon one market and what opportunities might exist for diversification; the East, from which Portugal was reaping such riches with trade in luxuries like pepper, cinnamon, nutmeg, cloves, camphor, teak, silk, sandalwood, copper and porcelain, grew more alluring; and the government during the reign of Edward VI was ready with encouragement. But in England's first surge overseas there were many casualties. Sir Hugh Willoughby and his crew froze to death aboard their ship in the wintry seas off Lapland, while Thomas Wyndham and most of his men perished of a fever on the pestilential coast of Benin. Nor was the process without diplomatic entanglements. Portugal protested as English ships nosed along the African coast, asserting her exclusive right to the area by virtue of discovery and conquest, and Spain stood ready to raise her voice when John Hawkins threatened to extend England's operations to the West Indies.

Hawkins's expeditions beyond the line added another dimension to the growing difficulties between Spain and England. Philip was already prepared to believe that the English had encouraged the Dutch rebels, and he knew that their privateers had taken commissions from the French Huguenots to attack Catholic shipping in the Channel. As yet the tension had its limits. On opposite sides of the religious divide though they were, Philip and Elizabeth had no desire for war. They both feared France too much to sacrifice a potential ally; their countries enjoyed some profitable trade; they had their hands full already, Elizabeth with Scotland, France and Ireland, Philip with the Mediterranean and the Netherlands; and neither had the resources to prosecute another major conflict. But John Hawkins's penetration of the blue waters of the Caribbean opened another rift between them, one which would deepen as the years passed. The integrity of the Spanish American colonies would be an issue between the two monarchs as long as either of them lived.[1]

John Hawkins bore a famous name. Born about 1532 of a family that hailed from Tavistock, he was often said to have been cousin to Francis Drake, but although we know from a letter of Hawkins's elder brother that there was a blood connexion between the two famous sailors, its exact nature is unknown. It was certainly sufficient to induce the Hawkins brothers to employ young Francis in a position of responsibility. John came of an enterprising seafaring stock. His father was William Hawkins, one of the few English merchants who had challenged Portugal's supposed monopoly of the African and Brazilian trades. In the 1530s he had developed a triangular run, trading in Africa for ivory and other commodities, and crossing the Atlantic to barter with the natives of Brazil. In these and other ventures William Hawkins had been successful, and he became one of Plymouth's leading dignitaries, serving the town as both mayor and Member of Parliament. More tangible than this prestige, he also bequeathed to his sons, William and John, a fleet of privateers and merchantmen. Of the brothers it was John who emerged the

---

[1] English overseas expansion of the period is covered by Williamson, *Age of Drake*; Ramsay, *English Overseas Trade*; Quinn and Ryan, *England's Sea Empire*; and Andrews, *Trade, Plunder and Settlement*.

more dynamic. He strutted in his extravagant dress and charmed the peers and diplomats of the court, but he was for all that a hard-headed, shrewd, calculating and methodical businessman, articulate and intelligent, and when Drake first sailed for him he had the assuredness of one who was at home on sea and land and had twice been out beyond the line.

About John Hawkins's voyages there has been great controversy. They were slaving voyages, the first in English history. Between 1562 and 1565 he had commanded two expeditions to Africa, where he acquired a few hundred Negroes and sold them to the Spaniards in the West Indies for American produce such as hides and treasure. Posterity has handled Hawkins roughly over the matter of the slaving, and not without reason. It was an inhuman trade, less offensive perhaps to the blunter sensibilities of the sixteenth century than it would be to us, but undeniable in its brutality to any but an insensitive observer. These objections do not seem to have troubled Hawkins or his backers, who simply asked that the colonial products brought back to Europe reap a sufficient profit. And among those backers were the highest in the land: London merchants like Sir Lionel Ducket and Sir Thomas Lodge; naval officials like Benjamin Gonson, William Winter, and the Lord Admiral of England; courtiers of the stamp of the earls of Leicester and Pembroke; and the queen herself, who contributed the 700-ton *Jesus of Lubeck* to Hawkins's second voyage.

Concern was expressed, however, at the diplomatic repercussions of these incursions into territories claimed by Spain and Portugal. The latter protested loudly that the African trade was her own, and alleged that Hawkins had even resorted to piracy, seizing slaves and other cargoes from Portuguese ships off the coast of Sierra Leone. In reply, the London merchants as vociferously denied that Portugal could exclude others from areas she had neither sufficiently subjugated nor occupied. Spain, too, denounced the voyages, embarrassed that her own West Indian colonies should profit from and perhaps collude with the interlopers. By Spain's imperial regulations the activities of Hawkins were plainly illegal. He entered the Caribbean without obtaining a licence to trade from Seville. He carried goods which had not been registered at Seville. And while he was 'trading' he refused to pay the local imposts upon the importation of slaves. The point was made several times, but Elizabeth chose to demonstrate her independence of Philip by ignoring his complaints about her seamen, and the voyages continued.

The Spanish Crown ordered its officials in the Caribbean not to treat with the English, but the colonies wanted slaves, and it is difficult to decide how far their resistance to Hawkins was genuine. Hawkins's practice was to demand a licence to trade from these officials (a licence which was in any case invalid since it was not issued in Spain) and to enforce trading by threats and a show of force. The procedures were exemplified by the case of Rio de la Hacha, a pearl-fishing and mining centre on the Spanish Main. The town was administered by a royal treasurer, Miguel de Castellanos, and when Hawkins arrived in 1565 the Spaniards refused to deal with him, having been expressly forbidden to do so by Santo Domingo. Nonetheless, 'trading' took place. Hawkins landed some men, dispersed the few Spaniards who turned out to resist him, and compelled Castellanos to be reasonable. But the Spanish show of resistance was unconvincing. In Spain it was said that Castellanos had colluded with the English, and that the fight had been a mere sham, designed to colour the treasurer's claim that his hand had been forced. Whatever the truth, poor Castellanos cannot have been ignorant of the rumours being spread about him, nor of the knowledge that one of his colleagues at Borburata had been arrested and sent home to face charges of trading with the English. The treasurer resolved that if Hawkins showed his face again Rio de la Hacha would demonstrate its loyalty to the Crown beyond doubt.

Young Francis Drake was inspired by the exploits of John Hawkins. These voyages into far seas, bearding the Spaniards in their own waters, promised excitement as well as profit. The doubts about the reception further English ventures would receive in the Caribbean, if they troubled him at all, possibly merely sharpened his interest, for he was an adventurous and fearless youth. He knew that Spain was protesting volubly to the queen, but Hawkins held the noise in small regard and soon had a further enterprise in hand. It is to be imagined that it was to Drake's unlimited pleasure that Hawkins signed him up for the very next voyage beyond the line.

The meagre details that survive of Drake's début in the Caribbean are instructive. One of his shipmates on the expedition was a Welshman, Michael Morgan, described as a stout, short man with a ruddy freckled complexion, from a farming family of Cardiff. He was in his mid-thirties and several years Drake's senior, but something of a waster. An experienced seaman with voyages to Lisbon, La Rochelle and Brittany behind him, Morgan was the father of two children, although he had lost his wife. Nevertheless, he was penniless when he joined the new Hawkins venture, having gambled away all that he had. From such an unlikely witness comes one of the first and most revealing glimpses of the young Drake. Regrettably the information was preserved through unpleasant circumstances, for Michael Morgan eventually fell into the hands of the Spaniards and suffered the tortures of the rack in Mexico City in 1574. In the resultant confession he admitted that it was Francis Drake who had converted him to Protestantism on the voyage of 1566-7. The full account is given here for the first time:

> He said . . . although at that time he [Morgan] could have found a priest to whom to confess he did not confess but to God in his heart, believing that such a confession was sufficient to be saved, and this he had heard said by Francis Drake, an Englishman and a great Lutheran, who also came on the vessel and who converted him to his belief, alleging the authority of St Paul and saying that those who did not fast should not say evil of those who did, and those who fasted should not speak evil of those who did not, and that in either of those two doctrines, that of Rome and that of England, God would accept the good that they might do; that the true and best doctrine, the one in which man would be saved, was that of England . . . On the deponent [Morgan] asking the said Drake whether his parents and forefathers would be lost for having kept the doctrines of Rome, he replied 'no', because the good they had done would be taken into consideration by God, but that the true law and the one whereby they would be saved was that which they now kept in England.[1]

[1] Confession of Michael Morgan, January 1574, Conway Papers, Cambridge University Library, Add. MS 7235.

The discussion involved only the two men, but it was evidently not the last they enjoyed upon that subject, for Morgan added that 'the said Francis Drake had taught him the Paternoster and Creed of the Lutheran Law and that he had also learned to recite the Psalms from a book.' Thus did the young sailor, fired by his zeal for the reformed church, employ the talents of his father and his own natural eloquence to bring an older man to embrace his simple faith.

If Drake went forth a strong and forthright Protestant, estranged from the Spaniards by his theology and the memories of his unsettled childhood, the voyage upon which he now embarked left him with more personal grievances against the servants of Philip II, and in it can be traced the roots of that deep enmity Drake held towards Spain for the rest of his life. The expedition was an unlucky one, and it sailed under a cloud, for Elizabeth had bent before Spanish protests about the earlier slaving voyages to the extent of forbidding Hawkins to leave England. But Hawkins was sure enough of his ground to allow his ships to slip out of Plymouth on 9 November, 1566, under a different captain, John Lovell. There were three vessels, the *Paul* of 200 tons under Master James Hampton, the *Solomon* of 100 tons under Master James Raunse, and the 40-ton *Pasco* under Master Robert Bolton. Drake was with them, probably serving as an officer, but upon which ship we cannot tell.

The ships were soon beyond any waters Drake had seen before, running before the prevailing winds towards the Guinea coast of Africa. There, in territory jealously guarded by the Portuguese, Lovell resorted to the pillage with which Hawkins had earlier been charged. At Cape Verde a Portuguese ship laden with wax, ivory, slaves and other commodities was seized by the English. February of the New Year saw Lovell off Santiago in the Cape Verde Islands, where he took two more Portuguese vessels, one reportedly worth 15,000 ducats and laden with slaves and sugar, and another valued at 600 ducats which had left Lisbon for Brazil. The first of these vessels was apparently taken into service by the English, for those of her crew who had not been killed while resisting capture were set ashore. Finally Lovell's piracy, for it was nothing less, took him to the Isle of Maio and the capture of two prizes with cargoes which were worth, overall, 7,000 ducats, or so it was said. These events illustrated the curious relations that existed among seamen of nations avowedly at peace in Europe once they were in contested colonial waters. The English were repudiating Portugal's pretensions, and the latter was prepared to defend them by force, capturing or sinking interlopers whenever she could. And lives, both black and white, were cheap in the greedy struggle for trade empire.

Lovell's attacks on the Portuguese ships were the first naval 'engagements' in which Drake had served. Whether they gave Lovell all the slaves he required is not known, but he was soon striking across the Atlantic with his merchandise, heading for the Spanish West Indies. Michael Morgan, our Welsh informant, told the Inquisition that the English visited Borburata on the Main and the neighbouring islands of Margarita and Curaçao, but the contemporary Spanish documents tell only of two contacts with Lovell, at Borburata and Rio de la Hacha.

At Borburata Lovell encountered a like-minded French expedition under Jean Bontemps. It, too, had collected Negroes from the Guinea coast and it had put into Borburata to sell them the day before Lovell arrived. Apparently the French and English conferred with the local authorities and offered to supply one hundred slaves to the royal treasury in return for a licence to sell a further two hundred with other goods. The matter was referred to the governor of the port of El Coro, but he was sensible of the Crown's attitude to the illicit traders and refused to issue the licence. However, the French, like Hawkins, had their own methods of dealing. Even before the governor's answer had been received they had seized some of the prominent citizens of Borburata as hostages and were threatening to carry them to France unless the Spaniards co-operated. After the arrival of the governor's refusal, Bontemps decided to make the best of a bad job. He released his prisoners, but kept 1,500 pesos which had belonged to two of them, and landed in return twenty-six Negroes. Whether Lovell himself benefited from this 'trade' and whether he had any other dealings at Borburata the evidence does not reveal.

At Rio de la Hacha Miguel de Castellanos was still fretting over his dealings with Hawkins two years before when the English reappeared. Castellanos had served his town for more than thirteen years. He was then its captain-general and royal treasurer, but he was an ambitious man and apprehensive lest the rumours of his collusion with Hawkins were injuring his credit. Ominously, the *Audiencia* of Santo Domingo had commissioned a judge to investigate the affair, and whatever the royal treasurer of Rio de la Hacha really thought of Hawkins, he knew that he would have to redeem himself with his superiors if the 'corsairs' returned. In May 1567 that day finally came. Bontemps arrived at Rio de la Hacha first, and Castellanos refused him a licence to trade and sent him on his way disgruntled, although not before the Frenchmen had advertised that an English squadron was also coming to the port. Lovell perhaps anticipated a better reception, for it was charged against Castellanos that he had agreed with Hawkins what goods the English would bring on their next voyage. Was Lovell expecting full co-operation, believing that the colonies were hungry for the goods in his ships and that he was fulfilling some kind of verbal contract made between Hawkins and Castellanos? If so, he was rudely awakened. His three ships and Portuguese prize were seen off shore on the eve of Pentecost, and there they remained for two days until Whit Sunday, when the weather admitted Lovell into the harbour. On Monday the captain, or a representative, went ashore to request permission to trade, and to the dismay of the English, Castellanos refused a licence.

Mortified, Lovell remained close by until Friday, uncertain as to how he should proceed, but occasionally sending men ashore to test the resolve of the Spaniards. Still they would not trade. On Friday a final interview with Castellanos failed to move him. According to the Spanish account Lovell asked if he could set some Negroes ashore in return for a receipt from the Spaniards, perhaps hoping that a mere acknowledgement that he had deposited slaves at the town would have given Hawkins a basis to demand payment upon some more auspicious occasion, but the royal treasurer would have none of it. He surmised that the English were not strong enough to coerce him, and he must have known too that Lovell's Negroes had endured a miserable voyage in captivity and that some of them would have been so ill that if they were not landed they would probably die. In short, the English were in a weak and desperate position.

An hour after nightfall on Saturday Lovell took the only choice open to him. He selected ninety-two of the blacks, old or sick and emaciated, and he set them down on the shore at a place where a swollen river prevented the townspeople from crossing to dispute the landing. Then, leaving the Negroes to fall into the hands of the Spaniards

21

free of charge, he sailed away in the darkness, poorer and wiser, steering along the coast and across towards Hispaniola. Nothing is known of his activities there, but he was back in Plymouth early in September, and it is hardly likely that Hawkins was satisfied with the result. His men had been rejected at Borburata and Rio de la Hacha, compelled to surrender more than ninety Negroes, and may not have made enough money to cover the cost of the voyage.

On the other hand, the officials of Rio de la Hacha were jubilant, and eagerly turned their handling of the English to their advantage. Did it not vindicate them of charges of collusion? Had they not demonstrated their obedience to their king? Indeed, the more they narrated the affair the larger it became. We have recounted the incident of Rio de la Hacha from the earliest reports, but in January 1568 Castellanos and his cronies were sending fresh accounts of it to the Crown and embellishing the story as they did so. Now Castellanos claimed that there had been a gun-battle with the English:

> A few days later another large fleet of English galleons and ships appeared, in command of John Lovell, and he made extensive preparations to trade in this town. Seeing that this was not permitted to him, they played many guns upon us, against which we defended ourselves so that we beat them into flight.[1]

Another version of the defeat of the 'large fleet' written about the same time by the town factor, Lazaro de Vallejo Aldrete, and Hernando Costilla, insisted that Lovell had brought his ships in shore and sent his men in four small boats towards a landing place to threaten the town. Although this letter contained no reference to firing, it maintained that the English made several attempts to disembark, but that they were always turned back. But a third revision of the tale, signed by officials of Rio de la Hacha, combined both Castellanos and Vallejo Aldrete and asserted that there had been firing and an attempted landing. This letter had Lovell bombarding the Spaniards from his ships and boats and dispatching the latter towards the shore, and it relates how the attack was repulsed.

Strange it is that the earlier letters contain no reference to these events, and, indeed, that the town expressly stated in its account of 23 June, 1567 that after Lovell had been refused a licence he retired to his vessels 'where he remained six days without daring to attempt anything further', and that he then landed his Negroes at night and left.[2] That letter does describe how the French had earlier been repulsed in an effort to land, before the arrival of Lovell, and it must be concluded that in their later descriptions the Spaniards conveniently confounded the two incidents in pursuit of political capital.

But English gunfire there was to be in Rio de la Hacha, for as the chastened Lovell sailed wearily for home there was one aboard his ships of greater spirit, and who nursed grievances sorely. Drake had watched impotently as Castellanos had cheated the English, but he was to return, soon.

---

[1] Castellanos to the Crown, 1 January, 1568, Wright, ed., *English Voyages to the Caribbean*, 107. This volume publishes the relevant Spanish documents for Lovell's voyage. English accounts are summarized in Williamson, *Sir John Hawkins*, 122-6, and the same author's *Hawkins of Plymouth*, 93-9.

[2] City of Rio de la Hacha to the Crown, 23 June, 1567, Wright, 95-100.

# CHAPTER THREE

# THE TROUBLESOME VOYAGE OF JOHN HAWKINS

An hundred iron pointed darts they fling,
An hundred stones fly whistling by his ears,
An hundred deadly dinted staves they bring,
Yet neither darts, nor stones, nor staves, he fears;
But through the air his plumed crest he rears;
And in derision 'scapes away . . .

Charles FitzGeffrey, *Sir Francis Drake*, 1596

JOHN HAWKINS WAS FITTING OUT ANOTHER EXPEDITION AT PLYMOUTH IN SEPTEM-
ber 1567, and Francis Drake was to be part of it. There were six ships in all, two
of them warships belonging to the queen, the *Jesus of Lubeck*, armed with a formidable battery of brass and iron pieces, and the smaller 300-ton *Minion*. This
time Hawkins would command in person, and he chose the *Jesus* as his flagship
and Robert Barrett to be her master, or navigating officer. Barrett was only young,
twenty-four years of age, but a local man from Saltash and one who had impressed
Hawkins while serving as a ship's master on a previous venture. Drake also sailed
aboard the *Jesus* as one of her principal officers, and among the convivial company
there he found not only his old friend Michael Morgan but Protestants as ardent as
himself, such as Henry Newman and Nicholas Anthony.

The *Minion* was captained by Thomas Hampton and her master was John Garrett. The other ships were the *William and John*, 150 tons, the *Swallow*, 100 tons,
the *Judith* bark of 50 tons, and the tiny *Angel* of 32 tons. Thomas Bolton commanded the *William and John*, and James Raunse, who had been with Lovell,
served as her master. It was not, overall, as impressive a collection as it looked,
although it was undoubtedly a far stronger force than Lovell had commanded, capable of bowling over the opposition at ports like Rio de la Hacha. The *Jesus* was a
large ship for the day, but old – she had been purchased from the Hanse in 1545 –
and in poor condition, rotting and unsafe, her huge poop and forecastle provided
to help repel boarding parties rendering her top-heavy and straining her ageing
timbers.

The sponsors of this, the fourth Hawkins slaving voyage, are imperfectly
known, although they included merchants of the City of London like Sir William
Garrard, Rowland Heyward and Sir Lionel Ducket, and probably once again the
admiral and naval official, William Winter. Members of the government were
alleged to have invested, and it seems that William Cecil, Elizabeth's chief minister, was one. As for the queen, her complicity is amply established by the use of
her ships. She assured the Spanish ambassador that Hawkins would not, as Spain
feared, intrude upon Philip's colonies, but her reassurance meant very little.
Originally, it was put about that the expedition intended searching for gold mines
in Africa, but the two Portuguese hired as guides absconded and Hawkins sub-

stituted a conventional slaving voyage instead, something he probably intended from the beginning. He promised the queen that his adventure could be made without offending any of England's allies or friends, a fatuous remark in view of his destinations, but one which might permit Elizabeth to deny that she had sanctioned his activities if they proved otherwise. Whatever words passed between the queen, Cecil and Hawkins did not retard his progress, and his voyage was soon under way.[1]

The ships left Plymouth Sound on 2 October, 1567, laden with cloth of various kinds, carrying 408 men, and bearing the red cross of England at their mastheads. It was, however, what Hawkins termed a 'troublesome' enterprise that he had begun. North of Finisterre the ships were scattered by a gale that lasted for four days, and only the diminutive *Angel* managed to keep company with the ailing *Jesus*. Already the flagship was betraying her years. Leaks opened in her decaying timbers, and one in the stern was so large that it had to be plugged with pieces of baize. The ship pitched and rolled alarmingly, and Hawkins had his men manning the pumps day and night to keep the water in her down. Eventually he took so pessimistic a view of their chances of survival that he summoned the crew for prayers, entreating the Lord to preserve the ship from sinking. Their prayers must have been heard, for at midnight on 10 October the wind fell and the weather began to clear. In the morning Hawkins again assembled his men and led them in a thanksgiving for their deliverance.

Pressing southwards, and finding the *Judith* along the way, Hawkins made for the Spanish colony of Santa Cruz de Tenerife, looking for shelter in which he might repair his damaged vessel. Spain had never closed Tenerife to foreign traders, but her governor can have had few illusions about Hawkins's eventual destination. Both sides eyed each other distrustfully. While his storm-battered vessels were refitting in an environment as potentially hostile as Santa Cruz, Hawkins was suddenly confronted with a quite different problem – dissension from within. Two of his officers, Edward Dudley and George Fitzwilliam, quarrelled and resolved to go ashore to settle their differences by a duel. Hawkins only heard about it after Dudley had left, but he immediately intervened and, refusing to countenance Fitzwilliam quitting the ship, he recalled Dudley forthwith. No display of disunity among his men would entertain the Spaniards while he was in command. Dudley was a hot-tempered man, and he stormed back to the *Jesus* where he fell into so violent an argument with his commander that the two resorted to blows and then drew swords. In a brief altercation both Dudley and Hawkins were wounded before

---

[1] The contemporary published narratives of this voyage, John Hawkins's *A True Declaration of the Troublesome Voyage of John Hawkins* (1569), Job Hortop's *The Rare Travels of Job Hortop* (1591) and Miles Philips's narrative, are reprinted, with summaries of the testimony given before the High Court of Admiralty in England in 1569, by Beazley, ed., *An English Garner*. More valuable is the anonymous account in the Cotton manuscripts of the British Library, published as an appendix to Williamson, *Sir John Hawkins*. Spanish materials have been printed in Wright, ed., *English Voyages to the Caribbean*, and Lewis's two articles, 'The Guns of the *Jesus of Lubeck*', and 'Fresh Light on San Juan de Ulua'. A wealth of unpublished detail can be found in the transcripts of the confessions of captured Englishmen contained in the Conway Papers of the Cambridge University Library. Additional valuable secondary accounts are Williamson, *Hawkins of Plymouth*; the over-dramatized Unwin, *Defeat of John Hawkins*; and Hair, 'Protestants as Pirates, Slavers and Proto-Missionaries'.

they were separated. Dudley had overstepped the mark, as he must have known as soon as he had calmed down, and he found himself placed in irons and hauled before Hawkins. The penalty for mutiny was death, and attempting to kill or wound the commander of the expedition admitted of no less a charge. Everyone knew it, and yet there was much sympathy for Dudley among the spectators, a feeling that if he had acted wrongly it had been in temper rather than malice and that he should not suffer the ultimate penalty. While Dudley pleaded for his life, Hawkins menaced him briefly with a loaded arquebus. Then, as tension mounted, the captain suddenly pardoned him. It was a humane gesture which greatly enhanced Hawkins's standing with his men, reinforced the point he desired to make, and saved him a valuable officer. Drake may have learned something about leadership by watching it.

Having disposed of his internal difficulties, Hawkins returned to the task of getting under way. As a precaution against attack the English ships had anchored behind a few Spanish vessels, masked from the guns of Santa Cruz, but one evening the covering merchantmen suspiciously shifted their position so that the castle guns had a clear line of fire. During the ensuing night Hawkins judiciously moved his vessels out of gun range, and soon afterwards he put to sea. At Gomera the *Minion*, the *William and John* and the *Swallow* joined company so that the squadron was complete as it approached the coast of West Africa. It encountered some Portuguese fishing caravels off Cape Blanco, but all but one of them had been evacuated, and the English heard that their crews had fled after a raid by Frenchmen who had entered these waters to barter with the Negroes for hides and ivory. Considering the abandoned vessels to be fair prize, Hawkins seized one of them to accompany his expedition.

Bent as they were upon piracy, slaving and illicit trading, the English yet demonstrated a simple but fiery piety. Every morning at seven or eight o'clock, and each evening when the night watch came upon deck to replace their tired fellows, and the hourglass was turned, Hawkins would assemble the men of the *Jesus*, both high and low, around the mainmast for religious services before a thundering quartermaster, whom Hawkins's young nephew and page, Paul, later described to the Spaniards as 'a notorious Lutheran, the greatest that existed in England.' According to the evidence of Michael Morgan, 'when a sufficient number of people did not gather round to hear what he preached he would order them to be rounded up with a rope's end.' Kneeling bareheaded the men recited the Psalms, the Lord's Prayer and the Creed in the English tongue, while the quartermaster's sermons defamed the Pope and denied that he, Our Lady or the saints could intercede between a man and his god.[1]

For all the overt righteousness aboard the *Jesus* and the other ships, however, it was a miserable business that Hawkins began at Cape Verde. He used two methods to gather his slaves: direct raids upon native villages and the plundering of Portuguese vessels for their Negroes. The latter was piracy. Portugal was at peace with England, and Hawkins had no commission for reprisals against her

---

[1] Criminal Suit against Paul Hawkins, 1573, Conway Papers, Cambridge University Library, Add. MS 7237.

shipping which could have authorized his proceedings. As for the slaving, undoubtedly many Elizabethans regarded the Negro as less than human and exempt from normal consideration, and discussion about the morality of the business was uncommon in England at that time. The issue was, after all, a new one for the English. But the conscience of Europe had already been pricked by the Spanish treatment of the American Indians, and some Spaniards were also raising their voices against black slavery. There is no reason to suppose that sensitive men can have been blind to the sufferings of the African natives they kidnapped and herded on to foul hulks for personal profit. Drake was in his twenties and did not question what his elders accepted, but he must share the blame, although in him, at least, there dwelt a capacity to sympathize with the blacks which time would one day draw out.

Hawkins's first attempt to gather slaves was a failure. Near Cape Verde he landed at night with about two hundred of his men and stole upon a slumbering Negro village, but the attack backfired badly. The surprise was incomplete and the natives resisted, wounding Hawkins and twenty of his men with poisoned arrows. Seven or eight of the injured contracted a mysterious ailment like lockjaw and died, a high price to pay for the nine Negroes who were captured.

Soon after this, when the English had put the Cape Verde Islands behind them, Drake received his first command under Hawkins. Some Frenchmen were encountered, the very same who had robbed the Portuguese fishing vessels off Cape Blanco. Indeed, with them still sailed a Portuguese caravel now commanded by a French sailor called Planes. Hawkins impounded the ship, the *Gratia Dei* (Grace of God), and installed as her new captain Francis Drake. Another of the French ships also joined the English, but voluntarily, apparently considering that Hawkins offered good prospects for profit. Between Cape Verde and Sierra Leone numerous rivers and inlets tumbled into the sea, and here it was that Hawkins hoped to gather the bulk of his slaves, using small, light-draught vessels and the ships' boats to explore the streams in search of native settlements or Portuguese craft carrying Negroes. While near to Cape Roxo at the end of November the English captured six Portuguese vessels in one river and seized their slaves. In another expedition the *Angel* took a caravel. According to Job Hortop, who wrote a narrative of the voyage at the end of 1590, Drake participated in one such foray in what is now the Cacheo River. It was not the happiest of adventures. Although a number of vessels were captured they contained no slaves, and the English were frustrated in an attack upon the Portuguese settlement of Cacheo. The *Swallow*, the *William and John* and Drake's caravel brought reinforcements up-river to join the advanced English already mustering for the assault, which was to consist of 240 men led by Robert Barrett, the master of the *Jesus*. Unfortunately, Negro levies turned out in support of the Portuguese and the raiders were beaten back. They had burned a few buildings and obtained some plunder, but four of their men were killed and they did not obtain a single slave.

The climax of these operations took place in January 1568, when Hawkins stormed a fortified Negro town on the island of Conga in the Tagarin River of Sierra Leone. At this point the commander had been unhappy with his progress, having only 150 slaves below hatches, and he was interested to receive an invitation from some chiefs of the Sapi peoples, who lived on the coast around the Sierra Leone and Scarcies rivers, to join them in an attack upon an enemy entrenched on Conga. The Sapi were being invaded by a Mande-speaking race from the east, in present-day Liberia, and it was a party of these tribesmen who inhabited the island town. Not slow to turn inter-tribal warfare to his advantage, Hawkins agreed to aid the chiefs against Conga providing he could keep the prisoners. Accordingly, Barrett was given ninety men to assist the Negroes in reducing Conga, but the English found it too strong, for it was surrounded by a log picket, defended by numerous warriors, and appeared capable of withstanding a long siege.

Hawkins had to come up-river with reinforcements. He directed his men to storm the defences and to fire the rude huts inside with torches carried on their pikes. As the shouting Englishmen breached Conga's walls, their Negro allies followed them inside, falling upon the defenders with a ferocity which amazed even the Europeans. The town was captured and large numbers of its occupants killed, some in battle, some by drowning as they sought to escape across the river, and some by the whim of the victorious natives. The conquering Negroes even ate a few of the prisoners. Nevertheless, the English secured about 250 slaves for the loss of only eight or nine of their men killed or fatally wounded, and now had enough blacks aboard to make the Atlantic passage.

By the beginning of February, therefore, Hawkins was much cheered. The first part of his voyage had been successfully completed, and with only slight casualties – a few killed in action, some lost by disease, and two drowned when a vessel was stoved by a hippopotamus. But as his squadron sailed westwards he may have been forgiven for frowning, for ahead lay only uncertainty. Times had obviously changed since Hawkins had last seen the West Indies, as he must have realized from what Lovell had described. A decidedly frosty reception might be in store for them. Colonial resistance to contraband trade had been stiffened, and local officials knew what penalties would be imposed for collusion with the English. Hawkins could still bank upon a demand for his wares, but he would have to contrive the means to sell them.

At first all seemed to go well. The English made their landfall at Dominica on 27 March, and after taking aboard fresh water and some wood they made their way to Margarita, where Hawkins announced that he was engaged in peaceful trade and exchanged some linen, cloth and iron for fresh victuals. No major dealing here, for it was at Borburata on the Main that he anticipated beginning his principal business. When he arrived off that port he approached the governor of the province by the agency of a courteous letter, in which the English acknowledged that Spain was enforcing its trade regulations but implied that they had come to these parts by misadventure and needed money to pay their soldiers. Would the governor be kind enough to let Hawkins sell a few wares and sixty Negroes so that he could overcome his difficulties? To soften the governor, the English commander hinted that a bribe would be available if negotiations were facilitated. The reply was disappointing:

*I am sure you know what straight charge the King of Spain, my master, hath given, that no stranger be licensed to traffic in no part of the India, the which if I should break, before my eyes I saw the governor, my predecessor, carried away prisoner into Spain for giving licence to the country to traffic with you at your last being here, an example for me that I fall not in the like or worse. I pray you therefore hold me excused.*[1]

In other words, the new governor had learned by the mistakes of the old, and Hawkins would have to look elsewhere. He stayed for a while at Borburata, and managed to supply a little cloth to Spaniards who cared less than the governor for the laws, but finally sailed at the beginning of June pondering whether this episode boded ill for what was to follow. After a brief landfall at the island of Curaçao, where the English secured further provisions, Hawkins turned to his second major prospect, Rio de la Hacha, where the treasurer, Miguel de Castellanos, had humiliated John Lovell two years before.

Drake must have relished returning to Rio de la Hacha, and perhaps Hawkins knew it. At any rate, he sent the *Judith* and the *Angel* ahead to prepare the way. Now, about this incident there is great confusion, but we must examine it because it concerns Francis Drake. The larger of the two ships was the *Judith*, and her captain was presumably the senior officer of the advance. It will be seen that in September, a few months later, the captain of the *Judith* was Drake, and because it was he who commanded the ship at that time writers have generally assumed that Drake was also in charge of her at Rio de la Hacha. This is likely, but the sources do not prove it. At the close of 1567 he commanded a Portuguese prize, as we have described, and obviously transferred to the *Judith* some time between then and the following September. But there is no indication of when that change took place. It could have been as late as August, when Hawkins may have reduced his force from ten vessels to eight, and if such was the case, Drake would not have commanded the *Judith* at Rio de la Hacha.

However, the behaviour of that little vessel at Rio de la Hacha so fits the personality of Drake that we are inclined to believe that it revealed his hand. This is how Job Hortop, then aboard the *Angel*, remembered it:

> He [Hawkins] sent from thence [Curaçao], the Angel and the Judith to Rio de la Hacha, where we anchored before the town. The Spaniards shot three pieces at us from the shore, whom we requited with two of ours, and shot through the Governor's house. We weighed anchor, and anchored again without the shot of the town; where we rode five days in despite of the Spaniards and their shot. In the mean space, there came a caravel of advice from Santo Domingo, which, with the Angel and Judith, we chased and drove to the shore. We fetched him from thence, in spite of two hundred Spaniard arquebus shot; and anchored again before the town, and rode there with them till our General's coming.[2]

Hortop was writing many years after the event, and his description may lack precision. There are substantial discrepancies between accounts of this arrival of the English at Rio de la Hacha, and a clear reconstruction is impossible. It seems that when the *Judith* and the *Angel* reached the port they applied for fresh water, but the Spaniards firmly refused it and opened fire, precipitating an exchange in which a ball penetrated

[1] Williamson, *Sir John Hawkins*, 518.
[2] Beazley, 225-6.

Castellanos's house, surely an action of Drake's if anything was! After retreating beyond the range of the harbour guns, the English virtually blockaded the port and drove a ship ashore, although rifling it they found nothing more valuable than some glasses and Indian pots.

Drake, if it was he, suffered some casualties during the proceedings. A participant's account in the Cotton manuscripts of the British Library implies that an Englishman was wounded by an arquebus ball as his ship traded shots with the enemy after the water was refused. However, some colleagues who were captured months later testified to the Spaniards that the English losses were incurred during the attack on the Spanish vessel. For example, Thomas Bennett deposed that 'in the port of Rio de la Hacha they found a Spanish ship the crew of which defended themselves; that in the fight the said Spaniards killed three Englishmen, among them the sergeant-major; that the crew of the said ship escaped on shore, which was very close; but the English found nothing on the said ship and left it.'[1]

Yet a further set of confessions made by English participants who were subsequently taken and interrogated maintained that the Spaniards drew first blood by firing with arquebuses upon two longboats sent ashore to request permission for the English to anchor, water and trade. In these statements the distinctions between the activities of the English advance party and of Hawkins's main squadron were blurred or eliminated entirely, so that it seemed that the longboats were dispatched by Hawkins himself with his full force in attendance and not merely by two forward ships. In one deposition that will stand for many, John Brown, a musician with Hawkins, declared:

> Thence they sailed to a port called Rio de la Hacha, on reaching which John Hawkins sent two boats on shore with his men to speak with the governor of the country requesting permission to provide themselves with water, but while the men were landing they were attacked by some Spaniards armed with arquebuses, who did not permit them to do so, firing at them and killing one of the Englishmen. Seeing this the party returned to the ships and informed John Hawkins of what had occurred, whereupon he put himself at the head of one hundred and eighty men, more or less, armed with arquebuses and crossbows, [and] went on shore.[2]

These latter accounts are almost certainly in error, and were probably deliberately distorted by the English to emphasize that they had only acted in self-defence at Rio de la Hacha, and that the Spaniards had unjustifiably fired upon small boats. It must be remembered that the witnesses who gave this information were in captivity and threatened with torture and execution, and their duplicity was eminently understandable. They disguised the fact that the *Judith* and the *Angel* had harassed the Spaniards for days before Hawkins arrived at the port, and provided an apology for his conduct.

Hawkins appeared off Rio de la Hacha on 10 June, and learned of the skirmishing between Castellanos and the English advance. In his characteristic manner Hawkins wrote to the royal treasurer reminding him of the loss he had suffered on account of

---

[1] Statement of Thomas Bennett, 1568, Conway Papers, Cambridge University Library, Add. MS 7257. This is substantially the same as an account given by William Sanders, to be found in the same volume.
[2] Statement of John Brown, 1569, *Ibid*, Add. MS 7260. Similar depositions, dated November or December 1569 were made by William Orlando, Michael Sol, George Fitzwilliam, Richard Temple, John Truslon, Thomas Stephens, Diego Hen, Anthony Goddard, Thomas Fowler, and others, for which see *Ibid*, Add. MSS 7258 and 7260.

Lovell's Negroes, but he did not pursue the matter. Instead he repeated what he had said at Borburata, asking licence to sell no more than sixty slaves so that he could pay his soldiers, and affecting that he had not intended visiting the West Indies but had been driven accidentally from his course. Perhaps he thought this letter could provide Castellanos with an excuse for dealing with the English, but the device was ineffective. The Spaniards dare not risk it. Castellanos had been sounding his trumpet about the defeat of Bontemps and Lovell, and he was not squandering his glory now. In effect he showed Hawkins the door.

The following day a number of small boats landed two hundred Englishmen, fully armed, who marched resolutely upon the town, towards the few modest fortifications that barred the road. Behind them the royal treasurer had assembled his forces, fewer than one hundred arquebusiers, twenty horsemen and some Negro and Indian auxiliaries. They were not a match for the English, and after firing a feeble volley which killed two of the attackers the Spaniards fled, scattering into the woods or racing into the town with their enemies on their heels. Once there, it was a simple matter for the English to occupy Rio de la Hacha and bring it under control.

What Hawkins had not reckoned upon, however, was the tenacity of Castellanos. The treasurer rallied his men, insisting that the loss of Rio de la Hacha made no difference to his decision. He set his followers to destroy any crops and provisions round about, so that the English could not use them, and when Hawkins threatened to burn the town if the Spaniards continued to obstruct him he sent an impudent note in reply, 'that though he saw all the India afire, he would give no licence.'[1] Angrily the English put torches to about twenty houses, including the governor's own.

For several days the deadlock continued. Hawkins held Rio de la Hacha, but could not obtain his licence, and though his purpose was trade the Spaniards refused to barter with him. Then an unexpected event changed the situation. A Negro, dissatisfied with his Spanish masters, defected to the English and promised that if they gave him his liberty he would guide them to the place where most of the Spaniards had hidden their valuables. He was as good as his word. In the night, about six miles from the town, the English discovered a cache of possessions, including some of the royal treasure, and triumphantly they bore it back in ox-carts. Here was the best bargaining tool Hawkins could wish for.

The townspeople soon forced Castellanos's hand. Alarmed by new English threats to carry all the captured property away, they clamoured for negotiations. 'Seeing this,' ran an official report, 'your Majesty's general, moved by his great commiseration for the said burghers, resolved to ransom them from the Englishman, that he might not carry out his cruel threat, and so they and all their goods and houses of the town which remained unburned, were ransomed for 4,000 pesos in gold.'[2] Discussions between Hawkins and Castellanos took place in an open plain, lest either side contemplated treachery, and some deal was made. Its nature is unclear. Castellanos maintained that he paid 4,000 pesos to prevent Hawkins killing some prisoners, destroying the rest of the town and stealing the valuables the English had discovered. Robert Barrett, a trusted officer of Hawkins, has it that the money was in payment for sixty Negroes

---

[1] Williamson, op. cit., 522.
[2] Lazaro de Vallejo Aldrete and Hernando Costilla to Philip II, 26 September, 1568, Wright, 116-19.

which the English delivered to Castellanos, and that such amicability developed between the two commanders that they exchanged gifts. In any case, the upshot was that Hawkins was able to unload two hundred of his slaves before sailing for Santa Marta at the beginning of July. And it is a mark against him that he left behind him not only a town fully chastened for the humiliation of Lovell, but the Negro whose flight to the English had facilitated their triumph. Instead of taking him along, Hawkins turned the wretched fellow over to the Spaniards, who forthwith put him to death.

Santa Marta was the next call. It was a small town of forty-five houses, too weak to resist, and in a conference ashore with the governor Hawkins agreed to feign an attack to provide the Spaniards with an excuse for trading. In accordance, 150 Englishmen disembarked, shot was fired over the houses and an old building was demolished. That done, Hawkins received his licence and trading was conducted with great courtesy by both parties, with 110 Negroes sold. The English believed that they could dispose of the remainder of their cargo at Cartagena, and they now set a course for that city on the Main. But it was far too powerful for Hawkins to coerce, and when he was again refused licence to trade he could do little more than protest with a futile demonstration. Exchanging fire with the shore batteries, he tarried thereabouts for a week, taking aboard some fresh water and provisions, but finding no further opportunities to sell his Negroes.

Hawkins probably doubted that any more could be done. It had not been easy dealing. Only Rio de la Hacha and Santa Marta had taken his slaves, and fifty-seven of them remained unsold in the English ships. But he also had aboard about £13,500 in gold, silver and pearls, and that was probably enough to yield a profit for the voyage. It was time to go home. The Frenchman who had voluntarily joined Hawkins at Cape Verde now went his own way, and the English scuttled one of their Portuguese prizes, no longer needed now that so many of the Negroes had been sold. With his eight remaining ships, the Jesus, Minion, William and John, Swallow, Judith, Angel, Gratia Dei and a caravel, John Hawkins turned on the homeward run, sailing northwards to pass around Cuba by the Yucatan and Florida channels and so into the Atlantic.

In any deep-sea voyage the weather is apt to overturn the most careful of calculations, to destroy a schedule or throw months, even years, of toil into jeopardy in an instant. The perils of the stormy tropical seas of the West Indies, where tempests might be whipped up with little warning, had brought disaster to many of the old-time sailing ships, as they do now to far better founded and sturdier vessels. Such an unforeseen trial now enveloped Hawkins's expedition, as it tried to weather Cuba, and wrought a decisive change in the English fortunes. On 12 August their ships were gripped by a violent storm.

The William and John was separated from her consorts, and eventually made her way alone to England, but the rest of the squadron ran helplessly before the gale, deep into the Gulf of Mexico where none aboard had ever been. For eight days the tempest scourged the ships, torturing the aged Jesus and prising open her seams so that on both sides of her stern the planks 'did open and shut with every sea.'[1] The gaps were such that fish were found swimming in her ballast. Hawkins's men returned to the work of

[1] Williamson, op. cit., 530.

the previous October, labouring desperately at the pumps and plugging leaks with cloth, and they cut away some of the ship's upper works to relieve her straining timbers. When the storm slackened, Hawkins found himself in a strange sea in need of a harbour where he could repair the broken *Jesus*, at least sufficiently for her to make the voyage home.

The English sighted land, and groped along the coast searching for shelter but finding none. On 12 September they happened upon a Spanish vessel, and inquired whether there was a port nearby. The Spaniard was bound for San Juan d'Ulua in Mexico, was the reply, but Hawkins frowned when he further learned that the annual *flota* from Seville was due to arrive there at the end of the month. The English were upon illicit business and in a bad way. Hawkins had no wish to encounter a powerful force of the king's ships in this condition, and he asked if there was any other port to leeward. There was not. Hawkins had no choice. Anxious at heart, he set a course for San Juan d'Ulua.

It was a modest enough place, although it served as the outlet for Vera Cruz, 15 or so miles away. The port was nothing more than a roadstead, about 250 yards long, running between the mainland and a low-lying bank of shingle off shore. There was little to justify San Juan d'Ulua's being called a town. On the island was a battery, and a chapel tended the few seamen and labourers whose huts were scattered around both mainland and bank. When the English arrived on 15 September they saw eight Spanish ships in the roadstead, their crews ashore. Hawkins was relieved. He had detained the few Spanish merchantmen he had encountered on the way to San Juan d'Ulua to prevent them alerting the authorities there, and he had clearly arrived before the *flota*. With luck the English might complete their repairs and leave before the Spanish fleet appeared.

Francis Drake had never seen San Juan d'Ulua before, but he would remember it all his life. Now he saw a small boat pulling out towards the English ships, aboard her the Deputy Governor of Vera Cruz, Martin de Marçana, and its treasurer, Francisco de Bustamante. They had hurried to the port to welcome the *flota*, not because its arrival was always an event of importance, but because in this instance it carried the new Viceroy of Mexico, Don Martin Enriquez, one of the two most powerful men in the Americas, come to take up his post. When the Spaniards saw Hawkins's ships they felt sure they were the first of the *flota*, and it was only when their boat got too close to the newcomers to flee that they noticed the faded royal standards of England at the mast-heads of the *Jesus* and the *Minion*. The Spanish party was brought aboard the flagship, where Hawkins received it politely and explained that he intended no harm and would leave as soon as he had refitted his squadron. In the meantime the Spaniards must remain with him for safe-keeping. The next day the *Jesus* led the English ships line ahead into the anchorage, provoking a brief surge of dismay among the observers, both afloat and ashore. It was not without difficulty that Hawkins was able to reassure them. He announced that he would pay for all necessaries consumed by his squadron, and released all his prisoners barring the treasurer to betoken his goodwill. And then he took control of the port, and settled down to preparing his ships for sea.

Dawn on 17 September brought a different prospect indeed, for thirteen sails could be seen out to sea – the Mexican *flota* was approaching already! Aboard was the viceroy, Don Martin Enriquez, but the command of the fleet, two warships and eleven armed merchantmen, was in the custody of Don Francisco de Luxan. It was a formidable array, greater than Hawkins had at his own disposal. The *Jesus*, his largest vessel, had twenty-six mounted guns; the *Minion* might hold her own; but the other English ships were small. The *Gratia Dei* had only eight guns mounted, and the *Swallow* and the Portuguese caravel some eleven between them, while Drake's *Judith* was so diminutive that witnesses later spoke of her as a 'tender'. Hawkins delayed not an instant. He deployed a force to occupy the island, and ordered new batteries to be erected upon it, using the Spanish guns available to enfilade the approaches to the roadstead. In the meantime the English ships were prepared for action, as a Spaniard remarked:

> Aboard these vessels they had many and very choice pieces of heavy bronze and iron ordnance, trained and loaded with powder and iron shot. Deponent saw the pieces loaded. He also saw many pikes and arquebuses and targets and corselets brought up and laid out upon the quarter decks and along the midship gangways of these ships. He saw many archers with bows and arrows and heavy stones take their places in the rigging. He saw them there, armed and ready to take either offensive or defensive. They made ready with such brevity and despatch that by 11 o'clock in the morning they had finished the land works on the island and cleared their ships for action.[1]

Hawkins believed that he had the strength to keep the *flota* out of harbour, but he could not be sure, and in any case he dared not do so. Without shelter from wind and weather, the Spanish fleet would likely have been scattered, and possibly shipwrecked. It would have created an outcry in Spain, and one the queen would have found difficult to explain. Rather than risk that, Hawkins determined to bargain with the Spaniards, trusting that he could bring them to terms – admission to the port in return for an armistice to last as long as Hawkins's stay. Consequently, he sent forward a boat with a Spanish official, Antonio Delgadillo, to apprise the *flota* of his position and to learn if the viceroy was willing to discuss terms of entry. Hawkins contended, with less than the truth, that he had harmed no Spanish citizen, but that after trading slaves and merchandise he had been driven into San Juan d'Ulua by bad weather. As soon as he had refitted his squadron he intended to leave.

Thus, within minutes of arriving in his viceroyalty, Enriquez was presented with a difficult problem. He was angry, perhaps even humiliated, that contrabanders should dictate terms to him from his own port. It was also his duty to destroy the English, who by Spanish law had no right to be in the Gulf of Mexico. But discussing the matter with his officers, Enriquez was cautious. It would be inadvisable to force his way into San Juan d'Ulua against the English guns, but nor could he permit his deeply laden merchantmen to lie exposed to adverse winds. In the afternoon Delgadillo returned to Hawkins with a message from the viceroy. Enriquez wanted to know the English terms. It took until the next day, and much shuttling to and fro by emissaries, to determine their nature. Both sides gave ten hostages to secure the conduct of the other, and Hawkins was to be allowed to complete his preparations unmolested. As another guarantee of their own safety, the English would continue to occupy the island and its batteries for the duration of their visit. This settled, the *flota* was free to enter. The weather was poor, and for three days the Spaniards lingered off shore, but eventually they crowded into the narrow anchorage. The ships sat uncomfortably side by side,

---

[1] Deposition of Francisco de Bustamante, 30 September, 1568, Wright, 146-52.

their bowsprits overhanging the island, within point-blank range of each other, the *Minion* nearest the Spanish vessels and the *Jesus* next to her.

On the face of it both parties were friendly, and ashore Englishman mixed with Spaniard, Protestant with Catholic, whiling away hours in polite and curious conversation. Nonetheless, treachery was afoot, for Enriquez had no intention of honouring his pact with Hawkins. He conspired with his officers upon the means by which the hated Lutherans could be destroyed, and a secret summons was passed to Vera Cruz calling 120 soldiers to San Juan d'Ulua. On the night of 21 September they were smuggled aboard the Spanish ships. A big merchantman lay nearest the English vessels, and Enriquez and De Luxan had it filled with 150 arquebusiers, rowed silently in the darkness from the other craft. Surreptitiously, the Spaniards also prepared the head ropes of the hulk so that at a given signal it could be hauled closer to the *Minion*. Enriquez was planning a soldiers' battle. At a signal his men would scramble aboard Hawkins's ships and take them in hand-to-hand fighting, while simultaneously Captain Delgadillo and Captain Pedro de Yebra would lead another force in an assault upon the English batteries on the island.

The English were not entirely deceived by these preparations. Although the greater perfidy was yet unknown to them, they had become alarmed at suspicious movements on the part of the Spaniards, and may have pondered the meaning of new gun ports being cut in some of the enemy ships. In fact, Hawkins was so concerned that on the morning of 23 September he twice sent Robert Barrett to Enriquez's flagship to complain. The first time Barrett returned with reassurances, but upon his second visit Enriquez had the Englishman seized and imprisoned in the hold. The viceroy was about to attack, and needed no further excuses.

Spanish accounts declare that their signal was given too early. De Luxan, who chose to command from the hulk closest to the English, the same that had been stealthily filled with soldiers, was supposed to signal the flagship that he was close to the *Minion* by waving a white napkin. In the event, it was a subordinate, Juan de Ubilla, who gave the signal – prematurely, because (according to his story) the English had realized what was happening and, indeed, had fired an arrow at Ubilla as he stood on the deck of the hulk. Anyhow, the napkin was seen aboard the Spanish flagship and Enriquez ordered his trumpeter to sound the attack.

The Englishmen heard that trumpet too. To their dismay they saw soldiers massing on the decks of the nearest Spanish ship, ready to board, drawing steadily closer to the *Minion* as the Spaniards heaved upon their hawser. Rowing boats appeared from various quarters, all bristling with armed men, some pulling frenziedly to the island, where the Spaniards quickly overran the English positions and cut down the defenders, and some bringing more boarders to attempt the sides of the *Minion* and the *Jesus*.

Hawkins called to his trumpeter, Thomas Johns, to signal a stand to arms, and as the enemy clambered over the sides of the *Minion* called to his men to repel the boarders. 'God and St George!' he shouted. 'Upon these traitorous villains, and rescue the *Minion*! I trust in God the day shall be ours!'[1] It took reinforcements from the *Jesus* to expel the Spaniards from the *Minion*. Once the ship had been cleared the English cut

[1] Beazley, 229.

the head fasts of both the *Minion* and the *Jesus* and hauled on their stern fasts to pull away from the Spanish vessels, dropping launches in the gap that opened so that their adversaries could not close again.

A thunderous cannonade then erupted on both sides. Ashore, the Spaniards turned the batteries upon the English ships with devastating effect, but the Spanish ships themselves proved no match for the queen's vessels, despite the heavy firing at close range. The guns of the *Jesus* and the *Minion* were trained not on the crowded hulk but upon the next two ships in the line, the Spanish flagship and its *capitana*, the only genuine fighting ships in the *flota*. They hulled the flagship on the waterline and saw her settle lower in the roadstead, the greater part of her crew abandoning her to flounder ashore, leaving Enriquez and only a few of his followers aboard. The vice-admiral's *capitana* suffered a direr fate. An English shot exploded a powder keg and the vessel burst into flames. Within a short time she had burned to the waterline with a loss of thirty-four men. Once the warships had been put out of action, the Spanish merchantmen received greater punishment and one of them also sank.

The shore batteries, for their part, were now ripping holes in the smaller English ships. The small *Angel* sank, and the *Swallow*, the *Gratia Dei* and the Portuguese caravel were battered into submission. Only Drake's *Judith*, which was virtually unarmed, got clear, probably because she was the outermost ship of the English line and the furthest from danger. From his position of safety Drake could see the Spanish guns turning upon the stricken *Jesus*, but he was powerless to help and could only stand by ready to move in as opportunity served.

The *Jesus* had already been in a poor condition before the attack, but as the batteries on the island found their range they riddled the great ship with shot, shredding her masts and sails to pieces. Job Hortop remembered Hawkins directing the fight from her deck:

> Our general courageously cheered up his soldiers and gunners, and called to Samuel his page for a cup of beer; who brought it to him in a silver cup. And he drinking to all the men willed 'the gunners to stand by their ordnance lustily like men!' He had no sooner set the cup out of his hand but a demi-culverin shot struck the cup and a cooper's plane that stood by the mainmast, and ran out on the other side of the ship; which nothing dismayed our general, for he ceased not to encourage us, saying, 'Fear nothing! For God who hath preserved me from this shot will also deliver us from these traitors and villains!'[1]

Yet Hawkins knew he could not save the *Jesus* as she agonized beneath the shot. His priority must now be the protection of the *Minion* and the removal of men, provisions and treasure from the doomed flagship. He signalled the *Minion* to shelter behind the *Jesus* and summoned Drake to bring in the *Judith*. Drake did as he was instructed, and received as many stores and men as he could, and perhaps a little of the treasure. Then he withdrew from gun range and allowed the *Minion* to take his place. 'At this stage of the fight,' recalled a soldier of the *Jesus*, 'John Hawkins went below where the ten Spanish hostages were detained and told them that since he had given his word to let them go in peace and free to return to their own land he would keep it, even though their Viceroy had broken his plighted faith of a gentleman, wherefore he wished them

[1] *Ibid*, 230.

farewell and Godspeed, and with this he left them in the disabled English flagship.'[1]

Returning to supervise the evacuation of his men to the *Minion*, Hawkins was greeted by the sight of another and potentially overwhelming danger, a fireship which the Spaniards had set adrift to bear upon the injured English vessels. The men of the *Minion* saw it too, closing upon them ominously, and, exhausted as they were by hours of hard fighting, their nerve now reached breaking point. They were overcome with what Hawkins called 'a marvellous fear'. Casting off the lines, they pulled the *Minion* away from the *Jesus* while their desperate comrades were still crowding upon the flagship's deck waiting to be taken off. Suddenly it was every man for himself, as the crew of the *Jesus* plunged towards the departing *Minion* in an attempt to get aboard. Some, like Hawkins himself, leaped from the bulwarks of the *Jesus* on to the *Minion* as she moved away. Some fell short, into the water. Some, like the boy Paul Hawkins, his arms clutching a rich goblet and some fine crystal plate set with precious stones and pearls, hesitated, frightened to jump, and were left behind. A few managed to follow the *Minion* in a rowing boat; most of those remaining on the *Jesus*, along with forty-five unsold slaves and the Spanish hostages, escaped the fireship, which was ultimately ineffective, but fell into the hands of the victorious Spaniards.

Towards evening, after a six-hour duel, the guns of San Juan d'Ulua fell silent. The *Minion* was sorely wounded and both she and the *Judith* were overcrowded. They lay beyond the range of the batteries, their men labouring to ready them for sea. Behind, the Spaniards chose not to pursue them. They had lost their warships, and their merchantmen were deeply laden and not a few damaged. Both sides were exhausted, and, balefully eyeing each other, gathered themselves for the next moves.

What happened next has never been adequately explained. Daylight revealed the tattered *Minion* alone at the mouth of the harbour, but of Drake and the *Judith* there was not a sign. Hawkins did not doubt that Drake had deserted him, and he held to this opinion after hearing his kinsman's explanation many months later. So bitter was he that when he wrote a narrative of the expedition, published in 1569, he had hard words for Drake, although he did not charge him by name. 'So,' he wrote, 'with the *Minion* only, and the *Judith*, a small bark of 50 tons, we escaped, which bark, the same night, forsook us in our great misery.'[2] Whatever Francis Drake said in his defence has not been preserved, and we are left to speculate about his reasons for leaving Hawkins. The weather conditions on the night after the battle offer part of the answer. After the engagement the wind was offshore, and both Hawkins and Drake used it to work further outside the range of the enemy guns, but the wind seems to have intensified in the night, threatening to run the two English ships upon the reefs about the coast. Drake, whose experience in West Indian waters was negligible, probably put out to sea where he was safe. In the morning he no doubt worried about Hawkins. Had he been shipwrecked? Was he still alive? It should have been Drake's business to find out, but his resolution, as far as we know for the first time, failed him. The *Judith* was certainly overcrowded, and probably under-victualled, and the voyage ahead was daunting for a man who had never guided a ship across the Atlantic before. The measure of Drake's

---

[1] Statement of Anthony Goddard, November 1569, Conway Papers, Cambridge University Library, Add. MS 7260.

[2] Beazley, 101.

difficulty is indicated by the fact that, although his bark was known to be a fast ship, she took four months to reach Plymouth. It is, therefore, conceivable that Drake felt his first duty was to bring his company home, and he must be complimented for doing so, but when he anchored in Plymouth on 20 January, 1569, he must have wondered how he would be judged if Hawkins ever returned.

The defeat at San Juan d'Ulua was not the turning point in Anglo-Spanish relations some historians have depicted, but it was decisive in the lives of the surviving English commanders. It marked the end of John Hawkins's slaving voyages. When Drake left him he was in a desperate position, with two hundred men crowded on the broken Minion and scarcely any food to maintain them. During the few days that followed the battle, the first fought by English-speaking people in the New World, the crew subsisted on what they could find, vermin from the hold, parrots, even hides which the men chewed to nourish their fragile bodies. So bleak seemed the prospect of surviving the homeward run that half the men asked to be put ashore; they would rather confront the Indians, the wilderness and the Spaniards.

With the remainder of his men, dying by the dozens along the way, Hawkins limped home. There was little to console him, although much, perhaps most, of the treasure had been saved in the Minion, enough to meet the costs of the voyage. But all but two of his ships had been lost, and further opportunities for trading in the West Indies dissipated, while between two and three hundred Englishmen never saw their native land again. Some starved in the forests or were murdered by Indians, and others, possibly the least fortunate, fell into the hands of the Spaniards, either at San Juan d'Ulua or after leaving the Minion. The Inquisition was not famed for its mercies, and the reports of the examinations of Hawkins's seamen make the grimmest reading. Most of those captured died in prison or in servitude. There was William Orlando of London, who died in the dungeons of Seville; Robert Barrett of Saltash, who perished in the flames of the Seville auto da fe; David Alexander, a Cornishman, who loitered in the isolation of a monastery; William Collins from Oxford, who laboured at the oars of the Spanish galleys; Michael Morgan of St Bridgets, Cardiff, who was tortured, whipped with two hundred lashes, and also sentenced to the galleys; George Ribley from Gravesend, who was strangled and his body burned at the stake . . . and many, many more. Sometimes over the years their stories filtered back to England to grieving relatives and friends, reopening the wounds of San Juan d'Ulua. Hawkins was close to despair when he brought his handful of survivors into Mount's Bay in Cornwall on 25 January, 1569. Reflecting upon his adventures, he told William Cecil that 'if I should write of all our calamities I am sure a volume as great as the Bible will scantly suffice.'[1]

The battle changed Francis Drake too. He was as yet a minor figure, even among the West Country seamen; asked by the Spaniards to name the captains of Hawkins's expedition, a captured Englishman, Noah Sergeant, did not even mention him. He had probably invested his small means in the slaving voyages, but he owed his current command to his family connexion with Hawkins rather than to wealth or even ability. Now even that patronage was doubtful. Lovell's voyage had been a commercial flop, but Hawkins's was a naval disaster, and Drake had barely received a command than he

---

[1] Hawkins to Cecil, Williamson, op. cit., 216.

had tarnished the little reputation he had.

But for all that Drake emerged a new man from the carnage and smoke of San Juan d'Ulua. He had reached a crossroads. Hitherto, his memories of the reign of Philip and Mary, the story his father had told of the family's flight from the Catholic insurgents in Devon, and his Protestant background had left him with little liking for the enemies of his faith and his country. He, like his shipmates, had joined in the extreme denunciation of the Pope heard aboard the old *Jesus*. All this was now sharpened by a deep sense of personal grievance. First there had been Lovell's discomfiture, and now far more mortifying the treachery of the Viceroy of New Spain. Drake had seen the fruits of a year's toil wither before Spanish gunfire, the English ships sink or surrender; and he had fled for his life. Good friends had died, and for all Drake knew as the *Judith* made for home Hawkins and the men of the *Minion* were among them. It can hardly be doubted that as he struggled over the wintry Atlantic swells Drake was coming to an important decision. The day of the contraband trade was over, smouldering in the ruins of that Mexican roadstead. It was time for another way, Drake's way. For the rest of his life Francis Drake pictured himself an avenger, bent upon rewarding the treachery of Don Martin Enriquez. It must have seemed a futile, an almost presumptuous decision at the time, but it put a fire into the obscure little sea captain, defeated and dishonoured. On the pitching *Judith*, brooding upon his misfortunes, Francis Drake declared war upon the King of Spain.

CHAPTER FOUR

# DRAKE'S WAR

Some think it true to say he did it in the Devil's name,
And none ever since could do the like again;
But those are all deceived, why should they doubt it,
They know each year there's some that go about it.

Anonymous verse on Drake, 1619

WHEN DRAKE REACHED PLYMOUTH ON THE NIGHT OF 20 JANUARY, 1569, HE hurried to William Hawkins to inform him of the fate of his brother's expedition. Hawkins listened gravely to the story the young captain brought him. He had already been disturbed by the blackest of rumours, a report that his brother had been trapped by the Spaniards in the Indies and killed, and Drake's inability to confirm the survival of the crippled *Minion* must have stimulated those fears anew.

Upon one matter Drake and William Hawkins agreed: the treachery of Don Martin Enriquez must receive its answer. Wasting little time, Hawkins wrote two letters, one to Elizabeth's Privy Council and the other to William Cecil, the queen's Secretary of State, informing them of Drake's return and soliciting redress. He suggested that either the queen issue commissions of reprisal authorizing Hawkins to attack Spanish shipping to recoup his losses, or that some of Spain's property then at Plymouth be sequestered in lieu. To colour his argument, Hawkins gave both letters to Drake and ordered him to carry them to London, where he could personally detail the affair of San Juan d'Ulua to the government.

As he rode along muddy tracks and roads to the capital, young Drake must also have pondered the events that had passed in England during the years he had been at sea, events that fitted comfortably with the plans for vengeance that were forming within him. The first gusts of a new wind were now troubling England, a wind that would create a storm large enough to blow the Armada to Albion's shores. In the recent past, the English had looked upon France, not Spain, as their traditional enemy. For centuries they had been stirred by stories of battles across the Channel, stories of Crécy, Poitiers and Agincourt. The oldest of them could remember the English invasion of north-eastern France in 1522, and rather more old King Henry's capture of Boulogne over twenty years later. Even Drake's generation could tell of the loss of Calais, England's last foothold on the Continent. Then, soon after Elizabeth had succeeded to the throne, Anglo-French rivalry had assumed a decidedly threatening character, for Elizabeth's cousin Mary, as the granddaughter of Henry VIII's eldest sister second in line to the English throne, was not only Queen of Scotland but also became Queen of France by her short-lived marriage to Francis II. Flanked as they were by two potentially hostile powers – Scotland and France – boasting a Catholic queen capable of plotting the death of the one person who stood between her and the throne of England, Drake's countrymen could be forgiven for uncertainty. They had feared for the integrity of their realm, for the life of their queen, and for their newly established Protestant faith.

But those dangers had diminished. Francis II had died, French troops had been expelled from Scotland, and after 1562 France herself was tormented by civil war. In Scotland a Protestant regime had been installed, and Mary herself was a prisoner in England, a focus of Catholic plots still, but not the danger she had been. English people had begun to realize that another and greater danger than France was clouding their horizon: Spain. Formerly there had been much to restrict hostility between Spain and England. They both distrusted France, and regarded each other as potential allies against the House of Valois. Nor did Philip wish to further French interests by raising Mary to the throne of England. He consistently blocked the Pope's efforts to excommunicate Elizabeth for that very reason. Then, too, England and Spain shared a profitable trade, and both had too many commitments elsewhere to relish additional military burdens: Elizabeth had confronted Scotland, France and internal rebellion, and the conquest of Ireland was going badly; Philip's brow was already wrinkled by the problems in the Netherlands and the Mediterranean. Yet despite all this, the bonds between England and Spain were weakening, even before Hawkins and Drake had left for the Guinea coast in 1567.

One difficulty, indeed, had been Hawkins's activities in the West Indies, which infringed the monopoly Spain claimed over that area. England did not recognize the sweeping nature of those pretensions, but the queen accepted that effective occupation and control of a region by a power did confer sovereignty. There was no doubt that Spain controlled the West Indies. However, did this justify her shutting the ports of those regions to foreign commerce? After all, both England and Spain permitted the vessels of other countries to traffic in their harbours in Europe. Why should these freedoms not be extended to the West Indies? Nevertheless, the queen and her Privy Council were not indifferent to the discomfort that Hawkins caused the Spanish Crown, and both Elizabeth and Cecil had promised – faithlessly as it turned out – that when Hawkins sailed on his next voyage in 1567 he would not visit the West Indies.

But Hawkins's voyages were not the main cause of the deteriorating relations between Spain and England. Far more serious was the problem of the Spanish Netherlands. There Protestantism was growing apace, hand in hand with native intolerance of Spanish rule, and in the 1560s much of the unrest was blamed upon the English traders who put into Antwerp. Annoyed also by restrictions that England had placed on the import of goods from the Netherlands, Spain's governess there imposed a temporary ban on English cloth entering Antwerp. Antwerp was still the most important outlet for England's major export, woollen cloth, and the ban brought immediate retaliation. By the end of 1564 England and the Netherlands had each closed their ports to the other and trade between the two was suspended.

The continuing crisis in the Netherlands and the turbulence of Spain's relations with her subjects in the Low Countries in turn weakened the economic links between England and Spain. As English merchants began to transfer their trade elsewhere, to Emden, Cologne, Frankfurt, and ultimately to Hamburg, Elizabeth's dependence upon both the Netherlands and Spain declined accordingly. Goodwill between England and Spain was also threatened by the presence of Philip's army in the Netherlands. Although charged merely with reducing those provinces to submission, the Duke of Alba was uncomfortably close to the English coast and revealed himself a man of ruthless resolution. In a six-year reign Alba's 'Council of Troubles' purged the Netherlands of over a thousand people suspected of disaffection, and has gone down in history as the 'Council of Blood'. Some Englishmen wondered whether Alba had it in mind to bring such terrors across the English Channel.

In November 1568, a few months before Drake's return from San Juan d'Ulua, five Spanish ships laden with chests containing £85,000 worth of treasure for Alba's soldiers in the Netherlands ran into dirty weather and Huguenot privateers in the English Channel. Four of them took refuge in Plymouth and a fifth in Southampton. Everyone knew the importance of those ships to Alba. The duke's soldiers had not been paid for months and were growing mutinous, and attempts to raise money by taxing the Netherlands were even then stiffening opposition to Spanish rule. The cargoes of the treasure ships were moved ashore for safety, while the Spanish ambassador to England, Guerau de Spes, begged Elizabeth, as the ruler of a friendly nation, to supply an escort which would enable Alba's money to reach its destination. The queen had her own ideas, however. She resented the pressure that the Spaniards levied on her by the arrest of English merchants in Madrid and Brussels, and when she learned that the Spanish money actually belonged to Genoese bankers who were loaning it to Alba she demonstrated her defiance. Her own government always needed money, and if the treasure was merely up for loan, she would borrow it herself! It would not proceed to Alba at all.

Whatever Elizabeth was playing at, she succeeded in raising tension to a new threshold. Alba's alternative to securing his treasure ships was a tax in the Netherlands that would multiply the outcry he had been sent to suppress. Just after Christmas, encouraged by the inflammatory De Spes, Alba delivered a counterstroke by seizing all English goods and ships in the Netherlands. However, there was a considerable amount of property and shipping belonging to the Netherlands in England at the time, and Elizabeth quickly replied by impounding it. The final round of the tit-for-tat reprisals was an embargo on English vessels in Spanish ports, but Elizabeth undoubtedly had the best of the exchange: she still had Alba's money, and with French privateers in the Channel, more Spanish ships were likely to fall into her hands.

Into all this came Francis Drake, fuming over the battle at San Juan d'Ulua and making his first appearance at court in his search for redress. Drake's plans seemed to fit into the deterioration of Anglo-Spanish relations, and he probably expected some support from the government. Still, the commissions of reprisal William Hawkins had requested were not issued. Perhaps in listening to this small, stocky sea captain from Devon, Cecil, always a prudent politician, sensed that he was dealing with men too full-blooded and bold for the sensitive situation in which England had found herself. Was it worth, in these circumstances, stretching Spain's patience further? As for San Juan d'Ulua, Cecil must have remembered the worthless promises that the queen had made to De Spes that Hawkins would not even enter the West Indies. If the destruction of Hawkins's flotilla was unfortunate, it was also embarrassing, for the English had been found red-handed where the queen had promised they would not sail.

Even when John Hawkins himself arrived in London in February 1569 to throw his influence into the argument, no commissions of reprisals were made out. It was not so much San Juan d'Ulua that marked the turning point in England's relations with Spain, but the matter of the Duke of Alba's treasure, and Hawkins's disaster did not affect the queen's policy. The significance of the battle lies rather in the impact it had in the West Country, upon the mariners who survived it, and upon the families who mourned the loss of their relatives and friends. It was they who would lead the onslaught against Spain, and they who were to find in Francis Drake their boldest leader.[1]

In February, while Alba's representative was on his way to England to negotiate an end to the trade deadlock, Drake was noting impatiently that his country's dispute with Spain had not immediately advanced his cause. Mounting dissatisfaction with the aftermath of San Juan d'Ulua hardened his resolve to attack Spain, with or without the government's permission. Years afterwards Drake spoke often of that Mexican harbour in which Hawkins's squadron had been destroyed, and he swore that he would recoup all that the English had lost there. The remarks seem incongruent in that much of the treasure acquired came home in the *Minion*, but losses there certainly had been in goods, ships and men. Drake exaggerated them in justification of his raids on the Spaniards, but probably what hurt and stirred him was less the material damage done by Enriquez than the viceroy's treachery itself. Memories of the battle and of the gruelling voyage home, the horrors he imagined must have been suffered by the prisoners left behind and uncertainty about their fate all exacerbated Drake's indignation. Spain was not only the enemy of his God and his country; she had treacherously destroyed his friends, and he himself had been fortunate to escape with his life.

The reunion of Drake and John Hawkins was not easy for either party. Hawkins must have learned of Drake's return from his brother, William, and presumably also of the younger man's version of the parting of the *Judith* and the *Minion*. Later, he must have also listened to Drake explain himself, but he was not convinced, and as we have seen the words of his narrative of the voyage, published in 1569, contained the thinly veiled charge of desertion. It cannot have pleased Drake that the first time his actions appeared in print they were tarred with inconstancy, irresolution, perhaps even cowardice. As far as we know nothing further passed between Hawkins and Drake about the incident, but it was remembered by others, and used against Drake by his enemies in later years.

Drake's movements during most of 1569 are unknown. We are encouraged to believe that he may have been busy somewhere, because when the High Court of Admiralty assembled in March and April to hear evidence from survivors of Haw-

---

[1] The best discussion of Elizabeth's foreign policy is Wernham, *Before the Armada*.

kins's voyage Drake was not called. It must be assumed that he was already planning his first reprisal against Spain, and that he was currying assistance from the maritime community in Devon. When the records reveal him to us again, however, Drake had a softer purpose – marriage.

Mary Newman is a shadowy figure, and very little of her life and personality have come down to us. A tradition asserts that she was Cornish, and today a cottage in Culver Road, Saltash, purports to be her birthplace, although the local parish registers do not bear out the claim.[1] Drake's cousin, John, told the Spaniards that 'he understands that the said Mary is a native of London', and it may have been so.[2] Francis married Mary at the newly built church of St Budeaux, near Plymouth, on 4 July, 1569, and the registers of that parish suggest that although the Newmans were then living there they had not been born in the parish. There are no baptisms, but the marriages of probable sisters of Mary are recorded: Maude to Lyon Worth in November 1552, Margaret to John Bodman in April 1560, Joanne to Robert Newman in August 1565 and Eleanor to John Sanders in September 1571. Margaret and John Bodman had at least one son, Zachary.[3]

Mary was Drake's wife for twelve years, but many of them she would spend alone while her husband was at sea. She lived long enough to become Lady Drake, but was probably at heart an unsophisticated girl from a humble background, a wife for an unknown sailor with a doubtful reputation. They had no children, although Drake seems to have wanted a son if we can judge from the patronage he bestowed on his young relatives. Soon he was to take as his protégé his cousin John Drake. Later it would be one Jonas Bodenham.

The marriages of Mary's sisters seem to shed new light on some of Drake's own relationships. They document another possible link between the Drake and Hawkins clans, for Maude Newman married Lyon Worth in 1552 and Stephen Hawkyn married Margery Worth in June 1555. In particular, however, Margaret Newman's marriage to John Bodman suggests a plausible solution to the mystery of Jonas Bodenham. During the admiral's later years Bodenham is rather like Drake's shadow, always unobtrusive but always there. Wherever we find Drake we are sure to find Bodenham, handling his master's financial affairs, witnessing his property transactions, serving as his lieutenant aboard the *Revenge* during his climactic duel with the Armada, succeeding to the captaincy of his ship *Defiance* after his death. Thomas Drake, Francis's brother, would later make the most serious allegations against him but Francis seems to have trusted him implicitly.

Although Bodenham was in Drake's service at least as early as 1581 we know next to nothing about his origins. In legal documents of 1597 and 1598 he describes himself as a gentleman. But at the same time Thomas Drake asserted that he was of mean parentage and that his brother had trained him 'up from his [Bodenham's] infancy in his own service', he 'having no other relief or maintenance.'[4]

---

[1] Parish registers of St Stephen's by Saltash, Cornwall Record Office, Truro.
[2] Deposition of John Drake, 1587, Eliott-Drake, *Family and Heirs of Sir Francis Drake*, 1: 381.
[3] Parish registers of St Budeaux, Plymouth, West Devon Record Office, Plymouth, 542/1. The marriage of Drake and Mary Newman was rediscovered by Vincent, 'Sir Francis Drake'.

Now the name of Margaret Newman's husband is written quite distinctly in the St Budeaux register as 'Bodman'. And Bodenham's name is often found abbreviated in contemporary records to 'Bodnam'. There is a strong possibility, then, that Jonas was John Bodman's son and Francis Drake's nephew. If further research could substantiate this identification it would solve many problems. It would explain, for example, why Francis took care of this penniless boy and why, if Bodenham abused his master's trust as grossly as the allegations of Thomas Drake suggest, he was so reluctant to admit to any fault in him.

Drake settled with his new bride in the town of Plymouth. His name appears in a list of freemen of the borough, dated 1570, the year after his wedding, an entry which tells us not only that he resided in the town but also that he commanded the right to trade enjoyed by all freemen.[1] A deed of six years later perhaps pinpoints the location of his property, for it announces that Drake, now styled a 'merchant', held land once known as Dubernon's chantry on the north side of Notte Street, Plymouth. Probably it consisted of a tenement and garden, as did the adjoining property which John and Charles Amadas sold to Stephen Wake in 1576, and is identifiable with the house later mentioned as belonging to Drake at the time he set out for his voyage around the world in 1577.[2]

At the time of his marriage Francis Drake was probably approaching thirty. Of no more than average height for the time, he was nevertheless strong and sturdy and he had a blustering cheerfulness that many found engaging. He was a skilled and experienced mariner. His complexion betrayed the weathers of many climates. Above all, he was bold, self-reliant and confident, a man well capable of using his own initiative. And if he styled himself a merchant it was certainly not trade that he had in mind.

In 1570 Drake's activities in Plymouth were interrupted by a raid that he made into the West Indies, the first known to have been conducted by an Englishman. It has been assumed that the Hawkins brothers put up the money for his ships, stores and equipment, but there is no evidence that this was the case. Drake used only two vessels, the *Swan* of 25 tons' burden and the *Dragon*, which was unlikely to have been much larger. Possibly, Drake outfitted the expedition himself, alone or in conjunction with its other leaders, using money he must have obtained from the slaving voyage with Hawkins. As for the seamen he needed, probably no more than fifty accompanied him, and it would have been compatible with the practice of the time if they had sailed without wages, relying instead upon taking a share from whatever plunder was taken on the voyage.

Drake was bent upon piracy. There was not a thread of authority for his raid, nor a commission from his government that would have made him a privateer. Privateers were authorized by governments to raid enemy shipping during war-

---

[4] Assignment by Drake of lease of two houses in Plymouth, 10 August, 1581, West Devon Record Office, 277/9; bill of Jonas Bodenham and answer of Thomas Drake (1597), Chancery proceedings, Public Record Office, C2/Eliz.I/B8-32; bill of Thomas Drake (1597), Chancery proceedings, C2/Eliz.I/D1/41; Bodenham indenture, 16 June, 1598, West Devon Record Office, T71/A22.

---

[1] Plymouth Black Book, West Devon Record Office, W46.
[2] Amadas bond, 21 September, 1576, West Devon Record Office, W625A.

time, and they were the common recourse of nations whose formal navies were weak. Lacking any such recognition from England, Drake was, in the legal sense, a pirate, but to condemn him as such, without qualification, would be to do him an injustice. Unlike later freebooters such as Avery, Roberts and even Lafitte, Drake was never an outlaw. His course was a desperate one, but many if not most Englishmen would have given it their approval, for he was striking at a country increasingly being seen as the supreme foe of both Protestantism and England. Whatever England's official relationships with Spain might be, a popular anti-Spanish xenophobia was in the making that would acclaim Drake as its hero. Nor, for that matter, was the English government over-concerned about what happened 'beyond the line', as events of the previous years had shown. A condition of informal warfare had been developing in remote places for some time. Hawkins had plundered Portuguese ships on the coast of Africa and he had bullied Spaniards into his contraband trade in the West Indies. Now Drake merely took the process further.

Occasional conflicts between Spain and France had drawn French privateers to the West Indies since 1528, but until Drake's arrival no Englishman is positively known to have entered the Caribbean intent on plunder. Here we must note the unusual genius that marked Drake's career, his opportunism, his perception of possibilities and the pioneering boldness with which he led Englishmen towards their realization. He was so alert to opportunities that he persistently out-thought both his rivals and his opponents. It would have been a simple enough matter for Drake to have obtained commissions from Huguenots, or from William of Orange in the Netherlands and to have attacked Spanish ships in the Channel, as some of his countrymen were doing. Fitted out by men like William Winter, the admiral and naval official, and Sir Arthur Champernowne, Vice-Admiral of Devon, small ships were sallying from south coast ports to prey upon Spanish vessels in the Narrow Seas. But Drake had seen the weaknesses and the wealth in Spain's West Indian possessions, and when the *Dragon* and the *Swan* quit Plymouth some time in 1570 it was to the shimmering waters of the Caribbean that they steered a course. Drake's war had begun.

The records are so silent about Drake's first raid that it seems that it can hardly have been eventful. During the previous year or two the French corsairs had been active again, sacking a village on the Spanish Main called Tolu in 1568 and 1569 and plundering some shipping. The year 1570, however, was apparently quiet in the Caribbean, despite the arrival of Drake. Spanish treasury records report that three ships were taken on the Main in 1570 and that two unsuccessful land raids occurred, but we cannot say whether any of these events concerned Drake.[1] Only one episode has been charged against him by the Spaniards, and there is doubt as to whether it belongs to 1570 or to 1571.[2]

---

[1] Hoffman, *The Spanish Crown and the Defense of the Caribbean*, 113.

[2] Wright, ed., *Documents Concerning English Voyages to the Spanish Main*, xxv, cites a Spanish complaint of 1575 that the English captured a frigate in ballast off the coast of Nombre de Dios in 1570, and that the ship belonged to Gaspar Hernandez. However, a similar, but not quite identical, document in the English state papers, a Spanish protest also of 1575, has this incident occurring in 1571 (Butler, et. al., *Cal. State Papers, Foreign*, 17: 500-3).

Many years later Drake apparently suggested that his purpose was recon-naissance, and it was probably true that this at least proved the most valuable re-sult of the voyage.[1] With his remarkable facility for detecting the strategic weak-nesses of his enemies, Drake probably fixed his attention quickly upon a route almost hidden in the fetid and pestilential jungle of the isthmus of Panama, a route that was, nevertheless, the most fabulous land-highway in the Spanish empire. He could not have found a region more vital to Spain's interests, nor a path richer in prospects, for it was Philip's Achilles' heel. The gold and silver from Potosi in Bolivia and from Chile and Peru, so fundamental to Spain's credibility in Europe, was shipped northwards to the city of Panama on the Pacific side of the isthmus. It was then transported by pack-mule into the jungle to Venta Cruces, a small outpost on the Chagres River that consisted of no more than fifty substantial houses with a wharf and warehouses by the riverside. Some of the bullion con-tinued by mule overland to Nombre de Dios, a town on the Caribbean coast, but the bulkier treasure was loaded into shallow-draught barks at Venta Cruces and proceeded down-river to the coast, and ultimately also to the treasure house of Nombre de Dios.

Nombre de Dios was the entrepôt for both the riches shipped from the Pacific and the merchandise and other goods that Spain exported to her colonies in Peru and elsewhere. It was the terminus not only for the treasure route across the steamy isthmus, but also for one of the two Spanish *flotas* that annually brought goods from Spain to the Americas. The *flota* arrived at Nombre de Dios to unload the Spanish exports, wintered in the harbour of Cartagena, and then returned to Nombre de Dios in the New Year to collect the treasure and carry it home. In the meantime the merchandise the fleet had previously unloaded had passed back across the isthmus to Panama, retracing the treasure route. It was taken by boats up the Chagres River to Venta Cruces, and thence by mule to the Pacific coast.

For all its importance to this two-way traffic, the communication line between Panama and Nombre de Dios was surprisingly vulnerable to attack, protected hitherto only by its geographical isolation from the interference of alien European powers. The road itself was a mere mule-path threading through a luxuriant rain-forest, while Venta Cruces and Nombre de Dios boasted little protection. At the time of Drake's appearance the area was described by Juan López de Velasco:

> The most frequented road of this district is that from Nombre de Dios to Panama, which is eighteen leagues across very rough mountain country, rivers and treacherous marshes, and by which, in the trains of five or six hundred mules normally used in this portage, and by the River Chagres in boats as far as the depots of Las Cruces, are carried the many goods brought from Spain to Peru and the silver and money brought thence. The city of Panama holds as public property a custom house or depot called Casa de Cruces, where the goods that come up the Chagres arrive, which is five leagues from the said city by a very bad road, hard travelling especially when it rains heavily. This place is maintained by the city, having a humid and sickly situation . . . It has forty-seven chambers, in which all the merchandise is locked up in the custody of a keeper . . . There is likewise maintained as public property another depot called Chagres, which is on the road from Panama to Nombre de Dios, six leagues from

[1] *Sir Francis Drake Revived*, reprinted in Wright, 254, is the only English reference to this voyage.

*Panama.*[1]

The town of Nombre de Dios might have been the treasure house of the world, as Drake once said, but it was not even properly fortified, although plans to erect defences there had long been topical. When Drake saw the town it had no more than a crude bulwark on the beach, behind which a few guns were mounted, a totally inadequate protection for a bay as open as that at Nombre de Dios. There was no regular garrison. Only when the *flota* was in port did Nombre de Dios spring to life as a raucous frontier settlement, capable of resisting a determined attack. For the rest of the time it languished sultrily in the heat, a humid, disease-ridden outpost of empire, periodically lashed by sharp tropical thunderstorms and consisting of perhaps two hundred mostly wooden houses.

French corsairs had already started to alarm Spain's servants on the isthmus highway, but there were other dangers too, from Indians, and most of all from the dreaded *cimarrones,* refugee Negroes who had bolted from the slavery of the settlements to live in the forest as outlaws. They had been brought to the West Indies by the slavers, Spanish, Portuguese and, more recently, English, and harnessed to a life of labour alien to their culture. The *cimarrones* ascribed their misfortunes to their Spanish masters and shared Drake's enmity towards that people. By 1571 their activities had created such concern that the Bishop of Panama recommended that no more Negroes be brought to the West Indies. The previous year a judge of the High Court in Panama also explained these difficulties to Philip II:

> *The matter which, in this kingdom, most urgently demands remedial action is the problem of dispersing the* cimarrones, *black outlaws in rebellion in its mountainous, unpopulated interior. They are numerous and (such is their daring and audacity) they come forth upon the roads leading from this city to that of Nombre de Dios, kill travellers, and steal what these have with them, if it be clothing and wine. So far they have not taken money.*
>
> *They threaten to burn these two towns, and have approached within an eighth of a league and frequently carried off Negresses at work washing clothes in the rivers . . . Similarly, they carry off Negroes sent out for fire-wood, and induce others to leave their owners, as they do every day.*[2]

Drake probably learned something of all this on his first independent voyage to the West Indies, and he must have ascertained the incompetence of the Spanish defences, both on the Main and elsewhere. A new West Indian squadron had been created by Spain to patrol in search of corsairs and contraband traders, but it was often burdened with convoy duties and drawn away from the coasts, and it was more likely to be encountered about the Antilles than off Darien. It was, in any case, a blunt instrument for frustrating the corsairs, for although the squadron consisted of oared galleons that were fast and manoeuvrable, they were unable to work close in shore or in rivers because they drew too much water, and these were the very places in which the French privateers were most likely to be found. There were also too few Spanish warships to discharge the enormous responsibility of defending an area as large as the

[1] Andrews, *Spanish Caribbean*, 18-19.
[2] Judge of the High Court in Panama to Philip II, 27 March, 1570, Wright, 9-10.

Caribbean. Only about five of the galleons were operating in that sea in the middle of 1570 when Drake made his appearance.

Later in the year Drake was in Plymouth again, preparing for a second voyage. Once more, his backers are unknown. Drake does not seem to have brought back much loot from his previous voyage, but he could speak of what he had learned and had the eloquence to tempt men bent on profit. According to a Spanish complaint made to the English government Drake was accompanied on his new venture by an Exeter merchant named Richard Dennis, and it is possible that Dennis and Drake between them raised the money from shipowners and sailors in Plymouth and Exeter. This Dennis is, however, an obscure figure, and cannot easily be identified. A Richard Dennis is mentioned in an inventory of lands and houses in Exeter in 1577, and since he was valued for a tax of £10 he was evidently a man of some substance. He may have been Drake's partner, and a member of the notable Dennis family that supplied two recorders of the city of Exeter.[1]

This time Drake used only one ship, the *Swan* of Plymouth, one of the two that had carried him upon his last adventure. He was in the West Indies in February 1571, and it must be assumed that he was timing his arrival to coincide with the appearance on the Darien coast of the annual *flota*, for it was then that the local traffic intensified. There was, of course, also a greater danger of being apprehended when the *flota* was about. It was commanded as usual by Diego Flores de Valdés, who was to remain for some time in 1571, guarding the area with two galleons and a shallop. Compared with the previous year, this was to be a lively one for the captain from Devon.

Even as the anchor of the *Swan* plunged into the clear water fringing the green shoreline of the isthmus, French corsairs were already attacking the communications between Nombre de Dios and Panama, recognizing, as Drake had done, the importance of that highway. Their leader was Nicholas des Isles, and he was a man with a mission. He had with him a Negro called Pedro Mandinga, who had been captured by the French in an earlier raid and taken to France, where he had obviously spoken of the treasure route across the isthmus. Now he had been brought back to lead the corsairs to Venta Cruces on the Chagres River, where they hoped to intercept either treasure from Panama or merchandise from Nombre de Dios. Nicholas des Isles may have been among those of his countrymen who had raided the mouth of the Chagres in 1569, and he was possibly not without personal knowledge of the area himself. But, if so, it was limited. Using a launch, he entered the Chagres, but before the Frenchmen reached Venta Cruces the Negro guide deserted, and they withdrew back downstream, capturing only a bark laden with silks and wine on their way. The stroke had failed, and worse still, when Nicholas des Isles and his men emerged from the mouth of the Chagres to rejoin their ship, *L'Esperance*, they discovered that the coast was in alarm, and Diego Flores was on their backs. The French fled northwards so quickly that their launch and ship became separated and the Spaniards recaptured three of the corsairs' prizes.[2]

---

[1] Rowe, ed., *Tudor Exeter*, 64.

[2] The few writers who have remarked upon Drake's voyage of 1571 have concluded that Drake co-operated with Nicholas des Isle's raid into the Chagres, but I remain unconvinced. The details of Drake's operations are drawn solely from Spanish documents, principally those published by Wright, xxiv, 11-35.

Diego Flores had not destroyed the raiders, but he had at least demonstrated that they could not threaten the isthmus with impunity. Perhaps he was not displeased with his efforts, but when he returned to Nombre de Dios it was to learn that a new adversary had appeared. Anchored close to Cativas Headland, a little to the east of the town, was the *Swan*, accompanied by a light-draught oared pinnace. Drake would prove himself a more tenacious and resourceful opponent than the French, but Nicholas des Isles had increased the difficulty for the English. The coast was more vigilant, and the Spaniards were even working to neutralize the one obvious advantage possessed by the corsairs: their use of vessels capable of managing shallows. The town of Nombre de Dios fitted out three oared vessels of its own to co-operate with Diego Flores against the raiders.

On the afternoon of Wednesday, 21 February, 1571, a Spanish frigate from Cartagena, bound for Nombre de Dios, anchored in a small port known as the Pontoons, between the mouth of the Chagres and their destination. The ship belonged to a burgher of Cartagena named Diego Polo, and aboard her were some local dignitaries, including Diego de Azevedo, a burgher of Santo Domingo, and his wife, Doña Joana de Estrada; the Licentiate Luys de Soto; and Canon Francisco de Talavera. A small pinnace, containing fifteen or sixteen of Drake's men and with two small culverins or guns mounted menacingly in the bow, pulled towards the frigate. The Englishmen were armed with bows and arrows and arquebuses. Although they protested later that they intended merely to parley, and they blew a trumpet perhaps so to signify, their behaviour was obviously hostile. The Spaniards could see them handling their swords and shields as the pinnace came alongside, and two of the visitors had powdered their faces, one black and the other red, as if to disguise their identities or to try to inspire fear among the people on board the frigate.

Sure enough, the Englishmen attempted to board, but they were resisted, although the Spaniards were poorly armed and it was later said that they had but two swords between them. The English opened fire, and three or four of the defenders were fatally wounded, including Diego de Azevedo, who was struck in the temple by an arrow, a seaman, shot through the body by a bolt, and a Negro slave, killed by a ball from a culverin. Others were also hit. The Licentiate Soto had his arm pierced by an arrow, and a female servant of de Azevedo's wife and three of her slaves were wounded. In retrospect, it is clear that the Spaniards would have done better not to offer resistance, for Drake's policy was to harm none who surrendered upon demand. However, the French had been noted for barbarities to prisoners, and the Spaniards had no intimation that in the hands of the English their fate would have been any easier.

In desperation now, the Spaniards cut their anchor cable and allowed the current to pull their frigate away from the corsairs' pinnace and run it upon the shore, where

These are difficult to interpret and repeatedly exhibit confusion as to whether the enemy corsairs were French or English. To some Spaniards all heretics were alike. However, the suggestion that Drake's men accompanied Nicholas des Isles does not seem to be supported by a closer reading of the evidence. An inside, and consequently better informed, account of the French expedition by the Negro Pedro Mandinga apparently contains no reference to the English (*Ibid*, xxxi-xxxii), and Diego Flores for one noted the presence of the English only after the French had been driven away: 'if the French and English combine I will seek them out together,' he wrote to the king on 16 March, 1571, implying that no such junction had yet taken place (*Ibid*, 18-19). The reconstruction of Drake's raids given in the text seems to be the most consistent with the material.

the crew and passengers were able to plunge over the side and wade waist-deep through a mangrove swamp to the safety of a small island. The English, in the meantime, had been diverted by the appearance of a second Spanish frigate, which they captured after its crew had also fled to the shore. For a day the corsairs plundered their two prizes, smashing open chests of goods, damaging cordage, and stoving in the bottom of the ship's boat aboard Polo's frigate. When the Spaniards eventually regained that gutted vessel they found that the corsairs had left a note for them expressing the contempt of the English for the galleons of Diego Flores:

> Captain and crew of this frigate:
> We are surprised that you ran from us in that fashion and later refused to come to talk with us under our flag of truce, knowing us, and having seen evidence a few days past that we do ill to none under our flag of truce, but only wished to speak with you.
> And since you will not come courteously to talk with us, without evil or damage, you will find your frigate spoiled by your own fault. And to any who courteously may come to talk with us, we will do no harm, under our flag. And who does not come, his be the blame.
> And do not think we were afraid of those ships [Diego Flores], nor of others. By the help of God it shall cost them their lives before they prevail over us.
> Now you have proof that it would have been better had you come to talk with us, for in the frigate you had not the value of four silver reals.
> Done by English, who are well disposed if there be no cause to the contrary; if there be cause, we will be devils rather then men.[1]

After making this somewhat specious justification, the English left for the Chagres River on Thursday, 22 February. Here was the fabled route by which rich merchandise passed to the Pacific and the bullion was brought the other way to support Spain's armies in Europe. Drake decided to go up the river, as had Nicholas des Isles, but although unguided he went further than any of his French predecessors, and reached Venta Cruces. Clothing and merchandise supposedly worth about 100,000 pesos was seized from the wharf, and four years later the Spaniards complained that the corsairs had also seized goods belonging to Lope Ruiz de Lezo and Balthasar Diaz from the inn at Venta Cruces. In addition, they captured three barks in the Chagres River, belonging respectively to Diego de Çaballos, Juan de Ciria and Alonzo de Paz, and sunk them so that they could not carry news of the depredations afield. These vessels do not seem to have been valuable prizes and were probably carrying little more than ballast.

By the first days of May, Drake had left the river and was operating off the coast between the Bastimentos Islands (near Nombre de Dios) and Puerto Bello to the west, intercepting barks bound to and from the mouth of the Chagres. Twelve or thirteen were captured, laden with clothing and merchandise valued at 150,000 pesos. Much of the plunder was loaded into two of the prizes to be taken away. There were some slaves taken, and, it was said, clothing and boxes worth more than 80,000 pesos.

The next victim was a frigate from Cartagena – no ordinary vessel, this, but an advice ship bearing the king's dispatches and correspondence for Peru and Panama. She was intercepted by a pinnace manned by twenty-three men off Cativas Headland on about 8 May. During the attack the English again encountered resistance, and they

---

[1] Note of the English corsairs, February 1571, *Ibid*, 11.

killed the ship's owner, one Salvatierra of Cartagena, and another seaman, and wounded seven or eight other Spaniards. The prisoners were put on an uninhabited islet nearby, from which they were shortly rescued by a Spanish ship, as Drake must have foreseen they would be, but the raiders stripped and abused a friar – a natural target for a crew that gave the Spaniards the impression they were all Lutherans – before they released him. Although the frigate was important, its cargo was probably far from lucrative, and after throwing the packages of letters overboard, Drake's men set her adrift. She was eventually recovered by a shallop from Nombre de Dios.

Later in the month the English turned again towards the Chagres River, and stealing once more upstream they encountered eighteen barks laden with bales of merchandise. Four of the vessels were seized. Drake had his men throw the wine casks of one of the prizes overboard to make room for the plunder from the other captures. Some Negro slaves were also taken by the English. A dispatch of 1571 valued the merchandise at 70,000 pesos, but a later complaint to England alleged that Drake had seized 'divers barks that were transporting of merchandise of 40,000 ducats, velvets and taffetas, besides other merchandise, with gold and silver, in other barks.'[1] The ducat was inferior to the peso, and the latter estimate was considerably more modest than the first. After pillaging the barks, the English pinnace left the Chagres with her prize to rejoin the *Swan*, which lingered among the islands near Cativas Headland with another capture.

With this exploit Drake's raid of 1571 came to an end. He had certainly made his name notorious along the Spanish Main, less for the damage he had done than for the bold strokes he had performed against the isthmus treasure route. Such attacks portended worse to come, perhaps even an attempt upon the most precious of Spanish assets – the treasure itself. Drake may have only been shredding the edges of Philip's empire, but he had found a vital artery, and for the first time the King of Spain began to read letters about this mean seaman and his private war. From Panama, officials complained to Philip on 25 May that Drake was 'so fully in possession of the whole coast of Nombre de Dios, Cartagena, Tolu, Santa Marta and Cabo de la Vela, that traffic dares not sail from Santo Domingo thither, and trade and commerce are diminishing between the windward islands and this Main.'[2]

The town of Nombre de Dios protested that efforts had not been wanting to arrest the career of this new corsair, for three expeditions had been sent against him. None of them had succeeded, and the imminent departure from the coast of the few naval vessels of Diego Flores would soon leave the town even more exposed. As Gonzalo Nuñez de la Cerde of Nombre de Dios wrote,

> In search of this corsair this city has sent out three expeditions on which were expended more than 4,000 pesos; and he has always had the luck to escape. Once the fleet is gone, when the town and port are deserted, it is plain we are going to suffer from this corsair and others, unless Your Majesty apply the remedy hoped for, by sending a couple of galleys to protect and defend this coast and the town, which is in the greatest danger.[3]

[1] *Ibid*, xxiv.
[2] Officials in Panama to the king, 25 May, 1571, *Ibid*, 31-5.
[3] Gonzalo Nuñez de la Cerde to Philip II, 24 May, 1571, *Ibid*, 29-30.

Drake's raid of 1571 has been almost overlooked by biographers and historians, but it was of considerable significance. It had been bold and successful, bold because no Englishman had made such an incursion before and because Drake had attacked the treasure road in the face of an alerted opposition, successful because it paid handsome dividends. The value of Drake's plunder cannot be estimated, for the sums claimed by the Spaniards, say 160,000 pesos' worth of merchandise, were likely much exaggerated, and the full value of what was taken was probably not recovered by Drake in the final disposal of the plunder. Even so, at 8s 3d a peso, 160,000 pesos were equivalent to £66,000 in Elizabethan money; the total Hawkins had obtained from his three laborious slaving voyages amounted to only half that sum.

The raid indicates how obsolete Hawkins's ventures had become, for as well as being only moderately profitable they had employed hundreds of men and squadrons of ships in long journeys. The outlay had been great and the risks were increasing now that both the Portuguese and the Spaniards were showing greater vigour in defending the monopolies they claimed in Africa and the Americas. The economic prospects for further voyages along such lines were bleak. And now Drake had shown his countrymen a quicker, more lucrative method. Inside a few months, with possibly no more than thirty mariners, and at little expense, Drake had netted enough to make himself a comparatively rich man. True, he had taken a step forward in lawlessness, but the rising anti-Spanish feeling in England was unlikely to condemn him too severely for that, and in the West Country it probably enhanced his status.

The voyage found immediate imitators. That accomplished admiral, seaman and gunner, William Winter, even then well into his life's work of transforming England's navy into a formidable fighting machine, sent three ships to the Caribbean before the end of 1571, perhaps influenced by what he had heard of Drake. They took a ship off Jamaica and at the turn of the year unsuccessfully attacked St Augustine in Florida. John Garret of Plymouth and James Raunse of the Isle of Wight got away in 1572, inspired by the stories of Drake's mariners, and Spanish records suggest that two others did the same, Lewis Larder of Plymouth and a Captain Trenel of Totnes. Thus, modestly, did the great age of British piracy in the Caribbean begin.

And Drake himself planned to return, his appetite whetted for a more ambitious campaign. Before leaving the West Indies for Plymouth he had sought out a secluded anchorage where he could refit his vessel and where he might deposit stores for a future expedition. Late in June 1571, somewhere on the Acla coast, east of Nombre de Dios but west of Tolu, the *Swan* had nosed into

> a fine round bay, of very safe harbour for all winds, lying between two high points, not past half a cable's length over at the mouth, but within eight or ten cables' length every way, having ten or twelve fathom water, more or less, full of good fish, the soil also very fruitful.[1]

Because of the multitude of birds in this hideaway Drake named it Port Pheasant. Unwisely, however, he had brought some Spanish prisoners with him, and when they were eventually released before the *Swan* sailed for home they carried word of the

---

[1] *Sir Francis Drake Revived*, 255-6. The exact location of Port Pheasant is unknown. Thomson, *Sir Francis Drake*, 341-2, considered the most likely location to be present Puerto Escoces, but that other alternatives were Puerto Carreto, also in Panama, and the Bahia Zarzurro near Cabo Tiburon, in Colombia.

refuge to the authorities. Even as Drake's little ship proudly rode the Atlantic swells for Plymouth his plans to return were being undermined.

But those problems lay ahead, and for the moment Drake's standing in his home town had risen. He had brought back wealth enough to reward mariners and investors, and had smote the Spaniards for the treachery at San Juan d'Ulua. There must have been envious rivals who attempted to resurrect that old charge of desertion, and others, more principled than Drake, who frowned upon his activities, but even enemies had now to acknowledge the courage and enterprise of the man. It seemed as if young Mary Newman had not married a loser after all.

For the first time since Drake's return in the *Judith*, there is evidence that the Hawkins brothers were again co-operating with the new talent they had nurtured. Among the vessels fitted out for his next expedition was the *Pasco*. She was a Hawkins ship, and Drake had seen her on Lovell's voyage a few years before. Her burden has been rated variously as between 40 and 80 tons, but she was probably about 70 and could carry as many as fifty men; according to a Spanish record there were twelve guns aboard her. Did Drake purchase the ship from the Hawkins brothers, or did it represent their investment in him?[1] We do not know, but Drake was certainly musing over an attractive financial venture. He was thinking about the isthmus again, and the treasure that flowed across it into Nombre de Dios, and he was remembering the weakness of that town, its open and ill-defended bay, and the wealth it so vulnerably contained. It was in Drake's nature to seize opportunities, and he saw one now. No more would he target the ships plying about the Main, plundering merchandise here and there. This time he would capture the treasure house of the world itself.

[1] *Sir Francis Drake Revived* calls this ship the *Pascha*. However, what appears to be the will of Drake's brother, John Drake, printed in Eliott-Drake, 1: 28, refers to her as the *Pasco* and thereby links her with the Hawkins vessel of that name (Williamson, *Sir John Hawkins*, 288-9).

CHAPTER FIVE

# 'THE MOUTH OF THE TREASURE OF THE WORLD'

Your general a valiant knight was never daunted yet,
But bravely made his foes recoil, when face to face they met;
Now is your bravery to be shown, there must you all take pain,
Else look for lasting ignominy when you return again.

Henry Roberts, *A Most Friendly Farewell*, 1585

PLYMOUTH SOUND, WHIT SUNDAY EVE, 24 MAY 1572. TWO SMALL SHIPS, THE *Pasco* and the *Swan*, worked their way towards the open sea carrying seventy-three men and boys bent upon a dangerous mission to the Caribbean. They were volunteers to a man, and all but one or two of them below thirty years of age, young and vigorous, capable of waging a new and deadlier phase of Drake's war. Francis Drake commanded from the *Pasco* while his younger brother, John, who had invested £30 in the adventure, was captain of the *Swan*. The desperate nature of the enterprise upon which they were bound was marked by the increased number of men Drake had recruited and the equipment he took with him: three pinnaces for inshore work, stored aboard in pieces; provisions for a year; and a plentiful supply of weapons and tools.[1]

The Atlantic passage was a good one, and on 29 June the ships could have been observed passing between the West Indian islands of Dominica and Guadeloupe, bound for the Main. After replenishing his fresh water from the fine mountain streams of Dominica, Drake set a course for Port Pheasant, where he intended to put his ships into good order and construct the pinnaces. On 12 July the *Pasco* and the *Swan* paused at the entrance to the quiet bay and Drake, after briefing his brother, clambered into a rowing boat with a few men to examine the landfall. As his boat pulled into Port Pheasant the captain saw the first sign of trouble – a thin trail of smoke rising from the woods close to where Drake had established his camp the year before. Drake had supposed Port Pheasant to be uninhabited, and miles from any Spanish settlement, but he summoned a second boat, filled with armed men, and led his party ashore to the remains of a fire that appeared to

---

[1] The standard narrative of this voyage was issued by Drake's nephew as *Sir Francis Drake Revived* (London, 1626). Composed from eye-witness accounts of the expedition now lost, it was written about 1592 by Philip Nichols, then Rector of Mylor, near Plymouth, at the instigation of Drake himself, and it was said that the admiral had improved the text 'by divers notes with his own hand here and there inserted.' The work contained a dedicatory epistle from Drake to the queen, dated 1 January, 1593, proclaiming it 'the first fruits of your servant's pen.' Obviously intended for publication, it lay neglected for many years before Drake's nephew put it into print. Although favourable to Drake throughout, the narrative checks consistently with the other documentation. An account of the voyage by the Portuguese, Lopez Vaz, can be found in Hakluyt, *Principal Navigations*, 10: 75-7. Some attacks made by Drake during the expedition are mentioned in a Spanish complaint of 1575, published in Butler, et. al., *Cal. State Papers, Foreign*, 17: 500-3. Wright, ed., *Documents Concerning English Voyages to the Spanish Main*, collects other Spanish depositions and dispatches and reprints *Sir Francis Drake Revived*. It is from this edition that quotations are made below.

be some days old. Nearby, nailed to a large tree, was a lead plate inscribed with a warning:

> *Captain Drake, if you fortune to come to this port, make haste away, for the Spaniards which you had with you here the last year have betrayed this place, and taken away all that you left here. I departed from hence, this present 7 of July, 1572.*
> *Your very loving friend,*
> *John Garret.*[1]

John Garret was a Plymouth man, an ex-slaver like Drake himself. He had been guided to this coast by men who had served on Drake's earlier raid, and was thus the first of many who would try to emulate the bold Devonian. Drake took note of Garret's information, but he did not allow the news to swerve him from his purpose. The pinnaces were brought ashore for assembly and the carpenters set to work on them, while the other men busied themselves felling trees and erecting a great stockade for security.

While sweating at this work the next day, the Englishmen were disturbed by three small craft entering the bay, but they were not enemies. One, a bark, was English, shipping out of the Isle of Wight under James Raunse, an old shipmate of Drake's, the same who as master of the *William and John* on Hawkins's last slaving voyage had missed the battle at San Juan d'Ulua; now, like Garret, he had been drawn into Drake's footsteps, and piloted to Port Pheasant by more veterans of the previous year's cruise. With him Raunse brought two Spanish prizes, a shallop and the *Santa Catalina*. Seeing Drake's men ashore in thatched shelters with their pinnaces a-building, Raunse asked that his small party might join them and increase the total English force to a little over one hundred men. The reinforcement was not unwelcome, for Drake, as he explained to Raunse, had in his mind the capture of Nombre de Dios itself.

With the three pinnaces, the *Lion*, *Bear* and *Minion*, finished, Drake quit Port Pheasant and sailed north-westwards along the rocky Darien coast to a small island called the Isla de Pinos, where he took two Spanish ships which had left Nombre de Dios laden with timber. Aboard the prizes Drake found a few Negro slaves from whom he tried to learn the strength of the town. To his dismay the Negroes said that Nombre de Dios lived in fear of an attack from the *cimarrones* and was daily expecting reinforcements of soldiers from Panama. These were certainly unpleasant tidings. Drake had no way of knowing that the information was erroneous, and that there were no soldiers on their way to Nombre de Dios. His men grew discouraged, but Drake released the blacks ashore ('willing to use those Negroes well') and bent himself to his task with greater urgency, trusting that he might surprise the town before it was reinforced.

East of Cativas Headland the captain divided his forces for what was undoubtedly the boldest stroke he had yet attempted. Raunse would remain behind with his own ship and the *Santa Catalina*, the *Pasco* and the *Swan*, while Drake would lead the attack on Nombre de Dios with seventy-three men in the three pinnaces and shallop. He got his assault force to an island at Cativas, where each man was issued a principal tool or weapon. There were six shields, twelve pikes, six firepikes which could also act

---

[1] *Sir Francis Drake Revived*, Wright, 256.

as torches, twenty-four arquebuses, sixteen bows, six spears, two drums and two trumpets. The men were drilled and briefed, and then on 28 July the raiders rowed silently onward, to steal upon the sleeping town of Nombre de Dios in the ensuing night.

Drake planned to carry the town in a sudden dawn onslaught, and brought his men to a point flanking Nombre de Dios bay where he waited for first light. His men were uneasy. They began to mutter anxiously about the size of the town and the soldiers supposed to be reinforcing it, and Drake sensed that further delay would only multiply their fears. He decided to act. Between two and three o'clock in the morning the moon scudded from behind the clouds and in the twilight the captain declared that dawn was breaking and it was time to attack. Once on the move, the men recovered their spirits, but the assault began shakily nonetheless. A ship conveying wine from the Canaries was anchored in the bay, and some of her crew saw the dim shapes of the English craft as they emerged stealthily from the gloom. The Spaniards instantly lowered a boat which tried to dash for the shore to raise the alarm, but Drake had anticipated the movement, and an English pinnace headed the Spanish boat off and drove her across the bay where she could do no more harm. Without further difficulty Drake landed and seized a battery of six guns from which the sole defender fled as fast as he could towards the town.

The success of Drake's operation depended upon how quickly and suddenly he could move, for if the Spaniards learned how few English were attacking them they would rally in numbers likely to be overwhelming. Consequently Drake paused no longer than it took to reconnoitre and to post a dozen men to guard the pinnaces and secure his retreat. Then he divided his men to storm the town. John Drake and John Oxenham were given sixteen men to approach the market-place from one of the flanks, and Drake himself advanced directly along the main street. As the parties set off they could already hear Nombre de Dios awakening before them in a cacophony of noise – shouts, drums beating up and down the streets, and the church bell pealing a frantic warning to the people of the town.

With the firepikes flickering eerily aloft, Drake's company brazenly marched forward to the sound of drum and trumpet as if they were a formidable array. At the south-east end of the market-place that served as the town centre the *alcalde*, Antonio Juarez, had assembled a body of militia to withstand the corsairs, and when Drake's men poured into view they were met by a volley of shot from the Spaniards. Most of the bullets struck the ground before the English, but one smashed into Drake's leg and another killed his trumpeter on the spot. The pirates replied with their own shot and arrows, and then surged forwards ferociously, brandishing their pikes. At the same time John Drake's company suddenly burst into the market-place from another direction. It was too much for the Spaniards. Terrified, they broke and fled precipitately from the town, some of them discarding their weapons as they ran.

Drake commanded the town, for the time being, but he must act quickly before the inadequacy of his force was discovered and the Spaniards counter-attacked. He reformed his men by a cross in the market-place and then commanded a few prisoners to lead him to the house of the town governor, where he expected to find a fair sample of the treasure that was brought into Nombre de Dios from Panama. According to the English account of the expedition, Drake was not disappointed, for there was discovered

> *a pile of bars of silver, of (as near as we could guess) seventy foot in length, of ten foot in breadth, and twelve foot in height, piled up against the wall. Each bar was between thirty-five and forty pound in weight. At sight hereof our captain commanded straightly that none of us should touch a bar of silver, but stand upon our weapons, because the town was full of people, and there was in the King's treasure-house near the water's side more gold and jewels than all our four pinnaces could carry, which we would presently set some in hand to break open, notwithstanding the Spaniard's reports of the strength of it.*[1]

Drake should have ordered his men to carry off some of the silver, but he was hungry for more valuable booty, gold and jewellery. The governor's residence was devoid of this particular treasure, so Drake decided to break into the waterfront strongroom where the treasure was stored before being transferred to the *flota* for shipment to Seville. There he was sure more was to be had. He directed Oxenham and John Drake to return to his pinnaces to reassure the men there that all was well, and led the main force towards the treasure house in the teeth of one of those sudden thunderstorms for which this part of the coast was notorious. By the time Drake's men reached their destination they were sodden, much of their gunpowder was useless, and even the strings to their crossbows were too wet to be efficient. The men would have to shelter and restore their weapons to order, and for more than half an hour Drake waited impatiently beneath a penthouse while the storm subsided, knowing that every moment that passed gave his enemies time to regroup. Not unnaturally the delay reawakened the nervousness among his men, and Drake had curtly to remind them that 'he had brought them to the mouth of the treasure of the world. If they would want it, they might henceforth blame nobody but themselves.'[2]

The whole adventure ended abruptly. When the rain eased John Drake, fresh from checking the pinnaces, was ordered to break down the door of the treasure house while his brother held the market-place. But as Drake stepped forward he became faint, and then it was that his men noticed the blood that covered one of his legs and stained the footprints that he left in the sand. The captain had hidden the wound he had received in the skirmish as best he could, unwilling to withdraw for attention lest it should damage the morale of his company. Now there was nothing more to be done. The sailors gathered around their fallen leader, bound his leg with a scarf, and despite his protests carried him back to the pinnaces, leaving the door of the treasure house solid and inviolate behind them. In the words of the contemporary narrative, they

> *so abandoned a most rich spoil for the present, only to preserve their captain's life, as being resolved of him that while they enjoyed his presence, and had him to command them, they might recover wealth sufficient; but if once they lost him, they should hardly be able to recover home.*[3]

A Portuguese account of the raid stated that the men Drake had left to defend the pinnaces had become so frightened that they had retired to the boats, and that Drake's party were compelled to swim or wade through the surf to reach safety. However, one way or another the whole force was embarked at daylight on the 29th, and as they left

[1] *Ibid*, 264.
[2] *Ibid*, 265.
[3] *Ibid*, 267.

the bay the English took the ship from the Canaries with them.

They withdrew to the Bastimentos Islands, west of Nombre de Dios, to refresh themselves, tend their wounded and overcome what must have been a crushing disappointment. Bitter must have been the thoughts at this time. They might have been on their way home, laden with treasure, bound for Plymouth and the best time they had known! But God had not willed it so, and Drake's mind wrestled with the consequences of the failure, at least thankful that he had brought provisions for a year in preparation for just such a misfortune. A new plan had to be formulated, and the men set to work to occupy their minds and prevent unprofitable reflection.

There was one sense, however, in which the sudden retreat from Nombre de Dios had salvaged rather than damaged the little captain's credibility. It is uncertain how much treasure was actually in the town that night of the attack, for the *flota* had left harbour a few weeks before and presumably with it had gone most of the treasure being stored for shipment to Spain. Obviously, Drake could not have contemplated assaulting Nombre de Dios while the fleet was in port – it would have been far too strong for that – but it may be doubted if much treasure lay behind that great door that John Drake was set to break down. And how would Drake's reputation have stood if the coffers had been empty? Paradoxically, Fortune may have been smiling on Francis Drake the day he attacked Nombre de Dios.

This was, of course, no consolation to the Spaniards, for whom such a daring raid upon the outlet of the treasure route was of the gravest concern. Some of the citizens of Nombre de Dios had been killed and wounded by the corsairs, although how many is unknown, so variant are the estimates in our sources. Many years later a Portuguese commentator reported that the only Spaniard killed was an unfortunate onlooker who was struck down as he peered from his window to ascertain the source of the racket! But a Spanish complaint of 1575 raised the fatalities to eighteen. Perhaps the severest version was given in April 1573 by an eye-witness, García de Paz. Recalling the eventful raid he testified that the English 'began to sound trumpets in the streets and to fire artillery (from four pinnaces which they had brought close in to the shore), and to discharge arquebuses and arrows through the streets; and they killed some men and women, white and black, and wounded many more, in all thirty-two persons.'[1]

The *alcalde* of Nombre de Dios was worried enough about his injured to send an envoy to the Bastimentos Islands to enquire of Drake if he was the same Drake who had raided the coast before. The emissary flattered the captain that he had earned a reputation for humanity, and asked if the arrows the English had used were poisoned. With the courtesy that many Latins commanded so easily, the Spaniard concluded his address by asking if he could serve Drake by supplying any necessaries required by the English. Drake replied with a braggadocio that was becoming his trademark:

> Our captain, although he thought this soldier but a spy, yet used him very courteously, and answered him to his governor's demands that he was the same Drake whom they meant; it was never his manner to poison his arrows; they might cure their wounded by ordinary surgery; as for wants, he knew the island of Bastimentos

[1] Deposition of García de Paz, 9 April, 1573, Wright, 57. The other accounts from Nombre de Dios and Panama, written in 1572 and 1573, place the number of men killed by the English at between two and nine.

*had sufficient and could furnish him if he listed, but he wanted nothing but some of that special commodity which that country yielded [treasure], to content himself and his company. And therefore he advised the governor to hold open his eyes, for before he departed, if God lent him life and leave, he meant to reap some of their harvest, which they get out of the earth, and send into Spain to trouble all the earth.*

When the messenger departed he was so burdened with English gifts that he protested he was never so much honoured of any in his life.[1]

Listening to the Spaniard's report, the *alcalde* of Nombre de Dios may have been forgiven for pessimism. The coast was badly defended, for although the West Indies fleet had patrolled the Main earlier in the year it had then retired to Cartagena to convoy the *flota* to Spain, leaving the Caribbean uncovered. The best that could be done was to summon assistance from Panama, and improve the town's defences. About a hundred soldiers were accordingly sent to Nombre de Dios. Earthworks were thrown up in the town, trenches dug near the beach, and a new battery of seven or eight guns erected on a commanding headland. Drake's failure was becoming a costly one. Not only was Nombre de Dios strengthened, but word of the presence of the corsairs was already on its way to Cartagena, Santa Marta and Honduras.

It was too much for James Raunse. When Drake returned to the Isla de Pinos and told him about it he refused to have anything more to do with Drake and shivered at the prospect of alerted Spaniards combing the coast for the pirates. Drake let him go, and cannot have been sorry; it was sterner material that he needed to meet the challenges ahead. To his remaining men, the faithful band he had brought from Plymouth, he proposed an audacious stroke against the shipping at Cartagena, the most important town on the Main. Cartagena was not strongly defended, but there was a stone tower and a battery of guns, and far too many defenders for Drake to contemplate the sort of attack he had made on Nombre de Dios. But it might be possible to surprise the ships in the harbour.

After dark on 13 August two English ships and three pinnaces stole stealthily into the bay of Cartagena and boarded a Spanish vessel anchored some distance from the waterfront. Another disappointment! Only one old man was aboard the prize, the rest of the crew having gone ashore to watch two men duel over a mistress, and he told Drake that the city already knew that Drake was on the coast, and that the shipping had moved in shore, beneath the protection of the shore batteries. One large vessel of about 240 tons was still within reach, however, behind the next point, and Drake led his pinnaces upon her, attacking her amidships with one boat while his consorts fell upon her bow and quarter. Scaling the ship's sides, the Englishmen quickly took possession of the ship, and they towed her towards the open sea with the hapless crew shut in the hold. This excitement now attracted notice ashore, and the townspeople gathered to watch Drake make his escape. They were powerless to stop him, although musketeers opened fire from the water's edge, the guns of the castle roared, and warning bells tumbled the militia from their houses. According to a Spanish account of the attack Drake pillaged his prize and burned it, carrying its owner, Bartolomeo Farina, to England, but this finds no verification elsewhere and was probably a deliberate invention to strengthen the case Spain was making against the English corsairs.[2]

---

[1] *Sir Francis Drake Revived*, 268-9.

The affair at Cartagena demonstrated the inability of either side to inflict a decisive blow upon the other. Drake had been foiled by the speed at which news of his attack upon Nombre de Dios had passed through the Caribbean. He could take neither Cartagena nor most of its shipping, and after seizing two more vessels the following day he retired to the nearby San Bernardo islands to refit. At Cartagena, on the other hand, Spanish efforts to arrest Drake's career proved futile, even when he virtually blockaded the city later in the year. The governor of the city was absent, and its defence was conducted by Alvaro de Mendoza and Martin de Mendoza. These worthies persuaded various shipmasters to put to sea in search of Drake but they merely made a fruitless voyage to Tolu and then refused to participate in further expeditions against the elusive raiders.

After this attempt upon Cartagena, Drake decided that, to keep his pinnaces fully manned and ready to steal into shallows, he could not afford to man both his ships. His brother's Swan would have to be sacrificed. The incident is interesting to us because it illustrates the guile and tact that Drake was capable of bringing to a problem. John Drake and most members of his crew loved the little Swan and Drake knew they would never agree to her being scuttled. In the San Bernardo islands he found an answer, and summoned the carpenter of the Swan, Thomas Moone, for a private conversation. Now, Moone's loyalty to Drake was unquestioned, but the instructions he received must have been as bewildering as they were unpalatable. He was sworn to secrecy and told to creep into the well of the Swan during the second watch and use a gimlet to bore three holes in the ship's hull, close to the keel. Then, placing an object against the leaks to prevent the water from gushing in too quickly, Moone was to withdraw and act as if he had done nothing untoward.

The morning after Moone had accomplished his furtive mission Drake rose early aboard the Pasco. He took a pinnace and pulled across to the Swan, where he called to his brother and asked him to join him for some fishing. John agreed, but told Francis to go ahead, for he must first prepare himself. He would follow as soon as he could. As Drake's boat drew away, he shouted to his brother again. Why, Drake asked innocently, was the Swan so low in the water? John cast his eyes over his sinking vessel in amazement, and ordered his steward to go below and investigate forthwith. In the words of the narrative, 'the steward hastily stepping down at his usual scuttle was wet up to the waist, and shifting with more haste to come up again as if the water had followed him, cried out that the ship was full of water.'[1] Drake affected great concern at this news, and offered to send men from the Pasco to help the leak, but John was proud of his company and maintained that the reinforcements would not be necessary.

He was wrong, for Drake's saboteur had worked well. All that day the men of the Swan struggled with the pumps, but even when some sailors from the Pasco were

[2] This charge, like others found in the complaint Spain made to Elizabeth in 1575, must be treated with caution. The same source had Drake capturing a caravel, bound for Havana from Seville with munitions. When the pilot, Francisco Ravano, refused to guide the corsairs to other ports, they threw him overboard. Such behaviour was certainly not beyond the English, but the episode cannot be identified from other English and Spanish accounts, and it was possibly concocted to blacken Drake's reputation and to sharpen the Spanish protest.

[1] Sir Francis Drake Revived, 273.

eventually ferried across to join the battle, the stricken vessel settled lower and lower in the water. John Drake was at a loss to account for the disaster, but he had to admit himself beaten. During the ensuing night the crew of the *Swan* transferred their belongings to the other vessels, and the empty shell of the ship was then set on fire to burn to the waterline and sink where none might salvage her. Drake had got his way, but to console his aggrieved brother he magnanimously gave John the command of the *Pasco* and shifted his own berth to one of the tiny pinnaces.

Having reorganized his force Drake was ready for another surprising and unprecedented move. If he could not capture the treasure at Nombre de Dios, he would take it before it reached the town, somewhere on the track that wound through the jungles of the isthmus of Panama. No corsair had attempted such an escapade before, but there were others who knew the interior well: the *cimarrones*, those Negro outlaws living about Panama, Nombre de Dios and the mountains of Vallano in the southern regions of the isthmus. If Drake could contact them they might serve him as scouts, guides and allies, for they shared the Englishmen's enmity towards the Spaniards.

It was at this point that Drake's attitude to coloured races began to change. Hitherto, he had probably seen blacks in the same light as did John Hawkins, as commodities for sale, like bales of cloth, but now they were emerging as individuals who shared a bond with himself – a grievance against the Spaniards, their common enemy. An instrumental figure in the transformation, and in the formulation of Drake's new strategy, was a remarkable Negro called Diego, who had defected from his Spanish masters to the English during the raid on Nombre de Dios. He attached himself to Drake as a manservant, and between the two developed a close friendship that benefited both. Diego had probably been born in Africa and shipped to the Caribbean as a slave, but he followed Drake to England and ultimately around the world, becoming possibly the first black circumnavigator. It was from Diego that Drake learned more of the *cimarrones*, of their knowledge of the treasure route between Panama and Nombre de Dios, and of their hatred of the Spaniards, from whose cruelties they had fled. Diego assured Drake that the *cimarrones* would help him, and the captain led his small squadron into the Gulf of Uraba, where he could perfect his new plan, reprovision his vessels and allow the alarm that had frustrated his attack upon Cartagena to subside.

On a quiet river Drake's party spent fifteen days repairing their pinnaces, using an anvil, iron and coal brought from England to set up a forge, and erecting shelters under the supervision of Diego. The men worked a shift system, with alternate days of off-duty in which games of skittles, quoits or bowls were played or arrows fired at butts.

As soon as the company had been restored to good order, Drake detailed John Drake and Diego to attempt to contact the *cimarrones* on the Darien coast while he took two pinnaces eastwards along the Main in search of provisions. It was his intention to establish a network of depots so that if some were discovered by the Spaniards others would survive to sustain the Englishmen. This prudence tempers the charge often made against Drake of haphazard organization and a dependence upon the inspiration of the moment. He was successful in his quest for supplies, topping up his reserves by trading with Indians on the coast and during the second week of September capturing six or seven enemy ships and seizing their provisions. Thus equipped, he was able to return to the Gulf of Uraba and construct four storehouses, some hidden on the mainland and others on islands, and while employed on this service Diego again drew the attention of his allies, this time by the rapidity with which he built the caches.

John Drake was also successful, for with Diego's help he had contacted the *cimarrones* while Drake himself had been probing eastwards for provisions. The free Negroes had been seen ashore, and, using Diego as an intermediary, John was able to arrange for fuller negotiations to be held shortly on a river between the Isla de Pinos and Cape San Blas. Now Drake could feel that his plans were shaping. Returning from the provisioning foray, he had spoken with two *cimarrones* John had brought back with him, and he learned from them that the Negroes not only knew of Drake's earlier voyages and his attack on Nombre de Dios, but that they would likely make common cause with him.

Drake did not want to waste time before cementing so vital an alliance, and he led his pinnaces westwards towards the rendezvous, leaving the *Pasco* secreted behind leafy islands, shoals and rocks off shore. On 14 September he met the *cimarrones* his brother had encountered, and ten days afterwards a second party of blacks. Eventually, Drake brought both groups aboard the *Pasco* 'to their great comfort and our content, they rejoicing that they should have some fit opportunity to wreak their wrongs on the Spaniards, we hoping that now our voyage should be bettered.'[1] Drake found them eager to discuss the movement of the treasure and was told that the process languished during the rainy months and was resumed some time before the arrival of the next *flota*. Drake calculated that this meant he would have to wait for five months.

The alliance with the *cimarrones* marked Drake as the most enterprising corsair the Spaniards had yet faced in the Caribbean, and later King Philip's officials repeatedly spoke of the terror it caused them. 'This league between the English and the Negroes is very detrimental to this kingdom,' commented the Municipal Council of Panama, 'because being so thoroughly acquainted with the region and so expert in the bush, the Negroes will show them methods and means to accomplish any evil design they may wish to carry out and execute. These startling developments have agitated and alarmed this kingdom. It is indeed most lamentable that the English and Negroes should have combined against us, for the blacks are numerous.'[2]

Drake had turned to the *cimarrones* as tools to his ends, but from the relationship he learned a respect for Negroes and coloured peoples generally that was in advance of most of the empire builders of his time. Working shoulder to shoulder with these black men, following them along jungle trails only they knew, confronting hazards together, and listening to their stories of the treatment they had received from the Spaniards, Drake thought that he understood their plight. He relied upon them as he relied upon his Plymouth lads, saw qualities in them as sterling as those he found in any whites, and they did not let him down. Interestingly, Diego figures more prominently in the English narrative of the voyage than any other individual, barring the two captain Drakes themselves. If the enslaving and slaughter of Indians in the West Indies and Central America and the introduction of the African slave trade were harrowing chapters in which the English had played a not unimportant part, it is pleasing to record the development of an unusual measure of racial tolerance in Elizabeth's great-

[1] *Ibid*, 281.
[2] Municipal Council at Panama to the Crown, 24 February, 1573, Wright, 48-51.

est sailor.

Drake established a forward base on an island about five leagues east of Cativas Headland, and built a fort there, protected by timber and earthworks and standing 13 feet high. He honoured the architect of the new alliance by naming the stockade Fort Diego.[1] Two weeks of labour, into which the *cimarrones* threw themselves with enthusiasm, saw enough of the task completed for Drake to leave his brother in charge while he made again for Cartagena with two pinnaces, evidently seeking more intelligence, provisions and prizes.

He would never see John again. Two days after Drake's force left, John was employing his remaining pinnaces collecting wood for the fort when a Spanish ship was seen close off shore. Had he been a cautious man, perhaps an older one, or had he not been a Drake, John might have let the Spaniard pass unmolested. The sailors left with him were poorly armed, and their leader relatively inexperienced. Now he allowed the clamour of his followers to persuade him into an ill-advised attempt to board the enemy vessel. As the English pinnace ran alongside its quarry it received a sharp volley of shot from the defenders. John, standing in the bow of the pinnace with nothing more than a broken rapier in one hand and a pillow as a shield in the other, was fatally wounded by a ball in his stomach, and a seaman standing beside him with a fishing harpoon also fell in his death agony.

Hastily the surviving pirates pushed away, but within an hour of regaining the *Pasco* John Drake died. He had not made a will, and in the closing moments of his life called his friends to witness the simplest provisions he desired for his young wife, Alice. His brother Francis was to be sole executor of his possessions, and would ensure that debts were met, but his share of any profits of the present adventure were to belong to his wife. Later, when Drake was back in England he attempted to fulfil these obligations and obtained probate, but for some reason the will was contested and pronounced null and void. Happily, Alice remarried quickly and secured letters of administration by which she claimed the full amount of her late husband's property.

Ignorant of his brother's death, Drake was merrily tormenting the city of Cartagena in the autumn of 1572. He chased some ships ashore, seized others, and almost blockaded the port, always taking care to put his prisoners ashore or into small boats, unharmed. Two vessels, perhaps the frigates of James Raphael and Sebastian de Proenca mentioned in a Spanish document of 1575, were intercepted by the English on 20 October just as they were trying to leave Cartagena. The Spaniards fumbled helplessly before Drake's impudent antics. The city's authorities negotiated with him; they tried to lure his men ashore into ambushes; and they sent out two armed ships to recover some of Drake's prizes. They failed to drive the corsairs away, but they were at least to be successful in preventing them from securing what might have been the richest prize Drake had yet encountered in the voyage. On 27 October the English ran a frigate ashore, where without rudder or sails she lay aground like a beached whale. Drake tried to board her, but four or five hundred mounted Spaniards thundered towards the ship and began a firing which kept the corsairs at a distance. The English were not particularly concerned, because they had no knowledge that the frigate contained a considerable amount of gold and silver as well as a more prosaic cargo of flour.

---

[1] Irene Wright identified the site of Fort Diego as an island in the Gulf of San Blas.

This, however, was the height of the Spanish achievement. The rest was frustration, particularly when they manned a large shallop and two pinnaces with soldiers and Indians and sent them out to engage the English, only to see Drake making light of them and forcing them to retire. But this could not go on, for Drake was desperately short of provisions, and when the weather favoured him on 3 November he quit Cartagena and set a course eastwards along the Main, proceeding as far as the memorable Rio de la Hacha. A prize was taken in the cruise, but not a valuable one, and the captain noticed ominous signs of discontent in his crew. He was probably not surprised, for the men were five months out of Plymouth and had little to show for their efforts. This time trouble was averted by an uncommon piece of good fortune, the discovery of a Spanish vessel of over 90 tons filled with the victuals so urgently needed by the English.

Drake summoned the stranger to surrender, receiving in defiance a discharge of their artillery. The narrative tells us:

> The sea went very high so that it was not for us to attempt to board her, and therefore we made fit small sail to attend upon her and keep her company to her small content, till fairer weather might lay the sea. We spent not past two hours in our attendance, till it pleased God after a great shower to send us a reasonable calm, so that we might use our pieces, and approach her at pleasure, in such sort that in short time we had taken her, finding her laden with victual well powdered and dried, which at that present we received as sent as of God's great mercy.[1]

The capture certainly alleviated the food shortage, more so in that her complement, eager to please their captors, guided them to further supplies of victuals and water near Santa Marta. After bartering with local Indians, Drake deposited his prisoners on shore and turned back for Fort Diego.

His return was not a comfortable one. First, he heard of John Drake's death, and then he lost another brother, younger still, Joseph Drake, who had been serving in some obscure capacity. The cause of this last tragedy, one of several, is not precisely known, other than that it was one of those terrible and feared epidemics which for centuries scourged seamen in the West Indies. Its sudden and spectacular onslaught – at the beginning of January 1573 some ten men were stricken and died within a few days – suggests it was yellow fever, a disease later christened Yellow Jack or the black vomit on account of its manifestations; it was capable of decimating whole crews with terrifying speed. It was not contagious, but arose from a virus associated with the mosquito. Drake and his comrades did not know that. They saw one man after another mysteriously struck down and wondered where it would end; at one time thirty men were sick, and when it was over about 40 per cent of the company had died.

The survivors argued the causes of the pestilence, speculating that it related to changes in the temperature or to the negligence of some sailors who had refilled water containers from a brackish estuary instead of up-river where the streams were purer. Drake could not contend with a problem he did not understand, even when his young brother died in his arms. With his usual decision he declared that he would open the body of one of the victims to investigate the origins of the sickness, and since the very

[1] *Sir Francis Drake Revived*, 290.

proposition filled the men with horror, he chose his brother as the subject of the autopsy. Unfortunately, the operation was futile, and left Drake no wiser. When the epidemic shortly passed, leaving the ravaged band at its weakest since it had left Plymouth, the men gave their island a new name, Slaughter Island.

As they foraged for provisions, or worked on the fort and the pinnaces, the thoughts of the sailors may have weighed upon the series of disasters that had overcome them, from the repulse at Nombre de Dios to the deadly fever, and some may have resigned themselves, with that superstition so common in seafaring men, to a belief that theirs was simply an unlucky voyage. It was when spirits were at such an ebb that the Englishmen were suddenly invigorated by the news for which they had been waiting. *Cimarrone* scouts arrived at the fort to inform Drake that Diego Flores's *flota* had arrived at Nombre de Dios and the treasure was moving across the isthmus.

CHAPTER SIX

# 'DESPITE . . . ALL THE SPANIARDS IN THE INDIES'

Oh thou who wast the greatest scourge of Spain, and who
To Philip's self wast source of fear and terror on the seas.

Latin Broadside commemorating Drake, 1596

FORTY-EIGHT MEN TOILED THROUGH THE TROPICAL RAIN-FOREST OF THE ISTHMUS
of Panama. Eighteen of them were English. They carried their weapons, but
were otherwise less heavily burdened than their comrades, the black *cimarrones*
who marched with them, laden with victuals which they supplemented by the
spoils of hunting. The forest was dark and quiet, only illuminated high in the tree
tops where brilliant macaws flitted among sunlit branches. In the gloom below it
was cooler. Lianas crawled up the thick, high boles, striving to reach the light.
Lizards scuttled in the undergrowth and wild pigs foraged among the ferns and
palms. Of fruit there was plenty, including lemons, mammee and palmetto.

The travellers marched purposefully, keeping where possible to the cool
uplands or the shade of the trees, but also sluicing across swift streams which
gushed on beds so stony that they cut shoes to pieces, or through tall and thick
grasses which lay open to the burning sun. Each day the march began at sunrise.
After some four hours the men rested until noon, and another camp was established at about four o'clock. Then the *cimarrones* would fashion rude shelters,
thatching plantain leaves between palmetto poles, and securing the dwellings
from water and the cold air which distinguished nights in the hills. During the day
four *cimarrones* broke trail ahead, while twelve acted as an advance to the main
party and another twelve formed a rearguard. The two remaining *cimarrones*, one
of them their leader, Pedro, accompanied the Englishmen in the centre.

Drake had acted quickly after learning of the arrival of the *flota*. He had sent a
pinnace towards Nombre de Dios to confirm the news, which it did, taking two
barks laden with provisions into the bargain. Then Drake had struck into the interior, leaving his ships, the sick, and the new Spanish prisoners (who needed protecting from the fury of the *cimarrones*) under the charge of Ellis Hixom at
Slaughter Island. By so doing he had already outwitted the Spaniards, for none of
them expected the corsairs to attack the isthmus highway close to Panama and
their eyes were seawards, not to the land. Diego Flores had been received at
Nombre de Dios with reports of Drake's activities, but he instinctively created a
convoy system for the barks plying between the town and the Chagres River, fitting out a brigantine and ordering the building of another oared vessel. Unfortunately for Flores, Drake was not interested in the barks this time; he intended
to cut the land highway between Panama and Venta Cruces and to intercept the
treasure-laden mule-trains as they plodded across the isthmus.

On the third day of their march Drake's party entered a *cimarrone* town, situated on a hillside by a river and protected by a ditch and a mud wall about 10 feet

66

high. The villagers furnished the corsairs with maize, fruit and meat, and regaled them with stories of Spanish atrocities, of how the year before the town had been sacked, and black men, women and children had been slaughtered or captured. In return the English captain could not resist proselytizing, as he had with that Welshman years before on Lovell's voyage. He encouraged the *cimarrones* to set aside their Catholic crosses and to embrace the 'true worship', evidently with some success.

Another four days brought Drake to 'a very high hill, lying east and west, like a ridge', and upon its summit an enormous tree into which the *cimarrones* had cut steps that they might ascend to the top, where a viewing platform had been established. The captain accompanied Pedro to the bower to behold a sight few Englishmen had yet seen. Lying to the west in the clear light, across the tree tops, was the mighty Pacific Ocean itself. Twisting round, Drake could see in the opposite direction the Caribbean that he knew so well. History and art have often dwelt upon this moment, sensing its significance and the inspiration with which it filled the English commander. Perhaps, with the benefit of hindsight, commentators have exaggerated the episode, but it was notable nonetheless. Drake saw a vision of the future here, the basis of another adventure. Just as he had led the corsairs to the isthmus highway, so he now grasped the possibility of unlocking the door to the Pacific, where none but the Spaniards and the occasional Portuguese had gone from Europe before, and which was still largely a mystery even to them. There and then Drake 'besought almighty God of his goodness to give him life and leave to sail once in an English ship in that sea.' And when he reached the ground John Oxenham, the Plymouth man who now stood as Drake's second-in-command, clambered up the tree to partake of the same exhilaration. A brave and respected man, but stern and grave, he seldom gave way to emotion, but now 'protested that unless our captain did beat him from his company he would follow him by God's grace.'[1] Both men would fulfil their pledge to furrow the Pacific, but, while to one it would bring glory, to the other it would bring death.

Soon after this incident Drake and his men reached the grassy hills about Panama, and working along the crests they gazed down at the city sitting on the edge of the greatest of oceans with the ships that passed to Peru nestling in its anchorage. About a day's journey from Panama the raiders found a grove in which to camp, remote enough to be secure from the casual Spanish traveller. Drake had penetrated a region unknown to other corsairs, and he did not intend that his presence should be discovered prematurely. At dusk he sent a *cimarrone* into Panama to gather information, and heard what he wanted. The treasurer of Lima himself, with his family, was due to leave the city with a mule convoy bearing gold and jewels bound for Nombre de Dios, while behind them would travel two more mule-trains laden with silver and victuals. After the news was confirmed by a Spanish prisoner, also brought in by the *cimarrones*, Drake set up an ambush.

He chose a spot a few miles from Venta Cruces, the small town on the Chagres River, and secreted half of his men in the long grass about fifty paces from one side

---

[1] *Sir Francis Drake Revived*, 299-300.

of the mule path and the other half, commanded by Pedro and Oxenham, on the other side, further from Venta Cruces. So that they might be distinguished in the dark the Englishmen wore white shirts on the outside of their clothing. According to Drake's plan, Oxenham was to allow the mules to pass his party. When the leading animals reached Drake's position he would rush forward and seize them while Pedro and Oxenham swooped on the rear of the train. Once the first and last mules had been forced to lie down the others, if they obeyed their training, would follow suit.

The next half-hour must have seemed longer than that to the men crouching by the wayside, wondering if all their travail was at last to be made worthwhile. Eventually, sure enough, the sound of the mule bells was heard in the still night, and the hooves of the animals struck sharp on the hard ground. The train was coming. But then there came another sound, not from Panama, but from Venta Cruces, in the opposite direction – the unmistakable hoof-beats of a single rider at a trot, with a page running at his stirrup. Drake trusted that his men would have the sense to keep their positions, and to allow this rider to pass, but as he listened he heard the Spaniard suddenly spur his horse forward in a gallop towards Panama and the oncoming mule-trains. Had Drake's ambush been discovered? He could only wait for the answer.

His suspicions were well founded. The fault lay in one Robert Pike, apparently a seaman of Oxenham's party. He had been drinking 'too much aqua vitae without water', in the words of the narrative, and stole close to the roadside in his eagerness to attack. Worse, when the Spanish rider approached from Venta Cruces, Pike rose from the grass in his white shirt like some dreadful spectre and was spotted before a *cimarrone* could pull him down and sit on him to prevent further disturbance. It was at this point that the rider broke into a gallop to warn the mule convoys ahead. He informed the escorts that he thought the pirate Drake was waiting for them along the path, and the Spaniards immediately turned back the mules carrying the treasure, which, it was said, was worth some £35,000. To engage the attention of the corsairs, however, the Spaniards sent forward the animals laden with silver and victuals so that the English would not suspect that their ambush had been discovered.

Thus it was that when Francis Drake's men leaped from their hiding places to secure the mule-train searches revealed no more than two horse-loads of silver and some food. A few bold Spanish drovers had volunteered to ride forward into the ambush, a sure indication that the Spaniards were convinced that it was Drake and not the *cimarrones*, whose savagery they feared, who lay ahead. From one of the prisoners the English learned how their plan had been frustrated, and black must have been the name of simple Robert Pike. Months of waiting and two weeks of stumbling across the isthmus had merely culminated in more bad luck, which now seemed inseparable from the expedition.[1]

The soldiers of Panama were sure to be told, and Drake had to get his com-

---

[1] The date of the attack is uncertain. Spanish accounts place it in the last days of January, but the English narrative has Drake leaving Slaughter Island on 3 February, viewing the Pacific from the tree in Darien on 11 February, and attacking the mule-train in the middle of that month.

mand away before it was destroyed. He consulted with his men and with Pedro, and decided not to retrace the route by which they had come across the isthmus, but to take the shortest way to the Caribbean, even though it passed through the small town of Venta Cruces. Drake reasoned that if he moved quickly he could capture it before its defenders could assemble. Addressing his men and the *cimarrones*, he convinced them of the necessity for the attack, and once they had replenished their provisions from the mules and released the animals and their drovers, the English plunged into the thick woods down a path that led to Venta Cruces.

As they approached the settlement they encountered a party of Spanish travellers, most of them Dominican friars on their way to Panama under military escort. Drake had been alerted by a few *cimarrones* in the advance party, and was able to issue a few brief orders before a Spanish voice called out, 'Que gente?'

'Englishmen!' Drake replied boldly.

The Spaniard ordered Drake to surrender in the name of Philip of Spain, to which insulting demand Drake answered, 'that for the honour of the Queen of England, his mistress, he must have passage that way,' and so saying he discharged a pistol in the direction of his enemies. There was a return volley from the Spanish soldiers, and Drake and some of his men were wounded, one of them fatally, but the captain blew his whistle as a signal to his men to fire. They delivered both arrows and shot, and then charged forward, the *cimarrones* bounding lustily to the assault with ferocious cries that sounded to the English like 'Yó pehó, Yó pehó!' In the brief skirmish that ensued a Spaniard skewered a *cimarrone* on a pike, three or four of the Spanish soldiers and a friar were killed and others wounded, and the rest of Drake's opposition fled.[1]

The raiders then swept into Venta Cruces and quickly made themselves masters of the small settlement, which consisted of no more than fifty houses, some storehouses, a commander's residence and a monastery. In one of the houses three women were convalescing after childbirth. Not unnaturally they were alarmed by the sudden appearance of the English, and more particularly by the *cimarrones*, nor were they reassured by the words of some of Drake's men that they would be safe. The captain understood the bitterness of the Negroes, but he endeavoured to curb their ferocity, enjoining them to harm no one who did not resist. It had been his aim to give the English a better reputation than the French enjoyed, for 'of all the men taken . . . we never offered any kind of violence to any, after they were once came under our power, but either presently dismissed them in safety or, keeping them with us some longer time . . . we always provided for their sustenance as for ourselves, and secured them from the rage of the *cimar*-

---

[1] Once again the Spanish casualties are given differently in the various accounts. The Municipal Council of Panama informed the Crown on 24 February, 1573 (Wright, *Documents Concerning English Voyages to the Spanish Main*, 48-51) that three Spaniards and a friar had been killed and five others, white and Negro, were mortally wounded. Depositions sent from Nombre de Dios indicate that three Spaniards and a friar were killed and others wounded. These depositions may be the basis of the Panama account (Miguel Ordoño to the Crown, 26 February, 1573, *Ibid*, 52-3). Lopez Vaz in the account published by Hakluyt in 1589 confused this attack on the mule-trains with Drake's later capture of a convoy outside Nombre de Dios.

rones."[1] However reprehensible the raids Drake was conducting, and whether it was patriotism, religion or the memory of Spanish treachery that was used to legitimize the violence, the casualties were those who resisted, and Drake waged his war with more humanity than anyone familiar with the barbarity of the religious conflict in Europe might expect. Now, when he learned of the apprehensions of the Spanish women, Drake visited them himself to convince them of their safety.

Guards were posted at the approaches to the town while the English and their allies refreshed themselves and added a little booty to the silver they had taken from the mules. Some buildings containing merchandise were burned some time before early the next morning, when the raiding party were marched out. The attack probably turned the men's minds from their disappointments, and as they retired to the coast Drake strode cheerfully forward, rebuilding the morale of his followers and assuring them that notwithstanding all the defeats they would not leave the Caribbean uncompensated. Once again Drake's fortitude and resourcefulness were on trial, as he must have known. If Nombre de Dios, Cartagena and the ambush outside Venta Cruces had spelled failure, he must think of some new audacity to retrieve their fortunes.

Jaded and footsore, the men force-marched towards the sea, tumbling into a village that the Negroes had newly established close to where Drake's ships were to call. Amid his tribulations, Drake must have taken consolation from the unswerving loyalty of the *cimarrones*, for those unusual men seemed equal to every situation. As the exhausted Englishmen rested at the village, the Negroes made new shoes for them and tended those who were sick. The English account of the voyage remembered it this way:

> These cimarrones, *during all the time that we were with them did us continually very good service, and in particular in this journey, being unto us instead of intelligencers to advertise us; of guides in our way to direct us; of purveyors to provide victuals for us; of housewrights to build our lodgings; and had indeed able and strong bodies carrying all our necessaries, yea many times when some of our company fainted with sickness or weariness, two* cimarrones *would carry him with ease between them two miles together, and at other times (when need was) they would show themselves no less valiant than industrious and of good judgement.*[2]

A *cimarrone* it was who now went ahead to signal to Drake's vessels that they could contact their captain at a nearby river. When the two parties of Englishmen met the one must have seemed strange to the other, for Drake's expeditionary force was gaunt and weak, and some of the men had been left behind to recover at the Negro town. The whole company was eventually reunited on 23 February, 1573, and embarked, still far from the riches they had sought with such ardent hopes. A few of the blacks left for home, but others were so enamoured of their new role that they accompanied Drake aboard the ships.

Drake knew that he must now mark more time to allow the Spaniards to think that he had abandoned his attempts to capture the treasure-trains for more lucrative

---

[1] *Sir Francis Drake Revived*, 326.
[2] *Ibid*, 310.

activities elsewhere. Then he planned to return, and to strike again at a place where vigilance would be lax. Discussing the problem with his comrades he found considerable disagreement as to which was the best course, and so divided his command to meet two of the proposals. Oxenham took the *Bear* eastwards in search of victuals, and Drake cruised in the other direction, hoping to snap up a prize or two among the treasure barks shuttling between Nombre de Dios and the mouth of the Chagres.

His own operation was not a success. Drake may have sailed as far as the mouth of the San Juan River and taken four vessels, but he acquired only a little gold and failed to surprise the harbour of Veragua. However when he rejoined Oxenham he was cheered to learn that the *Bear* had met with better fortune, and had secured a prize well-supplied in maize, hogs and hens, and stout and big enough herself to manage the Atlantic crossing home when the time came. The vessel was cleaned and fitted with guns and loaded with supplies, and for the time being Drake kept her crew prisoner. The raiders then repaired to Slaughter Island for an Easter feast during which they were cheered by the food they now had at their disposal and Drake's cavalier talk of further enrichment.

The twenty-third of March saw Drake with his new ship and the *Bear* off Cativas Headland hunting for more prizes. When a sail was seen to the west, he bore down upon it, merely to discover that the quarry was a Frenchman. Indeed, her captain was a Huguenot privateer, bent upon raiding the Spaniards, and he was out looking for Drake, for he was short of water and needed the support of an ally. Guillaume Le Testu explained that he had cider and wine aboard, but little water, and that some of his men were sick. Drake immediately sent some provisions across, and then bade Le Testu follow him to one of his depots where the French could be fully replenished. At anchor the Huguenot captain graciously sent Drake a case of pistols and a gilt scimitar that had been the gift of Admiral Gaspard de Coligny, the leader of the French Protestants. Not to be outdone by this Gallic charm, Drake awarded Le Testu a gold chain from his own collection.

Then there was serious talking. From Le Testu and his men the English learned the blood-curdling story of the massacre of St Bartholomew's Day in France. In August the previous year, the notorious Catherine de Medici, the queen-mother, frantic as she saw her son King Charles IX become the puppet of the Huguenot Coligny, and another son, the miserable Alençon, going in the same direction, had arranged for the assassination of Coligny. The assassin had botched the job, and Coligny was wounded, but not killed. Catherine became desperate; she persuaded King Charles that Coligny was a traitor, along with all Protestants, and prepared a death-list of the Huguenot leaders, including Coligny. But the political purge became mass-murder, and thousands of Protestants, in Paris and throughout France, were butchered in one of the bloodiest episodes of the period. Once again France was tortured by religious civil war. Drake must also have been stirred by news of the revolt in the Netherlands, where the Dutch, inspired by the capture of Brielle and Flushing by the so-called Sea Beggars, among whom were many recruits from the Netherlands, had at last broken into outright rebellion against Spain. Both tidings, indicative of the tensions developing between Rome and Geneva and between Spain and northern Europe, may have encouraged Drake as he chewed at the margins of Philip's empire.

Le Testu and Drake respected each other. The Frenchman had heard of Drake's exploits on the Spanish Main, and Drake would quickly have realized that Le Testu was no ordinary corsair: he was a middle-aged man of a seafaring family from Le Havre and had studied navigation at Dieppe; nor was he a stranger to American waters. Between 1550 and 1556 he had made three voyages to the New World with the monk André Thévet and had explored the Brazilian coastline; on the last of these occasions he had acted as pilot of a French expedition that had planted a small colony in Brazil and returned to Europe with tobacco, which Le Testu may be credited with having helped introduce to France. He demonstrated that he was no mean cartographer by producing a folio atlas of fifty-six maps, Universal Cosmography, based on his own experiences and completed in 1556; he dedicated it to Coligny. After further voyages to Africa, Brazil and North America and the revision of some of his cartography, and having received an appointment as Royal Pilot at Le Havre, Le Testu was drawn into the privateering that was unleashed by the wars of religion, cruising in the Huguenot interest. He was soon captured at sea, and imprisoned by the Duke of Alba at Middleburg in Flanders. Not until January 1572 was he freed, on the intercession of Charles IX to Philip II. Obviously, Le Testu had powerful friends – Coligny, André Thévet (then chaplain to Catherine de Medici), and possibly Philippe Strozzi, an important army officer who was planning a French expedition to the West Indies.[1]

Conceivably, it was Strozzi who was responsible for Le Testu's arrival in the West Indies. Possibly the seaman had been charged with reconnoitring for Strozzi's project. When Drake met Le Testu, although he could call upon the Negroes, his own force had shrunk to thirty-one, and his ships were small. The Spanish vessel that Drake was currently using was only about 20 tons' burden, and the tonnage of his pinnaces was not more than 10 each. Le Testu, on the other hand, had seventy men and a ship of over 80 tons. Drake may have viewed him as a potential threat, so superior was he in strength, or he may have regarded the Frenchmen as welcome reinforcements at a time when his own manpower was so depleted. Anyway, he struck a bargain with Le Testu. The two would join forces. Drake's plan of campaign would stand, and the corsairs would march inland to attack the isthmus highway using twenty Frenchmen, fifteen Englishmen and some cimarrones. Drake's Bear and Minion would land the raiders at the River Francisca, five leagues east of Nombre de Dios, while the rest of the ships would remain secluded in some quiet anchorage. It was agreed that the plunder taken would be shared equally between the French and English, half to each party; the cimarrones had little use for treasure and apparently supported Drake purely as another opportunity to strike their enemies.

This time Drake planned to cut the isthmus treasure route at a different place. Some of the bullion from Panama was loaded on to barks at Venta Cruces to be transported the rest of the way by river, but part of it continued by mule-train to Nombre de Dios. Drake reasoned that after so long and dangerous a journey the mule drivers and their escorts would begin to relax as the train approached its destination, and so he would intercept it at the Campos River, only two leagues from Nombre de Dios. He gave instructions to his pinnace captains to return to the Francisca River on 3 April to take off the expeditionary force.

[1] Lemonnier, Sir Francis Drake, 76-80, gives details of Le Testu's career from French sources.

On 31 March, 1573, the corsairs filtered into the woods, heading for the highway, a shorter march than that gruelling hike to Panama. The French were impressed both by the order and silence exhibited by the English and Negroes as they passed through the forest, and by the relationship that Drake had cultivated with Pedro and his followers. The raiding party arrived within a mile of Nombre de Dios, and were so close that local carpenters could be heard labouring in the port's shipyards. After a brief refreshment, the corsairs took up their positions on the Campos River and waited while some of the *cimarrones* crept towards the mule-path to watch. After so many disappointments the waiting was tense, but this time the discipline and determination of the men were rewarded. The following morning, 1 April, the Negroes reported that three mule-trains, nearly two hundred heavily laden animals in all, were coming along the path under an escort of forty-five soldiers. With the *cimarrones*, Drake probably outnumbered the Spaniards, and he had the advantage of surprise. He was also, it seems, better armed. Only some of the mule-train's escort carried arquebuses, and others bows, but some were so badly equipped that they marched barefoot. They hardly looked formidable opposition to men of the stamp of Drake, Oxenham, Pedro and Le Testu. As the mule convoy moved easily along the trail, with Nombre de Dios close by, the Spaniards had no suspicion that they were about to be attacked.

When it came the assault was sudden and swift. Drake's men bolted from the foliage and seized the first and last mules in the line, driving away the soldiers with surprising ease. A Negro arquebusier with the Spaniards discharged his piece at Le Testu, wounding him in the stomach, and a *cimarrone* was killed, but the escort was soon in flight. Greedily the corsairs leaped upon the baggage, and found an enormous prize in their hands, for the mules were carrying treasure worth more than 200,000 pesos belonging to both the king and private individuals. It was impossible to carry all of it away. According to what the French later told André Thévet some Negro drovers captured with the train told Drake where the more valuable treasure, the gold, was packed:

> Those who accompanied . . . Captain Testu took as much as they could carry; even the slaves leading the charges encouraged them to do so, through hatred of the Spaniard, showing them where the gold was so that they should not play around with silver. There were plaques of gold like two kinds of seals from the High Chancellery of France, some of Castillian ducats, others of pistoles.[1]

About 15 tons of silver were hastily buried, in burrows made by landcrabs, under fallen trees, and in the sand and gravel of the bed of a shallow river. The French interred some of it on a tiny island. More than 100,000 pesos in gold were actually carried back to the ships by the corsairs, including 18,363 pesos that were being shipped to the king from Colombia. This booty amounted to about £40,000 in Elizabethan money, equal to perhaps a fifth of the queen's annual revenue, and, according to the agreement made between Drake and Le Testu, half of it belonged to the English.

But first they had to escape, and here the disadvantage of striking so close to

[1] Translated from Lemonnier, 85. Lemonnier quotes a French manuscript by André Thévet, who claimed to have interviewed Le Testu's men ('as some of them have confessed to me'). The details are broadly compatible with those given by the English and Spanish records, but seem erroneous in some respects.

Nombre de Dios made itself felt. It would not take long for the routed gold escort to reach the town and declare their misfortune, and a posse of enraged Spaniards would soon be forming to pursue Drake's men. After two hours of looting, sorting, burying and packing treasure, the corsairs struggled into the deep woods with their winnings. Captain Le Testu's wound was a severe one, however, and he could not keep up with the retreat. Chivalrously, he remained behind, hoping to recover some strength, with two Frenchmen who elected to stay with him, while Drake led the rest of the party towards safety. The only other loss suffered by the party during the flight was that of a drunken Frenchman, Jacques Laurens or Lores, who wandered away from the march and was lost in the trees.

Burdened as they were with treasure, Drake's men pressed forward quickly for they knew that a determined pursuit might overtake them, or that the Spaniards could cut off their retreat by sea. In Nombre de Dios the alcalde, Diego Calderon, and Captain Hernando Berrio were indeed beating an alarm about the town and gathering soldiers for that very purpose. Drake's party marched for two days over difficult ground, enduring the intervening night when the forest was punished by a fearful storm. On 3 April they reached the mouth of the Francisca, the appointed rendezvous for the pinnaces, but it was not the welcome sight of their ships that greeted the weary travellers. The English pinnaces were nowhere to be seen. Instead, riding quietly off shore, were seven oared Spanish shallops with artillery and manned by eighty-five musketeers.

This was a desperate moment for the corsairs, and among them a sickening logic revealed what must have taken place. That drunken Frenchman they had lost must have been captured by the Spaniards and compelled to disclose where Drake was expecting to embark. The English pinnaces had been captured by this superior Spanish force, and Drake was now surrounded, by the shallops at sea and the pursuers behind. The imagination of the men dwelt upon one terrifying prospect after another. If the pinnaces had been taken it was only a matter of time before the Spaniards would learn where Drake kept his base. Even now Diego Flores might be on his way to destroy the Pasco, Le Testu's ship and Drake's Spanish prize, and with them any chance of returning home. Of what use was the treasure to them now, with their enemies on all sides and no means of escape?

It was a bad situation, but Drake's resource, resolution and equipoise did not fail him. Addressing his men, he reminded them that even if the pinnaces had been taken, as was supposed, it would be some time before the Spaniards could obtain the information about the base and mount an expedition against it. There would be a delay, and during that interval Drake must reach his ships and bring them away. But how, without the pinnaces? An overland march along the coast would have taken too long and was out of the question, so Drake set his men to make a small raft. They hauled fallen trees together, trimmed off their branches and bound them to each other; then they fitted a crude mast to the timbers and equipped it with a slashed biscuit sack as a sail. A rudimentary oar was fashioned from a branch. The craft was a crazy structure, large enough for only a handful of men, a fragile instrument to launch into the surf for a madcap voyage in a storm-prone, shark-infested sea. At least two men were required to manage her, and Drake declared that he would fill one place and called for a volunteer to accompany him.

John Smith offered himself, and two Frenchmen who were strong swimmers were also so insistent that Drake agreed to take them. Pedro, the *cimarrone* leader, begged that he might go too, but Drake would not have it so; he had too many for his raft already, and Pedro was not a good seaman. The captain and his three men waded out with their ridiculous craft, bent upon what must have seemed a forlorn adventure, a wild errand against Spaniards and the sea in which the chances of survival were not high. Yet every man there depended upon its succeeding. Drake knew that many doubted that he would make it or that they would ever see him again, and that they needed any reassurance his words could offer them. As he departed he turned to the solemn companions remaining on the shore, and 'comforted the company by promising that if it pleased God he should put his foot in safety aboard his frigate, he would, God willing, by one means or other get them all aboard, in despite of all the Spaniards in the Indies.'[1]

Fortune had so often defeated Drake, but this time she shone upon him brightly. The raft sailed three leagues, with the waves sweeping across it and surging up to the men's armpits. The salt on their bodies and the burning sun began to peel away parts of their skin, but a remarkable sight presently met their eyes – the pinnaces, the *Bear* and the *Minion*, which they had supposed had been captured. The Englishmen on board the ships did not see the tiny raft wallowing in the waves, and they put before a freshening wind into a cove for the night. Drake had to put his raft ashore and lead his companions across the point by land to advance from the trees towards the anchored pinnaces. At this moment his cheerful disposition found time for a joke. When the startled seamen recognized their captain among the four dishevelled men moving unevenly towards them their hearts sank, for it surely betokened another disaster, and as Drake climbed aboard one of the ships his grim aspect sustained their apprehension. Then, suddenly, he broke into a smile, and removed from his clothes a quoit of gold. Their voyage, he said, was 'made'.

Drake never pieced together the whole story of what had happened. The pinnaces had been prevented from reaching the Francisca River by a powerful westerly wind, and it was a Spanish force from Nombre de Dios that had arrived at the rendezvous instead. When news of the robbery first reached Nombre de Dios a party of foot soldiers had left for the Campos River, where they came upon the broken boxes that had contained the treasure. Some of the Spaniards under Diego Calderon remained to forage and discovered most of the loot hidden by the corsairs, while a small party under Captain De Berrio attempted to follow Drake's trail. In the woods they came upon Captain Le Testu and his two comrades. One of the Frenchmen fled, but the other, along with his gallant commander, was slain, and Le Testu's head was struck off that it might be displayed in the market-place of Nombre de Dios. Despite this success, the Spaniards gave up the chase before reaching the Francisca River because the storm on the night of 1-2 April wiped out the trail. Captain De Berrio's men therefore returned to the scene of the robbery where they busied themselves rooting for further caches of plunder.

If the land pursuit fizzled out, another by sea was soon under way. Two prisoners were eventually brought in by the Spaniards. One was the Frenchman who had wandered from Drake's party. He had been seized by some Negroes working on a dam

[1] *Sir Francis Drake Revived*, 320-1.

and turned over to the Spaniards, who summarily executed and quartered him. The other prisoner, a *cimarrone*, was forced to reveal Drake's destination. This information reached Nombre de Dios in the late afternoon of 1 April, and Diego Flores fitted out seven shallops, commanded by Captain Cristóbal Monte, and sent them to intercept Drake at the Francisca River. The vessels reached their station at dawn the next morning, and explored the lower reaches of the river without finding the corsairs. In fact, the Spaniards had arrived too early, for Drake was then still marching towards the Francisca. Had Monte's force remained in the river longer there might have been a skirmish. As it was, the Spaniards withdrew to stand off shore, preparing to leave, and were thus positioned when Drake arrived at the mouth of the Francisca to see them. Good luck was indeed with Drake upon this adventure. On 2 April a second posse of soldiers was led out of Nombre de Dios by Captain Antonio Suarez de Medina to renew the land pursuit, but whereas Monte's shallops had moved too quickly, Medina was too late, for he found that his quarry had escaped.

The night Drake found his pinnaces he had his men picked up, and their treasure was safely stowed aboard. Then he retired to the Cativas Headland to consolidate his position. The riches met all their expectations, and were divided between the French and English; the former then took their leave and sailed away after what had been an unusually profitable voyage. Drake prepared his Spanish prize for the journey home, and gave the old *Pasco* to his remaining prisoners to enable them to make their way to safety. After about two weeks he also judged it safe to return to the scene of his triumph for the unfinished business. He knew nothing of the fate of Le Testu and his two comrades, and wanted to try to pick them up, and there was the matter of the treasure that had been left hidden. The captain planned to send sixteen *cimarrones* and twelve Englishmen to retrace the line of their former retreat until they reached the scene of the robbery.

This expedition was not wholly fruitless. When the English reached the estuary of the Francisca and landed their party (commanded this time by Oxenham and Thomas Sherwell) it was hailed by a lone figure – the Frenchman who had remained with Le Testu until the Spaniards had arrived. He was able to tell Drake about the death of his captain and so to satisfy, if sadly, one of the mission's objectives. As for the other, a group of Englishmen did visit the site of the attack on the convoy and saw there the signs of the thorough searches the Spaniards had made. Nonetheless, thirteen bars of silver and a few quoits of gold repaid the men for their trouble and left them with but one remaining task, the voyage home.

Drake made a final cruise, taking a ship east of Cartagena, and both this and his own ship were then careened for home. They were tallowed and their rigging repaired, and the little pinnaces that had served them so well were burned and their ironwork turned over to the Negroes. The alliance of white and black must now come to an end. It had been the instrument of Drake's success and the aspect of his expedition that most troubled the Spaniards, who now feared that this intrepid Englishman would recruit an army of blacks and sack Nombre de Dios and Panama. None of Drake's fellow raiders, French or English, satisfactorily exploited the potential of the *cimarrones*, and for years Pedro and his followers remembered the little English captain. At their parting Drake invited Pedro and three other Negro leaders to rummage aboard his ships to choose gifts for themselves. As Drake was pulling out some silk and linen for the chiefs' wives, Pedro's eyes lighted upon the gold scimitar which Captain Le Testu had given his English ally. Drake would rather have kept it, but the *cimarrone* deserved no less, and Pedro received his sword.

More than a year had passed since seventy-three hopefuls had left Devon filled with dreams of Spanish bullion. Most of them were now dead, testimony to the dangers inherent in the game they had played. Two of Drake's brothers lay buried within the sound of the sea, on the small island in the Gulf of San Blas. But finally determination, audacity, careful planning and resourcefulness had been rewarded, and Drake was returning with wealth few Englishmen could have amassed in a lifetime. In value it may have been less than the plunder he had brought home in 1571, but this time the holds were filled with treasure, not merchandise, and their cargo had an immediate purchasing power.

Behind him Drake left a coast in great distress, and ringing again with tales of his exploits. Enormous as Drake's booty had been, it was only a minor loss in the totality of Spain's transatlantic trade, equal to only a twentieth of the annual value of the exports from Spain to the West Indies. But this corsair was not pottering haphazardly about the Caribbean; he was severing the artery through which the riches of the empire passed. He had captured two of the towns on the isthmus highway, Venta Cruces and Nombre de Dios, and threatened the third, Panama, and he had twice intercepted the mule-trains. Far more ominously, he had treated with the *cimarrones*, who provided both the knowledge of the bush and the manpower that the corsairs lacked. If Drake armed the Negroes the treasure flow might be stopped. As the Municipal Council of Panama told Philip of Spain:

> This realm is at the present moment so terrified, and the spirits of all so disturbed, that we know not in what words to emphasize to your Majesty the solicitude we make in this dispatch, for we certainly believe that if remedial action be delayed, disaster is imminent . . . These English have so shamelessly opened the door and a way by which, with impunity, whenever they desire, they will attack the pack-trains travelling overland by this highway.[1]

While Nombre de Dios clamoured for galleys to protect its coast, and Philip II, contemplating the insolence of this obscure corsair, instructed his Indies fleet to defend Darien, other Englishmen were following in Drake's wake. John Noble, Gilbert Horseley, Andrew Barker and John Oxenham would soon be exploring the Caribbean in quest of treasure. Oxenham, like Drake, had glimpsed something else too – the great Pacific Ocean and its totally undefended coasts from which the riches of South America were being shipped. As the King of Spain looked to improve his ravaged defences in the Caribbean, Drake was already ahead of him, dreaming of another and even more sensational stroke, where no corsairs had yet penetrated. A new phase of Drake's war was now in the making.

Plymouth, Sunday 9 August, 1573. The day had been quiet, as befitted the Sabbath, but a tremor of excitement shortly rippled through the congregation of St Andrew's church at an interrupting word from the harbour. Before long the preacher

[1] Municipal Council of Panama to Philip II, 24 February, 1573, Wright, 48-51.

was watching his flock desert the sermon to stream towards the waterfront. Francis Drake had come home.

# CHAPTER SEVEN

# SERVICES ASHORE AND AFLOAT

Seamen:    We give a shrewd guess how our quarrels have grown;
            For still when at land we are jointly designed,
            To the dainty delight of storming a town,
            You run to the plunder, and leave us behind.
Landsmen: Alas, our dear brothers, how can we forbear?
            But aboard when you have us, where wonderful gold,
            Is shovelled like ballast, y'are even with us there,
            We fight on the decks, whilst you rummage the hold.

William D'Avenant, *The History of Sir Francis Drake*, 1659

I F DRAKE WAS RICH AND THE HERO OF THE WEST COUNTRY MARINERS, THE HAVOC he had wrought on the Main had marked him as an enemy of the King of Spain, and it was singularly unfortunate that the corsair's return to Plymouth coincided with an improvement in Elizabeth's relations with Philip. In the Netherlands the Duke of Alba now had a full-scale insurrection on his hands, and he doubted that he could restore obedience while Elizabeth remained unfriendly and the English Channel was effectively closed to Spanish shipping. Nor was Alba alone in wishing an end to his damaging dispute with England. About the queen herself there was, it is true, a bellicose cabal of councillors headed by the Joint Principal Secretary, Francis Walsingham, who urged greater English intervention on the part of embattled Protestants in France and the Netherlands. But Elizabeth had burned her fingers in foreign adventures before, and instinctively shrank from extreme measures. Unofficially, she permitted her subjects to assist the Huguenots, but she would not commit herself any further to their cause.

Spain and England did the sensible thing, and came to terms. Both agreed not to harbour aliens unfriendly to the other, and Philip promised to afford the Netherlands greater liberties and to prevent the Inquisition further molesting English sailors. For her part, Elizabeth undertook to settle the matter of her seizure of the Spanish ships and to discourage her seamen from raiding Philip's commerce as pirates or privateers. The arrival of the most dangerous of her corsairs at such a time was, to say the least, impolitic. It appears that, soon after his return, Drake was advised to keep a low profile and that he was at sea and out of harm's way until the convention of Bristol had successfully restored a degree of amity between Spain and England in 1574.

Drake was so quiet, in fact, that nothing is known about his activities for almost two years after his triumphant return to Plymouth. When he did reappear it was as a supporting actor in the tawdry work that the Elizabethans were then undertaking in Ireland. This troubled land possessed an obvious strategic interest to England, for it guarded her vulnerable western flank, and were it to be occupied by a rival like Spain or France it would admirably serve them as a base for invasion. Unfortunately, the English found Ireland stubbornly resistant to their own influence. They administered 'the Pale', at that time a patch on the east coast embracing little more than Dublin, Kildare, Meath and Louth, but elsewhere a Gaelic society prevailed. This society was true to its own notions of succession, law and land tenure; a pastoral peasantry sustained itself by the raising and bartering of agricultural produce and livestock and was dominated by landed freeholders who recognized as their chieftain one of a ruling family, whether it be an O'Reilly of Cavan or an O'Neill of Tyrone. Even Irishmen of English descent, the so-called Anglo-Irish, frequently imbibed Gaelic rather than English traditions. Between the two very different communities, the Gaelic and the English, the Reformation added a religious wedge. In time Catholic Ireland was seen by the counter-reformers as a means by which England might be threatened through the back door.[1]

King Henry VIII had declared Ireland a kingdom united to the English Crown and had attempted to persuade the Irish chiefs to receive English title to the land they controlled, providing they introduced English law and religion and swore fealty to the king. But the 'surrender and regrant' policy, which sought to acculturate the Irish and bring them within England's orbit, made little progress, and more uncompromising methods were soon adopted. To the Elizabethans a combination of confiscation, colonization and plantation seemed an answer to the Irish problem. The lands of recalcitrant Irish would be seized and assigned to English adventurers, who undertook to settle the land with immigrants from England, grant them title, and develop in Ireland loyal communities which might support the English army against the Irish in times of difficulty.

It was a policy which bred conflict, of course. Across the Atlantic a similar practice later led to the dispossession and ultimate destruction of the aboriginal culture. In Ireland it created two communities nurtured in traditional hostility and ripe for discontent for centuries to come. Elizabeth had inherited in Ireland a land over which England had declared her authority but still exercised a fragile hold, and its conquest encompassed the whole of the queen's long reign. In so protracted a struggle it is not surprising that Drake, like so many other notable Elizabethans – Gilbert and Grenville, Ralegh and Spenser, Mountjoy and Sidney – became embroiled in the Irish campaigns. Of Drake's part little was said at the time. Edmund Howes, who may have obtained his information from the man himself, wrote that Drake voluntarily provided three frigates for the Earl of Essex's forces in Ireland, and that he served Essex with distinction by sea and land in the capture of 'divers' strong fortresses. This is an exaggeration, because familiarity with Essex's forays in Ireland reveals few encounters with stone houses, let alone enemy fortresses, and little in the way of naval action. There is one exception: the capture of Rathlin Island, and the records of Essex's expedition confirm that Drake was indeed engaged for that service and discharged soon after it was completed. The Irish interlude in Drake's life has been virtually ignored by biographers, and we here offer the first full account to be written of it.

---

[1] Valuable accounts of the Elizabethans in Ireland are Bagwell, *Ireland Under the Tudors*, and Canny, *The Elizabethan Conquest of Ireland*.

A man of about Drake's age, Walter Devereux, created the first Earl of Essex in 1572, was a rising star of Elizabeth's court, a dashing, commanding figure, elegant, brave, and, it soon appeared, ruthless. To strengthen his credit with the queen, he proposed to pacify and colonize Ulster, the most troublesome part of Ireland. The Crown granted Essex the lands in Ireland from Belfast Lough to Lough Sidney and the lower Bann, and the areas in the north-east known as the Glens of Antrim, the Route and Rathlin Island. He agreed to colonize the territory at his own risk, clearing away the rights of its Irish occupants and granting title to his English supporters who would bring over farmers and artisans to develop the settlement. It was typical of the queen and her parsimonious government that the conquest of Ireland was consigned to private enterprise. Essex invested his personal fortune in the expedition, and drew resources – capital, men and services – from the many who hoped to profit from his venture, including members of the government: William Cecil (now Lord Burghley and Lord Treasurer); Robert Dudley, Earl of Leicester; and Thomas Radcliffe, Earl of Sussex. The queen herself loaned Essex £10,000.

Essex's expedition sailed from Liverpool in August 1573, a few days after Drake's return from the West Indies. The earl spent the next two years trying to subjugate the area west of the Blackwater and the Bann rivers, but the Irish were slippery adversaries, avoiding full-scale engagements but adeptly using their knowledge of the woods, hills and bogs to ambush and harass the English. Eventually, Essex realized that only permanent garrisons could hold the country, but these were beyond his resources and he began to complain of inadequate support. Many of the gentlemen with him had been lured there by the prospect of quick returns, and the little enthusiasm they had displayed for the hard work of colonization wilted with the slow progress. Soldiers whose pay went into arrears grew mutinous. Essex asked the government to subsidize his efforts, but his pains obtained for him little more than the empty title of Governor of Ulster, and this he soon resigned in the bitter belief that while he was in Ireland he was being undermined by his enemies at court.

The principal resistance to Essex's 'plantation' came from the powerful lords of Tyrone, the O'Neills, who claimed sway in Ulster west of the Bann and Lough Neagh, and whose leader was Turlough O'Neill. There was also the problem of the mercenary Scots who had settled the Glens of Antrim, the Route and Rathlin Island, and who regarded as their head Sorley Boy MacDonnell, the son of the Lord of Islay and Kintyre. In 1575 Essex enjoyed some success against O'Neill, and turned upon MacDonnell, driving his Scots out of Clandeboy. It was at this point that Essex's attention focused upon Rathlin, a rugged, storm-swept island off north-eastern Antrim, which the Scots were using as a staging post between Ireland and Kintyre.

It was a craggy, L-shaped rock, four miles along one leg and three along the other, the home of thousands of seabirds – shearwaters, cormorants, razorbills, guillemots, puffins and gulls – but few people. Legend has it that the ancient castle that stood on the cliffs of its north-eastern shoreline had once been the refuge of no less a person than Robert the Bruce. Now Sorley Boy and his chiefs also considered Rathlin a safe sanctuary, and had sent their wives and children there, not without good reason, for the castle was assisted by considerable natural advantages. Thirteen miles from Scotland and three from Ireland, Rathlin was surrounded by waters that were notoriously dangerous, with eddies, currents and tides that even today not uncommonly claim their shipwrecks. In many cases the picturesque cliffs – white limestone crowned with contrasting black basalt under a wind-ravaged carpet of grass – rose sheer and smooth from the sea, up to 300 feet or more in height. And the castle itself, stretching from the summit of the cliffs, could only be approached from the west, and even there a swampy depression hindered any attack. Nonetheless, Essex reasoned that if he could seize and hold the island it would deal the morale of the Scots a hard blow, eliminate an enemy base, and cut communications between Sorley Boy's forces in Ireland and the Scottish Isles. It might also give him a concrete success to present to the queen. The enterprise demanded men, of which he had no shortage, and ships.[1]

The idea of creating a naval force had evolved late in 1574. On 8 October Essex had addressed a document to the Privy Council entitled 'My Opinion for the Government and Reformation of Ulster'. In it he made no reference to shipping, but remarked upon the problems of dealing with the Irish and Scots. To this the government responded with their own observations, of which the fifteenth read:

> *Item. What is to be thought requisite for the having of any shipping upon the sea, besides victuallers, to keep out ye Scots, for that no mention is thereof made in the plot [plan], and whether might not some of the galleys which the Scots use be thought meeter [more suitable] for those seas than the English pinnaces to stay [stop] the passages of ye Scots or take their galleys in their passages?*[2]

In other words, what ships was Essex planning to use against the Scots? Essex had already thought about this matter, and Drake was his answer. The earl drew heavy, perhaps his greatest, support from West Country men, and counted among his adherents such noted Devonians as Sir Peter Carew and Sir Arthur Champernowne, the latter then Vice-Admiral of Devon. Through some such connection, no doubt, Essex enlisted the advice and services of Francis Drake, who knew all there was to know about operating in the sort of shallows favoured by the Scottish galleys. Drake later said that he was recommended to Essex by John Hawkins, by which it may be assumed that the two seamen had settled their former differences. Howbeit, initially it was less Drake himself than the two Spanish prizes he had brought back from the West Indies that interested Essex.

Early in 1575 he responded to the Privy Council's 'doubts' about his plans for Ireland, and referred to Drake for the first time:

> *The shipping was not mentioned in the plot, but yet not unthought of, for I wrote unto my agents there to deal with my Lord Admiral, that ye shipping now here might be converted to buy certain frigates which one Drake brought out of [the] Indies, whereof one is in possession of Mr Hawkins [and] one of Sir Arthur Champernowne.*

---

[1] A useful history of Rathlin is given in Clark, *Rathlin-Disputed Island*.

[2] 'Doubts to be Resolved by the Earl of Essex', 1574, Additional MSS, British Library, London, Add. MS 48015: 319-20; Essex, 'My Opinion for the Government and Reformation of Ulster', 8 October, 1574, *Ibid*, Add. MS 48015: 314-18.

*The third [is] yet to be had, as I hearsay in Dartmouth.*

 *They were bought at easy prices. If two of these might be sent they might be kept with less cost than one ship and do much more service than any other vessel. They will brook a sea well and carry 200 soldiers, as I am informed, and yet they draw so little water, as they may pass into every river, island or creek where the Scottish galley may flee, and are of better strength [and] stowage than the others, for the galleys are made more slight and thin than the wherries upon the Thames. No shipping therefore [is] so good for this purpose in my opinion as the frigates. I have slight ordnance to furnish them, but I lack oars and such necessaries. Good choice must be made of mariners for these boats, for ordinary sailors love not to pull at an oar.*[1]

From this it seems that Drake had sold his Spanish prizes to Hawkins and Champernowne, who now offered them to Essex as light-draught ships suitable for service against the Scots. A third vessel was reportedly at Dartmouth, but since Drake returned from the Caribbean with two vessels, she likely had nothing to do with him. Eventually, Essex was able to secure the services of Drake himself, along with five or six vessels, for an expedition against Rathlin Island.

Three of the ships were described by Essex as 'frigates', and he also employed two transports – a flyboat and a hoy – and possibly another pinnace. The flyboat, the *Fortunate*, was evidently already in Ireland, commanded by Captain John Potter, who had been in that service since 1573. Two more ships and a hoy came from London through the agency of the government, which paid Captain James Sydae £40 to take them to Dublin. Of these, the *Reindeer* was described variously as a frigate and a pinnace, and belonged to the queen. The *Lymner* may have been one of Drake's old vessels, but she too seems to have crossed the Irish Sea with Sydae and was called either a pinnace or a frigate. Sydae's final vessel was a 30-ton hoy called the *Cork*. The arrival of these forces in Dublin on 8 May, 1575 enabled Essex to consolidate his squadron. Potter was transferred to the command of the *Lymner*; Sydae controlled the *Reindeer* and the hoy; while the flyboat passed to Master George Allen. To these were added one or two vessels under the command of Francis Drake, whose *Falcon*, described as a bark or a frigate, carried the captain himself, a master, pilot, boatswain, steward, carpenter, gunner and eighteen mariners, a grand total of twenty-five men, one of whom was apparently Drake's thirteen-year old cousin, John Drake. From the audit of Essex's accounts we also learn that the *Falcon* was accompanied by a small pinnace.[2]

The foregoing contradicts the claim made by Edmund Howes some years after Drake's death that the captain commanded, equipped and furnished with men and munitions three frigates for service under the Earl of Essex. Of the three 'frigates' assembled, only the *Falcon* and the *Lymner* may have once belonged to Drake, and there is no clear evidence that he commanded the full squadron. Drake, Sydae and Potter were paid at the same rate, 42 shillings a month, and in his dispatches Essex implies that each had an equal authority. Sydae, who had been serving in Ireland for two years, had the reputation of being a skilled seaman.[3] But we must not demote Drake

[1] 'The Answer of the Earl of Essex to the Doubts Conceived upon his Plot for the Reformation of Ulster', 1575, Ibid, Add. MS 48015: 329.

[2] Essex to Burghley, 8 May, 1575, State Papers (Ireland), Public Record Office, London, S.P. 63/51: 19-20; wages and victualling accounts for 30 April to 16 October, 1575, Ibid, S.P. 63/53: 114-15; audit of Irish accounts, Ibid, S.P. 65/8; Dasent, ed., Acts of the Privy Council, 10 April, 1575, 8: 366.

too severely, for he was clearly the most experienced and successful of the captains, and his ships had provided a nucleus for the squadron. He sank some of his resources into the expedition – a sailor later testified with exaggeration that he spent most of his money 'on certain islands over there towards Ireland' – and his services were retained longer than those of Sydae, Potter and Allen.[1] All were rated for pay from 1 May, 1575, but whereas Drake was kept until the end of September, the others were discharged on the 19th of that month.

Essex's original intention seems to have been to use his naval force to destroy the Scottish galleys plying between the Isles, Rathlin and the Glens of Antrim and the Route: 'Touching the guarding of the victuals from the Scots of the Rathlins,' he told Burghley, 'if the frigates come, there shall not a Scottish boat remain in the Rathlins, or in the Glens, or come upon that coast.'[2] But on reflection he decided that an attempt must be made upon Rathlin itself, which acted not only as a refuge and bastion for the Scots but also provided them with a base for freebooting along the coasts.

The squadron was assembled at Carrickfergus, which Drake would have found a squalid town, rife with typhus fever, but sporting a small harbour and a Norman castle. Drake might have compelled the Scots on Rathlin to surrender by a naval blockade alone, but Essex wanted a more dramatic and speedier result, and chose one of his ablest volunteers, John Norris, to take three hundred foot and eighty horse to the island to capture the castle there by storm. Norris was a captain of horse who had earned a reputation as a hard and ruthless soldier and whose talents had been honed in the bitter religious conflict in France, where he had served the Huguenots under Coligny. He was directed to take his troops to Carrickfergus and there to confer with the frigate captains about the suitability of wind and weather for a voyage to Rathlin. While Essex himself drew his army towards the Pale to suggest that he had no offensive afoot, Norris arrived in Carrickfergus, presented his letter of introduction from the earl to Drake, Sydae and Potter, and unfolded to them his plans. They agreed that the attack was feasible, and gathered all the small boats in the town to help transport Norris's army to Rathlin.[3]

Leaving a garrison at Carrickfergus, the frigates escorted the armada of tiny vessels out of the port on 20 July. At sea their flotilla was soon dispersed by the winds, but it successfully regrouped at the landing place at Rathlin on the morning of the 22nd. The site of disembarkation is not precisely known, but Arkill Bay on the eastern coast of Rathlin has been suggested, and the obvious alternative would have been Church Bay tucked inside the angle of the L-shaped island. In either case the troops faced a northerly march towards the castle on the north-east of Rathlin. The boats discharged the soldiers so quickly that they caught many of the island's inhabitants outside of the castle, and there was a brief skirmish as the English chased the Scots into their fortress. This part of the operation cost Norris his first casualty, one man killed.

---

[3] Notes for the Consideration of the Lords of the Council, 14 May, 1575, State Papers (Ireland), S.P. 63/51: 59.

---

[1] Deposition of John Butler, 1579, Nuttall, ed., New Light on Drake, 5-8.
[2] Essex to Burghley, 8 May, 1575, State Papers (Ireland), S.P. 63/51: 19-20.
[3] This account of the capture of Rathlin is drawn from Essex to Elizabeth, 31 July, 1575, Essex to the Privy Council, 31 July, 1575, and Essex to Walsingham, 31 July, 1575, Ibid, S.P. 63/52: 202-4, 206.

The siege began in earnest after Drake and his fellow captains landed two heavy siege guns, and fire was directed upon the castle walls. It took three days to knock a practical breach in the defences, but when Norris's men tried to storm the castle on the afternoon of 25 July they were driven back with losses of two men killed and eight wounded, although they had managed to fight their way across a bridge that passed over a ditch to the gate and even through the gate itself. The English consoled themselves in the belief that one of the principal Scottish leaders had been killed in this skirmish, and they resumed the bombardment, setting on fire some timber sections of the ramparts. Norris planned to make another assault the next morning, but just before daybreak on the 26th the Scots called for a parley.

The Scottish leader announced that he was willing to surrender the castle, provided that the inmates were allowed passage to Scotland. Drake would have accepted those terms, but Norris was in charge of the campaign, and he would have none of it. He knew, no less than the Scots, that the fall of the castle was inevitable anyway, sealed off as it was from food or reinforcements. Sooner or later the lives of the Scots would depend upon the clemency of the English, and there can have been few illusions about the disposition of Norris's troops. Ever since the 'Pardon of Maynooth' in 1535, when English soldiers had butchered the garrison of Dengen after its surrender, the propensity for unbridled violence upon the helpless had seldom been far from either side on this bitter frontier. Norris told the Scottish leader that if Rathlin immediately surrendered his life and those of his family would be spared; as for the rest, their lives, in the language of the day, would be placed at the courtesy of the English soldiers. They would have to take their chance upon the mood of the captors. The decision before the commander of the Scots was an unenviable one, but it is doubtful if he hesitated, for his own family stood to be lost if the English were forced to storm the castle. He surrendered.

The result was a bloodbath. The 'constable' of the castle, his family, and a prisoner being held by the Scots (he was the son of Alexander Ogg McAllister, an Irish chief) were secured, but the English soldiery – with or without the encouragement of Norris is uncertain – murdered every other Scot they could find on the island, men, women, children, the aged, the feeble and the helpless, without distinction. It is said that they had been enraged by the stiff resistance the castle had made and by the losses they had sustained. However, after butchering two hundred of the prisoners on the surrender of the castle, they roamed about the island for several days, rooting out several hundred more from their refuges in caves and among the cliffs, and chopping them down on the spot. In addition the soldiers seized 300 cows, 3,000 sheep and 100 horses, and they confiscated a large quantity of corn, sufficient, it was said, to have kept two hundred men for a year.

Barbarous it certainly was, and yet it affords an interesting insight into the sixteenth-century mind, for not one word of censure has survived. On the contrary, Essex boasted of the exploit in each of three letters sent respectively to the queen, to the Privy Council and to Walsingham, and he solicited in the same breath a letter of thanks from Elizabeth to the officers and gentlemen who had captured Rathlin. And he got it. The queen congratulated the earl and promised to remember Norris for his services. To be fair, we know that Elizabeth had once cautioned Essex against unnecessary bloodshed in the conquest of Ulster, but there is nothing to suggest other than that the government approved of the massacre as an object lesson to rebels. Essex proudly informed Walsingham, the great minister, that Sorley Boy MacDonnell himself had watched the destruction of his people from the mainland and that he had been driven to distraction.

It must be assumed that Drake neither approved of nor participated in the massacre at Rathlin. He probably assisted the besiegers in landing men, stores and guns at the beginning of the operation, and thereafter cruised off shore to ensure that no help reached the island. The frigates were apparently busy, for they captured and burned eleven Scottish galleys. Time would show that Drake had the capacity for ruthlessness of a kind, but he was not an inhumane man, and he had already shown in his raids in the West Indies that he would attempt to deal with prisoners as generously as circumstances permitted. He had never killed unresisting Spaniards nor prisoners, and he had protected them from the *cimarrones*. And Norris's murder of the Scots of Rathlin was not only not Drake's way; it was not his war. If he found the humanity to protect the hated Spaniards, whom he held responsible for the débâcle at San Juan d'Ulua, we cannot suppose he was the man to condone the murder of Scottish or Irish people against whom he bore no grudges.

The fall of the island did not bring Drake's services in Ireland to an immediate end, for Norris hoped to hold the castle for Essex, and, after repairing it with timber, bricks and lime brought from Carrickfergus, he installed a garrison of eighty soldiers and returned the rest to Carrickfergus for discharge. After handling these duties, the frigates found employment cruising about the island to keep its supply lines open and the predatory Scots at bay. Norris purchased a hoy and a small boat, perhaps the *Cork* and the *Fortunate*, for £60 and had them scuttle back and forth with provisions for the garrison under the screen provided by the frigates.

It was not until the end of September that the frigates were discharged. Essex had approved of the plan to hold Rathlin, and recommended that one hundred men be stationed on the island, forty of them to serve at sea. But someone spoke more loudly in Ireland than Essex now – the new Lord Deputy, Sir Henry Sidney, appointed in August 1575, and he thought differently. Sidney had a distant connection to Drake, for he was father-in-law to Drake's godfather, the Earl of Bedford. Whether the link was important we cannot say, but it was Drake who brought Sidney to Ireland to take up his new post, as seems evident from Sir Henry's accounts:

> Freight and transportation: to Captain Drake, with his bark, the Frigacie [Falcon], which carried my lord to Ireland, 12 Sept., 1575, with 10s for the mariners, £25 10s 0d. For a bark, the same time, with my lord's stuff, £24 10s 0d.[1]

Sidney was landed at the Skerries, north of Dublin, on the morning of 7 September, after a difficult passage. The calm weather which had blessed the embarkation had broken upon the point of sailing, and seas were so stormy that some of the vessels containing part of the Lord Deputy's train were separated and put into a creek two days' journey away. Dublin was wracked by the plague when Sidney arrived, but whether Drake accompanied him into the town is not known.[2]

The Lord Deputy's arrival marked the end of the Irish naval squadron. Essex had

[1] Hist. MSS Commission, *Report on the Manuscripts of Lord de L'Isle and Dudley*, 1: 427.

been instructed by the queen to maintain the garrison at Rathlin, 'and if you shall see any necessary continuance for the entertaining of the frigates until you shall confer with our said servant and counsellor, Henry Sidney, we can be content to allow thereof.'[1] In fact Sidney saw no necessity for either the frigates or the garrison on the island, and proved it by having all the captains except Drake discharged on 19 September. He cannot have been ignorant of the consequences, for without the screen the frigates had provided Rathlin's supply lines were open to incursions from the vengeful Scots. If the Lord Deputy was deliberately undermining the soldiers on Rathlin to justify their removal, his measures were effective, and Norris documented the result. He complained that

> my Lord Deputy that now is presently upon his landing there discharged the frigates, which the Scots having intelligence of and of their departure, upon the last voyage that the aforesaid hoy made for the revictualling of the castle, on their return assaulted, took and burnt her. My humble suit to your Honours is not to put this loss upon me . . . for had I not been assured by the Earl of Essex that he understood by certain [of] Her Majesty's letters to himself, her pleasure was the frigates should not have been discharged as long as the place was retained, I would more sufficiently have provided for the safety of the passage.[2]

Without naval cover Rathlin Island was difficult to provision, and there was no well in the castle there, so that even the water had to be brought from the mainland. Gradually but surely the garrison became untenable, with the remaining forty soldiers in the castle being reduced to eating horses and colts for food. Before the end of the year Sidney caused it to be abandoned, and the work, as well as the need for the naval squadron, was extinguished.[3] (There was to be at least one more occasion when England's navy was to make use of that storm-lashed piece of rock jutting from the grey seas north of the Irish coast, for in October 1917 a battle cruiser, mortally wounded by the torpedo of a German U-boat, limped into Church Bay where it capsized and sunk to the bottom. Its name? Most appropriately, H.M.S. *Drake*.)

For Essex, no less than for Drake, the Irish interlude was over. He returned to England and received some rewards for what had scarcely been in all a successful project. Even the victory of Rathlin had failed to suppress the MacDonnells, who mounted a counter-attack against Carrickfergus. Essex was back in Ireland in the summer of 1576, with the office of Earl Marshal, but he soon fell ill with dysentery and died with his dreams unfulfilled. Drake had lost a patron, but his heart had never been in the wretched and profitless business in Ireland. Throughout his service on these rainy shores he was nursing a grander design, a vision that had inspired him since he had climbed that tree in Darien some years before. He spoke of it to Essex, and to his friends in Ireland, like James Sydae of the *Reindeer*, and a soldier called Thomas Doughty who had formerly served Essex as an aide. And now that his Irish work was done, he proposed to bring his project, breathtaking as it was in magnitude, to frui-

---

[2] Sidney to the Privy Council, 28 September, 1575, Collins, ed., *Letters and Memorials of State . . . written and Collected by Sir Henry Sydney*, 1: 72-3.

---

[1] Queen to Essex, 12 August, 1575, Brewer and Bullen, ed., *Calendar of the Carew Manuscripts*, 21.

[2] John Norris to the Privy Council, 1575, State Papers (Ireland), S.P. 63/54: 126.

[3] Sidney to the Privy Council, 15 November, 1575, Collins, 1: 75-6.

tion. He would lead the English far from their own northerly seas, into the unknown, into the great South Sea itself.

# CHAPTER EIGHT

# THE SOUTH SEAS PROJECT

Well since that thou art going hence to take thee to the seas,
Forsaking wife and country both, thy costly cheer and ease;
To God thy voyage I'll commend, to whom I still will pray
To grant thee life and safe return to see that joyful day,
Wherein thou mayest behold again thy loving countrymen
Which wisheth well to thee, and prayeth for thy return again.

Henry Roberts, A Most Friendly Farewell, 1585

A N ENGLISH VOYAGE INTO THE PACIFIC! TO APPRECIATE THE BOLDNESS OF THE plan it is important to remember that, even to the Spaniards (the only Europeans to have used 'the South Sea' in any significant way), it was most imperfectly known, and their only direct sea route to it, via the Strait of Magellan, was so dangerous that it had fallen into disuse. During the sixteenth century Spain had reached the Pacific from across the isthmus of Central America. The sea route had been pioneered in 1519 and 1520 by the Portuguese navigator, Ferdinand Magellan, then in the employ of Spain and intent upon establishing that country's claim to the Moluccas by sailing west. Magellan was a mercurial figure, a consummate seaman, courageous and determined enough to set afoot the only voyage of circumnavigation yet accomplished, but his epic adventure had been a portrait in hardship. After surviving a serious mutiny in the Atlantic, Magellan groped his way southwards along the east coast of South America, discovering and, in a five-week battle, navigating the Magellan Strait to reach the Pacific. The size of the ocean itself, however, was greater than the explorers had anticipated, and their crossing was tormented by extreme thirst, starvation and scurvy. In 1521 Magellan brought the remains of his expedition to the Philippines, where he lost his life meddling in native feuds.

A second disastrous expedition, under Garcia de Loyasa, sailed for the Moluccas from Corunna in 1525. Of four vessels that passed through the Magellan Strait only two crossed the Pacific, in an appalling condition. The expedition disintegrated in the Moluccas with one crew mutinying and tossing the captain overboard to spear him with lances as he floundered in the water. This vessel was subsequently wrecked and her survivors murdered or captured by natives. The remaining ship was burned at Tidore, although some of her sailors succeeded in reaching the East Indies. In a third voyage through the Magellan Strait in 1540 only one of three vessels made Peru.

The travels of Magellan and Loyasa, crucial as they were to geographical discovery, illustrated vividly the perils of venturing into the difficult waters around the Magellan Strait and into the Pacific with men crowded in tiny ships. Mutiny, shipwreck, disease, deprivation and conflict with natives had been the common fare of both voyages, and of the twelve ships of the two expeditions combined, only one – Magellan's *Victoria* – actually returned to Spain. It is not surprising that the route to the South Sea which Magellan had pioneered was unpopular. As Lopez Vaz remarked, it was considered 'so dangerous, and the voyage so trouble-some, that it seemeth a matter almost impossible to be performed.'[1] The strait was undoubtedly a formidable test of seamanship, with its powerful currents and winds, awkward narrows and exposed anchorages, and it was practical for naviga-tion westwards only in the summer and midwinter months when the fury of the Westerlies declined. The coast of what is now Chile was also dangerous because of the onshore winds. But to these real hazards, Spanish imagination added perils of its own. The lands of those regions, it was said, were inhabited by giant savages, and although the strait was passable, albeit with difficulty, from east to west, the winds and tides completely precluded a return journey. The latter belief persisted despite two Spanish expeditions that successfully navigated the strait eastwards from the Pacific during the 1550s.

A modern reader pausing to inspect a map might ponder upon the sixteenth-century obsession with the Strait of Magellan, considering the open passage to the south by Cape Horn. Unfortunately, geography before Drake's voyage knew nothing of Cape Horn, where no European had been. Instead, it conjectured that a vast southern land-mass, Terra Australis, counter-balanced the continental areas of the northern hemisphere, and part of its coastline formed the southern flank of Magellan's Strait. The strait was thus seen as merely a channel between the continents of South America and Terra Australis, and was so depicted in 1541 by the influential Flemish geographer, Gerard Mercator.

The myth of the southern continent, fortified by tortuous interpretations of passages from the Bible and the writings of Marco Polo, exemplified the crude state of geographical knowledge of the Pacific in the middle of the sixteenth century. The Spaniards had eventually opened up a trans-Pacific trade between Mexico and the Philippines in 1564 and 1565, the return journey involving a rela-tively northerly voyage in which the ships made the coast of present California and followed it southwards towards Acapulco. Nevertheless, there was largely ignorance about what the ocean contained, to both the north and the south. Maps, including those of Ortelius, portrayed the Chilean coast as extending north-west, not north, from the Magellan Strait, a misconception arising from errors in the calculation of longitude, and, although by the 1570s the Spanish had ascertained the correct bearing of that coastline the information had not been made available to foreigners. In the north, the coast from Mexico to California was little known, and beyond that was a matter of pure speculation. No Christian had been further, but many dreamed about it, and argued that a counterpart of the Magellan Strait might exist there – a northern passage across America linking the Pacific and Atlantic oceans.

Like Terra Australis, the practical northern passage was mythical, and yet it

---

[1] Lopez Vaz in Vaux, ed., *World Encompassed*, 285. On early voyages to the Magellan Strait, see Wallis, 'English Enterprise in the Region of the Strait of Magellan', and Markham, ed., *Early Spanish Voyages to the Strait of Magellan*. It is sad that Samuel Eliot Morison did not complete his biography of Magellan, and more so that Viscount de Lagoa's *Fernão de Magalhães* (Lisbon, 1938), the best modern account, remains untranslated.

was a myth the English in particular found alluring, for it promised a convenient route from Europe to Cathay (China) and the East Indies and one that would not transgress the pretended monopolies of Portugal and Spain. During the 1550s the idea of a north-eastern passage from England across the north of Europe and Asia was in currency, but successive attempts to find it failed. Attention was now swinging towards the view that a short route to the East might be found by going north-west, across America. Geographers like Mercator, Ortelius and that en-igmatic Englishman John Dee, as well as sailors of the stamp of Cabot and Gilbert, believed in this waterway while disagreeing about its exact shape and location. Mercator and Ortelius thought that it ran from the Atlantic across North America and then through a strait (the Strait of Anian) formed by America in the east and Asia in the west. The idea that developed was that it passed north-east to south-west, with its Atlantic terminus situated in a higher latitude than its outlet into the Pacific, the last of which might be found at around 40° to 50° north or in what is the coast of present-day California and Oregon. Again, that these views re-mained unexploded illustrates the fragmentary nature of European knowledge about the Pacific in Drake's time.

If the Spaniards had grown wary of using the Strait of Magellan and knew rela-tively little of the great ocean beyond, the fitness of the English to dare those regions was even more to be doubted. The fact was that England had at that time limited experience in far-flung voyaging. Her fishing and trade were principally European in character, reaching at the furthest the banks of Newfoundland, Russia, the Mediterranean, the west coast of Africa, the Caribbean and Brazil. And although some foreign texts existed, including Portuguese sailing directions for the Strait of Magellan, they remained generally inaccessible. Richard Eden, who translated an account of the Iberian voyages of discovery and a manual of navigation into English in the 1550s and 1560s, complained of the 'ignorance . . . among us as touching cosmography and navigation, until I attempted . . . to open the first door to the entrance of this knowledge into our language.'[1] By the 1570s the efforts of Eden, Chancellor, Dee and others had improved this situation, but much of their work – including Dee's own Great Volume of Famous and Rich Dis-coveries, composed in 1577 – was unpublished, and when Frobisher sailed in search of the North-west Passage in 1576 he did not carry a single English work summariz-ing the current state of geographical knowledge of the Americas.

Not only did the English lag in geographical understanding, but they were far from all being masters of ocean-going navigation. There was a difference between the coastal pilotage or short-haul navigation employed by mariners in relatively brief runs about northern Europe and the skills demanded of blue-water sailors. The former was largely a matter of observation and experience and the ability to sound for depth, take bearings of landforms with a compass, and read a 'rutter', giving distances and steering directions from one place to another, or a chart. The pilot used his command of local landmarks, depths, currents and tides to plot a position on his chart and find his way by rule of thumb. Not so the deep-water navigator, who might be weeks on end beyond sight of any land that might guide

[1] Taylor, Tudor Geography, 21.

him or find himself driven far from the course he had hoped to steer.

The ability to fix a position upon the ocean demanded a more educated man. He still relied heavily upon 'dead reckoning' – the calculation of his position by relating the estimated speed of his ship to the time she had kept any particular course – but this was checked by calculating the latitude from observations of the stars or the meridian altitude of the sun with an astrolabe or cross-staff. It was a complicated process. Drake could do it, as could many a master mariner, but the task left many simple pilots nonplussed.

Finding a position far out at sea was always an inexact skill, perplexed by many unresolved problems. The sixteenth-century navigator had yet to discover a satisfactory means of estimating the variation of the compass, that is the disparity between true and magnetic north, or of assessing longitude. Such advances as had been made had been slow to percolate to the English, and in the mid-sixteenth century their ships were full of Ragusan, Genoese, Venetian and French pilots, so indifferent were the home-grown talents. London did not obtain its first professional instrument maker until 1553, and he was a native of the Low Countries. Martin Cortes's *Art of Navigation* had to wait ten years after its publication in Spain for an English translation in 1561, and the first English manual, abstracted largely from Cortes but couched in language more intelligible to the ordinary seaman, was not available until William Bourne's *Regiment of the Sea* was published in 1574. No original English work on navigation appeared until 1581.[1]

But all this was changing, and the pulse of English overseas endeavour was sharpening. The growing population stimulated the demand for exotic goods; the problems of the cloth industry encouraged the search for new markets; the benefit Portugal and Spain derived from their maritime empires inspired fear, greed and envy; the wealth from the rising value of land provided the means to invest in oceanic enterprise; the discoveries of other nations aroused curiosity and a spirit of adventure; and the growing conflict between England and Spain created a new breed of heretics willing to use the sea to distress their enemy. Drake was part of that change, and lived close to its heart in the West Country. He could feel it growing in pace and energy. Dangerous as a South Seas voyage might be, unique to the English as it was, Drake knew also that others beside himself were steeling themselves for that decisive thrust. A born opportunist, he understood that if he did not act quickly the glory would eventually pass to another.

Two other Pacific ventures were afoot, both of them in the West Country, one pivoting around Richard Grenville, and the other around Drake's old comrade, John Oxenham, who had once sworn that if Drake was not the first to sail an English vessel upon the South Seas then it would be he. As early as 1570 some Englishmen had considered establishing a colony near the Magellan Strait as a base for adventures in the Pacific, but the project took shape in 1574 when Grenville and a number of West Country backers petitioned the queen for permission to explore southward beyond the equinoctial, and proposed sinking £5,000 in providing four ships for the expedition. Just whither Grenville was actually bound is

---

[1] For Tudor seafaring see Waters, *The Art of Navigation in England in Elizabethan and Early Stuart Times*, and Taylor, *The Haven-Finding Art*.

now unclear. There is evidence that he intended settling the River Plate region of the east coast of South America before passing through the Strait of Magellan to discover new lands or islands in the Pacific and to claim them for England. He was considering less Terra Australis than the southern coast of present-day Chile, which at that time Spain had not yet occupied, and there was a suggestion that he would try to reach Cathay.

Such a voyage would have upset Philip, because the Spaniards regarded the region about and beyond the Strait of Magellan as their own, and no sooner had the queen issued Grenville his patent to explore the South Seas and traffic with Cathay than she had second thoughts. In 1574 relations between Spain and England were improving. Alba had been replaced in the Netherlands and there was talk of Spain restoring to the Dutch old liberties and privileges. In 1575 English Protestants were told that they might trade in Spanish ports without fear of molestation. Seldom had the queen's foreign relations enjoyed better prospect, and she decided that this was not the time for provocative incursions into the Pacific. Just as Drake had been told to keep his head down after returning from the West Indies, so now Grenville's scheme was scotched.

Grenville was too adventurous, high-spirited and determined to be put aside so easily. One of the country gentry, a man of learning known inside the portals of the Inner Temple, a soldier rather than a sailor, he was hardly the master mariner needed to negotiate the Magellan Strait, but he never lacked courage or ambition. Perceiving that interest was now switching to less antagonistic voyages to the north-west in search of the northern passage (Frobisher reached Baffin Island and discovered the Hudson Strait during three voyages between 1576 and 1578), Grenville resuscitated his South Seas scheme, but now he diverted the avowed purpose northwards, beyond territories claimed by Spain. He told Lord Burghley that Martin Frobisher and his backer, Michael Lok, were looking for the northern passage from the wrong direction – from the Atlantic, where the entrance to the passage was believed to lie in a high and difficult latitude. Far better to seek it from the Pacific amid warmer climes and seas. It seems that at this stage Grenville antic-ipated a voyage of the most ambitious kind, linking an exploration of islands about the Magellan Strait with a search for the northern passage and a voyage across the Pacific to Cathay.[1]

This revised plan was still before the government when Drake came forward with his own proposals, and Drake knew of it. He watched also, perhaps with greater interest, the activities of his friend, John Oxenham, who wanted to follow up the raid on the West Indies which they had shared some years before. Many times had the two friends spoken of the Pacific, which they had first seen from that tree in Darien, and of the opportunities that awaited anyone who might penetrate the South Seas. The Spaniards had now been alerted to the threat to their bullion as it crossed the isthmus of Panama, but they had never been troubled by corsairs in the Pacific, by men determined to intercept the wealth of Peru and Mexico on the west coast of the Americas before it even reached Panama. Oxenham planned to do so, but he would reach the Pacific across Central America rather than by

---

[1] Grenville's scheme is discussed in Rowse, *Sir Richard Grenville*, ch. 5.

way of the Magellan Strait.

In this instance Oxenham worked faster than his old captain, and sailed from Plymouth in April 1576 with two vessels and fifty-seven men, some of them veterans of Drake's expeditions to the West Indies. Just as before, the raiders sailed without government support, as pirates, willing to chance their lives for Spanish treasure. In Darien Oxenham renewed his acquaintance with the *cimarrones*, who still remembered Drake with affection, and recruited some of them for his expedition. For a while their luck held. Using a pinnace, the corsairs descended a river into the Gulf of Panama, and Oxenham realized his dream of leading the English into the Pacific. He was not the first of his nation to ride those broad waters. Magellan's master gunner had been English, and a merchant, John Chilton, had sailed on a Spanish ship from Panama to Peru in 1572. But no Englishman had commanded a vessel on the Pacific before. Now Oxenham had done it, and briefly reaped the rewards, collecting considerable booty from undefended ships he found in the Gulf.

But there the game turned against him. As Oxenham withdrew across the isthmus, Spanish forces closed around him. His men, black and white, were cut down, captured or dispersed, and the treasure lost. In 1578 eighteen Englishmen were taken as prisoners to Panama. Three boys were spared, and three men – Oxenham himself, John Butler and Thomas Sherwell – were sent to Lima in Peru for examination; the rest were hanged. Two years later John Oxenham and his two comrades paid the ultimate price of failure, and their execution in Lima vividly underscored the terrible risks attending the project Francis Drake now brought forward.[1]

In Oxenham's view no man was better qualified to pass the Strait of Magellan than Francis Drake, but Drake was of moderate means and relatively humble origins, and he needed more backing and the queen's support for so ambitious a stroke. This was a world in which patronage counted, and one of Drake's qualities was his ability to acquire and command such patronage when it mattered. His letters to the great men of the court and government seem to us obsequious, but he knew what he was doing. He courted and flattered them, he invigorated them with his entrepreneurial spirit, he appealed to their greed, their religion and their patriotism, and he usually had his way. So it was now.

Drake's own account of the birth of his great voyage tells how he carried a letter of introduction from the Earl of Essex to Francis Walsingham, the Joint Principal Secretary of State. Walsingham read that Drake was a useful man in any enterprise against Spain and sent for him, spreading a map before the stocky seaman and asking him how Philip might best be annoyed for offence he had lately given the queen. Drake remained astute in the presence of the great Secretary, and refused to put anything in writing, explaining that if misfortune should place the Queen of Scots upon Elizabeth's throne such a paper could cost him his head. However, he told Walsingham that Spain was most vulnerable in the west.

Something like this probably occurred, but Drake's story simplified the process

---

[1] The documents on Oxenham's raid are printed in Wright, ed., *Documents Concerning English Voyages to the Spanish Main*; for an excellent resumé, consult Williamson, *Age of Drake*, ch. 8.

and the scanty evidence that survives only affords the most conjectural reconstruction. The first people Drake involved in his plans are likely to have been the initial investors. Drake put up £1,000; John Hawkins, £500; Sir William Winter, £750; and George Winter, William's brother, £500. All were connected with the navy, and their association with Drake might have been made through Hawkins, whose father-in-law was then treasurer of the navy. From this base Drake proceeded to gather around his project a small band of influential courtiers and Privy Councillors: the Earl of Lincoln, Christopher Hatton, the Earl of Leicester and Walsingham himself. The syndicate backing Drake thus represented the navy and the court, but less the merchants, and this may be significant, for it suggests that Drake's intentions were not primarily concerned with trade.

The Earl of Lincoln, Lord Admiral of England, may have been influenced by Hawkins or Winter, but he also knew Sir Arthur Champernowne, Vice-Admiral of Devon, with whom Drake had dealt. Lincoln had full knowledge of Grenville's proposal, but he struck a good relationship with Drake and opted to support his scheme. Christopher Hatton was not only Captain of the Queen's Guard and a gentleman of the Privy Chamber, but one of the queen's favourite courtiers. Interested he was in maritime endeavour, but it is possible that he was drawn to Drake through the singular personage of Thomas Doughty. Doughty was one of Drake's newer friends; they had met in Ireland, where Doughty was in the service of Essex. A gentleman, Doughty was charming, articulate, impressive and educated, conversant with the classical languages, law and philosophy and a member of the Inner Temple. He was fond of exaggerating his influence and importance, and Drake may have seen him as a man worth cultivating. Anyway, Drake spoke to Doughty about the South Seas project and found him interested. Later, when Drake looked him up in London, Doughty had a new post as secretary to Hatton, and it may have been Doughty who broached the idea of supporting Drake to Hatton.[1]

But Drake's most powerful supporters were Leicester and Walsingham, two names that strengthen grounds for believing that the expedition was from the start anti-Spanish and not pre-eminently concerned with discovery and trade. For Philip had no more ardent foes in Elizabeth's court than these. In them Drake found companions of the soul. At forty-four years of age, Walsingham's long narrow face displayed the gravity of a Puritan frustrated by Elizabeth's moderation and afflicted by a sickly constitution. Like Drake a Protestant from childhood, he had left England during Mary's reign, but under Elizabeth had risen swiftly to power, second only to Lord Burghley in the influence he could command. Although a politician, he saw matters simply. The cause of England was the cause of Protestantism, and temporization with the Catholics, with the Queen of Scots and with Spain was useless. A decisive clash between the forces of the Reformation and Counter-Reformation would come, and England's true course was to ally herself with the Dutch and the Huguenots before they were crushed and to offer a

---

[1] This follows Doughty's account in Vaux, 171-2, but it must be used with caution. Not only was it contradicted by Drake at the time, but it is divergent from other evidence. Doughty claimed to have contributed £1,000 to the voyage, but this does not seem to have been the case.

united front against Philip. Elizabeth valued Walsingham's loyalty and the efficiency of his secret service, the tentacles of which permeated Europe, but she suspected his zeal and commonly ignored his counsel.

Yet Francis Walsingham's militance found strong support from Robert Dudley, Earl of Leicester, about a year the Secretary's junior, but more flamboyant about the court. Leicester had survived his dubious beginnings – a father executed for treason, a sister-in-law the pathetic Lady Jane Grey (the nine-day queen who died on the block), and his own efforts to support Jane's claim to the throne at the expense of Elizabeth and Mary – to emerge the queen's suitor. She never married him, but Elizabeth remained fascinated by Leicester, a gallant, choleric and bluff personality, a skilled horseman and administrator but indifferent soldier, and a powerful voice indeed for the strong line against Spain. These were the two men, Walsingham and Leicester, upon whom Drake would depend to argue his case before queen and government, and as long as they lived they never let him down. Their appearance now, and the absence of the more prudent Lord Burghley, indicates at the onset the provocative nature of Drake's mission.

This is worth emphasizing because some historians have contended that Drake was bent upon trade and that his voyage was not originally intended to serve aggressive purposes. Incongruent as this view may be with Drake's character and experience, it demands that we look more closely at the aims of this great voyage. Just what was Drake up to? There are probably three answers to that question. First, there was the public and ostensible reason for the voyage, designed to mask its real purpose from the Spaniards. Second, another and genuine motive was written down and known to Drake and his backers. And third, there seems to have been an understanding between the captain, his syndicate and the queen that Drake would raid Spanish shipping, but this purpose was, of course, far too dangerous even to commit to paper.

To provide a smokescreen for Drake's preparations, it was put about that a peaceful trading venture was under way. No one could hide the squadron of ships fitting out in Plymouth for a long sea voyage, but Spain's informers might be put off the scent. John Hawkins even wrote a detailed plan of the fictitious schedule, declaring that the *Swallow* and the *Pelican* were taking aboard Brazilian wood, tin, lead, cloth and steel for a trading voyage to Alexandria and Constantinople. The mariners were recruited on that basis. These devices seem to have worked, because it was not until after Drake had sailed that Spanish suspicions were aroused; even then none guessed his true destination. Scotland was mentioned, then the Caribbean, but not the Strait of Magellan.[1]

However, the strait did feature in a written proposal that Walsingham was to present to the queen. The document survives, but it has been damaged by fire and is only partly legible. From it we learn that Drake owned a bark, the *Francis*, and was storing in her six pinnaces ready for assembly, but that he needed another ship and was requesting the queen to supply her own *Swallow*. And his project? The memorandum cannot be fully transcribed, but the gist of it appears. Drake was to

[1] Skilliter, *William Harborne*, 19-21; Hume, *Calendar of Letters . . . in the Archives of Simancas*, 2: 544-5, 567-9; Butler, et. al., *Cal. State Papers, Foreign*, 1: 188, 319-20; Boulind, 'John Saracold'.

proceed towards

> the pole . . . the South Sea then . . . far to the northwards as . . . along the said coast
> . . . as of the other to find out . . . to have traffic for the vent . . . of Her Majesty's
> realms . . . they are not under the obedience of princes, so is there great hope of . . .
> spices, drugs, cochineal, and . . . special commodities, such as may . . . Her High-
> ness's dominions, and also . . . shipping a-work greatly and . . . gotten up as afore-
> said into 30 de[grees] . . . the South Sea (if it shall be thought . . . by the forenamed
> Francis Drake . . . to . . . far) then he is to return the same way . . . homewards, as
> he went out which voyage by God's favour is to be performed in 12 month. Although
> he should spend 5 months in tarrying upon the coast to get knowle[dge] of the princes
> and countries there.

This is a formidable document, but it appears that Drake was to reconnoitre the east coast of South America, pass through the Strait of Magellan and into the South Seas, and sail northwards along what is now Chile as far as 30° south. He was to make contact with the natives of those regions, who were not considered to be subject to a Christian prince (that is, Spain), and seek valuable trade commodities, such as spices. Having proceeded as far north as it was felt an English ship might legitimately go, Drake was to return the way he had come. The whole trip, it was anticipated, would take about a year to complete, and the trade elements in it were emphasized in initial estimates of the cost. Drake would carry £50 worth of presents for the natives and provisions to the value of £400. The wages of the mariners would total another £450, and £100 would be required to sheath the hulls of the ships to protect them from the ravages of the teredo ship-worm, which flourished in warm climates.[1]

The reader will not be unfamiliar with this plan, because it has appeared before, as part of the original submission of Richard Grenville. It will be recalled that Grenville's voyage had been abandoned for fear of offending Spain, and resurrected in Drake's hands it was no less provocative. England might not recognize the strait and southern Chile as Spanish territory, but Philip did. So what had changed? Fortunately for Drake, England's relations with Spain had changed – for the worse. Elizabeth's hopes of a satisfactory settlement in the Netherlands, one that would deny Spain full control of that strategic area and yet keep it beneath Philip's sovereignty rather than that of France – in effect one that would leave neither France nor Spain over-powerful across the English Channel – had crumbled. Instead of restoring the ancient liberties of the Netherlands, as he had promised, the new Spanish governor, Don John of Austria, prepared to batter the Dutch into submission by force. There was even a rumour that Don John intended turning Elizabeth off her throne once the Netherlands had been reduced to order. The queen was bitterly disappointed at the dissipation of what had seemed such fair prospects of peace, and she was willing to demonstrate her anger by loosing Drake. She gave her sanction to a voyage to the Strait of Magellan, as outlined in the written plan Walsingham put before her.

Indeed, she probably went further, and this is where the third and unwritten plan fitted in. If Elizabeth, Walsingham and Leicester intended doing nothing more than implementing Grenville's plan there was no reason why they should not have told the

---

[1] Wallis, et. al., *Sir Francis Drake*, 49; Taylor, 'Missing Draft Project of Drake's Voyage', and her 'More Light on Drake'. The best analysis of the draft project is Andrews, 'Aims of Drake's Expedition'.

enthusiastic Cornishman himself to hire some competent sailing masters and get on with it. But Drake was not only a master mariner himself; he possessed other experience, and was making other proposals. It cannot be doubted that the queen and Drake's backers privately agreed that an act of retaliation against Spain, an attack upon the undefended coast of Peru, where the treasure was shipped, was permissible. Whether Drake succeeded in making it the primary aim of the voyage, or whether it was something to which he might resort if the search for trade was unprofitable, is unclear, but Drake left England knowing that if he plundered the Pacific coast Elizabeth would stand by him.

Neither Drake nor the queen wanted anything in writing. He had refused to put his hand to paper; she would not issue a privateering commission. At some stage Walsingham arranged for Drake to meet the queen privately, for the first time. He found her a woman of moderate size, still blessed with a comely, well-shaped figure and a regal presence, with an olive complexion and golden hair. She was forceful and commanding, but so different from himself – moderate, careful, suspicious of both Catholics and Puritans, dedicated to preserving the security and prosperity of her country but unfired by the attractions of religious crusades, overseas empires and military glory. But she needed money, and she would not be dismissed or taken for granted by Philip of Spain. According to what Drake later said, she spoke bluntly. 'Drake!' she said. 'So it is that I would gladly be revenged on the King of Spain for divers injuries that I have received.' She asked his advice, and he suggested an attack upon shipping on the west coast of America. Elizabeth was convinced, and – so said Drake – she contributed 1,000 crowns to the venture.[1]

If this interpretation is correct, Drake was in effect a privateer, a licensed private man-of-war, an instrument of government policy, rather than a pirate, but with the difference that war had not been declared between England and Spain and Drake carried no commission; if he was captured he had nothing that would incriminate the queen. She even refused the use of her ship, the *Swallow*. The arrangement was devious, but not untypical of Elizabeth's relationships with her commanders. She was always willing to condemn publicly what she privately condoned, if necessity demanded it, and her officers were used to discharging secret instructions while the queen protested before the world that she knew nothing of their activities, which were wholly repugnant to her. As she once said of Drake, 'If need be the gentleman careth not if I should disavow him.'[2] William Winter, one of Drake's new backers and at that time the finest of Elizabeth's admirals, could have told of occasions when the queen had sent him away with a wink in her eye. He remembered taking the fleet to the Firth of Forth in 1559 and 1560 with orders to deal with the French expeditionary force there. He was to handle the business as if acting upon his own initiative, proclaiming that his sovereign 'was nothing privy' to his movements, and to assert that he had only arrived in the Forth by accident after running into a storm at sea.[3]

Drake had his expedition, and now he must prepare it. Ships were the first essentials. We have seen him providing vessels for Essex, and he probably had others, or the

---

[1] Vaux, 215-16.
[2] Sherley to Leicester, 14 March, 1585, Bruce, ed., *Correspondence of Robert Dudley*, 171-6.
[3] Glasgow, 'The Navy in the First Elizabethan Undeclared War'.

money to buy them. The profits from his West Indian voyages had been far from negligible, and he reaped additional income as a trader out of Plymouth. Occasionally, there are glimpses of him in this work. In 1576 we find one Acerbo Velutelli, a foreign merchant living in London, chartering two vessels for a trip to Zante, one from Drake and the other from Hawkins. The same year Drake donated 40 shillings towards the building of the New Quay at Plymouth, a tribute to the port's expanding business.[1]

It was during 1576, too, that Drake built his flagship, the *Pelican*. Not all ships were suitable for long voyages and rough weather. They were often top-heavy, with large masts or spars above and insufficient depth of hold below, or their hulls might be too weak for powerful ocean rollers. By early the next year the *Pelican* was ready, and Drake was applying to the queen for the allowance he had learned was available for the building of new ships for use within the realm. The *Pelican* was destined to make but one major voyage and yet to be remembered under another name as one of the most famous ships in history. Until recently the portrait of the *Pelican-Golden Hind* adorned the British halfpenny.

Surprisingly little is known about her. She proved to be a good sailer, responsive to her helm, and although she shipped some water in heavy seas (hardly a commendable feature in a vessel with an unplanked upper deck consisting of hatches), the auxiliary topgallant sails on her solid fore- and mainmasts assisted her mainsails and mizen sprit-sail to make the best of a favourable wind. Her hull was sturdy and sheathed with extra planking to defend her from rot, and she carried an armament of eighteen brass and iron guns. Nevertheless, by modern standards the *Pelican* was a diminutive craft indeed, of little more than 100 tons and only some 70 feet from her stem to her stern-post.[2] The other ships assembled for the voyage were the *Elizabeth* (80 tons, sixteen guns), brought from London by the expedition's second-in-command, John Winter, the son of George Winter, Drake's sponsor; the *Marigold* (30 tons, sixteen guns) captained by John Thomas; the *Swan* flyboat (50 tons, five guns) under John Chester; and the *Benedict* (15 tons, one gun), a pinnace entrusted to Drake's old shipmate, Tom Moone, once carpenter of the *Swan*. Four more pinnaces lay in pieces aboard the

---

[1] Williams, 'Ownership of Drake's *Golden Hind*', for this and the following paragraph; Risk, 'Rise of Plymouth', 356.

[2] The dimensions of the *Pelican* are not given in surviving contemporary evidence, and to the confusion of those who would estimate them her tonnage has been given as 100, 120 and 150 tons' burden. These last may not, however, be contradictory, since there was no standard formula for assessing tonnage in Drake's day, and the measurement for tons and tonnage is also distinct from tons burden. Naish, 'Mystery of the Tonnage and Dimensions of the 'Pelican-Golden Hind', demonstrates that tonnages of both 100 and 150 tons could have been calculated for a vessel of similar size by the use of different methods of estimating tonnage. The most important evidence relating to the dimensions of the ship is an estimate of the cost of a dock built to enclose her in 1581 (Anderson, 'The *Golden Hind* at Deptford'). It was envisaged that a wall some 180 feet in perimeter would be required, and that the breadth of the dock would be 24 feet to allow for a walkway around the ship. Assuming that the enclosure was open at one end, Anderson speculated that the dock would measure 24 by 78 feet, sufficient to contain a vessel 67 feet long, 19 feet wide, 9 feet deep and possessing a keel of 47 feet. He guessed that the tonnage might be as much as 107. Naish suggested that the dock might have had semi-circular ends, affording hospitality to a ship with a breadth of 18 feet, a depth of 9½ feet, a keel of 47 feet and a length from stem to sternpost of 68 feet. Others have estimated the size of the ship by comparing her to vessels of similar size. From such information Robinson, 'Evidence About the *Golden Hind*', suggested a keel of up to 59 feet, and Andrews, 'The Elizabethan Seaman', a total length of about 70 feet, a breadth of 24 feet, a depth of 12 feet and a tonnage burden of 160.

squadron, awaiting assembly when their services were required.

To man the ships, 160 or so men and boys were recruited, nearly all under the impression that they were bound for the Mediterranean. Drake regretted the deception, if only because it could lead to trouble as soon as the crews learned that they were sailing to the hazardous Magellan Strait. And discontent was contagious in crowded ships. The man to ton ratio of the expedition was high, over one to two; eighty people were packed in the little *Pelican*. But Drake could hardly have done other than mislead the crews, for his success and ultimately the lives of the company depended upon secrecy.

A diverse crowd the company was too. It included artisans – coopers, carpenters and a blacksmith whose forge was shipped aboard the *Pelican* – as well as mariners. One of the sailors, William Coke, had even been to the Pacific before, as a prisoner of the Spaniards. A number of gentlemen accompanied the expedition, perhaps ten or a dozen, some in search of adventure and at least one, Thomas Doughty, privy to its real destination and an investor in it. Doughty was accompanied by his younger half-brother, John, and a friend from the Inner Temple, Leonard Vicary. There was an amateur naturalist on board, Lawrence Eliot, a botanist who would one day furnish Europe with descriptions of newly discovered flora, and two or three merchants, one of them John Saracold, a member of the distinguished Company of Drapers. The parson was Francis Fletcher. A black man served Drake as his personal attendant – none other than Diego, who had stood by Drake ever since the raid on Nombre de Dios. Among other friends and relatives of Drake were his brother, Thomas; his fifteen-year-old cousin, John, who stood as page; and a nephew of John Hawkins. Anticipating long, tiresome days ahead, Drake also troubled to take with him a number of musicians – our first intimation of one of the captain's greatest pleasures, music.

Provisioning, furnishing, completing the tackle and loading the ballast continued right until sailing. Victuals for eighteen or more months were supposed to have been stowed away, beer and wine, vinegar, oil, honey and salt, cheese and butter, oatmeal, rice, biscuit, beef, pork, fish and water, all supplied by Drake's Irish comrade, James Sydae. There were carpenters' stores, like tar, pitch and rosin. A great miscellany of items was carried aboard: needles, nets, twine and cordage, hooks, plates, bowls, tankards, candles, cloth, shoes and hats, buckets, wood and coal. Spades and axes were required in case a fort had to be erected somewhere, and weaponry received careful attention. As well as regular small arms, like pikes, crossbows and muskets, and the powder and shot for the artillery, Drake carried an assortment of incendiaries, including projectiles containing powder, oil, pitch, sulphur, camphor and spirits that could be thrown like grenades or fired from a kind of rocket-tube. These weapons struck Spaniards who later saw them as unusual, although they seem to have been well-known to the English.

In his cabin Francis Drake carried a small selection of books and maps. The Bible was there, of course, and with it John Foxe's history of the Protestant martyrs and *The Whole Book of Psalms*, prepared for congregational singing by Thomas Sternhold and John Hopkin. But the seaman as well as the Puritan was represented. He had three books on navigation. One was either Eden's translation of Cortes's *Art of Navigation* or Bourne's *Regiment of the Sea*, another perhaps a French translation of Pedro Medina's *Arte de Navegar*, and the third an account of Magellan's voyage.[1] Of maps he had few that were useful. One was a world map, either by Mercator or Ortelius, with its Chilean coastline bearing north-west from the Strait of Magellan instead of north, and another had been specially made in Lisbon, possibly from a chart of Fernão Vaz Dourado, a Portuguese navigator. Unfortunately, while the Portuguese map may have given primitive details of the East Indies and the Indian Ocean, it must have been redundant for the Strait of Magellan and the Pacific, and neither the Portuguese nor the Spaniards had knowledge of some of the regions for which Drake was bound. Whatever else the expedition might be, it was undeniably a formidable test of Drake's seamanship.

At last it was ready. For most on board, a routine trading voyage, for some, privy to the truth, a giant step into the darkness. Thomas Doughty prepared for the worst, and on 11 September, 1577 signed his will. Francis Drake faced up to parting with Mary, his wife. How little she had seen of him, this husband now bound again upon a journey from which he might never return. Neither she nor Drake knew how great a journey it would become. For when the little ships slipped out of Plymouth Sound at five o'clock on the afternoon of 15 November, 1577, they had embarked upon the longest voyage man had yet made.

---

[1] On Drake's reading matter, Wallis, *Sir Francis Drake*, 40-3.

# CHAPTER NINE

# THE ATLANTIC VOYAGE

Nor can it be in vain that Francis Drake,
Your noble hero, recently sailed round
The vast circumference of Earth (a feat
Denied to man by many centuries),
To show how Father Neptune circumscribes
The continents, and wanders in between
To keep two worlds apart.

Stephen Parmenius, *An Embarkation Poem for* . . .
*Sir Humphrey Gilbert,* 1582

THE CAPTAIN OF THE *PELICAN,* THE GENERAL OF THE EXPEDITION THAT FORGED INTO the English Channel that night, had cause to ponder the questions hanging over his voyage. As well as the problems of finding and navigating the Strait of Magellan and the uncertainty of whatever might await him beyond, an enormous discipline problem confronted him. The men happily believed themselves on their way to Alexandria, and what would happen when they learned that Drake was taking them to the edge of the known world was anybody's guess. Far from land and the restraint of authority back home, discipline in those small ships sitting upon a gigantic empty ocean would rest heavily upon the General's shoulders. Deep-sea voyages, especially ones as fraught with danger as this one, invariably tried the tempers of crews and tested the firmness of command, and in this case Drake had not even his queen's commission to underwrite any action he might be compelled to take.

For the moment other problems were more immediate. Atrocious weather forced the expedition to retire first to Falmouth and then back to Plymouth for repairs. There, amid embarrassed reunions, recriminations flew about, and Drake, in some way dissatisfied with the provisioning of the voyage, dismissed Sydae. Not everyone was pleased. Walking with a carpenter named Edward Bright in Drake's garden, Thomas Doughty complained that Sydae had been essential to the success of the expedition. According to Bright, Doughty went even further. He began bragging about his own importance, and claimed not only that he had been instrumental in gaining Drake the command but also that the backers expected Doughty to share the General's authority. Drake, he said, had been ordered to consult Doughty on all matters. As Bright later reported it, Doughty began speaking obscurely. He told Bright that he would choose twelve men aboard 'that should carry the bell away, swearing that I should be one, and that he . . . would make me the richest man of all my kin if I would be ruled by him.'[1] Did the simple ship's carpenter consider that Doughty, one of the General's closest friends, was trying to raise a faction against the commander? If he

---

[1] Evidence of Bright, in Vaux, ed., *The World Encompassed,* 172. The principal documents relating to the voyage are found in this volume and in Penzer, ed., *The World Encompassed;* Taylor, 'More Light on Drake'; Nuttall, ed., *New Light on Drake;* and Wagner, *Sir Francis Drake's Voyage Around the World.* Wallis, *Sir Francis Drake,* is a valuable pictorial account.

did, Ned Bright said nothing to Drake about the matter, and held his peace, but he remembered Doughty's words and was to recall them another day.

On 13 December the expedition made its second start, and it was soon running south-westerly along the coast of north-west Africa by a shoreline of fine white sand fringing a rugged interior. By then it was plain that Drake was not interested in the Mediterranean, now rapidly being left behind. There was some discontent, and one mariner later complained to Captain Winter that 'Mr Drake hired him for Alexandria, but if he had known that this had been Alexandria, he would have been hanged in England rather than have come in this voyage.'[1] Still, the narratives of the voyage record no undue resentment at this time, and Drake steered for the Cape Verde Islands, his mind possibly on the extra provisions he might find there. They were occupied by the Portuguese and used as a source of fruit, vegetables and livestock and as a base for longer voyages to and from West Africa, the East Indies and Brazil.

Drake had no doubt about how he would obtain what he needed from the islands. England and Portugal had long fallen to blows in these waters, and Drake resolutely upheld the tradition. On the African coast he had already seized half a dozen Spanish and Portuguese vessels, and arriving in the Cape Verdes he sent a pinnace in pursuit of a ship off Santiago, capturing her despite a ragged fire from an onshore battery. The *Santa Maria* was a pleasing prize, for she yielded victuals and various other everyday commodities, an astrolabe, sailing directions for Brazil, and – more valuable still – a Portuguese pilot, Nuño da Silva, experienced in the voyage between Europe and South America and the owner of several nautical charts. Great navigator as Drake was, he knew there was no substitute for men schooled in the waters ahead, and he took not only the ship, putting her crew into a pinnace and bidding them farewell, but also Nuño himself. It was piracy, without a doubt, but Drake was not troubled. He needed the victuals to maintain a vigorous company free from scurvy, and Nuño would help him on the coast of Brazil. Captain Winter of the *Elizabeth*, Drake's immediate subordinate, was less accustomed to the informal warfare of West Africa, and when he later made a report he was careful to establish that he had acted only in accordance with his commander's instructions.

As it happened, the prize, now renamed the *Mary* (possibly after Drake's wife), brought with her the first flicker of the discontent for which Drake was ever on the watch. He appointed Thomas Doughty to captain the ship, but, soon after coming aboard, that gentleman was involved in a dispute with some of the men. Two accounts of it survive. John Cooke, a partisan of Thomas Doughty who has little to say in Drake's favour, has it that Doughty discovered the General's brother, Thomas Drake, had broken open a chest to forage through the Portuguese booty that it contained. Doughty declared that he would have to report the incident to the General, and so he did, the next time that Drake came aboard the *Mary*. By this version, Drake flew into a rage, and accused Doughty of undermining him by attacking his brother; he would hear no more of it. The tempers of both men flared, and Doughty's friend, Leonard Vicary, had to intercede to smooth the matter down.

So wrote John Cooke, Drake's enemy and Doughty's friend. But his story may be doubted, not only for its partiality but on account of its inherent implausibility. If Drake turned so vigorously against his comrade, it is strange that he next moved Doughty to the command of the *Pelican*, the flagship of the expedition itself. A more

[1] Report of Winter, 2 June, 1579, Taylor 'More Light on Drake', 150.

convincing account of the difficulty was provided by the preacher, Francis Fletcher, himself no friend to the General, and it puts a new complexion upon the affair. Soon after taking charge of the *Mary*, Fletcher relates, Doughty was accused by a few of the sailors aboard the prize of purloining some of the captured goods. Drake investigated, as he was bound to do in a matter so relevant to the maintenance of harmony and order, and found Doughty in possession of some gloves, a ring and a few coins. Doughty explained that Portuguese prisoners had given them to him, and we must presume that the General chose to believe the story because he demonstrated his continuing faith in Doughty by transferring him to the command of the *Pelican*. Drake himself took over the *Mary*, and no doubt hoped that the trouble would blow over.[1]

It did not, for now Doughty, perhaps upset by his experience on the prize, began sowing discontent on board the flagship. He worked on the master, Thomas Cuttle, and the carpenter, Ned Bright (the same we met in Plymouth), promising to reward them if they would do his bidding, and he seems to have hinted that whatever they did Doughty could square in England by bribing the queen and Privy Council. Doughty's will reveals that he was a considerable investor in the voyage, but his stake amounted to no more than £500, and there is no doubt that Doughty exaggerated both his authority in the expedition and his influence at home. For what purpose? He seems to have been trying to raise a party among the men, and there is a suggestion that he proposed abandoning Drake and taking the *Pelican* on a raid of Spanish or Portuguese possessions. If so it was at best desertion, and at worst mutiny.

How much of this came back to Drake in the *Mary* is not known, although it would be surprising if his friends on the flagship left him in complete ignorance of Doughty's activities. The latter's cause does not even appear to have been promoted with much tact. John Doughty, Thomas's younger brother, was alleged to have boasted that the brothers commanded powers of witchcraft, and that they could bring forward the Devil in the form of a lion or a bear, or poison their enemies by supernatural means. If these remarks were made they were injudicious in the extreme, because the Elizabethans credited and feared witchcraft, and in no community was that abhorrence more acute than among superstitious sailors. Equally tactless was a mysterious message Thomas Doughty sent to Drake, to the effect that the General would shortly 'have more need of me than I shall have of the voyage.'[2]

It was a small matter that finally snapped Drake's patience. He had sent his trumpeter, John Brewer, to the *Pelican*, and there an argument ensued between Brewer and Doughty. Shortly after the trumpeter's return to the *Mary*, Drake sent his boat to the *Pelican* to fetch Doughty. As Doughty prepared to climb aboard the *Mary*, Drake himself appeared at the side. 'Stay there, Thomas Doughty!' he called, 'for I must send you to another place.' And with that he commanded the oarsmen to take Doughty to the *Swan* flyboat, a storeship under the charge of John Chester.[3] There was no explanation, simply the stark demotion that said everything. When Doughty came aboard the *Swan*, he complained that he was being treated as a prisoner, distrusted as a conjuror and traitor, but that he would refute every charge in England.

---

[1] John Cooke's narrative, preserved by the antiquary John Stow, is published by Vaux, 186-218. Cooke returned to England on the *Elizabeth*, and his account ends with the passage of the Strait of Magellan. Only the first part of Fletcher's account survives, although he completed the voyage with Drake and spent his later life in Yorkshire, where he died about 1619. This account is given fully by Penzer.

[2] Evidence of Drake, Vaux, 173.

[3] Cooke narrative, *Ibid*, 194.

As the Doughty affair unfolded the expedition picked its way across the Atlantic, travelling south-westerly for more than sixty days without sight of land and crossing the line on 20 February, 1578. On 5 April they breathed the 'very sweet smell' of land at 31°30' south and reached the coast of Brazil.[1] Drake's instructions probably directed his attention to the area of the River Plate, reputedly rich and possibly the source of respectable trading prospects. But as the English crept southwards, with Drake scrupulously comparing the coastline with Nuño's maps, the General's interest was as much upon finding shelter from the turbulent weather now gracing their progress and places where supplies might be replenished and the ships repaired. Nearly two weeks were spent in the river itself, killing seals for fresh meat, refilling water casks and reconnoitring. Then Drake was at sea again, investigating bays, noting landmarks, searching for ships that had got separated, beating out to sea in foul weather to avoid shipwreck, and making contact with Indians. In an anchorage in 47°45' (in present-day Argentina) Drake eventually reassembled all of his squadron except for the *Mary*. The *Swan*, which had also parted company with the other ships for much of the time, had rejoined, and Drake was disappointed to learn that all had not been well aboard her. The trouble was Thomas Doughty.

He had been singing his familiar song, promoting his own authority at the expense of Drake's. Drake, he said, owed his advancement to Doughty, and even Lord Burghley himself had sought Doughty as his secretary. In England, indeed, Doughty's influence was such that the power to reward followers or to punish enemies would be his. Now after dinner one day, talk had fallen upon the rising discontent that Doughty's ramblings had encouraged, when John Saracold bluntly observed that if there were traitors aboard Drake should deal with them as Magellan had done, and hang them as an example to others. Saracold did not name Doughty, but the gentleman was plainly alarmed at the suggestion. 'Nay, softly!' he replied. 'His authority is none such as Magellan's was, for I know his authority so well as he himself does. And for hanging, it is for dogs, and not for men.'[2]

Doughty's pretensions had not been the only source of difficulty on the unhappy *Swan*, for the gentlemen on board were also manifestly failing to carry their share of the hard work, considering it beneath their station and dignity. In an expedition of this kind every hand was needed, and there was no place for the distinctions of rank of the Tudor class system. But as the mariners heaved upon ropes and scrambled about the rigging, the gentlemen idled. The divisions deepened, between supporters of Drake and supporters of Doughty, between mariners and gentlemen. It was the custom of the ship's officers to dine with the gentlemen, but so inflamed was the master, a man called Gregory, that one day he declared that he would no longer mess with Doughty and his friends but would rather eat with the common sailors. And he did so. What was worse, he used his authority to have the best victuals delivered to the mariners rather than to the gentlemen and other officers. Doughty complained to the captain, John Chester, expressing his surprise that Gregory's conduct was allowed, but when he got no satisfactory response he confronted the master himself. The argument blazed anew, with Gregory angrily telling Doughty that 'such rascals as he should be glad to eat the tholes when he would have it.' In other words, the gentlemen might eat the

---

[1] Narrative of Edward Cliffe, *Ibid*, 274. Cliffe served aboard the *Elizabeth* under Captain Winter, and his account, like that of Cooke, extends only to Drake's entry into the Pacific.

[2] Evidence of John Saracold, *Ibid*. 167.

ship's boat for food. Blows were exchanged, and Doughty again appealed to the captain. 'Master Chester,' he said, 'let us not be thus used at these knaves' hands. Lose nothing of that authority that the General hath committed unto you. If you will we will put the sword again into your hands, and you shall have government.'[1]

The most bloodcurdling of Doughty's innuendoes indicated that he was fomenting mutiny. He told four people, including Fletcher the preacher, that he would make the company cut one another's throats. The context of his remarks is unclear, but they clearly boded ill for the conviviality of the expedition. Whether Drake took up these matters while in the anchorage is not known, but certainly an argument occurred, and a furious one, for the General lost his temper. He struck Doughty and ordered him to be bound to the mainmast of one of the ships, a not uncommon punishment of the time. It was fortunate, perhaps, that the men had much else on their minds in the fortnight they spent in the bay, but as they butchered more seals and fowls for meat, loaded fresh water, and transferred stores from the flyboat, which Drake intended to break up, many of them must have sensed that Drake and Doughty would have to settle their differences soon. The quarrel had been afoot for more than four months and the dangers of the Magellan Strait and the South Seas, which now seemed the undoubted object of the voyage, lay not far ahead.

The Indians may have been a welcome diversion. They visited daily, growing friendlier the more they learned to trust the English. Drake's method of establishing rapport with the natives was the same used only a few years ago by the famous Villas Boas brothers in their historic efforts to contact remote tribes of the Brazilian rainforest. Presents were left on rods so that the Indians might approach them at their leisure and leave in return their own offerings. Then, gradually, relations were intensified. The native men proved to be ferocious-looking fellows, though hardly the giants depicted in Spanish myth. They wore their hair long, painted themselves red, white and black, and if they went largely naked they smeared their bodies with oil to keep out the cold. Bones or wood were thrust into their noses or lips. They fascinated the voyagers, who noted the Indians' love of music (especially the English drums and trumpets), their ability to produce a fire from two pieces of wood, their dances (in which, to the immense satisfaction of his men, Captain Winter participated) and their jollity. Amiable the Indians were, but the English also found them opportunist thieves, and one day as Drake was ashore an enterprising native snatched away his cap, a scarlet one with a golden band, and dashed away with it in triumph. The General understood the importance of good humour and patience in situations like this, and, in the words of a mariner, Edward Cliffe, 'would suffer no man to hurt any of them.'[2]

Drake's relative humanitarianism has been met before, and we have seen how he attempted to set better standards than the French in his dealings with Spanish prisoners in the West Indies. Likewise, he had learned much from the *cimarrones* – learned that they, like him, had suffered by the Spaniard, and that if their friendship was cultivated they made good allies. Fellow-feeling and self-interest alike dictated Drake's attitude to blacks. So now he approached the Indians of South America in a spirit of forbearance and friendship, hoping to give them an impression of the English that was better than the one they had of the Spaniards, and to prepare the way, if necessary, for

[1] Cooke narrative, *Ibid*, 196-7.
[2] Cliffe, *Ibid*, 277.

any future relationships in trade. We cannot suppose that Drake believed their religion equal to his own. He shared with other Europeans the assumptions of Christian moral superiority, and beneath his kindness lay thoughts of eventual profit. But there was, too, a genuine respect for peoples of another culture and colour that was absent in so many of the great discoverers, in Columbus, Pizarro, Da Gama and Hawkins. He constantly spoke of the *cimarrones*. One of Drake's men later told a Spaniard that 'those Negroes were the brothers of Captain Francis, who loved them dearly.' And a Spanish prisoner of Drake's remarked that 'he had heard Captain Francis say that he loved them, and that he spoke well of them, and every day he asked if they were in peace.'[1] This was an attitude, alas, that few of the English were prepared to live up to. Compare, for example, Richard Grenville's destruction of an Indian village as punishment for the theft of a silver cup at the landing of the first colonists in Virginia in 1585.

On 3 June the English at last quit the bay, having broken up the *Swan* in the interests of consolidating the squadron. Again there was an unpleasant scene, for when Drake ordered the Doughty brothers to ship aboard the *Christopher* Thomas refused. The General was now thoroughly tired of Doughty's behaviour, and cut the nonsense short by ordering Doughty to be lifted aboard with the ship's tackle. But he could also see the seeds of mutiny spreading among the men. Thomas Cuttle seized his arquebus and waded to the shore, turning in the shallows with the surf surging around him to declare that he would not return to see Doughty treated in such a fashion. Rather, 'I will yield myself into cannibals' hands, and so I pray you all to pray for me.'[2] Cuttle's bravado was only a temporary phenomenon: after the other men had been embarked Drake sent a boat ashore and the indignant mariner was persuaded to return. Nevertheless, it was a display of disobedience Drake could have done without.

The General's conviction that the Doughtys were fomenting disorder was plainly demonstrated shortly afterwards, when Drake disposed of the *Christopher* and transferred the brothers to the *Elizabeth*, where his vice-admiral might keep an eye towards them. Before the Doughtys came aboard Drake himself visited the *Elizabeth* and delivered a stern warning to her crew. He was sending them, he said, 'a very bad couple of men, the which he did not know how to carry along with him.' Continuing, he described Thomas Doughty as 'a conjuror, a seditious fellow and a very bad and lewd fellow, and one that I have made that reckoning of as of my left hand; and his brother, the young Doughty, a witch, a poisoner, and such a one as the world can judge of. I cannot tell from whence he came, but from the Devil I think.' If the men stood by Drake, he promised them wealth beyond their dreams, but they must neither speak to nor communicate in writing with the two troublemakers.[3]

Fort San Julian stood in 49° south, a little north of the Magellan Strait, its anchorage flanked on the south side by towering pillars of rock and sprinkled with small islands. Ashore stood a grim relic of fifty-eight years' standing, braving the powerful winds of these wild regions: the wooden gallows upon which Ferdinand Magellan had hanged one of his men for mutiny. As the *Pelican*, *Elizabeth*, *Marigold* and *Mary* stood into the anchorage on 20 June Drake was steeling himself for a more timely and no less

[1] Statement of San Juan de Anton, April 1579, Wagner, 365; deposition of Nicolas Jorje, 28 March, 1579, *Ibid*, 352.
[2] Cooke, Vaux, 199.
[3] *Ibid*, 200.

decisive resolution to the disaffection within his own ships. He had now reached a critical stage of his journey. His ships were further south than any English vessel had been before, and he could not afford to take on the formidable Strait of Magellan and the South Seas with his command torn by dissension. If there was to be a final confrontation with Thomas Doughty, it had to be here.

As if to proclaim the dark doings of Port San Julian, an unfortunate episode marked Drake's landing, two days after his arrival. The English hoped that their amicable relations with Indians would continue, but such was not to be the case. Drake and six men had rowed ashore. They were under-armed, having brought, apart from swords and bucklers, only one arquebus and bow between them. On the face of it this seemed perfectly adequate; only a few Indians appeared and their demeanour was reasonably friendly. It was one Robert Winter who haplessly transformed the scene. He was demonstrating the English bow to the Indians, matching it against their weapons, when the string broke. One of the aborigines, under the notion that the English were now devoid of fire-power, then fired an arrow into Winter's lungs, fatally wounding him. As Winter tumbled to the ground, a sailor named Oliver, who carried the only arquebus, discharged it at the offending warrior, but the powder was damp and the weapon misfired. The Indian slotted another shaft to his bow, and as Oliver fumbled with his priming the arrow smashed into his chest at close range with such force that the point protruded from his back.

Two of the English had been killed with impunity, and the Indians were now inflamed, shouting exultantly. From a distance they began to shower the remaining five white men with arrows. Drake was now fighting for his life, and he instantly took command of the situation. He ordered those of his men with shields to form a defence before the others, and as the arrows fell about them he had them broken into halves so that they could not be reused. Gradually, the fire slackened, as the Indians ran short of arrows. At this point, Drake snatched up Oliver's fallen arquebus, recharged it and turned it upon the Indian who had murdered his comrades, blasting 'his guts abroad', as Fletcher vividly put it.[1] At this reverse the Indians fled, and although Drake used the anchorage for a month they troubled him no more.

To protect his men from possible retaliation, Drake had them pitch their tents on a low sandy island in the bay, and amid his final preparations for the voyage to the Magellan Strait he attended to the problem of Thomas Doughty. On 30 June every man in the squadron was summoned to the island, where they found their leader in a grim mood and beside him, acting as clerk, Captain Thomas of the *Marigold*. Drake went straight to the point. Thomas displayed papers containing testimony to Doughty's mutinous talk throughout the voyage, and then Drake addressed the accused: 'Thomas Doughty, you have here sought by divers means . . . to discredit me to the great hinderance and overthrow of this voyage, besides other great matters wherewith I have to charge you withal, the which if you can clear yourself of, you and I shall be very good friends, where to the contrary you have deserved death.' The reference to the ultimate penalty so early in the proceedings was a spine-chilling indication of Drake's determination, and Doughty immediately denied the allegations. The General asked how he would like to be tried.[2]

---

[1] Penzer, 124.

[2] The only full account of the proceedings in Port San Julian is given by Cooke. Despite his partiality and the fact that the words he ascribes to his actors can only have been approximations of the original

'Why, good General, let me live to come into my country, and I will there be tried by Her Majesty's laws,' Doughty replied. He knew that if he could delay the trial any number of events might prevent it ever taking place, and if he had to answer the charges it was better that he did so before an impartial judge, and where influence might be brought on his behalf.

But Drake was having none of this. He could not continue his voyage with Doughty's mutinous influence festering aboard the ships, nor could he spare men to conduct the prisoner home. 'Nay, Thomas Doughty,' he said. 'I will here empanel a jury on you to inquire further of these matters that I have to charge you withal.'

Now, Doughty was not only an educated, articulate gentleman, but a lawyer, such a lawyer as few could master, according to Parson Fletcher. Having failed to delay his trial, he played his top card immediately and struck at Drake's weakest spot. Guessing that the General had no written commission from the queen, he questioned Drake's right to preside over the trial. 'Why, General,' he said pointedly, 'I hope you will see your commission be good.'

Drake began to bluster his way out. 'I warrant you my commission is good enough,' he said tersely.

'I pray you let us then see it,' Doughty chimed. 'It is necessary that it should be here showed.' If Doughty had any doubt about Drake's authority, he must have swallowed hard at this point.

Drake, however, had no answer; instead, he imperiously swept away the objection. 'Well, you shall not see it. But well, my masters, this fellow is full of prating. Bind me his arms, for I will be safe of my life.' And as some of Drake's men obeyed one wonders how impressed they had been with what had scarcely been one of their General's better performances. As for Doughty, he now knew that while he might possess greater knowledge and a sharper wit than Francis Drake, he had underestimated his ruthlessness and resolution in the face of danger.

In a brief altercation that followed, Drake accused Doughty of poisoning the Earl of Essex (for it had been rumoured, falsely, that he had so died) while Doughty replied with no greater accuracy that he had served the earl well, and that it was even Doughty who had introduced Drake to Essex. But now the lawyer was making a mistake. As long as he dwelt upon Drake's authority and the legality of a trial he could outfence the General, but once he began lying about simple facts within Drake's knowledge he was asking for defeat. The General merely repudiated Doughty's falsehood, adding that Essex had held Doughty in small esteem, 'for I that was daily with my lord never saw him there above once, and that was long after my entertainment with my lord.'

A jury was sworn, with Winter as its foreman, and Thomas read out the charges. Members of the company recalled Doughty's words, and he denied none of it until Ned Bright stepped forward and described how Doughty had tried to enlist Bright in his party, and how aboard the *Pelican* Doughty had hinted that he had a mind to break away from Drake and to use the plunder he obtained to bribe the government at home and earn indemnity for his conduct.

'Why, Ned Bright,' protested Doughty. 'What should move thee thus to belie me? Thou knowest that such familiarity was never between thee and me, but it may be I

statements, the source is convincing, and is supported in places by the other narratives. See also the examination of Nuño da Silva, 1 June, 1580, in Nuttall, 377-80.

said if we brought home gold we should be the better welcome, but yet that is more than I do remember.'

In the ensuing banter Doughty suddenly let out something that told significantly against him in Drake's eyes. He said that Lord Burghley, the Lord Treasurer, had knowledge – a 'plot' – of the voyage. Now, Burghley had not been involved in preparing for Drake's expedition, and apparently had been kept ignorant of it deliberately. Probably he would have disapproved of the venture as unnecessarily provocative, for he was neither militant nor fervoured. Drake's voyage bore the stamp of Walsingham and Leicester, not Burghley, and the queen, unusually, had taken their part without conferring with her most trusted public servant. Doughty had perhaps spoken innocently of the expedition to Burghley, unaware that so important an official had not been privy to the plans, but Drake did not interpret it so. As far as he was concerned Doughty had betrayed his voyage to the Lord Treasurer. When Doughty mentioned that Burghley had 'a plot' of the expedition, Drake denied it. Doughty insisted it was true, and Drake asked, 'How?'

'He had it from me,' replied Doughty artlessly.

'Lo, my masters,' exclaimed Drake, 'what this fellow hath done! God will have his treacheries all known, for Her Majesty gave me special commandment that of all men my Lord Treasurer should not know it, but to see his own mouth hath betrayed him.'

Realizing that he was treading into deeper water, Doughty tried to revert to the earlier debate about the legitimacy of the proceedings, and repeated his request to be tried in England. His friend and fellow lawyer, Leonard Vicary, pronounced Drake's actions illegal, but the General dismissed him peremptorily. 'I have not to do with you crafty lawyers, neither care I for the law, but I know what I will do.' He ordered the jury to deliberate upon the charges written down, and while they were talking he sifted through his papers to find material that would add colour to his authority.

After due consideration, the jury returned a verdict of guilty, although they remarked that Bright's character led them to doubt his particular evidence. It probably made little difference, for the tendency of Doughty's alleged remarks to Bright was similar to that others claimed to have heard. Drake accepted every word of the testimony, and waived the reservations about the carpenter ('Why, I dare to swear that what Ned Bright hath said is very true'). He then strode to the waterside, calling all but Doughty to accompany him, and there foraged through his papers. If Drake had a commission from the queen he would have produced it then. Instead, after searching, he exclaimed, 'God's will! I have left in my cabin that I should especially have had.' In lieu of the commission he displayed documents that established that it was one of the Hawkins brothers, not Doughty, who had recommended him to Essex; that it was through Essex and Walsingham that the present voyage had been organized; that he had the backing of Christopher Hatton, who had enjoined him to take aboard John Thomas and John Brewer; and that the queen had invested 1,000 crowns in the expedition.

And the sentence? 'My masters,' said Drake. 'You may see whether this fellow hath sought my discredit or no, and what should hereby be meant but the very overthrow of the voyage, as first by taking away of my good name and altogether discrediting me, and then my life.' It was obvious the General believed that Doughty was hatching a plot to kill him. 'And now, my masters,' he continued, 'consider what a great voyage we are like to make, the like was never made out of England, for by the same the worst in this fleet shall become a gentleman, and if this voyage go not forward, which I cannot see how possible it should if this man live, what a reproach it will be, not only unto our country but especially unto us, the very simplest here may consider of. Therefore, my masters, they that think this man worthy to die, let them with me hold up their hands.'

Drake had set out the alternatives. He could not go forward upon so dangerous an adventure with Doughty aboard to multiply the risks to its prospects. Nor could he return to England, and squander what had already been achieved and the goodwill and hopes of his promoters. Nor, for that matter, could he weaken his expedition by sending one of his ships home with Doughty. He had made up his mind: Doughty had to die, for the sake of the voyage, the safety of the company, the satisfaction of the backers, and perhaps the name of England itself. The argument evidently went home, for the men voted for Doughty's execution, and those who opposed it dared not advertise their dissent.

It was a hard decision, and Drake seemed to prevaricate, stating that if any could devise a means by which the voyage could be preserved without Doughty's life being forfeited he would listen. After Doughty had received the death sentence, he again added that 'if any man will warrant me to be safe from your [Doughty's] hands and will undertake to keep you, sure you shall see what I will say unto you.'

Doughty cast an appealing glance at Captain Winter, with whom he was apparently friends. 'Master Winter, will you be so good as to undertake this for me?' he asked.

Winter readily offered to keep Doughty safe aboard the *Elizabeth* and to guarantee his conduct, but Drake only pondered a short time. He would not do it. He could not risk Doughty, even through casual conversation aboard the *Elizabeth*, poisoning a ship's company against him, nor could he permit the *Elizabeth* to return to England with the prisoner and weaken the squadron. Doughty was told that he must prepare for death the day after next, on 2 July.[1]

The man met his end with dignity and courage. He chose to die under the axe, as a gentleman would die, and added a codicil to his will, dividing the money he had set aside for funeral expenses among his friends, of whom the principal beneficiary, Leonard Vicary, received £40. Before his execution, Doughty shared the sacrament with Drake, and then the two dined together, perhaps reaching some kind of reconciliation in these final moments of Doughty's life. They spoke alone for a few minutes, and then Doughty strode unfalteringly to the block and knelt before it in prayer, entreating God to protect the queen and grant success to the voyage. He prayed for his friends at home, and then begged the company to forgive himself and those of his associates on board. Drake promised that there would be no further reprisals. Then Doughty rose to embrace his General, called him his good captain, and bade him farewell – moments

---

[1] *The World Encompassed*, published by Drake's nephew in 1628, is the most extensive account of the voyage. It is highly favourable to Drake, and appears to have been prepared as a companion volume to *Sir Francis Drake Revived*. The date of its composition is unknown, although Quinn, 'Early Accounts of the Famous Voyage', has argued for an origin before 1589. It may be that it was drawn up at the instance of Drake himself. *The World Encompassed* depends upon Fletcher's full narrative, only part of which has survived, upon Cliffe's account, and perhaps also upon a log of Nuño da Silva. It contains a description of Doughty's trial and execution which is at variance with that of John Cooke, stating, for example, that Doughty himself chose to be executed, rather than to be set on the mainland or taken to England. I have followed Cooke as the more probable version, and that which is partly corroborated by Winter's report.

recalling the friendship that had bound them in better days. But the die was cast, and when Doughty's head was struck off, Drake had it held up in the manner of the time and called, 'Lo! This is the end of traitors!' Thomas Doughty was buried on the small island, close to the remains of Robert Winter and Oliver, far away from his home and the sheltered portals of the Inner Temple in which he had shone so brightly.

After more than four hundred years the motives that impelled Doughty to his miserable end remain a mystery. Why should a man who held so exalted a station in the expedition, whose money had been invested in its success, follow so destructive a course? What had he to gain by Drake's discomfiture? The question seems to have confounded contemporaries and historians alike, if we can judge by the marvellous theories it has inspired. Shortly after Drake's eventual return to Plymouth, local gossip averred 'that Thomas Doughty lived intimately with the wife of Francis Drake, and being drunk, he blabbed out this matter to the husband himself. When later he realized his error and feared vengeance, he contrived in every way the ruin of the other, but he himself fell into the pit.'[1] Yet this hardly fits the manner in which the quarrel developed. Drake's Victorian biographer, Julian Corbett, speculated that Doughty had been employed by Burghley to sabotage Drake's mission, but it seems unlikely that so loyal and solid a servant of the queen would have stooped to the undermining of her policies by the incitement of mutiny on the ships of her followers. Nor, for that matter, does Doughty appear to have shared Burghley's supposed pacific persuasion; the reverse, he seems to have been as bent upon plunder as Drake himself. Perhaps the best answer should be sought in Drake's style of command and Doughty's own complex personality.

Drake never enjoyed rigid command structures, in which orders passed strictly from superiors to subordinates. As long as he remained in control, he was apt to bypass key officers in order to instruct or enlighten the men below directly. Perhaps this informal management was not untypical of men who rose from the more egalitarian camaraderie of life aboard trading ships, and it was certainly attuned to Drake's readiness to pitch into the humblest tasks and labour beside the lowliest of sailors. But it carried the danger of upsetting officers accustomed to more formal methods of command, and what was worse, of making inferiors more acquainted with the leader's intentions than their superiors. Nor was this looseness in the chain of command the only difficulty experienced by Drake's officers, for at the very top the leader reserved and regularly exercised the right to plan and decide without or against the advice of his juniors, as he saw fit. On Drake's ships there could be no doubt whose voice held sway. Such practices had their advantages, but they were also capable of creating resentment in proud officers who felt their services or opinions undervalued.

Such a man was Thomas Doughty, whose inability to rescue his old companion from Ireland, Sydae, from dismissal at the beginning of the voyage has been noticed. Eager to make his way in the world, unscrupulous, fraternizing with the powerful, the conceited and the arrogant, he was, perhaps, jealous of Drake, a man he considered to be a social inferior, and hoped to wrest from him control of the voyage, or part of it, to reap the glories for himself.

If such was the case he misjudged Drake, whose easy affability masked an iron resolution. It is easy to blame Drake for the cold barbarity with which he removed Doughty. The trial was possibly illegal and certainly unfair; the accused was almost

---

[1] Donno, ed., An Elizabethan in 1582, 184.

'railroaded' to the block. But Drake's position must be taken into consideration. He was not at home and secure, in England. He was in regions unknown to himself and his countrymen, about to hazard his followers in waters of fabled treachery, and to beard the Spaniards in territory they claimed as their own. It was a project of supreme daring, and one Drake was unsure he could complete. Perils enough taxed his men, perils that called for unanimity and co-operation, not division and dissension. Doughty was agitating the men, and probably plotting mutiny. On deep-sea voyages, in which ships were remote from the common instruments of justice, mutiny was the most feared and extreme of offences. The service was hard, men were cramped in damp and miserable quarters for months on end, and discontent, frustration and anger were never far away. Tudor seamen were habitually quarrelling about victuals, plunder and the shares of work. In circumstances like these mutinous spirits soon infected others, and the history of the sea is full of the murders and strifes that ensued, and of the weak and irresolute captains like Dampier, Kidd and Bligh who succumbed to them. Drake's decision was a hard one, but it was the right one, the decision of a great commander. If Doughty's death is held against Drake, he must equally be credited with having taken men, ostensibly recruited for a pedestrian Mediterranean cruise, across the world in adverse circumstances without subjecting them to the agonies of a mutiny. That prospect he exorcized in a most timely fashion in Port San Julian bay.

Nor had Drake finished his task. Doughty was dead, but there were others aboard, his friends, who nursed additional grievances. There was John Doughty, the dead man's brother; Leonard Vicary, his companion; and Thomas Cuttle, Hugh Smith, John Cooke and other Doughty supporters who were unreconciled to Drake's dramatic reaffirmation of his authority. And there remained, too, the bitterness between the mariners and gentlemen engendered by the latter's failure to shoulder a fair share of the workload. Drake let it be known that old quarrels must be set aside and on 11 August assembled the whole company before him. Parson Fletcher made to give the customary sermon, but Drake motioned him away. 'Nay, soft Master Fletcher,' said he. 'I must preach this day.' Then he addressed the men:

> My masters, I am a very bad orator, for my bringing up hath not been in learning, but what so I shall here speak, let any man take good notice of what I shall say, and let him write it down, for I will speak nothing but I will answer it in England, yea and before Her Majesty.

He then called for unity in the face of the dangers ahead, impressing upon them what amounted to a social revolution, a demand that birth should carry few privileges in this service, and that none could be passengers:

> Thus it is, my masters, that we are very far from our country and friends. We are compassed in on every side with our enemies, wherefore we are not to make small reckoning of a man, for we cannot have a [nother] man if we would give for him ten thousand pounds. Wherefore we must have these mutinies and discords that are grown amongst us redressed, for by the life of God, it doth even take my wits from me to think on it. Here is such controversy between the sailors and the gentlemen, and such stomaching between the gentlemen and sailors, that it doth even make me mad to hear it.
>
> But, my masters, I must have it left, for I must have the gentleman to haul and draw with the mariner, and the mariner with the gentleman. What, let us show our-

*selves all to be of a company, and let us not give occasion to the enemy to rejoice at our decay and overthrow. I would know him that would refuse to set his hand to a rope, but I know there is not any such here. And as gentlemen are very necessary for government's sake in the voyage, so have I shipped them for that, and to some further intent, and yet though I know sailors to be the most envious people of the world, and so unruly without government, yet may not I be without them.*

*Also, if there be any here willing to return home, let me understand of them, and here is the Marigold, a ship that I can very well spare. I will furnish her to such as will return with the most credit I can give them, either to my letters or any way else. But let them take heed that they go homeward, for if I find them in my way I will surely sink them. Therefore, you shall have time to consider her of until tomorrow, for, by my troth, I must needs be plain with you. I have taken that in hand that I know not in the world how to go through withal. It passeth my capacity. It hath even bereaved me of my wits to think on it.*

Drake was relying upon the lure of Spanish gold, and perhaps the danger of a journey home without him, to keep most of the men with him when he made what he must have regarded a dangerous offer, threatening as it did the force at his disposal. However, the men agreed to continue. After some further ceremony, in which the General reminded all to whom they owed loyalty, he recounted for all how the voyage had been conceived and prepared.

*And now, my masters, let us consider what we have done. We have now set together by the ears three mighty princes, as first Her Majesty, [then] the Kings of Spain and Portugal, and if this voyage should not have good success, we should not only be a scorning or a reproachful scoffing stoke unto our enemies, but also a great blot to our whole country for ever, and what triumph would it be to Spain and Portugal, and again the like would never be attempted.*

He had reminded them of the magnitude of their task. He had disposed of the arbitrary distinctions of birth and privilege, and enjoined the gentleman to haul upon the ropes beside the common mariner. He had summoned them to their work in the name of queen and country and their own well-being. When they were dismissed, he willed them to be friends once more. And, throughout, he had created a basis upon which the venture could continue. For there was urgent work to be done. The *Mary* was burned, to reduce the size of the squadron and therefore the risk of the company being separated in storms, and on 17 August the *Pelican*, the *Elizabeth* and the *Marigold* quit Port San Julian and bravely stood towards the open sea on their way to the feared Strait of Magellan.

# CHAPTER TEN

# WAR COMES TO THE PACIFIC

The Dragon that over seas did raise his crest
And brought back heaps of gold into his nest;
Unto his foes more terrible than thunder,
Glory of his age, after-ages' wonder.

Robert Hayman, 'Of the Great and Famous . . .
Sir Francis Drake', early seventeenth-century poem

THE CAPE OF VIRGINS, MARKING THE ENTRANCE TO THE MAGELLAN STRAIT, WAS sighted on 20 August. Beyond looked defiant enough, great steep, grey cliffs rising bleakly from the pounding surf, and Drake lightened the moment with a ceremony. He had his ships salute the queen, held the inevitable religious service, and rechristened his *Pelican* the *Golden Hind,* a name that would be remembered in history alongside the *Santa Maria,* the *Mayflower* and the *Victory.* The new name honoured Sir Christopher Hatton, whose family crest was a hind, and we can guess why. Thomas Doughty had been Hatton's servant, and Drake probably wanted to flatter his patron and reassure him that, the execution notwithstanding, the General remained loyal to Sir Christopher. Drake realized that one day he might have to answer for Doughty's death, and Hatton was better a friend than an enemy.

Two days were spent awaiting a favourable wind from the north-east, and then the ships stood into the yawning mouth of the strait, keeping towards the centre of the channel to avoid shoals. On either side the distant shores first appeared to be low and flat, but the vessels shortly passed through two sets of narrows with scarcely a league of water from bank to bank, and the character of the landscape changed. Huge, craggy peaks, the highest of them still capped with snow in this southern winter, loomed behind thickly timbered lower reaches fissured with small streams. Then the passage opened and led southwards, but before proceeding Drake anchored by three islands, which he named after the queen, St George and St Bartholomew. A day or so passed in exploring and reprovisioning, during which the sailors stumbled across a human skeleton on St George's Island, but whose it was none could tell. For most of the time the men were busy bludgeoning penguins and storing them aboard for the arduous voyage ahead.

No one aboard the squadron, not even Nuño da Silva, the Portuguese pilot, had been through these straits before, and Drake's navigational skills must have been fully extended as he guided his ships along the 300-mile waterway, sounding as he advanced, and tacking to and fro. The current was with him for much of the way, but the winds varied, sometimes behind him, sometimes ahead or from either side, and they were so gusty that they occasionally whipped up whirlpools in the water. Depth concerned Drake too, for in some places there were shoals and rocks and elsewhere the strait was so deep it was impossible to anchor. When anchorages were eventually found, the bed was sometimes so rugged that it frayed the hempen cables by which the ships were held in position. A little more than half-way, the passage swung north-westerly, and the ships wove their way through a maze of scattered islands in the teeth of westerly winds funnelling between the mountains and with few anchorages that were safe. Nevertheless, Drake did it. He reached the Pacific – the fabled South Seas – on 6 September, after a journey of fourteen days. It was probably the fastest passage of the strait that century. Magellan took thirty-seven days, Loyasa four months, Thomas Cavendish forty-nine days and Richard Hawkins forty-six days.

Unfortunately, a greater test still awaited Drake. In compliance with the written plan of the voyage, he was bound for Peru, and accordingly instructed his captains that if they separated they should search for him at about 30° south. Emerging from the strait the ships turned north-westerly, assuming that the South American coast lay in that direction as the published maps then indicated. But after two or more days fighting wind, snow, hail and dense fog it became evident that the charts were wrong, and Drake was later to confirm that the true bearing of the Chilean coast from the strait was north, not north-west. It was his first significant geographical discovery, but not one Drake could ponder for long, for he had made only some 70 leagues when a ferocious storm from the north drove the squadron helplessly southwards.

Those terrible days that followed are vividly recalled in the narratives of the expedition: wild, relentless winds, sometimes threatening to crash them against the shore; occasional glimpses of dark, hungry crags grimacing through the fog and spray; black stormy skies and mountainous seas; and the looming peaks of the coastline, sometimes visible, sometimes only detected by the roar of the waves on the rocks. At times the ships were beating south-westerly into the open sea and at others clawing their way towards the coast. When they found shelter they were wrenched from their anchorages; at sea they were battered by the waves. Never, wrote Captain Winter afterwards, had he lived through such a storm.

Some were not equal to it. Towards the end of September the *Marigold* was lost, sucked down in the tempest with all twenty-nine men aboard her, including her captain, John Thomas, and the luckless carpenter, Ned Bright. For a time Drake hoped that she had merely parted company with the rest of his ships, and kept a lookout for her, but after her loss could no longer be denied Francis Fletcher swore that he and John Brewer had been on watch the wild night the *Marigold* had disappeared and that they had heard the 'fearful cries' of the wretched mariners as they were engulfed by the sea. The parson noted in his narrative, with a singularly ungodly satisfaction, that the Lord had taken his revenge against Ned Bright for his part in the conviction of Thomas Doughty.

Winter's *Elizabeth* gave up the voyage. One October night she parted company with the *Golden Hind* as they both hauled out to sea in 'fog and outrageous winter' to avoid shipwreck near the Magellan Strait. Finding a haven within the strait, Winter and his men took several weeks to recover from their ordeal, and when they sailed again it was not towards the Pacific. There is disagreement as to who was responsible for the decision to turn back. John Cooke and Edward Cliffe, mariners aboard the *Elizabeth*, said unequivocally that it was the captain's idea. He despaired of rejoining Drake and remarked that the winds were poor for a voyage to Peru. Winter's own report, on the other hand, has nothing of this. While admitting that he had small hope of reaching Peru or meeting Drake there, he insisted that it was his desire to sail to the Moluccas in the East Indies, and that Drake had voiced an intention to go there. But the ship's master disapproved of the plan, and influenced the crew to oppose it, and Winter was forced to sail for home.

Now, it is not unlikely that Drake had mentioned the Moluccas to Winter, because it was one of several routes he had in mind for his voyage home, but there is every reason to doubt the thrust of Winter's story. After all, when he arrived in England in a sound ship there would be those ready to accuse Winter of deserting Drake, and what more convincing defence than to blame the mariners for giving over the voyage? Better to admit that one could not control the ship than to own the greater ignominy of dereliction of duty or cowardice. We know that Winter had an eye to his survival when he related his adventures in England. He exonerated himself from wilfully plundering the Portuguese in the Atlantic, as has been noted, and he treated the matter of Doughty's execution gingerly, although he had been the foreman of the jury that returned the verdict. By emphasizing his offer to bring the prisoner home aboard the *Elizabeth*, he absolved himself, as second-in-command, of Doughty's death. On every culpable point Winter had his defence, and his report even declared that he was too afraid of Drake to oppose him: 'with the said Drake no justice would be heard.' On the whole, Cliffe's alternative testimony that the captain of the *Elizabeth* determined to sail home 'full sore against the mariners' minds' may be the closer of the two versions to the truth.[1]

Whoever prompted it, Winter made for England. He re-entered the Atlantic on 11 November, disproving once again the theory that powerful currents and winds made a west-east navigation of the Strait of Magellan impossible. His journey home was not without loss, however. Eight men disappeared in a pinnace, one was killed by a blow of the capstan, and two deserted to the Portuguese in Brazil. But the *Elizabeth* was back in Devon in June 1579, bringing tidings that Drake had passed into the South Seas, but with no certainty that he had survived the storms that had quenched Winter's quest for discovery.[2]

Of course Drake had survived, and his *Golden Hind* was now the sole English

[1] Winter's report, Taylor, 'More Light on Drake'. Cliffe, printed in Vaux, ed., *World Encompassed*, 281.
[2] It is worth referring here to the strange story of Peter Carder, which was published by Samuel Purchas, *Purchas, His Pilgrimes*, 16: 136-46. Carder claimed that after the separation of the *Hind* and the *Elizabeth* Drake had Carder and seven men man a small pinnace. The pinnace soon parted from the mother ship in the bad weather, but Carder and his comrades navigated her back through the Magellan Strait to north of the River Plate. Six of the men were captured or killed by Indians, another died, and Carder alone reached England in 1586 after spending several years with the Portuguese in Brazil. It is surprising that this far-fetched story has been believed so often. It is unlikely that Drake would have placed a few men in a small boat without a compass in weather so atrocious that two ships had already been lost; equally so that the party could have made their way to Brazil; and very improbable that such an incident should have escaped the narratives of those on the *Golden Hind*. Carder's story, in fact, seems to belong to the homeward voyage of the *Elizabeth*, not to the progress of Drake in the South Seas, and Carder turns up in Brazil for the very good reason that his pinnace was lost there. Edward Cliffe, who served aboard Winter's ship, records that off an island near Brazil a consort vessel disappeared: 'Here, by reason of foul weather,

vessel in the vast Pacific. After separating from Winter, he had retreated south-wards before the winds, occasionally finding brief but unsafe anchorages among the small islands of the archipelago of Tierra del Fuego. Yet, in the strange man-ner of fate, these untoward happenings enabled Drake to make the greatest geo-graphical advance of his voyage. He discovered that the Magellan Strait was not a passage between two great continents. South of it lay not Terra Australis, the southern land-mass, but merely a chain of broken islands with open sea beyond. If it existed at all, Terra Australis was much further towards the pole. Francis Fletcher recorded that the *Hind* was driven to the

> utmost island of Terra Incognita, to the southward of America, whereat we arriving, made both the seas to be one and the self same sea, and that there was no farther land beyond the heights of that island, being to the southward of the equinoctial 55° and certain minutes, to divide them; but that the way lay open for shipping in that height without let or stay, being the main sea.[1]

Just what that 'utmost island' was is difficult to say. Some of the best chroniclers of the voyage, Cliffe, Cooke and Winter, had departed with the *Elizabeth*, and the re-maining sources disagree about the island's position. Two depositions by John Drake, Francis's cousin, and *The World Encompassed* put it at 56° south, Parson Fletcher at 55° and Nuño da Silva 57°. The island may have been Cape Horn in 55°58', but Hen-derson Island in 55°36' has also been suggested. Either way, Drake saw enough to con-vince him that there was a passage between the Atlantic and the Pacific south of the Magellan Strait, and it is fitting that it bears his name to this day. Drake also formally claimed these southern islands for his country and called them the Elizabeth Islands. They were the first overseas possessions claimed for England during the current reign, preceding Drake's own attachment of Nova Albion (California) in 1579 and Gilbert's formal possession of Newfoundland in 1583. Both of Drake's claims were effectively beyond England's capacity to follow up or enforce, and they lapsed, but at the time the discovery of the Elizabeth Islands imparted to Drake a sense of achievement. Two stories come down to us that suggest this. First, Francis Fletcher landed on his 'utmost island' and set up a stone bearing the queen's name and the date. Second, the General himself, according to a story he later gave to Richard Hawkins and others, sought out the most southerly point of the last island the English reached and lay full length upon it, rising to claim that he had been further south than any European before him. This is exactly the sort of dramatic gesture in which Drake revelled, and it is entirely believ-able.

The great storm that had driven Drake south ended on 28 October. For more than fifty days the *Golden Hind* had suffered the violence of wind and sea, and the talents of her commander and master had been tested mightily. The *Marigold* and the *Elizabeth* were gone, and aboard the *Hind* many of the men were down with scurvy, a debilitat-ing disease caused by the lack of fresh fruit and vegetables that swelled the limbs and gums. Fortunately, all but two men recovered, and the wind eased and veered to the

we lost our pinnace, and eight men in her, and never saw them since.' (Vaux, 281-2) No doubt Carder, like David Ingram before him, found in his fertile imagination the means to embroider his adventures.

---

[1] Fletcher, in Penzer, ed., *World Encompassed*, 134.

south. Drake was able to make his way north again, revictualling with birds and seals at a small island, and then proceeding on a fair wind to Chile.

The plan written down in London enjoined Drake to reconnoitre the coast as far as 30° south, where it was free of Spanish occupation, but Drake's main contact with the natives nearly ended in disaster. On 25 November the *Hind* was anchored in twelve fathoms off the low-lying island of Mocha, situated in 38° south and not far from the Chilean coast. Taking about a dozen men ashore Drake was received by a party of Indians, who provided him with two Spanish sheep, hens and a kind of maize. Obviously these natives had seen Europeans before, and the English surmised that they had been driven from the mainland by the Spaniards.

They were probably members of the Araucanian peoples who lived south of the Biobío River in Chile, fiercely independent natives who practised a hunting, fishing and gathering economy, but who had already demonstrated a remarkable tenacity and versatility in confronting Europeans. The Spaniards had extended their influence southwards from Peru since 1535 and founded Santiago, La Serena, Concepción, Imperial, Valdivia, Villarrica and Angol in what is now Chile. Forts were established to hold the frontiers, near the coast and on the slopes of the cordillera. Despite the encroachment of Spanish power, the Araucanians resisted and a major contest between Spaniard and native American ensued in the 1550s. Three Spanish towns, Concepción, Angol and Villarrica, and as many forts were evacuated and burned before the native assault, and several detachments of soldiers, one commanded by the Governor of Chile, were defeated in the field. In 1557 the Indians menaced Santiago itself.

Their success was partly due to their ability to integrate aboriginal skills with new ideas borrowed from the Europeans. They made use of horses taken from their enemies, and developed weaponry to counter cavalry by lengthening their spears, strengthening their clubs, and creating a noose attached to a pole to ensnare the Spanish mounts. Some of the Indians even used arquebuses and cannon in the fighting. These changes were probably exaggerated by the Spaniards, along with the legend of the youthful Indian leader Lautaro, as an explanation for their defeats, but the Araucanians certainly proved themselves both capable and courageous. Their defeat in 1558 did not end their militance. Fifteen years before Drake entered the Pacific they inflicted further losses on the Spaniards; twenty years after his arrival they launched their most successful onslaught and cleared all of their enemies out of the region south of the Biobío.

Drake suspected but underestimated the hostility felt towards the Spaniards by the Araucanians when he appeared at Mocha, and he handled the situation badly. The Indians had given him their friendship upon his first landing, and he took only ten men with him when he rowed into a creek for fresh water the following day. None of the English carried firearms or bows, only swords and shields. As the boat grounded, Tom Brewer and Tom Flood stepped out to fill some vessels. Suddenly, they were set upon by Indians hiding in the reeds, and when Drake's men made to their assistance they found themselves confronted by overwhelming numbers of warriors, a hundred by one account, five hundred in another, and an unbelievable two thousand according to Parson Fletcher. Brandishing an array of weapons that caught the sun in an intimidating display, the natives seized the boat's mooring rope, and bombarded the crew with arrows and darts. There was no alternative to a retreat, and the English would have been massacred had not one of the seamen slashed the mooring rope with his sword and the others pushed off. As it was, the sailors lost four oars to Indians who splashed into the shallows after them, and every man was wounded, many several times, and two mortally. Drake himself received two injuries to the head, one from an arrow that struck him below the right eye.

When the boat returned to the *Hind,* and its bleeding occupants were removed, Drake had it reinforced with heavily armed men and sent in again to see what could be done for Brewer and Flood, but if Fletcher is to be believed the Indians were already butchering their prisoners and their strength was too great to allow a successful attack. There was a call aboard the *Hind* for the ship's artillery to be turned upon the natives, but with a compassion and understanding all the more surprising amidst such emotion and pain, Drake would not have it. 'We might have taken a revenge upon them at pleasure with our great shot out of our ship,' Fletcher wrote, 'but the General would not for special causes consent to it.'[1] It would not have saved Flood and Brewer, and Drake believed that the Indians had mistaken the English for Spaniards and had suffered enough by Europeans. He wanted to give his country a better record, a noble sentiment of which few of his successors were worthy. Nursing his wounded, Drake weighed anchor and sailed northwards towards the Spanish settlements of Chile and Peru.

Perhaps Drake's experiences with Araucanians and storms discouraged him from reconnoitring the Chilean coast more closely, but henceforth we see him in a more characteristic role, striking the Achilles' heel of Philip's empire along the west coast of the Americas. It was a logical extension of his previous work, when he had cut the bullion road across the isthmus of Panama. The thoughts that possessed him as he neared the part of the project nearest his heart are not fully recoverable. Conceivably he hoped to link up with John Oxenham, whom he knew would try to employ the *cimarrones* in an effort to cross the isthmus from the Caribbean to the Pacific. Perhaps he wondered if their joint forces might be enough to capture the city of Panama itself. As he worked northwards, however, he was to learn that Oxenham had been captured, and – no less painfully – that hopes of the *Elizabeth* and *Marigold* rejoining him could be dismissed. If he had pondered a surprise attack upon Panama, these tidings must have aborted the idea. Then more modest but scarcely less remarkable events occurred as Drake brought his war to Chile and Peru.

There was one legacy of this raid that possibly no one anticipated at the time. During those few months Drake took several prisoners, and it is their depositions and narratives, supplemented by the information of Nuño da Silva, the Portuguese pilot still aboard the *Hind,* that give us the clearest picture we have of Drake at sea. He had about eighty men with him, perhaps fifty of them fully fit. They were drilled to perfection – like veteran Italian soldiers, said one witness. Every man kept his firearm clean and ready for action. The General treated them kindly, bestowing favours with his usual generosity and joviality, but he was strict with those who transgressed his code and punished even minor offences. From them he demanded obedience and respect.

[1] *Ibid,* 140.

Not a man was allowed to purloin any of the plunder without the permission of the General, nor were they allowed even to address him bareheaded unless he bade them remove their hats. Drake realized that some distance between a commander and his crew was probably necessary on such a voyage, where the support of the promoters and the machinery of the state were far away, and where discipline could break under the extreme dangers to which men were exposed. He never lost the common touch, he toiled at ropes with the men and dug for water with them, but by little rituals he emphasized that he was also apart from them and would brook no challenge to his authority. And aboard the *Hind* most of the men responded loyally. 'I endeavoured to find out if the General was well-beloved and everyone told me that they adored him,' one prisoner wrote to the Viceroy of New Spain.[1]

This blend of formality and informality was evident in the daily routine of the ship. Drake dined with his officers and Nuño beside him, but none seated themselves until he said, and behind the General's chair stepped smartly his page, young John Drake. The meal was served on fine plates, some engraved with a coat of arms, and trumpets and oboes added entertainment. Drake loved music, and kept musicians at sea or ashore, and just as they serenaded the General at his midday and evening meals, so they were at hand at the religious services that invariably accompanied dining. In the last Francis Drake was truly his father's son, for he led the singing of the Psalms, read aloud from the *Book of Martyrs* and on Sundays appeared in his best finery and had pennants and flags hoisted at the masts.

One of these services was witnessed by prisoners off Guatulco in April of 1579. A table was placed at the poop with an embroidered cushion at its head, where Drake would conduct the worship. When he was ready, he flapped the table twice with the palm of his hand to call to attention those present. Nine men joined him at the table and sat bareheaded, and Drake knelt and prayed for perhaps fifteen minutes. This done, he read for an hour from a book and afterwards viols were brought forward to accompany the singing of Psalms. John Drake, ever on hand, concluded the ceremony with a dance. One of the Spaniards asked the General about his text, and Drake turned the pages of Foxe's *Book of Martyrs* to display the illustrations, one of them showing a man at the stake, engulfed in flames. 'Look at this book!' Drake commented. 'You can see here those who were martyred in Castile.' It was, he said, 'a very good book.' As usual he spoke strongly against the Pope in his conversation, but excused his own conduct by harking to that day ten years ago in a Mexican harbour he would never forget. 'You will say this man who steals by day and prays by night in public is a devil,' said Drake, but it pained him to plunder the property of ordinary Spaniards. 'I would not wish to take anything except what belongs to King Philip and Don Martin Enriquez . . . I am not going to stop until I collect two millions which my cousin, John Hawkins, lost at San Juan d'Ulua.'[2]

Looking at Francis Drake, Spanish observers saw a man well into his thirties, a man more gentle and refined than might have been expected in one of Drake's class and background. He was not more than medium in height, possibly even short, but he

[1] Francisco de Zarate to Martin Enriquez, 16 April, 1579, Wagner, *Sir Francis Drake's Voyage Around the World*, 377.

[2] Statement of Francisco Gomez Rengifo, 18 February, 1580, *Ibid*, 127.

was thick-set, robust and powerful, with broad shoulders and strong limbs. His head was round, with a high forehead, and his eyes large, open and bright, lending his face the 'merry' aspect that accorded with his demeanour. A profusion of short reddish brown curls that shaded into a full blond beard enclosed a ruddy complexion. Standing more closely, one might have noticed a small wart on the left side of his nose and on the right cheek a scar that marked the arrow wound he had received at Mocha. When he could free himself from the three hours a day he spent in worship, the attention he had to give to the handling of the ship and other matters, and the time he spent listening patiently to the council whose advice he seldom heeded, he found refuge in his cabin, studying charts and sailing directions, and – another unusual cultured touch – painting with cousin John. As a record of the voyage, he noted not only geography and navigation, but carefully painted the wildlife he had seen, birds, trees and seals. Nuño remarked of Drake and his cousin that when 'shut up in his cabin, they were always painting.'[1] Sadly, their work has not been preserved for posterity, for upon his return home Drake handed his material to the queen, and the details of his voyage were considered too sensitive to release at the time; since then they have been lost.

The most urgent concern of Spaniards who fell into Drake's hands was, of course, their own safety. Many expected to be killed, as was so often the manner of the day, yet they usually found the English commander to hate few Spaniards as individuals, and that they were treated politely, 'very courteously', as one prisoner recalled. Given that lives were at risk in any armed contest, Drake's raid on the Pacific coast of South America was remarkably bloodless. None of his prisoners was killed, although those who acted disingenuously, who attempted to withhold information or valuables, were sometimes dealt with severely indeed. Today, this brutality stimulates revulsion, but Drake lived in a world very different from our own, and he cannot fairly be judged by the ethics of the late twentieth century. We must locate his behaviour within the context of sixteenth-century conflict. It was a century that saw Vasco da Gama, the Portuguese pioneer, seal several hundred men, women and children into a captured ship and set it alight. It witnessed the whole populations of cities, towns and villages slaughtered by soldiery, at Naarden, Antwerp and elsewhere. It saw the Spaniards massacre French colonists in Florida in 1565, and behead or hang all the French prisoners they took in a naval battle off the Azores seventeen years later. It heard the cries of men executed by being torn apart between horses, of Protestant martyrs burning alive for their faith in Smithfield, and of prisoners put to bestial tortures by officers of the state across Europe. In that century Pope Gregory XIII celebrated the murder of several thousand, mostly unarmed, Huguenots in Paris by striking a medal. The English Puritan John Stubbs and his printer had their right hands sliced off for condemning their queen's relations with France's Catholic heir presumptive. In 1587 a Spanish admiral put to sea with orders to kill every man aboard any English ships he could capture. In 1596 the people of Faro sent an English commander the noses, ears and arms of some of his countrymen. This was sixteenth-century warfare, and by its standards Drake was far from cruel or brutal. Even when Spaniards resisted capture, and might have expected their lives to be forfeit, Drake generally received them with

---

[1] Nuño da Silva's narrative, *Ibid*, 348.

some respect and consideration.

Of course, they called him a pirate, even as some of them acknowledged his humanity, and in a sense he was, although the term 'privateer' would have been more appropriate at this time, since Drake was probably acting with authorization and in the interests of the Crown. The General was sensitive on the point, and boasted to his prisoners that he held the queen's commission. What is more, he even produced a document as proof, but only to Spaniards who could not read English! In full flow, Drake would go further in justification, for in his view it was the shipment of treasure from the New World that sustained Philip's standing in Europe and facilitated the suppression of Protestantism by fire and sword. Drake's war was not simply a squalid freebooting enterprise, but an arm of the fight against the Devil and his children. Like David, he was smiting the giant. At least, that was how Drake preferred to see it. 'The said Englishmen are Lutherans,' observed one Spanish prisoner, 'and their deeds and speech prove them to be such. They eat meat in Lent and on Friday, and do not keep the commandments of God as Christians do. They manifest themselves as being very much against the Pope.'[1] When they were told of the death of Don John of Austria, whose regime in the Netherlands had been as odious to the English as to the Dutch, the English sailors danced upon the decks of the Hind and celebrated with a banquet.

Drake would also speak of revenge, revenge for the treachery of the Viceroy of New Spain, still the redoubtable Don Martin Enriquez, he of San Juan d'Ulua. The property Drake had taken, he explained to the unfortunate victims, would partly compensate for the money lost by John Hawkins and for the three hundred men the English had left during and after the battle in San Juan d'Ulua. He exaggerated the loss, but not wholly in an effort to vindicate himself, for a steely bitterness crept into his conversation whenever he remembered Enriquez. Look at the testimony of Francisco de Zárate, whose ship was taken by Drake, in a letter to none other than the offending viceroy himself:

> I found him [Drake] walking about on board [the Hind], and went up to him to kiss his hands. He received me with good grace and took me to his cabin, where he made me sit down. He said to me, 'I am a good friend of whoever tells me the truth, but on the contrary I get very much irritated [if they do not], so to tell me the truth is the best course you can take with me. How much silver and gold has the ship on board?'
> I said to him that there was none, repeating, 'none, only some table service on which I am served, and some cups, altogether.' He was silent for a moment, and then turned to ask me if I knew your Excellency [Enriquez]. I told him yes. 'Is there on board any relative of his or anything that belongs to him?'
> 'No, Señor.'
> 'I would be more pleased to fall in with him than all the silver and gold in the Indies, and you would [then] see how [I would teach him how] to comply with the word of a gentleman.'[2]

To Francis Drake, Don Martin Enriquez was justification enough for all the depredations of the English.

Valparaiso, the port of Santiago in Chile, 5 December, 1578. The Spaniards aboard a

---

[1] Deposition of Domingo de Lizarza, Nuttall, ed., New Light on Drake, 176-9.
[2] Zárate to Enriquez, 16 April, 1579, Wagner, 374.

ship in the harbour observed a strange vessel entering, and a boat put out from her towards them. No cause for worry, this, because there were no foreigners in the Pacific, and the Spanish crew even drummed a welcome as the boat of the *Golden Hind* pulled alongside. They were not disillusioned until the abrasive Tom Moone clambered over the side, unnecessarily struck a Spaniard in the face, and called out, 'Go down, dog!' There was no further violence. The prisoners were herded into the hold (except for one, who jumped overboard and swam ashore to raise the alarm), and Drake then loaded two small boats with armed men and sent them to capture the little town. No opposition was encountered, for the inhabitants had fled, and in ecstatic abandon the Englishmen ransacked the port. From the ship they took a pilot, some wine and four chests containing perhaps 25,000 pesos' worth of gold. Ashore, the town warehouses and dwellings supplied meal and wine and the little church some silver. Drake left the following day, heading northwards with favourable tides and winds, and towing his prize behind him.

There was much to do before the raid was fully launched. A pinnace had to be built for cutting out prizes from bays and searching for the missing English ships, provisions needed gathering, and the *Hind* herself wanted repairs and her artillery fully mounted. At the same time, Drake could not afford to linger long. If the news of his presence on the coast passed north in advance of him it would frighten away shipping and allow the authorities at Lima or elsewhere to mobilize opposition. His force was too small to risk a major engagement with the Spaniards. He had to keep ahead of the news, descending upon his enemy by surprise. Already Rodrigo de Quiroga, the Governor of Chile, was in action. He fitted out a vessel with a hundred men to pursue Drake, fruitlessly as it turned out, and dispatched another boat towards Callao, the port of Lima, with word of the English raid on Valparaiso. Then, rather too late, he concentrated upon fortifying the ports of Chile in readiness for more attacks.

Drake's progress was retarded by his search for the *Marigold* and the *Elizabeth*, which he still hoped might meet him at the rendezvous in 30° south. For near a week he searched the area around the island of Tongoy. On 19 December he was anchored in a bay south of Coquimbo when he suffered his first losses to the Spaniards. A dozen or more men were at work on shore collecting fresh water. A superior party of Spanish horse and foot from La Serena, accompanied by naked Indian auxiliaries, appeared. The corsairs retreated into the surf to shelter behind a rock, but one, Richard Minivy, was shot down before they could be rescued by boats from the *Hind*. The English were then compelled to watch the Indians drag Minivy's body from the water and the Spaniards mutilate it by carving out the heart and striking off the head.

Drake then moved to Salada Bay, near Coquimbo, to complete his final preparations for the major part of his raid. A pinnace with a gun in the bow and large enough to take up to forty men was built, and while Drake took her out in search of his consorts some of his men set to work on the *Hind*, tarring and greasing the hull, trimming the sails and bringing the unmounted guns from the hold. Drake's quest for the *Marigold* and *Elizabeth* proved to be unsuccessful, but he dared not prolong it, and with the prize from Valparaiso still in company he made north.

A little plunder was taken along the way, a small boat or two here, some fish from the Indians there, even a llama-train laden with silver taken by a shore party. But the next important stop was Arica, a tiny settlement of about one hundred houses situated in 18° but nevertheless the entrepôt from which silver from the fabulous mines of Potosi was shipped to Panama. Here was the first port on the treasure route that led to Panama, Nombre de Dios and Spain, and Drake not unnaturally expected to profit from a visit. Yet it was disappointing. The English arrived on 5 February, 1579 and captured the two barks they found in the anchorage, one yielding thirty-seven bars of silver and a chest of silver coin, and the other merchandise and wine. One of the prizes and a pilot were commandeered, the other ship was burned, possibly by accident, and Drake set off for the small port of Chule.

It was a tiny place and the only prize there had nothing more valuable than a little water aboard. Worse, it now became apparent to Drake that warnings about the English were beginning to precede him, for he learned to his chagrin that a mere two hours or so before the *Hind's* arrival a considerable amount of bullion had been unloaded from the prize and was now stacked on shore guarded by a force of Spaniards and Indian archers. To rub in the point the locals jeered at the English from the waterfront, calling them thieves and deriding them for coming late. Drake's best weapon, surprise, had been destroyed by overland couriers, and if he wasted more time they would be carrying word into Lima, the capital of Peru, from which the viceroy, Don Francisco de Toledo, controlled Philip's South American dominions. In the next few days Drake set his prizes adrift, released all his prisoners except for two pilots, and steered for Callao, the outlet for Lima.

On the voyage he made more prizes, and obtained from the captain of one of them some information that quickened his pulse. Anchored at Callao, the Spanish captain said, was a vessel belonging to Miguel Angel, bound for Panama with silver. Better still, another ship, the *Nuestra Señora de la Concepción*, which the Spaniards irreverently rechristened the *Cacafuego*, had just left Callao for Panama richly laden with silver. And since she intended stopping at various ports for flour, Drake might just overtake her. Late in the evening of 15 February Drake passed stealthily between the island of San Lorenzo and the mainland into the harbour of Callao, which he found full of sail. Our sources disagree as to how many ships were there, but the lowest figure given is nine and the highest thirty. Anyway, Drake was reassured by the telling lack of vigilance in the port, and directed his pinnace and small boat to board and search each vessel in turn. The process was completed, but achieved little, for none carried treasure; Miguel Angel's ship was found not to have taken its silver aboard yet, for 200,000 pesos were then in the customs house ready for embarkation. Disappointed, the English decided to continue their chase of the *Nuestra Señora de la Concepción*. To prevent an immediate pursuit, they cut the cables of all the ships in Callao and hacked down the masts of the two largest vessels, and prepared to sail with only a quantity of linen and silk and a black leather chest containing some reals (coins) of plate for their trouble.

While Drake was so engaged another ship entered the harbour, the *San Cristobal* from Panama with merchandise for Peru. She anchored innocently, unaware of the English, and shortly received a boat from the customs house enquiring as to her cargo. It was in examining the *San Cristobal* that the Spanish authorities first noticed the *Hind* in the darkness, and assuming her to be another freighter the customs men pulled across, calling to the stranger to identify herself. Drake must have been relieved that Callao even then knew nothing of his arrival, and although he had a smattering of

Spanish, he ordered a sailor well versed in the language to reply that the *Hind* was Miguel Angel's ship from Chile. A crude subterfuge, certainly, but not an ineffective one, for the customs officers came alongside and it was only as one of them began climbing up the side that he gazed with growing alarm at the large and ominous guns of the English ship. This was no merchantman. The Spaniard pitched back into his boat and she was rowed back to the shore in panic, while her crew bellowed the alarm.

The flight of the boat was noticed aboard the *San Cristobal*, but she was intercepted by Drake's pinnace before she could escape to the open sea. A musketeer shot one of the privateers, but then the *Golden Hind* herself got under way, and the Spaniards bounded into their boat and bolted to the shore, leaving the English to swarm aboard the *San Cristobal* and bear her away in triumph.

At this juncture the attempts of the Viceroy of Peru to deal with Drake illustrate equally the ineptitude of Spain's defences in the Pacific and the completeness of the English strategy. The viceroy learned of the attack on Callao in the early hours of the following morning, and although it was still dark in Lima he had bells rung and officers hammering on door after door to raise a militia. About two hundred horse and foot were assembled and General Diego de Frias Trejo sped with them to Callao to find that the corsair was now standing insolently off shore rifling the luckless *San Cristobal*. Two ships were eventually secured and about three hundred men tumbled into them. Frias Trejo commanded the *Nuestra Señora del Valle* and Pedro de Arana the *Nao de Muriles* but neither of these impressive-sounding vessels was equipped with artillery and few of their crews had firearms. They would have been easy meat for the *Golden Hind*. Fortunately for them, the pursuers failed to catch up with their quarry, for when Drake saw two substantial ships coming towards him he cast off his plundered prizes, with all prisoners save Nuño da Silva, and headed northwards. Having achieved that much, the by now seasick Spaniards sensibly turned back. The viceroy certainly did not see it that way, and after fulminating against Frias Trejo he had two ships and a launch fitted out to finish the job, entrusting them to 120 soldiers with Pedro Sarmiento de Gamboa, a well-known navigator. Enjoined with following the corsairs to Nicaragua if necessary, they proceeded no further than Panama.

Drake's mind was in the meantime on something else – that treasure ship that was said to have left Callao for Panama. Could he overtake it? Would he find it in such an expanse of ocean? As he sailed along the coast he picked up one report after another of the *Nuestra Señora de la Concepción*. From a prize he learned that he was three days behind her, and at Paita, a port that he raided, that the treasure ship's lead had been cut to two days. It was during this search, which now took on the aura of Ahab's frenzied quest for the great white whale in *Moby Dick*, that Drake committed the first clear act of wanton brutality on his record. Among two ships taken after the English left Paita was a vessel owned and commanded by Bernito Diaz Bravo, captured at daybreak on 28 February, 1579. The mariners found eighty pounds of gold, some silver, food and ships' tackle in her, and Diaz Bravo later assessed his losses at 18,000 pesos' worth in gold and silver, and other goods to the value of 4,000 pesos. At one time it looked as though the ship would be taken as well, because the English tested her sailing qualities to see if they wanted her, and the crew were afterwards told to collect their belongings and go ashore in the English pinnace, which Drake would give them in exchange for their own vessel. Naturally distressed, Diaz Bravo pointed out to Drake that the ship was his only property. What would he do? The General usually made some kind of gesture when confronted with appeals of this nature, and so he did now. 'He . . . took me by the hand and led me to the bow, where he told me not to worry and promised by the God he worshipped to give me my ship and a cable from his own country, and said that even if he took her . . . he would pay me for her with a piece of the gold from Valdivia.'[1]

At this stage Francis Drake had behaved much to form, and Diaz Bravo's ordeal seemed to be over when the Englishmen eventually returned to the *Hind*. But they were no sooner gone than back again, and in an ugly mood, alleging that Diaz Bravo's clerk, Francisco Jacome, had been withholding some treasure. What had happened was this. Drake had taken some Negroes from the prize, not a surprising act since he often offered blacks the opportunity to join him and serve at the same rates of pay as the rest of his crew. About the time the Spanish ship was relinquished, one of the Negroes claimed that there was more gold aboard than had been revealed, and that Jacome was the author of the deception. Immediately the corsairs returned. Poor Jacome was hiding nothing, but the English did not believe him. A rope was put around his neck and he was momentarily hoisted from the deck to persuade him to talk. When no more information was forthcoming, he was allowed to fall into the sea, from which he was fished by the *Hind*'s boat. Drake was now satisfied that the clerk had been telling the truth, and had him returned to the prize, which was suffered to leave without further molestation.

Here we see Drake at his worst, torturing a helpless prisoner in pursuit of booty. There can be no denial of it. The ship's captain exaggerated the episode by claiming that he also was given a hanging, but, although this is obviously false, the facts gleaned from the other authorities, from Jacome's own statement, and the depositions of John Drake and Nuño da Silva, speak plainly enough. In the light of some of the atrocities committed upon prisoners by his contemporaries, Drake's action may have been of the milder kind, but it nearly cost Jacome his life. The English commander was not a man to be frustrated or crossed. Doughty learned it, and so did Jacome.

This unhappy episode over, the *Golden Hind* forged north of the Equator in search of the *Nuestra Señora de la Concepción*. Expectantly every horizon was scrutinized for a sight of the ship that represented a fortune. Drake offered a gold chain to whoever saw her first, and then, at noon on 1 March, the prize was claimed. The *Hind* was standing off Cape San Francisco when the lookout at the masthead, young John Drake, discerned a sail four leagues to seaward. Drake surmised that it was the treasure ship, and he was right. The *Nuestra Señora de la Concepción* of 120 tons, under Captain San Juan de Anton, had sailed from Peru without any knowledge of the danger closing upon her. She had made occasional stops at ports for flour, and even now her officers saw no reason to be alarmed at the appearance of a distant vessel on the same tack. And Drake would not alarm them. He had some pots filled with water thrown behind his ship and towed to act as a drag upon the *Hind*, a ruse that allowed her to keep her sheets out ready without closing the distance to the treasure ship too quickly.

Some nine hours later the two ships were within hail of each other. Drake had been attempting as best he could to hide the English pinnace behind the *Hind*, but

---

[1] Letter of Diaz Bravo, 7 March, 1579, *Ibid*, 355.

now he sent her to pull upon the port side of the treasure ship while he crossed her stern to engage her other flank. 'Englishmen!' the corsairs shouted. 'Strike sail!' They then called Anton by name and declared that if he did not surrender his ship would be sent to the ocean bed. For all her importance the treasure ship had no artillery and few firearms aboard, but momentarily Anton showed fight and refused to haul down his flag. In reply a whistle sounded aboard the *Hind*, a trumpet blew, and a volley of artillery fire brought down the treasure ship's mizen mast while a shower of arquebus balls and arrows wounded one of the Spaniards and sent all the others but Anton scuttling below in terror. Before long the pinnace had grappled alongside, and the privateers were scrambling over the enemy bulwark.

As was usual, the captain of the Spanish ship was taken to the *Hind*, where he found Drake removing his helmet and coat of mail. The English commander embraced Anton and politely remarked, 'Have patience. Such is the custom of war.' Patience was a quality Anton needed badly in the next few days as his ship was taken further out to sea and the dazzling cargo she carried was transferred to the *Golden Hind*. The boat moving it had to be loaded five times. There were thirteen or fourteen chests of silver reals, 80 pounds of gold, and 26 tons of silver bars! No Englishman had taken a prize like this before. The registered cargo alone amounted to 360,000 pesos, of which some 106,500 pesos belonged to Philip and the rest to private persons. In Tudor money that amounted to about £126,000, or about half the ordinary annual revenue of the English Crown! And this was not all, for there was also an unassessed amount of unregistered bullion, and San Juan de Anton's subsequent estimate of it at 40,000 pesos was probably an understatement. One thing was certain: Drake's voyage was truly 'made'.

During the week that Drake kept his prize, he spoke often with Captain Anton. The subject of John Oxenham came up, and Drake grew angry, for however far he had come he had no means to help the four Englishmen incarcerated in Lima. He bade Anton tell the Viceroy of Peru that if they were killed it would cost the lives of 2,000 Spaniards. Anton suggested that Oxenham and his men would not be killed; more likely they would be made to serve as soldiers, and, although he was wrong, his words gave Drake some comfort. Finally, the work was complete, and Drake sent the *Nuestra Señora de la Concepción* on her way. As Anton later reported:

> Before the Englishman turned loose my ship he gave certain articles to those whom he had robbed. In money he gave thirty and forty pesos to each one, and to some pieces of Portuguese linen and tools, such as pick axes and pruning knives, and two of his own decorated coats. To a soldier named Victoria he gave some side-arms; to me a musket, which he said had been sent him from Germany, for which reasons he esteemed it highly; and to the clerk a steel shield and a sword, telling us that he gave us these so we would seem to be men-at-arms. To me he gave two pipes of tar, six quintals of German iron, and a barrel of powder, and to a merchant named Cuevas he gave some sans with looking-glasses in them, telling him they were for his wife. To me he gave a basin of gilded silver with a name written in the middle of it which said 'Francisqus Draques', and at the time he turned me loose he gave me a safe conduct in English signed with his name, telling me that he gave it to me so that if the other two English ships which had been reported to be behind him should fall in with me they would not do me any harm or rob me again.[1]

Of course, Drake could afford to be generous. The safe conduct that Anton re-

---

[1] Relation of Pedro Sarmiento de Gamboa, *Ibid*, 366.

ceived is interesting to us, because although only the text of it survives and not the document itself, it is the first letter of Drake's that we have. In it he requested Captain Winter and Captain Thomas to pay Anton double for anything they wanted from the Spaniard's ship, and that Drake would make good any consequent loss later. He commanded them to do no one harm, and also reflected upon their situation, revealing once more the piety that sustained him in difficulty, 'beseeching God, the Saviour of all the world, to have us in his keeping, to whom only I give all honour, praise and glory.' Their fate, he reminded them, was in the hands of 'him that with his blood redeemed us, and [I] am in good hope that we shall be in no more trouble, but that he will help us in adversity, desiring you for the Passion of Christ, if you fall into any danger, that you will not despair of God's mercy, for he will defend you and preserve you from all danger, and bring us to our desired haven.' So it would be with all his letters. He signed this one, 'Your sorrowful captain, whose heart is heavy for you, Francis Drake.'[1]

Drake's main problem now was to discover a haven safe from the Spanish counterattack that was surely gathering, where the leaking *Golden Hind* could be cleaned of weed and barnacles and repaired for the voyage home. Fresh water and food were also now greater imperatives, for the ship might have to leave the coasts and strike out in a long travail across the ocean. He did not particularly need prizes, but off the coast of Nicaragua fell in with a ship belonging to Rodrigo Tello that had cleared Nicoya, a depot for the trans-Pacific trade to the Philippines. Drake secured some charts and sailing directions for this route, and hoped that the prize would furnish him with a pilot, for he kept a prisoner for that purpose, a man named Alonso Sanchez Colchero. Drake also wanted the ship herself, and placed the other prisoners into his pinnace with provisions sufficient to take them ashore.

Unfortunately, Colchero was unco-operative. According to his own statement – in which he was eager to ward off suspicions that he had collaborated with the corsairs – Drake tried to bribe him with gold and silver and even hanged him as Jacome had been hanged. However, this was probably a deliberate fiction designed to emphasize Colchero's sufferings in the Spanish cause, for while other accounts corroborate his story of the bribery none has anything to say about a hanging. Had it occurred it would surely have featured in the narratives by John Drake, Nuño da Silva, and Spanish witnesses, as the earlier atrocity had been. Colchero likely heard of how Jacome had been handled, and sought to exonerate himself the more effectively by pretending to have resisted similar persuasion.[2]

While Drake was having little success with Colchero he took another prize. Early in the morning of 4 April he surprised the ship of Don Francisco de Zarate. Most of the Spaniards were still asleep, and the few who saw a strange vessel coming upon them from the darkness were fooled when a voice identified her as the ship of Miguel Angel from the coast of Peru. The corsairs manned a boat, passed Zarate's vessel, fired small

[1] Drake to Winter and Thomas, March 1579, Vaux, 268.
[2] Among other things, Colchero said he refused to guide Drake into Realejo so the corsairs could destroy the town. He constantly professed his loyalty to Spain, and even made Drake say, 'You! You must be a devoted subject of your King Don Felipe, and a great captain!' However, he neglected to mention, as others did not, that he accepted fifty pesos in reals from Drake, and probably was afraid he would be charged with collusion (Colchero deposition, April 1579, Nuttall, 193-8).

shot into it, and called upon the Spaniards to strike their sails, which they did unre-sisting. The ship provided four chests of Chinese porcelain, some linen, taffeta and silks, water, food, a Negress, and a guide named Juan Pascual. Drake reckoned that Pascual could show him the way to fresh water, and exchanged him for the useless Colchero.

At first Drake believed, for some reason, that Zarate was related to the hated En-riquez. He told Colchero that 'if the said Don Francisco was related to the viceroy he wanted to hang him as such.' Fortunately, this misunderstanding was overcome, and Drake behaved as impeccably as the circumstances allowed. When the prize was re-leased, he mustered her captain and crew, and gave to each person a handful of reals as a gift, showing particular consideration to those who were sick. It is not surprising that some of the Spaniards, accustomed to tales of the barbarity that accompanied the raids of French corsairs in the West Indies and the ferocious warfare between Indians and Spaniards in the New World, wrote of Drake as a rather gentlemanly rogue. A rogue, yes, because he left them the poorer, but not wholly an unlikeable rogue.

His last call was at Guatulco, a small port in Mexico, where he remained for three days, from 13 to 16 April. A ship in the harbour, with her merchandise, was seized, and a party of men went ashore to ransack the town of fresh water, flour, biscuit, maize, hens, bacon, clothing, and a few thousand pesos of reals of plate, as well as a few items of wealth stripped from the local church. The few inhabitants who assem-bled to resist under the *alcalde*, Gaspar de Vargas, were soon driven into the woods, and the town remained in Drake's possession for the duration of his stay. During the pillage examples of the extreme Protestantism of the privateers were frequently on dis-play. One snatched a crucifix from a Spaniard and smashed it, alleging that idolators, not Christians, worshipped sticks and stones. In the church the images and crucifixes were broken, a picture on the altar torn and the altar-stone itself smashed, and a tall, hunchbacked corsair removed the bell from the belfry.

As for Drake, he remained on the *Hind* for most of the operation, riding gently at anchor in the harbour. The principal dignitaries of the town were invited aboard, and he conducted them around the ship. Over a glass of wine he made it clear that he would brook no interference with his work, and threatened to burn the ship he had taken in the port if his demands were not met. Before he left he also let out that he would visit Acapulco to burn the town. He may indeed have contemplated such an attack, or it may have been mentioned purely as a diversion. Certainly the Spaniards took the possibility seriously. Acapulco fitted out three vessels with two hundred men to give him a hot reception, and the militia was mustered. In fact, Drake showed no interest in Acapulco. He had his treasure, a fair stock of victuals and considerable water, and wanted nothing more than that secluded haven necessary for the careening of the *Hind*. To avoid being disturbed he was bound north and west, beyond the limits of Spain's settlements in the Americas.

Drake was thinking, too, about Devon, and the route he would take home. Should he try to reach the Atlantic by the fabled North-west Passage, the so-called Strait of Anian, or retrace his steps to the inhospitable seas of Tierra del Fuego, as had been originally planned? Could he cross the isthmus to the Caribbean, perhaps in small boats? Or should he ponder the almost unthinkable prospect of sailing west, across the Pacific and around the world? The Spaniards were working on that problem too. They had four vessels ready in the West Indies in case Drake came back that way, and efforts were being made to prepare the Strait of Magellan. They did not believe that he would hazard the Pacific voyage, nor did they take much cognizance of the Strait of Anian. But Nuño da Silva, whom Drake had ungraciously left at Guatulco, knew Drake better, and prophesied more truly: 'I think he will go on following the coast in search of the Strait [of Anian], and when he does not find it [he] will go home by way of China.'[1] The most formidable leg of the voyage was yet to come.

[1] Nuño da Silva, Wagner, 347.

CHAPTER ELEVEN

# THE WORLD ENCOMPASSED

Sir Drake, whom well the world's ends know,
Which thou didst compass round,
And whom both poles of heaven once saw
Which North and South do bound.
The stars above will make thee known,
If men here silent were,
The sun himself cannot forget
His fellow traveller.

Anonymous, circa 1616

FRANCIS DRAKE WAS HOMEWARD BOUND, BUT WHICH WAY SHOULD HE GO? HE had two ships, the *Hind* and Rodrigo Tello's frigate, with upwards of sixty or seventy people aboard, and a vast amount of treasure. The problem of how to get his fabulous hoard back to England must have occupied Drake's thoughts for many a day, and disturbed not a few nights. There were three alternatives that looked realistic. He could fulfil his original plan and return by way of the Strait of Magellan, or indeed even by Cape Horn, which he had discovered; he could seek the hypothetical Strait of Anian and attempt to circumnavigate the Americas and reach the Atlantic by the North-west Passage; or he might sail south-west, across the Pacific, to the East Indies and inscribe a girdle around the whole earth, as Magellan's expedition had done. Each course was desperate, and beyond the experience of any on board, but Drake quickly struck out one of the possibilities. He would not commit his heavily laden ship to the storms he had encountered in the region of Tierra del Fuego, or to the dangerous winds that blew on to the Chilean coastline in the southern regions. He had lost two ships battling those waters, and could afford no further casualties. Besides, Drake probably reasoned, the Spaniards would be on the watch for him on the west coast of South America, and might even be waiting for him at the Strait of Magellan. If that thought crossed Drake's mind, he was not entirely deceived, because Pedro Sarmiento de Gamboa was directed to take a detachment to the strait by the Viceroy of Peru for precisely that purpose, although not until after the English had quit the Pacific.

A voyage around the world was a terrifying option, but one Drake took more seriously, and he had mentioned it to Captain Winter and Captain Thomas, suggesting that if they accidentally separated from him they might meet him 'in the Portuguese Indies'.[1] There was no doubt, however, that if the Strait of Anian existed it represented the quickest way home, for it was believed that the western or Pacific entrance to it commenced in about 40° north. At least it seemed worth a try, and after leaving Guatulco Drake turned westwards to avoid contrary winds and then swung northerly towards the supposed location of the North-west Pas-

[1] Juan Solano to the Audiencia of Guatemala, 29 March, 1579, Nuttall, ed., *New Light on Drake*, 111-14.

sage. There has been some dispute about how far he sailed, but nearly all our creditworthy authorities – the version in *The World Encompassed*; the anonymous narrative that forms one of the better accounts of the voyage; the depositions of John Drake; and the opinions of men of the *Hind* who later accompanied an expedition under Edward Fenton – agreed that he reached 48° north, or a little south of what is now the Canadian border. This was further north than any European explorer of the Pacific had gone before, although the Spaniard Juan Rodriguez Cabrillo had got as far as present-day Oregon more than thirty years earlier.[1]

Shortly before the English reached their most northerly point the weather had turned cold, so cold, Parson Fletcher said, that cooked meat froze when it was removed from the fire, and the ropes and tackle became too stiff to manage without difficulty. For a while, Drake cheerfully urged them on, but on 5 June he ran towards the shore to anchor in a bay, where the ships were penetrated by violent winds and thick fogs. The weather was not encouraging, and Drake had also taken note that, if the Strait of Anian existed at all, it was not as the geographers commonly represented. Far from trending north-east from about 40°, the land was further west, and there was no indication that the entrance to a passage was imminent. It was time for the plans to be revised.

A trans-Pacific voyage was now inevitable, but so demanding an enterprise needed careful preparation, and Drake looked for somewhere to careen, clean and retallow the *Golden Hind*. Cruising southwards along a coastal plain, the English reached latitude 38°, and thereabouts, in what is now northern California, they found the sufficient anchorage they had been seeking. On 17 June the ships halted in a quiet harbour that has inspired more ink to flow than any other Drake found in the New World. One of the most prosperous communities in North America has since flourished in the area where Drake careened his ship, its centre the great city of San Francisco, currently the fourth most populated in the United States, and generations of diligent American scholars have searched for the site of the Elizabethan anchorage. Yet to this day no one can say certainly where that safe haven was found. From the latitudes given in the contemporary accounts and an identification of the language and culture of the Indians Drake met as that of the coastal Miwok people, we can place the English landfall somewhere in present Marin or Sonoma counties, but within that region three locations have been powerfully championed as the actual spot: Drake's Estero, in Drake's Bay, at 38°;

---

[1] In discussing the latitude Drake reached in the north Pacific weight has sometimes been given to the account published in Richard Hakluyt's *Principal Navigations* (1589), according to which the English found the air cold at 42° on 5 June, 'and the further we went, the more the cold increased upon us.' This narrative not only leaves unclear how far north Drake sailed, but cannot probably rank as a primary source. It was put together from Cooke's account, 'the anonymous narrative', and either Fletcher's narrative or an early draft of *The World Encompassed*. We do not know when the last was written. Quinn, 'Early Accounts of the Famous Voyage', in Thrower, ed., *Sir Francis Drake and the Famous Voyage*, 33-48, argues that Hakluyt used a version of *The World Encompassed*, which Quinn believes was written by Philip Nichols from Cliffe's narrative and the notes of Francis Fletcher. If this is correct, the Hakluyt story of Drake's voyage north was probably a carelessly transcribed derivation of *The World Encompassed*, and has no independent value. *The World Encompassed* states that Drake reached 42° on 3 June; that during the following night the weather became cold; that the *Hind* ran towards shore on 5 June in latitude 48°; and that he then turned south. See also the diary of Richard Madox, 13, 26-7 October, 1582, Donno, ed., *An Elizabethan in 1582*, 208-9, 215.

Bolinas Lagoon, in Bolinas Bay, at 37°55′; and an area inside San Francisco Bay, reached through the Golden Gate at 37°49′. None of these alternatives has been eliminated by even the most conscientious research.[1]

All manner of methods, from metal detecting to aerial photography, have been used to find the place where Drake built a fort near his anchorage, but searches in Drake's Bay, Bolinas Lagoon and San Quentin Cove in San Francisco Bay have all been unsuccessful. It is a testimony to the intensity of this search that more than eight hundred artefacts from sixteenth-century European ships have been discovered about Drake's Bay, most of them Chinese porcelain salvaged from the wreck of the Spanish *San Augustin*, which was lost there in 1595. Still, nothing that can positively be linked to Drake has been unearthed, although a number of hoaxes have been perpetrated. Three early English sixpences have turned up in Marin County, and in 1887 a sealing schooner was alleged to have pulled up an anchor inscribed with Drake's name! These reports probably reflect the charlatanism that has marked this particular controversy, a facet most obviously illustrated by the famous case of the Drake plate. The story is a digression, but worth telling.

In February 1937 a store clerk, Beryle Shinn, telephoned Professor Herbert Bolton of the University of California to inform him that the year before he had discovered a metal plate on a ridge overlooking upper San Francisco Bay and Point San Quentin. It bore the date 17 June, 1579, and an inscription claiming the land of New Albion for Elizabeth I, and it had the signature of Francis Drake. There was instant excitement, for some such plate is known to have been erected by the English in 1579, and when the artefact was examined it bore all the appearance of authenticity. The plate was solid brass, some five by eight inches, and it was punctured by a ragged hole in the bottom right-hand corner, large enough to admit an Elizabethan sixpence. Opinion was divided, but after metallurgical investigations supported those who contended that it was genuine, the plate was acclaimed a priceless Californian heirloom and strong proof that Drake had anchored in San Francisco Bay.

The 'finder', Shinn, eventually sold the plate to members of the California Historical Society for $3,500, but its mystery deepened when a chauffeur, William Caldeira, came forward to proclaim that it was he, and not Shinn, who had originally discovered the plate. He said that he picked it up in 1933 near Drake's Bay, but after carrying it for some time he concluded that it had no value, and discarded it about two miles from the spot where Shinn later came upon it. In time the argument about which possible anchorage the discovery of the plate favoured, and about the integrity of Shinn and Caldeira, became redundant, because renewed metallurgical and handwriting analyses, published in 1977, revealed that the plate was a fake. Thus the great memento of Drake's visit to California was

[1] The principal claims have been made for Drake's Bay (George Davidson and the Drake Navigator's Guild) and San Francisco Bay (John W. Robertson and R. H. Power). For an ingenious attempt to locate the exact site of Drake's anchorage in a small cove just inside Drake's Estero (Drake's Bay) and a reconstruction of the visit based upon that assumption, see Aker, *Report of Findings Relating to Identification of Sir Francis Drake's Encampment*. The whole controversy, with a judicious evaluation of competing claims and a comprehensive bibliography, is given by Hanna, *Lost Harbor*.

transformed into America's counterpart of the Piltdown Man, a cunning hoax that outfoxed the experts of the day to be exposed by the technology of a later age.

Drake's Estero, in Drake's Bay, was probably the scene of Drake's activities in California. This haven is the most immediately associated with the several miles of weatherbeaten white cliffs in Drake's Bay, which are surely those we know to have reminded Drake of the Seven Sisters near Dover in England, and which prompted him to name the country Nova Albion. The weather conditions typical around Drake's Bay correspond to those described by Francis Fletcher, and surely, if Drake had entered the Golden Gate to the substantial waterway within, would not the English have spent time exploring it? Would not their narratives have reflected their excitement at finding such an inlet, particularly since they had been searching for the Strait of Anian? Yet the contemporary sources are silent about all this, and so uninteresting were the waters surrounding Drake's anchorage in 1579 that when he did explore he marched inland. While San Francisco Bay cannot be ruled out, Drake's Estero seems to have the better of the argument.

The coast the explorers gazed upon seemed barren and forbidding, and their stay was attended by overcast skies, cold, and a mist that seldom permitted Drake to measure the altitude of the sun or the stars. Fortunately, the natives were more hospitable, and not long after the English arrived one of them brought a present, which consisted of a bunch of feathers and what may have been tobacco in a basket. For this he refused to be rewarded by more than a hat that was thrown to him from the ship, and which he successfully retrieved from the water. Drake was encouraged, but his experience at Mocha had made him more cautious in dealing with Indians. The *Hind* was leaking, and he needed to bring her close in shore so that she could be pulled over and her hull cleaned and repaired. In that condition the ship and her men were vulnerable to attack, so the General put his men ashore to erect tents and to throw up a fort for defence. The Indians came down a hill in a body to watch them, but although the warriors were armed Drake did nothing hasty or stupid. He could see that the native women were with their men, and guessed that their intentions were friendly, and when he motioned to the warriors to lay down their bows and arrows they did so. It appeared to the English that the Indians regarded them as gods; they were impervious to English attempts to explain who they were, but at least they remained friendly, and when they had received clothing and other gifts the natives returned happily and noisily to their village.

There were other visits, some made by Indians drawn a considerable distance by reports of the white curiosities, but far from offering any violence to the strangers the natives struck the English as 'a people of a tractable, free and loving nature, without guile or treachery.'[1] On 26 June a singular ceremony was performed. Two Indian messengers arrived at Drake's camp to inform him, by one means or another, that their chief was nearby, about to honour the English with a visit for the first time. Would Drake first demonstrate his goodwill by providing a present? He would, and an appropriate gift had no sooner been brought out than it was being carried away by the messengers. Aware that something unusual was

[1] Vaux, ed., *The World Encompassed*, 131.

going to take place, the sailors gathered round, and shortly they saw the Indians descending the hill towards them in full strength. At their head marched an official, holding a sceptre of black wood adorned with 'knitwork' crowns and chains manufactured from clam shells, and behind him, protected by his guard, the chief, attired in a head-dress and a skin cape, and followed by a throng of fiercely painted warriors, each one of whom bore a gift. The rear of the cavalcade was formed by the Indian women and children.

It looked a formidable array, and the English felt it prudent to retire into their fortress, but the precaution proved unnecessary. A short distance away the Indians halted and after a salutation fell silent while the sceptre-bearer delivered a speech that lasted half an hour. When it was over the children remained behind, while the adults completed their descent of the hill, and Drake, with his instinct for responding to the good intentions of native peoples, ordered the gate of the fort to be thrown open to admit them. In they came, and as the natives milled around them the Englishmen noticed that the women indulged in a strange ritual of self-mutilation, scratching their faces and scoring their cheeks until the blood flowed.

The point was that these Indians had never been close to white men before. True, Cabrillo had skirted the coast, but he had not landed on it north of the Santa Barbara Channel. Drake was bringing Europeans to new ground. At the time, the English could only think that the Indians were deifying them, paying homage to visiting gods, but anthropological research has come up with another explanation for the Indians' behaviour. In the culture of the Indians of central California self-mutilation was associated with mourning, and it is possible that the natives considered Drake and his men to be not gods but spirits returning from the dead. Either way, the English were treated with reverential awe and as the possessors of uncommon power.[1]

By gestures the Indians indicated that they desired Drake to sit down, and when he had done so they regaled him with a number of speeches, which the English interpreted to mean that the natives wanted the General to take 'the province and kingdom into his hand, and become their king and patron, making signs that they would resign unto him their right and title in the whole land, and become his vassals in themselves and their posterities.'[2] Drake had chains placed about his neck, a 'crown' rested upon his head, and a sceptre put into his hands as if he were being proclaimed the king of the coastal Miwok, a novel destiny for the son of a yeoman farmer from Devon!

If nothing else, the ceremony indicated that the English had nothing to fear from the Indians, and Drake felt it was safe to explore. Further inland, further from the booming surf, the English discovered a lusher country, abundant in deer and ground squirrels, and the site of several native villages, which were found to consist of wooden conical shelters covered with earth. It was remote from Europe, this place, and perhaps the safer for that, but Drake could not resist claiming it for England. His country's first possession in what is now North America was named

[1] Heizer, *Elizabethan California*, reviews the events of Drake's visit and reprints his two important papers analysing the English accounts in the light of the language and culture of the Miwok.
[2] *The World Encompassed*, 128.

Nova Albion, 'in respect of the white banks and cliffs, which lie towards the sea', and to proclaim it Drake had a post set up with a plate bearing his name and the date attached to it. It was this plate that Shinn claimed to have discovered over three hundred years later.

Now, this whole business introduced a new concept to the so far brief history of Anglo-American Indian relations, for Drake maintained that England's rights rested upon the voluntary surrender of the territory by its owners, the coastal Miwok. We have seen how Spain and Portugal had originally founded their rights to 'new' lands on papal grants issued by Alexander VI, and equally how England had repudiated any such claim. The English view was that discovery alone did not constitute ownership of territory; only effective occupancy or control by a Christian prince could do that. Thus, even Englishmen more scrupulous than Francis Drake felt little compunction about sailing in regions claimed by Spain, and Drake saw no reason why he should not annex the Elizabeth Islands or Nova Albion, unoccupied as they were by Christians, for his country. In this respect, then, the issue was clear – Philip II defended his rights by discovery, as legitimized by the Pope; Elizabeth contended that only occupied territories might be claimed, and that the Pope's authority had never extended to more than spiritual matters anyway. It had no relevance to matters of territory.

But what of the natives of these newly discovered lands? Where did the indigenous peoples stand in these squabbles over land which they had discovered long before the Europeans came, and in which they had supported themselves since time immemorial? In fact, there was already a growing body of opinion that the Christian nations had no rights at all to territories inhabited by aborigines. Francisco Vitoria of the University of Salamanca contended in 1532 that Spain's claims to the New World were valid only inasmuch as they applied to uninhabited country; inhabited land belonged not unnaturally to its inhabitants. Not only that, but even the idea that the natives could be conquered and compelled to surrender their title was being criticized, particularly in the light of Las Casas's arousal of much moral indignation at Spain's treatment of the American Indian. Pope Clement VI issued a bull in 1529 authorizing the conquest of the Indian as a means of converting him to Christianity, but it was rescinded in eight years.

That being said, then, as now, legalities were scarcely allowed to interfere with the sequestration of valuable resources held by the weak, and all sorts of justifications for dispossessing natives were trotted out. The most common were that they were only pagans and that many were merely rude hunters and gatherers, 'savages' who made little use of the soil. On either count they might be swept aside like the wilderness of which they were a part. It is interesting that in the case of Nova Albion we have recognition, of a kind, that the natives possessed title to their soil. Drake's view was that by giving him a sceptre and crown, the Indians had 'freely offered' him their 'kingdom', and conferred its possession upon England. At the same time he must have been aware how little the likelihood was that his country would ever be able to enforce its claim upon a land so remote as Nova Albion.[1]

For the rest of Drake's stay relations between the dusky Miwok and the barely lighter, weather-worn seamen remained good, and when the Hind was finally readied for sea the Indians exhibited great distress. Leaving the Spanish frigate broken up in the bay, Drake slipped out on 23 July, saluted by the forlorn natives who ran to the hill-tops to keep the ship in sight and kindled fires in what seemed to the English a strange form of final obeisance. Drake had plenty of water and wood, but he was short of food, and the following day he called at one of the Farallon Islands, south-west of Drake's Bay, and obtained birds and sea lions as provisions.

His next job was no light feat – the crossing of the great Pacific Ocean – but here the charts and sailing directions he had pilfered from Tello's ship proved invaluable, because they pointed out to him his best course and gave him some understanding of the distance involved, suggesting a longer passage than was indicated on any map he had brought with him. The real distance was greater still, but at least Drake was stocked for a long haul, and escaped the privations that had struck down Magellan's men. Equipped thus, the *Hind* carved her snowy wake south-westerly and then, a little north of the line, westwards as Drake took advantage of the northern trades and avoided the difficult currents of the Equator.

The English were sixty-eight days out of sight of land, long, monotonous days beneath the sun, with little more than the groan of the timbers, the creak of the rigging and the sounds of the ocean for company. But on 30 September they fell in with an island about 8° or 9° north, probably one of the Carolinian Archipelago, and possibly Palau, in which case Drake would have been its European discoverer.[1] Multitudes of Micronesians in dugout canoes swarmed out to receive them, and at first it looked as if friendly trading would be the order of the day. However, the natives soon began helping themselves freely to the sailors' possessions, and squabbling among themselves over whatever they acquired. The English tried to defuse the situation by refusing to trade further, but it got uglier, and the angry islanders began to bombard the *Hind* with darts and stones they ferried out in their canoes. Drake directed a gun to be fired as a warning, and frightened one group of natives away, but others were soon worrying the ship and he reluctantly administered a severer lesson. His artillery shot tore through the fragile canoes, mangling craft and bodies, and scattering the survivors in terror. Drake was not proud of his action, and the narrative he later had prepared carried only a veiled reference to the slaughter of the natives, but John Drake would tell the Spaniards that twenty of the islanders were killed. It was a bitter incident, and using the name Magellan had applied to the Ladrones, the English called their landfall 'the island of thieves'.

Drake next reached Mindanao, in the Philippines, and then at last passed out of the vast South Seas, southwards into the Celebes and towards the Moluccas. The Moluccas! How many Englishmen had dreamed of reaching these legendary

[1] That Drake's behaviour at Nova Albion did not reflect a consistent view of native rights is shown by his claim to the Elizabeth Islands at Tierra del Fuego, although they were inhabited by Indians with whom he had little contact.

[1] For a fascinating, comprehensive and rigorous identification of Drake's 'island of thieves' see Lessa, *Drake's Island of Thieves*. The same author's 'Drake in the South Seas', in Thrower, 60-77, complements the longer study.

regions, the rich spice islands, and of some northern passage that might unlock the way to them? What would Chancellor and Dee, Lok and Frobisher, Gilbert and Grenville have given to have been with Drake at that moment? The sense of occasion cannot have escaped the theatrical little commander of the *Hind* as he reached the frontier between the sea empires of Spain and Portugal.

Yet there was much to trouble him. Only fifty years before Spain had surrendered her claims to the Moluccas, which her sailors had reached by sailing west, to the Crown of Portugal, and now the Portuguese were entrenched in the islands, filtering eastwards from the Indian Ocean. Drake could count upon their resentment at the appearance of an English ship, and he had little knowledge of how many of the native peoples would welcome him, if any. Not only that, but his Spanish maps were now useless, and the other charts at his disposal did little justice to the elaborate maze of islands that spotted the seas in which the *Hind* now sailed. Drake was excited, proud that his ship was cutting the steamy seas of the Indian Archipelago that had inspired so much interest at home, hopeful that he might yet meet Winter or Thomas whom he had bade meet him there if they missed Peru, and fearful that after so much travail his expedition could still come to grief. Picking up two native fishermen who agreed to help him, he anxiously threaded his way through the Siau Passage and into the Molucca Sea.

Drake was in luck. He found the politics of the Moluccas entirely in his favour. The bulk of the rich clove trade was in the hands of the Sultan of Ternate, named Babu, and the sultan had no love for the Portuguese, who had killed his father. Indeed, Babu was desperately seeking to keep the Portuguese out of his islands of Ternate, Motir and Maquiam, and to dislodge them from Tidore, which alone rivalled Ternate in fame and opulence. For their part, the Portuguese were preparing to bring the maverick sultan to heel. Consequently, the arrival of a new power was important. Babu was not slow to understand that the English could serve his war against the Portuguese as well as provide him with an alternative European outlet for the cloves his islands produced. Thus, as Drake approached Ternate, the most northerly of the Moluccas, searching for victuals and water, he was contacted by an emissary from the sultan inviting him to the port of Talangam on Ternate, where an old Portuguese castle offered a home for the court of Babu. He was assured of a good welcome, and responded as munificently by sending a velvet cloak to the sultan.

The ostentation that awaited the *Hind* at Talangam immediately betokened the great wealth that flowed from the spice islands. Three galleys, each propelled by eighty oarsmen, stood out to greet the English, their decks full of soldiers armed with lances and bows and arrows, and sporting a piece of artillery seized at some time or another from the Portuguese. Encircling the seaworn ship in an impressive ceremony, the galleys eventually towed Drake towards the best anchorage, and as they did so the vessel of Babu himself appeared. The English commander was not going to be outdone. He had the sultan saluted with artillery and small-arms fire, and broke out his musicians to entertain him. In his best finery, Drake must have struck an odd contrast with the visitor. The Englishman was fairly short, but burly; Babu, tall, well built and imperious. Drake's European outfit seemed almost prosaic beside the sultan's. On one appearance his waist was girded with 'all cloth of gold, and that very rich.' Part of his legs were bare, but he wore red leather shoes, and precious stones and gold ornaments festooned his person; there were large gold rings on his headgear, a gold chain around his neck, a diamond, emerald, ruby and turquoise on the fingers of one hand and a turquoise and several diamonds on the other. Can we doubt but that Drake had some of that dazzling treasure from Peru brought up to demonstrate that he was no less magnificent a figure, although but a humble servant of his queen?[1]

The sultan allowed his vessel to be hitched to the *Golden Hind* and drawn into port by the galleys, and before he departed he promised Drake that the English would be supplied with all they required. And he was true to his word, for sugar cane, fruit, hens, rice, sago and clothing were brought aboard. More than that, Drake was able to get a trade agreement. According to a Spanish report of his activities,

> *Captain Francis went to the fortress of Ternate, where he was well received and provided with certain supplies. The King of Ternate soon opened negotiations with him, saying that he was not a friend of the Portuguese but an independent king, and that as Captain Francis had said that he was a vassal of the Queen of England, if the Queen desired to favor and help him to expel the Portuguese from that region, he would concede to her the trade in cloves, which up to that time the Portuguese had had. Captain Francis, on the part of the Queen of England, promised that within two years he would decorate that sea with ships for whatever purpose might be necessary. The King asked a pledge that he would as a gentleman comply with the word he had given in the name of the Queen of England, and Captain Francis gave him a gold ring set with a precious stone, a coat of mail, and a very fine helmet. The King gave Captain Francis other presents, but I could not make out what they were.[2]*

Perhaps the agreement was only a verbal one, but it was nonetheless one that both parties took seriously. Drake loaded six tons of valuable cloves upon his ship, while as late as 1605 Babu's son wrote to James I of England referring to a ring his father had sent Queen Elizabeth via Drake and explaining that Babu had long expected Drake to return with a force of ships. The islanders were by then anxious to preserve their relations with England, because Spain, which inherited Portugal's eastern empire in 1580, had within two years launched an offensive against Babu, and by 1605 the final conquest of Ternate was only a year away.[3]

---

[1] *The World Encompassed*, 144.

[2] Report of Dueñas, 1582, in Wagner, *Sir Francis Drake's Voyage Around the World*, 180. In 1580 Spain annexed the kingdom of Portugal, and the Spanish governor of the Philippines sent Dueñas to the Moluccas in 1581. He gathered information there about Drake's activities.

[3] Legend speaks of a disagreement between Drake and Babu. It is true that the sultan did not honour a promise to revisit the *Golden Hind*, and equally that Drake avoided a personal appearance at Babu's court for fear of treachery. Nor did the English remain at Ternate more than a few days. But the story that Babu wanted to kill Drake was introduced by Antonio de Herrera's *Historia General de Mundo* (1606) and elaborated by Bartolome Leonardo de Argensola's *Conquista de las Islas Malucas* (1609), who added that the sultan became annoyed because the English traded without his permission and was appeased by presents sent by Drake. Readers are cautioned about accepting information which appears so long after the event as this, and it should be noted that Herrera's only valid source on Drake's visit to Ternate seems to have been the depositions of John Drake, who makes no mention of the quarrel. Argensola lifted most of his material from Herrera. Neither historian merits serious attention on this point.

After leaving Ternate Drake wanted another peaceful anchorage to prepare his ship for her voyage through the Indian Archipelago and into the Indian Ocean. He found it in the Banggai Archipelago, somewhere off the north-eastern coast of Celebes, on a small and uninhabited island, but one wooded and watered, and commanding all the necessities of life. He sailed again on 12 December, 1579, leaving behind three Negroes, including one named Maria, who had been brought from Guatulco and had conceived a child aboard the ship. The so-called 'anonymous narrative' of the voyage complains that poor Maria was 'set on a small island to take her adventure' in the disapproving tone so characteristic of the account, but John Drake described the incident without condemnation. He said that the blacks were left to form a colony, with rice, seeds, and fire-making equipment. The island had been pleasing, and it is possible the Negroes elected to remain there. Harder judgements have charged Drake with dumping them to save victuals, but this would not only have been out of character, it would have made little sense. If Drake had wanted to spare food he would perhaps have left the blacks at Nova Albion, and not brought them across the Pacific at all. Diego, Drake's Negro friend, was still aboard, and the Negroes left at 'Crab Island', as the English called it, represented only a small proportion of the burden on victuals. Drake seems to have borne no ill will towards the Negroes he left behind, and renamed the island Isle Francisca in honour of one of them. Possibly he even believed he had served them, removing them from a life of servitude with the Spaniards and leaving them to make their own lives free from molestation.[1]

Whatever, Drake now sailed westwards, planning to pass around Celebes into the Celebes Sea and Makassar Strait. Ahead the greatest peril of the entire voyage lay quietly waiting for him. It was submerged beneath the warm green seas that washed the east coast of Celebes, its ragged crest only seven feet below the surface at low water: a long, steep-sided, sinuous reef. Nothing was more dreaded by sailors, nothing more terrifying than the destruction of those few planks of wood that protected them from the sea-bed. Drake had little knowledge of an area for which no reliable maps existed in any language, and was ignorant of how far to the south-east Celebes extended. Also, the prevailing north-east wind drove the Golden Hind south, instead of west, and the English found themselves in the maze of islands, shoals and finger-like peninsulas of the east coast of Celebes, confronting hazards more intricate than any yet encountered – 'inasmuch that in all our passages from England hitherto, we had never more care to keep ourselves afloat.' With 'extraordinary care and circumspection' Drake beat back and forth.[2] At one point, with the wind in their favour, the English believed that only open water lay ahead, and the ship was put under full sail, but as the men began the first night watch, about eight o'clock on the evening of 9 January, the Hind drove with a terrific shock upon the reef. Her fragile, life-saving timbers buckled upon the rock, and the sea surged into her hull.

No sooner had the frightened sailors recovered from the impact, than they were

---

[1] The anonymous narrative, Vaux, 178-86, covers the voyage from the passage of the Magellan Strait, and was possibly written after Drake's return to England by a participant. Depositions of John Drake, 24 March, 1584, 8-10 January, 1587, Eliott-Drake, *Family and Heirs of Sir Francis Drake*, 2: 343-401. There is not enough information about Maria to establish why she and the other two Negroes were left at 'Crab Island'.

[2] *The World Encompassed*, 151.

thrown to starboard as the ship, caught on her port bow, heeled over at an alarming angle. It seems that if a strong wind had not been blowing from the land, about 18 miles away, and counteracted the list the ship might have lost all semblance of being upright. But that wind also pressed the *Hind* more firmly aground, grinding her against the reef, and trapping her upon it. In the darkness the fears of the men multiplied. There was not so much panic as a deep despair.

The reef itself has not been identified. *The World Encompassed* put it at almost 2° south. Julian Corbett, Drake's Victorian biographer, identified it as the Mulapatia Reef, south of Peleng Island. An American scholar, Henry Wagner, agreed, pointing out that the context of the incident suggested that it took place near Tomori Bay. More recently, Vesuvius Reef or its neighbouring shoal have been mentioned. It made little difference to the sixty or so men aboard the *Golden Hind,* for at a stroke all the prospects of the voyage, even of survival itself, seemed to have been vanquished. They knelt in prayer, calling for their deliverance – a response typical of Drake – and then set to work on the pumps, trying to reduce the water in the hold so that the damage could be inspected more closely. Now came the first thread of hope. The timbers of the ship were found on the whole to have withstood the collision, and to be capable of repair, if the *Hind* could be worked from the reef without further damage.

Drake had a small boat lowered and ran an anchor to it. Then he was rowed out to the open water to starboard. He began sounding for ground in which he could wedge the anchor, because he might then have the men haul upon the cable and draw the ship towards the deeper water. But there was no ground. The reef must have risen sharply from a great depth, for even a boat's length from the ship Drake's line sounded over 300 fathoms and found no bottom. It was a dark situation indeed. If the *Hind* could not be brought off, she would surely break up, and what then? The nearest land was 18 miles away. There was one small boat, and it could accommodate only a third of the crew.

Throughout the rest of the night the vessel lay desperately fast, and at daylight Drake resumed his soundings with no better success. Fletcher once more led the men in prayers and gave them the sacrament. Then attempts were made to lighten the ship so that she could ride higher in the water, and three tons of cloves, victuals, ammunition, and two pieces of artillery were thrown overboard, but with no obvious result.[1] It seemed hopeless. Then, about four o'clock in the afternoon of 10 January, the wind suddenly slackened and shifted. It veered to the opposite direction, and pushed the *Hind* clumsily towards the deep water. She slid from the rock, lurched crazily upright, and then wallowed deliriously in the open sea.

This perilous episode had a singularly absurd epilogue that still invites explanation. Apparently Drake had taken exception to some remarks passed by Francis

---

[1] I have followed the anonymous narrative. John Drake's first deposition says that 8 pieces of artillery, 10 tons of cloves, 5 tons of ginger and pimento, and 2 pipes of flour were jettisoned. Argensola reported that the Sultan of Ternate had a heavy bronze gun salvaged from the bottom of the sea and mounted before his palace. It is not likely that the sultan learned of Drake's disaster, less that he was able to locate the exact scene and salvage the gun. Argensola is not an authority for this or anything else respecting Drake. Interestingly, Dueñas, who is an authority (although a poor one, since his material comes no more than second-hand) asserts that Babu displayed two of Drake's guns, one of them bronze, that were recovered from Colo Island. Colo Island was probably 'Crab Island', and although no English account refers to Drake leaving artillery there it is conceivable that he did so.

Fletcher during the crisis. He had the parson chained to a hatch in the forecastle of the ship, and excommunicated him. Sitting cross-legged upon a chest, the General imperiously addressed the miserable cleric in front of the assembled company: 'Francis Fletcher, I do here excommunicate thee out of the Church of God, and from all the benefits and graces thereof, and I denounce thee to the Devil and his angels.' About the parson's arm was affixed a notice, labelling him 'Francis Fletcher, ye falsest knave that liveth'.[1]

We do not know why Fletcher aroused so malignant a sense of humour in Francis Drake, but we can guess. Fletcher was apt to ascribe every calamity to the divine judgement of God. When, for example, the *Marigold* had foundered and Edward Bright, who had testified against Doughty, had drowned, Fletcher could not resist annotating his script with the observation that it was 'God's judgement against a false witness.'[2] It is not unlikely that he had similarly proclaimed the perils of the reef as God's revenge upon Drake for the execution of Doughty. If that was so, the General gave him his answer.

Drake's movements after his escape from the reef are difficult to interpret. It may be that he was driven eastwards into the Banda Seas by adverse winds, or that he decided to steer towards the Indian Ocean, south of Java rather than north of it so that he might avoid the Malacca Strait, which was controlled by the Portuguese. He re-fitted and replenished his provisions at an island that may have been Damma or Roma, and then slipped between the northern coast of Timor and various islands into the Samu Sea, and then westwards along the south coast of Java. Although the Portuguese were familiar with Java's northern coastline, and suspected that it was an island, Drake was the first European to navigate its southern shores and to prove to the western powers that Java was not part of the continent of Terra Australis.

Tjilatjap, in Java, proved to be a crucial haven for Drake, for the water and supplies he embarked there had to last for a long time. The *Golden Hind* sailed on 26 March, forging across the Indian Ocean. She came within sight of the African coast on 21 May and cruised around the Cape of Good Hope in June, searching anxiously for a further source of fresh water. If it had not been for the rain collected in casks set upon the deck the company would have been in difficulties, and when a landfall was made at Sierra Leone the supply was down to less than half a pint to every three persons. Surprisingly, the narratives are silent upon this extraordinary phase of Drake's voyage, a run of 9,700 miles from Java to Sierra Leone without a base or a reliable map, but experienced seamen marked it as among his finest achievements, and as late as the end of the eighteenth century reckoned it 'a thing hardly to be credited, and which was never performed by any mariner before his time or since.'[3]

There were sights for them in Sierra Leone, sights some Englishmen had never seen, such as elephants or the famous 'oyster tree' so beloved of contemporary travellers' tales. More important, water was at last taken aboard, as well as lemons and other fruit, all very necessary in the fight against scurvy, symptoms of which had probably

---

[1] Memoranda relating to the voyage in Harleian MSS, reprinted in Vaux, 176-7.
[2] Fletcher in Penzer, ed., *The World Encompassed*, 133-4. Fletcher, it should be noted, had himself signed some of the evidence against Doughty.
[3] William Anderson, *The Whole of Captain Cook's Voyages* (1784), quoted in Robinson, 'A Forgotten Life of Sir Francis Drake', 17.

begun to appear after so strenuous a trip. Home was now not far away, and everyone must have dreamed of it, of meetings with loved ones, of the fresh green hills of Devon, and of days free of the toil and danger with which they had lived for almost three long years.

But would reward and praise be waiting for them when they returned? That was what nagged at Drake as the *Hind* cut breezily through waters increasingly familiar to him. He had been away so long. He had plundered the King of Spain and the hold of his ship was full of treasure. He had set at naught the pretended monopolies of the Iberian powers. And he had done it on the basis of a private understanding with a spirited queen who might not even now be alive. What if the Catholic, Mary, the Queen of Scots, had succeeded to the throne? The thought made Francis Drake feel that his head sat loosely on his shoulders.

On 26 September, 1580, some fishermen at work with their nets in the English Channel saw a small, heavily laden ship picking her way towards the entrance to Plymouth Sound. As they passed her, a man aboard hailed the fishermen and asked a strange question. Was the queen alive? She was, and in good health, but a plague was raging in Plymouth itself. Then the fishermen watched as the *Golden Hind* sailed home.

# CHAPTER TWELVE

# THE GOLDEN KNIGHT

That ship whose good success did make thy name
To be resounded by the trumpet of Fame,
Merits to be beset with stars divine
Instead of waves,
And in the sky to shine.

Verse pinned to the *Golden Hind*, 1581

WHILE DRAKE WAS AWAY STORIES OF HIS EXPLOITS HAD PERIODICALLY TANTAL-ized Europe. There was a flutter of consternation when Winter came home in June 1579. The Portuguese ambassador to Elizabeth's court pressed for the res-titution of plunder taken from Nuño da Silva's ship in the Cape Verdes. At this stage the English government acted ambiguously. When Captain Winter visited London he was well received, and the queen was closeted with him for a long time, divining from him what progress Drake had made. But a year later the cap-tain's position was less than congenial, if not miserable, as he shifted uneasily under a burden of guilt. He had been party to seizing Portuguese ships. He had had a hand in the execution of Doughty, the gentleman. He had even deserted his commander. In June 1580 the Lord Admiral (himself an investor in Drake's voyage, mark you) ordered goods 'piratically taken on the seas by Francis Drake and his accomplices' to be restored to the Portuguese, in which process Winter was ingratiatingly co-operative.[1] The few items he had brought home that belonged to Nuño's vessel were given back, while Winter did his best to excuse himself by blaming everything upon everybody else, especially Drake. Now Fran-cis was not a forgiving man, but when he finally returned he was to intercede for the wretched fellow, who found himself imprisoned on charges of piracy. Perhaps Drake felt some responsibility for Winter's condition; certainly, he realized that the Winters were an influential family, and it was as well to keep in their good graces.

As proceedings against Winter took their course, news of the bigger fish fil-tered into Europe. In August 1579 the first of what was to be a stream of correspon-dence reached the desk of Philip II, informing him that his hitherto impregnable South Seas colonies were being ravaged by the same impudent corsair who had attacked the West Indies years before. 'it is a thing that terrifies one,' marvelled one informant, 'the boldness of this low man!'[2] Before very long, Philip had a bulky dossier in his hands, and was busily endorsing new papers with 'to be put with what relates to Drake.' He was angry and disturbed, but for the moment Philip bided his time. Vast as it was, Drake's haul was insignificant in comparison with the treasure shipments plodding across the Atlantic, and there were other,

[1] Commission of Court of Admiralty, 17 June, 1580, Nuttall, ed., *New Light on Drake*, 385-6.
[2] Don Miguel de Eraso y Aguilar to Philip II, 10 May, 1579, *Ibid*, 118-20.

weightier, matters at hand. It was the possible spin-offs of Drake's raid that worried the king. The magnitude of his success would inspire imitators, and Drake had exposed the weakness of the South Seas empire to the world. Some action was needed. The Strait of Magellan should be fortified. And Philip applied to the King of Portugal, urging him to intercept Drake if he tried to return home by way of the East Indies. As insurance, a claim for restitution of the booty was made to present to the queen if the corsair ever reached England.

On 3 September information about Drake's captures reached London, relayed by merchants of Seville. It was said he had taken 600,000 ducats. Bernardino de Mendoza, Philip's ambassador in England, complained, 'The adventurers who provided money and ships for the voyage are beside themselves for joy, and I am told that there are some of the councillors amongst them. The people here are talking of nothing else but going out to plunder in a similar way.'[1] That was the sort of news that concerned Philip. There followed months of waiting – for those, like Mary Drake, looking anxiously for their menfolk; for investors like Leicester and Hatton expecting the windfall of their lives; for the Spaniards scribbling their case for punishment and restitution; for English merchants trading with Spain, terrified of reprisals; and for the queen herself, enchanted by the reports of what Drake had taken but doubting whether she dared to keep it. All of it hinged on a tiny ship riding somewhere out there on the great ocean.

Drake was, however, only one piece of a much larger game being played out during those years. Far from diminishing, the colossus he had struck was growing mightier still: Spain was bringing the Netherlands under greater control, using a commander of exceptional military and political skill, Alexander Farnese, the Prince of Parma; and her empire took an enormous stride forward with the acquisition of Portugal. In January of 1580 the King of Portugal, an epileptic old bachelor, died leaving no obvious heir. Philip, who was the son of the king's eldest sister, enforced his claim with troops in the autumn of 1580, and the following year the Portuguese *cortes* recognized him as their king, provided that he guaranteed the liberties and privileges of the people. Thus at a stroke the two great imperial powers were fused into one. Portugal's domination of the African coast, the Indian Ocean, the East Indies and Brazil was now added to Spain's hold upon parts of Europe and the Americas to form the largest empire the world had yet seen. The riches of the spice trade that flowed into Lisbon reinforced the Atlantic treasure shipments to furnish Philip with a truly staggering revenue, arguably exceeding those of the rest of Europe combined. Furthermore, Portuguese and Spanish shipping together totalled over 250,000 tons. The man Drake and Elizabeth had dared to challenge was no longer merely the greatest monarch in Christendom; no one in history, not even the great Genghis Khan and his successors, had held sway over such an area, and Philip's naval resources were now six times those of England.

Confronted with such a giant, Elizabeth might have been forgiven for sacrificing Drake to improve her relations with Spain. She may have been passionate

---

[1] Mendoza to Gabriel de Zayas, 8 September, 1579, Hume, ed., *Calendar of Letters and State Papers . . . in the Archives of Simancas*, 2: 694-5. These volumes are the major sources for this chapter.

and impulsive, but the queen was inherently prudent in foreign affairs, unwilling to be drawn into reckless gambles with powerful adversaries. She was no longer young, and the wisdom of middle age reinforced her caution. But although she longed for peace, she was not bereft of means to manipulate Philip. She knew that if he was overmighty, his commitments were also great, and that he valued both England's trade and her neutrality while his relations with France remained uncertain and the Netherlands stubbornly held out. Elizabeth was also strengthening her alliance with France, equally concerned about Spain's growing power, even though that strife-ridden country was divided three ways, between the Catholic Guises who treated with the Spaniards, the Huguenots, and the court of Henry III. There was the possibility of a marriage between Elizabeth and the French king's younger brother, Francis, Duke of Alençon, her unprepossessing but amusing 'frog'.

Neither Philip nor Elizabeth was ready for a confrontation, but the political horizon darkened in 1579 when a papal expedition landed in Munster to foment an Irish rising against the English. September of 1580 saw a reinforcement join them, some of the soldiers recruited in Spain. The invaders had scant success, for the English soon penned them up in Smerwick and butchered them. Philip protested that the expedition belonged to Pope Gregory XIII, and owed little of its impetus to Spain, but the queen was able to accuse him of outright hostility to her realm. And it was as this disagreement was ripening that Drake anchored in Plymouth.

He did not immediately disembark. The town was still infected by the plague, and there was uncertainty about how Drake would be received by the queen. A few visitors, including Mary Drake and the Mayor of Plymouth, John Blitheman, who were rowed out to the *Hind,* briefed him on the present situation, and Drake dispatched John Brewer, Hatton's trumpeter, to London with word of his arrival. He also wrote to Walsingham, Leicester and the other investors in his voyage. They, he knew, would be his defenders in the troubles ahead.

London was soon humming with the name of Francis Drake, and amid mounting excitement the queen summoned her Privy Council. Five members managed to attend at the short notice. Lord Burghley was there, and the Earl of Sussex, but only one of Drake's supporters, the Earl of Lincoln, Lord Admiral. These worthies concluded that Drake's plunder might have to be returned, but first it would be registered and stored at the Tower of London. Then Drake's big backers opened fire. They were not in a hurry to lose a fortune. When the order to lodge the treasure in the Tower reached Walsingham, Leicester and Hatton they refused to sign it, believing that it was merely a preliminary to restitution. So the Privy Council was split and stalemated. In Plymouth, however, Drake's anxiety was relieved by a message he received from the queen. He should not fear for his safety, but come to court, bringing with him specimens of his adventure. This was encouragement indeed, for Francis Drake knew how to tempt a lady less indigent than Queen Elizabeth. He loaded some horses with gold and silver and took them overland to the capital.

What an interview it must have been! Sadly, we know little of it. It lasted for more than six hours, and must have embodied stirring stories that the queen did not fail to appreciate, great tales of adventure, of the Elizabeth Islands and Nova Albion, of the capture of the treasure ship and the trade agreement with Ternate, tales the like of which none had brought her before. She knew good service when she saw it, and resolved that if his treasure had to be restored to Spain he would not suffer by it. Drake was sent home with orders to register his treasure and send it to the Tower, and Edmund Tremayne, clerk to the Privy Council and formerly Member of Parliament for Plymouth, received instructions to help him. But Tremayne had some interesting secret orders. Drake was to be permitted to remove £10,000 for himself – unaided and alone, and before any of the plunder was registered.

It is not difficult to guess what was in Elizabeth's mind. Drake would take his reward, and none but he would know its full extent, and the balance of the treasure would be registered and stored as if it represented the whole of the plunder. If the latter had to be returned to the Spaniards, Drake's share would remain secure. It was vintage Elizabeth, and Drake took full advantage. He took his £10,000, a further £14,000 or so for his men, and probably more. Certainly the treasure lodged first in Trematon Castle at Saltash and later in the Tower fell far short of what had been taken in the Pacific, and the Spaniards knew it. There may have been some truth in Mendoza's complaint that Drake later presented the queen with £100,000 worth of treasure over and above that registered for the Tower. Neither Drake nor his queen was beyond such a subterfuge.

While Drake, Tremayne and Christopher Harris (another Devon dignitary) sorted out the treasure in the West Country, London was the scene of a complicated argument about its fate. Mendoza, Philip's ambassador, was refused an audience with the queen, and fretted and fumed, not only about the English but also about the interference of Pedro de Zubiaur, who equally argued for the restitution of the treasure but on behalf of the merchants of Seville, and who seemed to be forever getting under Mendoza's feet. Similar dissension divided Elizabeth's camp, some of the Privy Councillors suggesting that the treasure might be restored if Philip could explain the presence of his countrymen in Ireland, and others, like Leicester and Walsingham, steadfastly refusing to surrender a penny, unless it be to assist the Huguenots or other Protestant causes. It was said that, as there was no treaty between England and Spain forbidding Englishmen to sail to the Indies at their own risk, Drake had broken no laws.

The reply Elizabeth sent the furious Mendoza was insultingly deceitful. He had been complaining, she had heard, about Drake's voyage, but why she did not know, for she had made a diligent investigation and discovered that he had done Spain no damage! However, if the reverse was true, justice would be done. In the meantime, she would not receive Mendoza until she had got to the bottom of the Irish business. Mendoza's answer was only slightly less disingenuous, for among the documents he forwarded to refute Elizabeth's ridiculous statements were allegations that Drake had committed atrocities and cut off the hands of Spanish prisoners. Such monstrous falsehoods did Spain no service. In fact they enabled the English to avoid the issue at stake. Drake had visited London again at the end of October, but back in Plymouth he had Tremayne interrogate the crew of the *Golden Hind*, and forty-nine of them happily attested to the humanity of a commander they loved. The best refutation of Spain's charge, however, was not available to Drake – the depositions of the Spanish prisoners themselves.

On the seizures themselves, of course, Drake had no defence and was reduced to quibbling over details when copies of Mendoza's charges were submitted to him for an opinion. He denied what he could. Some of the treasure he had taken had no official existence since its owners had tried to avoid duties by shipping it unregistered. The Spanish, no less than the English, knew that Drake had a large amount of unregistered Spanish loot. But they could not put a figure to it. While Mendoza could document the extent of the loss of registered valuables, he could only vaguely intimate the balance. It was a loophole Drake quickly exploited. He said he had taken no unregistered treasure. If there had been any, he knew nothing of it, and suspected the mariners on the Spanish ships had stolen it themselves and blamed the loss upon Drake.

And so the year ran out, with Mendoza hectoring for an audience while Elizabeth held him at arm's length and postured about Ireland. She had reasons to give in. Mendoza was blustering about war ('He knows she loves not troubles . . . A war is easily begun, but not so soon ended').[1] England's Iberian merchants, haunted by the possibility of reprisals, pressed for the restitution of the plunder. Some of her most trusted councillors, and particularly Lord Burghley, disapproved of the whole business. But she dug her heels in. She was hearing Drake's name mentioned everywhere, and was not immune herself to the excitement and wonder that was making him an international hero, the great Protestant champion as well as discoverer of the unknown. She probably sensed the mood of the ordinary people of her realm, who were taking up Drake's cause, and if the raid in the Pacific had been an act of war, so had the papal expedition against Ireland. And, in the last resort, the dazzling hoard Drake had brought home at such peril was just too great to be sacrificed.

The total amount of Drake's booty is not known. About £264,000 worth was eventually deposited in the Tower, according to a memorandum of Burghley. The queen would loan £29,000 of it to the Dutch Protestants. Alençon and the newly formed Levant Trading Company each received £42,000, and a substantial deficit the government had incurred on recent Irish campaigns was extinguished. Nor was the treasure lodged in the Tower by any means the whole taken. Drake had deducted at least £24,000 before surrendering his cargo, and other sums had probably been diverted. Some of the reports undeniably ran wild. Seville merchants were reckoning the cargo of the Nuestra Señora de la Concepción alone at £330,000, exclusive of some silver bars and jewels (it was probably less than half that); in April 1581 someone put the total at over £600,000; and some years afterwards Edmund Howes came out with the astonishing remark that Drake's plunder was sufficient to defray the cost of seven years of warfare! In the seventeenth century Lewis Roberts declared that he had seen an account that showed the investors in Drake's venture made a profit of 4,700 per cent. Allowing for exaggeration, it must still have been a fabulous figure, and to appreciate its significance it is worth remembering that the queen's annual ordinary revenue, exclusive of extra-

[1] Mendoza's reply, 29 October, 1580, Butler, et. al., ed., Cal. of State Papers, Foreign, 14: 463-4.

ordinary grants that might be made by Parliament, was only about £250,000.[1]

By the New Year Drake's personal position, as distinct from the status of his pillage, was assured. The queen was not about to lop off his head, and he had sequestrated enough of his treasure to secure himself for many years. In achievement and fame he had suddenly eclipsed the sycophants that clung to the court like fat snails beneath a rockery. His name, which had once been feared only in the Caribbean and respected only among the sailors of the West Country, was now spreading through Europe as an object of wonder. Yet for all that he was still the son of a yeoman farmer, a man who had become a provincial merchant with a small town house, and his reputation was not of the type everyone admired. He was a new toy at court, but he was still moving in a world of alien people, of wealthy peers with great estates, of the articulate Renaissance men with whom he did not always find conversation easy, of men joined in webs of kinship and patronage. He was, in short, an outsider, tested by the sea rather than birth and privilege, and he aroused a compound of amazement, envy and contempt.

In Elizabeth's day the New Year was a time for gift-giving, and 1581 saw Drake at court, dispensing presents with a generosity that was part of his nature and a shrewdness he had learned. With gifts he also bought friendship, obligation and acceptance. Mendoza complained to Philip:

> Drake is squandering more money than any man in England, and proportionately, all those who came with him are doing the same. He gave to the Queen the crown which I described in a former letter as having been made here. She wore it on New Year's Day. It has in it five emeralds, three of them almost as long as a little finger, whilst the two round ones are valued at 20,000 crowns, coming, as they do, from Peru. He has also given the Queen a diamond cross as a New Year's gift, as is the custom here, of the value of 5,000 crowns. He offered to Burghley ten bars of fine gold worth 300 crowns each, which, however, he refused, saying that he did not know how his conscience would allow him to accept a present from Drake, who had stolen all he had. He gave to Sussex eight hundred crowns in salvers and vases, but these, also, were refused in the same way. The Chancellor got eight hundred crowns worth of silver plate, and all the councillors and secretaries had a share in a similar form, Leicester getting most of all. The Queen shows extraordinary favour to Drake, and never fails to speak to him when she goes out in public, conversing with him for a long time. She says that she will knight him on the day she goes to see his ship. She has ordered the ship itself to be brought ashore and placed in her arsenal near Greenwich as a curiosity.[2]

It was Drake's first major experience of the gaiety and noise of the court, which followed Elizabeth from palace to palace, Nonesuch and Richmond, Whitehall and Windsor, Greenwich, Hampton Court and Eltham. John Drake, Drake's young cousin, who accompanied him, probably found the histrionic burlesque of the court exciting. This was the playwright John Lyly's land of a thousand vain hopes, where he played the fool too long. Here was the trough in which hundreds of snouts were thrust, grubbing and jostling for preferment and attention, marketing their supposed skills in

---

[1] For Drake's plunder, Corbett, *Drake and the Tudor Navy*, 1: Appendix F; Scott, *English, Scottish and Irish Joint-Stock Companies*, 1: 78-82.

[2] Mendoza to Philip II, 9 January, 1581, Hume, 3: 73-5.

dancing, music, and tilting and their affected knowledge of affairs, literature and the arts, all for a claim upon the queen and her government. Drake had sailed to the world's end to outflank them, but he had learned the importance of patronage and bought as much of it as he could. He bribed and he flattered and played the courtiers at their own game.

Amid all the fawning around her, Elizabeth recognized an original when she saw one. Drake was regularly in her company, and once visited her nine times in one day. She listened to his blunt but cheerful provincial accent during leisurely walks about the gardens or long audiences indoors, and she ignored the envious whispers that he was nothing but a thief and a low-born upstart. And when he left the court, Drake met adulation of a different kind, the spontaneous acclaim of the ordinary people, who swarmed about the most famous of Englishmen at every appearance he made on the streets. With them he had the endearing common touch that marked a self-made man.

Francis Drake had always been a vain man, and perhaps inevitably his meteoric rise brought out the worst in him. He bragged and he boasted, and according to poor Mendoza daily berated the King of Spain. One evening in 1582, Drake was at a party holding forth upon his usual theme, when the Earl of Sussex, who had had enough of it, suggested that it was hardly a great feat to capture an unarmed treasure ship. Typically, Drake merely went further. Why, he answered, he was as ready to make war upon the King of Spain himself. The Earl of Arundel interposed that since the union of Spain and Portugal Philip was the equal of all the other monarchs united, but Drake meant what he said.

His proudest moment occurred on 1 April, 1581. He had brought the *Golden Hind* from Plymouth to Deptford so that the queen might see her in dry dock, and that day not only Her Majesty but a good proportion of London turned out to honour the great sailor and see him transformed into 'our golden knight'. So immense was the throng that after Elizabeth had crossed a plank on to the *Hind*, the flimsy bridge collapsed under the weight of those that followed her and something like one hundred people fell into the mud below. None was hurt, and there was more entertainment. Once aboard, the queen lost one of her garters, which slipped down her leg and trailed behind until the French ambassador, Monsieur de Marchaumont, on his best behaviour, darted out to retrieve it. The garter was purple and gold, and Elizabeth replaced it about her stocking in front of the ambassador and promised that when she had done with it she would send it to him as a keepsake.

After a banquet that was reportedly the most extravagant seen, the queen had Drake stoop before her. She had a gilded sword, she mused, and might strike off his head. Instead, she handed it to Marchaumont and bade him perform the ceremony of knighthood, cunningly involving France in a brazen act of defiance of Spain. The stocky seaman rose as Sir Francis Drake. Today, when knighthoods are distributed like postage stamps to nonentities, it is hard to appreciate the importance of this honour. The Tudors dispensed them freely to the privileged classes, but few men of Drake's background could have aspired to a knighthood. Even Walsingham, that devoted servant of state, earned no higher accolade. After the ceremony, Sir Francis was as munificent as ever, and presented 1,200 crowns to be divided among the queen's officers and a large silver tray and a diamond frog to Elizabeth herself.

The Elizabethans remained fascinated by the *Golden Hind*, and attempted to preserve her as a permanent symbol of endeavour and the new maritime stature that England had achieved, just as a later age protected the *Victory* at Portsmouth. A wall was built about the *Hind's* dry dock at Deptford, and she stood there for many years, until dry rot accomplished what three oceans had failed to do. In 1618 her battered hull was compared to the bleached skeleton of a horse, and half a century later she seems to have broken into fragments, some of which were used to make a chair still preserved in the Bodleian Library at Oxford.

Mendoza's claim for restitution of the treasure fared little better. Zubiaur, who had been empowered by the merchants of Seville to act for them, continued to irritate him, and although he laboured to present his case throughout 1581 and 1582 he was always being fobbed off with some excuse or tied up in bureaucracy. Sometimes the queen would not discuss Drake until Spain's interference in Ireland had been explained. At others the issue was reduced to the status of a private lawsuit, with the plaintiffs having to submit their memorials to the Admiralty court, which determined the propriety of seizures at sea. The witnesses against Drake had not been sworn in his presence (did they really expect San Juan de Anton to come to England?). The sailors accusing the English of taking their cargo could have purloined it themselves. The justices before whom the Spanish depositions were made were themselves among the plaintiffs. All as if the *Golden Hind* had never anchored at Plymouth loaded with Spanish treasure.

Drake simply got away with it. Although Zubiaur eventually secured the return of some of the money, most of it had been lost for good. There was one suitor, however, whom Drake may have listened to with greater favour. In May 1582 the ambassador from Portugal, Don Antonio de Castillo, passed through Plymouth, where he was courteously received by Sir Francis Drake. Castillo happily wrote that Sir Francis had promised that he would settle the suit of a Portuguese against him outside of the courts. We learn no more, but hope that it testified to a belated compensation of that most unfortunate, long-suffering and misused pilot, Nuño da Silva.

If the Spaniards got little satisfaction from Drake, no more did John Doughty, whose brother had been executed in Port San Julian. He had sailed around the world on the *Hind*, but remained throughout a lonely figure, distrusted by Drake himself and isolated in his hatred of the commander. Once he felt the turf of England beneath his feet again, he cast around for a means of avenging his brother, and received permission from the Lord Chief Justice, Sir Christopher Wray, and other judges of the Queen's Bench to proceed against Drake in the Constable and Marshal's court. Unfortunately, a regulation of that court required that such cases were to be heard by both the Lord High Constable of England and the Earl Marshal, and in 1581, for some reason, no one filled the former office. When Elizabeth refused to appoint a Lord High Constable for the purpose, she effectively quashed Doughty's suit, since the Constable and Marshal's court was the only instrument in which the relative of a deceased person might proceed against another for homicide committed outside the realm.[1]

Even worse was in store for the wretched brother of Thomas Doughty. In May 1582 Drake was complaining that at the time of his knighthood, Doughty had said that the

[1] Senior, 'Drake at the Suit of John Doughty'.

queen had honoured 'the arrantest knave, the vilest villain, the falsest thief and the cruellest murderer that ever was born.' Drake's witnesses said that Doughty declared he would repeat his words to the Privy Council.[1] At the same time, Walsingham's intricate spy system picked up one Patrick Mason, who confessed that Pedro de Zubiaur, the same who represented the merchants, had urged him to recruit John Doughty for an attempt to kill or kidnap Drake. Zubiaur had shown Mason letters indicating that Philip would give 20,000 ducats to anyone who did the deed. Whether Mason's story was true it is difficult to say but Doughty was arrested and thrown into the Marshalsea prison in London, where he remained at least as late as October 1583. Like the robberies in the Pacific, the execution of Thomas Doughty would not be avenged.

It was, indeed, Drake's day. He outshone the other stars of Elizabeth's realm. As Protestant hero and the ultimate authority on naval and maritime matters, he became a force in his own right as well as a folk myth. We can now see him clearly, in the more ample documentation for his career, and in the portraits that began to be copied and sold around Europe. Walsingham was once informed that

> Sir F. Drake's picture was brought to Ferrara [Italy] by a gentleman that came out of France this last week, which being given to a painter to refresh, because the colours thereof were faded in the carriage, was so earnestly sought after to be seen that in one day's keeping the same, the picturer made more profit by the great resort from all places to behold it than if he had made it anew.[2]

Basking in the glory of his circumnavigation, Drake probably sat for several portraits. The first fully authenticated likeness of him is an exquisite miniature of 1581 painted by Nicholas Hilliard. One version of it, done on the back of an ace of hearts playing card, was once owned by the Earl of Derby, but can now be viewed at the National Portrait Gallery in London, while another found its way during Drake's lifetime to the collection of the Archduke Ferdinand of Tirol. Whichever is the original, the portrait shows Sir Francis about the time of his knighthood, attired in the rich court dress he was now finding familiar, and peering augustly from an elegant ruff.

Copies of other portraits went abroad. In September 1586 the Spanish ambassador wrote that one sent to France was so popular that King Henry III had copies made for his leading courtiers. What picture this was he did not explain, but the story may not be unconnected with an oval engraving by Thomas de Leu, now to be seen in the British Museum. The pedigree of this portrait is impeccably French. The print was dedicated to England's ambassador to the French court, and was said to have been based upon an original made from life by the French artist Jean Rabel. The engraver, de Leu, had certainly been a pupil of Rabel, and was himself a Fleming domiciled in France. Although it is an admirable likeness of Drake, this head-and-shoulders portrait poses problems, since Sir Francis is not known to have visited France at this time,

---

[1] Evidence against Doughty, State Papers, Domestic, Public Record Office, London, S.P. 12/153: 48-50; S.P. 12/168: 19.

[2] Poole to Walsingham, 10 April, 1588, Butler, et. al., 21 (pt. 1): 572-3. The portraiture of Drake is controversial and involved, but there are grounds for regarding six surviving portraits as being painted from life or derived from paintings from life. See Hind, Engraving in England, 1: 158-60, 190; Strong, Tudor and Jacobean Portraits, 1: 68-71; and Sugden, 'Sir Francis Drake', for comment on these and a selection of the many other purported likenesses.

nor can Rabel be placed in England. The possibility therefore exists that Rabel's paint-ing was itself a copy, perhaps of the portrait sent to France in 1586.

Another foreign portrait of Drake is a Dutch engraving, sometimes said to be by Jodocus Hondius, and also in the collection of the British Museum. It carries an iden-tical inscription to the de Leu portrait ('Franciscus Draeck Nobilissimus Eques Angliae ano. aet. sue. 43') and portrays not dissimilar facial features, so it could be yet another copy of Rabel or of a portrait used by Rabel. It was not taken, however, from de Leu, because the Dutch print shows a feature absent in de Leu – the small wart on Drake's nose. This Dutch print is unsatisfactory as an image of the great sailor. The head is a respectable, but plumper, representation, but the upper half of Drake's body is bloated out of proportion and the diminutive arms flap at hip level as almost superfluous appendages. Conceivably the engraving was made from a head-and-shoulders portrait of Drake, with the deformed torso concocted by an over-imaginative engraver.

Curiously, while Drake's face was becoming familiar, details of his great voyage were not. He inspired a few celebratory pieces – a eulogy here, a panegyric there, the odd scrap of verse, even a dedication in Nicholas Lichfield's translation of Castanhe-da's history of the East Indies (1582). But the only notable piece of circumnavigation literature that appeared in the years immediately following Drake's return was a botan-ical tract published in Antwerp in 1582. It was written by Charles de L'Ecluse, under the pseudonym of Clusius. *Aliquot Notae in Garciae Aromatum Historiam Eivsdem* (Notes to Garcia's Treatise on Aromatic Plants) was graced by a Latin text with handsome drawings and descriptions of plants that had been collected on Drake's voyage by Lawrence Eliot. Some of these commodities were then little known: the Ternate bread fruit, the edible fruit of Batjan, Java papyrus, the aromatic bark of trees of the Magellan Strait, the nuts of Damma. Drake was interested in natural history, and spoke with L'Ecluse several times in London, supplying some of the information for his tract and presenting him with a specimen of the Peruvian bezoar stone.[1] Yet however pleasing it is to note this beginning of the partnership between the navy and natural science, a partnership that reached such an impressive culmination in the work of Joseph Banks and Charles Darwin, L'Ecluse's tract was no substitute for a connected account of the voyage.

For this – unless we count the garbled version in Holinshed's *Chronicles* – the public had to wait until 1589, when Richard Hakluyt managed to insert a six-page summary into most copies of his *Principal Navigations, Voyages and Discoveries of the English Nation.*

There are two possible reasons for this apparent neglect. First, it is conceivable that Drake hoped to write or sponsor his own account and that he actively attempted to discourage competitors. Certainly Hakluyt, as he tells us in his preface, was urged by friends to forbear from including Drake's voyage in his book so as 'not to anticipate or prevent another man's pains and charge in drawing all the services of that worthy knight into one volume.'[2] Who Hakluyt's rival was we do not know. His book was never published. But it was entirely in Drake's character to proclaim his own exploits.

---

[1] L'Ecluse, *Aliquot Notae in Garciae Aromatum Historiam Eivsdem*; Davidson, 'On Some Points in Natural History First Made Known by Sir Francis Drake'.

[2] Hakluyt, *Principal Navigations*; Wallis, 'The Pacific', in Quinn, ed., *The Hakluyt Handbook*, 1: 225-9.

In 1588 he would persuade Petruccio Ubaldino to write up the Armada campaign and four years after that he would employ Philip Nichols to pen what became *Sir Francis Drake Revived*. Drake did, of course, submit a journal and map of his voyage to the queen. And this brings us to the second possibility. These documents must have been crammed with sensitive information and valuable geographical data. Much of it would have been highly offensive to the King of Spain. It seems likely, then, that a policy of official secrecy prohibited public access to them. The queen may well have forbidden the publication of any accounts of the voyage at all. If so the ban was relaxed after the Armada, but Drake's journal has never since come to light and although his map was eventually displayed in the monarch's gallery at Whitehall it seems to have been destroyed by a fire in 1698.

Whatever the explanation, maps and published narratives of the time very inadequately served the magnitude of Drake's achievement. No one, for example, drew attention to the most remarkable fact that he had performed a three-year voyage across the greatest oceans but yet had so carefully preserved the health of his crews and secured them victuals and water that he had suffered no appreciable losses to scurvy. This most dreaded scourge of the seafarer had tormented Magellan's expedition before Drake's time and would decimate Anson's one and a half centuries later.[1]

There was much contemporary uncertainty, too, about Drake's important geographical discoveries. Winter had reported the archipelago south of the Magellan Strait upon his homecoming in 1579, and Drake confirmed it a year later. The Spaniards might fortify the strait, he said, but 'they would find themselves deceived, as it was not continents but very large islands, and there was the open sea beyond Tierra del Fuego.'[2] However, neither this nor his discoveries in the northern Pacific received much publicity. What appears to be a copy of Drake's own map, made after 1586, shows these and England's new 'possessions' of Nova Albion and the Elizabeth Islands, but it was again left to Hakluyt to supply an early comprehensive printed interpretation, in an edition of Peter Martyr's *Decades* published in 1587. This, with a French map engraved about 1583 by Nicola Van Sype and a map struck upon a silver medallion by Michael Mercator in 1589, recorded Drake's contributions, but after the third circumnavigator, Thomas Cavendish, failed to confirm the archipelago south of the Magellan Strait, geographers began to doubt the accuracy of Drake's observations. Thus, within his own lifetime, Drake's discoveries were called into question and it was not until 1617 that the Dutchmen Le Maire and Schouten finally authenticated them.[3]

Yet everyone knew that Drake had made a difference. As a feat of navigation alone his voyage was unsurpassed by any of the great age of discovery. Thomas Blundeville estimated in 1594 that the expedition had traversed 36,000 miles, or the equivalent of more than one and two-thirds circuits of the Equator. It dwarfed any of the voyages of Columbus and Vasco da Gama, and was substantially longer than either the first or

---

[1] Years later Drake patronized the work of Hugh Plat, who produced for him a pasta 'in the form of hollow pipes' that was supposed to retain its freshness for years. Drake used it on his last voyage in 1595. Another idea of Plat's, adding vinegar to water to preserve it, was also tried by Drake. Quinn, *England and the Discovery of America*, 206.

[2] Mendoza to Philip II, 20 April, 1582, Taylor, ed., *Troublesome Voyage of Edward Fenton*, 37-40.

[3] For this aspect, Wallis, 'The Cartography of Drake's Voyage', in Thrower, ed., *Sir Francis Drake and the Famous Voyage*, 121-63.

third circumnavigations by Magellan or Cavendish respectively; and it had not been done by Iberian seamen, the acknowledged masters of oceanic exploration, but by Englishmen who had never before broken the bounds of the Atlantic.

Although Drake had used rutters, maps and local pilots, and although he left the routine handling of the ship to his subordinates (Simon Wood and William Hawkins, two of his men, said that the commander often retired to his cabin at eight in the evening and that he would stir thereafter for neither wind nor rain), the bulk of the credit for the navigation belonged to Sir Francis. No pilots had served him on those mighty hauls across the Pacific and Indian oceans; none of his charts or rutters gave more than an inkling of the intricacies of the Strait of Magellan or the Celebes Sea; and for many regions he had had no guidance whatsoever. He had found his maps as much misleading as helpful. When pilots were available, Drake preferred his own judgement. As he told one of them, the pilot need do no more than point out the landmarks, for he would see to the rest. The best navigators of the day, men like the Spaniard Pedro Sarmiento de Gamboa, the Portuguese Nuño da Silva, and the Englishman John Davis, attested to Drake's mastery of their trade, and, of course, none was more aware of this than Drake himself. He boasted 'of being such a good sailor, so learned, that . . . there was no one in the world who understood better the art of sailing.'[1] In public estimation the voyage proved him right. Edmund Howes, in an edition of William Camden's *Annals*, saw Drake as 'more skilful in all points of navigation than any that ever was before his time, in his time, or since his death. He was also of perfect memory, great observation, eloquent by nature, skilful in artillery, expert and apt to let blood and give physic unto his people according to the climates.'

The significance of the voyage lay primarily in its suggestion that England had come of age as a maritime power and in its inspiration of further Elizabethan endeavour. But even here we must be careful not to exaggerate its impact. Philip responded, not for the first or the last time, to Drake's opportunism, and in 1581 sent an expedition of some 3,500 men in twenty-three ships under Diego Flores de Valdes with orders to occupy the River Plate region and the Strait of Magellan and to reinforce Chile. The venture was disastrous, for few of the men saw their native land again, and it took only a few years to reduce the colony at the strait to a pathetic, starving remnant. Nevertheless, it deterred the English from developing a trade with Brazil. Rather better service was done Spain by a new royal South Seas fleet that was established in the 1580s. In 1587 Thomas Cavendish, trying to emulate Sir Francis, but without his flair or luck (he lost thirty men skirmishing with the Spaniards, and for fewer rewards), slipped through, but the squadron was in place for the next intruder, Richard Hawkins, and forced him to surrender on the coast of Ecuador in 1594.

If one result of Drake's success was that Spain improved her defences, England was unable to carry out her ambition of following up Drake's great voyage. There was plenty of spirit, true enough. Mendoza complained that 'at present there is hardly an Englishman who is not talking of undertaking the voyage, so encouraged are they by Drake's return.'[2] But success was not forthcoming. Humphrey Gilbert and two of his ships' companies perished in the icy seas of the north Atlantic attempting to colonize

---

[1] Report of Gaspar de Vargas, 14 April, 1579, Wagner, *Sir Francis Drake's Voyage Around the World*, 381.
[2] Mendoza to Philip II, 16 October, 1580, Hume, 3: 54-6.

Newfoundland. Davis's search for the North-west Passage in the 1580s likewise failed, and Ralegh, who took up Gilbert's patent and tried to establish settlements in what is now Virginia, was ultimately no more successful. Captain Fenton's efforts to capitalize on Drake's agreement with Ternate ended in a shambles, and he returned to England empty-handed and his expedition in pieces. If Drake had proved that Englishmen could sail anywhere, his countrymen waited long to demonstrate that the great voyage had not been something of a freak, an unusual stroke of genius aided by good fortune. Until Drake himself put to sea again and Cavendish made the third circumnavigation there was little enough for English expansionists to exult about. The disappointing years that immediately followed Drake's voyage around the world, the inability of the English to transform their triumph into a regular South American or East Indian trade, left the promise of the voyage unfulfilled but its status as a symbol of individual en-deavour the greater. Against its context, it shone brighter still.

# CHAPTER THIRTEEN

# 'WHAT HAS BECOME OF DRAKE?'

... he that sings of matchless Drake had need
To have all Helicon within his brain,
Who in his heart did all heaven's worth contain.

Charles FitzGeffrey, *Sir Francis Drake*, 1596

IN THE MONTHS AFTER HIS KNIGHTHOOD DRAKE MADE A MAJOR ADJUSTMENT. THE step from privateer to international folk hero, from master mariner to a knight of the realm, was a vast one. Sir Francis had now to carry himself among the rich and the great, without losing touch with the common people he had left behind. He must live in a style commensurate with his new status, and appropriate to the company he was now keeping. He had outgrown the little house in Plymouth, and he must find a family coat of arms, that indispensable testimonial to the dignity and honour of his line.

The queen moved quickly to secure Drake's social standing. In 1581 she assigned him a coat of arms consisting 'of sable a fesse wavy between two stars argent, the helm adorned with a globe terrestrial upon the height whereof is a ship under sail, trained about the same with golden haulsers by the direction of a hand appearing out of the clouds, all in proper colour with these words, "Auxilio Divino".'[1] Put more simply, Sir Francis was to have a shield emblazoned with a horizontal undulating line. Above and below the line was a silver star, each representing a pole of the earth. Above the shield was a crest, a knight's helmet surmounted with a globe, upon which rode a ship under sail, moored with a golden hawser to a hand from the clouds, and inscribed with the words quoted.

Drake fussed over this coat of arms like a child with a toy. Those jibes about the upstart, the social climber, were having some effect, and Sir Francis's initial reaction was to deny his humble origins, and insist that his family had, after all, been distinguished. As the Clarenceux King of Arms put it, Drake protested that he was 'well born and descended of worthy ancestors such as have of long time borne arms.'[2] The upshot was that while he was happy with the shield granted by the queen, he remained dissatisfied with the crest. He had come up with what he said was a family crest, a red-winged dragon, which he almost certainly had borrowed from the Drakes of Ashe in East Devon. Accordingly, a patent for his coat of arms was drafted that included the dragon, but when the final design was submitted to Drake, he found that for some reason it had been deleted. Possibly Sir Bernard Drake of Ashe had objected to the Clarenceux King of Arms that Sir

---

[1] Statement of Robert Cooke, 20 June, 1581, Wallis, *Sir Francis Drake*, 102.

[2] Corbett, *Drake and the Tudor Navy*, 1: Appendix G. Drake, 'Drake – The Arms of His Surname and Family', argues that the Tavistock Drakes had been using the dragon symbol before 1581. Worth, 'Sir Francis Drake', strikes me as the more authoritative discussion. The story that Sir Bernard Drake and Francis Drake fell to blows over the family crest is apocryphal. Whatever difficulties there may have been the two men seem to have remained friends, and Sir Bernard borrowed £600 from Drake in 1585.

Francis had purloined his crest. At any rate, Drake did not like his patent, and experimented with the whole design. He was wont to divide the shield into quarters, in two of which were the stars and fess, and in the other two his dragon. The crest troubled him greatly. Sometimes he depicted the demi-wyvern, or dragon, in the ship on the globe, and at other times he dispensed wholly with the ship, globe, hand and clouds and simply used the dragon upon a helmet. By 1591 he was so uncertain about his crest that he had it missed off the coat of arms inscribed upon a portrait for which he was sitting. It was not until the end of his life that he felt secure enough to forgo fretting about whether his family had had a crest or not. His last portrait, painted in 1594, contained the crest as originally granted, and at least one of his surviving seals, made of silver and ivory, did not display the dragon.

So much for the coat of arms. Now, what about property? He needed a country house where he could entertain his elevated guests and play the local squire. He did not have to look far – only some four miles north of Plymouth, to the old monastery of Buckland Abbey, built by Cistercian monks in the late thirteenth century in what must have then been a lonely spot conducive to a life of contemplation. For two and a half centuries the monks had ruled Buckland, and some of them were buried beneath the stone floor of the nave. Then, during the Dissolution in 1539, the abbey had passed to lay hands, and in 1541 it became the property of the Grenville family. Old Sir Richard, the Cornish knight, secured the building itself and that portion of the Cistercian estate bounded by the Tavy and a stream that emptied into it at Lopwell. His successor went down in the *Mary Rose* in 1545, and Buckland was acquired by the younger Richard Grenville, he of the South Seas project and the *Revenge*, who was then but an infant. In time Grenville expended effort and love in developing the property, and it was to his dedication that the transformation of it from church to house was due.

The building itself betrayed the simplicity and strength of its origin. The long nave, the chancel and the square, low central tower, were strong, with walls built of stone, flecked in green and brown, hewn from local quarries, but they lacked the ornamentation and stained glass favoured by more ostentatious monastic orders. Grenville changed all that. He pulled down the two transepts to streamline the building, leaving the roof marks to commemorate their passing. He built an east wing with two floors to house kitchens and the domestics. In the church itself he fixed three wooden floors, and partitioned them into rooms. The nave became three reception rooms, a drawing room and some bed chambers. Above all, Grenville enjoyed himself in creating a great hall out of the choir. Over the fireplace was inscribed the date 1576, and a plaster frieze was erected there symbolizing Justice, Prudence, Temperance and Fortitude. Along the length of the west wall ran another frieze that depicted an allegory of the retirement of a warrior – a knight forsaking his profession of arms to reflect upon a skull and an hourglass, his armour discarded upon the ground, his shield hung upon a tree, and his war-horse turned out to graze nearby. Perhaps it was to escape the introspection induced by the frieze that Grenville made a bowling green outside.

When Richard Grenville left Buckland Abbey it was L-shaped in plan with the shorter wing facing towards the north-east. To the north, beyond the small village of Buckland Monachorum, the River Walkham ran towards the Tavy, striking it only a little below Tavistock, where Drake was born. Westwards the sheltered valley of the abbey descended to the timbered bottoms of the Tavy itself, the way marked by orchards that had been planted by the monks. Eastwards, the house was overlooked a mile or more away by the gorse-covered and windswept Roborough Downs, and in the south the Tamar was just visible. About were parks full of deer, and the waters were rich in fish. Here was everything that the Elizabethan gentleman could desire.

Why did Grenville part with something into which he had poured his soul? The truth is probably that he was speculating in land and needed money to discharge various mortgages. Indeed, it is conceivable that he was raising money on Buckland but hoped subsequently to redeem it, because when he sold the house, partly furnished, with five hundred or so acres of land and fishing rights granted by the Marquis of Winchester, he agreed that if the buyers were dissatisfied he might repay the purchase price of £3,400 in two years' time and repossess the property. This sort of agreement was not an unusual form of borrowing at the time, but in this instance the loss was permanent. On 19 December, 1580 Richard and Mary Grenville conveyed Buckland to Drake's agents, John Hele and Christopher Harris. It took another year or two to complete the formalities of the transfer, but Drake and his wife may have taken residence as early as the following summer, because on 10 August he assigned the lease of two houses he had been using in Plymouth to his friends, Tremayne, Hele and Harris. The whereabouts of these town properties is not clear, although Drake had held the lease from a certain Thomas Edmonds, gentleman.[1] One of the houses may have been the one Drake had in 1576, which we presume Mary had occupied in the long years her husband had been at sea. Whatever, Buckland was to be his official seat thereafter, and he was content with it. It was a country retreat in the valleys he had explored as a child, but close enough to Plymouth to serve his public business, and it required no further modification. Grenville had left one minor problem outstanding, for a charge against him of illegally enclosing nearby wood pastures was before the Court of Exchequer, but he had paid Drake's agents £300 as security against any confiscation that might arise from the proceedings and had thus acted honourably.[2]

Buckland Abbey still stands, with its large tithe barn, managed by the National Trust as a monument to the monks who created it, to Grenville who transformed it, and to Drake, for whom it was mute but tangible attestation to his upward mobility. In Drake's day property, particularly land, was the basis of

[1] Assignment by Drake of lease of two houses in Plymouth to Tremayne, Hele and Harris, 10 August, 1581, West Devon Record Office, Plymouth, 277/9.

[2] Youings, 'Drake, Grenville and Buckland Abbey'; Gill, *Buckland Abbey*; Morton, ed., *Calendar of Patent Rolls, 1580-82*, 115. On Grenville's method of borrowing, Drake similarly assisted Captain James Erisey in 1585, when Erisey was raising money to fit out the *White Lion* for Drake's expedition of that year. On 6 September Erisey mortgaged his manor of Pensignance in Gwennap and Kea to Drake for £220, the terms being that if Erisey failed to redeem the sum at Sir Francis's house at Michaelmas in 1586 the property would pass to Drake (Andrew, 'Sir Francis Drake and Captain James Erisey'). The manor did eventually pass into Drake's ownership because in 1595 he sold it to Richard Carew for £250 (Indenture between Drake and Carew, 27 August, 1595, West Devon Record Office, 277/11).

power, privilege and prestige. A few were lucky enough to inherit land; even fewer converted wealth acquired by other means, such as trade, into land as soon as possible, as Drake had done. Land legitimized status and the right to influence. For a few years, indeed, Drake was obsessed with property, and amassed it by reward or purchase at a remarkable rate. The queen was still being generous to him, and sending him gifts – a pendant jewel of sardonyx and pearls, a richly decorated green scarf and matching silk cap, and a number of cups; but the most important rewards were properties. On 12 January, 1582, she granted him the manor of Sherford, in Devon, about three miles from Plymouth, another of those houses pilfered by the Crown through the Dissolution, this time at the expense of the monastery of Plympton St Mary. Drake held it from the queen for the service of one-twentieth of a knight's fee, medieval jargon that was now little more than a form of words.[1]

Sir Francis quickly found this acquisition looked better on paper than in reality, for while the ownership of it now passed to him, and he was obliged to pay John Stanning 6s 8d per year to act as bailiff there, the house had sitting life tenants in John and Walter Maynarde. However, the queen also assigned other properties to her hero, and a handsome list they made too: the manors and patronage of Gayhurst and Stoke Goldingham in Buckinghamshire; land in Little Stainton, in the bishopric of Durham, that had once been part of the estate of Blanchland Monastery; some territory in Buckland Newton in Dorset formerly possessed by Glastonbury Abbey; land and two houses, Burstone House and Burgoin House, in the parish of St Martin, Stamford Baron, Northamptonshire, late of Stamford Priory; and tracts in Morton on Swale, in Yorkshire, that had previously been allocated to supply the stipend of a schoolmaster for the village of Bedale.

There was a snag. Every one of them was granted in *reversion*, that is to say they would only pass to Drake upon the deaths of the present occupiers, and it is possible that he derived no benefit from some of them at all, or indeed that the prospects of doing so were so slight that he renounced his claims upon them. That not one of these properties other than Sherford is mentioned in Drake's subsequent marriage settlement and wills affords reason to believe that he quickly disposed of them. But, knowing Drake, he found some means of gaining advantage. On 13 January, 1582, for example, only a day after receiving the grant, he sold Burstone House in Northamptonshire to Sir Thomas Cecil, the son of Lord Burghley.[2]

Records for 1581 and 1582 show that Drake was investing and speculating heavily in real estate, and that he was hobnobbing with those for whom it was second nature. Sir Arthur Bassett of Umberleigh, Devon, a West Country Puritan and associate of the Earl of Bedford and Richard Grenville, was one of them. Sometime Member of Parliament for Barnstaple and Devon, Bassett had inherited no less than eleven manors when he came of age. In 1582 Drake and Bassett were

---

[1] Royal letters patent, 12 January, 1582, granting manor of Sherford to Drake, West Devon Record Office, 277/14.
[2] Morton, 289; Wyvern Gules, 'Hele and Harris', 183.

involved in mysterious transactions concerning the manor, barton and lands of Boringdon and the areas of Brixton Barton and Brixton, all situated just west of the River Plym and a little way from Plymouth. Possibly they merely acted as agents. It appears that John Hele, Thomas Brewerton and Thomas Walker conveyed the properties to Bassett, Drake and Anthony Monk, who (with John and Mary Hele and Jerome and Catherine Mayhow) forthwith transferred them to Humphrey Selwood and Anthony Mapowder.[1]

Nonetheless, if Sir Francis secured no lasting benefit from that deal, he soon secured two more Devonshire manors, Yarcombe, north-east of Honiton, and Sampford Spiney, west of Tavistock. Yarcombe had passed through several hands since the Crown had obtained it during the dissolution of the religious houses. In 1581 Leicester sold his rights in the property to Richard Drake, the younger brother of Sir Bernard Drake of Ashe, and the following year they were transferred to Sir Francis himself, who promptly acquired title to the remainder of the property by accepting the nominal obligation of knight's service to the Crown.[2] He then completed his acquisitions in the countryside by obtaining Sampford Spinney from the Earl of Devonshire.

This sweep of available country estates gave Drake four properties upon which to found his dynasty: Buckland Abbey, Sherford, Yarcombe and Sampford Spinney. On 20 October, 1582 he moved into the urban market with a single but gigantic investment of £1,500 that made him the third largest landlord in Plymouth, inferior only to the Hawkins family and the town corporation itself. For this sum William Hawkins and John Hele sold him forty separate freeholds about the town. Twenty-nine of them were houses, some of which included taverns and shops and one a bakehouse; four of the properties were gardens, two were stables, and five were warehouses or stores. In addition to these, the Hawkins brothers surrendered to Drake a half share in the old Plymouth tide mills at Millbay, and he got 50 per cent of the manor of Sidbury in East Devon, which he was to sell to Richard Hawkins ten years later. Finally, the deal apparently involved Drake in providing a mortgage. Jerome Mayhow agreed to settle his estates on the family of his prospective son-in-law, Edmund Parker, in return for £3,000 advanced by Parker, drake, Bassett and Monk. The properties in question are not specified, but in 1592 after Mayhow's death P arker owned Thornhill, in the tithing of Compton Gifford. He let it to Drake, and it is conceivable that the rents were offset against the mortgage, or that Drake's tenure owed something to the agreement of ten years before.[3]

When Sir Francis rode about Plymouth he was now a man to whom many were bound by favour and financial obligation. We know little about his many tenants, but they included friends, relatives and camp-followers. One of two properties he had in the High Street was occupied by his brother, Thomas. A newly built house with an attached garden on the corner of Looe Street, one of several properties Drake had in that street in the heart of the town, was leased in March 1587 to

[1] Morton, 174, 266.
[2] *Ibid*, 27; Eliott-Drake, *Family and Heirs of Sir Francis Drake*, 1: 62-3.
[3] Barber, 'Sir Francis Drake's Investment in Plymouth Property'.

Edward Gilman and his sister Florence. Gilman commanded the *Scout* for Drake in 1585, and Sir Francis once generously acknowledged that he was a greater mariner than Drake himself. During the Armada year one Anthony Plott, who had assumed responsibility for repairs to the premises and who married Florence, was admitted to that particular lease for 10 shillings a year. Other tenants may have had no connections with Drake. His only house on Southside Street was occupied by a 'painter', Robert Spry.[1]

Drake released some of his town properties, and at his death his holdings were said to be eighteen messuages, as many gardens, and 34 acres of land. But his standing in the community was secure and the immediate dividend was his selection to be the Mayor of Plymouth for the year beginning September 1581. The stipend was only £20, but the honour great, for Drake now held sway over his home town with the aid of twelve aldermen and twenty-four common councillors. He set up a compass upon the Hoe and passed a regulation controlling the local pilchard trade, and after surrendering his office to Thomas Edmonds in 1582 Sir Francis continued to act as a justice. His interest in law and order is reflected in a donation he made towards the maintenance of the city gaol about 1581, and his order for the arrest of a man who had killed another citizen on the Catdown in 1586 or 1587.[2]

In all of this there was, perhaps, a flaw that troubled Drake. He had no heir for his estate. An attractive anecdote, preserved by Robert Hayman, at one time Governor of Newfoundland, attests to Drake's love of children. Sir Francis was probably visiting Nicholas Hayman, Member of Parliament for Totnes in 1586 and 1587, and came upon young Robert outside the door. Recalling his childhood encounter in a poem, 'Of the Great and Famous, Ever to be Honoured Knight, Sir Francis Drake, and of my Little, Little Self', Hayman wrote:

> This man when I was little, I did meet,
> As he was walking up Totnes's long street.
> He asked me whose I was. I answered him.
> He asked me if his good friend was within.
> A fair red orange in his hand he had.
> He gave it me, whereof I was right glad,
> Takes and kissed me, and prays, 'God bless my boy,'
> Which I record with comfort to this day.[3]

That vacuum in his life, which he filled with his young cousin, John, whom he regarded as a son, was suddenly, immeasurably, extended. He lost them both, first John, on a voyage shortly to be described, and then Mary, his wife. She had been beside him in the worst of times, when he had been publicly tainted with cowardice when they had first married, and in those days of uncertainty when he had returned from his great voyage and waited to hear how the queen would receive him. The local sailor's wife had become Lady Drake, dined with her husband at the expense of the Plymouth Corporation, and been driven in a carriage to a house that must have seemed from another

---

[1] Worth, ed., *Calendar of Plymouth Municipal Records*, 79-80.
[2] *Ibid*, 18, 123, 127; Risk, 'The Rise of Plymouth as a Naval Port', 355.
[3] Callender, 'Drake and His Detractors', 104.

world. And then, almost as if to protest at the social revolution in which her husband had engulfed her, she died, of what no records tell. Her burial is registered for both the church of St Andrew's and that of St Budeaux for 25 January, 1583, and beyond there is silence. Sir Francis could do little more. But he took as his own his late wife's nephew, and as he served and protected Jonas Bodenham perhaps in some way he held fast to her memory.[1]

There was one man who got nervous when information about Francis Drake dried up. Philip II knew Drake, his restless energy and his determination to injure Spain, and he jostled his negligent ambassador. 'Tell me what has become of Drake and what you hear of arming of ships . . . It is most important that I should know all this.'[2] The king's fear was not misplaced, because Drake's mind teemed with plans to Philip's detriment. He was no sooner back from his circumnavigation than talking about a new voyage in which every pound invested would yield sevenfold. Scant details sketch a proposal for him to serve as the life governor of a company that would search for new territories in South America, but there were also rumours that he was bound for the Moluccas with ten ships and that he would rendezvous there with another force to come by the Strait of Magellan. The haze clears to reveal a new figure who had entered Drake's life, the mercurial pretender to the Crown of Portugal, Dom Antonio.

He has been dismissed as a footnote, this enigmatic figure, but he was a barb in Philip's side for fifteen years. Dom Antonio, the prior of Crato, had been the other claimant to the Portuguese throne after the death of King Henry in 1580. Although the king had recognized Philip as heir, many Portuguese, suspicious of Castilian supremacy, acclaimed Dom Antonio, Henry's illegitimate nephew, and he had been sufficiently dangerous for the Spaniards to attempt to buy him off. Neither bribes nor the advance of Alba's army into Portugal quenched the pretender's spirit, but the Spanish conquest was unstoppable. Only Setúbal, Cascais, Oporto and Lisbon offered resistance, and while 10,000 Portuguese turned out for Dom Antonio in defence of the capital they were not soldiers and were quickly dispersed. The pretender himself was wounded in the brave but futile stand.

There followed a period in which Dom Antonio acted the part of a sixteenth-century Bonnie Prince Charlie, roving in disguise through remote mountains with a few loyal supporters, hiding in reed beds, and eventually shipping out on a Dutch vessel despite a price that had been placed on his head. He went to France, and then to England, full of promises for anyone who would give him back his kingdom. Dom Antonio's cause did not die with his flight, for Terceira in the Azores still held out for him, and there was unrest in the Cape Verdes that might be fanned into rebellion. It was in connection with these islands that England was drawn into the pretender's plans. Neither Elizabeth nor the French king, Henry III, was interested in seeing Philip's power augmented by so rich a prize as Portugal, and the prospect of keeping the Azores out of Spanish hands and a potential source of insurrection against Philip on the Portuguese mainland was alluring. Besides, Dom Antonio was offering trading concessions in return for help, and English merchants had long wanted a foothold in

---

[1] Worth, 124.

[2] Philip to Mendoza, 24 April, 1581, Hume, ed., *Cal. Letters and State Papers . . . in the Archives of Simancas*, 3: 102-3.

1. *Francis Russell, 2nd Earl of Bedford (1528-85), godfather and patron of Drake. This eighteenth-century engraving was made from a portrait in the family collection at Woburn.*

2. *John Hawkins (1532-95), kinsman and backer of Drake, as he appeared in 1581. (National Maritime Museum, Greenwich)*

3. ABOVE *The church of St Budeaux, Plymouth, where Drake married Mary Newman in 1569. (Devon Library Services)*

4. LEFT *Walter Devereux, 1st Earl of Essex (d. 1576), painted shortly before he employed Drake in Ireland. (National Portrait Gallery, London)*

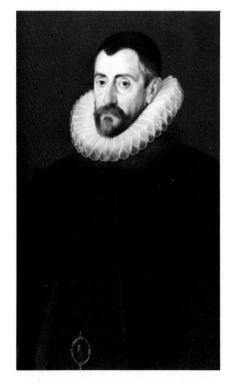

5. TOP LEFT *Sir John Norris (d. 1597), who co-operated with Drake in Ireland, Spain and Portugal. Engraving from a portrait by F. Zucchero.*

6. TOP RIGHT *Edward Clinton, Earl of Lincoln (d. 1585), the Lord Admiral who supported Drake's plan to enter the Pacific.*

7. LEFT *Sir Francis Walsingham (1532-90), Secretary of State, Drake's fellow Puritan, and his principal supporter in government. (National Portrait Gallery, London)*

8. TOP *Elizabeth I (1533-1603), in a portrait attributed to J. Bettes. (National Portrait Gallery)*

9. ABOVE *Abraham Ortelius's world map (1570), showing geographical misconceptions about the southern continent, the Chilean coast and the Northwest Passage before Drake's circumnavigation. This edition of 1579 has been marked with Drake's route. (By permission of the British Library, 920.[327])*

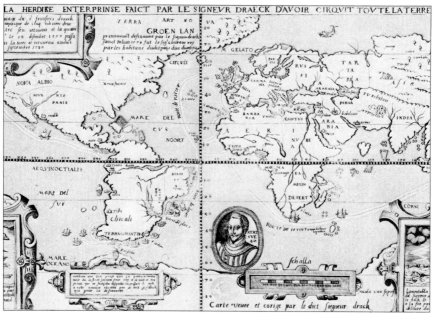

10. TOP *Philip II (1527-98), by Pantoja de la Cruz.*

11. ABOVE *Nicola Van Sype's map of Drake's voyage around the world. Produced about 1583, it was apparently based on a map given by Drake to the Queen. The insets show the Golden Hind. (By permission of the British Library, Maps C.2.a.7[1])*

12. ABOVE *Sir Francis Drake by Nicholas Hilliard, 1581. This is the earliest authenticated portrait. (National Portrait Gallery, London)*

13. LEFT *Sir Francis Drake. An engraving by Thomas de Leu from a painting by Jean Rabel, this is the best of two distinct prints showing Drake shortly after his circumnavigation.*

14. ABOVE Buckland Abbey, Drake's country seat. (Devon Library Services)

15. LEFT An alleged portrait of Elizabeth Sydenham in 1583, before her marriage to Drake. (National Maritime Museum, Greenwich)

ANTHONIUS *de 1. Coninck van Portugael en Algarben.*

16. ABOVE Combe Sydenham House, home of the Sydenhams, now open to the public. Note the front (right) with Sir George Sydenham's coat of arms above the door, and the only surviving wing (left) and tower. (Combe Sydenham Hall, Monksilver)

17. LEFT Dom Antonio (1531-95), claimant to the Portuguese throne, who persuaded Drake to invade Portugal. (National Maritime Museum, Greenwich)

18. *Robert Dudley, Earl of Leicester (1533-88), who used his enormous influence at court to promote Drake's voyages. (National Portrait Gallery, London)*

19. ABOVE *A contemporary map by Baptista Boazio, showing Drake's attack on Cartagena in 1586.*

20. LEFT *Charles, Lord Howard of Effingham (1536-1624), Lord Admiral during the campaign against the Armada in 1588. (National Maritime Museum, Greenwich)*

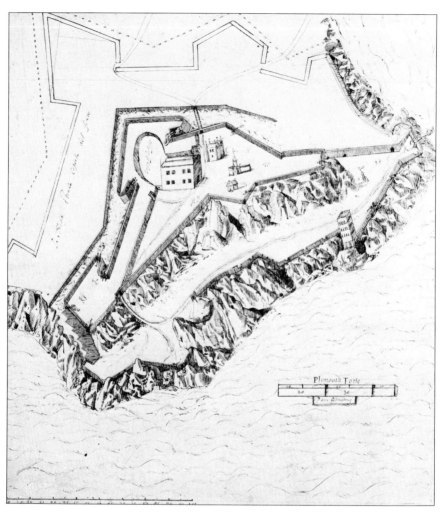

Plimouth Forte

21. Plymouth Fort, which Drake pressed the government to build, shown in a drawing of 1602. Note the extension of the fort to the foot of the cliffs. (By permission of the British Library, Cotton Ms. Augustus I.i,42)

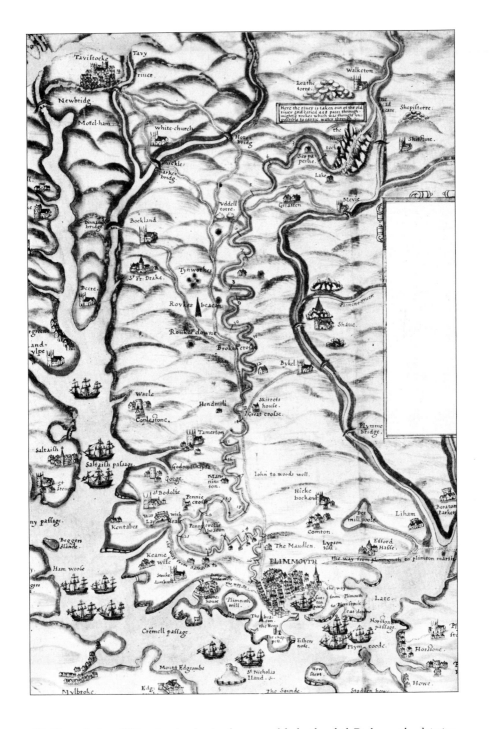

22. Plymouth about 1590, a drawing showing the course of the leat by which Drake was then bringing fresh water into the town. (By permission of the British Library, Cotton Ms. Augustus I.i,41)

23. *Sir Francis Drake in 1591, a portrait attributed to Marcus Gheeraerts. Uncertain about which crest to use for his coat of arms, Drake omitted it from the painting. (National Maritime Museum, Greenwich)*

24. ABOVE *Terence Morgan in the title role of the Sir Francis Drake television series, 1961-62. Employing 16 scriptwriters, it successfully exploited Drake's appeal to the audiences seeking high adventure. Also shown is Jean Kent as Queen Elizabeth. (ITC Library Sales Ltd)*

25. LEFT *A replica of Boehm's statue of Drake, erected on Plymouth Hoe in 1884, when the admiral was regarded as the founder of England's naval greatness. (Devon Library Services)*

*26. Seymour Lucas's nineteenth-century view of the inspiring story of Drake's game of bowls. (National Maritime Museum, Greenwich)*

the islands, so strategically placed in the path of the African, East Indian and trans-atlantic trades.

And so Dom Antonio and his retinue flitted stealthily about the court, lobbying for English support. A man of about fifty years of age, small, dark, thin-faced, with green eyes, his beard streaked in grey, the pretender did not cut an impressive figure. His talents were modest, and his cause doubtful. But there was undoubted charm in the man once he spoke, a certain gallantry in his manner, and there could be no question about his courage, determination or ability to inspire loyalty in his followers even in difficult circumstances. He began to make headway. Elizabeth was not prepared to go to war over Portugal, but she was well aware of the advantages to be gained if 'King Antonio' could be maintained in the Azores. Her councillors wrestled with trying to devise some way in which aid might be given Dom Antonio without constituting an open breach between England and Spain. One possibility was getting France to do the dirty work, and negotiations were opened with Henry, with the English suggesting that as their merchants were vulnerable to reprisals from Spain it would be better if Elizabeth merely underwrote a quarter of the cost of a French expedition to the Azores. Henry was still interested, but tried to make his support conditional upon Elizabeth agreeing to the French marriage. Talks began to flag.

Another possibility involved Sir Francis Drake. The English had not forgotten that Philip had allowed the Pope to recruit Spaniards for an expedition against Ireland. Very well then. Since England recognized the legitimacy of sovereignty by possession of territory, and since Terceira plainly adhered to Dom Antonio, what was to stop Elizabeth permitting the pretender to recruit Drake in its defence? No treaties would be broken, because there were none between England and Spain that concerned the islands, and if necessary the whole operation could be conducted under Dom Antonio's flag. But even this plan depended upon French support in order to create a fleet large enough to defend the Azores.[1]

In April 1581 a band of politicos and naval men, Walsingham, Leicester, Drake, Hawkins, Winter and Richard Bingham (who had the distinction of having served not only under Winter but with the Spaniards at Lepanto), discussed sending eight ships, six pinnaces and perhaps a thousand men to the Azores. Drake would command, and some of Frobisher's associates like Edward Fenton, Gilbert Yorke and Luke Ward, as well as Captain Brewer and Captain Gregory, were named as possible captains. Soon ships were being fitted out at Plymouth in 'frantic haste', as Mendoza reported to Philip. On 26 April Dom Antonio had provided his own view of the expedition. He wanted it to sail on 15 June, victualled for four months, and proposed to pay for a quarter of the costs of Drake's fleet within two months, and high interest payments on the balance. The English would receive 75 per cent of Spanish prizes, and could keep any Portuguese ships that refused to declare for Dom Antonio. As for trading privileges, the pretender promised to license English merchants to trade with the Azores for two years, and they would be obliged to pay only half-duties. The only discordant note was Dom Antonio's request that the fleet be ready to intervene on the mainland ('If the Kingdom of Portugal needs succouring they shall do it'), a requirement that was

[1] Articles to be considered relating to Drake's proposed voyage to the Azores, 21 August, 1581, Lansdowne MS 102, article 104, British Library.

likely not authorized by the English government.[1]

There was a strong profit motive in the venture, for once installed in the Azores Drake would have a base from which to intercept Spain's ships from the West and East Indies, using letters of marque issued by Dom Antonio. Much has been written about these divergent goals of profit and national interest; it is important to understand that the two were not always incompatible. Philip's ability to make war in Europe depended upon his credit with European financiers. His resources, from the ecclesiastical contributions of his dominions, the taxes in Castile and the American silver, were becoming inadequate against his enormous commitments, and his dependence upon the Genoese bankers, for all their high rates of interest, had been demonstrated five years before when Philip attempted to renege upon his debts, only to find his soldiery in the Netherlands breaking out in mutiny. In a sense the bankers, rather than Philip, ruled Europe, and although Spain's principal revenues came from taxes, their confidence in her ability to redeem their loans rested heavily upon the regular and substantial shipments of treasure. Drake believed that cutting the silver route served both man and mammon.

There was still some uncertainty about the plan, but Drake intended landing on Terceira and throwing up a fortification. After that, one idea was to cruise about until the end of September in the hope of catching the *flota*, or failing that to attack the West Indies. The alternative was less provocative, and involved sailing from Terceira to Brazil and the East Indies. A cost of £10,320 was mentioned, and the use of some of the queen's ships, including the *Swiftsure*, as well as private vessels like the *Galleon Oughtred* and the *Primrose*. In the summer Drake was in London, discussing the details with his principal confederates, Walsingham, Leicester, Hawkins and Winter, and with Dom Antonio himself. He found the pretender impatient, and had to tell him that the expedition could not be readied as quickly as he demanded, but finally Drake got away, and left for Plymouth with Hawkins and Dom Antonio's agent, Juan Rodriguez de Sousa. Back in the West Country he did the best he could. Firearms, armour, weapons and ammunition were purchased, some of them by Dom Antonio; artillery and other arms were brought from the Tower; wagon-loads of victuals left London for the outports; Drake lobbied the merchants for money and ships, and it was said that twenty-five vessels in all were fitted, at Plymouth, London, Southampton and Bristol; Portuguese pilots were recruited for their local knowledge and to add a national colour to the voyage; men were raised in the west, and captains appointed, although none was apprised of their destination; and for a while it seemed that Drake was about to lead out the largest long-distance naval strike in English history.

And then, suddenly, it fell through. The expenses rose like a mountain, and when they topped £13,000 everyone felt they had reached the limits of their purses. The queen had contributed £5,000 but was being pressed for more. Drake and Hawkins,

[1] Terms granted the English fleet, 26 April, 1581, Butler, et. al., ed., *Calendar of State Papers, Foreign*, 15: 132-3. For source materials on the Azores expedition, see Lansdowne MSS 31, articles 81-3, and 102, article 104; Taylor, ed., *Troublesome Voyage of Captain Edward Fenton*; Donno, ed., *An Elizabethan in 1582*; Hist. MSS Comm., *Calendar of the Manuscripts of the Marquis of Salisbury*, 2: 420; Digges, ed., *The Compleat Ambassador*; Klarwill, ed., *Fugger News-Letters*, 2: 50-65; Brown, ed., *Calendar of State Papers . . . in the Archives and Collections of Venice*; Murdin, ed., *Collection of State Papers*, 351-60. A recent discussion of Dom Antonio is McBride, 'Elizabethan Foreign Policy in Microcosm'.

who had put up money, could go no further. Dom Antonio was using his jewels as collateral; he had given one to the queen and used others to buy three ships, commission a few privateers, and provide some necessaries. But much of his spending was on credit, and what was worse, credit dependent upon the successful outcome of the voyage. Linked with the strait circumstances of the English side of the adventure was the increasingly evident reluctance of the French to give firm assurances of support. At the end of July Walsingham himself went to France to negotiate with Henry and Catherine de Medici. England's contribution, he was to explain, would be 'indirect', by which Elizabeth possibly meant that it would be one for which she might disclaim responsibility if the need arose. She may also have been wavering about the prudence of using armed force at all. Catherine, whose own distant claim upon the Portuguese throne Philip had brushed aside more imperiously than Dom Antonio's, was prepared to assist the pretender, but no more desired to incur Spain's wrath alone than did Elizabeth. The English were given the impression that if the queen would marry the Duke of Alençon and thereby commit herself more vigorously to French foreign policy a joint expedition to the Azores might be undertaken. Elizabeth, of course, had no intention of making any such commitment and acute observers must have doubted if the impasse between the positions of England and France could be negotiated away.

As late as 20 August it was intended that Drake's expedition should sail as planned. But the next day, when Drake and Hawkins attended a conference with Burghley and other leading English participants, they found their backers tormented by doubts and misgivings. How would the King of Spain react? Would he send fresh support to Ireland? Would he take reprisals against English vessels trading in Spanish ports? Or would he interpret Elizabeth's sanction of the enterprise as an outright declaration of war? They decided that the expedition must be contingent upon French support. Even then Drake's freedom of action would be carefully circumscribed. Although he might relieve Terceira and attempt Madeira or 'any other island that did belong to Dom Antonio as King of Portugal' he could not justifiably attack Spanish shipping or colonies. But yet, if the Spaniards were not to be plundered, how could the adventurers realistically hope to make a profit?

Drake had little patience with such timorous talk. And certainly neither he nor Hawkins had any wish to preside over the demise of their Terceira project. So in order to salvage something from the preparations they eagerly endorsed a proposal for an immediate but reduced expedition. Burghley's minutes tell us that it was suggested that 'three ships and a bark might be presently sent to the isles to do service there, whereunto Drake & Hawkins assent, and think thereby great service may ensue, and in this case the rest of the ships may be reduced to a smaller charge, and yet remain in readiness, upon knowledge from France.'[1]

After this meeting the two seamen conferred with Dom Antonio again. But when they broached the idea of a reduced expedition under William Hawkins and John Norris the pretender would have none of it. That very month the Spaniards were attempting to reduce Terceira and greater forces were already being mustered to finish the job. The Azores, he contended, needed help, substantial help, now. Drake and Hawkins must have been dismayed. They would have pointed out that in the circumstances this

---

[1] Articles to be considered, etc., 21 August, 1581, Lansdowne MSS 31, article 81, and 102, article 104.

was the best offer Dom Antonio was likely to get, but he was adamant. A marginal annotation, added subsequently to Burghley's minutes of 21 August, reads simply: 'The King Antonio will not assent hereto, as to bear any charges thereof.'

King Philip himself hammered the last nail into the coffin of the Azores expedition. On 14 August he instructed his ambassador to leave no doubt that if Dom Antonio sailed from England against him Spain would regard it as a declaration of war and he followed this up with a stern letter to Elizabeth to the same effect. If the queen ever believed that she could have unleashed Drake without making that great step, she now had her answer.

The men were discharged, the provisions and munitions sold. Dom Antonio demanded that the queen return his jewel and then, in September, followed his agent, Francisco, Conde de Vimioso, to Paris. To Drake, who had believed in the project so much and who had striven so mightily to realize it, it was all a terrible disappointment. He even failed to recoup all the money he had expended upon the preparations. But, more important, he subscribed fully to the view that Spain's war effort rested upon the import of American silver. Ever the opportunist, Drake had seen in Dom Antonio a chance to acquire the perfect base from which he might strike at the treasure fleets. And how he would have relished the prospect of taking a *flota*!

It would have been a worthy sequel to his circumnavigation, but in fact neither Drake nor anyone else would accomplish that dazzling feat in his lifetime. Even the relief of the Azores proved to be more than the simple task Dom Antonio represented it to be. Stimulated by the pretender's arrival, the French bungled it twice. In July 1582 a French fleet, commanded by Philippe Strozzi, was defeated in a five-hour sea battle. Some English vessels appear to have served in a private capacity on the French side. After the failure of a second French expedition, Dom Antonio skulked between France and England pressing for a third attempt, but for the moment no one could be persuaded, and Terceira was eventually captured by the Spaniards. Dom Antonio's cause was not entirely crushed by these misfortunes, for he continued to proclaim himself the true King of Portugal and commissioned privateers to attack Spanish shipping, but his prospects certainly lost lustre. Philip strengthened his hold upon Portugal and the islands by tact as well as force. For perhaps a few Portuguese Dom Antonio symbolized independence of Castile, but most became reconciled to Philip, who avoided unnecessary interference in their internal affairs and kept the country's offices out of the hands of Spaniards.

The collapse of the Terceira project left Drake with time on his hands. His letters of the autumn of 1581, barely one year after his return in the *Golden Hind*, reveal a man already itching for further action. 'I am very desirous,' he told Leicester in October, 'to show that dutiful service I can possibly do in any action your good Lordship vouchsafeth to use me.' There is no doubt that he was still hoping for a revival of the Azores venture. In November we find Sir Francis advising Leicester that 'the bark which I sent of late to the island [of] Terceira is returned, by whom I have received certain letters . . . wherein your Lordship shall understand the state of that place more effectually than I can signify by writing'.[1] But he was soon occupied in the pre-

[1] Drake to Leicester, 14 October, 1581, Cotton MSS, British Library, Otho. E. VIII f. 98; Drake to Leicester, 7 November, 1581, *Ibid*, f. 102.

parations for a different if equally ill-starred enterprise – a trading voyage to the East Indies that would exploit the openings he himself had made with Ternate and use some of the ships and men originally assembled for the Azores.

Leading courtiers and members of the government, like Leicester, Walsingham, Hatton, Carleil (Walsingham's dashing son-in-law) and the Earl of Lincoln, merchants from the Muscovy Company eager to expand their trade to the east, and Frobisher, Drake and other seamen pitched into the investment, Drake to the tune of £666 13s 4d. Leicester was the expedition's principal organizer, but Drake was its inspiration and leading adviser. He indicated places where trade might be had and advised that some of his old crew be shipped to help with navigation, watering places and means of preserving health aboard ship. Upon his recommendation, more than a dozen of his old comrades joined the voyage, including both his young protégés, Jonas Bodenham and John Drake. Cousin John, barely twenty years old and high spirited, was now striking out on his own for the first time as captain of his cousin's 40-ton *Bark Francis*, manned by about thirty-five men, some – like himself and the sailing master, William Markham – veterans of the *Golden Hind*. Sir Francis also interviewed for other appointments. Richard Madox, a preacher preferred by Leicester, recorded that on 15 January, 1582 he was examined in Muscovy House in London before a panel that included Drake and the merchant and alderman, George Barnes. When Madox was asked what remuneration he would demand for his services, he manfully declared that his only wish was to assist his country.

The leader of the East Indies voyage was to have been Martin Frobisher, but the cantankerous Yorkshireman stepped down when the Muscovy Company pressed him to accept Edward Fenton as his second-in-command. Fenton moved smartly into Frobisher's place, and a bad move it was, for Fenton was little enough of a sailor and demonstrated an inability to control difficult crews. His vice-admiral was Luke Ward. Fenton raised his flag on the *Leicester Galleon*, a merchantman Leicester had purchased from another investor, Henry Oughtred, and there were three other ships, the *Edward Bonaventure*, the *Elizabeth*, and the *Bark Francis*. The rendezvous was Southampton, and we have a picture of Drake visiting the port on 22 April to encourage the officers with typical extravagance. And it was obviously impressive, for three people sat down to write of it the same day. First, Fenton himself beseeched Leicester 'to be thankful to Sir Francis Drake for his good counsel towards me and persuasions to his companies for their obedience to that effect.' Then the earl learned from the minister of the *Edward Bonaventure* that 'the right worshipful Sir Francis Drake hath used me with the greatest friendship that any might desire, both in instructing me for the voyage and in dealing with me and my fellow preacher, for the which thanks.' Richard Madox noted in his diary that 'Sir Francis Drake was at Southampton and dealing liberally many ways. [He] gave M[aster John] Banister 50, and 50 more between me, M[aster John] Walker and M[aster] Lewis Otmore, but in that also M. Banister made himself a part.'[1] Francis Drake was a man who made friends as easily as he earned enemies.

The expedition sailed in May 1582, but was little favoured. Drake had to help it out almost immediately by sending extra tackle with some wine out of Plymouth to

[1] Fenton to Leicester, 22 April, 1582, Taylor, 41-2; Walker to Leicester, 22 April, 1582, *Ibid*, 43-4; Madox diary, 22 April, 1582, Donno, 117. Banister and Otmore were surgeons on the expedition.

Torbay. In the Atlantic the winds were unfavourable for a voyage around Africa, and many of the sailors, including the fiery John Drake, demanded that the instructions be thrown over the side and the ships run through the Strait of Magellan to plunder Peru as Sir Francis had done. Some of Fenton's squadron reached Brazil, where they engaged three Spanish ships in battle and sank one, but they were refused trade and further separated. Despairing of any success, Fenton sailed for home, and when he reached the Downs in June 1583 he found that his vice-admiral had returned to England before him. It had been a fiasco, and for Drake worse, for John Drake remained missing.

As months passed, Drake's anxiety for his cousin remained unrelieved. John never came home. In 1587 it was learned that he had been captured by the Spaniards, and although Drake must have prayed that John would survive and somehow find his way to England as a few other enslaved Englishmen did, the hopes dimmed with the years. Spanish records have told us a little of his fate. After parting from Fenton, John ran for the Magellan Strait, but was shipwrecked at the River Plate. Some of his men were killed by Indians, and others, including the captain, fell into the hands of the Spaniards. A long, miserable life awaited him. After his identity was discovered, he was interrogated at Santá Fe and Lima, and years of imprisonment brought him to repent his Lutheranism and to walk in the *auto-da-fe* of 1589, adorned with the red cross of the penitent. Although he escaped the grosser torments of the Inquisition, John lived out his life among his country's enemies, far from home. Possibly our last glimpse of him is as a pathetic, shambling old man of about eighty-eight, for a John Drake participated in the *auto-da-fe* held in Cartagena in December 1650. If this was Drake's cousin, the decades of captivity and humiliation must have contrasted vividly with the brilliant days of his youth, when he claimed the golden chain for sighting the treasure ship, sailed around the world with Sir Francis Drake, and excited wonder in the gaudy court of Gloriana.

Fenton's voyage failed to fulfil the heady expectations of an England aroused by Drake's circumnavigation, but in that it was apiece with other adventures of the time – with the efforts to find the North-west Passage and the first faltering steps to colonize America. Drake, like others who invested in oceanic endeavour, counted Fenton's voyage as one of several losses. In November 1582 his *Matthew* was one of five vessels that sailed under old William Hawkins to the Cape Verdes and Brazil, hoping to capitalize upon Elizabeth's support of Dom Antonio. But their reception in the islands was so frosty that the expedition was abandoned, and Hawkins tried to recoup its costs by dredging pearl oysters off Margarita and plundering the Caribbean.[1] Nearly two years afterwards Leicester, Drake, the Hawkins brothers and the Raleghs were preparing another voyage to the East Indies, proposing a force of eleven ships, four barks and twenty pinnaces to be fitted at a cost of £40,000, but nothing came of it. England would have no maritime successes to celebrate until Sir Francis put to sea again himself.

The years 1580 to 1585 are often portrayed as a lacuna in Drake's life, but they were crammed not only with planning new expeditions but also with public service. His

[1] Williamson, *Sir John Hawkins*, 402-5, and *Hawkins of Plymouth*, 218-25; Taylor, 1v.

opinion on seafaring matters was eagerly sought by all parties. We find him subscribing £20 down plus an annual stipend of the same amount to Richard Hakluyt's unsuccessful attempt to endow a lectureship in navigation. We see the Privy Council in 1581 requiring him to assist John Hawkins, Winter, Hakluyt, Thomas Digges, William Aborough, a Master Dyer, and the comptroller of the navy, William Holstocke, in considering how the crumbling pier in Dover harbour might be repaired. Two years later charges that the queen's ships had decayed under the treasurership of John Hawkins and that Winter and other naval officials had been misappropriating money and materials or paying contractors excessive prices led to the establishment of a five-man committee under Burghley to investigate the navy, and Drake was one of eleven men named as possible assistants, although whether he actually served is unknown. The same year the Privy Council called upon Sir Francis to arrest some Dutch ships, and on 31 July, 1584 he was commissioned with the Lord Admiral and Carew Ralegh to apprehend pirates. The government was also finding Drake an efficient man in handling local business in the West Country, and began to unload upon him the duties generally associated with the Lord Lieutenants of the counties. His name, with those of members of the Champernowne family, is found appended to assessments of rates and musters of forces for South Devon.[1]

Perhaps the most testing of Sir Francis's new obligations was his entry into Parliament, for it demanded of him skills in a combat different from any he had known and thrust him into the heart of the privileged society in which he now moved. Here, directly or through friends and relatives, Drake had access to everyone who mattered in Elizabeth's England, and here, too, he exercised the power to oblige both the rich and the humble. The speed with which he entered this fraternity is surprising. When Parliament opened in January of 1581, only months after his return from the circumnavigation, Drake was part of it, because on 17 February he was granted leave of absence on account of 'his necessary business in the service of Her Majesty.' His constituency is not known, but he must have been slotted into some by-election, and Camelford, a Duchy of Cornwall borough in the parish of Lanteglos, has been suggested as the seat. It returned two Members, and one of them was nominated by none other than the great magnate Francis Russell, Earl of Bedford, Drake's own godfather. Now, for the first time perhaps, that connection was gathering its rewards. Bedford's influence was profound. He was warden of the stanneries, Lord Lieutenant of Devon and Cornwall, and controlled several parliamentary seats, all of which he assigned to friends and relatives who would assist him in promoting his particular cause in government, the Puritan faith. Sir Francis Drake satisfied Bedford on all counts. He was the son of an old family tenant; he was his godson; he was a national hero; and he was an unbridled Puritan, a patriot who cheerfully signed the Devon Instrument of Association in 1584, proclaiming unreserved support for the queen and the Protestant succession, and who symbolized the nation's rising pride and confidence. A vacancy at Camelford occurred after the death of one of the constituency's Members in 1576, but although a by-election was organized in 1579 there is doubt about whether a return was made, and it

---

[1] Waters, *Art of Navigation*, 542-3; Dasent, ed., *Acts of the Privy Council*, 13: 80; Williamson, *Sir John Hawkins*, 347-51; State Papers, Domestic, Public Record Office S.P. 12/162: 33, S.P. 12/172: 38, S.P. 12/183: 33-4.

is possible that it was the seat provided Drake in 1581.[1]

However, Drake had little to do with the Commons at that time. He was too busy with the treasure he had brought home, and the parliament was in its last days. Three years later another opportunity arose, for the general election of 1584 introduced a new parliament in which only one-fifth of the 460 Members returned had previous experience in the Commons. Sir Francis was elected one of the two Members for Bossiney, in Cornwall, on 28 October. His indenture was signed by a mere nine persons, creatures of Bedford, who controlled both the Bossiney seats, and simply presented the electors with their representative.

The Commons, which assembled in St Stephen's Chapel of the Palace of Westminster, brought Drake to London again. He was used to the city now, familiar with its few principal arteries and its narrow garbage-ridden alleys, accustomed to watching the swans upon the Thames. Perhaps he lodged with friends, or rented a town house. A letter of the previous June suggests that Drake was then living in a house belonging to the father of Julius Caesar, the augustly named judge of the Admiralty court, in Cheapside, a well-paved area that was the pride of the capital. Drake and Caesar had a reasonable relationship, good enough for Sir Francis to intercede with the justice on behalf of deserving individuals (we find him entreating Caesar to assist 'this poor man and divers others who have endured . . . much wrong at this Powell's hands' in 1584), and for the Caesars to provide for Drake as he confronted the unseemly hubbub that then, as now, passed for debate among the ignoble Members of the House.[2] Hardly had he taken his seat than on 27 November he was appointed to a committee to consider the first bill of the session, for the better preservation of the Sabbath.

The matter had long troubled churchmen – a year before eight people had been killed when a platform collapsed at a Sunday bear-baiting pit in Paris Green – and the committee was stacked with the devout, kindred spirits to Drake, among them the Chancellor of the Exchequer, Sir Walter Mildmay, Sir John Higham of Suffolk, Sir Richard Knightley, William Grice, Robert Beale, Peter Turner, William Strickland and Edward Lewkenor, Puritans every one. After labouring the subject in the Exchequer during the afternoon of the same day and late into the night, this fervent gathering had little to show, but by 3 December they had concocted a harsh bill that prohibited games, bear-baiting, hawking, hunting, wakes and even the rowing of barges on a Sunday. When an amended version eventually appeared before the queen, she considered it so extreme that she refused to sign it.

It is difficult to imagine Drake being impressed by the tiresome argument that was inextricably part of parliamentary business. By nature masterful and decisive, he preferred action to words, but he earned the reputation of an eloquent and bold speaker in the Commons, and was much in demand for the committee work that prepared bills for submission to the House. In December he was appointed to four more committees, all involving maritime affairs. The first, chaired by Sir Edward Dymock, the Sheriff of and Member of Parliament for Lincolnshire, was appointed on 7 December and met

[1] Hasler, The Commons, 1: 123-5, 2: 54, a valuable discussion of Drake's parliamentary career; D'Ewes, Journals of All the Parliaments, summarizes house proceedings.

[2] Drake to Caesar, 12 February, 1584, Lansdowne MS 158, article 37; see also Lansdowne MS 158, article 32, and Additional MS 12,507, f. 117, British Library, for other occasions on which Drake lobbied Caesar in favour of various parties.

three days later to discuss the importation of fish and ling. On the 19th Sir Francis was required to consider the maintenance of the navy and on the 21st the preservation of Plymouth harbour. When this last committee convened in the Middle Temple the following February, Drake found himself with local men he probably already knew, including Peter Edgcombe, who represented the Cornish borough of Liskeard.

Unquestionably the most famous of the committees was organized on 14 December to report upon the issue of a licence to Walter Ralegh for the colonization of Virginia. Among its members were the poet Sidney, Hatton, Drake, Sir Richard Greenfield, Sir William Mohun and Sir William Courtenay. There can have been little doubt that Ralegh's patent would be approved, although Drake was not passionate about colonization. But he was ready to endorse it, and even presented verses for Sir George Peckham's tract promoting Gilbert's plan to settle Newfoundland, published in 1583. It was to Sir Francis that the explorer John Davis wrote in October 1585, relating his discovery of an island that promised handsome yields of furs and leather. For Drake was not only a respected authority on all matters of the sea, but his approval and support were actively sought as invaluable assets to any oceanic enterprise. In the case of colonization there was one component that could not have failed to excite his interest, and that was the possibility of using a Virginian colony as a base for raids upon the Spanish West Indies.

The parliamentary session lasted until March 1585, with Drake joining Mohun, Edgcombe and others on the 15th of that month in his final committee, considering the manufacture of Devonshire kersies. Shortly afterwards, while Drake was preoccupied with his next great voyage in 1585 and 1586, he lost the seat at Bossiney. Partly it was because he was otherwise employed. Partly it arose from the death of Bedford in 1585. After his patron's death, the control of the constituency fell between William Peryam and John Hender, who slipped relatives, John Peryam and William Pole, into the two seats in 1586. Yet, brief as it was, Drake's experience in the Commons had been valuable, strengthening his power and widening his circle of influential friends. An impressive array of gentlemen had floundered with him in the committees – Sir Drew Drewry, Sir William Herbert, Sir Robert Germin, Sir Thomas Manners, Sir William Moore, Sir Nicholas Woodroofe, Sir Henry Neville . . . and on and on, all of them potential supporters, some possible investors for future voyages.

Sir Francis further advanced his new status in 1585. He married again, but the bride, young Elizabeth Sydenham, was very different from the wife he had lost two years before. Mary had belonged to the society from which Drake himself had sprung, from people who lived a step ahead of want and insecurity, and whose world was dominated by their economic betters. Elizabeth, by contrast, was no simple sailor's wife, but the sophisticated and elegant heiress of one of the wealthiest men in the West Country, a member of an influential family accustomed to privileged company. The difference between Mary and Elizabeth measured the distance Drake had travelled.

Elizabeth was many years his junior. According to legal proceedings held at Tavistock in 1598 she would have been born about 1562 and was in her early twenties at the time she married. Of her appearance we perhaps have an indication. Dedicating a poem to her in 1596, Charles FitzGeffrey called her 'the beauteous and virtuous Lady Elizabeth', but since dedications were then made by permission and often to solicit favour, and since the poet's patrons were the Rouse family of Halton, Elizabeth's trustees, we may excuse FitzGeffrey if he was merely being gallant. Two portraits, however, would bear him out, although neither is fully authenticated. They show a regal lady in the full and elaborate dresses then fashionable, slender and trim, with long, sensitive hands, dark hair, and an oval face displaying a firm narrow chin and a petite mouth betokening some humour.[1]

Nothing tells of how they met, but it may have been at Fitzford, in the parish of Tavistock, not far from Buckland. Drake knew the Fitz family, and at one time acted as trustee for another of their properties at Lewisham, and the wife of John Fitz, head of the household, was Mary Sydenham, one of Elizabeth's four aunts. Or perhaps he met her through the many social occasions that brought the West Country élite together. Certainly, Miss Sydenham was well connected and made a good marriage. Her paternal grandfather had been Sir John Sydenham, Sheriff of Somerset, and his wife, who survived until 1608, was Ursula Bridges, the sister of John, first Lord Chandos. Their extensive brood were significant local figures. The oldest of Elizabeth's five paternal uncles, Sir John Sydenham, inherited the estate of Brympton d'Every. An aunt, also called Elizabeth, married the Sheriff of Devonshire.

The father of Drake's bride was Sir George Sydenham, sometime Sheriff of Somerset, who had inherited from his father the estate of Combe Sydenham in the same county and had added to it since. In 1561, for example, he had purchased the manor of Sutton Bingham from Sir William Kayleway of Rockborne. He played the local benefactor, providing £15 a year from his properties at Combe Sydenham and nearby Stogumber for the upkeep of six cottages he had donated to poor widows, and was a pillar of the county administration, regularly mustering the local levies at Bridgwater. Sir George's wife, Elizabeth, was of no less distinguished a lineage than the Sydenhams. She was the daughter of Sir Christopher Hales, once Attorney-General to Henry VIII and the prosecutor of Wolsey, More, Fisher and Anne Boleyn.

As the only child of such a formidable union, Miss Elizabeth Sydenham had a most secure future long before she met Sir Francis Drake. She stood to inherit a battery of family properties, and in time she did so: the house of Combe Sydenham; the manors of Sutton Bingham and Bossington; tracts of land in Bossington, Selworthy, Luccombe, Porlock, Sutton Bingham, Coker, Wester Colcombe, Combe Sydenham, Stogumber and Monksilver, all varying in size and tenure, some held from the Crown and others from the Dean and Chapter of Bath and Wells; and the patronage of the rectories of Stogumber, Monksilver, Puriton and Woolevington. No ordinary bride, indeed.[2]

The remains of the world of the Sydenhams are discernible today for those who journey, as Drake must often have done, into the deep and picturesque wooded valley in western Somerset where the house of Combe Sydenham, Elizabeth's parental home and a family possession since the fourteenth century, still lies hidden. Not all of it stands now, but enough to give an impression of how it appeared to Sir Francis as he came to court his lady there centuries ago. Built of stone and remodelled by Sir

[1] One portrait, attributed to George Gower, now hangs in Buckland Abbey. The other, supposedly coming from Elizabeth's family home of Combe Sydenham but purchased by the National Maritime Museum from the Heathcote Collection in 1938, is inscribed 'Anno. Domi. 1583/aetatio suae: 22', and (in a later hand) 'Elizabeth, 2nd wife of Sir Francis Drake'.
[2] Sydenham, *History of the Sydenham Family*, gives details.

George, the house possessed several towers and was E-shaped, with the south-facing front exhibiting a central doorway and the three wings, only one of which survives, to the north. As Drake passed through the wooden doors of the gatehouse, and arrived at the front door of the house, he may have paused before entering to gaze at the Sydenham coat of arms set in stone above the porch and the Latin inscription beneath the device that read, 'I this door shall always be open to all your friends, noble George, but an open doorway is closed to unwelcome spirits'. Sir George's initials and the date 1580 were engraved at the top of the pilasters on either side of the porch. Inside, a screen passage passed to the rear courtyard, with access on the right to kitchens and ultimately to the east wing that once housed the sleeping quarters, and on the left to the great hall, a room that once extended to the roof but for a minstrels' gallery, but which was eventually (perhaps before Drake's day) divided into two storeys by the insertion of a new floor. Today visitors can pass through the hall to the one surviving tower and into the ruins of the western and only remaining wing. Outside we can picture Sir Francis and Elizabeth lingering about the fish ponds set out south of the house, or riding into the little valley that contained what some believed to be the remains of a medieval hamlet, or further, into the rolling hills of western Somerset.

Drake may have been the most famous man in England, but Sir George Sydenham was not about to let his only daughter go without striking a hard bargain. On 9 February, 1585 a marriage settlement was signed by which Drake granted his manors of Yarcombe, Sherford and Sampford Spiney, and Buckland Abbey to Elizabeth, himself and their heirs forever. The document reveals that the marriage had then already taken place, but no record of it has been found.[1] Anthony Rouse of Halton, Cornwall and William Strode of Newnham were named as trustees of the agreement.

The couple retired to Buckland Abbey, and Elizabeth accompanied her husband to Plymouth and dined with the Corporation, as Mary had done, and with Harris and Strode and their other friends. By the middle of that year Sir Francis Drake could review his progress since the circumnavigation with considerable satisfaction. He had a title, a coat of arms, wealth and honour. He had the prospect of founding a dynasty, and of leaving to any children properties scattered across Devon and Somerset. He had served as the Mayor of Plymouth and Member of Parliament, and was courted by high and low. He was recognized and mobbed as a hero in the streets. In need he might call upon a network of powerful friends in all quarters. There was no better example of the self-made man. Yet Sir Francis was never complacent. He remained true to his faith, and continued to scheme for the downfall of King Philip of Spain. And in June 1585 another opportunity came.

---

[1] A letter of Sir Philip Sydenham, written in 1717, states that Drake's marriage occurred on 18 June, 1585 at the church of Monksilver, near Combe Sydenham, with Archdeacon Barret of Exeter officiating. There was a small church of medieval origin at Monksilver, with a rector named John Pope, but the register does not survive. In any case, the date ascribed to the marriage by Philip Sydenham is disproved by the marriage settlement of 9 February, which speaks of a marriage 'already had and solemnized between himself and Elizabeth'. Sir George Sydenham and his wife were eventually laid to rest beneath stone effigies and an elaborate canopy next to the altar of the neighbouring church of St Mary, in Stogumber, but the registers at the Somerset Record Office in Taunton contain no reference to Drake's marriage. The couple may have been married in London, where Drake was generally attending Parliament at the turn of 1584 and 1585.

# CHAPTER FOURTEEN

# PLAYING THE DRAGON

The general minding to depart
Commands his men in haste aboard,
Then lifting up both hands and heart
Most thankfully they praise the Lord,
For giving them such victory
Without bloodshed or jeopardy.

Thomas Greepe, *True and Perfect News of . . .
Syr Frauncis Drake*, 1587

THE WAR WAS COMING. MOST ACUTE OBSERVERS COULD SEE THAT. PHILIP II WAS
not always a decisive man, and his removal to the monastery of San Lorenzo
de Escorial, the great palace at the base of the barren Sierra de Guaderrama,
seemed to emphasize his need for an isolated place in which to contemplate, to
worship, and to plan. But as he sifted through the enormous piles of papers
beneath the magnificent ceilings of the Escorial, or kissed the relics of the saints
that he so assiduously collected, even he understood that a decisive confrontation
between England and Spain could not long be avoided. He thought he knew how
to handle it, too. Time seemed to be on his side. The union with Portugal had
given him the basis of a fleet that could challenge Elizabeth's navy, the beginnings
of a vast armada, and Santa Cruz's defeat of Strozzi and capture of Terceira suggested that at least he knew how to use it. The caution that had once warned
Philip against antagonizing England while France was still a powerful rival also
diminished as the French slid towards another civil war. After the death of Elizabeth's French sweetheart, Alençon, his brother, the king, had no obvious heir except the Huguenot Henry of Navarre, and the Catholic League and the influential
Duke of Guise were willing to accept Spanish money to oppose him. Divided,
France was less of a problem. And the Netherlands? The champion of the Dutch,
William of Orange, was dead, struck by an assassin's bullet in 1584, and Parma's
mixture of diplomatic and military skill was slowly reducing the rebellious provinces to order. Even now he was poised for his most dramatic achievement, the
capture of Antwerp, one of the last pockets of resistance south of the Maas. A
conviction was growing in Europe that the war in the Netherlands was reaching its
finale, one which would leave England bereft of useful allies and staring across the
Channel towards a hostile coast, standing almost alone in the path of Spain.
Then, Philip reckoned, would be the time to deal with the heretical queen and
her pirates.

In England that summer of 1585 Dutch envoys begged for help to save Antwerp, urging Elizabeth to intervene more decisively in Europe while there was still
time. As a monarch she might resist encouraging rebellion against a legitimate
king; as a housekeeper she shrank from the expense of war; but as a patriot, a

sovereign of her realm, could she see the Dutch fall for want of friends when the result would have been England's isolation? She wavered, but then in June a little London trading bark, the *Primrose*, returned home with a fearful tale of Spanish treachery that raised outrage throughout the country. Like many another foreigner, the *Primrose* had been exporting grain to Spain, where the crops had failed, but in May Philip suddenly declared an embargo on English vessels in Spanish ports, and had them stripped of their arms, munitions and tackle to equip his fleet at Seville and Lisbon. The *Primrose* was boarded in the Bay of Bilbao, but fought free and escaped, and when she reached England her crew were able to show a document they had captured, which was no less than Philip's instructions to Spanish officials for the seizure of English ships.

In the rising indignation Elizabeth was pushed into action. She did not declare war, at least not directly, for she clung to the increasingly tattered notion that acts of war need not necessarily mean war. They might be legitimate but limited reprisals for injuries, such as Philip's embargo or the involvement of his ambassador, Mendoza, in a recent plot against the queen's life, and yet fall short of all-out conflict. But she went further than she had ever done before: she agreed that an army must be sent to the Netherlands to prop up the ailing Dutch rebellion until Philip would grant satisfactory terms, and she unleashed Sir Francis Drake upon the Spanish coast. Now, for the first time, the great sailor was given the queen's commission, signed on 1 July, 1585 and authorizing him to visit the ports of Spain to release the English ships and crews impounded by Philip. Better still, as far as Drake was concerned, commissions of reprisal were issued to merchants whose property had been lost in Spain, enabling them to recoup their losses by plunder. Under their colour, Drake could rove in search of booty and honour wherever he chose.

A document endorsed 25 April, 1586, but probably prepared the previous November, suggests the itinerary Sir Francis had tentatively set himself. He planned to raid the Cape Verde Islands, cross the Atlantic and reprovision at Dominica before the end of November, and then capture Margarita, Santo Domingo, Rio de la Hacha and Santa Marta in the next month. During January and February he might be able to reduce Cartagena, Nombre de Dios and Panama, the last with the help of 5,000 *cimarrones* Drake hoped to recruit in the isthmus, and the fleet would conclude the campaign with the capture of Havana. Since most of the English ships seized by the Spanish had been released before Drake reached the Spanish coast, there seemed to be more time for what was, in fact, an overimaginative and overcrowded schedule that left no room for misadventure.

Ambitious it was. And it exemplified the combination of strategic and economic motives that underlay so much Elizabethan endeavour. If it succeeded, Spain would be virtually ripped out of the Caribbean by the roots, and there was even a suggestion that the English might leave a permanent garrison in Havana themselves. The profit motive also ran through the entire document, which bristled with optimistic allusions to the expected returns: Santo Domingo would yield 500,000 ducats; Cartagena, a million ducats; Panama, a million ducats, and so on. This mercenary footing was inevitable in an expedition that cost more than £60,000 to outfit and was funded by private enterprise, but it was not, it should be noted, incompatible with strategic or national interest. Although sometimes described as a grand privateering raid, Drake's voyage was not motivated by purely commercial ends. Money was needed by the queen to finance her new initiative in the Netherlands; very well then, let Drake supply it. And, with Philip starved of his American treasure, it was supposed that his military offensive in Europe would come to a halt. 'That,' chirped Leicester to Burghley, 'is the string that toucheth him indeed, for whiles his riches of the Indies continue, he thinketh he will be able with them to weary out all other princes. Those taken away, himself will quickly fall. And I know by good means that he more feareth this action of Sir Francis than he ever did anything that hath been attempted against him.'[1] Drake and his collaborators were fully attuned to the political dimension of their new project.

The composition of the fleet Drake assembled between June and September reflected the entrepreneurial side of the enterprise. It would be a joint-stock venture, in which the queen contributed two naval vessels, the *Elizabeth Bonaventure* of some 600 tons and 250 or more men, and the *Aid* of 250 tons. The *Bonaventure* was not new. Purchased from a Hull merchant in 1567, she had been rebuilt, but painted in black and white, and, the largest ship in the fleet, she looked impressive, 'the best conditioned ship of the world,' thought Thomas Bayly.[2] Drake took her as his flagship, and appointed as her captain Thomas Fenner, one of the famous seafaring family, and a thorough professional. The *Aid* was commanded by Edward Winter, son of Sir William and cousin to the John Winter who had sailed with Drake to the Strait of Magellan.

As usual court and peerage were well represented. The earls of Rutland, Shrewsbury and Bedford seem to have invested money in the venture, and Shrewsbury supplied the *Talbot* bark. Leicester contributed the *Galleon Leicester*, commanded by his brother-in-law, Francis Knollys, and the tiny *Speedwell*. Some of the main investors were connected with the navy. Sir William Winter provided the *Sea Dragon*; the Lord Admiral, now Charles, Lord Howard of Effingham, the *White Lion*, captained by James Erisey, a West Country man; and the Hawkins brothers, the *Bark Bond* (Captain Robert Crosse), the *Hope*, the *Bark Hawkins* (Captain William Hawkins the younger), probably the *Galliot Duck* (Richard Hawkins), and possibly also the *Bark Bonner*, whose captain, George Fortescue, had been one of Drake's circumnavigators. A number of the vessels, fitted by Drake himself, reflected the names of their owner's family. The *Thomas Drake* (formerly the *Bark Hastings*) was commanded by the brother whose name she bore. Thomas Moone of Plymouth, who shared all of Drake's voyages, took charge of the *Francis*, and the *Elizabeth Drake*, often called 'the little Elizabeth' to distinguish her from the *Bonaventure* and captained by John Varney, proclaimed Drake's new lady to the world.

Most of the remaining ships belonged to the merchants of London and Ply-

---

[1] Leicester to Burghley, 29 January, 1586, Butler, et. al., ed., *Cal. State Papers Foreign*, 20: 330-2. The principal documents dealing with this voyage are contained in Corbett, ed., *Papers Relating to the Navy During the Spanish War*; Keeler, ed., *Sir Francis Drake's West Indian Voyage*; Wright, ed., *Further English Voyages to Spanish America*; and Palencia, ed., *Discurso de el Capitan Francisco Draque* (appendices).
[2] Bayly to Shrewsbury, 27 July, 1586, Owen, ed., *Bath MSS*, 5: 71-2.

mouth. The Town Corporation of Plymouth ploughed some money into the voyage, but the most important merchantmen were the *Primrose* and the *Tiger*, both apparently the property of the City traders. The 400-ton *Primrose* served as vice-admiral under that hard-nosed seaman ('harsh and violent' someone called him) Martin Frobisher, while the 150-ton *Tiger* was commanded by a stepson of Walsingham, Christopher Carleill, the lieutenant-general of the expedition. All in all, it was an imposing fleet, some twenty-five ships and eight or more pinnaces, the largest England had ever sent from home waters.

Drake was equally satisfied with his personnel. The captains of the *Thomas Drake*, *Francis*, *Bark Bonner*, *Bark Hawkins*, and *Benjamin* had sailed with him around the world, and he could vouch for them, while others, like Edward Gilman of the *Scout*, James Erisey and Richard Hawkins, were well known to him. The twelve companies of soldiers, who formed a great part of the two thousand or more who composed Drake's force, were largely inexperienced and unskilled, but Carleill knew his business, and with his sergeant-major, Anthony Powell, and two 'corporals of the field', Matthew Morgan and John Simpson, would soon knock them into shape. Prima donnas were less welcome, however, and Sir Francis suddenly found himself lumbered with two men who epitomized everything in Elizabethan gallantry: poets, politicians, courtiers both, Sir Philip Sidney and Sir Fulke Greville, hotfoot from London to Plymouth and waiting to sail. Drake's heart must have sunk.

Sidney had sat with Drake in Parliament and was, besides, Master of the Ordnance, so Drake knew something of him. He also remembered Sir Philip's father from his service in Ireland, and even better the poet's uncle, none other than Leicester himself. Sidney's spirit and generosity probably appealed to Drake, but was he capable of the serious business in hand? Besides, the queen knew nothing of her favourite's flight, and was sure to take it badly. Sidney and Elizabeth were not on the best of terms. He was disappointed at her failure to appoint him Governor of Flushing, and rather than kick his heels at court in pique he wanted to sail away without the courtesy of consulting his sovereign. Not only that, but neither Greville nor Sidney was likely to remain unobtrusive. Somehow Greville got himself named as captain of the *Hope*, and Sidney began interfering by insisting that one of his protégés should replace old William Hawkins as captain of the *Sea Dragon*. Drake's instinct for survival in a world of patronage, and his unfailing attention to the great, forced him to make the switch, but to salve the old man's feelings he took Hawkins aboard the *Bonaventure* as his own assistant. He owed far more to this veteran sea dog than ever he would owe Sidney.

As if Sidney and Greville were not enough, there now turned up another recruit, the mercurial Dom Antonio, fresh from adventures in France and ready to meddle anew in English affairs. Drake unloaded both Sidney and the pretender on his wife at Buckland Abbey, and while Lady Elizabeth played hostess he grappled with the problem of getting rid of them. He dare not offend the queen by taking Sidney. Twice before, in 1581 and early in 1585, he had laboriously set voyages afoot which Her Majesty had suddenly suppressed for one reason or another. And so he prosecuted his preparations with the greatest speed, and – if Greville's reminiscences are to be believed – secretly allowed the queen to discover that Sidney was with him. As he anticipated, she immediately recalled him, and without waiting longer than it took to disembark Greville and Sidney from the flagship Drake sailed from Plymouth with a fair wind on Tuesday, 14 September, 1585. His departure was so hurried that victualling had not been completed and at least one captain, John Martin, had his commission signed the same day. However, while the courtiers returned to Buckland, which both they and Dom Antonio shortly left for London, Sir Francis led his expedition unfettered into the Channel.[1]

For the first time Drake was trying his hand at managing a large force. The afternoon of sailing he assembled his principal officers aboard the *Bonaventure* to determine procedures to govern the fleet, and the next day the captains and masters received their sailing directions. Drake developed the practice of using them as advisers while confiding more closely in his vice-admiral and lieutenant-general. 'For my own part,' admitted Carleill of his commander, 'I cannot say that ever I had to deal with a man of greater reason or more careful circumspection.'[2]

Everyone knew that the first priority was supplies. Because of the military character of the expedition, the total man-tonnage ratio was high, one man to one-and-a-half tons, and the hasty sailing had prevented the completion of watering and provisioning.[3] Drake would not risk putting into an English port in case even there the queen's caprice aborted his adventure, and trusted to finding a haven in France or Ireland. His luck held. On the 22nd the *Bonaventure* and *Tiger* tried to outsail each other in pursuit of a Biscayan ship laden with fish, and it was Carleill who overhauled her. Equipped with her cargo, Drake had enough food to run for Spain, where he planned with his usual bravado to force his enemies to make good his shortages. Within a week of the capture of the Biscayan the English were sheltering near the mouth of the Vigo River in north-western Spain, where Sir Francis submitted two questions to the local governor at Bayona: was Spain at war with England, and why had Philip impounded English ships?

Don Pedro Bermudez had a problem indeed, for here on his doorstep was the most feared of Englishmen with a great fleet at his disposal. The towns of Vigo and Bayona were at his mercy, and Drake was obviously considering an attack. Some of his men were landed on an island, where they destroyed the images in the chapel, while the admiral himself took Carleill in a rowing boat to inspect the defences of Bayona. But Bermudez was not ready for a showdown, and replied courteously. He knew nothing of a war, he said, and although English shipping had been seized he announced that they had now been released. He went further still, and sent provisions to the English to signal his goodwill – bread, wine, oil, grapes and marmalade.[4]

Drake remained in the river, for the weather was stormy, and on the 28th the sea was so difficult that when the admiral's skiff was sent out in emergencies her

---

[1] Dispatches refer only incidentally to the Sidney affair. A full, but late and probably unreliable account is in Greville, *Life of Sir Philip Sidney*. See also Corbett, *Drake and the Tudor Navy*, 2: 16-21.

[2] Journal of the *Tiger*, 17 September, 1585, Keeler, 73. Drake was considered to be both admiral and general of the expedition, but I have used the former term to avoid confusion.

[3] For the man-tonnage ratio, Andrews, *Drake's Voyages*, 102.

[4] In addition to the above sources, see Bermudez to Santa Cruz, 7 October, 1585, Brown, ed., *Calendar of State Papers . . . in the Archives and Collections of Venice*, 124-5.

crew were promised extra pay. Some of the ships lost their cables and were in danger of running ashore, so they put out to sea and one of them, the *Speedwell*, returned to England. As the weather improved, Drake moved his force up-river to threaten the town of Vigo and seize a small number of boats and caravels. Fearing the worst, the governor assembled about 1,000 horse and foot on the shoreline where the English fleet rode at anchor, and agreed to confront the formidable corsair face to face. There followed a curious pantomime. Drake sent two volunteers, Captain Erisey and Captain Crosse, to the Spaniards as hostages, and Bermudez was then pushed off in their boat and rowed towards the ships. A handkerchief was raised at the water's edge as a signal, and another small boat appeared, pulling from the *Bonaventure*. In it was Francis Drake. He met Bermudez midway between the fleet and the shore, and they parleyed for two hours in the admiral's boat, rising and falling upon the swell. When it was over Drake had what he wanted. He had agreed that the English would leave Bayona and Vigo alone, provided his men could provision and water ashore without molestation.

It must have been an unusual sight, the fraternization that ensued between Englishman and Spaniard, Protestant and Catholic. Drake's men went ashore and rubbed shoulders with the natives, gathering their provisions, while a few Spaniards visited the ships to discover that the terrible dragon of the sea was far from inhospitable. Then, on 11 October, the fleet was gone. Behind it Spain fumed at the humiliation. That Drake should dictate terms on Spanish soil was bad enough. That he should secure Spanish provisions so that he could threaten Spanish possessions made it worse. The king was ill, but his council debated the matter for three consecutive days. Philip's admiral, Santa Cruz, was also in a sweat. Drake, he said, might sweep the Brazilian colonies, raid the Pacific or ravage the West Indies, for there was no force in the whole of the Americas equal to the one he had brought from England. Panama, Santo Domingo, Puerto Rico, Cartagena, Havana and Nombre de Dios – Spain's key strongholds in the Caribbean and on the isthmus – were all at risk. The communications between Spain and the West Indies could be severed, and the *flotas* commandeered. The trouble was that no one knew whither he was bound. Philip, when he addressed the problem, could do little to solve it. He prayed that the *flotas* would reach his kingdom safely, and sent word to the West Indies that Drake was loose. He ordered the convoys bound for the west to remain in Seville, and directed Santa Cruz to defend the coasts of Spain. But the truth was that once again Drake had exposed the weaknesses of Philip's empire. Spain had certainly improved her defences, both in the Pacific and the Caribbean, enough to contain the sort of corsairs that had hitherto troubled her colonies. Yet there was nothing that could handle a fleet such as Drake commanded. By raising the scale of the operations and the level of potential violence, Sir Francis had remained ahead of the game.

For a time it seemed that he might achieve the unthinkable, and capture a homeward-bound treasure *flota*, but he had tarried too long. That bad weather that had penned him in the Vigo River and the necessary but lengthy provisioning had cost him the opportunity. His remarkable good luck deserted him. The Mexican *flota* had sailed in July, tired of waiting for the Peruvian fleet to join it at Havana, and slipped home in September. The Peruvian *flota* was among the richest known, but it ran late, and did not reach Terceira in the Azores until 7 October, when Drake was at Vigo. However, it made San Lucar in the middle of the month as the English were cruising several miles to the north-west, off the Portuguese coast. Drake had missed his prey by a short run indeed, according to his own estimate by a mere twelve hours!

It was a decisive misfortune nonetheless, for it left the admiral without his richest prize. All he could do now was to descend upon the West Indies after the bird had flown. The afternoon of 3 November found the fleet off the Isle of Palma in the Canaries. After conferring with his officers Drake made an attempt to capture the town there, but rough seas and the vigilance of the enemy promised a resistance too stiff for this stage of the voyage. Several pieces of artillery were fired at the ships as they approached. The first shot passed over the *Bonaventure*, but the second was a direct hit. It swept between the admiral's legs, passed Frobisher and Carleill who were walking with him, and smashed into the wooden gallery throwing out splinters which slightly hurt another officer, George Barton. Other shots struck the *Aid* and the *Leicester*, and the flagship received a second ball, close to the waterline. Drake judged it injudicious to attempt a landing, and sailed instead for the Cape Verdes.

His descent upon these Portuguese islands, now united with the Crown of Castile, has been described as a diversion, although since no comprehensive plan of the voyage survives it is difficult to say whether it was part of Drake's itinerary or not. In any case, it was fairly usual for Elizabethan voyagers to make the Atlantic crossing from the Cape Verdes. Having said that, Sir Francis maybe had something else in mind. He was a man who nursed grievances, and constantly justified his private war against Spain by reference to the treachery of San Juan d'Ulua. Against Santiago, the capital of the Cape Verdes, he also had his complaints, for in 1582 the ships of William Hawkins, in which Drake had invested, had been rebuffed there, apparently through some kind of deceit. Little is known of Hawkins's defeat, but it was said that English lives had been lost, and it would be entirely in Drake's character to have decided that the time had come to square the account.

Santiago was situated on the south-western side of the isle which bore its name, and consisted of several substantial houses and a population of perhaps 2,000 people. It lay in the mouth of a low narrow valley, flanked by cliffs and hills, with the sea towards the south. There were numerous gardens, rich in coconut and date palms and fig, lemon and orange trees, but the island's economy was much dependent upon sugar cane, cotton and silk. As for defence, looking seawards there were two batteries near the harbour, and a third covered the western approaches to the town. In all, these 'forts' mounted fifty to sixty pieces of artillery, most of them brass, but they were not in good shape and the town was vulnerable, especially from the east, where no effective works had been established.

Santiago had been unfortunate these past few years, for it had fallen not so long since to French corsairs. Drake dealt it a far harder fate. In the evening of 17 November he landed some 1,000 men under Carleill, east of the town, where they could strike at its weakest point. Then, while his soldiers were scrambling through the darkness over the difficult ground towards Santiago, he took the fleet to menace the harbour and divert the attention of the defenders from the true point of the attack. As it happened the army was not needed. The shore batteries opened fire upon the English ships, but the defence was ill spirited and the towns-people were soon fleeing westwards with their valuables, leaving behind only a few civilians and about twenty-six sick Negroes in the hospital. When Carleill's force reached the town they found that the opposition had fled, and it took but a little time to raise the flag of St George over the principal buildings.

There was little plunder to be had. Seven ships in the harbour were deprived of various commodities and one of them was added to the fleet. Ashore, Drake's men took off the artillery, along with powder, oil, cotton, silk, victuals, fruit and water, even the bells of the steeple. But Drake hoped for a better return by ran-soming the town, and sent a Portuguese who had appeared under a flag of truce to find his governor, with the message that unless negotiations were opened to decide upon what sum would be paid to save Santiago he would raze it to the ground. There was no response to his threat, and Drake did not hesitate to carry it out.

While his men occupied the town, Drake led six hundred soldiers to a nearby village called Santo Domingo. It was a tiring, fruitless episode, for its inhabitants had fled into the countryside taking everything of value with them. The English burned the village, and trudged back to Santiago, Drake and Carleill looking not a little ridiculous as they took turns riding an ass. Parties of enemy horse and foot hovered around, too weak to interfere, but they did pounce upon a straggling English boy and cut off his head and carved out his insides. The next day, 28 November, Drake dispatched another force to march upon Porto Praya, a settle-ment of less than a thousand inhabitants east of Santiago, and then supervised the evacuation of the city itself. With unflinching severity he ordered it destroyed, sparing only the hospital, a warning to those who would not treat with him that he meant his word. Harsh it was, although understandable. Drake's expeditions owed their existence to investors looking for a financial return, and he needed to impress his adversaries that they would have to pay to save their homes. His single-mindedness on the subject was seen soon afterwards, when the fleet reached Porto Praya on the 29th. His men had taken the town, but obtained nothing more worthwhile than two pieces of artillery, and the inhabitants had fled. Drake ordered that it, too, be put to the torch.[1]

To account for such booty as they had acquired, Drake had already laid down instructions governing the conduct of the land forces, enjoining that neither chest nor door be broken open without the authorization of Drake or an appointed officer, and that officers ensure that none of the plunder be purloined for private use. One article will suffice to indicate the flavour of the regulations:

> *Item, for as much as we are bound in conscience and required also in duty to yield an honest account of our doings and proceedings in this action . . . persons of credit shall be assigned, unto whom such portions of goods of special price, as gold, silver, jewels,*

---

[1] The violence to property admitted, there are few grounds for charging Drake with injury to persons at this stage. The journal of the *Primrose* remarks that two prisoners were abused by 'a certain kind of torment' (Keeler, 188), but this is at least vague and possibly exaggerated. One of the prisoners, Octavius Toscano, left a deposition that suggests that he suffered nothing worse than being made to serve at the table.

*or any other thing of moment or value, shall be brought and delivered, the which shall remain in chests under the charge of four or five keys, and they shall be committed into the custody of such captains as are of best account in the fleet.*[1]

Drake may have been an entrepreneur, hungry for profit, but his fault mirrored that of the Elizabethan government, court and city that had backed him, and to which he owed his command. Private enterprise, encouraged by the State, had delivered his voyage, and he must perforce satisfy its expectations.

It was in connection with his regulation of the fleet that Drake experienced the insubordination that always infuriated him, and again at its root were men of birth accustomed to privilege and command. The disaffected coalesced around Francis Knollys, captain of the *Galleon Leicester*, a man of impeccable connections, the son of the Treasurer of the Household, and a blood relative of the queen herself. By marriage he was also related to Leicester. Knollys was not without experience of the sea, but he owed his appointment to the expedition to patronage, and evidently considered himself indispensable to its success. Perhaps Knollys believed that he should have had more to do with the running of the fleet than Drake allowed. He had not always been privy to the admiral's decisions, nor been included in all the councils. That the journal of his ship, written by one of his supporters, has such harsh words for Drake and Carleill is indicative of the jealousy he bore them.

While the fleet was at Santiago Knollys found fresh fuel for his resentment. The *Leicester* journal records that Drake had disposed of the cargoes of the ships taken there no one knew how, and that Carleill had distributed unequal shares of plunder among the soldiers and quartered himself and his land captains in the best houses. If Knollys had originally taken offence at the lack of deference paid to his position, his anger had spilled into charges of corruption. We hear from his ship's journal that much personal plunder was carried aboard the fleet at Santiago. Again, the complaint is clear: the regulations were being flouted, and Drake and Carleill were to blame.

But perhaps it was a curious ceremony of 20 November that first alerted Drake to the problem. He had asked his chaplain, Philip Nichols, to draw up oaths of loyalty which acknowledged the sovereignty of the queen, bound Carleill and the fleet captains in obedience to Drake, and the men in a like condition to their captains. There is no suggestion that Drake produced the oaths other than as a routine assertion of his authority, and highly unlikely that he considered that any of them would be found offensive, for they simply acknowledged the authority structure that already existed in the fleet. However, after Drake had read out the articles of the oaths, he found one captain, and only one, who demurred to swear to them. Francis Knollys declared that he would surely swear to the supremacy of Her Majesty, but he would put his name to no other oath. Drake was probably surprised, particularly inasmuch as Knollys could offer no explanation for rejecting an oath that simply bound him to serve his admiral. The obvious inference was that he did not consider it his duty to obey Drake. We can imagine the fiery Devonian's eyes narrowing at the thought.

For a while the Knollys episode was the talk of the fleet. There was an altercation between Nicholls and Knollys, in which the latter murmured incoherently about oaths 'dangerously like to hazard many men's souls', as if there was a religious dimension to

[1] *Leicester* journal, Keeler, 130-1.

his opposition.[1] The chaplain was not impressed, and the next day, 21 November, being a Sunday, gave him his platform to reply before the whole company. During his sermon Nichols remarked that any who refused to take the oaths were unworthy of the enterprise upon which they had all embarked. This stung Knollys to the quick. After dinner he confronted the chaplain in Drake's presence, assisted by one of his friends, Master Thoroughgood, but the admiral brought the argument to an end by an outburst of fury. He swore that while he could speak for the loyalty of his chaplain, he had no faith in Knollys and Thoroughgood, who had refused the oaths and now sowed sedition and faction. Thoroughgood hardly knew the memories conditioning Drake's thinking, but protested that he was as ready to serve as any. Drake would not have it, and accused Knollys of raising a party against him. 'Yea,' he said. 'You are their defender and maintain them against me.'[2] The affair had become ridiculous. Drake was looking at Knollys and seeing Thomas Doughty, unable to understand his objection to the oath. For his part, Knollys could no more explain it. It was probably an emotional response, a gesture of non-co-operation that arose from his resentment at being slighted during the voyage, but one he found difficult to justify in rational terms. Confronted by a choleric display on the part of the admiral, he assured Drake of the loyalty of his men and suggested that it might be better if they were given a ship to go their own way.

Sir Francis's instinct told him to deal decisively with the matter, and the following day he had every man of the *Leicester* assembled before him and the other captains of the fleet. To them Drake put only one question. Would they stay or return to England with Knollys? Most of them agreed to remain, but Knollys found forty or fifty in his support, and Drake forthwith declared them exempt from further service. He said that he would provide them with a vessel, the *Francis*, and dismiss them. And yet he was unhappy with this solution. He was satisfied that he had unearthed the core of the opposition, but the more he thought about them sailing away, beyond his control, perhaps alerting the Spaniards by plundering, perhaps being captured and revealing what they knew about Drake's intentions, the less he entertained the idea. On the 23rd he sent Knollys three articles to which he required written answers. Would he place his company at Drake's disposal? Was he resolved to leave this service of the queen? And if he was relinquished would he return directly to England? Drake wanted a written acknowledgment that the captain had surrendered his command to the admiral, and returned of his own free will, and he wanted a guarantee that Knollys would not loiter where he could do harm.

On the first and last points Captain Knollys's reply was satisfactory, but the response to the second article was more equivocal. He was unwilling to depart, he affirmed, but rather than be considered 'a mutinous or faction person' and thereby 'an hinderance' to an expedition 'which I desire God to bless and prosper', he desired 'not only to be out of the society but under the waves as deep as there is any bottom.'[3] Drake was still unhappy. Knollys was, after all, not uninfluential in England, and the admiral was reluctant to send him home under a cloud. Although the decision had

[1] *Ibid*, 141.
[2] *Ibid*, 144.
[3] *Ibid*, 146. The account in the journal of the *Leicester* is the only detailed source for this affair.

been endorsed by some of his principal officers, Drake decided to delay enforcing it. Instead, he divided Knollys's supporters among the other ships, where he hoped they could hatch no mischief. The details of this affair have only recently been brought to light, and sharpen our understanding of Thomas Doughty's legacy. The events of Port San Julian weighed heavily upon Drake's shoulders. His extreme sensitivity to insubordination indicates how deeply his emotions ran. Now, at Santiago, those emotions had driven him to engineer a 'mutiny' that should never have occurred. There had been no need of the oaths of loyalty. If they had ever been necessary, they should have been administered in Plymouth, where dissenters could have stepped back without detriment to the voyage. They had simply created and advertised a situation in which up to fifty men had been forced into an act of public disobedience. Probably it would have been far better to have permitted the petulant Knollys to fester privately for the duration of the voyage. But it could not be undone.

There was soon a more serious matter to hand, for after quitting the Cape Verdes the fleet was struck with a virulent disease, and as the ships made their way across the Atlantic it advanced alarmingly. At one time a hundred men were down with it on the *Bonaventure* and sixty aboard the *Primrose*, something like a third of their companies. Two or three hundred men died in a few days, and many others were debilitated, left temporarily weak in body and mind. It was assumed that the disease had been caught at Santiago, but its cause is obscure, and some of the symptoms, the feverishness and spots, indicate that it may have been typhus fever and the product of the insanitary and crowded conditions on board ship rather than a tropical contagion. Drake monitored its progress, and counselled each ship about its management, but it pursued him to the West Indies. A landfall was made in the Leeward Islands, where valuable supplies were loaded, and then the fleet halted at St Kitts. It was uninhabited, and the men could be brought from the fetid ships to rest ashore while cleaning and fumigation took place. The fever began to recede, but even so twenty men were buried on the island.

Despite his reduced force, Drake decided to attack the city of Santo Domingo, situated on the estuary of a river in south-eastern Hispaniola. 'The flower of the west', a contemporary called it; it was the oldest Spanish city in the New World, once the capital of Spain's colonial empire and still comparable in size to most cities in the mother country herself. Santo Domingo was partly sustained by the island's substantial sugar and cattle industry. It boasted sedate and elegant buildings, a cathedral, three monasteries and two nunneries. Yet there was another face to Santo Domingo, one of decline and complacency. It was no longer part of the bullion route, and functioned largely as an administrative and legal centre, and the enervating sunlight in which it lazed revealed the decay of many of its houses. It had been fortified for more than a century, enough to deter the grosser ravages of the corsairs, but it was only strong towards the sea, where a bar protected the harbour and a fort. One governor proclaimed the fort among the strongest in Christendom, perhaps because it sported more guns than any other in the West Indies, but it possessed neither a regular garrison nor an adequate supply of powder. The little powder that was available was so poor in quality that it could scarcely project shot as far as the waterfront. Another battery had been established on the sea front in 1571, but on the whole the city's defences were a fair reflection of Santo Domingo itself: an ageing façade waiting to be exposed.

The governor and captain-general, Licentiate Cristóbal de Ovalle, President of the *Audiencia*, had no professional soldiers to defend the city and depended upon a civilian militia, about eight hundred in the town and its environs, and more in the interior of the island. The numbers that opposed Drake are not known. A Spanish officer, but not one who was present when the English appeared, said that 'there were more than 3,000 men, burghers and transients' capable of being mustered.[1] The governor himself was reluctant to admit so high a figure, and reported that about 1,500 met Drake's attack. Whatever the number, they had no will to fight. Most of them fled, and the bare two hundred or so who gave the principal resistance were poorly armed, many of them carrying only rusty pikes and swords. As for the naval force at Santo Domingo, there was only one galley, and it was unseaworthy.

Away from the sea the situation was even worse, despite the fears some citizens harboured of a rebellion by the several thousand blacks, mixed bloods and Indians who inhabited the island. The Spaniards had started walling the western and northern boundaries of the town, but the work was unfinished, dogged by financial problems and disputes about how far to the west and north the wall should actually run. In any case, some did not take the threat of attack from the west, at least from Europeans, very seriously. A practical landing place surely existed ten miles in that direction, at the mouth of the Hayna River, but it was only approachable through dangerous reefs and a heavy surf, and the path from the Hayna to Santo Domingo threaded through difficult jungle. So complacent were the Spaniards that when Drake arrived the wall amounted to only a few short stretches flanking the western gate, and there was no regular watch at the Hayna.

These were serious flaws to present to a man like Drake, who had spent fifteen years wiping smiles from smug faces. Now it was the turn of the West Indian cities to learn that lesson, and as his fleet passed through the Caribbean he had a useful piece of good fortune. From two or three prizes made on his way to Santo Domingo, he captured a useful pilot and the letters Philip II had sent to the West Indies warning them of Drake's approach. Santo Domingo was caught napping. The city had heard that an English force had put to sea, but knew not where it was bound. And although a fishing boat reported seeing a large fleet nearby on 31 December, it was not until nightfall that an investigating frigate returned with the fearsome tidings that the ships were probably English. By then it was too late.

Santo Domingo fell in one New Year's Day. In the early hours, while it was yet dark, Sir Francis Drake personally piloted his soldiers through the difficult shoals and surf at Hayna, and landed them from pinnaces and small boats before returning to his fleet to lead it to the city.[2] There the governor was dithering nervously. A force was rudely assembled during the night, and Ovalle's officers strengthened the harbour by sinking three ships on the shallows of the bar and positioning the solitary galley where her guns could rake an intruder. Earthworks were erected ashore, one with a parapet and cannon. Yet so little confidence did the Spaniards have that many began fleeing the city before it was light. When the sun rose that 1 January, 1586, it revealed Drake's

---

[1] Alonso Rodriguez de Azebedo to Diego Fernandez de Quiñones, 22 January, 1586, Wright, 25-7.

[2] Corbett's view that Drake contacted the *cimarrones* of Santo Domingo, who finished off the watchmen by the Hayna so that Drake could land unopposed, is founded only upon an unsupported intelligence report and is likely incorrect (Corbett, *Spanish War*, 79-80).

fleet tacking into position off the bar, while westwards, and still undiscovered by the enemy, were Christopher Carleill and his men, marching purposefully to the admiral's support.

Now Sir Francis realized how weak this great city was, for when the supposedly formidable forts opened fire their shot fell short, apart from one that crashed through the *Bonaventure*. Even when the English pressed close to the waterfront and began sweeping the town's defences with their artillery – one cannonball killed a Spaniard in his house – they suffered nothing in the reply. While Drake worried the city, drawing its attention, Carleill brought his men forward in good order, and it was not until noon that his approach was detected. A scrappy force of horse and foot came out to skirmish, but they were driven back by English arquebus fire. Then the Spaniards drove a herd of cattle towards the invaders, hoping to break their formation, only to see the frenzied animals scatter into the brush. Before long Carleill's troops were gazing upon the gates to the city. There were two of them on this west side, the Lenba or main gate, and another, nearer the sea side, and they were pitifully defended by the few Spaniards who had not already fled, possibly less than two hundred indifferently armed men. They proved no match. Carleill led a part of his force against the main gate, while Captain Powell's column stormed the other, and neither met appreciable opposition. Casualties did not exceed four killed on either side before the English surged through into the town, scattering the Spaniards before them. By the end of the afternoon St George's ensign was fluttering above the royal palace and the church of Santa Barbara, and the city's officials had fled, including the governor. Ovalle had been conspicuously absent during much of the fighting, and it was said that his horse had fallen in a muddy street and he had gone to his house for a change of clothes. Nevertheless, when he quit the town he left his wife and nieces behind. The only remaining pocket of resistance, the fort, held out until nightfall, but it was not prepared for an attack from the land, and the men evacuated it during the darkness, some flying up-river in boats and a few becoming captives of the English.

Drake had his men erect defences and batteries to deter any counter-attack, and made his headquarters in the cathedral. The privateers set to looting, rifling private homes and public buildings, desecrating the churches of the hated Papists and gutting the cathedral of its ornaments and images, its crucifixes and bells, and turning two of its chapels into common gaols. It did not take long to discover that the wealth of Santo Domingo had been overestimated. A good deal of plunder was obtained – hides, victuals, wine, vinegar, oil, olives, livestock, and some money, including 16,000 ducats from the royal treasury – but the haul was disappointing. However, there was still the matter of a ransom. On 12 January the High Sheriff of Santo Domingo, Juan Melgarejo, came to see Drake, authorized by the homeless *Audiencia* to negotiate a sum to save the city from destruction. Drake's opening bid was one million ducats, but although talks went into the night Melgarejo insisted that that sort of money was simply unavailable. Sir Francis wanted to make sure that he was not lying, and after the sheriff had left he began to apply a grim form of pressure. First he had a chapel a mile north of the town set on fire, and then he detailed men to begin a systematic destruction of Santo Domingo itself. The work was hard, because most of the buildings were of stout stone, and days were passed in laborious toil.

But there shortly came the king's factor, Garcia Fernández de Torrequemada, to reopen the discussions. Argument and counter-argument followed, and the factor was allowed to send someone to assess the worth of the remaining houses. At the end of it Drake could only get 25,000 ducats, and he had to threaten to suspend negotiations to secure even that amount. It was not an inconsiderable sum, and, with the money from the royal treasury, raised the English takings to an equivalent of £11,275, but it was far less than the privateers had anticipated.

While he was haggling with Drake, Philip's factor was able to observe the most legendary of Englishmen at close hand, and later committed his impressions to paper:

> Francis Drake knows no language but English, and I talked with him through inter-
> preters in Latin or French or Italian. He had with him an Englishman who under-
> stood Spanish a little and sometimes acted as interpreter. Drake is a man of medium
> stature, blonde, rather heavy than slender, merry, careful. He commands and
> governs imperiously. He is feared and obeyed by his men. He punishes resolutely.
> Sharp, restless, well-spoken, inclined to liberality and to ambition, vainglorious,
> boastful, not very cruel. These are the qualities I noted in him during my negotiations
> with him.[1]

Who will gainsay that it is not an accurate portrait! One remark, in particular, calls for attention: that Drake was 'not very cruel'. The significance of it can only be gauged from the fact that it was written by a man who must have been familiar with the most barbaric act of Drake's career. Despite it, Torrequemada recognized that, within his context, the English commander was not inhumane.

There are three accounts of the ferocious incident that occurred during Drake's occupation of Santo Domingo. The central figure in it was a black boy attached to the English side. He may have come with the fleet, or been one of the galley slaves Drake liberated when he captured the city. He may even have been among a number of blacks who came from the interior to join the English. With exaggeration it was re-ported in Europe that Drake 'behaved with such humanity to the Indians and Negroes that they all love him and their houses were open to all English.'[2] Whoever he was, the boy was sent by Drake to the Spaniards to carry a message under a flag of truce. One of them took offence. Perhaps he recognized a former slave. Perhaps he merely condemned the envoy because he was a black man. He took a lance and thrust it into the boy's body. Mortally wounded, the messenger struggled back to the city and died at Drake's feet.

The admiral rose in the grimmest fury, and nothing he ever did matched the feroc-ity of his vengeance for the Negro boy. He had a few prisoners in the cathedral, and he ordered two Dominican friars, harmless, innocent men both, to be brought out and hauled to some gallows he had caused to be erected on a spot visible to the Spaniards. They were both hanged, and Drake released a third and more fortunate prisoner to go and explain to the Spaniards why he had done it. Two prisoners a day would be exe-cuted, he told them, unless the murderer of the black messenger was surrendered or punished. It was enough, for the offender was hanged by his own countrymen. It may be that some of them were ashamed of what he had done, and one eye-witness gave out that Drake had hanged the friars because they had opposed the teachings of one of

---

[1] Torrequemada to the Crown, 4 February, 1587, Wright, 220-5.
[2] Vincenzo Gradenigo to the Doge, April 1586, Brown, 155-6.

the English Lutheran parsons!

In handling his own men, Sir Francis appeared in a happier mood. He even found a solution for the Knollys problem, which had been left simmering all the way across the Atlantic. Now the unfortunate subject of the argument was pressing Drake to make a decision, and at one time the *Bark Hawkins* was being prepared to ship Knollys and his malcontents back home. But on 10 January the admiral attempted a reconciliation with his errant captain. Fenner was hosting a dinner, and Drake used the occasion to draw Knollys and Captain Winter into a private room, where he declared that if only Knollys would accept the oath of allegiance he would be used as well as any man – nay, better, for Drake would allow him to act as rear-admiral. This was a generous offer, and one Sir Francis must have found difficult to make, but it struck to the root of the problem by raising Knollys's status in the fleet. Remarkably, the stupid man rejected it, and still insisted on returning on the *Bark Hawkins* as originally planned. It took several weeks for him reluctantly to accept the suggestion and bury the miserable squabble for the rest of the voyage.

By the end of January 1586 the ransom for Santo Domingo had been paid, and the English, much behind their schedule, were ready to leave. Behind was left a sorrowful sight, the humiliation of a proud city, the worst blow Philip had yet suffered in the New World. A third of the houses had been destroyed, along with the churches, monasteries, nunneries and the castle. The governor's house had been stripped of anything valuable and the cathedral was an empty shell. The naval galley and twenty or so small barks had been burned, and a few captured ships had been taken away, to replace three discarded English vessels, the *Hope, Benjamin* and *Scout.* As the inhabitants drifted back to their broken homes in the smoking city there was much anguish and despair. Torrequemada bewailed that 'this thing must have had Divine sanction, as punishment for the people's sins.' Another official informed Philip that 'the destruction of this, Your Majesty's city, and the evils which have befallen us, Your Majesty's servants and vassals, cannot be recounted without tears.' And yet another inhabitant put it more simply still. 'Nothing remains,' he said, 'but life itself.'[1]

---

[1] Rodrigo Fernández de Ribera to the Crown, 30 June, 1586, Wright, 178-80; deposition, 20 February, 1586, Klarwill, ed., *Fugger News-Letters*, 1: 89-93.

CHAPTER FIFTEEN

# 'A FEARFUL MAN TO THE KING OF SPAIN!'

> Ulysses with his navy great
> In ten years' space great valour won;
> Yet all his time did no such feat
> As Drake within one year hath done.
> Both Turk and Pope and all our foes
> Do dread this Drake where'er he goes.
>
> Greepe, *True and Perfect News of . . .*
> *Syr Frauncis Drake*, 1587

DRAKE'S NAME WAS RINGING THROUGHOUT EUROPE, AND RUMOURS CASCADED from dispatches and newsletters in speedy succession. Many dealt only in the marvellous, and credited the most extravagant fictions, while their numerous contradictions fed uncertainty and generated excitement from England to Italy. He had liberated 12,000 slaves and inspired a black rebellion in Hispaniola by one account, and been attacked by the Negroes in another. He passed through the seas like a conqueror, leaving gutted cities and ravaged ships in his wake, said some; he had met disaster in the Canaries and his fleet was decimated by disease, countered others. There were reports that he had been defeated at Havana, or indeed achieved nothing at all; and others that not an important town in the West Indies had escaped destruction and ransack, and that he had gathered great wealth. It was said that the flagship of the Peruvian *flota* had been taken, and twenty-six ships and 300,000 ducats off the coast of Portugal. The truth was that no one in Europe knew. Everywhere there was a state of expectancy and apprehension. Ailing as he was, Philip summoned Santa Cruz to the Escorial for his counsel. And in the Vatican the Pope reflected upon this bold English heretic. 'God only knows what he may succeed in doing!' he protested.[1]

The fall of Santo Domingo sent a shockwave through the Caribbean, creating a general state of confusion and fear. Men were mustered and defences inspected, even in Santa Fé de Bogatá, the capital of New Granada (Colombia), where it was believed that Drake might march into the interior. However, it was Cartagena, the principal city on the Spanish Main, that he was after. An important port used by both the outward- and homeward-bound *flotas*, it was smaller than Santo Domingo, but better defended. Moreover, before Drake's arrival it had received warnings of danger, first from Seville and then more directly from Santo Domingo, which advised the city that the English were on their way. There was no question

---

[1] Giovanni Gritti, Venetian Ambassador to the Doge and Senate, May 1586, Brown, ed., *Calendar of State Papers . . . in the Archives and Collections of Venice*, 168. There are numerous contemporary reports in Butler, et. al., ed., *Calendar of State Papers, Foreign*; Hume, ed., *Calendar of Letters and State Papers . . . in the Archives of Simancas*; Klarwill, ed., *Fugger News-Letters*; Lemon, ed., *Calendar of State Papers, Domestic*; Corbett, ed., *Papers Relating to the Navy During the Spanish War*.

of Sir Francis surprising the Spaniards here. They had evacuated their non-combatants from the city, removed everything portable that was valuable, and improved their defences. Men had been raised from Cartagena, Tolu and Mompox, pikes had been renewed and arquebuses repaired. The city itself was not easy of access. It rested on the coast, but there were few places nearby suitable for disembarking soldiers, and frequent north-easterly winds made it difficult for ships to maintain a position off shore for any length of time. The land to the east of the city was swampy, and the Spaniards had made some defences there. The obvious place from which to launch an attack was the harbour, a mile or more west of the city, for it presented a safe haven for the fleet and gave direct access to the town, and it was there that Drake headed on the afternoon of 9 February, 1586. To reach it the fleet sailed impudently past the city, with the governor and his forces drawn up on the beach as spectators to its progress, and through the Boca Grande passage which led into the outer of two harbours that served the town. Drake anchored, unable to get closer. The Boquerón Channel that linked the outer and inner harbours had been sealed by a strong chain, and was defended by a stone fort, and when Sir Francis later sent Frobisher to tease the garrison with a diversionary attack his ships were forced to retire. Unlike Santiago and Santo Domingo, this was going to be a battle only the army could win.

For opposition, Governor Don Pedro Fernandez de Busto had between 1,500 and 2,000 men, of whom some 600, half of them slaves, were aboard two fighting galleys, the Santiago (Captain Juan de Castaneda) and the Ocasión (Captain Martin Gonzales), moored in the inner harbour. Ashore, he had upwards of 1,000 more defenders, consisting of about 600 Spaniards and free blacks, including 50 horse under Captain Francisco de Carvajal, and perhaps 400 Indian levies, armed with bows and poisoned arrows. It was by no means a contemptible number, but a weak force nonetheless, relying upon a civilian militia with little stomach for fighting. The men were well armed, and had recently completed drill, but they continued to perform manoeuvres badly. In this they were not dissimilar to the English, and Captain Alonso Bravo, whose company failed to set up firing lines in the actual battle, believed that Drake's men were clumsier than his own. The crucial difference was morale. The fate of Santo Domingo had chilled the Spaniards, and although the governor and his military adviser, Pedro Vique y Manrique, had mustered them for inspiring exhortations, they could instil no spirit into them. When the fighting started the English were prepared to press the attack; their adversaries were not.[1]

The other decisive problem bedevilling the Spanish defence was its dispersed

[1] Dean of Cartagena to Alonso de la Tome, 16 February, 1586, Wright, ed., Further English Voyages to Spanish America, 29-31; Martin Gonzales deposition, 27 April, 1586, Ibid, 70-80; account enc. by Don Luis Guzman and Alonso de Tapia, 1 June, 1586, Ibid, 150-60; Vique y Manrique to the Crown, 5 April, 1586, Ibid, 62-4; return of the forces, Corbett, 19. In addition to the forces on the galleys there was a small crew aboard the oared Napolitana. Estimates of the numbers of defenders on shore vary greatly. The dean gave 650 Spaniards and 800 Indians. Vique y Manrique (deposition, 3 May, 1586, Wright, 100-15) made the Spanish land force 589, including 25 blacks. The official return has 624. Captain Bravo's deposition (Ibid, 115-29) gives 550, and the governor and Diego Hidalgo Montemayor put it lower still, at 450 (Montemayor to the Crown, 23 May, 1586, and De Busto to the Crown, 25 May, 1587, Ibid, 129-47).

nature. The governor had to cover numerous points against which an attack might be made. Fifty of his men were holding the fort at the Boquerón Channel. Others were guarding Hanged Man's Swamp, to the east of the city, and San Francisco Bridge, which linked Cartagena with its hinterland to the south-east. And the largest single force was waiting grimly at the Caleta, the narrows of a neck of land that extended westwards and formed an arm that enclosed the lagoon from which the two harbours were made. To cover all the options, therefore, the Spaniards were divided between several places too far apart to provide mutual support. Drake, on the other hand, could concentrate the bulk of his men into a single thrust.

Cartagena's material defences, like those of Santo Domingo, successfully deterred the ordinary freebooter, but were scarcely an obstacle to Drake. For this the governor bore some responsibility. Old, resistant to advice, and preferring chess to fighting, De Busto's twelve years in office had failed to impress upon him the importance of defence. He had replaced a few of the city's iron guns with bronze ones, and secured a few more, but the most essential fortifications had been neglected. The only strongpoint was the eight-gun fort overlooking the Boquerón Channel. There were no works on the point of the land encircling the harbour, and the Caleta was walled only for part of its width. Word of Drake's approach had driven the Spaniards to throw up batteries and entrenchments in the streets leading to the waterfront, but the only substantial recent improvement in defence had been the supply of the *Santiago* and *Ocasión* galleys in 1578, and even these were now of doubtful utility. With another oared vessel, the *Napolitana*, and a tender, the *Santa Clara*, they lay sealed inside the inner harbour, defended by the fort and the chain across the Boquerón Channel, totally incapable of contesting a fleet such as Drake's.

During the night of 9-10 February Sir Francis landed Carleill with nearly 1,000 men on the point and left them to march upon the Caleta while the fleet made as impressive a display as it could. As the soldiers made their way through the darkness they found that the enemy Indians had driven poisoned stakes into the path, and had to bypass them by occasionally wading through the shallows by the beach. Ahead was the Caleta, a neck of land only some 150 paces across from the harbour in the south to the sea on the north side. Here, behind a wall with an outer ditch, was the principal Spanish force with a four-gun battery, but the defences were flawed because of an incredible thirty-yard gap in the wall, from its northern extremity to the sea-side. True, it had been plugged by a crude barricade of wine butts filled with sand, but it was on the wrong side of the Caleta to be effectively supported by fire from the ten guns of the galleys in the inner harbour.

About three hundred Spaniards and two hundred Indians, dubiously supervised by the governor, manned the wall at the Caleta. Some of them ventured out to try to ambush the advancing army, but when they gauged its size they soon scuttled back, protesting that they would not commit suicide. It was about an hour before dawn, on the blackest of nights, that Carleill's column eventually reached

---

Figures for the Indian force are most disparate, with the return given by Corbett stating 100 and an eyewitness ('the sack of Cartagena', Wright, 46-52) 1,000. Vique put it at 400.

the Caleta, stealthily moving forward in the darkness like an enormous caterpillar. Then someone struck a match and the light was seen from one of the Spanish galleys resting close by. As the English emerged from thickets on the beach they were greeted by a burst of artillery and small-arms fire, first from the galleys and then from the wall, and in the ensuing uproar a brief exhilaration enthused the Spaniards. 'Come on, heretic dogs!' called one.[1] But the galleys were firing too high, and Carleill's attack was made on the other side of the Caleta, where he threw his men against the flimsy wine-butt barricade with a cry of 'God and St George!' So impetuous was the assault that the Spaniards at the wall had no time to recharge their arquebuses. There was a brief clash of pikes, and then the defenders broke, running pell-mell towards the city with the English on their heels. A few examples of Castilian courage occurred. Captain Alonso Bravo, one of three captains of infantry, was taken prisoner after being wounded six times, while a standard bearer stood his ground until Carleill himself cut him down. Most simply followed the example of their governor, and ran for their lives.

As Spaniard and Englishman tumbled into the city together, the hastily improvised redoubts guarding the streets were abandoned in panic. A few Indian bowmen inflicted casualties upon the invaders by firing poisoned arrows from houses, and a detachment of defenders under Captain Martin Polo briefly rallied at San Francisco Bridge, but neither was able to retard Carleill's progress, and the town was soon in his possession. In the harbour the position of the galleys was now hopeless, for they were trapped behind a chain that had been designed to protect them. Captain Gonzalez aboard the *Ocasión* made a run for it, promising his galley slaves reduced sentences of servitude if they would take him out to sea. His vessel did reach the chain, but there it had to wait while someone went to the *Santiago* to fetch a key to unlock it. Unfortunately, Captain Castaneda had problems of his own. Momentarily inspired by Polo's stand at the bridge, he tried to land men to reinforce him, but as the hopelessness of further resistance became apparent, the disembarked crew simply scattered into the countryside. The ship was then run aground near the fort and abandoned. Fear now spread to the trapped *Ocasión*, and her men were soon out of control, despite the captain who tried to reduce them to order with a sword in hand. In the confusion a powder barrel was ignited and the ship was enveloped in flames. Some of the sailors plunged into the water, while others piled into an overloaded skiff to pull for the shore, beating the swimmers away from the boat with their oars. Less lucky, three or four galley slaves burned to death. As night fell the remains of both galleys lay aground and deserted, and Vique sent detachments to complete their destruction so that Drake could not capture them. The English did not, however, go entirely empty-handed, seizing the *Napolitana*, *Santa Clara*, and a few other vessels they cornered in the harbour.

It took another day to force the Spaniards in the fort at the Boquerón Channel to evacuate their position, and on 11 February Drake was master of Cartagena, a city he had merely taunted in his early raids along the Main. He had taken sixty or more brass ordnance, and used them to entrench his men in the town, while he

[1] Deposition of Pedro Vique y Manrique, Wright, 100-15.

took for his own headquarters the house of his prisoner, Alonso Bravo, reputed the best residence in the area. Reflecting upon the cost of his victory, he cannot have been dissatisfied. Twenty-eight of his men had been killed and others wounded. The Spanish losses may have been even lighter, for not more than nine Spaniards died in the fighting. A few galley slaves perished in the flames of the *Ocasión*, and the Indians probably sustained casualties, but it is doubtful that in all the enemy losses were higher than Drake's. About ten Spaniards were taken prisoner.

With Alonso Bravo reluctantly serving as host, Sir Francis now held court, attending to the details of the occupation. Sickness had reappeared in the fleet, and he ordered wells to be dug in a search for clean water. To protect the numerous captives of the Spanish whom he released Drake issued 'a general commandment given for the well usage of . . . Frenchmen, Turks and Negroes', and he recruited several into his forces.[1] A hundred Turks accompanied the fleet back to England, where the government sent them home by the Levant Company, and used them as a basis for a rapprochement with the Ottoman Porte. There was also the crucial matter of plunder. Although the Spaniards had stripped the city of valuables, Drake was bargaining upon raising a respectable ransom.

The process began with individuals, such as Alonso Bravo, himself a wealthy city burgher. From him Sir Francis wanted 5,000 ducats covering his release and the preservation of his house and neighbourhood. Between these two men, of conflicting nationality and creed, a rough understanding developed. The Spaniard accepted the misfortunes of war, and knew that Drake must have his money, but he saw much sympathy in the English commander. Bravo's wife, Elvira, who had left Cartagena before the battle, was gravely ill, and Drake granted him leave to visit her, first for a day, and later for longer as the woman's condition deteriorated. With the integrity of the best Spanish gentleman, Bravo always returned, as good as his word. When Elvira died, Bravo asked permission to bury her in a Franciscan priory then held by the English, south of the town. Perhaps Sir Francis was remembering Mary, sleeping in that Plymouth churchyard. Anyway, he understood. The funeral took place according to the Spanish custom. Drake attended, and had his men drawn up; flags were reversed; drums muffled; and a volley fired in honour of a soldier's wife. Sir Francis had wanted 3,000 ducats from the Spaniards to save the priory from destruction, but he assured Bravo that he would not desecrate Elvira's resting place, and reduced the demand to a nominal 600 ducats.

Negotiations for the city's ransom formally opened on 15 February. The governor and a bishop, Fray Don Juan de Montalvo, appeared at Drake's insistence, but Cartagena was generally represented by others, including the lieutenant-governor, Diego Daca, and a merchant named Tristan de Oribe Salazar. Sir Francis fired off a demand for upwards of 400,000 ducats, and the Spaniards countered by offering a mere sixteenth of that amount. As talks faltered, the English resorted to the pressure that had wrung a settlement from Santo Domingo, and Drake set his men to burn parts of the city. After 248 houses (two-thirds of

---

[1] *Leicester* journal, Keeler, ed., *Sir Francis Drake's West Indian Voyage*, 169; Lorenzo Bernardo to Doge and Senate, 1 April, 1587, Brown, 261-2; Dasent, ed., *Acts of the Privy Council of England*, 14: 205-6.

them masonry and tile, and the rest thatch and palmboard) had been destroyed a ransom of 107,000 ducats in bullion was agreed early in March, and for several days heavily laden mule-trains tramped to Captain Bravo's house to discharge the debt. The total sum obtained is unknown. Drake's haul for Bravo, the city, the priory, and a small estate on an island totalled 113,000 ducats' worth, and apparently gold ducats too, equal to up to £48,000 in English money. Yet there were other payments, for Drake dealt with various individuals for their houses and possessions, and some of the prize ships were redeemed by their owners. He refused to treat for the artillery, which was carried off, and he destroyed the fort. The money Drake had taken from Santo Domingo and Cartagena was thus raised to over £50,000, but it was still short of his rosy predictions.[1]

In treating with his enemies, Drake was as courteous, affable and hospitable as usual. His conversation was quick-witted, but full of the bravado so many found irritating, and when he spoke of Philip and the Pope he grew angry and bitter, sparing none of the feelings of the Spaniards about him. The Pope was a dissolute tyrant, and what right had Philip to call Drake a pirate when he himself oppressed so many in Europe and America? But he had no fear of this king, he boasted. He would assemble some pinnaces and ascend the Chagres to destroy Panama, and as for a Spanish fleet that was reportedly being sent after him, he would rather fight it than not. He was not afraid of it.

Behind the façade, Drake was nevertheless far from confident. He was probably depressed by the loss of one of his closest friends, Captain Tom Moone of the *Francis*, the same who had followed him in jungles in Darien and around the world. One day two Spanish barks had innocently entered the harbour, and Tom manned a pinnace with John Varney of the *George* and a few sailors. With two other English boats, they pursued the barks into the shallows of a small island, where one ran aground and its crew leaped over the side to splash ashore. There was no resistance as the first pinnace, under John Grant of the *Tiger*, came alongside and her men boarded the prize to rummage around. When Moone and Varney arrived Grant refused to allow them aboard, perhaps wishing to reserve the credit for the capture to himself. While Moone and Varney stood in their boat remonstrating with Grant a shot was fired ashore. Some Spaniards were seen lurking in the undergrowth, and Varney raised his piece to reply, bidding Moone hold a shield before him as he fired. Then both suddenly received a volley from the island. Varney and Moone fell, each, as it turned out, fatally wounded, Varney in the head and Moone in the right thigh, and four or five other men were injured. Bold John Grant and his comrades now bolted, tumbling into their pinnace and pushing away to safety, and it was left to Captain Fenner, who came up in a third pinnace, to try to flush the Spaniards out by firing into the thickets. Moone lingered a few days and died. His death must have been keenly felt by Drake, for this Plymouth man had not only been one of his oldest shipmates, but a man of unequivocal loyalty. The admiral buried his old comrade in the cathedral of Car-

---

[1] Presumably the 25,000 ducats obtained at Santo Domingo were silver ducats, worth about 5s 6d each. The ransom at Cartagena seems to have been valued as gold ducats, which would have made it worth at least £40,000. For valuations of the ducat see Keeler, 259-60.

tagena, with all the captains in attendance and a volley of shot to salute the passing of one of the most courageous of the Elizabethans.

There was far worse, for a sickness had returned to the fleet, perhaps a re-emergence of the earlier pestilence or possibly dysentery. During the two months that Drake occupied Cartagena it claimed one hundred deaths, among them that of Captain George Fortescue of the *Bark Bonner*. On 27 February the land captains had a meeting to consider whether Cartagena might be held as a permanent English base in the Caribbean. It was desirable, for such a colony would facilitate the disruption of Philip's bullion route, and it might be done, they thought, if provisions were maintained. However, they did not like the idea. Only seven hundred men were fit for service, and disease was still at work. Besides, the voyage had not provided the dividends anticipated, and the force was probably now too reduced to attempt Panama or Havana, especially with a Spanish fleet supposedly on its way.[1] The land captains declared that they would follow Drake whatever he decided, but they suggested he go home. Drake was certainly behind schedule, and was probably no less alarmed about the distemper torturing the expedition than were his officers. He would certainly have been concerned about the dissatisfaction among his men, many of them adventurers who had been in it for the rewards. In view of the problems of maintaining and victualling a healthy force in the area in the face of possible Spanish retaliation, Drake's decision to follow the recommendations of his officers was probably sensible. After a false start he got away from Cartagena in the middle of April and headed for England.

Cartagena was no longer the strongpoint of the Main. It had not a gun to defend itself, and the damage Drake had dealt it was assessed at 400,000 ducats. In wiping eggs from innumerable faces, the citizens had to explain why their city had fallen so easily. Everyone blamed somebody else. Martin Gonzales was explaining the abandonment of his galley, the *Ocasión*. Don Pedro Vique y Manrique, commander of the galleys, was explaining why he had not even been aboard them. Captain Pedro Mexia Mirabel had reasons for his evacuation of the fort, and the treasurer and accountant was looking for reasons to excuse his payment of the city's ransom from Crown funds. The lieutenant-governor exonerated himself for the failure of his men to defend an important bridge and the Franciscan priory. One by one, in depositions and letters, they bailed themselves out by sniping at others, and particularly at the governor, who at least had the wit to warn his sovereign beforehand that it would be so. Considering his own role in the inept defence of the city, De Busto was indeed remarkably frank in his letter to the *Audiencia* of Panama: 'I do not know how to begin to tell your lordship of my misfortune . . . I can only say that it must be God's chastisement of my sins and of those of others.'[2] In that, at least, he had a convincing argument.

At Cuba the English landed to dig wells for fresh water, and the admiral, who never lost the common touch, 'helped to load, and went into the water to his armpits, fully clothed and shod, carrying barrels and demijohns of water.'[3] Then the

---

[1] In fact, the Spanish fleet was so ridden with disease that it put back without ever reaching the West Indies.

[2] De Busto to the Audiencia of Panama, 12 March, 1586, Wright, 52-7.

expedition skirted the east coast of Florida, bound to call upon England's new colony at Roanoke Island, off what is now North Carolina, until on 27 May a Spanish watchtower was observed on shore, marking the proximity of Philip's oldest town in Florida, St Augustine. Drake regarded it as a threat to Walter Ralegh's infant settlement, and the next day disembarked with some of his men and marched up-river until he found himself gazing across the stream at the timber fort of San Juan. Inside it Governor Pedro Menéndez Marquez commanded only seventy to eighty effectives, but he fired upon the English and dispersed them temporarily among the sandhills until Drake could bring up some ordnance. That done, the fort was incapable of effective resistance, and in the night the Spaniards stole away, leaving the English to take possession without more opposition than that of a few bullets fired by the rearguard and a brief demonstration launched in favour of the Spaniards by local Indians. Sir Francis discovered that the governor had fled so quickly that he had left behind a strongbox containing £2,000 worth of money that had been sent from the nearby town to the fort for safe-keeping! Daylight also revealed a number of useful artillery pieces that the English greedily purloined.

A short way upstream reposed the town of St Augustine, a diminutive collection of wooden houses sheltering less than three hundred civilians, all of whom had fled before Drake's men arrived on the 29th. Both town and fort were completely destroyed, including the adjacent orchards and cornfields, but Drake did not harm the Indian village close by, although some warriors had turned out to defend the Spaniards and cost the English a man. Instead he went on his way, north-eastwards, looking for Roanoke, where Ralph Lane commanded the first group of colonists lodged in America under the patent of Walter Ralegh. He did not know exactly where it was, because Richard Grenville, who had shipped the settlers to Roanoke, had not returned to England before Drake had left, but he suspected that it lay about 36° north.

He reached Roanoke on 9 June, and since the anchorage was unable to admit his fleet he had his ships ride outside. Nevertheless, some of the men rowed ashore, and Drake was able to confer with Lane about the progress of the colony. All was not well. Lane's men were largely soldiers, not artisans and farmers. They were interested in exploring, but lacked the skills and knowledge to form a sustainable community, and to provide for themselves they badgered the natives for food and waited for supplies from home. Understandably, the Indians had begun to resent the colonists, while Richard Grenville, who was supposed to have returned with provisions at Easter, had failed to show up. After listening to Lane's woeful story, Drake offered him a choice: the settlers, all 105 of them, could return to England with the fleet; or Drake could give them a ship, pinnaces, some seamen and provisions sufficient to help them find a more suitable harbour, or, if unsuccessful, to come home. Lane wanted to persevere, and the admiral readied the *Francis* with some small boats, food for four months and one hundred men. Unfortunately, the preparations were interrupted by a storm that lasted for three days, and some of the ships, including the *Sea Dragon, Talbot, White Lion* and the

[3] Deposition of Pedro Sanchez, 1586, *Ibid*, 212-14.

important *Francis* were driven out to sea and separated. A few made their own way across the Atlantic.

Hastily revising his plans, Drake offered a substitute vessel, the *Bark Bonner*, and what further provisions he could spare, but Lane and his men had now had enough. They wanted to be taken home. On 18 June the fleet weighed anchor, thus writing an end to yet another English attempt to colonize America. Ironically, within days Grenville at last appeared. He left a few men behind, but none of them survived.[1] Drake himself abandoned a plan to raid Spanish fisheries around Newfoundland because of contrary winds, and made straight for England, reaching Portsmouth on 27 July. He announced his return to Lord Burghley with a typical blend of swagger and piety, praying his voyage would be the foundation of greater deeds. 'My very good Lord,' he wrote, 'there is now a very great gap opened very little to the liking of the King of Spain. God work it all to his glory.'[2]

Financially the expedition had failed, and there were embarrassing delays in due payments while committees sifted the accounts. Drake got an advance to discharge the men, but as late as September Sir William Winter and others were being asked to investigate complaints from the crews and to authorize necessary remuneration. Nor did that silence the discontent. Drake's accountant had died on the voyage, and his records were in disarray, so the general audit by a committee under Winter and John Hawkins was protracted. It eventually reckoned the total proceeds at about £65,000, of which £45,000 represented plate, bullion and pearls, a figure that seems to have been rather too low. However, a third went to the crews, and the investors, including the queen, had to be content with an initial dividend of 15 shillings in the pound. Far from providing money to finance Elizabeth's increasingly expensive foreign policy, the expedition had left its promoters out of pocket. It all worried Sir Francis, because he wanted another voyage to complete the work left undone, and to maximize the return of the investors he refused to claim the not inconsiderable expenses he had sustained in fitting out the fleet. As the commissioners acknowledged, Drake 'dealeth very liberally and truly with the adventurers, and beareth a very great loss therein.'[3] If he had to work within the framework of private enterprise that the queen and her council insisted must govern naval operations, if he had to turn his voyages to profit, at least he was not the man to put his own gain before the public service.

Nor had the expedition been without other difficulties and costs. Some of them were embedded in the structure of Elizabeth's navy, like the underfunding that made voyages such as Drake's dependent upon joint-stock profit seekers and threatened to subordinate strategic to economic goals. Then there had been the problem of the gentlemen, ready to fight at the drop of a hat, but not only unwilling to share with the common seamen the mundane burdens of seafaring but also resentful of being commanded by their social inferiors. Drake had never had any use for such distinctions aboard ship. The sea tested all men equally, irrespective of birth or privilege, and he himself always laboured with his mariners cheer-

[1] Documents and valuable commentary on Drake at Roanoke in Quinn, ed., *Roanoke Voyages*, 1: 243-313; see also Bayly to Shrewsbury, 27 July, 1586, Owen, ed., *Bath MSS*, 5: 71-2.
[2] Drake to Burghley, 26 July, 1586, Corbett, 83-5.
[3] Statement of Accounts, 11 March, 1587, *Ibid*, 86-92.

fully. They were his own people. Back in England the issue between Drake and Knollys resurfaced, and it was the talk that Sir Francis would never be allowed to command gentlemen again. The upshot of the affair is not known, although Knollys was placed temporarily under arrest.

Drake's expedition had also raised another, and even more important problem: the disease that invariably wasted those who adventured into pestilential tropical seas with large numbers of men packed into tiny ships. Here it had curtailed his schedule and ruined many of his prospects, and it would reappear in all the great campaigns that lay ahead. It would take two centuries and more, and the work of Blane, Trotter and other eminent physicians, to find means by which a large navy could keep to the sea and remain healthy. We should not blame Drake too severely for his failure to find answers to the problem in 1586. Indeed, on the whole, Sir Francis had not handled his first large-scale expedition too badly. He had overcome the command and organizational problems, and succeeded in directing the offensive spirit on an ambitious scale.

If the plunder was disappointing the voyage had been successful as an act of war. The capture of Santo Domingo and Cartagena proclaimed to the world how weakly Philip's American empire was defended, how vulnerable were its principal cities and the treasure flow that depended upon them. The king's credit, upon which his military campaigns were founded, temporarily collapsed, and he was rumoured to be almost bankrupt. The bank of Seville broke, and that at Venice tottered. The Pope and the dukes of Florence and Savoy refused Philip a loan of 500,000 ducats, and in the Netherlands 'the most contemplative' of Parma's paymasters 'ponder much over this success of Drake', and tightened their purses. The man from Devon had dealt his enemy an enormous blow to morale. 'Truly,' declared Burghley, 'Sir Francis Drake is a fearful man to the King of Spain.'[1]

Conversely, throughout Protestant Europe spirits soared. The Spanish complained that 'every gentleman' in the English court 'buildeth a ship or two to send after Sir Francis Drake.' The predatory and patriotic instincts of Elizabeth's subjects reached new heights, as the voyage 'inflamed the whole country to adventure unto the seas in hope of the like good success.'[2] Even more than the circumnavigation, Drake's West Indian raid was commemorated in literature. Captain Bigges, a participant, wrote the first full-length account of any of Drake's expeditions in his *Summary and True Discourse*, while Henry Roberts chided his countrymen for neglecting the subject and compared Drake to David and Alexander in his *Most Friendly Farewell*. A Spanish poet, a priest of New Granada, Juan de Castellanos, was less fortunate with his six-thousand line 'Discurso del Francisco Draque', recounting the sack of Cartagena, for it was held unconducive to his country's morale and had to wait more than three centuries to find a publisher.[3]

---

[1] Corbett, *Drake and the Tudor Navy*, 2: 61.

[2] Spanish advertisements, Corbett, *Spanish War*, 77-9; John Hooker in Quinn, 1: 312-13.

[3] In this context reference should be made to a late sixteenth-century French manuscript called 'Histoire Naturelle des Indes', acquired by the Pierpont Morgan Library of New York in 1983. Containing 134 leaves, principally depicting the flora, fauna and natives of the West Indies, the manuscript appears to have been the work of different artists and writers, probably Huguenots. It is sometimes called the 'Drake manuscript' because of the claim that it 'almost certainly derives from Francis Drake's West Indian

There were other consequences of this voyage, more far reaching than the immediate blow to Spanish national prestige. For fifteen years Drake had been advertising Spain's imperial weaknesses, and Philip had never failed to respond. So it was now, for in 1586 he sent an engineer and a campmaster to the West Indies to assess their defences. The mission of Juan Bautista Antonelli and Juan de Texeda was the beginning of the effective fortification of the Caribbean, but it cost Philip sorely, and forced him to pare down his efforts in Europe.

And it was just as well that it did, for Drake's expedition set in motion another, and deadlier, policy. In Spain the maritime classes, grown prosperous on American trade, were clamouring for an end to the English threat. Drake's achievements would attract imitators, many of them, who cumulatively would inflict greater damage than he had ever done. Privateers, financed by merchants, the navy and the court, were already beginning to sally from English ports with commissions of reprisal, the harbingers of an industry based upon plunder, and a substitute for the old trades with Brazil and the Iberian Peninsula that fell victim to the worsening relations between England and Spain. Drake's expedition was a signal to Spanish merchants that decisive action was necessary to avert possible ruin. Whether or not Elizabeth had genuinely hoped that she could release Drake without starting a war, for Philip the raid was the last straw. Encouraged by his leading counsellors, Juan de Idiaquez and Cristóbal de Moura, he recognized that even though Parma had captured Antwerp, even though Leicester's English army had achieved little to halt the Spanish tide in the Netherlands, Spain's communications with both the Low Countries and the Americas depended upon defeating England. It had to be done, for God and Empire. From the different proposals submitted to him by Santa Cruz and Parma came the king's great crusade against England. Around the Portuguese galleons inherited in 1580 and the ships of the West Indian guard, a mighty Spanish fleet was already assembling, and Santa Cruz would take it to England and wrest the narrow seas from Drake. When he had done so, he would link with Parma and ship his army across the Channel, where it would overthrow the heretical queen. From Spain's humiliation and frustration over Drake's raid emerged a greater strength of purpose, and before the end of the year the new Pope, Sixtus V, had joined the crusade, promising Philip a million crowns after Parma's army had landed in England.

Across Europe the reverberations of Philip's new plans were heard, and the great Armada formed. Ships were commandeered or hired in Spain, in Italy and in the Baltic regions. Naval stores and provisions poured into Spanish and Portuguese ports. Guns were cast in Italy and Germany, and troops raised in Milan,

---

voyages' (Klinkenborg, *Sir Francis Drake and the Age of Discovery*). Valuable as the manuscript is, the link with Drake seems questionable. It contains two references to Drake, one a vague aside on his visit to the Moluccas, and another asserting that the Indians about Roanoke were skilled warriors and had fought the English under Drake in 1586. Unfortunately, the contemporary accounts of Drake's visit to Roanoke in 1586 do not mention any such conflict, and the reference is probably either an outright error or a confusion of Drake with some other commander, such as Grenville. The 'strongest link' between Drake and the manuscript is said to be geographical. It mentions many places in the West Indies connected with Drake. But French corsairs were in the Caribbean before Drake, and almost certainly knew its geography as well as the English. Until more is known about the evaluation of the 'Drake manuscript', authoritative judgement must be withheld.

Portugal and Naples. The dockyards throbbed to the new schedule. In February of 1587 the king's secretary wrote: 'The intervention of the English in Holland and Zeeland, together with their infestation of the Indies and the Ocean, is of such a nature that defensive methods are not enough to cover everything, but forces us to apply the fire in their homeland.'[1]

Drake's war had become England's war now. But Drake held a torch too, and with it he would singe the King of Spain's beard.

---

[1] Lynch, *Spain Under the Habsburgs*, 315.

CHAPTER SIXTEEN

# 'STOP HIM NOW, AND STOP HIM EVER!'

> Whether to win from Spain that was not Spain's,
> Or to acquite us of sustained wrong,
> Or intercept their Indian hoped gains,
> Thereby to weaken them, and make us strong.

Charles FitzGeffrey, Sir Francis Drake, 1596

TIME WAS RACING NOW, HEADLONG TOWARDS THE COLLISION BETWEEN ENGLAND and Spain. In 1586 Walsingham and his agents unravelled a Catholic plot against Elizabeth's life, and it implicated the Queen of Scots. Mary paid for it with her life in February 1587 at the block in Fotheringay Castle. Her death eased Protestant fears about the succession, because it left as the most likely heir to Elizabeth Mary's son, James, who had been raised apart from his mother as a Calvinist. Yet for all that it brought the Armada closer. While Mary had been alive Philip had sometimes doubted the wisdom of overthrowing Elizabeth, heretic though she was. The restoration of Catholicism would have put Mary on the throne, with all her ties of blood to the French, and strengthened the bonds between England and France. Philip had not wanted that. But now such fears had fallen from the block with Mary's head. Indeed, Philip himself stood forward as the legitimate Catholic heir to Elizabeth's crown, claiming the legacy bequeathed him by his former wife, Mary, the last Catholic Tudor. His Armada would restore a rightful religion, and a rightful king.

None saw that coming Armada more clearly than Francis Drake. Few were so reluctant to see it as Elizabeth. How different they were, the aggressive, fiery zealot and the cautious, war-weary monarch. For Drake life was approaching its climax, the ultimate contest for which he had been preparing all these years – a decisive clash of armour not just between England and Spain but also between God and Antichrist. Far from shrinking from it, he thirsted for the action, supremely self-confident, guided by temperament as well as logic to the opinion that Elizabeth must strike first, disorient her enemies and disrupt their preparations. No sooner was he home than he was canvassing for another expedition.[1]

Elizabeth listened to Drake because she recognized his unswerving loyalty and understood his value, and perhaps because she often found his hearty and frank conversation entertaining. But every time she saw the burly little seaman swaggering forward she knew what he was going to say. He wanted money, ships and men to hit Philip hard. Strike Spain now, before the Armada could sail! His message was always the same, and there were always those, like Walsingham and Leicester, who would echo it.

---

[1] The state papers contain several estimates for fitting out a fleet in September 1586, and one indicates that Drake may have been earmarked for command, although it appears it should have referred to William Winter. State Papers, Domestic, Public Record Office, S.P. 12/193: 26, 29, 35, 42, 49.

And yet she feared to let them have their way. She could not comprehend the depth of their hostility to Spain and the Pope, and she took a broader view of the international scene. To her it was not purely a matter of Spain and England. She could not forget that France was her closest neighbour and had long been her rival. How would it serve England to destroy Spain, the one country capable of curbing the power of France? Not only that but a war, any war, would fracture her hard-won and fragile solvency. She had only to review the annals of her father's reign to learn how money squandered on foreign adventures could beggar the Exchequer. Despite the legacy of her extravagant forbears she had paid her debts, revalued the debased coinage and created a reserve fund, but with a gross income of less than half a million pounds a year her government was already in trouble again. Everybody wanted money. Drake wanted it for ships. Leicester wanted it for his Netherlands army, although it had performed little and had exceeded its allocated budget of £126,000 a year. The Dutch wanted money, and so did the French Huguenots. With chagrin Elizabeth saw her chested reserve fall by four-fifths between 1584 and 1588 to a mere £55,000, less than it would take for the full mobilization of her fleet. She had looked for dividends from Drake, but however successful his raid of the West Indies had been militarily it had failed her financially. There was an alternative, one she should have taken, but she hated to use it. She could ask Parliament to raise taxes. Elizabeth's perennial stringency reflected less a lack of wealth than a reluctance to tap it. The propertied escaped lightly under her regime. Her take from the national income may have been as low as three per cent and custom rates remained low. This was one reason why so many merchants were able to sink funds into privateering. The queen's reluctance to tax more heavily was, in the light of growing national danger, probably irresponsible but not unreasoned. Taxation caused unrest, and it increased Elizabeth's dependence upon Parliament, which alone had the right to grant it. She resisted putting herself in the hands of those whose judgement she distrusted. And she resisted a more oppressive taxation. So she prevaricated and stalled while the storm brewed about her, grasping the flimsiest straws to preserve peace, clinging to hope after it had gone. Drake and Elizabeth were bound by a common patriotism, but they exasperated each other whenever they discussed policy.

In the autumn of 1586 Drake was bothering her with a new plan to assist Dom Antonio, who as usual had been talking about the thousands of followers who were going to flock to his standard the moment he set foot in Portugal. Replying in kind, Elizabeth fobbed the pretender off with another familiar line: she would act if he could find someone to share the burden. Consequently, that October Sir Francis Drake found himself bound for Rotterdam and Middleburg with eight ships, carrying troops and money for Leicester and a brief to curry support for Dom Antonio from the Dutch. He was only partly successful. Officially, the Dutch would not commit themselves, but they gave out that private shipowners were free to co-operate with Drake if they wished, and it was said that Holland and Zeeland eventually offered to place thirty or forty armed transports at his disposal. The visit also enabled Drake to exchange news and gossip with Leicester – the earl's man, Robert Otheman, once found the two seated at chess – and then to bring him home with a handful of Dutch deputies in November. Drake called upon

Dom Antonio at Eton to acquaint him with the result of his mission, and in December was lobbying the Privy Council for leave to fit out ships. Apparently he had some success, too, for soon Spanish agents had letters flitting across the Channel with news that disturbed Philip greatly: Drake was preparing for sea again.[1]

Drake was seldom happy with precise planning. Like every great opportunist he preferred a flexible schedule that he could tailor to circumstance, and his ideas about the voyage shifted considerably over the winter and spring. By February 1587 he had dropped the Dom Antonio scheme in favour of a replay of his West Indian raid, involving attacks upon the Main between the island of Trinidad and Puerto de Caballas in Honduras, and a strike at San Juan d'Ulua at a time when the ships of the Mexican *flota* would be beached there.[2] Whenever Drake started talking about treasure, mouths began to water, but on this occasion national security demanded his presence at home. There was no question of England's greatest seaman crossing the Atlantic when provisions and ships were converging on Lisbon for the invasion of the realm. The West Indian proposal, if it was ever more than a tentative suggestion, was short-lived, and in its place was advanced a pre-emptive strike against Philip's Armada.

On 15 March, 1587 Drake's new commission was signed, and it was entirely to his satisfaction. Strategic purposes dominated this new adventure. He was instructed to impede the flow of ships and supplies from Andalucia and Italy to Lisbon, to distress the enemy fleets within their own havens if possible, and – here was the sop to private enterprise – to intercept heavily laden homeward-bound ships from the West and East Indies. If Drake discovered that the Armada had sailed before he reached Spain, he was to confront it and 'cut off as many of them as he could, and impeach their landing' in England.

Once again it was a joint-stock operation. The principal investor was the queen, who supplied the *Elizabeth Bonaventure* (Drake's flagship), the *Golden Lion*, which served as vice-admiral under William Borough, the *Dreadnought* under Rear-Admiral Thomas Fenner, and Henry Bellingham's *Rainbow*, as well as two pinnaces. Next came the London merchants, with whom Drake signed a contract on 18 March. They provided about a dozen ships and pinnaces, including some substantial vessels such as the *Merchant Royal*, *Susan* and *Edward Bonaventure*. The names of the merchant investors survive: Thomas Cordell, a wealthy mercer, member of the Levant Company, and formerly engaged in the Spanish trade; the Banning brothers, Paul and Andrew, grocers who had turned to privateering after the collapse of their trade with Spain, and who also had interests in the Levant Company; Edward Holmeden, a grocer trading with the Levant; John Watts, clothier, another fugitive from the Spanish trade; and Richard Barrett, Hugh Lee, William Garraway, Robert Sadler, John Stokes, Robert Flick, Simon Borman and others who, whether grocers, haberdashers, fishmongers or drapers, were men of substance all. The balance of the fleet was provided by Drake and Howard of Effingham, the Lord Admiral. Drake's four ships commemorated his family, and

[1] Motley, *History of the United Netherlands*, 2: 98, 137.
[2] Statement of a voyage projected by Drake and Hawkins, enclosed with Mendoza to Philip, 18 February, 1587, Hume, ed., *Calendar of Letters and State Papers . . . in the Archives of Simancas*, 4: 20-3.

included the *Drake*, the *Thomas Drake* and the *Elizabeth Drake*, and Howard supplied the *White Lion*. As an indication of the relative contributions, as determined to apportion prize money, it was reckoned that the queen provided 2,100 tons and 1,020 men; the merchants 2,100 tons and 894 men; Drake 600 tons and 619 men; and Howard 175 tons and 415 men.[1]

After signing the contract with the merchants, Drake left with his wife for Dover to take ship for Plymouth, where the expedition was to be assembled. It was the largest he had commanded, and after Thomas Fenner led in the London contingent at the end of March it numbered twenty-four ships and about 3,000 men. According to Fenner, Drake

> with all care doth hasten the service, and sticketh not to any charge to further the same . . . The General spareth not in great charge to divers men of valour, as also layeth out great sums of money to soldiers and mariners to stir up their minds and satisfy their wants in good sort. There is good order and care taken for preservation of victual, and men very well satisfied therewith, the General encouraging them.[2]

Notwithstanding his efforts, Drake still fretted. There had long been a paranoid element in his character, a darkness instilled into him by Doughty, Knollys and the world of plot and counterplot that formed such an important part of the Elizabethan political scene. This time he noted the unusual number of men who defected from his forces while they were waiting in port, and suspected that it was due to the machinations of his enemies. He was reassured, however, by his officers. 'I thank God,' he wrote to Walsingham, 'I find no man but as all members of one body to stand for our gracious Queen and country against Antichrist and his members.' To all appearances Borough, Fenner and Bellingham were 'very discreet, honest and most sufficient.'[3] The other matter troubling Drake was the queen's notorious habit of altering her mind. Pinning Elizabeth down was like nailing jelly to a wall. He had prepared expeditions to see her abort them, and had had to scurry from Plymouth leaving his provisions ashore rather than risk awaiting her recall. So it was now, for even as Drake was sailing the queen had further thoughts about those instructions. As if the Armada were an illusion, and Philip's intentions were not thoroughly transparent, she decided she must not unnecessarily provoke him. New orders were sent to Plymouth, forbidding Drake from entering Spanish ports or threatening their property ashore; he must confine himself to seizures at sea. But it was too late, for Drake had foreseen the change of heart.

His ships were already at sea. On 2 April from his cabin on the *Elizabeth Bonaventure* he wrote a farewell to Walsingham that expressed the sense of urgency on the eve of this, his most brilliant adventure:

[1] Statement by William Stallenge, 24 October, 1587, State Papers, Domestic, S.P. 12/204: 46; sureties provided by Drake's partners, 31 October, 1587, *Ibid*, S.P. 12/204: 52.

[2] Fenner to Walsingham, 1 April, 1587, Corbett, ed., *Papers Relating to the Navy During the Spanish War*, 97-100. The English documents for this voyage are given in this volume and in Hopper, ed., 'Sir Francis Drake's Memorable Service . . . Written by Robert Leng'. The 'Brief Relation' given by Hakluyt is largely cobbled from dispatches and is not in itself a primary source.

[3] Drake to Walsingham, 2 April, 1587, Corbett, 102-4. Drake's accounts for the voyage refer to the apprehension and imprisonment of men, possibly for desertion (State Papers, Domestic, S.P. 12/204: 27-9).

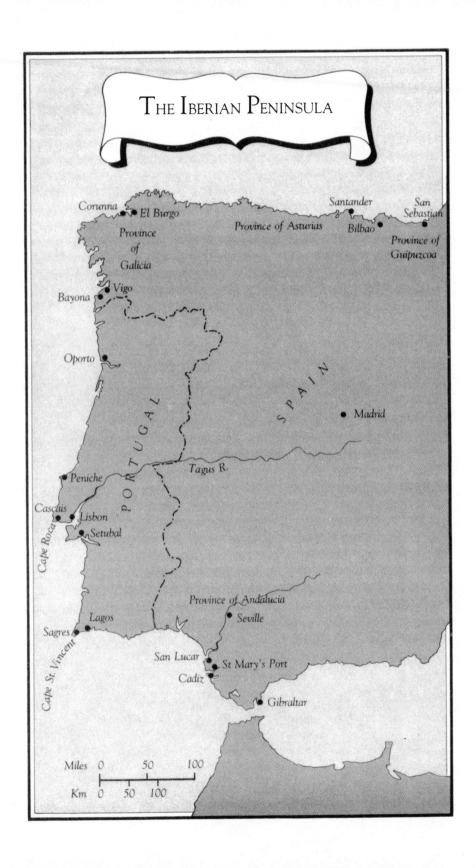

# THE IBERIAN PENINSULA

Corunna • • El Burgo
Province
of
Galicia

Province of Asturias

Santander
Bilbao •

San
Sebastian •

Province of
Guipuzcoa

Bayona • • Vigo

Oporto •

P O R T U G A L

S P A I N

• Madrid

Tagus R.

Peniche •

Cascais •
• Lisbon
Cape Roca • • Setubal

Province of Andalucia

Lagos •

• Seville

Sagres •

San Lucar •

Cape St. Vincent

Cadiz •

• St Mary's Port

• Gibraltar

Miles  0      50      100
Km   0   50  100

*The wind commands me away. Our ship is under sail. God grant we may live in His fear as the enemy may have cause to say that God doth fight for Her Majesty as well abroad as at home . . . Let me beseech your honour to pray unto God for us that He will direct us the right way . . . Haste!*

Wasting no more time than to commandeer two privateers, seize a few prizes and round up his fleet after it had been hammered by a week long storm, Drake bowled to the Spanish coast with the intention of taking it by surprise.[1] He moved so quickly that when he arrived off Cadiz on 19 April much of his fleet was trailing behind. Drake would not wait for them. He did not even wait to reconnoitre the port and its defences. It was crowded with shipping and provisions for the Armada; the wind was fair for an attack, and after a perfunctory council in which the vice-admiral counselled caution, Drake bore down on his enemies like one possessed.

William Borough was horrified at Drake's action. A brilliant navigator, whose reputation rested solidly on his charts of the White Sea and work on the variation of the compass, Borough was nevertheless a plodding, conservative and quarrelsome naval commander who had stood out against the revolution in warship design that Winter and Hawkins were bringing about. Now the rash attack of Drake's was too much for him. There were, indeed, grounds for apprehension. Cadiz had two anchorages formed by an offshore island at the south-eastern end of the bay, but the only entrance was dominated by several batteries – at the point, in the castle and by the harbour – and beset by difficult shoalwater, while the passage between the outer and inner havens was only a half-mile across and could easily be secured by the positioning of guns at the narrows. However, as usual Drake was a step ahead. The port was unsuspecting, the batteries weak, and most of the sixty ships and many smaller vessels inside the harbour were unarmed. Some were storeships destined for the Armada, and others had provisions for it. Still more were innocent merchantmen caught in a war that was not of their making. Drake had caught them unawares and would not afford them time to seek sanctuary beneath guns, behind shoals or up creeks. Without flying any flags or distinguishing pennants, the English ships were led by the *Elizabeth Bonaventure* past the batteries and into the outer anchorage.

No one contested them. As an apparent eye-witness admitted, 'the nonchalance that there was was so great and the confidence that no enemy would dare to enter the bay, as they were so little accustomed to see sea-going ships dare to do so, nor had it been heard in many centuries previous of any having such daring to break through the gates and entrances of their port.' It was the same old Drake, doing what was not so much difficult as unthinkable. Two Spanish war galleys, long and rakish, were eventually propelled forward by banks of oars to investigate the intruders. Galleys had dominated warfare in the Mediterranean since ancient times, but they were no match for the hardier deep-sea sailing ships Drake had brought, with their stout timbers and superior artillery. As soon as the galley commanders realized that the newcomers were unfriendly, they fled without firing a shot. The queen's ships now raised their flags and fired after the retreating galleys, putting a ball through one of their midship gangways and killing several of the oarsmen. When some of the other eight galleys that were in the port also bravely advanced, the English scourged them with shot and drove them

[1] Dasent, ed., *Acts of the Privy Council of England*, 19: 455-6.

to shelter.[1]

Panic now overwhelmed the defenceless shipping in the outer harbour. Some fled for refuge in the adjoining river estuaries of St Mary's Port and Porto Reale, others were abandoned, and one, a big thirty- or forty-gun Genoese ship estimated at 1,000 tons, made a fight of it. Drake would have liked to capture her, but she was stubborn and fought until she was sent to the bottom of the harbour with a rich cargo of merchandise. On shore the Spaniards thought Drake intended sacking the city, and rushed terrified into the castle, suffocating or trampling to death about twenty-six fellow citizens in the crush. It was some time before the Corregidor, Juan de la Vega, restored order and soldiers reoccupied the town square, set up a guard and covered possible landing places, while the galleys drew up in battle formation at the waterfront. Messages for help fanned out, to Seville, Jerez, San Lucar and elsewhere.

Apprehension was not confined to the Spaniards. William Borough was more impressed with Drake's vulnerability than the town's, and that evening called upon the admiral on the *Bonaventure*, apparently to urge him to withdraw. As he left Drake's cabin he met Captain Samuel Foxcroft and ruefully told him that he could drum no sense into his superior. In fact, far from quitting, Drake was only getting into his stride. The night was cold and dark, but the English set it aglow as they began removing cargoes from their prizes and putting a light to the empty ships. Then, in the early hours of 20 April, Drake led a flotilla of ships' boats into the inner harbour, where they found the greatest warship in Cadiz, a 1,500-ton galleon belonging to Santa Cruz himself, the leader of the Armada. She was laden with iron and had no guns mounted, and Drake shortly set her ablaze. Poor Vice-Admiral Borough was in dismay. He again called on the *Bonaventure*, while Drake was leading this new attack, and unable to find the admiral had himself rowed forward to Robert Flick's *Merchant Royal*, which was stationed in an advanced position by the entrance of the inner anchorage. There he learned that Sir Francis was further still, attacking Santa Cruz's galleon. It seems that Borough then began to take it upon himself to initiate a withdrawal in the admiral's absence, for he spoke to Captain Flick 'in fearful sort' and urged him to retire a little, 'for he thought it better to be gone than to stay there.' Flick believed that his vice-admiral was afraid of the galleys.[2]

When Drake returned from his incursion into the upper anchorage he met Borough. There are fundamental disagreements about what happened next, but the most likely explanation is as follows. The batteries in the castle and the town and the galleys had been ineffective, but on the 20th the Spaniards established another battery on a commanding height and it opened fire upon Borough's ship, the *Golden Lion*, sending a shot through her timbers below the waterline and breaking the leg of a gunner on board. According to Drake, Borough then came to him trembling with fear and whining about the possibility of one of the queen's ships being dismasted. This is probably exaggerated, but certainly the vice-admiral returned to his vessel and without

[1] Two Spanish relations of the attack on Cadiz are given in Maura, *El Designio de Felipe II*, ch. 10. One is an eye-witness narrative, and the other a retrospective version from the archives of the dukes of Medina Sidonia. Both were translated for this biography, and copies of the translations have been deposited in the National Maritime Museum, Greenwich, and the Plymouth Public Library. The quotation is from the account of the anonymous eye-witness, published in Maura, 185-203.

[2] Further articles against Borough, 29 July, 1587, Corbett, 156-64.

orders from Drake withdrew about two miles from the rest of the fleet, off St Mary's Port. More remarkably he tried to persuade others to join him, using his authority to instruct Captain Bellingham to follow suit. Captain Henry Spindelow, who was aboard Bellingham's *Rainbow* that morning and saw her captain returning from Borough's ship, said that Bellingham told his master to weigh with the *Golden Lion* if Borough stood further out. Spindelow could not resist the sarcastic remark that in his opinion the vice-admiral was far enough from the action already.[1]

Nevertheless, Drake could not let Borough stand alone off St Mary's Port, and authorized six ships, including the *Rainbow*, to support him. It was true, as Borough later pleaded in extenuation, that so positioned he could secure Drake's rear from the galleys, if indeed it needed protection, but he also forced the admiral to weaken his force deeper inside the harbour. Fortunately, the Spaniards could do little to arrest his progress. During the night of the 19th and throughout the 20th some 6,000 men had arrived in Cadiz in response to the calls for help, and the Duke of Medina Sidonia came from San Lucar to take command, but they could only watch flames enveloping Drake's remaining captures. 'With the pitch and tar they had, smoke and flames rose up, so that it seemed like a huge volcano, or something out of Hell . . . A sad and dreadful sight,' said one.[2] How many ships were destroyed or captured is in dispute. Drake claimed thirty-nine: two galleys sunk, along with the Genoese ship; Santa Cruz's galleon and thirty-one other vessels of between 200 and 1,000 tons burned; and four prizes brought away. Fenner spoke of thirty-eight sunk or brought away, including fourteen or fifteen Dutch ships, five Biscayans, Santa Cruz's galleon, a shallop, three flyboats and about ten barks. Spanish sources suggest serious but slighter losses, of which the lowest estimate appears to be twenty-five ships, worth 172,000 ducats.[3]

When his work was done Drake prepared to leave, but at the critical moment the wind fell and left his ships becalmed, and it was not until early the following morning, while it was still dark, that he led them out, 'as well as the most experienced local pilot,' marvelled a Spaniard. In the bay the wind deserted the English again, and the galleys took advantage of it by attempting a sortie against them, but they were quite unequal to the task. The superiority of the armed sailing ship over the galley had been demonstrated in earlier naval operations, but never more effectively or definitively than at Cadiz.

Drake's destruction of the shipping in Cadiz, his 'singeing of the King of Spain's beard', as he put it, rightly stirred Europe. Not even Philip's own cities and fleets were free from humiliation at the hands of this arrogant Englishman. The impudence, dash and damage of the raid even raised doubts as to whether Spain, albeit the greatest power on earth, could handle England besides her many other commitments. Reflecting inaccurately upon the subject the Pope exploded in admiration for his foes:

---

[1] There are difficulties in accepting alternative versions. Borough's own claim that he visited Drake to discuss victualling seems unlikely. Some evidence does suggest that the *Golden Lion* was hit while Borough was absent and that it was the master who decided to warp her further out, but even if this was correct, Borough obviously endorsed the decision when he returned.

[2] Anonymous eye-witness, Maura, 185-203.

[3] A letter by Thomas Fenner to his cousin appears to be the basis of the uncredited account published by Hopper, as well as of that in Haslop, *News out of the Coast of Spain*. See also Lippomano to the Doge and Senate, 9 May, 1587, Brown, ed., *Calendar of State Papers . . . in the Archives and Collections of Venice*, 273-5; Duro, ed., *La Armada Invencible*, 1: 334-5.

*The King goes trifling with this armada of his, but the Queen acts in earnest. Were
she only a Catholic, she would be our best beloved, for she is of great worth! Just look
at Drake! Who is he? What forces has he? And yet he burned twenty-five of the
King's ships at Gibraltar, and as many again at Lisbon. He has robbed the flotilla
and sacked San Domingo. His reputation is so great that his countrymen flock to him
to share his booty. We are sorry to say it, but we have a poor opinion of this Spanish
Armada, and fear some disaster.*[1]

Exhilarated as Drake himself felt about the victory, he knew it was merely a good
beginning. He had destroyed ships and provisions at Cadiz that had been destined for
the Armada, and he had inflicted tremendous psychological damage, but there were
other contingents, at Passages and Lisbon, and in the Mediterranean at Gibraltar,
Cartegena and Italy. And everywhere he saw evidence of Philip's determination to
invade England. As he made his way to Cape St Vincent to disrupt the co-ordination
of these movements, he wrote home to Walsingham, warning him of the danger and
begging him to force the queen to a strong stand. 'I dare not almost write unto your
honour of the great forces we hear the King of Spain hath out in the Straits,' he wrote.
'Prepare in England strongly, and most by sea. Stop him now, and stop him ever!'[2]

Cape St Vincent, a promontory more than 100 miles south of Lisbon, was Drake's next
destination. By stationing his fleet off this strategic headland he could intercept shipping bound for Portugal from Andalucia and the Mediterranean and disrupt communications. First, he needed a base from which to sustain the vigil, a safe anchorage
for his ships, and a place where the men could land to refresh and reprovision themselves, and he decided to seize the Cape itself. It was an idea that brought Vice-
Admiral Borough to boiling point.

Borough, it is true, was an irritable, conservative man, but no more than Doughty
and Knollys was he entirely to blame for the difficulties that were developing with
Drake. Part of it lay in Drake's arbitrary and sudden decision-making, his habit of
listening to others only to ignore their counsel, and his rapid changes in direction as
circumstances altered. Ultimately, he depended upon his own judgement and initiative and needed no reinforcement. Nor did Sir Francis fully understand how to nur-
ture proud subordinates who were his social or professional peers. While he was able to
inspire devotion among many officers, like Fenner and Crosse, he lacked the ability to
make all men feel they mattered, the skill in teamwork that later distinguished
Nelson. Any resentment Doughty and Knollys bore a commander of inferior social
status had been sharpened by the disregard he too frequently showed for their
opinions. Borough was no high-born gentleman. He was not of the stamp of Knollys or
Doughty, but he was older than Drake and more than a thoroughly professional seaman. He had participated in the early voyages to the north-east and deserved his reputation as one of the pioneers of Elizabethan overseas endeavour. Yet his counsel had
been ignored outside Cadiz; he had not been informed of the foray into the inner harbour there; and now the first he heard of the plan to seize St Vincent was when he
came aboard the flagship on 29 April and heard some common soldiers speaking about
it by the helm. They knew more than the vice-admiral of the fleet!

---

[1] Giovanni Gritti to the Doge and Senate, 20 August, 1588, Brown, 379.
[2] Drake to John Foxe, 27 April, 1587, Hopper, 30-1; Drake to Walsingham, 27 April, 1587, Corbett, 107-9.

Borough was upset, and rightly so, but he acted unwisely nonetheless. Returning to the *Golden Lion*, he addressed a long letter of complaint to the admiral, protesting that the officers were mere 'witnesses to the words you have delivered', entertained perhaps by Drake's 'good cheer', but nevertheless dismissed from meetings 'as wise as we came'. The admiral was 'always so wedded to your own opinion' that he regarded criticism as offensive. As for this attempt upon St Vincent, that was far too bold a stroke for Borough, and he bombarded Sir Francis with objections: there was neither a suitable landing nor watering place at the Cape; Drake's instructions prohibited him from setting foot on Spain's territory; there was no advantage to be gained, except as bravado; the place was impregnable; the coast was already alert and ready for the English; and galleys from Cadiz or Gibraltar might separate landing parties from the ships by using the shallows, or even attack the fleet if it became becalmed. On and on he went.[1]

We can imagine Drake's contempt upon reading such a letter as this. It bore testimony to the gulf between the two men, for had Drake been a Borough he could never have been a Drake. The admiral saw the weaknesses as well as the strengths of his enemies, and profited by them. He was hardly a man to quake at the prospect of assaulting the remote strongholds on a Cape now central to his purposes or of meeting galleys he had already discredited at Cadiz. And as for instructions, he had always exceeded them, and sometimes knew that the queen and Walsingham expected him to do so. Borough enjoined Drake 'to take this in good part', but hardly knew the man before him. Nothing provoked the admiral more than insubordination. Nothing stirred those dark suspicions that always lingered in his head faster. Drake now minded how Borough had hung back at Cadiz, advised him to delay the attack, and retired prematurely from the hottest action. Bottling his fury for the moment, he handed the letter to his chaplain, Philip Nichols, and to Fenner for their opinion. They decided that it was prating in tone and that it charged Drake with inefficiency ('You also neglected giving instructions to the fleet in time and sort as they ought to have had, and as it ought to be,' Borough had written). Although Borough rushed an apology to the admiral as soon as he learned of the offence his letter had caused, it was too late. Drake deprived him of his command and confined him to cabin, naming the sergeant-major of the soldiers, John Marchant, as the new commander of the *Golden Lion*. It was a sad day for a seaman of thirty-five years' standing, a middle-aged man whose accomplishments had made him the comptroller of the queen's navy.

Having disposed of the unhappy Borough, Drake returned to his search for a base. He made a stab at Lagos, east of St Vincent, but found it too strong, and then struck at the four forts at Sagres and Cape St Vincent. This time he led the attack in person. On 5 May about eight hundred arquebusiers and pikemen were disembarked on the beach of the Bay of Belixe and wound their way up the cliffs towards the fort of Valliera. It was defended by six brass pieces, but the garrison withdrew immediately to Sagres Castle to the south-east, the strongest of the forts. Sagres Castle occupied about 100 acres of ground and was a position of some strength. Its garrison was small, only about 110 Portuguese soldiers, but its location was formidable. It was perched defiantly upon the summit of towering cliffs, which fell from its walls on three sides and made it

---

[1] Borough to Drake, 30 April, 1587, Lansdowne MS 52, article 39, British Library.

approachable only from the north by a path some 180 paces across. The castle walls themselves, judged to be around 10 feet thick, rose another 30 or 40 feet, and the one across its front zig-zagged so that no part of it could not be covered by the arquebusiers and bowmen on the battlements. Eight pieces of artillery enfiladed the approaches.

Drake had his men exchange shots with the garrison at Sagres and then summoned it to surrender. When the Portuguese refused he sent to his ships for wood. Eventually all was ready, and the admiral detailed his arquebusiers to pin down the defenders while he led the advance upon the great wooden gate, piled the faggots against it and set it alight. Briefly the garrison resisted, killing and wounding a few of Drake's assault party, but perceiving the determination of the English and, according to one report, running short of ammunition, they called for a parley. Drake let them depart with their baggage and then occupied the castle, and the following day turned his attention to the two remaining forts, one a fortified monastery and the other another castle. Neither offered resistance, although one commanded seven brass pieces and the castle, like Sagres, could only be reached along a single path.

Drake now controlled the bays on both sides of Sagres headland, and his men spent two days gutting the monastery and forts and a nearby village, and pitching the captured guns over the cliffs for collection by the sailors on the beach. Once again, the symbols of the hated Catholicism received special attention. A Spanish account recorded that

> the nefarious English entered the holy convent [of the monastery]; they carried out their customary banquets and drunken revelry, their diabolic extravagances and obscenities; they stole all they could get their hands on and set fire to the place. Likewise, they carried out a thousand acts of contempt and profanities on the images of the saints, like unadulterated heretics; because, just as darkness is offended by light, so these infernal people abhor radiant brightness.[1]

Meanwhile, Drake's ships were already at work, scouring the local bays and destroying every vessel they could find. By Fenner's count forty-seven caravels and barks laden with hoops, pipe-boards, planks and oars were burned. These were the materials that Santa Cruz needed to make casks to store provisions for the fleet, and when the Armada eventually sailed the following year the rot that prematurely afflicted its supplies was in no small way due to the Spaniards' having to use unseasoned wood for casks after Drake's raid destroyed so much of their supply of seasoned timber. In addition, Fenner reckoned that between fifty and sixty fishing boats with their nets were also destroyed. Drake took little satisfaction from this ruin of the local tuna fisheries, and tried to explain to the bereft Portuguese mariners that he could not help the exigencies of war. But he also knew that he was reducing the food supplies available to the Armada.

During these operations Drake had the effrontery to appear off Lisbon, where Santa Cruz's fleet was assembling, and blockade the port for two days, driving vessels ashore and capturing a caravel. He dared the old admiral to come out and fight. Santa Cruz was no milksop. He had made the transition from galley to sailing-ship warfare, having fought against the Turks at Lepanto and defeated Strozzi off the Azores. How-

---

[1] Anonymous eye-witness, Maura, 185-203.

ever, the guns had not been mounted on his ships and he had few men for them, while the galleys at his disposal were no contest for the queen's ships. The old Spaniard could only fume in humiliation. Truly the Venetian ambassador in Madrid wrote, 'The English are masters of the sea, and hold it at their discretion. Lisbon and the whole coast is, as it were, blockaded.'[1]

While Drake held the coast the ships and supplies that had been converging on Lisbon were paralysed. Ten war galleys that met him near Lagos only escaped by retreating behind rocks and shoals. Soldiers being shipped from the Mediterranean to join Santa Cruz dared proceed no further than Cadiz, where they were put ashore and told to continue their journey overland. Much of the local carrying trade was suspended. It seemed as if Drake might rampage at will for months, starving Santa Cruz of reinforcements and provisions, and meanwhile in England four of Elizabeth's ships and twelve merchantmen were being fitted out to join him off Cape St Vincent. Then, suddenly, Drake was gone. It may be that he doubted his ability to maintain the station because his men were sickening, but the most likely explanation of his abrupt departure is that he had heard of rich ships for the taking, somewhere near the Azores, and meant to have a share of them.

Some historians have been strongly critical of Drake's voyage to the Azores, and cited it as an example of his alleged willingness to subordinate the national interest to naked profit-seeking. Going further, some have dismissed Sir Francis as an innate corsair, a predator pure and simple, for whom plunder was the principal objective. While none would deny that Drake was always interested in money, at sea or ashore, these criticisms have been taken too far. Drake's letters reveal that religion, even more than gold, dominated his mind, and for Drake the causes of God and England were one. It is difficult to believe that this fiery, almost fanatical zealot would have betrayed them.

It must also be remembered that the navy of Elizabeth I was not financed like that of today. The Crown provided less than half of the funds that created Drake's expeditions. All Elizabethan naval commanders were more or less dependent upon private finance, and had to ensure a financial return if they wanted similar backing in the future. Even the queen's investment was often made with a view to profit. The men who led her fleets were generally corsairs as well as admirals. Plunder, whether it detracted from strategic aims or not, was inextricably built into the system. If it was a failing, it was an institutional rather than purely a personal one. Sir Francis Drake could not operate outside this context. He had to respond to his paymasters, and as those paymasters were primarily private investors looking for gain he must necessarily seek the means to satisfy them. When Drake sailed for the Azores in 1587, far from neglecting his duty, he was doing it. To condemn him as a mere mercenary on these grounds is to condemn him for the circumstances that controlled him, and indeed for being an Elizabethan.

That Drake remained a corsair does not preclude him from also having been an admiral. To some extent these same conditions had influenced naval operations throughout the century. Even the Duke of Albuquerque, who secured for Portugal control of the Indian Ocean, and whom many regard as the finest naval strategist of the day, launched plunder raids to compensate for the shortcomings of the funds sent

---

[1] Lippomano to Doge and Senate, 21 May, 1587, Brown, 276-7.

by his sovereign. In 1514 he abandoned an expedition to Aden and the Red Sea to attack Ormuz, the wealthy entrepôt at the mouth of the Persian Gulf, for precisely that purpose. Yet no historian has dismissed Albuquerque as a mere corsair. Although Drake rose from the ranks of the corsairs, and plunder remained a strong imperative in his career, no more does the term justly account for the complexity of his motivation and the range of his operations.

An ugly incident marked the beginning of Drake's dash for the Azores, and the *Golden Lion*, now commanded by Marchant but with Borough still aboard, was at the heart of it. The crew of the ship were in poor shape, debilitated by the blockade and reduced victuals, and when a storm dispersed the fleet it seems to have been the last straw. They demanded that Captain Marchant take them home, and when he refused put him in a pinnace so that he could return to the admiral. The *Golden Lion* herself made for England, and Borough went with her. His part in the mutiny is unclear. He had been deprived of his command, but had addressed the men, telling them that their best course was to lay their grievances before Drake. How earnestly he tried to return the company to its duty, and how far he feared for his life if he protested too loudly, is uncertain, but the admiral's reaction to the news of the defection of the *Golden Lion* was predictable. Without hearing any important evidence, he convinced himself that Borough had not merely done insufficient to stop the mutiny, but was part of it, and empanelling a jury, he had a verdict returned and the death sentence pronounced upon Borough and some of his officers. Not one of the men charged was present to answer the allegations.

The storm and the flight of the *Golden Lion* left Drake with only nine ships, but he led them to the Azores and raised the island of São Miguel on 8 June. Towards dark a large sail was spotted beneath the land, and it was surmised that she was a man-of-war. Early the following morning a ship was seen again, probably the same one, and Drake steered for it. Shortly the improving light revealed a great red cross emblazoned on the ship's sail, and the English realized that they had stumbled upon one of the fabled East Indiamen that shipped the riches of the Indian Ocean to Europe. In fact this Portuguese carrack, the *San Felipe*, was even more than that. She was the king's own ship, reputedly among the greatest in the East India fleet, and carried a double cargo, for she had taken aboard the goods of the *San Lorenzo*, which had sprung a leak and foregone the voyage. It was said she had twenty-two brass guns, many iron ones, and 659 passengers.

This was a magnificent prize, certainly, the greatest taken by the English since Drake's capture of the Pacific treasure ship eight years before, but no easy conquest, for the *San Felipe's* tonnage exceeded that of the three largest English vessels combined. The admiral closed upon her without distinguishing colours, and when he was within range suddenly raised flags, pennants and streamers to declare his identity, and called upon the carrack to yield. There was an exchange of gunfire in which the smaller English ships slunk beneath the great Indiaman's shot to cling on her flanks and bow like mastiffs worrying a baited bull, firing into her hull as she lurched about, trying to defend herself with her guns and the incendiaries that she probably projected from mortars or periers. Surrounded, and with six men killed and others wounded, the *San Felipe* was forced to surrender.

When the English came aboard her they were astonished at the wealth they found

– great quantities of pepper, calico, cinammon, cloves, ebony, silk, saltpetre, jewels, reals of plate, china, indigo, nutmeg, gold and silver – everything that had made the East fabulous. Drake sent her crew, including the black slaves, away in one of his ships, and started for home with his prize, there being no further question of returning to Cape St Vincent with such a reduced force. The capture of the *San Felipe* had 'made' the 1587 voyage. The attack at Cadiz and Drake's brilliant work off St Vincent may have disrupted Spanish preparations for the Armada, but in the eyes of most English contemporaries the dazzling fortune brought home in the carrack was the perfect consummation of the adventure. It stimulated anew the desire to reach the East, and it was Drake's backers who were to become leading lights in the formation of the East India Company at the turn of the century, Paul Banning, William Garraway and Thomas Cordell becoming directors and John Watts its governor.

But the diversion to the Azores was not only a commercial success, for it, rather than the operations off the Spanish coast, postponed the sailing of the Armada for a year. Remarkable as Drake's offensive had been, the naval campaign had only frustrated Santa Cruz temporarily. It was the sudden departure of Drake from the coast and the fears it raised in Spain for the safety of the opulent ships coming home from the East and West Indies that did the long-term damage. To protect them Santa Cruz was bullied into scraping a fleet together and putting to sea in June in search of the English, but by the time he did so Drake had gone. The Spanish admiral cruised uselessly to the Azores and back, returning in October, his ships in disrepair, his men sick and his stores depleted. Philip had planned to launch the Armada against England in 1587, but the debilitation of Santa Cruz's fleet during the Azores voyage made it impossible. It would have to be postponed until 1588, and Elizabeth had gained a valuable year in which to prepare for it. Drake had proved that this time at least commercial profit and national security were not incompatible.

Drake arrived in Plymouth on 26 June, dispatched Fenner to the court with a preliminary report, and shortly followed with a casket from the *San Felipe* as a present for the queen. The mere beginning of a long inventory of its contents suggests the wealth Drake had brought home:

> *Six forks of gold; twelve hafts of gold for knives, to say, six of one sort and six of another; one chain of gold with long links and hooks; one chain of gold with a tablet having a picture of Christ in gold; one chain with a tablet of crystal and a cross of gold; one chain of gold of esses, with four diamonds and four rubies set in a tablet; one chain of small beadstones of gold . . .* [1]

It was said that Elizabeth was displeased that Drake had committed such open acts of war as the seizure of forts and the entry into Cadiz, and her notorious reluctance to goad Philip too far as well as her attempt to amend Drake's instructions before sailing indicate that this was so. At least, it was diplomatic to affect to be annoyed. Yet Drake's fleet had done her great service, buying her time and providing some of the money she desperately needed. She did well out of the sale of the great carrack. Commissioners to assess its value, including Sir John Gilbert and John Hawkins, were appointed on 1 July, and eventually they reckoned the cargo, exclusive of ship and

[1] Inventory, July 1587, Hopper, 52-3. For capture of the *San Felipe* see also *Fugger News-Letters*, 2: 138-9.

guns, to be worth a staggering £112,000. It took seventeen ships to carry it from Plymouth to London and more than a year to realize the proceeds, but in December 1588 the queen was apportioned £50,000 and Drake himself must have netted around £20,000.[1]

Amidst discharging his men and shipping the cargo of the carrack to London, Drake still found time to pursue the mutineers of the *Golden Lion*, who had reached England in June. Sir Francis did not accuse the whole of the ship's company of desertion, and even sought £350 for the wages of those whom he believed had been against it, but he had no comfort for Borough. The month after Drake's return, he provided charges against the former vice-admiral ranging from maintaining a poor state of discipline on his ship and over-caution ('if Sir Francis Drake would have been advised by Mr Borough, there had been no service done') to outright cowardice ('Mr Borough was so afraid of the shot as he could not tell where to ride with the ship'), and thirty officers, including ten captains, swore to the truth of the allegations. The matter had to be taken seriously, and the Privy Council appointed Sir Amyas Paulet and Mr Secretary John Wolley to consider the charges. Drake himself attended an early session of the hearings at Burghley's house Theobalds on 25 July.

The affair did credit to neither of the contending parties. Drake had misinterpreted Borough's original letter of complaint and allowed his emotions to get the better of his judgement, thinking no more clearly than in his ridiculous trial of the offender *in absentia* after the desertion of the *Golden Lion*. There were no sufficient grounds for convicting Borough of mutiny, but while he survived the inquiry he had clearly blotted his record. He had retired from an advanced position at Cadiz and counselled against the attack on St Vincent, thus setting himself apart from the great achievements of the voyage, and he had come home with a crew of mutineers, by implication either a deserter himself or incapable of controlling the men he had once commanded. Poor Borough. When the Armada finally reached England in 1588 there was no place in Drake's fleet for this fine old seaman. Instead he captained Elizabeth's solitary galley and pottered futilely about the Thames.

Drake never forgave Borough, and was disappointed that he had escaped so lightly, but there were graver matters at hand. After his voyage of 1587 attitudes hardened in both England and Spain. The Venetian ambassador wrote from Madrid that 'all Spain is in earnest' and united in a determination to expunge the humiliations Drake had dealt, 'for they declare that the Queen of England and Drake are obscuring the grandeur of this Crown and the valour of the Spanish nation.'[2] Philip's crusade was now not merely a matter of religion and empire, but necessary for the redemption of national honour.

---

[1] State Papers, Domestic, S.P. 12/204: 37, 39, 40; Hist. MSS Commission, *Calendar of the Manuscripts of the Marquis of Salisbury*, 3: 281-2; Rodger, 'A Drake Indenture'.

[2] Lippomano to the Doge and Senate, 16 May, 1587, Brown, 275-6.

CHAPTER SEVENTEEN

# 'THE SOONER WE ARE GONE,
# THE BETTER WE SHALL BE ABLE TO IMPEACH THEM'

> And Bartolo my brother
> To England forth is gone
> Where the Drake he means to kill,
> And the Lutherans everyone
> Excommunicate from God.
>
> Contemporary Spanish Ballad

SOME WOULD CALL IT 'LA FELICISSIMA ARMADA', THAT FLEET PHILIP CAUSED TO BE assembled for the enterprise of England. There were nine great Portuguese galleons, ten smaller ones from the Indian guard, four ships of the *flota*, four Italian galleasses, four Portuguese galleys, and forty-two armed merchantmen, in all a fighting force of seventy-three vessels, attended by over fifty freighters, dispatch boats and lighter craft, and they carried some 2,400 guns and nearly 30,000 men. Its keynote was faith. For the crews' day began to the sound of Salve Regina and the sunset was serenaded by Ave Maria. Their watchwords were Jesus, Holy Ghost, Most Holy Trinity, Santiago, All Saints, the Angels and Our Lady. They were told that theirs was the most important mission 'undertaken for God's church for many hundreds of years. Every conceivable pretext for a just and holy war is to be found in this campaign . . . This is a defensive, not an offensive, war, one in which we are defending our sacred religion and our most holy Roman Catholic's faith; one in which we are defending, too, the land and property of all the kingdoms of Spain, and simultaneously our peace, tranquillity and repose.'[1] Before they finally sailed every man aboard was confessed and communicated. Their standard was reverently brought from its resting place at the altar of the cathedral of Lisbon, its banner inscribed with the arms of Spain, the Virgin Mary and the Crucifixion, and the words, 'Arise, O Lord, and vindicate thy cause.'[2]

Faith, indeed, had to be a basis for an adventure in which so many lacked confidence. Once he had committed himself to it, Philip II drove the project forward with a rare and almost pathological resolution. No excuses and no difficulties could swerve him from it. Not even the pessimism of his commanders deterred him. When his leading admiral, Santa Cruz, died in February of 1588 the responsibility for the fleet passed to the Captain-General of Andalucia, Don Alonso Perez de Guzman el Bueno, seventh Duke of Medina Sidonia. We have met him before, helplessly watching Drake gut the harbour of Cadiz, and on the face of it he seemed a strange choice. He had neither battle experience nor self-confidence,

---

[1] Elliott, *Imperial Spain*, 288.
[2] Of the older studies of the Armada campaign, Mattingly's *Defeat of the Spanish Armada* is the best. A plethora of works on the subject accompanied the quadri-centennial of 1988, but two are outstanding: Martin and Parker, *The Spanish Armada*, and Rodriguez-Salgado, et. al., *Armada, 1588-1988*.

and he was sure the Armada would fail anyway. He said so, with brutal frankness. Besides, complained the anxious grandee when Philip first threatened him with the new post, he had few proven qualities of leadership; his health was poor and he would be sea-sick on the voyage; he had no personal fortune to spend on the fleet; he did not understand its business; and while he would serve if the king so ordered him, he would certainly make a mess of it! Few commanders have approached a task in such a spirit of self-denigration. Yet Philip would not have it otherwise. He knew that whatever Medina Sidonia's shortcomings might be, he was an efficient administrator who had fitted out fleets before and who could bring some order to the chaos Santa Cruz had left behind. His loyalty, diligence and courage were beyond question, and he had something even more important – the social status to rule the more experienced naval men who had been appointed his subordinates and whose counsel would redress the commander-in-chief's weaknesses. Surrendering to the inevitable, Medina Sidonia reluctantly took the appointment, but while he slowly nurtured the great fleet into being, he continued to harbour doubts about its fitness for the work at hand.

But if Medina Sidonia fell back upon his faith, so too did the other leader of the enterprise of England, Alexander Farnese, Duke of Parma. There had been times when he had suggested that Philip call the whole thing off. He had complained until the king had refused to hear more of it. Yet he was no less important to Philip's plans than Medina Sidonia, for he was to command the army that would invade England. In its final form, Philip wanted the Armada to seize control of the Channel, take up a station off Margate, and hold the narrow seas while Parma's troops were shipped from Flanders to Kent. Medina Sidonia was ordered to fight the English fleet only if necessary, if it approached or followed him, and to attack it unprovoked only if it was encountered piecemeal and vulnerable. If his first attempt to join hands with Parma failed, Medina Sidonia might capture the Isle of Wight and use it as a base for a second effort. No one knew the flaws in this plan better than Parma. Certainly he had gained control of the coast of Flanders, excepting Ostend. And certainly he had a chain of canals from Sluys to Dunkirk along which his men might be brought in light-draught invasion barges to points of embarkation. It was also true that his 17,000 men, reinforced by the soldiers the Armada would bring, would be more than a match for the English levies Elizabeth had belatedly mustered. But he had no deep-water port capable of sheltering the Armada, and Medina Sidonia's ships would have to ride off shore, vulnerable to attack and storm. Not only that, but if the Armada could not reach the army, no more could the army reach the fleet, for the two-hundred odd transport barges Parma had assembled were wholly unsuitable for use at sea, and as soon as they emerged from port among the shallows and banks that skirted the coast the Dutch would pounce upon them, with Medina Sidonia, confined to the deeper waters beyond, powerless to intervene. Even supposing the Armada did pass by Drake (the Spaniards always considered the English fleet synonymous with Drake), and supposing a miracle enabled Parma to cross the Channel into Kent, Medina Sidonia would still have to hold the seas to prevent the English ships cutting the Spanish army's communications behind. It was an enormous gamble. As late as March 1588 Parma was complaining that while the enemy was alert, his assembled troops were being ravaged by sickness. He, a man who had captured Antwerp, who had many times achieved the doubtful and the hazardous, now seemed dispirited and strangely lethargic and irresolute.

There were other pessimists too, including the Pope, Sixtus V, whose ardour for the crusade against England was tempered by forebodings that Drake would defeat the Armada. Philip, however, was not listening. Between bouts of illness he prosecuted the campaign vigorously, suppressing any fears he might have entertained as ruthlessly as he flattened the protests of his commanders. Like Sixtus he was troubled by deep anxieties. He grew irritable, depressed and unreasonable, but he continued to grasp the nettle. This time, Philip was determined to fight.

Sir Francis Drake was no less spoiling for action. He had few doubts that the Armada would sail, and perhaps fewer that England's best course was to meet it head on. But unlike Medina Sidonia and Parma, Drake rippled with confidence, indeed with over-confidence. He knew that Elizabeth's warships were the best in Europe, and his successes had fed him with scant regard for the fighting abilities of his opponents. His men, it was said, were boasting that one English ship was the equal of three Spaniards. In the year after he returned home with the *San Felipe*, he saw war fever rising in England. Invasion was the talk of the land, and even the government was eventually forced to make preparations. Drake sat on Burghley's war council, co-ordinating defences with soldiers such as Sir John Norris and Sir Roger Williams. County lieutenants, including Drake's father-in-law, Sir George Sydenham, who acted for Somerset, were instructed to raise, arm and train the militia, and two armies came into being, one of 20,000 men under Leicester at West Tilbury on the Thames, and another in reserve to defend the queen. Beacons were constructed on hill-tops to carry word of the Armada's approach across England. Everywhere, a sense of tremendous anticipation was abroad. The general opinion was that the battle would be won or lost at sea, and it was to Drake and the Lord Admiral, Howard of Effingham, that the country looked for leadership in their moment of crisis.

Throughout, Drake argued that the best defence was attack. He stood on his record. He had created turmoil and dismay on the Spanish coast, and promised to do it again if the Privy Council would allow him to make a pre-emptive strike against the Armada to forestall its preparations. From September 1587 the stocky seaman was hammering his views home at court and winning some converts. Briefly there was talk of Drake sailing for Spain with part of the fleet, or even reinforced by Howard, but for the moment the idea was too bold or expensive for the Privy Council to adopt.[1] It took an alarm, false as it transpired, that the Armada was about to sail to push Elizabeth into a general mobilization of her fleet in December. Four days before Christmas Howard got his commission as overall commander of the English fleet, empowering him to attack, invade and sequester the territories of Spain, instructions that thus preserved the option of offence as

[1] Wroth to Burghley, 5 September, 1587, Hist. MSS Commission, ed., *Calendar of the Manuscripts of the Marquis of Salisbury*, 3: 279; Hist. MSS Commission, ed., *Foljambe Papers*, 26. Other publications containing English documents on the Armada are Laughton, ed., *State Papers Relating to the Defeat of the Spanish Armada*, and Naish, ed., *The Naval Miscellany*, vol. 4. This last prints a narrative of the campaign prepared for Drake by Petruccio Ubaldino.

well as defence. The Lord Admiral was already at work. He tested his ships for sea-worthiness and took them into the Channel, and he scuttled between the fleet and the court discharging his duties to the utmost. Unlike Medina Sidonia, Howard was no spreader of gloom and despair. From the beginning his dispatches overflowed with the national confidence that Drake's exploits had helped to create.

Howard's appointment as overall commander may be surprising. After all, although he was a great noble he was relatively unknown, untested by battle, and Sir Francis Drake was a legend, the most celebrated Englishman of his time. How-ever, Drake could not have been placed in total command of Elizabeth's fleet. The option was never open. In an age in which even the monarch found it expedient to keep the influential peers satisfied, the position of Lord Admiral was a mono-poly of the nobility. In 1585 when it became vacant after the death of the Earl of Lincoln the only credible successor had been Howard of Effingham. His pedigree was impeccable, for his family was among the greatest in the realm, and he had served on the Privy Council and as Lord Treasurer. Three of them, including Howard's father, had already been Lord Admiral, and Howard himself was cousin to the queen. His status was betokened by a spectacular rise: a Member of Parlia-ment at twenty-six, commander of horse at thirty-three, and admiral at thirty-four. But that was not all. Howard's spare figure, his courtly background, his love of finery, and his tales of his youthful prowess in the lists did not disguise another qualification of this ageing dandy: he was also a sailor, with a genuine love of ships and the sea. True, his record had been pedestrian. He had never seen a battle, and most of his sea time had been spent shuttling dignitaries back and forth across the Channel, but he had trod the decks more than most nobles of his day. As a sailor with immense social prestige, a man bred to command, Howard was the obvious choice for Lord Admiral. Had a national crisis not arisen, he might have done little more than intersperse his routine administration of the navy with local voyages, but now that the country faced invasion it was naturally expected that he would lead the nation's fleet into battle.

In 1588 Howard was still something of an unknown quantity. Over fifty, he had never been far from home, and even the Atlantic was largely foreign territory to him. He was also unbloodied. Time would prove him a competent Lord Admiral, diligent, tactful and firm, but his great strength lay in his educability. None knew better than Howard that the Lord Admiral was under-qualified, and while he never relinquished a jot of his authority, he listened and learned from his subordinates, and particularly from Sir Francis Drake, who became his vice-admiral.

Even if Sir Francis had not been debarred by birth from assuming Howard's position, there would have been a good reason to appoint someone else to the supreme command in 1587. The most brilliant and experienced English officer, Drake was also viewed by many as a vulgar, low-born upstart, too fond of his own ideas, too contemptuous of regular form and too easily the focus of controversy. Doughty, Knollys, Borough . . . who would be next? John Hawkins had been big enough to accept his eclipse by the younger man, but Martin Frobisher, the quar-relsome and unimaginative Yorkshireman who had once served as Drake's vice-admiral was no admirer of Sir Francis, and was honest and fearless enough to say so. On reflection the queen's command structure worked well. As vice-admiral of the fleet, the leading fighting man on the English side, and Howard's principal counsellor, Drake got his way with a Lord Admiral very aware of his own inexperience; and, as Lord Admiral, Howard could rely upon Drake's energy and ideas, and employ his own noble standing, natural dignity and administrative skills to create the teamwork necessary for success. The two made a perfect complement.

In the early days that happy outcome might not have been predicted, for Drake, who was so much the greater seaman, was known to be a difficult subordinate. Indeed, Howard hesitated to tackle him. We can sense the Lord Admiral's perplexity in a letter written to Walsingham on 27 January, 1588. Drake, Howard learned, had been drilling his gun crews, and Howard fretted about the shortage of powder. Yet how to broach it with Sir Francis? It was better that Walsingham, Drake's friend as well as a member of the Privy Council, did the job. Thus the Lord Admiral wrote to Walsingham: 'There happened a mischance in one of his [Drake's] ships at Portsmouth, that a piece broke and killed a man, with some other hurt. If you would write a word or two unto him to spare his powder, it would do well.'[1] The letter has often been used as evidence of Howard's weakness, but it also denoted a strength – his diplomacy. He could not afford difficulties with the man upon whose reputation, experience and ability he must fundamentally depend, and the recourse to Walsingham neatly side-stepped the problem.

At the time that Howard was designated commander of the fleet, the Privy Council envisaged dividing their ships between the Lord Admiral and Drake, giving them an eastern and a western squadron respectively. In their instructions to Howard, dated 15 December, they were anticipating that Drake would ply between Ireland, the Scilly Islands and Ushant, guarding the entrance to the Channel and poised to intercept any attempt to menace Ireland or Scotland, while Howard would patrol the narrow seas, watching Parma. If, however, Howard learned that the Armada was too powerful for Drake, or that it had forced its way into the Channel, the Lord Admiral was to order Drake to fall back upon the narrow seas or to send him reinforcements.

A poorer plan could not have been devised, because it divided the English fleet before a powerful enemy for no good reason. Parma's flat-bottomed boats and barges hardly needed Howard's fleet to contain them. Even the Privy Council understood that: 'for . . . the forces of the Duke of Parma will not be such but that you may with a convenient number of our own ships be able to impeach and withstand anything that he shall attempt either against this realm or Scotland.' That being the case, there was no reason to leave Drake undermanned in the west, for whether the Armada threatened Ireland, the western peninsula or forced its way into the Channel that was where it would have to be met. The correct place for Howard was not in the narrow seas but in the front line with Sir Francis Drake at Plymouth. Equally remarkable was the Privy Council's notion that if the Armada was too strong for Drake's force Sir Francis might retire upon the eastern fleet –

[1] Howard to Walsingham, 27 January, 1588, Laughton, 1: 48-50.

thus leaving the south-western part of the country exposed to a possible Spanish landing! The plan was dangerous, but few besides Drake seemed to realize it, and it remained the basis for the government's thinking until the spring.[1]

As part of the plan, on 23 December Drake received a commission to command a western squadron of thirty sail, to consist of seven of the queen's ships (the *Hope, Nonpareil, Aid, Swiftsure, Revenge* and two pinnaces) and a number of merchantmen and privately owned vessels called into service to meet the emergency. The names of some of these ships may be remembered from Drake's previous campaign. Robert Flick's *Merchant Royal* and James Lancaster's *Edward Bonaventure*, owned by Thomas Cordell, had been with Drake before. Sir Walter Ralegh provided the *Roebuck*, and Drake himself the 60-ton *Elizabeth Drake* (Captain Thomas Cely) and the 200-ton *Thomas Drake* (Henry Spindelow). Aboard the fleet would be an estimated 2,820 men.

The Privy Council remained uncertain as to how they wanted Drake to perform. That he was to guard the western approaches was obvious, but Drake was constantly badgering them to authorize him to attack the Spaniards on their own coasts. Half persuaded, the Privy Council included in the admiral's commission orders to distress enemy ships in their own ports, providing he proceeded with caution and avoided risk. If he met the Armada at sea, Drake was to send a warning home and then obstruct the Spaniards' advance, attacking them if opportunity served, but again only if the assault might be made with impunity. These instructions were not unsatisfactory to Drake, if somewhat restrictive, and he apparently secured the approval of the Lord Admiral, who accompanied him as far as Rochester on his trip back to Plymouth at the beginning of January 1588.

Philip II's efficient intelligence system soon had the gist of the English plans. Drake, it was believed, would attempt an offensive, but if the Armada reached the Channel before he could do so Howard would advance to reinforce him in the west, leaving Vice-Admiral Sir Henry Seymour with a reduced force to watch Parma. It was a reasonable statement of the English position, and Drake himself probably could have been little more precise. As his scouts sailed out to reconnoitre, his ships assembled, and powder, shot, provisions and men were found for the new campaign, his mind probably turned over a number of possibilities with one common principle: attack. The exact target, he decided, would have to be selected once he was on the Spanish coast, where he could assess the local circumstances.

But for the time being there was to be no campaign. Barely had Drake begun work than the queen thought better of it. She was, as we have seen, most reluctant to enter the war, and reached for the feeblest glimmers of peace. When it was learned that the Armada was not as ready as reports had once indicated, Elizabeth felt the expense of mobilizing her own fleet was not justified, and orders were given that half the ships be paid off and Sir Francis be prevented from sailing. The admirals were furious, even Howard, who complained to Walsingham that 'we are like bears tied to stakes.'[2] Yet worse was to follow, because in February of 1588

[1] Instructions to Howard, 15 December, 1587, *Foljambe Papers*, 109-10.
[2] Howard to Walsingham, 1 February, 1588, Laughton, 1: 56-8.

Parma made some transparent peace overtures, knowing the queen well enough to predict that she would find them irresistible. He was not disappointed. Elizabeth's commissioners were soon on their way to the Netherlands to negotiate with him, while her admirals remained stymied and the Spaniards bought time. In the event the queen gained little by her vacillation, but she aroused the distrust of her Dutch allies, who suspected that she meant to betray them. Throughout the ensuing crisis the co-operation between the English and Dutch navies was far from exemplary, and important ships from Howard's fleet were detailed to guard Parma, a job entirely within the interests and resources of the Dutch.

Drake's plan to attack the Armada was frozen. 'The stay that is made of Sir Francis Drake going out I am afraid will breed grave peril,' wrote Howard.[1] Nor, with the mobilization truncated, could Drake use the time for a thorough outfit of his force, although he did his best. As the queen's ships that had been assigned to him arrived at Plymouth he had old William Hawkins use the spring tides to careen and tallow them, and he set his principal officers to selecting their berths. For his own flagship Drake chose the *Revenge*, perhaps the most famous of all Elizabethan warships. Built in 1577, she was one of the improved vessels the Navy Board had been producing, and had a length of 92 feet, a beam of 32 feet and a tonnage of about 470. She carried up to forty guns and 250 men, and was strikingly painted in a green and white harlequin design.[2] John Gray was Drake's master and Jonas Bodenham served as the ship's lieutenant. Thomas Fenner, vice-admiral of the Western Squadron, raised his flag aboard the *Nonpareil*, and Robert Crosse took command of the *Hope* as rear-admiral.

While the impatience and frustration of Howard and Drake were understandable, Elizabeth has been both accused and vindicated for her refusal to allow an early mobilization of the fleet. In her defence it may be said that her ships had been mobilized very quickly the previous December, and perhaps they could be counted upon to do the same again, and that some of them needed dry-docking for refit. More important still, to have sustained a full mobilization for several months would have risked the spread of disease among the crews. As it was, the Armada found England's ships in good shape and her men sufficient and healthy enough to man them. No doubt Elizabeth's decision to pay off half the fleet had had little to do with these considerations. She was more interested in saving money, but her stringency may not have been without beneficial consequences.

Nevertheless, there were losses as well as gains in keeping a battle fleet idle. Centuries later Napoleon also endorsed the misconception that his fleet was better in port, secure from the rigours of the sea, while the British blockading squadrons were being battered to pieces by constant service. But he was wrong. The experience gained by the British at sea honed their skills of seamanship and gunnery to levels unattainable by adversaries who were recruited for specific cruises and then laid off, and it was these very skills that proved decisive in combat. Time and again French or Spanish ships, superior in design and strength, more heavily armed and generously manned, were overwhelmingly defeated by British oppo-

---

[1] Howard to Walsingham, 9 March, 1588, *Ibid*, 1: 103.
[2] Glasgow, '*Revenge* Reviewed'.

nents. It became obvious that material advantages were easily offset by skills that Continental crews, inexperienced and often sea-sick, lacked. Of course, the two situations are not strictly comparable. By Nelson's time copper-sheathing had improved the durability of ships, and scurvy was at last being mastered. But this much can be said. The seamanship and teamwork of crews and the rates of fire and accuracy of gunners were never improved by ships sitting in port, and the fleet that fought the Armada was hardly a crack force. Fortunately, neither was the Armada.

No one was more mystified by the queen's reduction of the fleet and her negotiations with Parma than Drake, for they occurred at a time when his own misgivings were increasing. The reports of the preparations in Spain and Portugal made a nonsense of Parma's overtures. In an effort to induce his government into action, Drake kept forwarding intelligence of the Armada's progress, and in March sent some prisoners taken by one of his scouts so that the Privy Council could hear for themselves. Some of these accounts were much exaggerated, such as the story that Lisbon sheltered 450 ships and galleys and nearly 90,000 men, but in March they convinced Drake that the various detachments of the Armada had been concentrated and would make a harder nut to crack. Originally, he had hoped to catch the different divisions of the Armada at various places about the Spanish coast, before they could unite, but now he was forced to consider tackling the bulk of the enemy fleet.

It is possible that the Spanish consolidation not only had Sir Francis revising his tactics but that it intensified his fears for the safety of Devon and Cornwall. That month Drake had joined a committee that underscored how exposed they were. Since it 'is unlikely that the King of Spain will engage his fleet too far within the sleeve before he has mastered some one good harbour', Drake and his colleagues agreed that Plymouth, Portland or the Isle of Wight were likely landing places for Spanish troops brought by the Armada. They recommended that 2,000 men be raised immediately for the defence of Plymouth, with the further 4,000 of the trained bands of Devon and Cornwall held as a reserve.[1]

All of this raised Drake's concerns about England's defence. With the fleet divided between Plymouth and the Straits of Dover, Sir Francis had the strength neither to attack the concentrated Spanish fleet nor to defend the West Country from it. He had to have more ships. And once again he began to speak out.

At court opinion was already divided about Drake's ideas. The queen was as cautious as anybody, and it was with great difficulty that she could be brought to allow her fleet beyond her ken. In January she reportedly blew up about it to old Leicester, reminding him that 'my ships have left to put to sea and if any evil fortune should befall them all would be lost, for I shall have lost the walls of my realm!' On the other hand Burghley was coming out with some irresponsibly bold ideas. He remained committed to the division of the fleet, and even spoke of Drake getting in the rear of the Armada, following it and trapping it between himself and Howard. So much for concentration. There were stranger suggestions

[1] Brushfield, 'The Spanish Invasion of 1588', 276-9.

still – that while Howard defended England against the Armada, Drake might sneak behind to mount a counter-offensive against Spain, possibly by landing Dom Antonio to foment a rising in Portugal or by cruising to the Azores. Such a strategy would, of course, have separated the English at the very time that unification was most needed. It was preposterous.[1]

Nevertheless, towards the close of March the Privy Council seems to have decided that Drake should do something, even though the negotiations with Parma continued, for it issued a royal warrant authorizing him to purchase victuals for 2,900 men over a two-month period beginning 24 April. Yet they were unprepared for the additional demands Sir Francis now clapped upon them. On 30 March he addressed a letter to them, couched in his most obsequious style, but calling for a concentration of shipping and an offensive that would raise morale at home and disrupt Spain's preparations:

> My very good Lords, next under God's mighty protection, the advantage and gain of time and place will be the only and chief means for our good; wherein I most humbly beseech your good Lordships to persevere as you have began, for that with fifty sail of shipping, we shall do more good upon their own coast than a great many more will do here at home, and the sooner we are gone the better we shall be able to impeach them.[2]

When the queen asked for more details, Drake refused to commit himself to a precise plan. Now that the Armada appeared to have gathered in Lisbon, he was unsure about what could be achieved, although he envisaged a blockade of the coast and an attempt to harass or disrupt the Armada when it emerged from port. To Elizabeth he merely wrote that once he was upon the Spanish coast he would decide how best to serve her, and added with irresistible venom that much would depend upon the calibre of his men, for 'one such flying now, as Borough did then [in 1587], will put the whole in peril.' In short, she must trust him, but he needed four more of her warships and the sixteen ships and pinnaces then fitting in London to add to his existing thirty sail if he was to make the voyage:

> If the fleet come out of Lisbon, as long as we have victual to live withal upon that coast they shall be fought with, and I hope, through the goodness of our merciful God, in such sort as shall hinder his quiet passage into England . . . The advantage of time and place in all martial actions is half a victory, which being lost is irrecoverable. Wherefore, if your Majesty will command me away with those ships which are here already, and the rest to follow with all possible expedition, I hold it in my poor opinion the surest and best course; and that they bring with them victuals sufficient for themselves and us, to the intent the service be not utterly lost for want thereof.

To rub in the last point, Drake noted that the two months' victuals he had been awarded were insufficient for such an expedition, and remarked that 'here may the whole service and honour be lost for the sparing of a few crowns.'[3]

[1] Tilton, 'Lord Burghley and the Spanish Invasion, 1588'; Advice from England, January 1588, Hume, ed., *Calendar of Letters and State Papers . . . in the Archives of Simancas*, 4: 190-1.
[2] Drake to Privy Council, 30 March, 1588, Laughton, 1: 123-6.
[3] Drake to the queen, 13 April, 1588, *Ibid*, 1: 147-9.

Early in May Elizabeth summoned him to court. Rumours of the Armada's sailing were then so rife that, shortly after the admiral left for London, Fenner moved the western fleet to a more forward anchorage in Plymouth and ordered that the seamen must remain aboard and the soldiers close by, in readiness for immediate service. French mariners were saying that they were surprised that Medina Sidonia was not already in the Channel. As he sped towards court, therefore, Drake knew that something very important underlay the call. He found the Privy Council humming with plans for the offensive Drake had demanded, but in a quandary as to what had to be done. Dom Antonio had been stirring it up again, and insisting with might and main that if he could be landed in Portugal with a few thousand soldiers the people of Lisbon would rally to his support. The pretender, as always, sounded convincing, and there were those, like Sir Walter Ralegh, with whom Dom Antonio had recently been consorting, who pointed out that if Lisbon rose against Philip it might be possible to attack the Armada as it sheltered there. Apparently Drake and Essex also favoured the idea, and it was said that Sir Francis and the pretender began meeting at the dead of night so that they could work out the details of the plan without arousing the suspicion of spies. But even Leicester and Walsingham had their doubts about Dom Antonio's scheme. How many soldiers would be needed to attempt Lisbon at a time when it was bristling with arms, men and ships belonging to the Armada? Could they be raised in time? No, the matter was dropped. However, Drake's more modest proposals for a voyage to Spain were more successful.[1]

In fact he succeeded too well, for the queen moved even more shipping to Plymouth than he had wanted, and the Lord Admiral to boot. On 13 May Howard was ordered to shift his fleet to Plymouth, leaving a token force under Seymour to guard the Straits of Dover, and 'to dispose of our navy . . . in placing of the same between the coast of Spain and the west parts, as may best serve to impeach the great navy now prepared in Spain.' Seymour was told that Howard was required to 'lie upon the coast of Spain.' Sir Francis Drake, who had returned to Plymouth, can only have been disappointed. His strategy had triumphed, and the English fleet – the combined force of Drake and Howard that would fight the Armada – was to be grouped in the west. But he had not bargained for the transfer of so many ships, nor for the arrival of the Lord Admiral. Once Howard reached Plymouth, Drake would lose his independent command, the emoluments that went with that position, and, most important of all, the complete control of his own expedition. Drake must have frowned, for Howard had been at court with him earlier that month, and had spoken against the offensive against Spain. The queen had backed the opinion of her greatest sailor, but it remained to be seen how far Howard would co-operate with a plan he had personally opposed.[2]

Howard, flying his flag aboard the *Ark Royal*, arrived at Plymouth with a detachment of sixteen ships, nearly 4,000 men and a month's victuals on the morning of 23 May. Undoubtedly he was apprehensive at assuming command over Sir Francis Drake and a force that had learned to be loyal to him, but as the Lord Admiral approached

[1] Among several references to the plan to use Dom Antonio, see the intelligence of Antonio de Vega, 17, 21 May, 1588, Hume, 4: 298-300.
[2] Queen's letters to Howard and Seymour, 13 May, 1588, *Foljambe Papers*, 116; Lord Talbot to Shrewsbury, 7 May, 1588, Owen, ed., *Bath MSS*, 5: 90-1.

the Sound he was greeted by a remarkable sight. Drake led some forty sail in three files, with banners streaming and music playing, to meet the newcomers, and escorted them into port in a style that would have befitted the queen. He had no intention of playing dog in the manger, and a few weeks later a relieved Howard was able to inform Walsingham that 'I must not omit to let you know how lovingly and kindly Sir Francis Drake beareth himself, and how dutifully to Her Majesty's service and unto me, being in the place I am in, which I pray you he may receive thanks for by some private letter from you.'[1]

Drake's own fears were no less unjustified, for the Lord Admiral was willing to learn from his deputy, and after a council of war that lasted through 24 and 25 May, in which there was some opposition to Drake's ideas, he proclaimed them as proudly as if they were his own. 'Sir,' Howard admitted to Walsingham, 'you know it [has] been the opinion both of Her Majesty and others, that it was [the sur]est course to lie on the coast of Spain. I confess my error at that time, which was otherwise, but I did and will yield ever unto them of greater experience.' Drake's opinion had prevailed not only over the government and Lord Admiral, but over the leading seamen Howard had brought with him. Howard wrote:

> The opinion of Sir Francis Drake, Mr [John] Hawkins, Mr Frobisher, and others that be men of greatest judgment [and] experience, as also my concurring with them the same, is that [the] surer way to meet with the Spanish fleet is upon their own [coast], or in any harbour of their own, and there to defeat them.

During the ensuing weeks an excellent relationship developed between the two commanders of the English fleet, with Howard acting on Drake's advice ('it hath pleased his good Lordship to accept of that which I have sometimes spoken,' said Drake), and the Lord Admiral shoring up his own credibility by reference to the vice-admiral's authority. Now we find Howard writing such phrases as 'Sir Francis Drake and all here do think', and even soliciting a testimonial from the vice-admiral on a letter he had written defending himself from imputations of negligence. There is nothing in the correspondence that indicates that at this time Drake and Howard worked other than in complete harmony.[2]

Shortly after his arrival, Howard formalized his advisory council, the men who would manage the campaign. Sir Francis Drake was there, of course, and with him John Hawkins of the Victory, serving as rear-admiral of the combined force, Martin Frobisher of the Triumph, and Thomas Fenner. There were, besides, three other members whose inclusion had to be defended to the government. Sir Roger Williams, a veteran of Sluys, was needed to advise upon land matters, Howard explained, and the remaining two were 'gallant gentlemen, and not only forwards, but very discreet in all their doings.' This could not hide the obvious nepotism behind the Lord Admiral's last nominations, for one was his cousin, Lord Thomas Howard of the Golden Lion, and the other his nephew, Lord Edmund Sheffield of the White Bear. Neither had much to contribute. Lord Thomas was only twenty-seven and Lord Sheffield still younger at twenty-five, and both were inexperienced. Yet their inclusion had practical value to

[1] Howard to Walsingham, 14 June, 1588, Laughton, 1: 199-202.
[2] Howard to Walsingham, 13 June, 1588, Ibid, 1: 256-8; Drake to Walsingham, 11 August, 1588, Ibid, 2: 101.

Howard, for both men could be counted upon to support him in a vote. Howard needed the advice of the sea-dogs, but he was careful to avoid being dominated by them. He was the Lord Admiral, in act as well as name.[1]

Drake's offensive had conquered opinion, but other obstacles proved more stubborn. The shipping was mercifully in order. This was a service that promised hard fighting rather than financial return, and it had not been outfitted on the old joint-stock basis. In the national emergency the government had placed an embargo on ports, requiring them to furnish vessels for the fleet and to maintain them with a local tax. The towns affected naturally complained, but Drake had got his ships, from havens on both sides of the western peninsula. Nor was manpower deficient, despite the indifferent wage of 10 shillings a month paid to the seamen. Victuals, however, were a different matter. Sir Francis and other officials had been impounding munitions, powder, stores and provisions from ships trading with the enemy since the previous year, in Falmouth, Plymouth and elsewhere. While unjustified seizures were restored, some confiscated victuals found their way to the English fleet. But for the most part Drake and Howard depended upon royal warrants that authorized the purchase of provisions. Unfortunately, the increased demand stretched local supplies and inflated prices, and some merchants were reluctant to deal with so poor a payer as the Crown – three merchants who supplied goods totalling £1,481 in value were still claiming payment two years afterwards. Worse still, the government consistently sent their warrants late, forcing the fleet to eke out threadbare supplies. As we have seen, Drake had been victualled up to 24 June, but the arrival of Howard's ships, predictably under-provisioned, meant he had exhausted his victuals by 15 June. There was no prospect of going to Spain in those circumstances.[2]

It was a combination of the weather and victualling problems that effectively postponed Drake's attack. An unseasonal wind from the west and south-west blew gustily into the teeth of the English and prevented them sailing for the best part of a month. They tried to break out on 30 May but were beaten back within days, and it was while they sat in port fuming at their bad fortune that the remaining victuals were extinguished to no purpose. Drake had the feeling that his chance of pre-empting the Armada was slipping away. According to the crew of a ship from San Lucar that the English had encountered in their attempt to get out of the Channel Medina Sidonia was already at sea with two hundred ships. In reporting it to Burghley, Drake marked that 'either we shall hear of them very shortly or else they will go to the Groyne and there assemble themselves.'[3] It was his latter estimate that proved correct, and created the final opportunity for him to anticipate the Armada.

The prospect suddenly improved in the third week in June. The gales subsided and at midnight on the 22nd fifteen ships from London arrived with the needed victuals. The fleet broke into a frenzied activity, as the men laboured through the rest of the night by torchlight and during the following day to load enough of the new stores to put to sea. The air of expectation and excitement was increased as important fresh news suggested that Medina Sidonia had in fact put to sea but that his fleet was in dis-

[1] Howard to Walsingham, 19 June, 1588, *Ibid*, 1: 208-12.
[2] For seizures at sea, Dasent, ed., *Acts of the Privy Council*, and Butler, ed., *Calendar of State Papers, Foreign*, 21 (part 4): 485. Claims of merchants, *Salisbury*, 4: 52-3, 79.
[3] Drake to Burghley, 6 June, 1588, Owen, 2: 28.

array. Some mariners reported that about 19 June they had come upon nine large Spanish ships between the Scilly Islands and Ushant. To Drake and Howard it suggested that the gales had broken the Armada into companies, and they surmised that if they sailed immediately they might find the Spanish ships scattered along the French coast, vulnerable to attack. It was an opportunity they dare not forego. Without waiting to stow all the new provisions aboard they darted from Plymouth like hungry wolves running down stricken deer.

They were too late. Medina Sidonia had left Lisbon with 151 ships on 18 May, his flag aboard the *San Martin*, but winds had first driven his ships south and then scattered them, so that only a few reached the appointed rendezvous off the Scillies. They remained long enough to alert the English to the Armada's predicament, and then turned back. Medina Sidonia got most of his fleet into Corunna, where they spent a month refitting, replacing bad food and water, and discharging the sick. The duke was close to despair, and again appealed to Philip to consider whether the campaign should be prosecuted further, but with no greater success than before. Sail the Armada would, insisted the king, and Medina Sidonia dutifully obeyed. Piecing his fleet together, he eventually led some 130 sail from Corunna on 12 July and steered towards England.

As Drake and Howard made their dash upon the Armada it was already retiring towards Corunna, and when the English reached the Scilly Islands they could find no trace of the Spaniards. The wind also turned foul again, swinging to south-south-west, and retarding further headway. Clawing his way along the French coast with a detachment of ten ships and three or four pinnaces, Drake came upon a Dublin bark that had brushed with a large Spanish force 15 leagues off the Lizard on 21 June. This confirmed the earlier reports, but it seemed clear to Drake that the enemy had since withdrawn, and he therefore proposed that the English press on to Spain at the first favourable wind. For two days Howard threw a screen of ships between Ushant and the Scillies to satisfy himself that the Spaniards had indeed retired, but time only vindicated Drake's opinion and various French and English vessels they encountered gave out that the Armada had been dispersed into different havens. Here seemed the opportunity Drake had longed for prior to the concentration of Medina Sidonia's fleet at Lisbon, an opportunity to attack disparate fragments of the enemy force or to frustrate its regrouping. The seventh of July saw the wind northerly and Howard and Drake forging towards Spain, but it was to no avail. The fickle elements veered powerfully to the south-west and there was nothing the English could do but run before them back to Plymouth.

This was the last of Drake's efforts to intercept the Armada, and those in the English fleet who had imbibed his confidence were intensely disappointed. It is impossible to estimate what would have been the result had the encounter he had wanted taken place. The English did not doubt that they could give the Spaniards a drubbing and that their ships and gunnery were superior, but the battles ahead were to prove that they underestimated the Armada, and that it took far more powder and shot to deal with than they had bargained for. In a full-blown action off Spain, Drake and Howard could have exhausted their ammunition and been reduced to following Medina Sidonia ineffectually into the Channel. On the other hand, this may be an unduly pessimistic view. On many occasions the Spaniards had been in vulnerable positions. In March the Armada was in a chaotic state following the death of Santa Cruz, and some of its ships were in Cadiz and elsewhere. In June it had been scattered by storms, with portions of it as close to the English as the Scillies, while thereafter until 12 July most of the Spanish ships sheltered in Corunna, a haven Drake was to breach in a year's time. And even if the English had met Medina Sidonia's force at sea it is probable that Drake and Howard would have used the superior sailing qualities of their ships to keep the weather-gauge (i.e., remain in the windward position) with the prospect of picking up stragglers or falling upon groups of ships that became isolated. The fact is that Drake was denied his chance, and speculation about the possible outcome of the conflict is specious. Drake's own optimism was as much the product of temperament and instinct as a careful evaluation of respective fleets. We can no more imagine him sitting happily at home waiting for Medina Sidonia than we can see Nelson pottering about Europe in 1805 awaiting the return of Villeneuve. Action and excitement, no less than salt, were in his blood.

Just what were the differences between the Spanish and English fleets in that momentous year of 1588, as Europe held its breath? Did the advantages lie with Howard or with Medina Sidonia? Nineteenth-century Britons thrilled to a tradition that told of a David and Goliath contest in which small English ships overwhelmed the great galleons of Spain, but like so many patriotic myths it disguised the reality. It is true that on the whole Philip's fleet was composed of larger vessels, and their visual impact was enhanced by the huge stern- and forecastles that many of them carried as well as by the presence of four 600-ton Italian galleasses, which employed banks of blood-red oars to supplement their sails. The Armada must have been a terrifying sight. By comparison the English ships were lighter. Although England's fleet had greater numbers of smaller vessels, it could dispose only fifty-one ships in excess of 200 tons' burden against the ninety-three Medina Sidonia brought to the Channel. But the Armada was a giant that rested on distinctly shaky foundations. Its fighting core was deficient in speed and manoeuvrability, in guns and gunnery skills, the qualities that were to prove decisive in the battles ahead.

The nucleus of the English fleet was formed by the queen's ships, twenty-five of which were over 100 tons' burden. Created in the reigns of Henry VIII and Mary Tudor, and maintained thereafter, England's navy had evolved into the best in Europe. Oared galleys, once the basis of Mediterranean sea power but quite unsuitable for mounting broadside guns or for service in the heavy rollers of the Atlantic, had been discarded, and only one survived in 1588. As we have seen it was assigned pedestrian duties in the Thames under William Borough, who had run afoul of Drake the year before. Even the design of the sailing ships that now constituted England's fleet had undergone a period of experimentation and development by the time they fought the Armada. The changes have been attributed to John Hawkins, who became treasurer of the navy in 1578, but they had an older history and were evident from the first years of Elizabeth's reign. If credit must be attached to particular individuals, it would more justifiably rest with William Winter, who had been surveyor of the navy from 1549, and with the royal shipwrights, Richard Bull, Peter Pett and Matthew Baker.

Whoever was responsible, the changes produced a new breed of ships, nimbler, faster, and capable of mounting substantial numbers of broadside guns. The large

231

superstructures on the bows and sterns, traditionally the home of the soldiers who were expected to board enemy vessels as they grappled side by side, were reduced, and the low waists removed. The hull was lengthened in proportion to its breadth, until the ratio of the one to the other was a little under three-to-one; and the draught was deepened. The result was a long rather than a 'round' ship, more streamlined, more stable, handier, and able to sail closer to the wind. The new ships were generally smaller than their predecessors, but their main instruments of combat were broadside guns, and they did not need to carry large numbers of soldiers. They heralded a new and revolutionary mode of naval warfare. The ship should not be a mere transport, loaded with men, and placed beside an opposing vessel so that the battle could be decided by boarding. It was itself an agent of destruction, able to manoeuvre for position so that its guns could be used to defeat the adversary at a distance.

Slowly, from the beginning of Elizabeth's reign, these new ships had developed, and most of them were with Drake and Howard: the *Elizabeth Jonas, Hope, Triumph, Aid, White Bear, Foresight, Dreadnought, Swiftsure, Revenge* and *Ark Royal*, to name the largest. Some vessels bought from the merchant service and incorporated into the navy, such as Hawkins's *Victory* and the *Elizabeth Bonaventure*, had been partially re-built along the new lines, as had older vessels such as the *Golden Lion, Nonpareil, Swallow* and *Mary Rose*. They gave the English an important advantage during the Armada battles, because the Spaniards had not only been slower to develop a purpose-built navy but had substantially embraced the older tradition of naval warfare, in which the soldier rather than the ship or the gun was the instrument of combat. Drake's raid of 1587 had led them courageously to scrap their substantial galley fleet, which they recognized would be of little assistance in an artillery duel, but their sailing ships – for the most part armed merchantmen – were generally stubbier and clumsier than the queen's ships. Indeed, instead of reducing the sterns and forecastles of their vessels during the months before the Armada sailed, the Spaniards provided loftier super-structures for ships they considered to be under-endowed. No, Medina Sidonia might have the larger vessels, but his principal fighting ships were seriously deficient in sailing qualities compared with the vessels of the queen's navy.

Nor was this all, for there was a still more important difference between the two fleets. The Armada was heavily manned, but had both fewer and lighter guns than its opponents. Overall, the weight of metal it could fire was probably about a third less than that available to the English. At all ranges the Spaniards were at a disadvantage, and a massive disadvantage it was, because it was compounded by the inadequacy of their gunnery skills. They were still wedded to a battle of boarders rather than guns, and did not develop techniques of continuous fire. Rather, soldiers were drilled to dis-charge the pieces and then disperse to boarding stations, and so little attention was paid to recharging and refiring processes that the artillery was lashed to the ships' sides and mounted on unwieldy carriages. When more regular firing did become necessary, the Spaniards found the larger guns too difficult to manoeuvre and resorted to the smaller pieces, thus exacerbating their own lack of fire power. And as if this was not enough, because the Armada's guns came from foundries across Europe and had little standardization of bore, the supply of a sufficient quantity of appropriate shot was diffi-cult to ensure. By comparison, however indifferent the English gunnery may have been (and Howard's fleet had neither the battle experience nor the regular practice that could have made it more efficient), it was far superior to the Armada's. The English depended upon the gun, not the soldier, and had long since mounted their pieces on smaller, more manageable carriages, easier to recharge and fire, and it was the duty of their gunners to maintain continuous fire. The advantage that this conferred upon them was invaluable. Even broadside for broadside Howard and Drake outgunned their opponents, but when they could deliver several discharges for every one of the enemy's they were almost undefeatable.[1]

Summing up, both fleets brought to the conflict weapons that reflected the tactics they intended to employ. Philip himself understood that, and in March had reminded Medina Sidonia that the English would have an advantage in artillery, and would endeavour to keep the battle at a distance, firing low into the hulls of the Spanish ships to sink them. The Armada, on the other hand, should try to close with the enemy vessels, grapple and board them. Accordingly, Drake and Howard's ships were swift, better armed and manned by professional gunners; Medina Sidonia's enjoyed a superiority in manpower, and carried generous reserves of soldiers. It was the English, however, who held the initiative. Their superior sailing qualities could dictate the course of the action, keep the fight at a distance while their guns pounded the Spanish ships, and deny Medina Sidonia the opportunity to employ his boarders.

The commander of the Spanish fleet was not even impressed by his own men, and bluntly told Philip so:

> To undertake so great a task with equal forces to those of the enemy would be inadvisable, but to do so with an inferior force, as ours is now, with our men lacking in experience, would be still more unwise. I am bound to confess that I see very few, or hardly any, of those on the armada with any knowledge of or ability to perform the duties entrusted to them. I have tested and watched this point very carefully, and your Majesty may believe me when I assure you that we are very weak.[2]

Perhaps Medina Sidonia exaggerated. He, like Howard, was a grandee rather than a battle admiral, but there were some tough, experienced officers to hand, men such as Juan Martinez de Recalde, the second-in-command, and Miguel de Oquendo, both of whom had served in the great battle of the Azores in 1582. It is often forgotten that the English themselves had little experience in full-blown naval warfare. England had no professional navy, no cadre of naval officers inured to years of combat, not a single man seasoned in fleet action. The men of 1588 were not naval commanders in the modern sense. They were traders, explorers or privateers, few of whom had seen sustained gun action. They were fine seamen, certainly, confident and brave, but largely unprepared for what lay ahead of them. George Fenner might speak of his victory over the Portuguese in 1567; John Hawkins remembered the battle in San Juan d'Ulua; and

---

[1] For ship design, guns and gunnery I have drawn upon Martin and Parker; Rodriguez-Salgado; Glasgow, 'The Shape of the Ships That Defeated the Spanish Armada'; and Thompson, 'Spanish Armada Guns'. It must be presumed that Drake approved of the improved design of English warships. In 1590 three more ships were built for the queen, the Merhonour, Garland and Defiance. Their keels were just under three times the length of the beam, and depths nearly half the beam. These would seem to have been regarded as the ideal hull proportions. The ships were designed by a committee composed of Drake, Winter, Hawkins, Howard, Borough, Fenton and the royal shipwrights. That Drake and Hawkins were satisfied seems to be implied by their choice of two of these new ships as flagships for their last voyage in 1595.

[2] Medina Sidonia to Philip, 24 June, 1588, Hume, 4: 317-19.

Drake, Thomas Fenner and Robert Crosse had done violence to various Spanish galleys during their cruise of 1587. But none of these actions approximated in scale or circumstance to the great conflicts in the Channel.

It was with a tremendous sense of occasion, of participating in a momentous episode in history, that Europeans on both sides of the religious and political divide waited for the clash that could determine not only the fates of England and the Netherlands but also the fortunes of the Reformation. Some shuddered at ancient prophecies that foretold 1588 as a year of cataclysm and revolution in which 'empires will dwindle and from everywhere will be great lamentation.'[1]

For the English fleet the days that followed the abortive expedition to Spain were occupied by refitting and revictualling the ships. The government continued to press supplies forward with reluctance, waiting until the middle of July to authorize the purchase of a further twenty days' provisions, and were so late to ship extra powder from the Tower that it did not reach the fleet in time for the first engagement.

On the morning of 19 July Captain Thomas Fleming was cruising with some thirty men off the Lizard in his 50-ton *Golden Hind*. He may have been reconnoitring for Drake and Howard, but hard words have been said of him. William Monson, then a young officer aboard one of the queen's ships, described him as a 'pirate' who was out 'a-pilfering' that summer morning, and although the remark has generally been dismissed, perhaps it was true. On 7 June the Privy Council had ordered his arrest for the taking of Thomas Nicolls's 80-ton hoy, the *Hope* of Newhaven. Whatever, some time that morning he saw several ships in the distance, towards the Scillies, their sails struck as if they lay waiting for consorts to come up. Gradually, the Englishmen distinguished large crosses emblazoned on the sails of the strange vessels. Spaniards! It may have been the duty of the queen's officers to seize Fleming if he put into port, but he promptly put about to carry the news to Plymouth. And soon alert watchers on the Cornish cliffs were lighting beacons to relay the same news. The great Armada was sailing into the Channel.

---

[1] Mattingly, 160.

# CHAPTER EIGHTEEN

# 'IT WAS IMPOSSIBLE TO COME TO HAND-STROKE WITH THEM'

And in your fighting evermore, think you are Englishmen,
Then every one of you I hope will slay of Spaniards ten,
Or any else whatever they be, that shall disturb your peace
And seek by any kind of mean your quiet to decease.

Henry Roberts, *A Most Friendly Farewell*, 1585

IT IS ONE OF THE MOST ENDURING STORIES IN BRITISH HISTORY. CAPTAIN FLEMING, or some other breathless messenger, found the commanders of the English fleet quietly playing bowls on Plymouth Hoe. His announcement that the Armada was on the coast created a whir of excitement, perhaps even of panic, as the captains began to hustle to their ships. Yet Sir Francis Drake himself was unmoved. 'There is plenty of time to finish the game and beat the Spaniards too,' he remarked, and so saying he continued his bowling and restored equanimity among the observers. It is one of the most popular stories in history, but among others comparable to it that tell of Robert the Bruce and the spider, King Alfred's burning cakes and George Washington and the cherry tree, it is not true. There is no credible authority for it.

It was not until 1624 that a shred of evidence for it appeared, and that of the most unimpressive kind. A pamphlet called *Vox Populi*, printed in Goricum, quoted the alleged words of the Duke of Braganza to the Spanish Cortes, a boast to the effect that the Armada had approached England 'so cunningly and secretly' that when it reached the coast 'their commanders and captains were at bowls upon the Hoe of Plymouth; and had my lord Alonso Guzman, the Duke of Medina Sidonia, had but the resolution . . . he might have surprised them at anchor.' Thus the point was not Sir Francis Drake's unperturbability, but the incompetence of the Spanish admiral. The English admirals were not even mentioned by name. A century had to pass before William Oldys, in a *Life of Raleigh* (1736), added to the tradition the story that 'Drake would needs see the game up, but was soon prevailed on to go and play out the rubbers with the Spaniards.' In Oldys's version, therefore, Drake was overruled. Tytler, borrowing from Oldys for another book on Ralegh, published in 1832, seems to have suggested the modern wording, for he had Drake insisting 'that the match be played out, as there was ample time both to win the game and beat the Spaniards', but the story continued to be embellished and achieved great currency during the Second World War, when England faced invasion once more.[1]

On such flimsy foundations rests the most famous of all yarns about Sir Francis Drake. It was not contemporary, its origin was Spanish rather than English, and

---

[1] Lloyd, 'Drake's Game of Bowls'; Tytler, *Life of Raleigh*, 88-9.

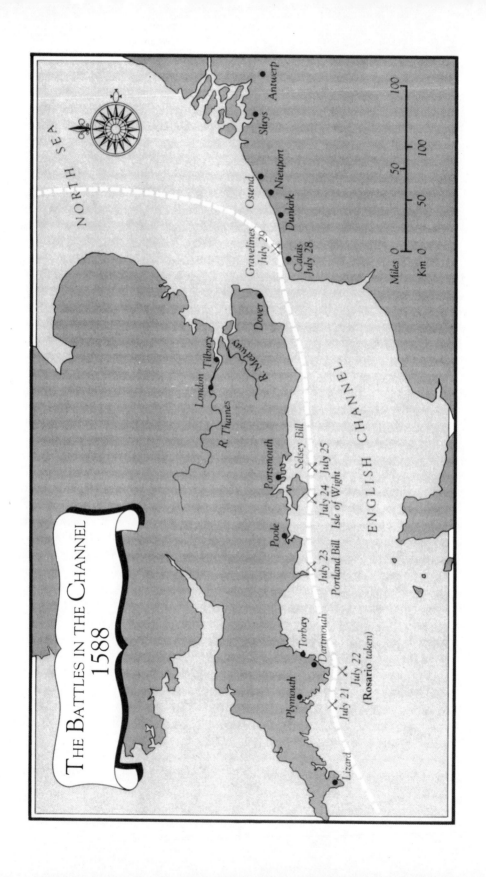

THE BATTLES IN THE CHANNEL
1588

NORTH SEA

Antwerp

Sluys

Nieuport

Ostend

Dunkirk

Gravelines
July 29

Calais
July 28

Dover

London
Tilbury

R. Medway

R. Thames

Selsey Bill

Portsmouth

July 25

Poole

July 24
Isle of Wight

ENGLISH CHANNEL

July 23
Portland Bill

Torbay

Dartmouth

July 22
(**Rosario** taken)

Plymouth

July 21

Lizard

Miles 0        50        100

Km 0        50        100

its point was that the Armada had caught the English napping, and had Medina Sidonia been formed of sterner stuff he might have destroyed Drake in Plymouth. What really happened that 20 July, 1588, when the Armada lay off the Lizard with the wind at south-west, favouring a Spanish advance towards Plymouth and dead set against the English?

The possibility of an attack upon Drake seems to have come up in a council of war called by the Duke of Medina Sidonia. As far as the Spaniards knew, Sir Francis, the dreaded 'El Draque', was in the Sound and Howard still to the east in the narrow seas. Don Alonso Martinez de Leiva, commander of *La Rata Santa Maria Encoronada,* and named in secret orders as successor to Medina Sidonia, urged an attack upon Plymouth to eliminate part of the English fleet. But Medina Sidonia did not like the idea, and reminded his admirals that such an attack would not only be difficult, for Plymouth was not easy of access, but contrary to Philip's orders, which cautioned the fleet against unnecessary diversions and fixed it firmly upon the great task of linking with the Duke of Parma. No, it would not do to risk a crippling battle so early in the campaign and so far from the true objective. It was obvious, however, that the Armada might need shelter, from the weather if not from enemy action, and there was no satisfactory port beyond the Isle of Wight. The council of war apparently decided that if necessary the Armada might use the Isle of Wight before making the junction with Parma. In the meantime it would press on – but prepared for battle.

And onwards it came, sighting the English mainland the same day and slipping past the green shores, from which, on headland to headland and hill to hill, the beacon fires could be seen kindling, carrying the word across the realm, faster than the fastest horse. Within hours grim northerners as far as Durham knew that the invaders were here, and the spirit of '88 was abroad. During those next summer days many men rode along the roads to the coast, not all of them young men, but men enthused with the fervour of Protestant England, men hoping for their chance to fight the Armada. And in the ports little ships were being fitted out. Most of them had never seen battle before, and it was to be doubted if they could be of significant service, even if Howard and Drake wanted them. But they were determined to fight, and to pour from their havens to play their part in the epic and stand a turn in history.

It was a magnificent sight, the great fleet that imperial Spain had sent against England, about 125 ships forming a front of two miles when in battle order, the large fore- and stern-castles on some of the vessels giving them a bulky appearance compared with the smaller English ships that would issue out to meet them. It seemed a more formidable array than it was, with fighting galleons from Spain and Portugal, lumbering Italian galleasses and big armed merchantmen, mixed with numerous freighters and dispatch boats, and massed with 19,000 soldiers armed with arquebuses, muskets and pikes as well as 8,000 sailors. Medina Sidonia's battle formation resembled nothing so much as the head and horns of a gigantic steer, with the duke's principal force, including his own 1,000-ton *San Martin,* some of his warships and the galleasses, composing the head, while on each flank stretched some twenty ships forming the horns, Leiva commanding the left, and the right handled by the Armada's second-in-command, Recalde, the most experienced admiral in the fleet, flying his flag aboard the *San Juan de Portugal*. In principle the head was supposed to engage the enemy, allowing the horns to sweep round to encircle them, and drew for inspiration upon the standard Spanish galley tactics of the Mediterranean. Yet for all that the Armada was already displaying some of the weaknesses that would undo it. It was a convoy, shepherding large numbers of transports, and could move only as fast as its slowest member, and its advance was far too ponderous to have caught the English in Plymouth, even if Leiva's plan had been adopted.

Medina Sidonia did not come close to bottling up Drake and Howard. They must have heard of his approach on the afternoon of 19 July, when the tide was running into the Sound and the wind was at south-west. Getting out would call for seamanship of the highest order. When the tide began to ebb, the English put out boats to tow their ships from harbour against the wind, and it was not until late that night that the movement was under way. Drake had dispatched a messenger, William Page, to speed to the queen with the news, but during the morning of the 20th he was with Howard and fifty-four sail, beating out towards the open sea. In the afternoon they were off the Eddystone rocks when they saw it: an ominous wall of shipping to windward, the Spanish fleet at last. They had seen nothing like it before and Howard could not contain his amazement. All the world, he later said, never saw such a force as this. But there was no time to waste, for the Armada would soon be threatening Plymouth, and as the rain reduced visibility the English spent the remainder of the day and night striving to gain the weather-gauge – the attacking position.

In naval engagements of the sailing ship era opponents might fight from either the windward (or upwind) or the leeward (or downwind) position. Those in the windward position were said to have the weather-gauge. With the wind behind them, they possessed the advantage of being able to attack at their convenience, and to manoeuvre more efficiently, but even if they seriously disabled an enemy vessel by dismasting her they were not always able to make a capture, since an injured ship could generally retreat before the wind to leeward. In the last years of sailing-ship tactics enterprising British admirals attempted to solve the problem by attacking from the windward position, but once engaged passing to leeward to seal off an opponent's retreat. Dawn of 21 July, 1588 showed that Howard and Drake had got around the Armada to gain the weather-gauge, ready to launch their first assault upon the Spanish rear. How they achieved this position no one knows, whether by working westwards inshore or by striking across Medina Sidonia's front and passing to his rear around his right flank. Yet it was a considerable feat, only revealed to the Spaniards by daylight. Far from being bottled in Plymouth, or waiting to be attacked from leeward, there was 'El Draque' bearing down behind them! If any of the Spaniards had had doubts about English seamanship, they must have shed them that first morning of battle.

Surprisingly, these important naval engagements in the Channel are ill documented from the English point of view. The commanders were evidently too busy fighting to write full dispatches, and the one sustained narrative, given by Howard to Petruccio Ubaldino, is disappointingly scant in its details of Drake. One reason for this is that Howard simply did not know what Drake was doing. In the first two battles, off Plymouth and Portland Bill, the movements of the English ships were somewhat unco-ordinated, with ship's commanders acting much on their own initiative. The situation proved unsatisfactory, and on 24 July the English endeavoured to obtain greater control by dividing the fleet into four squadrons. Frobisher, in the *Triumph*, was at the head of one of them, closest inshore; Howard in the *Ark Royal* had another squadron on Frobisher's right flank; Hawkins came next; and Drake commanded the seaward wing of the English fleet. Yet even this device gave limited control, for the squadrons operated almost independently, with Drake neither taking orders from Howard nor giving any to Hawkins or Frobisher. In these circumstances the Lord Admiral had no clear idea of what was happening amid the smoke of battle. We find him speaking very satisfactorily of his own exploits, and a little about Frobisher, but he had less to say about Hawkins and nothing of Drake, who for the most part operated independently far to the south, beyond Howard's cognizance.

There is the possibility, too, that by the time the Lord Admiral was working with Ubaldino he had conceived some jealousy for his vice-admiral. Rumour had it that the public considered that what credit there was in defeating the Armada belonged to Drake, and that Howard resented the idea. Conceivably, the story was without foundation, but it is strange that Howard's narrative omitted all reference to the engagement of 24 July, when Drake's division fought a considerable battle with the Armada just off the Isle of Wight and dealt it higher casualties than it had sustained in any previous action. On that day, said Howard, 'there was little done.'[1] That he should draw a veil over an encounter described in many Spanish accounts implies something less than objectivity in his account.

Reconstructing Drake's movements in the Armada battles is not, therefore, straightforward. Apparently Sir Francis himself recognized the want of information, because when Petruccio Ubaldino – the same concocting an account for Howard – approached Drake for further details, the vice-admiral was happy to redress the deficiency, but his revisions seem to have been interrupted and add little new perspective to the engagements themselves. In consequence it is not to the English, but to the Spanish accounts that historians have looked for the most complete picture of the conflict, and in those Sir Francis and the *Revenge* emerge more clearly, if still obscurely, from the gunsmoke.[2]

This was to be a new battle for every one of the participants. It was more than that, for these encounters in the Channel amounted to the first major naval battle that emphasized sails and guns rather than oars and boarders. It marked the beginning of the great age of fighting sail as surely as the ruins of the Turkish fleet at Navarino two and a half centuries later denoted its end. Drake and Howard, Recalde and Medina Sidonia, professional and amateur, all were in for surprises in these fierce clashes. The first belonged to the Spaniards, as they saw the English fleet behind them on the morning of 21 July, south of Plymouth.

---

[1] Howard, 'A Relation of Proceedings', Laughton, *State Papers Relating to the Defeat of the Spanish Armada*, 1: 1-18. The relation is unsigned, but evidently was composed from Howard's information.

[2] Spanish accounts can be found in Duro, ed., *La Armada Invencible*; Hume, *Calendar of Letters and State Papers . . . in the Archives of Simancas*, vol. 4; and Oria, *La Armada Invencible*. Naish, *Naval Miscellany*, prints the Ubaldino narrative adapted by Drake.

The wind, which had been south-westerly, was veering to west-north-west, and Howard and Drake had the Armada to leeward, between Plymouth and themselves. But inshore, still working their way to windward of the Spaniards, were some English stragglers, including a few galleons, and although these eventually passed westwards to join their comrades they formed the initial focus of the battle of Plymouth. The royal standard fluttered to the foremast of Medina Sidonia's flagship, and the Armada shuffled into battle formation. Hauling in their sheets, the Spaniards steered towards Plymouth, possibly to cut off the English ships that were still to leeward, possibly, as far as Drake and Howard knew, to enter the Sound. The English admirals had little more than fifty of their ships available, but they had to drive the Armada beyond Plymouth, and they plunged after it.

Yet now the English inexperience showed itself. They could not have been skilled gunners, as we have seen, but the little sustained gunnery they remembered had been in unusual circumstances. They had sunk ships by gunfire at San Juan d'Ulua and Cadiz, but then their opponents had been in confined anchorages, unable to manoeuvre from the shot, pinned down beneath a point-blank hammering. In open water it was different, as targets moved in and out of range or in front of or behind other ships, and as the attackers had to pause to go about to bring their guns to bear again. During battles of this kind it was extremely difficult to sink ships by gunfire alone, and even the terrible ship-smashing batteries mounted by Nelson's ships seldom won victories that way; rather they killed or maimed so many of the enemy's crew or disabled their ship so badly that it could be successfully boarded or compelled to surrender. Drake and his comrades hardly knew this. They noted those soldiers gathering on the decks of Medina Sidonia's ships and decided to keep their distance at all costs, apparently believing that their artillery alone could do the job. Instead of moving in close and using their heavier armament to maximum effect, relying upon their superior sailing abilities to get them out of trouble, the English chose to pop away almost harmlessly at a distance. Howard was quite frank about it: 'we durst not adventure to put in among them, their fleet being so strong.'[1]

In the first battle off Plymouth it was at once evident that the English ships were too nimble for the plodding Spaniards, but no less so than that the fire of Howard and Drake was having little effect. The weather-gauge conferred an advantage on the English, for as they attacked the Armada's rear the Spaniards found it difficult to beat back against the wind to support their hindmost consorts. Howard struck at Medina Sidonia's left flank, firing upon Leiva's *La Rata Santa Maria Encoronada*, while Drake led an attack upon the other wing, where Recalde's *San Juan de Portugal*, itself more than twice the tonnage of the *Revenge*, was the leading flagship. Recalde made no attempt to escape, but bravely turned to face the assault, and received the fire of Drake, Hawkins, Frobisher and others for the best part of two hours before some of the heavy Armada ships were able to swing round to rescue him. The English then sheered off and after about four hours the battle of Plymouth came to an end.

Drake had been impressed by Recalde's courage, and decided to warn Lord

[1] Howard to Walsingham, 21 July, 1588, Laughton, 1: 288-9.

Henry Seymour who lay ahead in the narrow seas. As he put it, an exchange had taken place between 'some of our fleet and some of them' and 'as far as we perceive they are determined to sell their lives with blows.' There were above 'a hundred sails, many great ships; but truly, I think not half of them men-of-war,' he added shrewdly. Howard, too, was beginning to gauge the metal of his opponents, and called for more powder and shot, remarking, 'This service will continue long.'[1] The action had been a testing time for both fleets, but while Howard had harried Medina Sidonia beyond Plymouth and demonstrated that his leading warships handled better than the Spaniards, he may have sensed the inadequacy of the English performance. Not a single Armada ship had been taken or destroyed, and Medina Sidonia's formation had remained basically intact. He did not know it, but even Recalde's *San Juan*, which had taken such punishment, had sustained relatively minor damage: torn rigging, a damaged foremast, a cut forestay and a number of dead, fifteen by one account. It seemed as if the English had not only been firing badly, but too high, for little if any injury had been visited upon the hull. Don Pedro de Valdes, admiral of the Andalucian squadron and commander of the *Nuestra Señora del Rosario*, put it into a nutshell: 'There was little harm done because the fight was far off.'[2]

The Armada had successfully repulsed the first attack, and proceeded on through the Channel, edging towards the rendezvous with Parma, but two accidents now cost it the first losses. Recalde wanted to repair his ship in case the English renewed the assault, and called for assistance. As Don Pedro de Valdes made towards the *San Juan* to help her, his ship collided twice with Biscayans, and lost her foreyard, bowsprit, halyards and forecourse. The *Nuestra Señora del Rosario* was a big 1,150-ton *nao*, a multipurpose vessel now armed for war, and carried about 450 crew and fifty-two guns. Her men struggled to fit a new forecourse and contain the other damage, but the sea grew rougher and the wind intensified, and the foremast suddenly cracked close to the hatches and crashed against the mainmast. The ship was now in real distress, and Don Pedro fired three or four guns to signal his plight, begging Medina Sidonia to wait for him. But the admiral had the fleet to think of, and although his efforts to have the *Rosario* taken in tow failed, he held his eastward course and gradually left her to the rear.

She was no mean vessel to lose. Apart from being one of the largest and most heavily armed in the fleet, and the flagship of one of the Armada's leading officers, one whose reputation was probably only surpassed by those of Recalde and Oquendo, the *Rosario* stored about a third of the Armada's money. Her captain, Vicente Alvarez, said she carried 52,000 of the king's ducats in a chest, 4,000 reals, [about 400 ducats] belonging to Alvarez and other gentlemen, and a store of precious jewels and apparel. Don Pedro, who served in her as admiral, gave a more modest figure: 20,000 ducats, and silver vessels worth another thousand. In either case there were few ships in the fleet so wealthy.

The other accident cost Medina Sidonia a second prime warship, one of Miguel de Oquendo's Guipuzcoan squadron, called the *San Salvador*. For some

[1] Drake to Seymour, 21 July, 1588, *Ibid*, 1: 289-90.
[2] Don Pedro de Valdes to the king, 21 August, 1588, *Ibid*, 2: 133-6.

reason – whether through accident or sabotage was never established – she caught fire and the great quantity of powder she carried went up in a vast explosion that ripped away her stern and two decks and killed about two hundred men. Boats were ordered to her rescue, and the fire was extinguished, but all that remained was a burned out shell, stinking of charred wood and bodies. Most of the survivors of her crew were evacuated, but with the English fleet closing, the Spaniards abandoned the *San Salvador* to the winds and current with some dreadfully injured men still aboard her.

Although neither loss had been directly caused by English action, and the Armada was pressing relentlessly onwards, Medina Sidonia may have thought more seriously about the possibility of a haven such as the Isle of Wight. There would be more battles, more casualties, and no one could guess what shape the Armada would be in when it reached Parma. Drake and Howard were worrying about it too, and talking it through in council. They were short of powder and shot, and the action off Plymouth suggested that they were going to need more of it than they had believed. It was likely that there would be a greater battle off the Isle of Wight, if Medina Sidonia threatened to run into Spithead, and although the English had now been reinforced by the ships that had not managed to quit Plymouth in time for the first débâcle, it was unwise to press the Armada too closely at this time. Yet they must follow it and look for opportunities, and it was decided that Sir Francis Drake should lead. During the night of 21-22 July he would keep his stern lantern alight to mark the course for the rest of the fleet.

During the darkness Sir Francis dogged the rear of the great Armada, as it bore slowly along, past Start Point and the Skerries Rock, and through Start Bay. Then something happened. The watch of the *Revenge* reported lights to the right, perhaps three or four ships sailing abreast, but what ships? And to what purpose? One possibility was that some of the Spaniards were working to windward of the English in the dark, just as Drake and Howard had done the previous night, and Drake deemed it his duty to investigate. Since he did not wish to lead the whole of the English fleet from their course, he ordered the lantern of the *Revenge* to be extinguished, and put about towards the strange vessels, bringing with him only the *Roebuck* and one or two pinnaces.[1]

[1] Some writers, eager to attack Drake, have accepted at face value Martin Frobisher's unsupported insinuation that Drake abandoned his position for the sole purpose of capturing the *Rosario*, and that Sir Francis's story about the freighters was invented. It is worth remembering that Drake could not have known of the wealth aboard the *Rosario* before he captured her, and that his account is fully supported by Matthew Starke (deposition, 11 August, 1588, Laughton, 2: 101-4). Frobisher's allegations (recorded by Starke) were stimulated by jealousy of the vice-admiral and a fear that he, as the captor of the *Rosario*, would claim the full amount of the prize money for the *Revenge* instead of sharing it with the fleet (petition of the officers of the *Margaret and John*, August, 1588, *Ibid*, 2: 104-7). No one else seems to have raised the charges, and Howard thought so little of them that he allowed Drake to hold the watch for the fleet on subsequent occasions, including the night after the decisive battle off Gravelines. Further vindication of Drake's story is provided by the deposition of Hans Buttber, who seems to have been skipper of one of the freighters Drake investigated on the night of 21 July (Klarwill, *Fugger News-Letters*, 2: 168). Buttber stated that he was bound for Hamburg from San Lucar, when Drake intercepted him on 21 July, 'just after the latter had had an engagement with the Spanish Armada.' Sir Francis told Buttber to attach himself to the English fleet for safety, and the German was present at the capture of Don Pedro. On 26 July Drake allowed him to proceed on his journey, providing he took a message with him for Seymour's squadron off

The quarry turned out to be harmless, merely German freighters, and Drake eventually started back to rejoin the fleet, probably feeling not a little chagrined. But he did not return empty-handed, for at dawn of 22 July he came upon Don Pedro's great *nao*, *Nuestra Señora del Rosario*, which had dropped out of the Armada and lay to the south so that the English fleet had passed her by. Don Pedro was in a poor position indeed. His ship was powerful, and her tonnage exceeded the *Revenge* and *Roebuck* combined, but he was virtually without sails, his mainmast was damaged and his foremast and bowsprit had gone. A few ships and pinnaces had tried to take the *Rosario* in tow during the night, but fear of falling behind Medina Sidonia as well as poor weather and big seas frustrated their efforts, and the last of them had made off about nine o'clock the previous evening, when an English ship appeared. Captain John Fisher, of the 200-ton *Margaret and John*, found the *nao* without lights, but as he ranged alongside, her towering castles defied boarders, so he fired some arrows and musket balls at her from close range to test for a response. Two or three Spanish guns replied, Fisher delivered a broadside, and then the English ship withdrew and lay to, close enough to hear the voices of the Spaniards despite a brisk wind. The *Rosario* was far too strong a ship for the *Margaret and John*, and after a while Fisher set off to return to Howard.

Then, at dawn, Drake arrived. Sir Francis wasted no time. He summoned Don Pedro to surrender, and when the Spaniards asked for terms, told them he had no time to parley, but they had the word of Francis Drake that they would be well treated. This was enough for Don Pedro. Even though he had a superior force, there was no shame in surrendering to the greatest seaman of the age, and the Spanish admiral and several of his officers were taken aboard the *Revenge*, where they were received with trumpets and music. Don Pedro kissed Sir Francis's hand and complimented him upon both his exploits and his humanity, and the stocky Englishman then embraced his vanquished foe, and directed him to make use of his own cabin, where a banquet was shortly served.[1]

Nearly twenty years later, in depositions taken before the Barons of the Exchequer, some of Drake's old crew recalled the capture of the *Rosario*. With a fierce loyalty to the memory of their little captain, they highlighted his gracious treatment of Don Pedro. James Baron told how the grandee had come aboard the *Revenge* for talks after Drake had pledged his safe return to the *Rosario* should he decide not to yield.

> The said Sir Francis entertained the said Don Pedro in his cabin, and there, in the hearing of this deponent, the said Sir Francis Drake did will his own interpreter to ask the said Don Pedro in the Spanish tongue whether he would yield unto him or no and

Dover. It seems to me that the evidence supporting Drake's explanation is stronger than any opposing it. See also Benson, 'Drake's Duty. New Light on Armada Incident'.

---

[1] For details of the capture of the *Rosario* I have drawn upon the Drake Ubaldino narrative, an account in Purchas, *Purchas, His Pilgrims*, 19: 488-9, and the depositions taken in the lawsuit *Drake v. Drake* in 1605, Public Record Office, E.133/47/3-5. The latter, although containing a good deal of *Rosario* material, are not as informative as might be supposed. The depositions were taken seventeen years after the event and much of the testimony, in any case, was hearsay. The intention of the witnesses, moreover, was to shore up the claims of one or other of the contending parties (Francis Drake of Esher and Thomas Drake), not to leave an objective record of events for posterity.

*further to tell him if he would not yield he would set him aboard again. Whereupon the said Don Pedro paused a little while with himself, and afterwards yielded unto the said Sir Francis Drake and remained with him as a prisoner.*

George Hughes, another Drake hand, remembered that when they had encountered the *Rosario*, 'straying and distant a little from the rest of the Spanish fleet', they had willed it to yield. Don Pedro had accordingly

*sent some of his captains unto Sir Francis Drake to show him upon what conditions he would yield, but Sir Francis Drake not accepting of any such conditions & Don Pedro distrusting the danger ensuing, [Don Pedro] came voluntarily into the said Sir Francis Drake's ship and yielded himself prisoner unto him, together with his own ship & company. And after that this deponent [Hughes] heard it commonly reported in the ship that the said Don did say & give out in speech that since it was his chance to be taken he was glad that he fell into Sir Francis Drake's hands.[1]*

It was only after the capture of the *Rosario* that Drake learned of the wealth that she carried. He decided to transfer it to the *Revenge*, where he could keep his eye on it, rather than risk its shipment to port, but how much actually came into his possession no one can say. Some of the booty was undoubtedly purloined by the sailors who found, broke open and emptied the treasure chest. What remained was passed down in thin canvas bags into the skiff. There more of it probably went astray during the confusion of the passage to the *Revenge*, so many men piling into the boat that it was in danger of capsizing as it laboured through a rough sea. George Hughes even accused the Spaniards of plundering the treasure themselves when they perceived that they must be captured, 'for that he heard . . . that one of the Spaniards that was taken at that time had of the gold as much about him as did afterwards pay for his ransom.'[2]

---

[1] There is a transcript of the deposition of James Baron of Stonehouse, Devon, 7 October, 1605, in the papers of Lady E. F. Eliott-Drake: Drake Papers, Devon County Record Office, Exeter, 346M/F534. I have not seen the original. The deposition of George Hughes of Tottenham Court, Middlesex, 13 November, 1605, is in the Public Record Office, E.133/47/3. Both Baron and Hughes sailed in the *Revenge* during the Armada campaign. There are also accounts of the surrender of Don Pedro in the depositions of Simon Wood of Bushe Lane, London, 9 November, 1605, and Evan Owen of Esher, not dated, at E.133/47/3 and E.133/47/4 respectively, but both are at best secondhand. Wood served in the campaign, but aboard the *Leicester Galleon*. Owen, who took no part in the campaign at all, purportedly deposes to what he had heard 'from Don Pedro's own mouth'.

[2] Deposition of George Hughes, 10 February, 1606, E.133/47/4. Since the total amount of money carried by the *Rosario* is not known it is impossible to estimate how much went astray. Drake surrendered 25,300 ducats of it to Howard. Hughes said that Drake delivered the plunder to the Lord Treasurer and that the queen later authorized Howard and Drake to 'bestow some of the same treasure upon the commanders, gentlemen & others that were in that voyage, whereof this deponent had a part'. It does indeed appear that a reward of 4,667 'pistolets' (ducats) was shared amongst the fleet (Hist. MSS Commission, *Calendar of the Manuscripts of the Marquis of Salisbury*, 3: 364). After Drake's death, the Drakes of Esher, disappointed at the fruits of their legacy from Sir Francis, tried to obtain money from Thomas Drake (the admiral's brother and heir) by preferring a bill against him in the Exchequer Chamber alleging that Drake had embezzled some of the money from the *Rosario*. These accusations were vigorously contested by Thomas, but ultimately the prosecution collapsed because of his death. Although it is unlikely that Drake did not secure a respectable reward for his capture of the ship, nothing like a convincing case was ever made out for his dishonesty. Although the men of the *Roebuck* were suspected of purloining plunder from the *Rosario*, there appears to have been no contemporary allegation that Drake did not surrender such money as had come into his hands (Dasent, ed., *Acts of the Privy Council*, 16: 363).

Sir Francis did, however, successfully persuade the queen to allow him the privilege of ransoming Don

Once the treasure had been removed, the prize was conveyed to Torbay by Captain Jacob Whiddon of the *Roebuck*. Drake rejoined Howard later on the 22nd. The morning had been eventful for the Lord Admiral. Lacking Drake's light some of the English ships had been following the stern lights of straggling Spaniards during the night, while others had hove to. Dawn found them in disorder, with Howard's *Ark Royal*, the *Mary Rose* and the *Bear* so far forward that the nearest Spaniards were within gun range, off Berry Head, and the rest of Elizabeth's fleet well behind. As for Drake, he was nowhere to be seen. Howard and the advanced ships battled back to their main body, where the Lord Admiral had his second surprise of the day: Sir Francis Drake returning to the fleet with a Spanish admiral as his prisoner, one of the enemy flagships as his prize, and a fortune in booty! If Howard listened soberly to Drake's adventure, and entertained Don Pedro whom Sir Francis introduced, he may have smiled to himself, for who in the fleet but Drake would have been likely to pull it off?

Drake's independent action on the night of 21 July may have given the English their first and richest prize of the campaign, but it had also endangered the fleet and it triggered a wave of envy among the ship captains. It was unclear whether the spoils would be distributed to the immediate captors, Drake and Whiddon and their men, or to the fleet as a whole. Fisher of the *Margaret and John* protested that he had a claim, but none was more enraged than Frobisher, who fulminated with unbridled passion against Drake's good fortune. He shouted that Drake 'thinketh to cozen us of our shares of fifteen thousand ducats, but we will have our shares, or I will make him spend the best blood in his belly, for he hath had enough of those cozening cheats already.' Sir Francis heard about it, and had Frobisher's comments written down, possibly with a view to acting against him, but nothing came of it, and others saw the whole matter differently. When news of the *Rosario*'s capture reached London bonfires were lit in celebration.

There was one unlooked-for and less constructive consequence of the fall of the *Rosario*: it reinforced the excessive caution of the English fleet. Don Pedro's ship was one of the most powerfully armed in the Armada, with some fifty-two guns, most of

---

Pedro. Most of the Spaniards who had come aboard the *Revenge* with the Spanish admiral were conducted to London by two of Drake's associates, Thomas Cely and Tristram Gorges, but Don Pedro and a few others remained with Sir Francis until the fighting was over, when they were landed at Rye. Don Pedro and two companions were eventually housed at Esher at Drake's expense. Simon and Margaret Wood, then both in Drake's service, later deposed that Sir Francis paid Richard Drake of Esher £4 a week for the grandee's diet. Margaret, for example, stated that Richard's servants came weekly for the money to Drake's house in Dowgate, 'where this deponent then dwelt'. (Deposition of Margaret Wood, 9 November, 1605, at E.133/47/3.)

It is worth mentioning that Don Pedro was humanely treated by Drake. Because of the Spaniard's high status, the queen was reluctant to release him before the war ended, and he remained with the Drakes until early in 1593, notwithstanding Sir Francis's efforts to get him exchanged and sent home as soon as possible. During those years Drake attended to Don Pedro's complaints, and sent him provisions. There are references to Don Pedro walking in St James's Park with Sir Francis and the queen, hunting, and meeting Lady Drake, Dom Antonio, Sir Horatio Palavicino, Sir John Norris and other notables who visited Esher. When he was finally ransomed for £3,550 (plus maintenance at £400 per annum), sums that Sir Francis allowed the Drakes of Esher to keep, the Spaniard was given a farewell banquet by the Lord Mayor of London. See Martin, *Spanish Armada Prisoners*, ch. 5. This book provides an excellent account of the disposal of the prisoners and plunder from the *Rosario*.

them heavy-shotted pieces capable of delivering a fearsome close-quarter broadside. Although mounted on unwieldy carriages, those guns still gave a deceptive picture of the Armada's strength, a picture unfortunately supported by the *San Salvador*, the other Spaniard that fell into Howard's hands through mishap. Neither ship was at all representative of the Armada generally, but together they gave the English a vastly inflated opinion of Medina Sidonia's fire power. Drake had no doubt that the Spaniards would be beaten, but he was playing for enormous stakes, and did not intend to take unnecessary risks. He and his colleagues continued to believe that their best plan was to stay at a distance, knocking the Spanish ships to pieces and risking close action only when single enemy vessels or groups of vessels could be mobbed and overwhelmed. The plan was certainly safe, but it was also inadequate to inflict serious damage on the Spanish fleet, let alone defeat it. Indeed, Medina Sidonia was rearranging his fleet to make those tactics even more difficult. The horns of the Armada, vulnerable to splintering before a determined assault, were brought in to give a more solid, compact formation consisting of main and rear bodies. Whatever lessons the contending fleets had learned from the first exchange were soon to be put into practice, because as dawn broke on 23 July they prepared for a furious second round off Portland Bill.[1]

The wind had gone to north-east, presenting the Armada with the weather-gauge, and in the first light Howard led his fleet north-westerly towards the shore to try to regain the attacking position. But Medina Sidonia anticipated the move, and headed the English off, forcing Howard to go about and turn eastwards on the opposite tack towards the sea. Now was the time for the Spaniards to attack, with the wind in their favour and the Lord Admiral's ships straggling to leeward, and they tried to do so. But they were far too slow. The dexterous English ships slipped nimbly away, leaving their foremost attackers astern.

Nevertheless, Howard's manoeuvre had failed, and he had got himself into a difficult spot. He could not outflank Medina Sidonia and fell back to leeward to reform, but in doing so he left a detachment of his ships behind, inshore, close to Portland Bill. They included Martin Frobisher's *Triumph*, the largest ship in the English fleet, and Flick's *Merchant Royal*. The Spanish admiral ordered up his four big fifty-gun galleasses to attack them, and Hugo de Moncada led them forward propelled by 1,200 oarsmen. Now, however, Frobisher's gunners found their mark. Their smaller, handier gun carriages enabled them to run out the pieces, discharge them, pull them back in for reloading and run them out again fast enough to maintain a constant fire, and they had an obvious target – the massive banks of oars on the galleasses as they crept menacingly forward. Soon the English shot was ravaging Moncada's vessels, splintering the oars and maiming rowers, and the much-vaunted galleasses faltered, and yet

---

[1] Martin and Parker, *Spanish Armada*, 212, were the first historians to develop the connection between the capture of the *Rosario* and English battle tactics in succeeding engagements, but I cannot agree with their conclusions. They contend that the *Rosario* suggested the weaknesses of the Armada, and encouraged the English to adopt more aggressive tactics. Inasmuch as the prize carried some fifty bronze and two iron pieces of artillery, and was unusually heavily armed, I infer that it conveyed a false picture of the Armada's strength and reinforced *caution* in the English fleet. And far from the succeeding battles of Portland and the Isle of Wight displaying improved tactics on the part of the English, I believe that they showed no significant advances on the tactics employed off Plymouth. I must add, however, that I depart from the judgement of Martin and Parker only with the greatest hesitation.

still Frobisher and his comrades were in danger. For seeing Moncada wilting before the superior fire power of the English, a number of other Spanish captains began to bring their guns to bear upon the small group of enemy ships.

The wind saved the stubborn Yorkshireman from further punishment, for about ten o'clock in the morning it shifted to south-south-west, restoring the weather-gauge to the rest of the English fleet and enabling it to counter-attack. Drake, who had apparently led about fifty ships out to sea, now suddenly threw himself into the battle, launching a vigorous assault upon the Armada's southerly flank, 'so sharply,' says the presumed Howard narrative, 'that they were all forced to give way and bear room.' Medina Sidonia's attack on Frobisher was now diluted, as he transferred ships from inshore to meet Drake's division, and Howard came forging forward with the wind behind him to rejoin the combat.

The battle had now swung the other way, and it was the Spanish admiral, and no longer Frobisher, who was in danger of being overwhelmed. Towards Medina Sidonia's *San Martin* came Howard's *Ark Royal*, Robert Southwell's *Elizabeth Jonas*, George Fenner's *Leicester Galleon*, Edward Fenton's *Mary Rose*, Sir George Beeston's *Dreadnought*, John Hawkins's *Victory*, Richard Hawkins's *Swallow*, Lord Thomas Howard's *Golden Lion* and others in line-ahead formation, even eventually Drake and his followers who had no sooner seen the Armada's southern flank reinforced than they switched their attention elsewhere. In turn they entered the action, blasting away into the *San Martin*, riddling her with no less than five hundred shot, according to the chief purser of the Armada, Pedro Coco Calderon. The Duke of Medina Sidonia could not get his ship round to make use of both broadsides, and replied with eighty balls from one side of the flagship only. For an hour the English pummelled the *San Martin*, enveloping her in so much gunsmoke that the other Spaniards could not see her, but in the middle of the afternoon the fight ended. Frobisher had been released, and Medina Sidonia and his ships slipped away to leeward. Howard did not chase them. His fleet had fired off most of its shot, and was probably exhausted.

The action off Portland Bill revealed in stark relief the incapacities of both sides. It had been fully joined, hard fought – no partial encounter such as Plymouth had witnessed. There could be no doubt that both sides had made a serious attempt to break the other, and the Howard narrative emphasized that

> it may well be said that for the time there was never seen a more terrible value of great shot, nor more hot fight than this was . . . the great ordnance came so thick that a man would have judged it to have been a hot skirmish of small shot, being all the fight long within half musket shot of the enemy.

The battle had not only been well sustained, but at various times produced favourable circumstances for both sides. It had opened disastrously for the English, with Howard beaten off and Frobisher isolated, but the change in the wind and Drake's attack had changed the complexion of the fight, and facilitated the heavy assault on the *San Martin* and its immediate consorts. And yet to what purpose? Neither fleet had sunk or crippled an enemy, and at the end of the cannonade the Armada was bearing away before a strong evening breeze at the south-west while the English were almost out of ammunition. Under-armed, the Spaniards had inflicted little damage upon Elizabeth's ships, and even the *Triumph*, for much of the time the prime target for the Armada, was so little injured that she could fight just as hard two days later. Even more remarkably, however, the Spanish *San Martin* suffered only peripheral damage: a few holes to be plugged in the hull, some rigging and a mainstay cut, and a flagstaff missing! In all the Spaniards reported a loss of only fifty killed in the engagement.

The conclusions are inescapable. If the Armada's armament and gunnery were unable to do the English much harm, no more was that light shot fired by Howard and Drake doing much to Medina Sidonia. Admitting some exaggeration of the closeness and ferocity of the encounter by the witnesses, and the indifferent gunnery of the English ships, the result of the battle of Portland Bill clearly denoted a need for new tactics on the part of Elizabeth's admirals. They would have to move in close and give their guns some hitting power, and they needed a manouevre that would break up that tight Spanish formation.

Make no mistake about it, Portland Bill was a victory for Medina Sidonia, if a poor one. It must be remembered that his task was to proceed through the Channel to link with Parma, and that was what he was doing; it was the job of Howard and Drake to stop him, to splinter or destroy his fleet, and in two engagements they had failed to accomplish it. And another shuddering thought may have occurred to Sir Francis, for ahead lay the Isle of Wight – the next danger point – and here he was, trying to replenish his powder and shot with the rest of his fleet, and wondering what to try next.

He could not leave it like that, and at dawn the following morning he tried again, committing his division without the support of the rest of the fleet, just as the Armada approached the Isle of Wight. This first battle of the Isle of Wight, on 24 July, was totally ignored in the Howard narrative but features in several Spanish accounts, of which the fullest was given by Captain Vanegas:

> On Wednesday, August 3rd [New Style], once it was daylight, the enemy once again pounded our rear-guard, and then came to our help the good Oquendo and the good admiral, and Don Alonso de Leiva and Bertendona, and two galleasses and the Duke of Florencia's galleon, and the leading storeship, on board which was the good Guan de Medina, leader of all the armada's storeships, and two other galleons of the squadron that came from Castile. The Duke ordered the admiral's ship to put about to help the rearguard, and as the enemy saw our royal ship turn it turned in flight and it was understood that it had received quite some damage. This was realized more by the fact that it only wished to fight from outside the range of the artillery. That day our vice-admiral's ship fired one hundred and thirty cannon shots, and in both armadas more than five thousand cannon-balls were fired. In our armada they killed sixty people and wounded another seventy. The leading storeship was embayed on a lee-shore and more than forty cannon shots were fired at it. The enemy's flagship had its main lateen-yard smashed by a shot which our vice-admiral's ship fired at it. After the enemy had withdrawn it put to sea beamside for about four hours, getting itself ready.[1]

Even this garbled and exaggerated account permits two important conclusions: Drake fought a considerable action that day, causing (if the figures can be believed) greater casualties than the Spaniards received at Plymouth, Portland Bill or the succeeding

[1] Translated from Duro, 2: 384-5. Other accounts of this battle may be found in Pedro Estrade's narrative (Oppenheim, *Monson*, 2: 299-308); Jorge Manrique to Philip, 11 August, 1588 (Hume, 4: 373-5); Pedro Coco Calderon narrative (*Ibid*, 4: 439-50); and Medina Sidonia's relation (Laughton, 2: 354-70).

battle off the Isle of Wight, but, notwithstanding, the English remained wedded to the tactics of harassing stragglers or small units with a relatively ineffective fire over long distance.

The battle had begun about dawn and lasted for up to two hours. With the wind in his favour, Drake led an assault upon the Armada's rearguard, under Recalde and Leiva, singling out for particular attention *El Gran Grifon* (Juan Gómez de Medina), the flagship of a squadron of hulks, a pitching merchantman armed with thirty-five guns and carrying 279 men. The English beset her as wolves bait a wounded bison, putting (it was said) forty shot into her, but other Armada ships were also engaged, including fighting galleons and galleasses. Initially, the Spaniards preserved their order, deigning to reply to the English only with their stern guns, but eventually Medina Sidonia decided that a more positive response was necessary and began to put about. Drake discreetly retired. The wind was beginning to fail, he may have sustained some damage (the Spaniards thought they had slashed some of the *Revenge*'s rigging and brought down a yard), and he was probably low on ammunition and powder. The evidence does not suggest that the attack was much more successful than the fiasco off Portland Bill. Medina Sidonia's progress had been unchecked, and even the wretched *El Gran Grifon* lived to fight another day, but what was worse, the battle gives no indication that Sir Francis had learned anything from his previous engagements.

It is possible to imagine a furrow across the brow of Sir Francis Drake after this latest attack, for he knew a critical moment in the campaign was approaching. Hours ahead lay the Isle of Wight, which had often seemed the logical first step in any invasion of England from across the Channel. Little more than forty years before it had been occupied by the French. Now, its governor, Sir George Carey, had been improvising land defences, and was even then dispatching some ships to reinforce Howard's fleet. Ammunition, provisions and supplies, all badly needed, were also passing to Elizabeth's ships, and spectators had begun to gather on nearby cliffs to watch their fleet manoeuvre against the Armada in what would be a crucial contest. Would Medina Sidonia try to enter the Solent and seize the Isle of Wight? Could Drake and Howard drive him beyond, further into the Channel, or destroy him utterly? Those questions were worrying Drake too. Three battles and still the Armada held its formation, drew closer to its goal. Three battles, and yet Medina Sidonia's only loss by enemy action had been the *Rosario*, and that more through accident. Sir Francis was thinking hard, getting his ship refitted, going over in his mind the local tides, currents and shoals. He had sailed these waters many times, ever since he was a boy, and he wondered how they could serve him. If the Armada made for the Solent, it would be by the eastern passage, and a little beyond lay some dangerous shallows . . . the Owers Banks.

The dissatisfaction of the English commanders found tangible expression on 24 July, as Howard reorganized his fleet into four divisions to give it greater co-ordination. Perhaps the disciplined order of the Armada had been some inspiration, but the difficulties of handling such large numbers of vessels would have pinpointed the problem anyway, for the Tudor navy had no efficient method of signalling and captains were more frequently working as individuals than as members of a team. Now Frobisher was promoted to the position of squadron commander, and placed in shore, while Drake took the seaward wing, from his point of view by far the best position since it gave greater freedom of manoeuvre. Howard and Hawkins commanded the centre.

On 25 July the new system was blooded. Both fleets were south of the Isle of Wight, and now if ever the Duke of Medina Sidonia must decide whether he wanted to try for the Solent. But the beginning of the day was sluggish, for dawn found the ships becalmed off Dunnose Head, and without wind Drake and Howard were denied one of their principal advantages – the speed and mobility of their ships. The Spaniards, however, could again call upon their galleasses, although their commander, Moncada, must have still been reflecting upon his disastrous showing off Portland Bill.

Conditions on that important day seemed slightly to favour the Armada, but it had a shaky start, for two of the ships were straggling, the Portuguese galleon *San Luis* and an armed merchantman, the *Santa Ana*. Nearest to them was the squadron of John Hawkins, and the calm did not deter the old veteran from making an attack. Boats were lowered, and slowly some of Hawkins's great ships were towed towards the Spaniards. As they got close a musket fire from the Armada ships began to spatter upon the long boats, and drove them away, but the warships they had tried to bring to action remained in an advanced position. Moncada's time had come, and the galleasses ominously advanced, their blood-red sweeps rhythmically cutting the water beneath red upper works and loose sails adorned with the 'bloody sword'. In their support edged Leiva's *Rata Encoronada*. Howard, whose squadron was next to Hawkins, took up the challenge and his boats pulled the *Ark Royal* and *Golden Lion* into a position to support Hawkins. From both sides the guns rumbled, but despite the roar and banks of powder smoke little damage was done. The galleasses rescued the Armada stragglers and brought them into the fleet, but no more, and Howard had the satisfaction of blowing away one of the enemy's stern lanterns!

When the wind freshened it blew from the south, and Medina Sidonia advanced in support of Leiva and Moncada. For a while he paid the price of his boldness, for the duke took the fire of several English ships. His mainstay was cut and some men were killed, but then his temerity paid dividends, for as his rearguard came to join him the English centre retired. Only one English ship was left in danger by these actions – predictably Frobisher's *Triumph* which had crept too far forward inshore during the poor wind and was now being left to leeward by the most westerly of the Spanish ships. Some of Frobisher's followers realized their mistake and withdrew in time, but their commander was virtually cut off, the eastward tide running alongside the Isle of Wight pressing him further into danger. This time Martin Frobisher was seriously worried. Although the *Bear* and the *Elizabeth Jonas* were close enough to fire in his defence, he was in danger of being overwhelmed, and lowered his ensign to signal for assistance and fired distress guns. Small boats were put out, eleven in all, to try to tow him away.[1]

At this stage the performances of both sides had been lack-lustre, but the Armada was in the stronger position. It had the largest of the English vessels in difficulties, and there appeared nothing to prevent Medina Sidonia entering the eastern channel of the

---

[1] For tides, see Williamson, *Age of Drake*, 334.

Solent if he desired. Unfortunately for the duke, winds are commanded by no man, and a freshening breeze suddenly rescued the English. As the sails of the *Triumph* began to fill, Frobisher was able to demonstrate the superior sailing qualities of Howard's fleet, for he called in his boats and retired so quickly, according to a Spanish eye-witness, that by comparison the fastest ships of the Armada seemed to stand still. That same wind enabled the English to make a desperate bid to drive Medina Sidonia beyond the Isle of Wight. Sir Francis Drake had been quietly working his way out to sea with his division, waiting for his opportunity, and now he launched a vigorous charge upon the seaward flank of the Armada, marked by the Portuguese galleon *San Mateo*, and began crowding the whole Spanish fleet north-easterly towards Selsey Bill. Some of the Spaniards believed he was trying to corner the Armada, but Medina Sido-nia seems to have realized the frightening import of Drake's manoeuvre, for just ahead – directly in the path of the Spanish fleet – there appeared signs all seamen learned to heed from their first days afloat, signs of dangerous and extensive shoals, the treacher-ous Owers Banks. 'El Draque' was running the Armada aground! The wind, which blew from the south-west, and tides were in league with him, and Medina Sidonia had but one safe escape: to put about and steer south-south-east with all speed, forgetting any plans to enter the Solent. Before the end of the morning the Armada had saved itself, but ploughed solidly eastwards, with the Isle of Wight astern.

The battle was over, and in one sense it was a victory for the English, for they had successfully protected the Isle of Wight. Howard began knighting some of his officers, Hawkins and Frobisher, Lord Thomas Howard and Lord Sheffield, his kinsmen, and a few others (Drake, of course, he had no power to reward), but in truth neither side could take too much credit for what had been, Sir Francis's manoeuvre excepted, a rather scrambling, undistinguished encounter. Nothing could disguise the fact that four battles had left the Armada more or less unscathed, and that the English tactics of using light artillery at less than point-blank range, and of concentrating largely upon straggling or isolated groups of ships, had failed. In the last engagement none of Medina Sidonia's vessels had been seriously damaged and he had lost only about fifty men killed. Drake and Howard had won some strategic victories, but had been unable to break the Armada's order or prevent its passage along the Channel. The English admirals sent ashore for more powder, shot and supplies, and looked forward to a re-inforcement from Lord Henry Seymour and Sir William Winter, whose squadron lay ahead, but above all they needed a new plan of battle.

Yet Medina Sidonia, Recalde and their officers were no less perplexed, and an air of desperation was creeping into the duke's letters to Parma. Whether the duke had really intended to seize the Isle of Wight is not known, but after Drake's attack he had no adequate port before him, and while the English had been repelled the Armada had been able to do no appreciable violence. The enemy gunfire was weak, but the Spanish reply was far, far worse, and the Armada's main weapon, its soldiers, had re-mained redundant. 'It was impossible to come to hand-stroke with them,' reported Medina Sidonia's journal. To Parma the admiral wrote, 'The enemy has resolutely avoided coming to close quarters with our ships, although I have tried my hardest to make him do so. I have given him so many opportunities that sometimes some of our vessels have been in the very midst of the enemy's fleet, to induce one of his ships to grapple and begin the fight, but all to no purpose.' Another officer sadly reflected that the English 'displayed some signs of a desire to come to close quarters, but did not do so, always keeping off and confining the fight to artillery fire. The Duke endeavoured to close with him, but it was impossible in consequence of the swiftness of the enemy's vessels.'[1] It was unfortunate, but from the Spanish point of view, it is difficult to see how a *closer* action, other than a boarding action, could have done anything but multiply their misery, for the handiness of the ships would have simply permitted the English artillery to reap greater slaughter at point-blank range. It was almost impossible for the Armada to defeat Howard's fleet severely.

This meant that the overall prospect for the Armada was extremely bleak, for if Drake and Howard could not be neutralized, how could they be prevented from interfering with the passage of Parma's army across the Channel, and perhaps from destroying it? Medina Sidonia forlornly pinned his hopes upon Parma, and after his last battle wrote to the general begging him to come out and help the Armada push back the English, and perhaps at last to seize the Isle of Wight. In any case, he wanted forty to fifty light-draught flyboats to help him defend any anchorage he might find for the fleet.

But Parma can only have judged the letter somewhat pathetic. His river craft could barely serve at sea, let alone take on Drake. It was the Armada's job to clear the passage, not the army's, even though the tone of the admiral's letter suggested that the task was beyond him. Parma set in motion some fresh supplies of ammunition for the Armada, and on 28 July left Bruges for the coast to supervise the embarkation of 16,000 men at Nieuport, Sluys, Antwerp and Dunkirk, all flattering themselves they were bound for England. It is doubtful if the general himself believed it. The Armada did not look as if it was capable of making a way for him, and even if the English were held off there were still those Dutch ships waiting to spring on Parma's barges in the shallows, where Medina Sidonia's warships could not sail. But Philip had ordered, and Parma must go through the motions.

So must the Armada, and in growing despair it steered for Calais.

---

[1] Medina Sidonia to Parma, 4 August, 1588, and Manrique to Philip II, 11 August, 1588, Hume, 4: 360, 373-5.

# CHAPTER NINETEEN

# 'GOD HATH GIVEN US SO GOOD A DAY'

Post: From Dover cliff we might discern them join;
Twixt that and Calais; there the fight began.
Sir Francis Drake, Vice-Admiral, was first to give the onset.
This Drake, I say, . . .
Gave Order that his squadrons, one by one,
Should follow him some distance; steers his course
But none to shoot till he himself gave fire.

Thomas Heywood, *If You Know Not Me*, 1606

TOWARDS MIDNIGHT ON 28 JULY, 1588, IN A FRESH WIND AND OCCASIONAL RAIN, several dark shapes gathered ominously in the gloom outside Calais Road and hesitated. They were ships, eight of them, eight ships of 90 to 200 tons, and they were in line abreast, with their sails set and their bowsprits pointing the course taken by both the wind and a strong tide, straight into the anchorage. Aboard them skeleton crews quickly secured the ships' rudders, tying them fast, and then briefly went to work at the bows before running to the sterns, tumbling over them into small boats and pulling furiously away, out to sea, to safety. Abandoned now, the eight ships ran swiftly forward with wind and current, towards Calais about a mile and a half to leeward, and as they did so first one and then another sputtered into flames. Fireships! In the high wind they flickered fiercely, throwing an eerie orange light across the roadstead that intensified as they came, feeding not only on the timber, rigging and canvas of the ships themselves, but also upon the pitch, tar and faggots stored aboard. When the flames licked around the loaded ordnance explosion after explosion tore open the night. Like gigantic fire-crackers, the burning vessels swept towards the anchorage, towards the large concentration of shipping shifting there, the fleet of the Duke of Medina Sidonia.

It was a fresh attempt on the part of the English to break the Armada's iron formation, and although fireships were seldom effective (indeed, they had failed miserably to dislodge Drake in Cadiz the previous year), here they promised some success, for Calais offered little shelter. The Armada had anchored in this neutral French port on 27 July, and had not moved since. Howard and Drake, whose proximity to home was not the least of their many advantages in this continuing battle, had replaced their sick with new recruits, including merchants such as Palavicino, nobles of the stamp of the earls of Cumberland and Northumberland, as well as many gallants hot in their nation's cause, and scraped together enough shot and powder to fight another battle. Their victuals were meagre, especially after forty ships under Lord Henry Seymour and Sir William Winter joined them in Whitsand Bay on the evening of the 27th, bringing the English fleet up to its full strength of 140 ships, but sufficient for a few days.

On the morning of the 28th, a Sunday, there had been a council of war aboard the *Ark Royal,* and the decision to use the fireships was made. Winter, who joined Howard's committee with Seymour and probably Sir Henry Palmer of the *Antelope,* put his influence behind the idea, but provision had already been made for it, and vessels were even then being prepared for the purpose in Dover. Sir Francis certainly favoured the idea. According to Thomas Cely, he was an expert in smoke and incendiary devices, and so enthusiastic was he that when the admirals decided to fit up fireships from the fleet rather than wait for those from Dover, Drake offered his own *Thomas Drake* as one of them. The English hoped that their blazing vessels would either force the Armada out of Calais in disorder, or ground some of the Spanish ships on the shoals to leeward of the anchorage. If the attack was successful, the Lord Admiral would lead Elizabeth's fleet into battle, and his division would be followed by Sir Francis Drake.

The Spanish commanders were just as aware of the inadequacy of Calais as a haven, but there was no port beyond that could be of service, and Medina Sidonia's pilots assured him that to venture further, without some plan to join with Parma, would risk being carried by the currents into the North Sea. Calais was neutral, but its governor, Girault de Mauleon, Seigneur de Gourdan, was believed to sympathize with the Catholic League. He had no great love for the English, and had lost a leg getting them out of Calais thirty years before. While the Spaniards anchored there, they were allowed to buy provisions ashore and to send messengers to Parma, urgent dispatches calling upon the general to be ready to assist the fleet. The replies, when they came, were the first Medina Sidonia had received from the army he was supposed to meet, and they were crushing. Parma would not be ready for several days, and it seemed from the messengers that the troops at Dunkirk and Nieuport were in no state to embark.

The hopeless futility of the whole plan now bore down relentlessly upon Medina Sidonia and Parma. The Armada could get no closer than Calais to the little ports Parma was using, those small shallow havens hiding behind extensive banks off shore. For its part, the army's barges would have to run the gauntlet of the Dutch warships before reaching deep water, and would even then be totally unequal to helping the Armada fight a battle with the English. Philip himself, apprised of the difficulty by Parma, shuddered at what seemed an insurmountable obstacle. 'Please God,' he wrote in the margin of the duke's letter, 'let there not be some slip-up here.'[1]

But a slip-up there was, and now Medina Sidonia was sitting in an open roadstead, waiting for Parma to gather himself for a run through the shoals, vulnerable to attack. The Armada ships were each moored by two anchors to hold them in place, but they were directly in the path of the current entering Calais that night of 28-29 July. The Spanish admirals suspected that an effort would be made to dislodge them with fireships, and had detailed a number of small boats to intercept such vessels and tow them away. But when the attack came most of the English fireships got through, and drifted upon the crowded Spanish shipping. It seems that the guns that discharged aboard the oncoming craft convinced the Spaniards that they were not dealing with ordinary fireships, laden with combustibles, but

---

[1] Martin and Parker, *The Spanish Armada,* 184.

explosion ships, floating mines liable to detonate at any minute and destroy every-thing close by. Fresh in the memories of the Spaniards were stories of the 'hell-burners' of Antwerp, the explosion ships launched by the Dutch against a bridge of boats Parma had thrown across the Scheldt in 1585. Only one of the two had reached the target, but it smashed away part of the bridge, killed about eight hundred soldiers and wounded many more, including Parma himself. Now, as the English fireships advanced upon the anchorage, burning vividly and occasionally erupting in the thunder of artillery, some of the Spaniards also remembered that the inventor of those Dutch hellburners, Federigo Giambelli, had gone to England, and might, for all they knew, even then be in league with 'El Draque'. The small boats kept their distance, and six of the fireships reached the Spanish anchorage and threw it into disorder.

The flames, the gunfire and the darkness would have created total confusion in a fleet less capable and disciplined than the Spanish Armada. As it was they wrought great damage. Captains severed their cables, leaving their anchors behind, and spread sail to escape the hellburners, manoeuvring to avoid their fel-lows, and for the most part struggling out to sea. Only Medina Sidonia's San Mar-tin, Recalde's San Juan and three of the Portuguese galleons, more judicious than the rest, preserved their anchors, shifted position and then remoored in safety. But the flag galleass, Moncada's San Lorenzo, was less fortunate, running afoul of another vessel, losing her rudder and taking the ground beneath the guns of the fortress of Calais. The fireships did not destroy a single Spanish ship, and ran upon the banks east of Calais, where they burned themselves out; but they had done something the English fleet had failed to do in four battles: they had scattered the Armada, driving all but the San Martin, her four consorts and the beaching San Lorenzo alongside the intricate banks of Zeeland, north-east of Calais.

At dawn the Duke of Medina Sidonia, Recalde and the three Portuguese gal-leons with them weighed anchor, and with the wind at south-west quit Calais to join their fleet off the banks, hoping to be able to reform it before the English attacked. It was Monday, 29 July, 1588, and the decisive battle of the campaign, the battle of Gravelines, had begun.

In the opening stages of the action, when it was imperative for the English to fall upon the scattered Armada ships before Medina Sidonia and Recalde could reach and reform them, Howard made an enormous error of judgement. He seems to have had little understanding of the opportunity that lay before him. For Howard success meant, as he once said himself, plucking the Armada's feathers one by one, and the San Lorenzo, incapable as she was to influence the battle, was a prize plume. And so he led some twenty ships, including the important Ark Royal, Golden Lion and White Bear, the pick of his squadron, out of the main battle to perform in an unnecessary and as it transpired largely futile sideshow at a time when they were badly needed elsewhere.

It was the only boarding action of the campaign. As the smaller of Howard's ships crept to the San Lorenzo, Moncada worked his ship further inshore, ground-ing her more firmly on the sandbanks so that she heeled over and her artillery could not be used. The English shot was, as usual, too distant to inflict much damage. According to a French report, and it was the French who eventually secured the prize, 'not one of the English cannon shots had pierced the hull of the ship, but only her upper planks above the oars. She was therefore still very sound.'[1] The matter was decided by boarders. Boatloads of them now pulled towards the Spanish ship, and, rather than fight, the Spaniards leaped into the water and floundered ashore, leaving behind their gallant commander, Hugo de Moncada, shot through the head by an English musket ball. However, the English did not enjoy their prize for long. The Governor of Calais insisted that she fell within his jurisdiction, and when the English demurred, the French drove Howard's men off the galleass with shot from the castle. The Lord Admiral eventually returned to the centre of the action, but after about a third of it, some three hours, was over.

As Howard dropped away to tackle the *San Lorenzo* Sir Francis Drake led the rest of the English fleet against the Armada. Ahead he could see the *San Martin* and the four galleons with her offering battle. Never lacking in courage, Medina Sidonia had chosen to meet Drake's attack and gain time for the balance of his fleet to reform. He signalled the Armada to beat to windward and join him and then stubbornly put his five ships in the face of the oncoming English. Now, with the advantage of numbers on their side, Elizabeth's captains closed to point-blank range, directing their fire horizontally into the Spanish hulls. First came Drake's *Revenge*, then Fenner and the rest of his squadron, and then the divisions of Hawkins, Frobisher and Seymour, pouring shot into the five Spanish ships at less than musket range.

But the punishment they took was not without purpose, for although Drake soon left Medina Sidonia's small squadron and passed to leeward to open fire upon the Armada ships beyond, the Spaniards there doggedly manoeuvred around, turning into the wind to their admiral's support and eventually aiding Medina Sidonia to bring his ships up to the main body. That inspiring discipline that had so often stood them in stead once again sustained them, allowing them to develop a ragged formation in the shape of a half moon, the head of the steer with the horns trailing behind. On this occasion, however, the English continued to press the attack, concentrating their fire upon the ships around the *San Martin*, Portuguese galleons such as Recalde's *San Juan*, the *San Felipe*, and the *San Mateo*; big armed merchantmen including the *San Juan de Sicilia*, *La Trinidad Valencera*, *La Maria Juan*, *La Rata Santa Maria Encoronada*, and *La Regazona*; Castilian galleons such as the *Nuestra Sēnora de Begona*; and hulks such as *El Gran Grifon*. In some respects the engagement resembled earlier battles, with the Armada conducting a fighting retreat, and the English warships trying to exploit the gaps that opened up, but this time Drake and his comrades blasted away at close range, creating so much gunsmoke that Medina Sidonia had to climb to his fighting tops to ascertain what was going on. And this time that shot was telling.

One of the most exposed of the Spanish ships was the *San Felipe*, under Don Francisco de Toledo. Galled by the fire of several English opponents, Toledo gamely tried to run his ship amongst his enemies, searching desperately for a way

---

[1] Advice from Rouen, 11 August, 1588, Hume, ed., *Calendar of Letters and State Papers . . . in the Archives of Simancas*, 4: 376-8.

to employ his boarders. Yet the English refused to grapple, only darted away from the ponderous galleon as she lunged forward, and then returned to slash her with a fierce fire, piling her decks with dead and wounded men and the debris of shattered masts and spars and shredded sails, and riddling her hull. The *San Mateo* endeavoured to assist her, only to come under a similar pounding, and both ships were soon so badly damaged that they fell further behind and were almost cut off, encircled and pummelled by the bulk of the English fleet. And they were not alone. The *Maria Juan* was reduced to a sinking condition. An Italian ship was observed severely battered and 'all full of blood'. One witness, Pedro Estrade, recalled:

> This day was slain Don Philip de Cordova, with a bullet that struck off his head and struck with his brains the greatest friend that he had there, and 24 men that were with us trimming our foresail. And where I and other four were, there came a bullet and from one struck away his shoe without doing any other harm, for they came and plied so very well with shot. And in the afternoon as I was below discharging my artillery there was a mariner that had his leg struck all in pieces and died presently. Many misfortunes have happened, I cannot recount them all.[1]

English participants also recorded intense action. It was said that Winter's *Vanguard* fired five hundred great shot within musket range. A more remarkable story still, and almost certainly exaggerated, came from Drake's *Revenge*:

> That day Sir Francis Drake's ship was pierced through by several cannon balls of all sizes which were flying everywhere between the two fleets, seeming as thick as arquebuses usually are. It is true that his cabin was twice pierced by cannon balls and there was an occasion in which two gentlemen, who towards evening had retired to rest a little, after the battle, and one of them lying upon the bed, when it was broken to pieces under him by a saker ball, without his taking the least hurt. And shortly afterwards the Earl of Cumberland . . . and Sir Charles Blount were resting on the same bed in the same place when it was again hit by a ball of a demi-culverin which passed through the cabin from one side to the other without doing any harm other than scrape the foot, taking off the toes of one who was there with them.[2]

Late in the afternoon the action drew to a close. The English were running out of ammunition, and the weather was turning squally, with the wind at north-west, threatening to press the fleets against the Zeeland shoals. For the Armada the ensuing hours proved no less critical, and as darkness fell Medina Sidonia's ships were still striving to avert disaster, their exhausted men wrestling with broken timbers and ropes, trying to repair the worst of the damage, plug the shot holes and shorten sail to haul the vessels away from the threatening banks.

Some did not make it. The Biscayan *La Maria Juan* settled so low in the water that boats from other ships began to evacuate her crew, but only one got away before the vessel went straight to the bottom with the remaining men on board, the first Armada

---

[1] Narrative of Pedro Estrade, Oppenheim, ed., *Monson*, 2: 307-8.

[2] Ubaldino narrative, Naish, ed., *Naval Miscellany*, 72. Although this narrative was seen by Drake, and the *Revenge* certainly sustained damage during the battle, this account was exaggerated. The statement that the cabin was pierced 'towards evening' and 'after' the battle cannot be accurate. If there was a basis to the anecdotes, it probably occurred in the afternoon.

ship to be sunk by gunfire. Two of the Portuguese galleons, the *San Felipe* and the *San Mateo*, were driven on to the banks, one near Nieuport and the other between Ostend and Sluys, both falling into the possession of the Dutch. The Spaniards had tried to re-pair the ships, and a diver had plugged the holes in the *San Mateo*, but both were so battered that they had no sooner been brought by the Dutch to the Scheldt than they sank. As for their crews, some of the men from one of the ships were taken off by the *Doncella* hulk, but the rest became prisoners of the Dutch, who reportedly murdered about three hundred of them. Exultant Zeelanders capered in the streets of Flushing, attired in costumes plundered from the Spanish ships, and celebrating a triumph cheaply won.

Thus, at least four ships – the Biscayan, two Portuguese galleons and the galleass *San Lorenzo* – were lost by Medina Sidonia in the battle of 29 July. Many more were seriously damaged, without anchors (which had been cut away in Calais), shot-ridden, and loaded with wounded or debilitated men, and the flagship herself was almost lost. She had taken, it was said, two hundred shot on her starboard side, many of her guns had been dismounted, and the sea was leaking through holes below her waterline. At one time it seemed that nothing could be done to save her from falling helplessly on to the sandbanks. Early the next morning Medina Sidonia called to the pugnacious Oquendo, commander of the *Santa Ana*, flagship of the Guipuzcoan squadron. 'Senor Oquendo, what shall we do? We are lost!' But the other petulantly referred him to Diego Flores de Valdes of the *San Crístobal*, who had been named the admiral's naval adviser. 'Ask Diego Flores,' he snapped. 'As for me, I am going to fight, and die like a man. Send me a supply of shot!'[1]

The wind helped spare the Armada further losses. It changed to the south-west, and enabled the crippled ships to bear north-eastwards, away from the shoals, from the English and from Parma. The Armada was in poor shape, and had possibly lost as many as 1,500 men killed, drowned and captured and some eight hundred wounded in the fight off Gravelines. Some sizes of shot appear to have been in short supply. Yet for the moment the English did not renew the attack, but rode gently to windward, threatening, shadowing, but keeping their distance, for their reserves of powder and shot were even more precarious, hardly sufficient for another battle. As long as the Armada kept her course into the North Sea, leaving Parma's superfluous barges still at their embarkation points, Drake and Howard could bide their time. The crucial moments of the campaign had passed.

Sir Francis Drake's spirits had risen after the battle of Gravelines. That evening he wrote to his friend Walsingham that 'God hath given us so good a day in forcing the enemy so far to leeward as I hope in God the Prince of Parma and Duke of Sidonia shall not shake hands this few days.'[2] In council the following afternoon it was decided that Seymour would remain with his squadron in the Narrow Seas, covering Parma's ports, while Howard and Drake pursued Medina Sidonia northwards. When Sir Fran-cis addressed another letter to Walsingham, on the last of the month, he was almost cheerful:

[1] Calderon narrative, Hume, 4: 446.
[2] Drake to Walsingham, 29 July, 1588, Laughton, ed., *Defeat of the Spanish Armada*, 1: 341-2.

*We have the army of Spain before us, and mind, with the grace of God, to wrestle a pull with him. There was never anything pleased me better than the seeing the enemy flying with a southerly wind to the northwards. God grant you have a good eye to the Duke of Parma, for, with the grace of God, if we live, I doubt it not but ere it be long so to handle the matter with the Duke of Sidonia as he shall wish himself at St Mary Port among his orange trees.*[1]

He obviously wanted another battle, and we can see why. Behind his obvious relief at the frustration of the Spanish plan to link with Parma lay some dissatisfaction with what the English had achieved. They had, it appeared, ultimately won victory from those running battles through the Channel. Excluding the *San Salvador* (which had been abandoned because of mishap and evacuated of all but a few seriously wounded men), but including the *Rosario* (taken substantially intact with a full complement and battery), and the *San Lorenzo* (run ashore at Calais), the English action had cost the Armada in all five fighting ships and perhaps 2,100 men dead and prisoners. The English had damaged other vessels and wounded several hundred men, and they had suffered insignificant hurt in return. Yes, it was a victory, but hardly an impressive one. If we can borrow some boxing terms, it was a bare win on points rather than a knock-out. For the Armada was still intact as a fighting force, shorn of a few important plumes perhaps, but largely as formidable as it had been before the fighting began. Indeed, it would be impossible to regard the English victory as decisive, but for one fact: Medina Sidonia's intention of facilitating Parma's invasion of England had been frustrated.

The truth was that if the English performance can be deemed satisfactory, it was far from a good one. The English had displayed brilliant seamanship, and sometimes superb courage, and they had identified the weapons that would dominate naval warfare in succeeding centuries: the sailing ship and the gun. But they had not learned how to use those weapons efficiently. Their inexperience showed ashore and afloat. They had not prepared the ammunition necessary for sustained gun action. Their artillery was too light, and only effective at close range. Their tactics were, with one exception, unable to break the Armada's formation and were too restricted to mobbing stragglers or small groups of Spanish ships that became isolated. Despite the superior fire power and sailing qualities of their ships, and the impunity with which they could assault their under-armed opponents, they generally failed to understand the importance of close-quarter action. Their gunnery skills were almost certainly deficient. No, Drake cannot have been satisfied. An opportunity had been missed, and he felt it personally. No one had done more than Drake to defeat the Armada. He had led the attack on Recalde off Plymouth, captured the *Rosario*, launched vital counter-attacks on the Spaniards at Portland Bill and the Isle of Wight, and taken his division unsupported into one battle. He had led the fleet into the decisive action off Gravelines. And yet he felt he had done less than was expected, and that all his bragging had not been fulfilled.

He wanted another battle, but for the moment the fleet had too little ammunition to risk an unnecessary encounter. As they trailed the Armada northwards the English held several councils, and eventually decided to follow Medina Sidonia into Scottish

[1] Drake to Walsingham, 31 July, 1588, *Ibid*, 1: 364-5.

waters and then run into the Firth of Forth for supplies, leaving two of their ships, the *Advice* and a caravel belonging to Drake, to continue watching the retreating Spaniards. It was not a bad decision, for the English were low on all kinds of provisions, and the Armada seemed intent only on flight. Initially, Medina Sidonia and his officers had wanted to turn back towards the Channel for another attempt to meet Parma, but by 2 August, when the English planned to enter the Forth, the idea was less practical. The Spanish ships were full of sick; their water and food were stale, and the men were showing the symptoms of combat fatigue and the effects of a long sea voyage. Drake guessed the state the Armada was in, and even foretold that it would suffer losses on its homeward run.

But the English ships too were foul, and disease was spreading as it always did in such large fleets. Less than sixty Englishmen had died in the Channel battles, but the threat of pestilence promised far greater mortality. Contrary winds prevented Drake and Howard from reaching the Forth, as they had planned, and they headed for the North Foreland instead. Off the Norfolk coast their ships were scattered by a storm, and made what ports they could. Drake was in Margate on the evening of the 8th.

There was a deep belief among the commanders that from first to last their effort had been blunted by inadequate support from the government, and that with greater reserves they could have attacked the Armada after the battle of Gravelines and continued the pursuit beyond 2 August. So strongly did the senior officers hold these views that they signed a joint memorandum to that effect. The government could not be acquitted of tardiness, and well knew it. 'Our half doings doth breed dishonour and leaveth the disease uncured,' Walsingham admitted.[1] During the fighting only about 60,000 pounds of powder had been sent to the fleet by the Crown. At the same time, shortages were not all down to the government. There had been misadventure, problems of supply ships reaching the fleet, and not least the enormous squandering of powder and shot to little advantage in futile cannonading by English ships.

Nevertheless, the queen and Privy Council behaved abominably in their treatment of the mariners who had saved their country. Disease, probably typhus fever, had been troubling the English ships, particularly those of Howard's division, for some time, but after the fleet's return the losses reached alarming proportions, welcomed only by the enemy and, almost incredibly, some members of the government who saw it merely as a saving on wages. The men had not been paid and could not, therefore, be fully discharged, and they began dying daily on the ships and in the ports, their miseries multiplied by deficiencies in clothing and what seems to have been a form of food poisoning occasioned by the consumption of contaminated victuals. The admirals entreated the government to help, and Howard and Drake went to court soon after their return, but were unable to resolve the matter. Sir Francis was probably not surprised, but Howard was disgusted throughout. It broke his heart 'to see them that have served so valiantly to die so miserably', and although he began fairly to insist upon the Privy Council doing its duty, he also dived into his own pocket to discharge some of the most vulnerable.[2] In two more years Howard would join Drake, Hawkins and others in founding the first naval charity.

---

[1] Walsingham to the Lord Chancellor, 8 August, 1588, *Ibid*, 2: 69-70.
[2] Howard to Burghley, 10 August, 1588, *Ibid*, 2: 96-7.

The admirals were not only angry with the government, but with less justification began to set about each other. Seymour was castigating Howard for detaching him to watch Parma when the rest of the fleet followed Medina Sidonia north, and Frobisher fulminated against Drake in an almost hysterical manner. He accused Sir Francis of cornering the reward for the capture of the *Rosario*, and even charged him with cowardice off Gravelines. At Harwich he exploded in public. 'Sir Fra. Drake reporteth that no man hath done any good service but he; but he shall well understand that others hath done as good service as he, and better too. He came bragging up at the first, indeed, and gave them his prow and his broadside; and then kept his luff, and was glad that he was gone again, like a cowardly knave or traitor – I rest doubtful, but the one I will swear.'[1] It was as well that when essential visits to the court had been completed, and Howard and Drake met their council in Dover on 21 August, Frobisher was absent, because he was still at loggerheads with the vice-admiral as late as November.

There were some rumours that Howard, too, resented popular acclaim being assigned to Drake at his expense. On the Continent, certainly, the English fleet was almost personified by the character of the burly Devonian, and little was said of any other. 'Have you heard how Drake with his fleet has offered battle to the Armada?' demanded the Pope in conversation one day. 'With what courage! Do you think he showed any fear? He is a great captain!' One infuriated Spaniard, seizing an arquebus to show his friends how he would serve 'El Draque' if he saw him, grew so excited that he accidentally shot one of his listeners dead.[2] The letters of the Lord Admiral and his deputy do not betray such jealousy, and when Drake left again for court (for the second time that August), Howard plainly expected Sir Francis to speak well of him. Nonetheless, the Lord Admiral can only have felt undervalued, because Drake and not he had been summoned to discuss plans for a new expedition. Vice-admiral or not, Sir Francis was still the nation's leading seaman.

Some of the irritation may have arisen from the initial sense of disappointment that pervaded the fleet. 'If I have not performed as much as was looked for, yet I persuade myself his good Lordship will confess I have been dutiful,' sighed Drake on 11 August.[3] Whatever the merry crowds gawping at the captured Spanish banners exhibited on London Bridge might say, there was uncertainty as to whether Medina Sidonia might return, and early in the month the queen herself turned out to review the troops at Tilbury and declared that she would fight beside her soldiers if need be. It was stirring stuff – Elizabeth cantering on her white gelding, and protesting that within the 'body of a weak and feeble woman' there lived 'the heart and stomach of a king, and of a king of England too', one that scorned 'that Parma or Spain, or any prince of Europe should dare to invade the borders of my realm.' They were bold words in the state of continuing apprehension, for the Armada was still within striking distance and Parma had not yet dismantled his invasion flotilla.

During the following months the full extent of the Spanish disaster unfolded, as Medina Sidonia's care-worn ships attempted the long and miserable voyage home,

---

[1] Deposition of Starke, 11 August, 1588, *Ibid*, 2: 101-4.

[2] Giovanni Gritti to Doge and Senate, 3 September, 1588, Brown, ed., *Calendar of State Papers . . . in the Archives and Collections of Venice*, 383-4; Edward Palmer to Walsingham, 19 September, 1588, Lemon, et. al., ed., *Calendar of State Papers, Domestic*, 12: 254-6.

[3] Drake to Walsingham, 11 August, 1588, Laughton, 2: 101.

through hundreds of miles of cold grey seas around the north of Scotland and the rugged western shores of Ireland. The Armada separated, and within the space of two months suffered ferocious losses on the Irish coast. The *Santa Maria de la Rosa* was disembowelled on a rock in Blasket Sound, and there was but one survivor. The *Gran Grin* ran ashore off Clare Island, and the part of her crew that got to the shore was murdered by the Irish. Off the Giant's Causeway the *Girona* galleass, packed with survivors from two other ships, including Don Alonso de Leiva, went down with over 1,000 men. There were more losses, many more. It was said that twelve hundred bodies were counted on a beach in Donegal Bay.

Elizabeth's Lord Deputy in Ireland, Sir William Fitzwilliam, wanted no Spaniard to stir the Irish against his own puny forces, and callously ordered his subordinates to put survivors from Armada shipwrecks to the sword. The complement of a ship lost in Tralee Bay struggled ashore only to be caught and hanged by the English. Sir Richard Bingham, the Governor of Connaught, had hundreds of Spaniards executed. Only one officer refused to obey Fitzwilliam's orders – Drake's old comrade, Christopher Carleill, then governing Ulster – and it was to his credit that he sent his Spanish prisoners to neutral Scotland and paid for their transportation out of his own pocket.

Slowly and painfully the remnants of the once-mighty crusade limped home, broken in body and spirit. Hundreds of sick were disembarked in Spanish ports. Medina Sidonia led a small weary squadron into Santander in September. One hundred and eighty men aboard the flagship had died during the voyage home, and many more were ill, including the duke himself, who had to be carried ashore in a litter. All he wanted was a quiet retirement from further service. Oquendo got back, but was dead within six days of his arrival at San Sebastian. Among the last there arrived at Corunna the brave Recalde, and he, too, was dying. As the catalogue of disasters multiplied the English celebrated, Elizabeth arranging for her 'Armada portrait' to be painted and having a medal struck, the first to be minted by an English sovereign in commemoration of an historical event.

Philip's fortitude, even that which he embraced most, his faith, began to quail. It became clear that if the core of his royal ships had survived (all of his Castilian and seven of his Portuguese galleons), the losses had otherwise been horrific. Studying a report sent from Corunna by Recalde, he remarked, 'I have read it all, although I would rather not have done, because it hurts so much.' In all some sixty of the 130 ships that had sailed for Spain had been lost, and, no less troubling to a monarch who genuinely felt for many of his servants (unlike Elizabeth, Philip insisted that his veterans be paid), the toll in dead, prisoners or dying probably rose to 15,000 or more. By November Philip's grief was extreme. 'If God does not send us a miracle . . . ,' he wrote, 'I hope to die and go to Him . . . which is what I pray for, so as not to see so much ill fortune and disgrace . . . Please God, let me be mistaken, but I do not think it is so.'[1]

It was what Sir Francis Drake had always wanted. The spirits of the King of Spain had reached their lowest ebb.

[1] Martin and Parker, 258.

# CHAPTER TWENTY

# 'THIS WILL CAUSE AN EVIL SUMMER'

You follow Drake, by sea the scourge of Spain,
The dreadful dragon, terror to your foes,
Victorious in his return from Inde,
In all his high attempts unvanquished.
You follow noble Norris, whose renown,
Won in the fertile fields of Belgia,
Spreads by the gates of Europe to the courts
Of Christian Kings and heathen Potentates.

George Peele, *Farewell . . . to . . . Sir John Norris
and Sir Francis Drake, 1589*

DOM ANTONIO DREAMED NIGHT AND DAY OF BEING RESTORED TO THE THRONE OF Portugal, and the destruction of Philip's great Armada spurred him to dizzier fantasies. England and Spain had at last cast aside their masks and locked horns, Philip had suffered a mighty disaster, and now was the time for him to press his adventure. With hindsight we can see what the pretender refused to see – that his cause was, simply, hopeless. He had failed to hold Portugal before, and fled his country a fugitive, and there were few grounds for believing he could do better now that Philip had entrenched his position. The Spanish king had courted rather than antagonized the proud Portuguese, confirming their control of much of their country's administration, and some of Dom Antonio's more extreme supporters had been flushed out. Even Terceira in the Azores, which had held out longest for the pretender, had been subdued. No, what had been impossible in 1580 was no more likely to succeed in 1588. If Dom Antonio had somehow seized Lisbon, he could hardly have held it against the strength of Philip II.

But he dreamed on, and his fair words beguiled the English. Strategists saw in his schemes an opportunity to open a front in the Iberian peninsula itself, one that would employ Spain in the defence of her own frontiers and drain from her the resources she could otherwise devote to troubling England or the Netherlands, much as the 'Spanish ulcer' later bled Napoleon. Merchants rubbed their hands at the prospect of the rich trading privileges Dom Antonio would bestow upon those who restored him to his kingdom. And in their enthusiasm they made light of the difficulties. Sir Roger Williams, that conspicuously bold veteran of the Low Countries, the hero of Sluys whom Leicester had said was worth his weight in gold, had no doubt that 'half our forces, well entrenched [in Lisbon] with victuals and munitions, will not be dislodged with all Spain.'[1]

---

[1] Williams, 6 March, 1589, Wernham, ed., *The Expedition of Sir John Norris and Sir Francis Drake to Spain and Portugal*, 103-4. This volume provides a comprehensive but not exhaustive collection of the English documents relating to the expedition. The most important omission is the diary of a soldier on the voyage, published as *Ephemeris Expeditionis Norreysii & Draki in Lusitaniam* (1589), which has not been used by

Sir Francis Drake wanted to believe it too. He had always reached for the stars, realized ambitions that some might have considered chimerical, and probably it was only a matter of time before, like others who dared, he overreached himself. That time had finally come. He must have had his doubts, must have wondered whether a foothold in Portugal was really sustainable, but in his eagerness to deal Philip a crippling blow that would preclude a further attempt against England, he allowed himself to be carried along by the words of Dom Antonio, words that admitted of no uncertainty. 'Dom Antonio is so confident that they will restore him to Portugal that he looks upon himself as already there,' wrote one observer.[1]

In that summer of 1588 the pretender had been encouraged by his contacts with Spain's traditional enemies, the Moors. Muley Hamed, whose kingdom of Fez viewed Spain across the Straits of Gibraltar, eventually promised that if the English attacked Philip they might victual from his ports. Furthermore, Fez would commit thousands of soldiers and a considerable amount of money to the battle, providing that once Dom Antonio was King of Portugal he would recompense his allies for their trouble. The pretender jumped at these offers. He sent his youngest son, Don Cristobal, to Fez as a guarantee of his good faith, and threw himself into promoting an expedition from England.

The queen and Lord Burghley were no less interested than Walsingham and Drake in exploiting their victory over the Armada by some counterstroke, while Philip's forces were in disarray, but their views differed from Drake's. It was debated whether an attack might be made on the returning Armada ships, or if it was worth trying yet again to intercept a *flota* about the Azores. If Fez assisted, support for Dom Antonio was not out of the question, and on 5 August Walsingham had spoken of Elizabeth's 'resolution' to assist the pretender, but neither Burghley nor the queen accorded that alternative the priority it received from Drake. They were interested in the destruction of Spanish naval forces, but less in opening another front in the peninsula when they could barely sustain the conflict in the Netherlands and France. Their aim was primarily to secure England from a further invasion attempt and to force Philip to terms over the issue of the Dutch.

Sir Francis was unwell, but before August had passed he was called to court to discuss possibilities. He did not think the ships ready for an immediate voyage to the Azores, but he argued, as always, for another offensive, and probably mentioned Dom Antonio. If it had not been for his cautious performance against the Armada, one might suppose that Drake's habitual self-confidence had reached

previous biographers, probably because it was printed in Latin. For a translation, see Sugden, 'Diary of the Expedition of Drake and Norris, 1589'. Other useful primary sources can be found in Dasent, ed., *Acts of the Privy Council*, vols 16-17; Hume, ed., *Calendar of Letters and State Papers . . . in the Archives of Simancas*, vol. 4; Brown, ed., *Calendar of State Papers . . . in the Archives and Collections of Venice*; Klarwill, ed., *Fugger News-Letters*, vol. 2; and Butler, ed., *Calendar of State Papers, Foreign*, vols 22-3. The expedition has aroused great controversy. Corbett, *Drake and the Tudor Navy*; Oppenheim's *Monson*, 1: 177-225; Cheyney, *History of England*, 1: 153-89; and Tenison, *Elizabethan England*, 8: 1-178, exculpate Drake and Norris at the expense of Elizabeth and her government. Wernham, 'Queen Elizabeth and the Portugal Expedition', and McBride, 'Elizabethan Foreign Policy in Microcosm: The Portuguese Pretender, 1580-89', tend to reverse the argument. Hume, *The Year After the Armada*, presents an anti-English view and draws upon two Lisbon diaries of the period.

[1] Antonio de Vega, 8 December, 1588, Hume, 4: 493-5.

dangerous levels. The truth was probably that he completely overestimated the support Dom Antonio commanded. It was not his first miscalculation, but it was certainly to be his costliest.

The plans discussed are evident from a note written by Burghley that September. Three objectives were listed: first, the destruction of surviving Armada shipping in Seville and Lisbon; second, the capture of Lisbon itself, as part of the fomentation of an uprising in favour of Dom Antonio; and third, the seizure of the Azores, also in the name of the pretender, as a base for intercepting the *flotas*. Later, when it was learned that many of the Armada ships were in Santander and San Sebastian, rather than Seville and Lisbon, the voyage was lengthened, but it still contained the germ of a brilliant plan.

The bugbear was Lisbon. If that unattainable item had been struck out, and Drake had been charged with destroying the shipping and then invading the islands, there might have been a resounding success. For by wiping out Spain's surviving naval strength the English could the more easily have taken and defended the Azores. These islands were familiar to the English, through trade and war, and Terceira had only recently yielded its allegiance to the pretender. If they fell, they could have been defensible by sea power long enough to enable the English privateers to disrupt the treasure flow that used the Azores as a stop-over on the voyage to Spain, and possibly even to capture some of it. After all, Philip's navy would have been disabled, and where were his greatest seamen – Santa Cruz, Recalde, Leiva, Oquendo and Moncada? Dead or dying, every one, destroyed by the wasting voyage of the Armada. The idea, then, was not without merit, and Philip took it seriously enough to set in hand the fortification of his vulnerable Atlantic islands.

The immediate problem was not the nature of the plan, but the difficulty of finding money to outfit the venture, and in the task Drake found a partner in his old Irish comrade, Sir John Norris. Sir John, known as 'Black John' (on account of his dark complexion rather than the ruthlessness with which he had dealt death to military opponents in Ireland and the Low Countries), was a fighting man if ever there was one, the eldest of three soldier-brothers, decisive, frank and incurably brave. His experiences in the Dutch campaigns had raised him to the position of England's foremost soldier. Knighted in 1586 for breaking Parma's lines at Grave, Norris had been serving Leicester as a kind of chief-of-staff at Tilbury during the Armada crisis. He embraced the new adventure heartily, and greatly advanced its cause, for now Sir Francis had on offer what appeared to be an unbeatable team, the nation's greatest men of action as joint commanders of the expedition, and at Drake's disposal was Black John's not inconsiderable influence. Norris's parents were friends of the queen, and he knew a formidable number of military men, at home and abroad.

The queen would contribute, but even so great an undertaking as this must be financed largely by private individuals and merchant companies. Three years of war had stripped Elizabeth's meagre resources to the bone. The war was forcing her to improve her revenue, by parliamentary subsidies, the sale of royal property and an unwise recourse to loans, but these efforts had been too recent and, arguably, too limited to release naval expeditions from dependence upon the private purse.

Once again her commanders went cap-in-hand to the monied, soliciting investors with stories of good prospects; once again they harboured incentives to underestimate costs and cut corners to win royal approval for their venture. Norris and his friends offered £20,000; Drake was put down for £2,000, his friends for £6,000, and the syndicate of merchants that had financed his 1587 voyage for £5,000; the City of London, envisaging plunder and perhaps a breaching of the lucrative Portuguese trade, promised £10,000; and a number of individual shipowners and courtiers were interested. Elizabeth herself agreed to supply £20,000, six ships and two pinnaces, victualled and furnished for three months, a siege-train and other equipment, and to authorize the towns and counties to supply provisions, ships and men. This was to be no mere hit-and-run raid, but a veritable counter-armada, the greatest expedition yet mounted by Elizabethan England, and one with the potential seriously to affect the war, perhaps to end it.

Drake and Norris received their commission as joint commanders in October, and the dreary and often distressing task of organizing the expedition began. Sir Francis gathered the shipping at Plymouth around a core of the queen's ships, the *Revenge* (which still flew Drake's flag), *Dreadnought*, *Swiftsure*, *Nonpareil*, *Foresight* and *Aid*, dealt with the provisions for the mariners, and had six pinnaces built. Norris raised and armed the soldiers. At the turn of the year the southern counties were being summoned to furnish men through London and the outports. The men sent were far from the best: often they were ill equipped, with neither coats nor weapons, and many were the 'idle and loose' whom local authorities had been glad to see go. One 'gentleman' had fled from debt, and Drake and Norris were forbidden by the Privy Council to take him. Others, having been put down for the voyage, found themselves in prison in London and Westminster, and had to be released by an application from the commanders. In late September Sir John had gone to the Low Countries in search of experienced soldiers to stiffen the ranks of these raw English levies. The Dutch had defence problems of their own, but a meeting of the States General in December gave Norris what he wanted: 2,600 foot and horse from those men England had undertaken to maintain in the Low Countries; ten Dutch companies; five fully furnished ships of war; and provision for the English to hire more vessels as transports. Momentarily the course of the great counter-armada ran fairly smoothly.

But not for long. When the English began to withdraw their forces from the Low Countries the Dutch flew into a 'passion'. Far fewer of Elizabeth's troops remained than Norris had agreed. The queen made matters worse by giving out that she expected the Dutch to replace the forces Norris had taken with their own men, and that she intended to abandon Ostend. Eventually she compromised, redeploying her soldiers in Brielle and Flushing to the more threatened towns of Bergen and Ostend and reducing Norris's contingent by five hundred men. But her commander in the Netherlands, Lord Willoughby, continued to press the Dutch to use their own troops to fill the vacuum created by Norris, and there was a disastrous breakdown in Anglo-Dutch co-operation. The promised Dutch warships did not arrive, and few of the transports. Some 2,000 Walloons did appear but refused to serve. And such of the English soldiers as were shipped from the Low Countries were slow in arriving. To these major delays were added less serious if no less irritating frustrations. Elizabeth prevaricated about putting her seal on the commanders' commission, and some investors grew discouraged and withdrew, including the Earl of Northumberland, who was down for £2,000. The longer the expedition took to prepare the more valuable those subscriptions were, for the cost of maintaining men sitting in port inflated relentlessly the expenses of the voyage. Both the government and the remaining investors had to find more money, a great deal more, but even so it seems that provisions for the force were skimped.

The queen's detailed instructions were dated 23 February 1589, and embraced an extensive plan, not unsound if somewhat impractical. The fleet was expressly ordered to attend first to the enemy ships of war in the ports of Guipuzcoa, Biscay or Galicia, and to destroy them that they might not interfere with the further operations. Thus, for the queen, the most crucial objective of the voyage was the elimination of the remaining Armada ships in Santander, San Sebastian and Corunna. Only when that was completed should Drake and Norris try their fortune at Lisbon. Nor had Elizabeth been swept off her feet by Dom Antonio's smooth talk, for she did not fully endorse his visionary plan of capturing the city. Her commanders were cautioned not to attempt the town unless they had assessed the amount of opposition, ascertained that the Portuguese would rise in their support, and were satisfied that they could be successful. If the hazard seemed too great, Drake and Norris were to confine their attacks to the shipping.

However, the last part of the plan, to seize the Azores with a view to intercepting rich prizes, was given greater priority and listed with the attack on Armada shipping as a principal objective of the expedition. Drake and Norris had equal authority, but a council was appointed to advise them, and secret instructions named Thomas Fenner and Sir Roger Williams to succeed the commanders in the event of their deaths or illness. In addition, the queen's special representative, Anthony Ashley, was sent aboard to keep a record of the events and ensure that the government's views were fully expressed.

The plan was ambitious, but not injudicious, despite its inclusion of the Lisbon enterprise, which ought to have been completely left out. Drake and Norris, however, did not share the government's priorities, and had their minds fixed upon Lisbon. About the time they had their instructions from Elizabeth, they worked out an agreement with Dom Antonio. The pretender called himself the King of Portugal and spoke breezily of the welcome his people would give him, but he readily admitted that his finances were negligible. Indeed, they were so depleted that it was said that Sir Francis had to lend him money for his armour, Essex had to give him a carriage and the queen had to equip his retinue, who had but three shirts to each of their backs. Little wonder, since he had been treading the political wilderness for nearly a decade, dependent upon the goodwill of Spain's enemies and the charity of the few loyal Portuguese who stood by him. But he assured Drake and Norris that once he was in control of his country all would be different. Ten days after their army was disembarked in Portugal, he would begin to pay and provision the troops regularly, and given six months he would indemnify the adventurers for the full cost of the expedition. Apparently he pinned his hopes on raising money from Fez as well as from his own subjects.

The agreement between Antonio and the commanders shows that the 'king' expected that several thousand of Norris's soldiers would be at his disposal in Portugal for at least three months. He also made it clear that his was a war of liberation, not conquest, and that his people were not to be pillaged. Preferring reconciliation to revenge, he had hundreds of pardons printed to circulate to Portuguese who had worked with the Spaniards, and he demanded the English respect liberty of conscience and religion, and that they refrain from looting either churches and hospitals or civilians. If individual Portuguese were taken in arms they were to be surrendered to Dom Antonio, who would compensate the captors, and Portuguese shipping should not be commandeered. As a reserve plan, Dom Antonio said that if he could not be landed with the whole force in Portugal, he might be taken to the Azores, in which case he requested that ten ships and 4,000 men be left with him there to enable him to secure his position. There is no doubt that Dom Antonio's priorities for the voyage were not the same as Elizabeth's.

It was not until March 1589 that the final stage of the preparations were under way. The commanders took their leave of the queen, and Norris travelled overland to the West Country, while Sir Francis left London for Dover where he would meet the ships fitted out in the Thames and take them to Plymouth. An excited Dom Antonio, with his son Dom Emmanuel, his aide Diego Botello (whom he had rewarded with a dukedom) and a few retainers, travelled by boat for Gravesend and then by horse to Dover to join Drake. On 16 March the fleet sailed for Plymouth, and Sir Francis had the fortune to intercept immediately sixty or seventy Dutch flyboats, most of them bound for Spain or France. Even at this stage, he was short of transports for his troops, so he happily impounded the lot.

Drake and Norris were soon ready to leave, but the south-westerlies kept them in port with an obstinacy that must have reminded Sir Francis of those days when the same winds prevented him from sailing to pre-empt the Armada. The time was not entirely wasted, for Norris used it to drill the soldiers ashore, but it ran down the victuals that should have been carrying them to Spain. Volunteers were also still arriving, and Norris bundled as many of them as he could into his forces. Since the Low Countries had failed to supply all the veterans he wanted, perhaps he felt they were necessary, but they contributed to the run-down of stores. The commanders had foreseen the problem, and had secured a promise from the queen to pay for extra victuals that might be needed in precisely such an emergency, but now she became difficult, and responded indifferently to the appeals she began to receive in April. The government waited for an estimate of the price of the required victuals, and, after a fortnight had elapsed since Drake and Norris's first request, authorized purchase. Unfortunately, the expedition had sailed that very day.

It did so woefully under-supplied. For this Drake and Norris were partly at fault for accepting last-minute increases in manpower, but the government was also to blame. The fleet had made some seizures in the Channel (one, the *Sea Rider*, was brought into Plymouth by Drake's brother, Thomas) and sold some goods to buy victuals, but these were mere palliatives. On 3 April Sir Francis reckoned he had only enough rations left for five weeks, and a few days later Norris more frankly told Burghley that 'we never received any favourable answer of any matter that was moved by us, were it never so just or reasonable', and threatened that if the voyage had to be abandoned the countryside would be filled with outraged and disorderly soldiers and sailors.[1] This finally did the trick, but not before the damage was done and the fleet had sailed with threadbare supplies.

It is impossible not to sympathize to an extent with Elizabeth. Her contribution to the expedition already far exceeded the £20,000 she had agreed to spend and Marmaduke Darrell, who was Drake's surveyor of the victuals, did not send his estimate of the cost of the needed supplies until 8 April. But in this instance her sluggish response to the matter of the victuals was thoroughly destructive to the prospects of the voyage. Arguably, the shortages now precluded the commanders from attempting the whole of their instructions. Those orders, as we have seen, had been extensive, enjoining a detour deep into the Bay of Biscay towards Santander before a voyage to Lisbon and the Azores. Given the uncertainties of tides, winds and battle, this was entirely beyond the duration of the provisions Drake had aboard. In effect, the commanders would now have to make choices, choices between what had to be performed and what might be left, and their priorities did not coincide with the queen's. She had emphasized the destruction of Armada shipping, but she was not the sole paymaster of the fleet. It must respond also to the private investors who had brought it into existence, and upon whose satisfaction any further ventures depended. If choices had to be made, commercial imperatives directed the fleet away from the Armada ships, in which there was little profit, and towards Portugal and the Azores. Many merchants who had invested in the venture thought only of restoring Dom Antonio, and through him of gaining access to the opulent Portuguese trades with Brazil, Africa and the East; of reviving a once rewarding Anglo-Iberian trade; and of the immediate indemnification of the investment promised by Dom Antonio. Not only were their voices urging Drake to Lisbon, but both of the commanders were convinced, quite wrongly, that Portugal was the true strategic target. When the victuals dictated priorities, they would not be Elizabeth's.

In more than the question of victualling did the queen permit her ships to sail without the means to fulfil their instructions, for she had also denied the fleet the siege-train that Drake and Norris had requested as early as September. Considering the powerful forts at Santander, Corunna and Lisbon, this was a gross oversight, and one it is surprising that Norris tolerated. None knew more than he what was needed to batter holes in European castles, and he was not a man to bide his tongue when aroused. Yet almost unbelievably he sailed without his guns, and the expedition would suffer because of it.

Before it quit Plymouth, Drake's counter-armada was in trouble. For there were other, more marginal problems, too. One of them was Robert Devereux, the second Earl of Essex, son of Drake's old patron, an impetuous, generous but foolish youth, striking in manner and looks. He was in debt, and trusted to win money as well as honour with Drake ('If I speed well, I will adventure to be rich; if not, I will never live to see the end of my poverty'), but he stole from the court secretly at night and headed for Plymouth by the fastest horses, fearing the queen would call him back.[2] It was reminiscent of Sidney's escapade of three years before, and per-

[1] Norris to Burghley, 8 April, 1589, Wernham, 126-7.

haps Essex remembered how that had ended, for he had no sooner reached the fleet than he persuaded the captain of the *Swiftsure*, one of the queen's ships, to carry him to sea, beyond the reach of either Elizabeth or his own friends, who thundered after him. Sir Francis was left with the embarrassing job of explaining that while he regretted the temporary loss of one of his best ships, and of Sir Roger Williams, who was aboard her, he was entirely innocent of conniving at Essex's escape. He was no doubt glad to get to sea.

The great fleet finally sailed at the first usable wind on 17 and 18 April. It was such a force as Elizabeth had not sent to sea before. Some 13,000 soldiers were aboard in fourteen regiments, one of which Drake himself commanded, and there were about 4,000 mariners and 'pioneers' and 180 sail – the queen's ships, substantial contingents of armed merchantmen from London and the outports, and numerous freighters. Behind him Sir Francis left his redoubtable subordinate, Captain Robert Crosse, who was charged with assembling further provisions and following him. And ahead?

Sadly, even the Spaniards knew. No effort to mask Drake's activities, not even the nocturnal discussions between Drake and Dom Antonio, could have shrouded preparations on such a scale. But in any case, Philip's intelligence system was efficient and his spies had penetrated the closest councils of the enemy. The English ambassador to France, Sir Edward Stafford, was in Spanish pay and leaking inaccurate details of Drake's force at the beginning of the year. Dom Antonio's retinue was riddled with Philip's agents, Portuguese who now despaired of their master's success and sold secrets to the enemy in the hope of reconciling themselves to Spain. Manuel de Andrada was one of the pretender's most trusted servants, and attended Drake's house when Diego Botello went over the Portuguese contract with the English admiral, yet he regularly passed information to the Spaniards under the code-name 'David'. When Antonio grew depressed, he was wont to confide in Antonio de Escobar, another spy. And Dr Rodrigo Lopez, a follower of Dom Antonio who became the queen's physician, actually ended his life on the Tyburn gallows for attempting to take her life by poison. In September 1588 Philip knew that a counterstroke was afoot; soon after, that it involved an assault on surviving Armada ships and support for Antonio; and early in April the Spaniards had full possession of the substance of Drake's instructions of February! The news, indeed, was all over Europe. A report from Cologne, preserved by the Fugger banking house, reported that February that Drake's fleet was only waiting for wind and weather to sail, but that it would 'cause an evil summer'.[1]

But aboard the fleet itself there was hope. 'It was hardly believable with what great alacrity the cry went up from everyone: "Spain! Spain!"' wrote a diarist. One man in particular set the doubts firmly aside. 'Dom Antonio is determined to be the first to set foot ashore,' wrote 'David'. 'He takes with him some black bullet-proof armour, the helmet being also proof. He intends to leap ashore fully armed, Don Alonso carrying before him a Christ raised from the dead.'[2] And well might

[2] Essex to Knollys, *Ibid*, 133.

---

[1] Report from Cologne, 23 February, 1589, Klarwill, 2: 186-7.
[2] Advice from 'David', March 1589, Hume, 4: 522-6; *Ephemeris Expeditionis*, 11.

he be excused his excitement. For after years of exile, Dom Antonio was going home.

Sir Francis wanted to go straight to Lisbon, and make as much of a surprise of it as he could, but he was unwilling to flout Elizabeth's instructions so blatantly, at least without having come to some private understanding to do so. He had been ordered to destroy the Armada ships, which various reports placed in Santander and Corunna, and he now endeavoured to achieve that end, although without his usual determination and commitment. His vast fleet was soon scattered by the poor weather – 'being tossed in all directions by uncertain winds and violent tempests,' says an anonymous journalist – and thirty sail parted company, a problem that was to continue to trouble Drake. Over the ensuing weeks ships from the expedition were putting into La Rochelle and the ports of Devon, Cornwall and Dorset, and not always because of storms. In one case the men simply refused to go further. Although the Privy Council dealt severely with such defections, which were apparently stimulated by the deficiency of victuals, the losses reduced Drake's strength.

By the time Drake had collected his forces after the first spell of dirty weather the wind was too far easterly for the voyage to Santander, and he ran to Corunna, encouraged by rumours that two hundred sail were sheltering in the ports of Galicia and Portugal. Or so Drake and Norris plausibly explained later, and it seems reasonable to suppose that the voyage to the capital of Galicia was an attempt to some extent to fulfil the instructions to distress ships 'in any of the ports either of Guipuzcoa, of Biscay or Galicia.'[1]

The arrival of the English on the afternoon of 24 April was so sudden that Corunna was taken by surprise. It was perched upon a promontory, with a higher and strongly fortified section towards the end of the peninsula and the principal residential area below on the low ground towards the mainland. Across the neck of the promontory and protecting the lower town from attack by land was a fortification, while the high town received additional cover from guns on the offshore island of San Antonio. The Governor of Galicia, Don Juan de Padilla, Marquis of Ceralba, had relatively few men under arms in Corunna, for most of his soldiers were off duty, and he was forced to rely upon a few hundred trained reserves and local levies.

Drake was disappointed to find that Corunna, where the Armada had reassembled the previous year, now contained only a few ships: Recalde's great San Juan, once vice-admiral of Medina Sidonia's fleet; two men-of-war; two large freighters laden with provisions; two war galleys; and a few small boats. This was scarcely the prize he had hoped to find, but he must make the best of it. He knew that the enemy might still be injured by the destruction of naval stores and provisions, especially as Spain was then enduring a famine, and his own fleet badly needed the victuals. There was desultory fire from the fortifications, but that night Drake landed Norris with several thousand soldiers a mile from the wall across the lower town. They soon reached it, pushing back a few Spaniards who resisted

[1] Instructions to Drake and Norris, 23 February, 1589, Wernham, 82-8.

271

them, and then camped outside among some convenient buildings. The next morning Sir John was troubled with fire from the Spanish ships, especially the *San Juan*, which sheltered near shore batteries, but some artillery was eventually landed from the English fleet, and at least the offending galleys were driven beyond range. All was then prepared for a major assault upon the lower town.

The immediate obstacle was the wall across the neck of the promontory, but early the following morning (26 April) Drake launched 1,500 men in small boats against landing places on the Spanish side of the fortification, while Sir John's men threw themselves upon it from outside, using scaling ladders to clamber over or taking advantage of the low tide to wade out around the edges of the defences, which they discovered did not extend far into the sea. Beset from both sides the defenders broke in an hour and fled towards the town with the English in hot pursuit. The news swept through the streets of Corunna, and the people ran in terror towards the castle or high town at the end of the promontory or scattered into the countryside. Some did not make it. Norris's soldiers knew the custom of war, that resistance earned its reward, and they mercilessly cut down about five hundred Spaniards they found in the town. 'Glad was the Englishman that could kill one,' gloated one witness.[1] Other prisoners had the wisdom to surrender to officers and received protection, one of whom was the military commander of Corunna, Don Juan de Luna, who hid in his house until the next day.

Later that morning the Spaniards also abandoned their ships, except for the galleys, which pulled out of danger. Recalde's once proud galleon, the survivor of that fearsome barrage off Gravelines, was now run ashore and set on fire by her crew. Consternation also spread to the heavily fortified upper town of Corunna, as refugees from the lower town told and retold their stories and the cries of the English looting below accompanied the fires that sporadically appeared as stores and war material were destroyed. Ceralba gathered his forces to resist attack, but he had little confidence in a successful defence, and sent his wife and daughter to flee the town on foot. A few thousand local peasants who rallied to help him were quickly dispersed by the English soldiers as soon as they made their appearance.

At this point Drake and Norris seem to have lost full control of some of their men, who fell to ransacking houses for plunder and breaking open wine cellars to swallow their contents, wantonly destroying provisions badly needed for the ships. The commanders wanted to remove or burn any supplies that might furnish another fleet for Philip, and both in the town itself and in the surrounding countryside the English sequestrated or destroyed everything of value, scattering Spanish detachments that opposed them. According to one report 6,000 oxen, 15,000 cantaras of biscuit, 3,000 hogsheads of wine and 6,000 barrels of powder were taken. Fish and corn were also impounded, along with thousands of ropes and other naval stores and 150 pieces of ordnance, many of them bronze and none of which Spain could afford to lose. For Anthony Ashley, the queen's representative, this was an excellent result. 'Our coming hither hath marvellously hindered the King's preparation of his navy, especially in his provisions,' he wrote.[2]

---

[1] Report of the voyage, *Ibid*, 242.
[2] Ashley to the Privy Council, 7 May, 1589, *Ibid*, 148-50.

It seemed as though the fleet's victualling problems might be over, for although much had been wasted during the fevered pillage of Corunna and some of the food found, such as corn, was not in a form in which it could be used, wise captains had the sense to stock their ships as fully as they could. Drake was perhaps remiss in not insisting that all did so. It may be that he tried, and if the expedition had sailed immediately the supply could have carried the fleet on to other work.[1] But no man could command the wind and tides, whatever superstitious Spaniards might say about Drake. For on the 26th, as the essential job at Corunna was done, the wind began to blow strongly towards Corunna harbour, sweeping across a heavy sea, and the expedition was confined to port. It was to remain there for two weeks, two weeks that wiped out the extra provisions the English had found in the town and restored them to their former predicament. Drake's fleet had thus spent more than a month cornered by the wind, either in Plymouth or Corunna, consuming supplies to little purpose.

During the delay Norris turned his attention to the high town of Corunna, where he believed additional munitions and stores were kept. The governor refused to surrender when summoned, and Norris opened a formal siege, firing with some effect upon the walls using two culverins and two demi-culverins, the best battery he could bring to bear in lieu of the siege-train the queen had denied him. In time the town would have fallen, but Norris had little to spare and hoped to force a speedy end to the contest. He decided that two parties would storm the town simultaneously, one using a hole his little guns were gradually knocking into the wall, and the other attacking a tower that the English 'pioneers' had mined. On 4 May the assault took place. But the mine failed to demolish the tower completely, and as Norris's heroes tried to fight their way through its shattered remains, gallantly led by Drake's regiment (Sir Francis himself being with the ships), the surviving structure collapsed on top of them. Some twenty men were killed or buried beneath the rubble, including one of Drake's relatives, Captain John Sydenham. The colours of the regiment themselves would have been lost but for a lieutenant who recovered them when the ensign holding them was shot down. Badly shaken, the attackers recoiled, only to be joined by the other assault party, also in retreat, and both retired through a narrow lane beneath a galling musket fire. The total English loss was about sixty.

Norris was facing up to his lack of adequate guns, for his progress was torturous. However, if the siege would have to be foregone there remained one piece of glory for Black John. Word reached the English that part of a relief army was gathering a few miles to the south-east under the Count de Andrada. At first it was believed to be 15,000 strong, but Norris did not hesitate to meet it, believing that to withdraw before its approach would be to encourage charges of cowardice. Leaving Sir Francis to guard Corunna, he set off on 6 May with nine regiments,

[1] Captain Wingfield, in his narrative of the voyage, said that Corunna could easily have provided for all of the English ships. However, that some captains were able to victual themselves fully does not establish that all could have done so. In their dispatches Drake, Norris and Fenner acknowledge that the captured provisions had ameliorated their problem, but the commanders and Ashley continued to press the Privy Council to hasten forward a further supply of victuals. This suggests that Corunna failed to meet the deficiency for much longer than the fleet was in that port.

and about four miles from the town, near El Burgo, came upon 8,000 or more Spaniards strongly entrenched across the River Hero. Norris was outnumbered and the Spanish camp was difficult to attack, being accessible only over a narrow stone bridge, about 80 feet long, that spanned the river, but the English were in a fighting mood and probably guessed that most of their opponents were not trained or experienced soldiers, but civilians hastily armed for the emergency. Sir John hurled his men against the bridge, and, bravely led by Sir Edward Norris, the general's brother, they bowled over the opposition, which met them half-way across, bulldozed them back to their own bank, and put the entire Spanish army to flight. Probably the action was not as sharp as the English remembered, because only three of their men were killed, but the enemy loss, particularly in the pursuit of the broken army, was severe. 'The fields were strewn with arms, the slopes covered with bands of fugitives in clusters, some swimming in the river and others submerged, still others up to their necks in the marshes, and some stuck in the weeds and slime, and some slinking along the fences and amidst the wheat. What more? Over seven hundred of the enemy soldiers had been slaughtered, and twice as many as on our side . . . The enemy lost its royal standard, its camp and all the equipment, the table silver and utensils, the uniforms, weapons and provisions,' wrote one participant.[1] Norris reckoned the Spanish dead at 1,000, and another at two hundred. Certainly there was considerable butchery, and one group of Spaniards found hiding in a monastery were hauled out and killed on the spot and the cloister burned. The English then ravaged the countryside with uncommon delight. 'You might have seen the country more than three miles compass on fire,' remarked Captain Wingfield.[2]

It was now time to be gone, for the wind had improved and the capture of the high town was not an immediate prospect. There had been some profit in the raid on Corunna, as Drake wrote to Sir John Wolley: 'We have done the King of Spain many pretty services here at this place, and yet I believe he will not thank us.'[3] The destruction of valuable Spanish stores and a few ships, the indignity Philip must have felt at the sack of one of his chief ports, and the loss of upwards of 1,000 men, all advertised Spain's weaknesses. It was said that the king railed that the mistress of half an island, a corsair and a common soldier such as Norris should bait the master of a huge empire. But the result was far from satisfactory for the English. The amount of Spanish shipping destroyed had been small, and the largely futile days in harbour between 26 April and 8 May had depleted the English rations. More yet, for that other scourge of the large-scale ocean voyage – disease – had now raised its formidable head. Was it the excessive drinking during the sack of the lower town, the crowding aboard the ships, or the hot, sultry air? No one knew for certain, but it was there like a spectre, almost intangible at first, but intensifying into terrifying proportions. The captains had seen it before, and knew how it had decimated the fleet that defeated the Armada and sapped the strength of Drake's West Indian voyage. They knew that it could ruin this ex-

---

[1] *Ephemeris Expeditionis*, 19.
[2] Wingfield's narrative is in Wernham, 246-90.
[3] Drake to Wolley, 8 May, 1589, Tenison, 8: 114.

pedition too.

Disease and reduced stores declared a new urgency, for the attack on Corunna had left none of the fleet's objectives fulfilled. They had not finished off the Armada ships; they had not visited Lisbon; and they had not taken any of the Atlantic islands. In their letters home the English, hiding the doubts that must have been stealing over them, made the best of the recent operation, and repeated their calls for more men, victuals and siege guns, pleas that were not answered. Privately they probably knew that hard choices had to be made. The men were embarked from Corunna on 8 May, but where were they to go?

A sensible course would have been a return to Santander to attempt the ships there, even though it was said that the port was protected by powerful fortifications that would have been proof against the ordnance Norris had available. The want of siege guns may have prevented a success, but if the English had taken Santander a severe blow could have been dealt Spanish naval power. So still thought the queen, who raged at the failure of her fleet to attack Santander, but whose tardy support in guns and victuals was still reaping its reward. A voyage from Corunna to Santander was not straightforward, however, and when Drake consulted the leading masters and captains they said that 'it was a thing unfit and most dangerous, in respect there was no safe harbour upon that coast where such a fleet might ride in safety before the army should have landed, the wind being westerly.' One journal of the expedition recorded that they were 'violently opposed' to it.[1] That was enough for Drake and Norris. They probably feared their victuals were not up to trips to both Santander and Portugal, and that the disease attacking their fleet would bring a premature end to the expedition even if a deficiency of supplies did not. A choice was made – Portugal.

It was the wrong decision, but a courageous one, for Drake and Norris knew that the premier objective of the queen had not been met. They gambled that the capture of Lisbon would sink all criticism into oblivion, and none had more often vindicated severe risks by an eventual success than Drake. But this time he had miscalculated, and worse, he had run out of luck. He needed a quick passage to Portugal, but instead it was a difficult one, beating back and forth against the wind for days while one man after another went down sick. On the way they encountered the missing Swiftsure, which had absconded from Falmouth with the runaway Essex on board. The earl was there, 'welcomed with the greatest applause and joy by everyone,' it was said, and eager to be unleashed upon the Spaniards, and so was the even more ferocious Sir Roger Williams.[2] They had been cruising for some time off the Iberian coast, picking up a few prizes and waiting for Drake to arrive. An upstart and meddler Essex may have been, but Sir Francis was not without affection for the son of his old patron, and Williams was a first-class fighting subordinate. Point him in the right direction and he would fight till he dropped. As for the Swiftsure, she greatly stiffened the quality of the fleet. All in all, Drake was happy to see the reinforcement, especially after disease and the dispersal of some

---

[1] *Ephemeris Expeditionis*, 20; answers to charges against Drake and Norris, 23 October, 1589, Wernham, 291-4.

[2] *Ephemeris Expeditionis*, 20.

of the ships in the bad weather had drained the strength of his command.

A council of war held at Cape Roca at the estuary of the Tagus decided that Peniche, north of Lisbon, would serve for a landing. Norris would march his army the 40-odd miles to the city and menace it from the north-west, while Drake would simultaneously appear before it from the waterfront, by passing the forts of Cascais, St Julian's and Belem and ascending the Tagus. It was a doubtful plan. Conceivably, Lisbon might fall, for despite lengthy preparations Spain's defences there were poor. The city was controlled by Philip's nephew, Cardinal-Archduke Albert of Austria, and he had only a few hundred horse and foot stationed in the most vulnerable parts of the town. He supplemented these detachments by mustering several thousand militia, but most were Portuguese and their loyalty, like that of the native population at large, was questionable. It was possible that Dom Antonio's appearance might spark a rebellion, and the cardinal-archduke perhaps dwelt upon the 10,000 Portuguese who had defended Lisbon for the pretender in 1580. Anyway, he dealt with the problem by oppression. Suspect Portuguese were removed or imprisoned, and any found colluding with Dom Antonio were subject to execution. Propaganda depicting the English as destructive self-seekers was circulated, and it was broadcast that Don Fernando de Toledo was collecting troops in Spain to march to the city's relief. Probably there was much sympathy for Dom Antonio in Lisbon, but most Portuguese would be reluctant to commit themselves to the pretender's cause unless the English secured a clear-cut advantage. A military setback for the cardinal-archduke could have upset his precarious control and turned Lisbon over to Antonio, but even if the English had taken the city it would still have been difficult to regard the plan of Drake and Norris as other than unsound.

From their point of view the chance of success was slim. If Lisbon was weak, it was arguably too strong for a pestilence-ridden army deficient in powder and without siege guns to batter the city's strong walls. Even from the harbour the castle was out of effective gun range. Norris and Drake simply lacked the resources to compel Lisbon to surrender by siege or storm, and could only trust that a spontaneous uprising by the Portuguese would win the day. Yet even had they taken it, they could not have preserved it from recapture. Still, they persisted, and in the afternoon of 16 May the English boats pitched in the ferocious surf at Peniche as the landing took place. It was difficult. One of the boats was capsized with a loss of twenty-five men, while even the more fortunate had to wade the last few yards waist-deep beneath shot from the castle on the cliffs above. Essex and Sir Roger Williams, vying to display the greatest valour, led the way. 'The Earl of Essex,' recorded a diarist with the soldiers, 'a man with a great and outstanding spirit, when he saw the enemy shake their pikes, brandish their swords and threaten us, seized his weapons and impatient with the delay, was the first to jump into the sea. He was immersed up to his chest, not without the greatest risk to his life.'[1] Eventually enough troops had been put ashore and led to the top of the steep cliffs to clear away a Spanish force that tried to dispute their passage. The town of Peniche, abandoned by the terrified inhabitants, was soon seized and the following

---

[1] *Ibid*, 21.

day the first encouraging event occurred, for upon learning that 'King Antonio' was with the invaders, the Portuguese in the castle surrendered.

Dom Antonio had a toehold on his kingdom, but that was all. It remained to be seen how Lisbon would react. A council of war planned the next move:

> The officers called in the Earl of Essex and the commanders and took counsel on what seemed the most opportune thing to do. With a unanimous decision and vote, they decided that Norris should proceed with an army to Lisbon, which was but 8,400 paces from Peniche, that Drake, with his fleet, his arms, provisions and equipment, should approach him and remain at Cascais [a town and castle defending the northern approach to the Tagus], in order to see whether there were any there sympathetic to King Antonio, whether there were any there to assist the army at its coming, whether any passage [up the Tagus] was possible, and whether any help from Lisbon would be precluded. They shook hands, and Norris took charge of the army and Drake of the fleet.[1]

Norris would lead fourteen regiments of a little under 6,000 fit men across the hills to Lisbon, with Dom Antonio, now again on his home soil, as their figurehead. A guard would be left at Peniche to secure his rear, but Drake was bound for the Tagus, and may have promised to meet Norris in Lisbon. The English soldiers must have wondered, for although they marched against a big city they were without siege artillery and had only such food, arms and powder as they could carry upon their backs. To some extent they must have depended upon Drake – to bring up more supplies with the fleet, to land their diminutive battery near Lisbon, and perhaps not a little to inspire terror amongst their enemies by his appearance in the harbour. It is difficult not to believe, however, that Norris and Drake pinned their hopes of taking Lisbon primarily upon Dom Antonio's assurances of a Portuguese rising, that they fully understood that their forces were inadequate to take the city without such a rising, and that they had no intention of mounting a full blown attack unless there were solid manifestations of support for the pretender.

To encourage the natives and to counter the frightening stories the cardinal-archduke had been spreading about the heretical English, Norris forbade his men to molest or pillage the villages they passed through. As the general led them from Peniche on 18 May, Sir Francis climbed to the top of a nearby hill and 'with a pleasing kindness took his leave severally of the commanders of every regiment, wishing us all a most happy success in our journey . . . with a constant promise that he would, if the weather did not hinder him, meet us in the river of Lisbon with our fleet.'[2] Then Drake made for the Tagus, arriving at Cascais on 20 May. The wind was fair for passing up-river, but Drake wanted to deposit his sick and the least serviceable vessels and transports at a base and test the feeling for Dom Antonio before attempting a potentially hazardous voyage to Lisbon past the forts of St Julian's and Belem. Accordingly, on the 21st he took some men ashore and led them into the town unopposed by more than a few shots from the castle. The citizens began to flee into the countryside with their valuables, but Sir Francis dispatched a Portuguese to assure them that if they accepted Dom Antonio as king they had naught to fear, and when the inhabitants

---

[1] *Ibid*, 22.
[2] Wingfield, Wernham, 267.

gave him the assurances he requested he directed that the town be left unmolested. Indeed, once rapport had been established, the English even received fresh food from the townspeople, for which Drake was careful to ensure immediate payment was made. So far so good. But then messengers were sent overland to ascertain what progress Norris and Dom Antonio were making, and Sir Francis sat down to await the answers.

Drake has been criticized for his conduct at Cascais. It has been said that he broke a bargain to meet Norris at Lisbon by not pressing up-river at the first opportunity. But Norris himself advanced no such charge, for, whatever Sir Francis's bluff optimism may have led him to say by way of encouragement to the officers, he acted fully in accordance with the plans he had worked out with Norris and the senior commanders at Peniche, plans which enjoined him to risk the fleet in the Tagus only after he had assessed the prospects at Cascais. In short, Drake was to test the support for Antonio before hazarding heavy losses. Nor, indeed, was Norris doing much more. He refused to take more than 6,000 men, and had no artillery and little powder. There was no question of his storming Lisbon with such a force, but it remained to be seen whether it would encourage a movement in favour of the pretender. In short, both commanders were gauging the worth of Antonio's claims, and that entirely fulfilled their instructions from the queen. 'We would have you carefully and substantially to inform yourselves before you proceed to attempt anything,' they had read. 'You may proceed to make a descent there without any great hazard' and 'We expect at your hands that you will have a special care' for the 'preservation' of the men, 'down to the meanest person.' Elizabeth had made it completely clear that an attack upon Lisbon would be dependent upon a considerable show of support for Antonio, and it was upon that above all else that her commanders relied.

The problem was that neither the English nor any latent loyalists for Dom Antonio were willing to stick their necks out. Unless the Portuguese rallied, the English would not attack; but unless the English attacked, and showed the ability to overturn the cardinal-archduke, which Portuguese were going to risk imprisonment and execution by declaring for the king? There was a crucial leap to be made; perhaps Drake might have been capable of making it, for if his fleet had appeared before Lisbon there was a chance, if a thin one, that the Portuguese may have been encouraged. But he waited too long. A plodding caution had come over Sir Francis, not necessarily injudicious, but in marked contrast to the man at his best form. This was not the Drake who had raided Nombre de Dios with a handful of Devon men, nor the admiral who had dashed into Cadiz before his fleet had come up with him. Some scholars have argued that Drake was in poor health. Certainly he told Sir Julius Caesar, in a letter dated January 1589, that he had been confined to his room by pains in his body and legs. But the correct dating of Elizabethan documents is tricky. The start of the new year, for example, was then commonly reckoned from Lady Day (25 March) and this means that Drake's letter could have been written in January 1590 – not before, but after, the Portugal expedition. In any case there is no reason to suppose that a physical problem in January 1589 should affect a matter of judgement four months later. Whatever the cause, Drake remained at Cascais.[1] It was not until the morning of 25 May that he learned that Norris's army was at Lisbon (in fact it had entered the suburbs two

---

[1] Drake to Dom Antonio, 21 May, 1589, Tenison, 8: 136-7.

days before) but even then he waited until the following day to summon a council of captains and masters to discuss whether the fleet should ascend the Tagus.

Only in that meeting did a little of the admiral's old spirit flicker into life. All manner of objections were raised to a voyage up-river. Sickness had deprived the fleet of necessary manpower, and there were the many guns at St Julian's and a dozen galleys beneath them. Another fort was situated at Belem, and the shipping in Lisbon harbour would probably be armed. Drake listened to all this, and then swept it aside, commanding that two-thirds of the fleet – the best ships and fittest men – would follow up the Tagus at the first good wind. Yet it was too late. That very evening fresh news arrived: there had been no rising and Norris was in full retreat.

Black John had marched upon the city with scant supply, threatened but never really opposed by the Spanish forces the cardinal-archduke sent to worry him. The sickness intensified, however, occasioned, it was believed, by the consumption on the way of honey or stagnant water. Weary, depleted and under-supplied the English seized the suburbs of Lisbon on the 23rd, and waited for the Portuguese to demonstrate enthusiasm for the return of their king. It did not happen. On the march a few of the clergy, Dom Antonio's greatest supporters, and some of the poor turned out to speak with the man who had come to claim his throne. A few brave Portuguese, daring to defy the Spaniards, arrived to comfort and support the pretender, but it was hardly the army Dom Antonio expected, 'only a company of poor peasants, without hose or shoon, and one gentlewoman who presented the King with a basket of cherries and plums.'[1] In Lisbon the Spaniards had withdrawn their forces inside the city, leaving the suburbs to the English, after removing or destroying as many supplies as they could. They also demolished houses situated just outside the walls so that they could not shelter the enemy, and guns that could not be brought away were pitched into the river. As Antonio and Norris passed through the suburbs they found the houses shuttered and quiet and the streets empty – but for a few beggars who called out 'Viva el Rey Dom Antonio!'

The following days had underscored the hopelessness of Norris's position. His enemies made the occasional sortie against him, only to be beaten back, but the skirmishes cost a few men and valuable powder, match and lead for the muskets. It became clear that a further supply would be essential if the English were to be able to fight a major action, either against those in the city or against any force that might try to relieve them. There was no artillery, few victuals, and disease was cutting the soldiers down. The fleet had not appeared, and Dom Antonio's supporters, if they existed, were cowed by the fearful rewards of 'treason' that the cardinal-archduke was handing out. A few horse and foot did assemble in the pretender's name, but, sighed Captain Wingfield, 'all his horse could not make a cornet of forty, nor his foot furnish two ensigns fully.'

The English were reduced to bravado, with Essex boldly leading a party to the walls of Lisbon and rapping on the gates, but their manpower and means were weakening while the Spanish garrison received reinforcements from Oporto. There were eventually more soldiers defending the city than attacking it. Dom Antonio begged Sir John to wait a little longer, promising that his countrymen would come, but an

---

[1] Fenner to Anthony Bacon, 1589, Wernham, 236-41.

army could not live on dreams, and after four days in the suburbs Norris began to fall back to Cascais, travelling westwards down the Tagus, the Spanish horsemen now issuing boldly from the city to butcher or seize the sick or stragglers. From the river the galleys also tried to annoy the retreating army, although their fire had no greater effect than to blow a man's leg away and kill a mule. Disease caused severer losses. A diarist of the expedition estimated that by the time Norris rejoined Drake at Cascais a third of his force had gone.

It had been a fiasco and blame was freely if not openly cast about. Some charged Antonio for his misguided optimism; Dom Antonio blamed the queen's instructions for not permitting the expedition to go straight to Lisbon in order to surprise it; others blamed Drake for failing to make a rendezvous with Norris; and Ralph Lane, a petulant colonel of one of the regiments, attacked both of the commanders as 'two so overweening spirits, condemning to be advised and disdaining to ask advice.'[1] But they had done as they had been commanded. They had threatened Lisbon, and tested Antonio's predictions to find them wanting. And having done so they had retired without a major contest and the hazards it would have entailed.

The castle at Cascais surrendered shortly after Norris arrived. Seven bronze pieces were left to the English, but the small garrison was suffered to depart for Lisbon with its baggage. On 29 May Norris mustered 4,000 men to leave camp to meet a Spanish army that had advanced to menace them, but the enemy scattered as soon as Black John approached. Another, and more important service was performed in the first days of June as Drake's fleet, riding off the Tagus, snapped up some sixty prizes from a fleet of Hanseatic and French ships that were carrying corn, copper, wax and naval stores into Lisbon. Drake was able to dismiss the Dutch flyboats he had impounded off Dover and send them to England with cargoes of corn for their trouble.

Nonetheless, this stroke could not dispel the gloom that was enveloping the expedition, for victuals were almost exhausted, the men reduced to about 4,000 effectives, and none of the principal purposes of the voyage had been achieved. Corunna had not yielded the Armada shipping expected, and Drake and Norris's gamble to retrieve the expedition by an attempt upon Lisbon had also failed. At this moment word at last reached them from England. The queen, it appeared, was furious that no attack had been made on Santander, but once again she failed to provide the siege equipment Norris needed. On the other hand Essex was recalled, for which Drake may not have been ungrateful, and at least there was news that Crosse was on his way with the victuals that had been authorized as long ago as 17 April. What was to be done? There remained the Azores to try, and the commanders decided to bend their course towards them.

On 8 June, with the wind northerly, the fleet quit Cascais to look for Crosse, having tried to withdraw their men at Peniche (regrettably, the Spaniards had got there first) and gathered the remains of their forces together. The Spanish galleys, now reinforced by nine from Andalucia to about twenty-one in number, exploited the calm weather of the next two days to pounce upon some of the weaker English ships lagging behind, destroying two of the Hanseatic prizes but scattering when Drake himself bore up and opened fire from the *Revenge*. But Crosse joined company with fifteen grain

[1] Lane to Walsingham, 27 July, 1589, *Ibid*, 218-21.

ships, and although the quantity of provisions he brought was disappointing the fleet endeavoured to steer for the Azores.

To the last the expedition was dogged by baffling winds, and it had to reassemble in Bayona, where Drake had first bearded the Spaniards on their own ground four years before. Two weeks of battling hostile winds had sorely tested the frail constitutions of Drake's remaining crews, and bodies had been cast overboard daily, so that only 2,000 effectives could be mustered at Bayona. On 20 June Sir Francis ordered Fenner to demonstrate off shore, while he and Sir Roger Williams attacked the town of Vigo from opposite quarters. Strong barricades had been erected, but the Spaniards fled before the onset and Drake occupied the settlement and destroyed it with its immediate hinterland. Then, when the fractured fleet had been more completely reunited, he made one last effort to reach the Azores. Leaving Norris at Vigo, he put to sea with the best men and ships, only to encounter a savage storm.

In dribs and drabs the remains of the great counter-armada struggled home. Aboard Thomas Fenner's *Dreadnought* only three of three hundred men had escaped contamination; 114 were dead, and only eighteen were fit when she reached an English port. The smaller *Gregory* of London had only four effectives left, while the *Griffin of Lubeck*, one of the transports taken near Dover, eventually reached Sandwich with 'none that were well and able to hoist a sail when it was down, but were sick and dead, and [there] were not in the ship five or six men well. The master died since the ship's return, and out of 50 soldiers that were on board, they hurled overboard 32 or 33, and about 20 came home very sick, and 2 of them died as soon as they came to Sandwich.'[1] Drake and Norris had lost relatively few men in battle, and suffered a negligible loss in ships, but arguably as many as 10,000 who sailed on the expedition died abroad or shortly upon its return. As a fighting force it had disintegrated.

It has been said that the Drake-Norris expedition failed as miserably as the great Armada of 1588. If Medina Sidonia, his force greater than the English under Norris and Drake, had lost half as many men as he did and only a few ships; if he had burned part of Plymouth and taken three or four other towns, landed men who had routed the trained bands, and menaced London; if he had captured scores of merchantmen and great quantities of ordnance and provisions, that comparison would have had validity. But if the English expedition had not left its commanders bereft of some claims to attention, it had undeniably and spectacularly failed to accomplish its ends. It had missed a great opportunity to destroy the surviving Armada ships, and with them the core of Spain's naval strength, and it had demonstrated that Drake was as incapable of delivering a knock-out punch as Philip. The Venetian ambassador to Spain remarked that 'everyone sees that the attack on Portugal has brought loss to the English in persons and reputation, and to Dom Antonio because it has shown how feeble are the foundations on which he builds.'[2]

For the first time in his life Drake tasted failure, and failure for which he must fairly accept blame. He had taken more volunteers than he could feed, and contributed to the deficiency of victuals that clouded the fleet's operations. After quitting Corunna he had opted for a voyage to Lisbon rather than Santander and San Sebastian, perhaps

[1] Henry Gayney, July 1589, *Ibid*, 210-11.
[2] Tomaso Contarini to the Doge and Senate, 10 July, 1589, Brown, 460-3.

in response to the commercial interests of the expedition, but more probably in hopes of opening a front in Portugal – a strategy that rested more upon Dom Antonio's glib tongue and Drake's ardour to damage Spain than upon a cool assessment of the situation. And even his naval operations themselves had lacked the vigour and decisiveness of his earlier campaigns. That dithering at Cascais was the first indication that Sir Francis Drake was changing. The speed, resolution and daring that had once singled him out was beginning to fade. Was it age or responsibility that was breeding this new, pedestrian indecision? Or had the furious battles with the Armada damaged his confidence, or exhausted him, as they had seared the King of Spain? There are no answers to these questions. But the facts remain. Portugal had seen a man well off his form, and he would never recover it. Sitting alone in Buckland, Sir Francis must have often pondered the 'ifs' of the largest adventure he had ever put upon the sea. If he had eschewed the queen's instructions, and made straight for Lisbon . . . If the fleet had anchored in Lisbon harbour . . . If he had taken less notice of Dom Antonio. He probably knew he had been at fault, and when Norris and Williams roared in defiance of criticism and bragged of their achievements, Sir Francis Drake said nothing at all.

In truth none of the principals emerged from the Portugal expedition with much credit, not Drake, Norris or Williams, nor the queen or Burghley, nor the discredited King of Portugal. It was not true, however, that the commanders returned in disgrace. Norris sent his brother to London and informed Walsingham that 'if the enemy had done so much upon us, his party would have made bonfires in most parts of Christendom.'[1] Ashley wrote to the same effect, and the queen's letter to her commanders, written on 7 July, showed that her anger was behind her and that she considered 'there hath been as much performed by you as true valour and good conduct could yield', while the men had exhibited 'as great valour as ever nation did.'[2] Nor was that all, for the government was minded to employ Drake and Norris again immediately. Ashley was sent back to Plymouth to enquire of the two 'what enterprise they think fittest to be presently undertaken by them for the most advancement of her Majesty's service and the greatest annoyance of the enemy', using the better part of the forces they had available. The Privy Council was contemplating another raid on the Armada shipping or Spain's Atlantic convoys, but Drake and Norris discouraged the idea. Sir Francis knew that neither men nor ships were ready for such an adventure. The town of Plymouth was infected by diseased soldiers and mariners, and Drake may have wanted to remain at Buckland, for his own wife was ill, although on what account is not known. As for Black John, he was still spitting with fury at the government's tardy support of the expedition. Complaining to his brother, he said, 'We must be better used before I enter into any new service.'[3] When he came to London at the end of July he was grumbling about the 'crosses and disgraces' he had had to bear.

The voyage was long winding up, and Norris found greater grounds for dissatisfaction during the proceedings. The Privy Council's initial orders to local officials to assess and store the cargoes of the prizes and to sell perishable goods and sufficient of the rest as was needed to discharge men, care for the sick and remunerate the ship-

[1] Norris to Walsingham, 4 July, 1589, Wernham, 199-200.
[2] Queen to Drake and Norris, 7 July, 1589, *Ibid*, 200-1.
[3] Norris to Sir Edward Norris, 13 July, 1589, *Ibid*, 206-7.

owners, were, said Sir John, in breach of the commission given the commanders. He claimed that only Drake and himself could dispose of the prize goods and pay off the ships and men. We can see why the government was cautious. Most of the prizes belonged to neutrals like Denmark and the Hanse towns, and, while Elizabeth was prepared to confiscate goods being carried to Spain in aid of Philip's war effort, she had to ensure that they were condemned by due process of law. Furthermore, it was known that prizes were being rifled before the cargoes could be examined, and such profits as the voyage had made were passing into private pockets. The Privy Council explained that the commanders would indeed handle the disposal of the booty once it had been declared lawful prize.

With undue haste the commanders then had Nicholls, a justice, condemn the prizes, and they began to sell the cargoes and discharge the ships and men. The Privy Council had appointed their own commissioners to examine the seizures, and reacted sharply. Rumour had it that boatloads of goods from the ships had been embezzled, and that £7,000 in gold coins had been discovered hidden aboard a London ship, the *Unity*. The Council strove to curb the irregularities, and declared the sales invalid. Sir Edward Norris was even ordered to return some goods to a hulk, and Ralegh to restore a French ship he had purchased.

Norris and Drake were not blind to the claims of the neutrals, but they wanted to protect their conceived prerogative to dispose of the captured cargoes and to discharge the men as soon as possible. The ports were full of noisy and turbulent soldiers and sailors screaming out for their wages, and many of them descended upon London, where they created disturbances at the Royal Exchange and elsewhere. Two proclamations were issued to restore order in the capital and the counties; arrests were made; and four men were hanged, one of them protesting that thus he was rewarded for serving his country. The needs of the sick also demanded attention, as indeed the government acknowledged. Drake and Norris had them quartered in different places, but the locals refused to tend them for fear of infection. The Privy Council had to provide money to establish new shelters for the sick in places accessible to wood and water.

For many months the repercussions of the voyage were heard. Drake and Norris furnished accounts for examination before the end of the summer, but the cases of the Hanseatic prizes dragged on into 1590, and as late as the following year some debts contracted on account of the expedition remained unpaid. When the books were finally closed it was probably to record a loss: financially, too, the venture had failed. A growing sense of the voyage's shortcomings led in October 1589 to the Privy Council's charging Drake and Norris with mishandling the business. The commanders gave their answers without blaming each other, and the matter was dropped. Black John was commanding another army within a year, and while the war of the Atlantic lapsed into small-scale privateering and Drake was not employed at sea, he was entrusted with valuable local work.

One man felt the failure more than most, certainly more than Norris and even Drake – Dom Antonio, the plucky but unfortunate pretender. Those few of his countrymen who had supported him had now to face the anger of their Spanish masters. A Portuguese nobleman discovered sending money to Antonio had been executed. Some sixty monks from a Lisbon monastery occupied by the English had been hanged. The 'king', for so he continued to call himself, had to write dolefully to one of his closest adherents that he had hoped to be able to summon him to Lisbon to receive the rewards of a grateful sovereign, but God had deemed it otherwise; now he must say that he had brought Estaban Ferreira de Gama's wife and child out of Portugal with him, because he feared for their safety at home. Antonio's own son, Dom Cristobal, was held a prisoner by the Moors of Fez, his ostensible allies, for four years.

In fact the 'king' was in a wretched condition, condemned for the folly of the expedition, penniless, and living as a recluse in a village outside Plymouth. On his better days his spirits rose, and he protested that but for the wasteful diversion at Corunna, but for the lack of seige guns, he would have yet been master of his realm. None of his people had opposed him, he was quick to point out, and Spain had been too weak to prevent the English marching about their territory and drubbing their forces. All it needed was another, stronger expedition, and if the queen would not supply it he would apply to the Turks of Constantinople or Barbary.

But privately Dom Antonio sank into despondency, unburdening his fearful resignation to Antonio de Escobar:

> The end of it is, in short, that we have returned to this port of Plymouth, which is a just recompense for my sins. I recollect very often what you told me about an astrologer who said that a great victory was in store for Philip, and I confess it has grievously troubled me ever since . . . I am in such a state of mind that I cannot talk, and hardly know what I am saying, but this I can assure you: that 4,000 Englishmen are equal to 8,000 Spaniards, and whenever I can embark with them again, I shall gladly do so, especially if Sir John Norris and Sir Francis Drake be amongst them, for by my faith they are gallant gentlemen![1]

[1] Dom Antonio to Antonio de Escobar, August 1589, Hume, 4: 553-5.

# CHAPTER TWENTY-ONE

# LAST YEARS ASHORE

The irksome drought that Plymouth felt,
Full long all parts distressed;
Industrious Drake by bringing home
Fresh waters here redressed.

A.W., 1592

ONE OF HIS BIOGRAPHERS HAS WRITTEN THAT AFTER THE DISAPPOINTING voyage to Portugal Drake did what all sensible men do: he returned to his own place and his own people. That is true, for Drake spent most of the next six years in his native Devon. Writers have also seen these years as another hiatus in the admiral's life, an uneventful period in which Sir Francis lived in official disgrace, looking longingly out to sea where lesser commanders handled the war with Spain. That is less true. For far from being idle, Drake was never busier than in the years after he returned from Portugal, and far from being in disgrace, he was considered so valuable to the government that he was overburdened with important administrative and defence responsibilities.

The truth is rather that 1589 discredited less Drake and more the ambitious large-scale campaigns he advocated, and the queen saw no immediate need for his services. The Armada and counter-armada had proved that neither England nor Spain could deliver a knock-out punch, and both began to direct their attention elsewhere. Although Philip was reviving his navy and nursed plans for more armadas, for the moment he invested in fortifying the West Indies, in subduing the Netherlands and in giving military assistance to the French Catholic League. With the relaxation of fears of invasion, England lapsed into a reliance upon privateering, which proved profitable in terms of money and experience – from 1589 to 1591 some three hundred prizes taken were possibly worth £400,000 – but which inflicted limited damage upon Spain. Hawkins tried to elevate the business by proposing a permanent blockade, using relays of naval squadrons to patrol the waters between Spain and the Azores to intercept the treasure ships, but the idea was never fully implemented and would likely not have worked. Fast frigates, capable of eluding the English vessels, began to ship Philip's treasure, while the queen's squadrons were so weak that they could be brushed away by powerful Spanish convoys. So Philip continued to receive his treasure, and, while naval operations remained on a low key, Francis Drake remained in Devon.[1]

But not in retirement. The range and diversity of Drake's activities were remarkable. He was a Member of Parliament, acting Deputy Lord Lieutenant, military and civil engineer, entrepreneur, magistrate and prize commissioner. Drake had lost his old seat in the House of Commons in 1586, and had to wait until the

---

[1] The nature of privateering, which remained a basis for England's naval activity, is treated by Andrews, *Elizabethan Privateering*.

parliament of 1593 to secure another constituency. At that time the mayor and aldermen of Plymouth returned Sir Francis as the senior Member for the borough, with Robert Bassett, the son of Arthur Bassett, Drake's associate, as the junior Member for Plymouth. In addition, Drake, along with Sir John Gilbert and Sir William Courtenay, drew an allowance as Deputy Lord Lieutenant for Devon. William Bourchier, Earl of Bath, stood as Lord Lieutenant, with responsibility for preserving the peace, superintending the magistracy, and mustering and preparing the county's defences, but although provision for the official appointment of a deputy had been made in 1585, the government was so pleased with Drake's industry in that direction that it was not until his death that the Privy Council formally filled the vacancy.[1]

Both positions, that of Member for Plymouth and that of acting Deputy Lord Lieutenant, reflected the tremendous local standing and influence Drake now commanded, and, while he never lost his ability to relate to the common mariners, his time was increasingly spent with the West Country well-to-do. Time and again the same names appear in the records of his activities. There was Sir John Gilbert, brother of the colonizer, Sir Humphrey, and Vice-Admiral of Devon, who lived near Dartmouth; and Piers Edgecumbe, Member for Cornwall, son of the noted Cornishman Richard Edgecumbe but now beginning to fade from public life under the embarrassment of heavy debts. Connected to the Edgecumbes by a sister of Piers was another distinguished Cornish family who formed part of Drake's circle – the Carews of Antony House: Richard, a justice and Vice-Admiral of Cornwall, but best remembered as the historian of his native county; and George, the Member for Saltash whose position as the clerk responsible for writing pardons for outlawry earned him numerous and lucrative perquisites. On the Devonshire side of the Tamar estuary resided two of Drake's closest associates, Christopher Harris of Radford and John Hele. Harris, who had himself once been Member for Plymouth, lived at Plymstock, overlooking the Sound. Hele would shortly become a sergeant-at-law (eventually the queen's sergeant) and sit in the Commons for Exeter, but at this time he was a formidable upwardly mobile man of business, a moneylender whose increasing fortune, pride and arrogance left an unpleasant taste. Contemporaries described him as 'insufferable in our country', 'odious and ridiculous', 'greedy and insatiable', 'a great drunkard' and a brawler, and perhaps not without cause, for in 1603 he was imprisoned in the Fleet Prison for extortion.

Not all of Drake's business associates were close friends, but among the latter were certainly the Champernownes, a remarkable brood with mixed local and seafaring interests, related to the Edgecumbes. The late Arthur Champernowne of

---

[1] Privy Council, 19 July, 1593, 31 May, 1596, Dasent, ed., *Acts of the Privy Council*, 24: 406-7, and 25: 425; Gilbert to the Privy Council, 26 September, 1592, Hist. MSS Commission, ed., *Calendar of the Manuscripts of the Marquis of Salisbury*, 4: 228-9. The letters, reports and instructions that form the basis for this chapter are too many and scattered for individual citation, but may be found principally in the State Papers, Domestic (Public Record Office), S.P. 12/163, 230-56 passim; Dasent, vols 19-25; Hist. MSS Commission, ed., *Salisbury*, vols 4-6; D'Ewes, *Journals of All the Parliaments*; and Worth, ed., *Calendar of Plymouth Municipal Records*. Additional documentation, where necessary, and the sources of specific quotations are given below.

Modbury and Dartington had served several Devon constituencies in Parliament, and as Vice-Admiral of the county had known (and possibly helped) young Francis Drake long before he had become an international figure. His son, Gawen, testified to his regard by bequeathing Sir Francis a ring. A son of Gawen's cousin, Richard Champernowne, was also Drake's friend and shared his love of music – indeed, needed it, for like Saul Richard was deeply troubled by depression and found solace in listening to the choir he kept at Modbury. It became so legendary that Sir Robert Cecil tried to poach one of the choirboys, and Sir Francis Drake had once to warn Richard that the story was going round the court that the voices of his choir had only been preserved so well because he had gelded the boys. "Tis false!' declared the maligned gentleman indignantly, for no Christian could act in such a manner.[1]

Among the families Drake may have met through the Champernownes none was more prestigious than the Blounts, who were connected by the marriage of Catherine Blount, sister of the fifth Lord Mountjoy, to John Champernowne. In 1592 the seventh Lord Mountjoy leased Sir Francis fishing rights on the Tavy between Lopwell and Denham Bridge for a minimal two shillings a year, and his younger brother, Charles, was a volunteer aboard Drake's *Revenge* during the Armada campaign. Lord Arundell, who married Lady Mountjoy's niece, also willed a ring to the admiral.

One of the wealthiest of Drake's newer colleagues was undoubtedly Sir William Courtenay of Powderham, who acted in conjunction with Sir Francis as Deputy Lord Lieutenant. In 1588 Courtenay was one of twelve knights whose 'great possessions' helped recommend them for elevation to baronies, and when he died in 1630 he owned twenty manors in Devon. Drake worked with Courtenay, but whether he liked him is uncertain. He was a Catholic, which hardly endeared him to the sailor, and an ungenerous foe, as survivors of the Armada ship, the *San Pedro Mayor*, discovered. The vessel had been wrecked in Hope Cove, near Salcombe, where Courtenay had some of his land. A few Spaniards who fell into Courtenay's hands were imprisoned and set to labour, for years, sustained by a diet of broth, bread and water, while extortionate ransoms were demanded. Drake had a prisoner too, the unfortunate Don Pedro de Valdes, but he was humanely treated, and the delays in his release were due to the prevarications of the queen and Council, rather than to those of Sir Francis. Courtenay was, besides, a notorious womanizer, who sired seven sons and three daughters by his first wife, Lady Elizabeth Manners, daughter of the Earl of Rutland. Bath, the Lord Lieutenant, certainly thought little of Sir William, 'a man who, though he gives himself out to all vice, as drinking, whoring, etc., yet he neither wants wit to devise, nor might to practise how to strengthen himself and weaken others.'[2] Maybe Courtenay's eyes were roving over Lady Drake too, because little more than a year after the return of the admiral's last expedition with its word of his death, he married her.

These, then, were the men with whom Drake now consorted. They joined

---

[1] Richard Champernowne to Sir Robert Cecil, 26 March, October, 1595, *Salisbury*, 5: 155, 437-8. Eliott-Drake, *Family and Heirs of Sir Francis Drake*, contains much relevant information about Drake's immediate relations.
[2] Hasler, *The Commons*, 1: 664.

him at receptions and dinners and transacted public business with him in London and Plymouth. Their activities in this context are well documented. About the admiral's private life – and the people who shared it – we know much less.

Drake was a man of robust constitution and immense energy. It is ironic, therefore, that one of the only personal letters from him that we possess describes a breakdown in his health. It was the one written to Sir Julius Caesar and dated 23 January, 1589. The general practice before 1752, however, as we have seen, was to reckon the start of the year from Lady Day (25 March), and hence the letter may properly belong to 1590.

> Good Sir,
> 
> Being touched with some grief before my coming out of London, with a strain I took in quenching the fire, I found my travel so much increase the same as I had much to do to recover Sir George Sydenham's house, where I have ever since continued and in my chamber for the most part. And notwithstanding I have and do use all possible good means by physic, following the advice of Doctor French, I do yet find little ease, for that my pain not tarrying in one place, is fallen now into my legs and maketh me very unable to stand without much grief, and therefore yet uncertain when I shall be able to travel but I hope it will not be long. And at my coming up touching Mychellart's matter, I will willingly do him all the furtherance I can. Thus, with my very hearty commendation, I commit you to God's favour, from Combe Sydenham, this 23rd of January 1589.
> 
> Your assured loving friend,
> [signed] Francis Drake.[1]

Lady Drake accompanied her husband whenever he attended social functions, and so serving she appears briefly in the records. Their relationship is largely a mystery, but we know that they never had children, and towards the end of his life Drake began to worry about the great inheritance he had created. The obvious heir was his brother Thomas. In his prime Thomas Drake was a short, broad-shouldered man with a pale complexion and scant red beard. By his wife, Elizabeth Elford, he had produced two children. Undoubtedly Sir Francis would have liked to bequeath the bulk of his estate to Thomas because that would have preserved it in the hands of the Drake family. The difficulty was that Buckland Abbey and the manors of Sampford Spiney, Sherford and Yarcombe had been assigned to Lady Drake by the terms of her marriage settlement and there was thus a very real danger that on Drake's death they would pass to the Sydenhams. This awkward situation was further complicated by Drake's wish to provide for Francis Drake of Esher and Jonas Bodenham.

Francis, the son of Richard Drake of Esher, was Drake's godson. Drake had evidently promised Richard that one day he would settle an estate upon the boy. We are told a few details about this – and about the difficulties it had imposed upon Sir Francis – in a deposition made nearly ten years after Drake's death by a certain Samuel Pomfrett of Esher, gentleman. Pomfrett recalled a visit that young Francis Drake of Esher and he himself had once made to Drake's home at Buckland Abbey, apparently about 1593. There they had been 'most kindly entertained' by Sir Francis. They had stayed

---

[1] Drake to Caesar, 23 January, 1589 (90?), Additional MS 12,507, f. 17, British Library. There is another reference to 'Mychellart' or 'Michelett', equally mysterious, in Drake to Caesar, 16 September, 1586, Addit. MS 12,504, ff. 303-4.

for twelve weeks and when the time came for them to return home Drake had given his godson 'a jewel and money in his purse.' More, he had repeated his promise of some settlement of land upon him in the future:

> . . . after that the said defendant [Francis Drake of Esher] had remained there with Sir Francis Drake about some xii weeks and [was] ready to return home again the said Sir Francis called this deponent [Pomfrett] unto him and requested him to desire the defendant's father, terming him his very good cousin, that he would not think amiss in that he had not at that point assured to the defendant some lands as he had promised, alleging that he had to his father-in-law Sir George Sydenham, knight, whose only daughter he had married, and doubting lest if he should make over any lands in the lifetime of the said Sir G. Sydenham, that it would not be to his liking, and for that cause did defer to assure any lands at that time, saying further that some assurance of lands should be made hereafter to the good contentment of the defendant's father and for the great good of the defendant himself.[1]

Drake also considered himself obligated to make some provision for Jonas Bodenham. The exact relationship between the two has never been satisfactorily explained but it seems likely that Bodenham was a younger son of Mary Newman's sister Margaret. Thomas Drake and Bodenham grew to detest each other. If accusations levelled by Thomas against Bodenham in 1597 are to be credited the origins of their feud lay in the latter's repeated embezzlement of Sir Francis's money.

Thomas's allegations tell a sorry tale of avarice, deceit and betrayal. Drake had trained Bodenham up from his infancy in his own service. For many years he employed him as his factor and special dealer, entrusting him with sums 'amounting at several times near to a hundred thousand pounds at least.' These funds Bodenham regularly misappropriated. He was 'very magnificent in his expenses.' He squandered at least £2,000 at cards and dice. He loaned £1,500 to Dom Antonio in his own name. And he expended another £1,500 on the purchase of an estate in Ireland, apparently as 'a place of refuge in time to come.' Drake, of course, frequently solicited accounts. But Bodenham always seemed to have a plausible excuse for not producing them and when at last he 'could not well defer his accounts any longer by ordinary persuasions' he burned them, fobbing Drake off with some fable about an accidental fire in his chamber.[2]

It is difficult now to gauge the truth of these assertions. Bodenham always denied them. And certain it is that Drake himself never lost faith in him because he made Bodenham a major beneficiary of his will and appointed him to succeed to the captaincy of his last ship, the Defiance. Even Thomas was obliged to concede this. Sir Francis, he tells us, believed Bodenham's story of the fire. Furthermore, when Thomas apprised him, not long before he sailed on his last voyage, that Bodenham had used his money to buy for himself an estate in Ireland, Drake 'would not be then persuaded that the complainant [Bodenham] had made any such purchase.' Thomas's animosity

---

[1] Deposition of Samuel Pomfrett of Esher, gentleman, 7 November, 1605, Public Record Office, E.133/47/5. Perhaps Pomfrett had accompanied young Francis Drake of Esher to Devon as his tutor. When he made the deposition he was about 58 years old.

[2] Bill of Jonas Bodenham and answer of Thomas Drake (1597), Public Record Office, C2/Eliz.I/B8/32; Bill and replication of Thomas Drake, and answer of Jonas Bodenham (1597), C2/Eliz.I/D1/41. For the proceedings in Drake v. Bodenham, see Public Record Office, C33/93-8.

towards Bodenham had doubtless been sharpened by the latter's competing claim to a share in Drake's estate and it is probable that he exaggerated the case against him. Nevertheless, he is unlikely to have publicly made such serious allegations unless there was some truth in them. Generous to a fault, Sir Francis was perhaps unwilling to admit, even to himself, that a relative of his first wife could have treated him so shabbily.

Whatever private contentions simmered in family gatherings, Sir Francis appeared before the public at the peak of his reputation, at home and abroad. The mere rumour that he would sail again set the court humming, preparations afoot along the length of the Iberian coasts, and ships finding shelter on both sides of the Atlantic.[1] He sat for his most impressive portraits at this time, perhaps twice to Marc Gheerarts the younger. One of the possible Gheerarts pieces bears the date 1591, and another, painted three years later, hung for a long time in Buckland Abbey. A third portrait belonged to Trinity House in London before being destroyed in the Second World War, but the half-length portrait currently on display in Buckland Abbey is apparently a copy of it. The original may have been painted by one of the Segars, for a likeness attributed to Segar is mentioned in an inventory of portraits made in 1590.[2]

Drake continued to visit the court, but with the deaths of Leicester and Walsingham he had lost his greatest supporters in government. Blustering Leicester lived long enough to see the Armada defeated, but died of a fever in September 1588, on his way from the capital to his home in Kenilworth, and Walsingham died in London in the April of 1590 after a lifetime of poor health. They had not only been Drake's friends, but the buttress of his influence in the Privy Council, and he could ill afford to lose them. Nevertheless, when he took his seat for Plymouth in the parliament of 1593 he brought with him some hopes of returning to the front of the political stage. At the end of 1592 he had been well received at court, and he was putting the finishing touches to a narrative of his voyage of 1572 that had been ghosted by Philip Nichols. Its publication, he probably anticipated, would help recall his former services, and he even dedicated it to the queen.

While in London Drake lived at 'The Herber', a large old house with adjacent land on the east side of Dowgate Street, near the church of St Mary Bothaw. It belonged to the Company of Drapers, of which Drake had been made an honorary freeman after the Armada's defeat, but was customarily leased out. Drake bought the lease from Sir

[1] Anthony Rolston to Anthony Bacon, June 1593, *Salisbury*, 4: 349-50; Klarwill, ed., *Fugger News-Letters*, 2: 246-7.

[2] Callender, 'The Greenwich Portrait of Sir Francis Drake', advances the view that the three-quarter length Buckland Abbey portrait of 1594, reproduced as the frontispiece in Corbett, *Drake and the Tudor Navy*, was a spurious copy of the Greenwich portrait of 1591. There seems no reason to believe this. Neither is signed, but both may have been the work of Gheerarts the younger, and it is possible that the 1594 portrait was either a final version of the earlier likeness, or the product of a separate sitting. In 1591 no crest was painted above Drake's coat of arms, but three years later Drake seems to have become reconciled to the crest granted by Elizabeth I, for it appears on the painting of 1594. The assumption that the original of the half-length portrait now in Buckland Abbey, badly reproduced in Thrower, ed., *Sir Francis Drake and the Famous Voyage*, 92, was the Segar painting cannot be established. There are other portraits of Drake, including a head-and-shoulders and a full-length in the National Portrait Gallery, a painting once attributed to Zucchero and engraved by Holl, and a work once owned by the Marquess of Lothian, but there are grounds for believing them all to be spurious, barring those described in an earlier chapter.

Thomas Pullison in November 1588, but hardly had the house been readied for occupation when one Edmund Neville contested possession, claiming that the house was his according to a legacy of one of its former occupants, Margaret, Countess of Salisbury. Although Neville brought a suit of trespass against Drake's servant, he did not have the chance to press it effectively, for he was then imprisoned in the Tower, accused of treason. 'The Herber' served Sir Francis well enough for the duration of the parliamentary session, and when it was over he sold the lease for £1,300 to Paul Banning, on 28 May, 1593.[1]

The parliament ran from February to April, and Drake was busy throughout the sitting in committee work, considering the details of bills before the House. The span of subjects he tackled was wide, among them being the regularity of the election of the Member for Southwark, recusancy, salted fish, poor relief and vagabondage, aid for injured soldiers and sailors, fresh water projects for Plymouth and Stonehouse and the assize of bread. He chaired the committee dealing with abuses in the manufacture of cordage and other naval matters. On some of these issues Drake's feelings ran deep. Three years before, his disgust at the government's callous abandonment of maimed mariners of the Armada campaign had led him to join Howard and Hawkins in founding one of the first welfare insurance schemes, in which working seamen paid a portion of their wages to the 'Chatham Chest' to fund their aged, wounded or disabled fellows. But it was the question of the subsidies to be granted the queen that moved him to speak both in the committee room and upon the floor of the House. No one knew better than he how severely England's scant resources had endangered her security; no one would have agreed more with Sir Robert Cecil's complaint that England had been 'slack in provision' in 1588. Supporting the demand for extra subsidies in his only known speech before Parliament, 'Sir Francis Drake described the King of Spain's strength and cruelty, where he came, and wanted a frank aid to be yielded to withstand him, and he agreed to three subsidies.'[2]

It was typical of the man. The Armada had come and gone, but Drake's war had no end. He would never relax his guard, nor pull his punches. He might be on the beach, a sailor ashore, but he was still active in his country's interest, and for the most part in the danger zone too. With the exception of the parliamentary session of 1593 and a few other short periods, Drake spent most of his last years in the West Country, where the threat from Spain seemed very real indeed. The memory of the battle fought with the Armada off Plymouth was proof enough of Philip's ability to strike at those shores, and in 1590 Spanish troops entrenched themselves in Brittany while the king's alliance with the Catholic League was giving him access to important areas of the French coast – ever closer. There had been many stories that year, wild, fearful stories, some of them. It had even been said that Parma wanted to induce Sir Francis Drake into Spanish service! But none could take lightly the prospect of an enemy squadron attacking Plymouth, Torbay or Dartmouth. Although Drake's biographers have given scant notice to his efforts to strengthen Plymouth and develop it as a major port at a time when it was so essential to England's defences, it was not the least of his many

---

[1] Johnson, *Worshipful Company of Drapers*, 2: 152-3, 232; Kraus, *Sir Francis Drake*, facing page 171; and references in Dasent for 1592.

[2] D'Ewes, 492.

achievements and deserves our attention.

At the beginning of 1590 the Privy Council was so alarmed by the vulnerability of the West Country that it decided to put Devon and Cornwall on a war footing and to charge Sir Francis Drake with defending Plymouth, a position readily acknowledged to be weak. Drake did what he could. He assembled some small vessels and combustible materials that could be turned into fireships to dislodge any enemy impudent enough to anchor in the Sound, and stacked enough muskets, armour and pikes for 350 men on the fortified island of St Nicholas that dominated the entrance. Several pieces of artillery were borrowed to improve the town's batteries. Drake had thirteen guns placed on the Hoe, four on the towers of an obsolete medieval castle that stood before the town, and twenty-three on the island. On May Day the Hoe shook to the drill of 1,300 men, and a nightly watch was set, with Drake leading the first.

For all that it was a weak defence and Drake knew it. With John Blitheman, the mayor, he petitioned the Privy Council to supply brass artillery and to contribute towards the building of a fort on the Hoe:

> This fort being once erected, the town and whole country should be more resolute and safe, which would be a great encouragement to the realm, and the enemy, knowing the artillery to be out of danger, would with less boldness enterprise that way. Now the harbour lying without any defence to make long resistance, the town upon this late report was stricken with such fear that some of them had conveyed their goods out of the town, and others no doubt would have followed if they had not been stopped by the coming of Sir Francis Drake who, the more to assure them, brought his wife and family thither, so that if the enemy had made his approach in his absence he had assuredly taken the town without resistance and carried away their ordnance. [1]

Knowing the financial stringency of the government, Drake suggested that if the queen would supply £1,000-£1,200 towards the fort local subscriptions would meet the rest of the cost. There can be no doubt that he fully endorsed the plan to fortify Plymouth. He pledged himself to contribute £100 to the fund and sent a plan of the proposed fort to Burghley, urging him to favour the town's petition. But Drake was Drake and he could not resist feeding the Privy Council his old idea that attack was the best of all defences. If a Spanish fleet was coming to Plymouth, well then, he was ready to go out and fight it as he had done two years before:

> There was an intent in me . . . finding so many meet men and willing minds for such a purpose to have followed the Spanish fleet to the eastward, in hope enough to have done some service upon them, but they are not come and the wind too much easterly. It may please your Lordships to signify your pleasure whether I shall continue at this town or pursue the fleet if they shall haply pass from Plymouth to the eastwards. [2]

Was there a yearning for action in this offer? A venturesome spirit searching for release from the pedestrian toil of the administrator? If so, the Privy Council did not respond. But they were persuaded that Plymouth's defences had to be improved to the point where the town could withstand an attack long enough for support to arrive,

[1] Drake and Blitheman to Privy Council, 3 May, 1590, British Library, Lansdowne MS 65, article 12.
[2] Correspondence of Drake, May 1590, Hist. MSS Comm., ed., *Twelfth Report*, 1: 13-14.

and, after a year's delay, called upon a local commission, consisting of Drake, Sir John Gilbert, Piers Edgecumbe, George and Richard Carew, Gawen Champernowne, Christopher Harris and John Hele, to present a plan of the necessary fortifications and an estimate of the expected cost. Drake and his fellows responded with a proposal to build an elaborate wall and ditch about the town and a rectangular fort on the south-east corner of the Hoe, above the cliffs, for £5,000.

Although the Privy Council anticipated financing the project by a tax on the local pilchard trade, they predictably jibbed at so expensive a recommendation and sent their own expert, Robert Adams, to Plymouth to confer with Drake and others and suggest amendments 'either for the more strength or the less charge.' In fact, Adams's scheme proved more costly still. The fort would be extended down the cliffs to the sea and eastwards to give shelter to any who might try to reinforce it from the quay. He recommended a town wall and 20-foot wide ditch 380 perches long and a fort 96 perches in circuit at a total cost of £5,005.[1]

The plan was thus approved in 1592. The queen authorized the use of £100 a year from the customs receipts of Devon and Cornwall, half the value of confiscated exports, and levied a tax on pilchards exported from Plymouth. Donations were solicited from the London merchants whose ships used the port, and Drake and Harris were set to organizing a local subscription, a job they delegated to William Stallenge. The Lord Lieutenant, the Earl of Bath, set an example by subscribing £100 and exhorting the county magistrates to support the project, but Drake repeatedly had to complain to the Privy Council that donations were slow and as late as August 1593 few had come from outside Plymouth itself. Even the pilchard tax was being evaded as fishermen began to ship their produce from ports other than Plymouth. Stimulated by Drake's reports, the Privy Council did its best to spur the local effort, recording the names of those who failed to subscribe as well as those who did, but progress on the fort remained painfully slow.

Drake could see one reason for Devon's indifference. He tried unsuccessfully several times to persuade the Privy Council to invest the control of the fort, when it was built, in the town authorities rather than in Crown officials. This, he said, would encourage support among the townspeople. Even in 1595 he was confident that he could block a Crown appointment to the command of the fort. 'Doubt not,' he wrote to the mayor, George Baron, from court, 'but whilst I am here I shall stop it.'[2] Arthur Champernowne, Carew Reynell and other local men jostled for the post, but just after Drake sailed on his last voyage the Privy Council placed their own man, Sir Fernando Gorges, over both the fort and St Nicholas Island.

Drake worried about the security of his beloved Plymouth to the end. In one of his last surviving letters, written on 21 July, 1595, a month before he embarked upon that

---

[1] In addition to the sources listed on p. 286, n.1, especially the State Papers, Domestic, and the Acts of the Privy Council, the fort is treated in Preston, *Gorges of Plymouth Fort*, ch. 4.

[2] Drake to Baron, 20 January, 1595, Worth, 197-8. In the State Papers (S.P. 12/254. 20ii) is a statement of the money raised and expended upon the fort from 17 July, 1592 to 11 October, 1595. The Crown had contributed £1,241 17s, the City of London £29 and Plymouth itself £40. Sir Francis Drake, the Earl of Bath and the Lord High Admiral had each pledged £100 and had made part payments of £60, £60 and £50 respectively. The other private donors were Sir John Hawkins (£60); Sir Francis Godolphin, Sir Thomas Denys and George Carey (£10 each); William Strode (£6); Sir William Bevill, Anthony Rouse and Jonathan Trelawney (£5 each); John Wray (£2 10s).

final voyage, he joined with George Carey to urge further measures upon the Privy Council for the protection of the town, 'especially when this fleet of ships shall be departed.' They wanted the Privy Council to order the training of 'those companies that are appointed to guard and succour Plymouth' and the repair of all bulwarks and trenches on the sea coast that had not been repaired since 1588. And they recommended that any prisoners brought in by privateers should be 'presently sent away' or imprisoned at the expense of their captors in order to prevent them from going 'at large as they do' to see the fortifications and coastal defences. A postscript reads: 'We have already given order for the watching and warding of the beacons and likewise that all men with their armour and weapons to be in perfect readiness.'[1]

The fort was not finished until after Drake's death. Despite fear of Spanish attacks – and the Spanish actually raided Cornwall in 1595 – it had progressed so slowly that in 1594 the government had put five hundred men in Plymouth until the works were completed. Perhaps because of the inadequacy of local subscriptions the idea of the town wall was abandoned altogether. But the Hoe eventually got its fort, nearly 600 yards of stone wall almost five feet thick at the base and 13 feet high, its guns commanding the Catwater, Sutton Pool and the Sound.

Drake's contribution to the fort has long been forgotten, but an old Plymouth tradition once commemorated an allied project – the bringing of the water into the town in 1591.

Every August a 'fishing feast' used to be held in which the mayor and corporation drank water at the weir-head 'to the pious memory of Sir Francis Drake.' The achievement thus honoured was not an inconsiderable one, although Drake was by no means its only hero. Fresh water was of incalculable importance to a town like Plymouth. It served the domestic needs of the growing number of inhabitants and was important in checking disease and insanitation, and it was indispensable for watering the ships that put into the haven and supplying them with corn. Without more fresh water, the port could not grow. Yet its estuary was polluted from the filth of settlements on the upper Tamar and Tavy, and the few alternative streams and wells could not meet demand. For many years the corporation had wanted to bring fresh water into the town, but it was not until 1584 that a bill proposing to divert water from the upper Meavy to Plymouth was presented to Parliament. Drake was then Member for Bossiney, but as a seaman, and a Plymouth freeman to boot, he had an obvious interest in the project. Moreover, he had just leased two corn mills at Millbay from the corporation and water supplies were essential to their operation. On several counts, therefore, Drake was willing to assist the Members for Plymouth, Harris and Henry Bromley, in forwarding the bill.[2]

On 21 December it had its first reading and was passed to a committee, chaired by Robert Wroth, representing Middlesex, but containing such good West Country men as Drake and Piers Edgecumbe. They met in the Middle Temple, and endorsed the bill with one proviso that surely betrays the hand of Drake, newly embarked as he was on a career as millowner. Before the project could proceed all millowners who would be

[1] Drake and Carey to Privy Council, 21 July, 1595, British Library, Cotton MSS, Titus B. V, f. 109.

[2] The most authoritative study of the leat is Worth, 'Sir Francis Drake', but it is unnecessarily prejudicial to Drake. Also useful are Risk, 'Some Recent Revisions of the Drake Chronology', and his 'The Rise of Plymouth as a Naval Port', and Gill, *Plymouth*, 207-8, 233. For the primary documents see p. 286, n. 1.

affected had to consent to it. The Plymouth water bill then went through another reading and received the royal assent on 29 March, 1585.

For several years the Spanish war prevented the town going further, but in 1590 Sir Francis was on hand to troubleshoot the venture, and Mayor John Blitheman furnished him with £300 to perform the work, a third of which sum was intended to compensate the owners of grazing land through which the leat, six feet wide and two feet deep, would be cut. Drake took no part in assessing these awards. Two leading justices, Sir Edmund Anderson and Thomas Gent, were engaged for the work, advised by Christopher Harris, William Crimes, William Strode and other local dignitaries, most of them justices of the peace and all cronies of Drake. In 1592 over eighty persons were awarded payments ranging from a few pence to 17 shillings, based upon the value of the land at sixteen years' purchase. The names of the beneficiaries survive, and include many of Drake's friends, such as the Elfords of Shepstor, into whom Thomas Drake married, Walter Pepperall, under whose mayoralty in 1590-91 most of the work was done, Hele and Baron. Drake himself received 17 shillings on account of land he was renting from Edmund Parker.

There are unanswered questions about the compensation, and Drake's name has been dragged through the mud because of them. The awards totalled £60, and, although there may have been other expenses, it seems that Drake made a handsome profit from the £100 he had been allocated for the purpose. Nothing wrong with that perhaps, but some of the landowners, such as Thomas Wise, Walter Elford and William Creese, claimed that they did not receive their compensation ('little or nothing,' someone said), and the corporation had to find more money to still their complaints. But it is unlikely that Drake was in any great default. Some of the protests came from his business rivals, and the townspeople generally, who had access to more information than we do, continued to regard their first citizen with confidence. Indeed, the corporation named him Member for the town a year after the first complaints were made.

The leat was financed by private donations. Its course was planned by Robert Lampden in 1590, and starting below Shepstor it meandered 17 miles, close to its source passing 448 paces through a channel blasted or chipped from hard rock, and then twisting right and left like an enormous serpent, around hills and over heath, until it reached the north-west of the town. Legend proclaimed that as Drake sped across the moors to Plymouth the water followed his horse's tail! Entries in the town's account show that 24 April, 1591, the day the water was brought in, was only a little less remarkable. Four mounted trumpeters were commanded to the head of the leat. There was wine, a dinner, and a gun salute, and another trumpeter rode with the rushing water to herald its arrival.

Sir Francis Drake was never at a loss to earn some quick cash, and no sooner had the leat been opened than he erected six grist mills on it, two at Crownhill Widey in Eggbuckland parish, and four about the town, at Mill Lane and what became known as Drake's Reservoir, some of the last with two adjoining closes of land. These replaced his older mills, which had apparently fallen into disuse and depended upon a sixty-seven-year lease from the corporation. By September 1591 four of the new mills were grinding corn. Drake's mills created an immediate hubbub among local tradesmen. Some tinners and rival millowners contended they drew too much water from the leat, and even sent a private bill to Parliament in 1592 to protest at Drake's action. They should have known their man better, or understood his tremendous influence. After its second reading the bill was referred on 29 March, 1593 to a committee consisting of Piers Edgecumbe, Sir Thomas Conisby, James Dalton, Henry Boucher, Richard Broughton, Sir Thomas Denys and Sir Francis Godolphin. Its chairman? None other than Sir Francis Drake himself. Not surprisingly, the bill did not survive, although the same committee did approve a leat for Stonehouse and the reclamation of Marsh Mills at Plympton, both near Plymouth.

In the popular mind Drake's bringing of the water was a laudable act of public utility, and it formed part of a dedication to Drake in Kempe's *Art of Arithmetic*, published in 1592. It was complementary to his work for the fort, since both increased the importance of Plymouth as a naval base and port. If Drake's time had always been so profitably consumed he would have had cause for satisfaction, but a stream of orders from the Privy Council were brought at a gallop to his door, and many, while matters of some heat and fury then, seem less significant to us now. Whenever the government was confronted with a difficult local dispute, they called upon Sir Francis. Examples of the problems he handled are the disputes about the local pilchard trade and the building ambitions of William Strode, a landowner of Plympton and Newnham.

The pilchard controversy may seem a storm in a teacup, but it was a serious matter for local fishermen. Pilchards were the basis of the diet of the Plymouth region, especially since three days a week had been designated fish-days to promote the industry, and they were a lucrative export. That, indeed, was the trouble. Lured by profits, bigger merchants from Cornwall began large-scale 'seine' fishing, using large nets from groups of boats, storing the catches in cellars at Cawsand Bay on the west side of the Sound, and exporting fish and oil to the detriment of the local Plymouth fishermen. The seiners cornered the bulk of the stocks, reduced the catches of the Devon men and forced up the price of pilchards in Plymouth. Thomas Cely even complained to Burghley that pilchards were being exported to the enemy abroad while people in Plymouth went without. The controversy continued for many years, as Richard Carew wrote, 'the takers jarring and brawling, one with the other.'[1]

Drake had tried to solve this problem before, when he was Mayor of Plymouth in 1581, by restricting the number of pilchards any one person could land, sell or buy, and by placing particular restrictions upon foreigners engaging in the trade. Several subsequent efforts, by the town corporation and the Privy Council, enjoyed no greater success. To some extent the issue was one between Devon and Cornwall. When Drake, Edgecumbe, John Fitz and Harris were appointed to investigate the affair, the Cornish people complained that they were under-represented, and had two of their deputy lord lieutenants, Richard Grenville and Richard Carew, added to the committee. Notwithstanding, in 1588 the Privy Council came down on the side of Plymouth. In line with the thinking of Sir Francis Drake and John Hawkins, they ordered that no more cellars or storehouses should be built at Cawsand, that two-thirds of the pilchards taken by the seiners must be taken to Plymouth, and that the export of the

---

[1] This controversy is discussed by Rowse, 'The Dispute Concerning the Plymouth Pilchard Fishery, 1584-91'. See also State Papers, Domestic, S.P. 12/193: 27, and Risk, 'Rise of Plymouth as a Naval Port', 357.

fish be temporarily suspended in favour of local consumption.

The Cornishmen simply ignored the order, and Drake and John Gilbert sent four of the culprits to answer for it before the Privy Council at the end of 1590. The 1588 order was reaffirmed after another consideration of the case, along with some amendments negotiated between the Mayor of Plymouth and the Cornish Members of Parliament that limited the use of drift nets and prohibited the production of oil until fish stocks rose. Six commissioners were named to enforce the new order, three (Drake, Gilbert and Harris) representing Devon and the others, Carew, Thomas Wray and Anthony Rouse, standing for Cornwall. It is a measure of the Privy Council's confidence in Drake that of the four commissioners required to be present at the landing of the pilchards, Sir Francis alone was required always to be one of them.

These provisions proved to be impossible to uphold. In 1591 the government permitted the export of pilchards to be resumed, providing they passed to friendly powers, but the tax levied on such exports in Plymouth to raise funds for the fort simply encouraged the seiners to use other ports. Drake and his colleagues could not be on hand everywhere, and the regulations continued to be flouted.

But the admiral had rather more success in the matter of William Strode, the ubiquitous landowner. Strode had infuriated the residents of Plymouth by threatening to build on some land on the waterfront, although it was pointed out to him that he would obstruct both the harbour and the new fort. So strong was the town's feeling that its representative, John Sparke, appealed to the Privy Council in January 1595, asking it to intervene. Burghley sympathized with their case, but the lords could find little justification for denying Strode the use of his own land. However, Drake, who was in London, was asked for an opinion, and appointed to a committee of local notables, consisting also of Gilbert, one of the Champernownes, Edward Seymour (Member for Devonshire), Thomas Peyton and George Carey of Cockington, he who displayed such a talent for aggravating others but who was declared by the painter Isaac Oliver to be 'free from all filthy fraud'. The committee found in Strode's favour in April, but Drake found a way to settle the dispute more favourably. He had words with the offender and persuaded him not to build on the land, but instead convert it into gardens. It was probably the last service Sir Francis Drake did Plymouth before leaving on his final voyage.[1]

Pressure of business kept Drake constantly moving between Buckland Abbey, London, Plymouth and other West Country ports. His own commercial enterprises continued to flourish. Although he had sold some of his properties in Plymouth, he still held eighteen messuages, eighteen gardens and 34 acres of land there, while the ships he owned continued to sail for trade or plunder and his new mills began to produce in 1591. Of his public affairs, legal proceedings absorbed as much time as anything, for Drake was appointed a prize commissioner, and as Deputy Lord Lieutenant he supervised the justices of the peace. Thus, when the question of Catholic justices came up in 1592, Bath, Drake, Gilbert and Courtenay assembled the county justices in Exeter Castle on 24 November and administered, along with the customary oath, another

---

[1] Report of Harbord and Bampfield in Bridgeman and Walker, ed., *Manuscripts of the . . . Twelfth Earl of Lindsey*, 5-6, in addition to sources on p. 286, n.1.

acknowledging 'Her Majesty's Supremacy'. Drake, Gilbert and Courtenay began by taking the oath themselves (Bath being exempt), and then thirty-four justices followed suit in open court.[1]

This legal work involved Drake in varied and often complicated but interesting cases. We find him investigating the theft of corn at Saltash and Millbrook and taking up the complaints of the aggrieved – of Thomas Lymberry, one of his old mariners, who was usurped from his property in Plymouth by wealthy citizens and feared to enter the town, and of the yeoman Robert Palmer, whose family had been terrorized in their home in Kingstone. The most infamous and intriguing human tragedy that concerned Drake was the Page murder case, which has been unnoticed by other biographers, but attained in its day a rare and enduring status as a classic crime of passion. The subject of at least one contemporary tract and three ballads, it inspired Ben Jonson and Thomas Dekker's drama *Page of Plymouth* in 1599, and as late as the eighteenth century Lyne Brett's *The Merchant of Plymouth*. Acute public sympathy was aroused, less for the unfortunate victim than for the two lovers who conspired his end that they might be together.

Drake must have known the principals well. He may have patronized the shop in Tavistock where the romance of Ulalia Glandfield, the daughter of the owner, and George Strangwich, the shop assistant, began. George had learned his trade under a Master Powell of Bread Street in London. A capable workman, he was soon managing the shop for old Master Glandfield, who, so it was said, 'took so good a liking to him, being a proper young man, that it was supposed he should have had his daughter in marriage.' But the mutual attachment of Ulalia and George was due to be disappointed. Glandfield planned to move to Plymouth, and have his daughter close by, and he soon saw a better match for her in a respectable but elderly widower and merchant of Woolster Street, Master Page of Plymouth.

The girl married Page, but continued to see Strangwich when he came down from Tavistock on visits. She decided to dispose of her husband, and during the first year of their marriage made several unsuccessful attempts to poison him, each time underestimating the strength of his constitution. The desperation of the lovers increased, and when Ulalia was delivered of a stillborn child she believed that she would never have successful progeny by Page. A crazy plot was fomented. One of Ulalia's servants, Robert Priddis, was paid to dispatch Page, and promised a further £7 when the deed was done, while Strangwich hired a young man called Tom Stone to assist him. Stone was due to be married, and may have been in need of extra money.

About ten at night, evidently on Wednesday, 10 February, 1591, Page lay in his room, undressed for bed, but still awake, and naked but for a head kerchief. He was alone, for his wife was convalescing in a separate chamber. Furtively, Priddis unlatched the door of the house to admit the accomplice, Stone, and together they entered the old merchant's room and sprang upon him in the dark. Page perished miserably. Dragged to his knees on the floor, he was strangled with his own headscarf, clawing so violently at it with his fingernails that he lacerated his throat. When the body fell limp the murderers broke its neck against the bed. Then they stretched it upon the bed as if sleeping, spread out the old man's clothes ready for dressing, and

[1] Hamilton, 'Justices of the Peace for the County of Devon'.

left.

Priddis reported to Ulalia, and they thought to wait until daylight, but once Stone had quit the house the servant began to lose his nerve and fancied he could hear Page groaning. He called up Mistress Page and begged her to go in to see if her husband was still alive. Ulalia summoned her maid, a totally innocent party, and attired in her petticoat led the way to Page's room with a lighted candle. As if afraid to look upon her handiwork, she hesitated outside the door, and sent the hapless maid inside to see if the master was ill. In the darkness the poor maid discovered Page on the bed, fumbled across his face, but could not rouse him, and was then instructed by Ulalia to put a warm cloth about his feet, for he must be ill. It was only as her fingers fell upon the legs of the corpse that the maid realized that they were cold and stiff, and that Page was dead. The hapless girl was sent forthwith to bed highly distressed, while Priddis ran through the empty streets to summon old Master Glandfield. Page's sister, Mrs Harris, was also awoken and told that she must come at once, for her brother was dying of a disease everyone knew as 'The Pull'.

Mrs Harris it was who first became suspicious that all was not as it seemed. She noticed blood on the dead man's chest and traced it to the wounds about his throat, and further examination revealed that the knees had been scuffed and the neck snapped. The mayor and justices were soon on the scene, and Priddis was hauled to the town gaol, blabbing all he knew and accusing Stone of being the principal actor. Stone was arrested the next day, in the midst of his own marriage ceremony at a local church!

The mayor, Sir Francis Drake and some other justices had the sad duty of examining poor Ulalia, and unravelling the whole story, for she confessed everything, asserting boldly that she would rather die with Strangwich than live with Page. Strangwich himself was arrested as he returned from a visit to London, and proved equally resigned, but he begged clemency on the grounds that he had repented of hiring Stone and Priddis, and had even written to them from London, calling upon them to abandon their task. But it was too late, for Page and for Strangwich. There could only be one result. Priddis, Stone, Strangwich and Ulalia Page were imprisoned at Exeter and hanged together at Barnstaple on Saturday, 20 February, 1591. The ballads found a theme of thwarted love irresistible. In one, alleged to have been 'written with her own hand, a little before her death', Ulalia is made to address Strangwich:

> And thou my dear, who for my fault must die,
> Be not afraid the sting of death to try;
> Like as we lived and loved together true,
> So both at once, let's bid the world adieu.

And 'The Lamentation of George Strangwidge' echoed a similar sentiment:

> Farewell, my love, whose loyal heart was seen,
> Would God thou hadst not half so constant been;
> Farewell, my love, the pride of Plymouth town;
> Farewell, the flower whose beauty is cut down.[1]

Surviving records allow few cases to be known in as much detail, and some of them surface tantalizingly briefly among the more mundane minutiae preserved in municipal records. The town's accounts contain occasional glimpses of Sir Francis Drake, dining on venison with John Sparke, William Hobbes and three justices in Plymouth, taking wine during a visit to the tinworks, or receiving messages from the corporation at Buckland Abbey. One interesting entry for 1594-5 reads: 'Item, paid for hue and cry made after Sir Francis Drake's musicians, 2s 6d', and conjures up images of Drake's musical accompaniment being pursued across the Devon countryside.[1]

As the Spanish war progressed, prize court proceedings occupied more of Drake's attention. Captured vessels were regularly being brought into English ports with cargoes of fish, hides, silk, cotton, gold, silver, jewels, sugar, spices, brazil-wood and other luxury commodities, and many of the captors were needy men, glancing over their shoulders at trade depressions and poor harvests. The crews sailed for a third share of the cargo and as many of the goods above deck or on the captured mariners and passengers as they could find, and looting and piracy were seldom far away. The regulation of privateering became a major problem for the government. Neutral shipping had to be protected from illegitimate seizure, and the men who manned the privateers prevented from purloining excessive portions of legitimate plunder at the expense of the shipowners.

Inevitably, the problem descended upon Drake, on account of his standing in and knowledge of the maritime community and his general usefulness to the Privy Council. A particularly delicate case, but one that illustrates the difficulties involved, seems to have first enmeshed him in the frustrations of prize administration in 1590. A privateer commanded by John Davies and owned by the London merchants Thomas Middleton and Erasmus Harvey captured two ships off the Portuguese coast, a Florentine, the *Mary Margery*, and a Venetian vessel, the *Ugiera Salvagina*, both laden with sugar, pepper and ivory. They were ostensibly neutral, but shipped Spanish and Portuguese goods that were legitimate prize, and Davies brought the whole home. There was an immediate and strong diplomatic protest, both the Grand Duke of Tuscany and the Doge of Venice personally complaining to the queen and demanding restitution. A further complication was that before the prizes arrived in the West Country much of the cargo had been purloined by the privateers, and in the spring of 1591 Davies himself was reported in Falmouth, bragging of the spoils he had spirited away.

The Privy Council turned to its stalwart servants in the west. Sir Francis Drake was commissioned a justice of the Admiralty Court in November 1590, and ordered to collaborate with Gilbert, Harris, Richard Carew, the Mayor of Plymouth (Pepperall), Peter Edgcombe and Anthony Rouse in sequestrating the prizes and cargo landed at Dartmouth, Plymouth and Weymouth, making an inventory of the proceeds and storing them pending court proceedings, and apprehending Davies if he made an appearance. Under considerable pressure to resolve the case, the government closely monitored progress, giving full powers of search to the justices ('you may not spare to break open doors').

---

[1] *A True Discourse of a Cruel and Inhuman Murder* (1591) supplies the detail. The ballads, 'The Lamentation of Master Page's Wife of Plymouth', 'The Lamentation of George Strangwidge', and 'The Sorrowful Complaint of Mistress Page', were reprinted in Hindley, ed., *Roxburghe Ballads*, 2: 191-201.

[1] Worth, 137.

But the matter was a stubborn one. The slippery Davies remained at large, and as late as July 1593 Drake and the Mayor of Dartmouth were being ordered to arrest him in that town. Nor was the abjudication straightforward. Philip Corsini and Scipio Borsany claimed the cargo as the property of Italian merchants with whom England had no quarrel, while the captors as vociferously insisted that much of it in fact belonged to Spaniards and Portuguese who were shipping it under neutral cover. In the meantime, Drake and his colleagues deposited such of the plunder as they could recover with Admiralty commissioners, John Hart and Richard Salconstall, until a decision could be made. Eventually, a provisional distribution between Corsini and the captors was arranged, upon the presentation of securities to cover any goods delivered. But even here there were recriminations, for Harvey was detected trying to embezzle twenty-five bags of pepper that had been assigned to the Italians. By the spring of 1593 the cause had been heard no less than sixteen times, sometimes by such august individuals as the senior justices of the Admiralty Court, William Aubrey and Julius Caesar, and by the Lord Admiral and Burghley. Although Corsini succeeded in recovering some of the cargo for his clients, the case damaged relations between England, Florence and Venice and underscored the necessity for a close regulation of prize.[1]

Drake was principally involved in recovering, accounting and securing the cargoes, and in apprehending mariners guilty of pilfering from them, and evidently gave some satisfaction because he was used time and again when similar services were required. In 1591 we find him beset with a multitude of duties. He was to accompany Gilbert to Dartmouth to check the 'foul outrages' reported to have been perpetrated by sailors and 'other loose and dissolute persons' in the instance of prizes taken by some London privateers.[2] He was charged with assisting Sir Henry Palmer in disentangling the claims of thirteen French fishing vessels intercepted on their return from the Newfoundland banks, and determining which belonged to the Catholic League and constituted legal prize. He was involved in the searching of neutral flyboats to discover whether they were carrying war material to the enemy in violation of the safety passes granted them by the Lord Admiral. And on it went, year after year.

Nothing justified the government's concern about the disorderliness of the mariners more than the capture of the great Portuguese carrack, the *Madre de Dios*, in August 1592. She was taken near the Azores by a swarm of privateers, belonging variously to the queen, the Earl of Cumberland, Sir Walter Ralegh and others. This prize was the richest ever taken, wealthier even than Drake's Pacific treasure ship and *San Felipe*, and the captors ran wild with excitement, spending a night in ecstatic pillage, raiding the cabins of passengers, breaking open chests, and running off with much of what was due the investors and shipowners. Even the mariners were at each other's throats, some angry that Cumberland's men had rifled precious stones and other goods at will before they themselves could get aboard. The carrack was brought triumphantly into Dartmouth in September amidst tremendous tumult and concern. London jewellers had agents galloping to the port to purchase gems from the returning

---

[1] This case runs as a thread through the State Papers and acts of the Privy Council, but see also Butler, ed., *Calendar of State Papers, Foreign*, 11: 399-403.

[2] Privy Council, 25, 27 October, 1591, Dasent, 22: 37-8, 44.

sailors, and crowds of riff-raff gaggled about the dockside to steal from the cargo as it was being unloaded. Thomas Middleton, the Receiver of Customs, complained, 'We cannot look upon anything here, except we should keep a guard to drive away the disordered pilfering bystanders that attend but a time to carry away somewhat when any chest is opened.' In fact, the scenes were so riotous that when Drake and other commissioners tried to secure and recover the cargo they had difficulty gaining control of the ship, and it was only after many weeks, and the appointment of additional commissioners, including Sir Robert Cecil, that they were able to restore order, inventory the plunder, examine the mariners, and finally ship some £141,000 worth of cargo to London.[1]

And so the years slipped by, busy, sometimes frantic years, in which Sir Francis Drake punctuated the travails of Elizabethan administration with precious moments at home, fishing in the Tavy, hunting for deer about Buckland, or relaxing with his young wife. A prevalent view that they were years of idyllic retirement is unjustified. Drake was a greying man in his middle fifties, and could no longer expect abundant time ahead, but he remained too energetic, too restless to retire. Yet he can hardly have been satisfied. Although he was leaving Plymouth the stronger, his vendetta against Spain had progressed little, and he apparently missed the thrill of action and, like all good seamen, the feel of timbers and swell beneath his feet. Probably he felt it most in the summer of 1594, when he prepared some of the shipping for an attack upon the Spanish fortifications near Brest, and piloted it from Plymouth to the rendezvous in the Channel Islands. But the assault was to be directed by others, including Sir Martin Frobisher, who was fatally wounded, and Drake returned with his zest for battle more enhanced than appeased.

Then, at the end of the year, it all changed. The sea once again reclaimed its own.

[1] An account of this episode is in Bovill, 'The "*Madre de Dios*" '.

# Chapter Twenty-two

# 'Into a Waste and Desert Wilderness'

England, his heart; his corpse the waters have;
And that which raised his fame became his grave.

Richard Barnfield, *The Encomium of Lady Pecunia*, 1598

IT WAS AUGUST 1595 AND THE SHIPS WERE AT LAST READY TO DEPART. THERE WERE twenty-seven of them, six provided by the queen – the two new flagships, Drake's 550-ton *Defiance* and Sir John Hawkins's 660-ton *Garland*, the *Hope* (Gilbert Yorke), *Elizabeth Bonaventure* (John Troughton), *Adventure* (Thomas Drake) and *Foresight* (William Winter the younger). The rest had been put together by merchants and shipowners, such as John Watts of London. It was the old joint-stock operation again, but on a grander scale. Some 2,500 men had eventually been recruited, about two-fifths of them soldiers. After six years ashore, Drake's name had lost none of its magic, and once mobilization had got under way volunteers had come forward briskly. There had been delays in organizing the army, and it had not been until May that its colonel-general had been appointed. Drake found Sir Thomas Baskerville, as well as other senior officers, through Essex, the new patron he had been so successfully cultivating. Baskerville was the son of one of the first Earl of Essex's servants, and had been both a soldier in the Low Countries and a Member of Parliament under the patronage of the Devereux family. A greedy, self-centred and opinionated man (what Sir Nicholas Clifford called 'a true lover of himself'), Baskerville drove a hard bargain for his services, but he was a spirited professional, pugnacious and energetic. Now, on the eve of sailing, Drake had a powerful force, and he was bound for the oldest of his hunting grounds, the Spanish Caribbean.[1]

On the face of it the prospects seemed fair. Spain's defences in the West Indies had been improved since 1586, but there was doubt about how far the fortifications proposed by Bautista Antoneli had gone, or how well they would meet the challenge of invasion on an increased scale. After all, Drake had done this before. By 1585 the Spaniards had raised sufficient defences to counter the customary raids of small bands of corsairs, only to be overwhelmed by a fleet of unprecedented strength that Drake had brought from England. Now he had a larger force still, and again threatened to overpower all that the Spaniards had prepared.[2]

Despite that, the voyage had had a painful birth. It had been mooted as early as 1593 and finally put in hand before the end of the following year, but it had not been organized to Drake's satisfaction. The principal problem was the divided

---

[1] Clifford to Essex, August 1595, Andrews, ed., *The Last Voyage of Drake and Hawkins*, 34. This volume, which presents a selection of English and Spanish sources with a penetrating analysis, is the principal foundation for this chapter. It contains full reference to additional sources.

[2] The improvements in the fortification of the West Indies appear to have figured marginally in Drake's attack upon Puerto Rico, but hardly at all in his attempt upon Panama.

command, for Drake and Sir John Hawkins had received a joint commission with
equal authority. Such commands seldom worked, and hardly ever when the
leaders were men of such contrasting temperament, and stiffened by a pride that
suffered no subordination. The idea can hardly have been Drake's, and it arose
perhaps from the view that the management style of Sir Francis had created too
much dissension in the past and needed the restraint of Hawkins. It was, however,
an unhappy situation, in which both commanders believed themselves fettered by
the other. Sir Francis Drake was no longer a young man, but still alert and capable
of some vigour, but Sir John, then in his sixties, had grown slow in age. Thomas
Maynarde, who knew them both well, has left a portrait of the two great sailors as
they embarked upon their last voyage:

> Sir Francis Drake . . . a man of great spirit and fit to undertake matters. In my poor
> opinion better able to conduct forces and discreetly to govern in conducting them to
> places where service was to be done, than to command in the execution thereof. But
> assuredly his very name was a great terror to the enemy in all those parts, having
> heretofore done many things . . . to his honourable fame and profit. But entering into
> them as the child of fortune, it may be his selfwilled and peremptory command was
> doubted, and that caused Her Majesty (as should seem) to join Sir John Hawkins in
> equal commission, a man old and wary, entering into matters with so leaden a foot
> that the other's meat would be eaten before his spit could come to the fire, men of so
> different natures and dispositions that what the one desireth the other would com-
> monly oppose against . . . whom the one loved the other smally esteemed.[1]

If the queen and Privy Council harnessed Hawkins to Drake in the interests of equanimity they made an error, for from their decision evolved, in effect, two fleets within
one. Both commanders raised and victualled their own squadrons, and manned them
with officers loyal to themselves. It was a recipe for discord.

Nor had this been the only difficulty with which the admirals had contended.
Almost until sailing they had been threatened with an unwelcome diversification of
objectives. The main target of the expedition seems to have been Panama, entrepôt
for the Pacific treasure ships, which Drake intended to approach by the River Chagres,
but the queen had grown increasingly alarmed at the extensive naval preparations in
Spain. It was feared that another armada was in the making, and that it might strike at
Ireland or England. In July a Spanish raiding party from Brittany burned the villages of
Penzance, Newlyn and Mousehole in Cornwall and fuelled such speculation. Elizabeth
did not relish facing a crisis of that magnitude without Drake, Hawkins and their fleet,
and in August she ordered the admirals to switch the focus of their operations to European waters, reconnoitring the Spanish and Irish coasts in search of enemy fleets, and
awaiting the return of the *flota* before making a transatlantic voyage. Moreover, they
could not be spared longer than eight months and must return by May.

The new instructions had not been dispelled without passionate argument. The
commanders had said that men would have to be discharged, pinnaces already stored
away for river work disembarked, and that considerable reorganization would be necessary. They had entreated Essex to dissuade the queen: 'we humbly beseech your good
Lordship that if Her Majesty do alter our first agreement, that you stand strongly for us

[1] Narrative of Thomas Maynarde, Andrews, 86.

that the whole charge may be borne by the Queen, else look we for nothing but the like discontentment or worse than that of the Portugal voyage.' Baskerville, whose money had been invested in the Caribbean adventure, lobbied the earl no less urgently: 'I am already half ruined, and shall be wholly if the journey go not forward according to the first plot.'[1]

In the end it had not been argument that had suddenly shifted the queen back to the West Indies alternative, but the lure of treasure. The flag galleon of the home-ward-bound treasure *flota*, the *Begona*, dismasted and her rudder damaged in a storm, had separated from her consorts and put into Puerto Rico on 30 March, carrying, it was said, two and a half million ducats' worth of cargo. Drake and Hawkins had hap-pily sent the news to Elizabeth, who promptly dropped her objections to a direct voyage to the West Indies and cleared the way for sailing. Puerto Rico was still a diver-sion, but one less incompatible with the expedition to Panama, although the queen continued to insist that the campaign be a short one.

Prevarication about the aims of the voyage had not, however, been the principal cause of the long delay in readying the fleet for sea. According to Howard (the Lord Admiral), Drake and Hawkins had promised to leave Plymouth by 1 May, but here they were more than three months later still hurrying to complete preparations. Prob-ably provisioning had not been straightforward, for Drake spent much of July out of town searching for victuals, and when he sailed his supplies remained inadequate. There had been at least two unfortunate consequences of the delay. The cost mounted, and Spanish intelligence of the fleet's destination deepened.

According to her original agreement, Elizabeth had contracted to supply six ships and contribute two-thirds of the other costs, including the hire of private vessels and the wages of the men. When all was done the Exchequer authorized the payment of about £28,000 on the expedition, and Drake and Hawkins together paid out perhaps more than half as much, Sir Francis finding it expedient to sell a Cornish manor (Pensengnance) to Richard Carew for £250 to help with last-minute fitting out. To economize the admirals had resorted to granting the soldiers and shipowners shares in any plunder taken in lieu of orthodox remuneration, thus placing their contributions upon a 'no prey, no pay' basis.

The other consequence of the delay was potentially more serious. No one could have prevented the Spaniards from investigating the preparation of a large fleet under Drake, and in February warnings had been sent from Spain to the West Indies that they might expect trouble. Yet at that time Philip's agents had merely been guessing at Drake's destination. Thousands of people had soon been fleeing from Lisbon in the belief that 'El Draque' would shortly return to the Tagus. In May the Spaniards decided that the English were bound for the Caribbean, and further alarms went across the Atlantic, and in June prisoners taken in the Americas from Ralegh's expedition to the Orinoco blurted out the exact target of Drake's fleet: Panama. None of these tid-ings permitted the Spaniards to raise insurmountable obstacles to a force as large as Drake's, but compounded with other circumstances they helped tip the balance against him.

---

[1] Drake and Hawkins to Essex, 13 August, 1595, *Ibid*, 27-8; Baskerville to Essex, 13 August, 1595, *Ibid*, 28-9.

In those last days in England Sir Francis Drake's mind grappled with the embarkation of supplies and men, the winding up of his public business, and the settlement of personal affairs. There were things forgotten or neglected, but not his faith. Psalters were purchased for the ships, and instructions drawn up for the captains of the fleet, of which 'the first is to observe divine worship and to keep this rule twice daily unless for some special reason you are unable to do so.' Another injunction forbade gambling with cards or dice aboard, 'by reason of the many quarrels which usually arise from this.'[1]

He reflected, too, upon his own mortality, perhaps as the aged knight pondered upon the skull in the frieze at Buckland Abbey, and made an effort to untangle the problems around his estate. Since he was 'now called into action by Her Majesty, wherein I am to hazard my life as well in the defence of Christ's gospel as for the good of my prince and country', it was time to write his will. Yet everything was in conflict: the obligations to his wife and father-in-law, the promises he had made to the Drakes of Esher and Jonas Bodenham, and the desire to establish the Drake line through his brother; none of it could be comfortably reconciled. But it could be postponed no longer. He fumbled indecisively with it, setting out a statement that satisfied Lady Drake, but failing to sign it. After a characteristic bequest of £40 to the poor of Plymouth and its neighbourhood, the will granted Buckland Abbey and its contents, with the leases of the corn mills, to his wife. Thomas Drake, who would perpetuate the line, received the tenements, gardens, parks, cellars and other properties in Plymouth, including a house in the High Street in which Thomas then lived, and was no doubt dissatisfied. Bodenham retained the confidence of Sir Francis to the last, and sailed aboard the *Defiance* with him, but the will awarded him a mere £100, while Drake's servants received various sums of between 40 shillings and £100 each. The document was witnessed by Bodenham, Charles Manners, Thomas Webb, William Maynarde and George and Roger Langsford.[2]

Nothing was said about the manors of Sampford Spiney, Sherford and Yarcombe for the good reason that the terms of Drake's marriage contract already guaranteed those properties to Lady Drake for the period of her life. Two of the three executors of the will, Strode and Rouse (the third was Christopher Harris), had been named trustees of the manors at the time of the marriage and possessed full information about the agreement. A trust deed also empowered the executors to operate Drake's land and mill leases in his absence, or in the event of his death for a further five years, and to apply the proceeds to any debts.

To the Drakes of Esher the will would have been a disappointment, for they failed to secure the properties for which they had lobbied Sir Francis for some time. Drake had permitted them to keep the ransom paid for Don Pedro de Valdes, but obviously the family expected more. The admiral knew it, but did not see how he could fulfil his promises and deal honourably with his wife. He simply left the pot simmering, taking the unsigned will with him, and perhaps hoping for inspiration.

The essence of this voyage should have been speed and surprise, and both had once been Drake's trademarks. Materializing out of the twilight at Nombre de Dios,

[1] Drake's instructions to the fleet, August 1595, *Ibid*, 177-8.
[2] Drake's will, Nichols and Bruce, ed., *Wills from Doctors' Commons*, 72-9.

emerging from the brush outside Panama, breaching the Pacific without a warship to resist him, or charging almost impetuously into Cadiz – this had been the Francis Drake of days gone by, the man who had made himself a legend. This had been the 'El Draque' who had terrified the Spaniards. Those qualities were needed now, for a squadron of five fast Spanish frigates under Don Pedro Tello de Guzmán was being fitted to sail for San Lucar to collect the treasure at Puerto Rico. The ships eventually weighed anchor on 15 September for a race across the Atlantic, and success depended much upon Drake preceding them, for if Don Pedro reached Puerto Rico before the English his strength would provide a valuable reinforcement to the Spanish defences. As for Panama, as yet little had been done to enhance its ability to protect itself, but word of Drake's intentions was spreading and measures were already under way. A quick passage and sudden and resolute onslaught would have probably bowled both of them over, and the Drake of ten years before would likely have done it.

But Sir Francis was older now, perhaps too old, and like many a master losing his touch he was the last to find out. Even in Portugal he had displayed an unusual caution, a certain diffidence that seemed a curiosity in the context of brighter days. But that same strain was to reappear again and again in this final voyage. Where once he had been bold, nimble and surprising, he was now hesitant, ponderous and predictable. He refused to believe it, and said the Indies had changed. But it was not that. It was he who had changed. The conclusion is inescapable: Sir Francis Drake had lost his spell.

The fleet quit Plymouth on 28 August. After only a few days there was a council aboard the *Garland* in which Drake declared that he had three hundred more men in his division, and that Hawkins should take some of them to spare Drake's provisions. Sir Francis had under-supplied his force, but Hawkins now aggravated the mistake by refusing to help. Perhaps for the first time in years the two old sea-dogs were at loggerheads, and the voyage continued with undiminished contention. As one participant wrote, there were 'divers meetings with our generals [admirals], where passed many unkind speeches, and such as Sir John Hawkins never put off till death.'[1] Drake had been at fault in provisioning; even when not hamstrung by government stringency or the need for a hasty departure, it had never been his strong point. Sir John's attitude, however, was also unreasonable. The result was costly, for Drake had to make a diversion to Grand Canary to water his squadron.

The fleet reached Las Palmas on 27 September and after a careful but protracted reconnaissance Drake tried to land a force to take the town. His approach was too slow, and the islanders were able to organize resistance and employ artillery against the English boats, killing a number of men. The wind was also indifferent and the sea heavy, and Drake seems to have doubted his ability to support or re-embark any party he landed, and gave up the attempt. He retired to another part of the island to complete his watering, and even here a few men were killed and captured by the local inhabitants. The débâcle at Grand Canary set a pattern for the voyage. It wasted valuable time and was ineptly handled by the English. Drake had beaten Don Pedro's frigates to the Canaries by two days, but his activities there cost him his lead, and the

[1] John Troughton's journal, Andrews, 109.

Spaniards and English reached the West Indies about the same time. Even as Drake and Hawkins made their way across the Atlantic the balance was tipping further against them.

The fleet reached the Antilles on 27 October, but there another and no less instrumental delay occurred. Two small English pinnaces, the *Francis* and the *Delight*, which had become separated from the main force, ran into Pedro Tello's ships and the *Francis* was captured. The *Delight* brought word of it to Drake at Guadeloupe on the 30th. This was a matter of much importance, for Don Pedro would surely learn from his prisoners that Drake's first objective was Puerto Rico and make there in double quick time. His arrival was certain to put the governor, Pedro Suárez Coronel, on immediate alert, and increase the men and guns available for the island's defence. Drake was for giving instant chase to the frigates, crowding on all sail, but this time it was Sir John's turn to prevaricate. He wanted the English ships refitted, their additional guns mounted and some pinnaces built before risking an encounter, and would not stir from Guadeloupe. Sir Francis ought to have overruled what was a thoroughly bad decision, but he relented in an unfortunate act of charity to his ailing partner. As one witness put it, 'Sir John prevailed for that he was sickly, Sir Francis being loth to breed his further disquiet.'[1]

For three more days the English tarried at Guadeloupe, losing invaluable time, and then the fleet made north-west to the Virgin Islands, where the army was landed and exercised. On 12 November the English reached Puerto Rico, and they had no sooner done so than old Sir John died. He had not made a good end, and left his fleet living with the consequences of his sluggish advance, but his loss accentuated the gloom that was enclosing the expedition, for, Drake excepted, no English mariner symbolized the age more than the man who lay dead.

Pedro Tello had reached San Juan, the capital of Puerto Rico, nine days before, bringing the islanders their first tidings of Drake's intentions. In the ten days that followed the Spaniards raised the city's defences to unprecedented levels, using the fortuitous reinforcements on the *Begona* treasure galleon and the five frigates. The fortifications, which had been neglected, ill manned and under-gunned, were supplied with artillery and men from the ships, and in all about 1,000 men were put under arms and seventy pieces mounted on shore. The town was situated on a small island off the northern shore of Puerto Rico, and was approachable from the south by flanking the island on its western or eastern ends. Both passages were protected. In the east a narrow causeway linked San Juan with the mainland, and four small forts or batteries mounted fifteen guns between them. The principal channel was by the west of the island, but it fed through shoals and rocks and beneath now resuscitated batteries, notably the thirty-two gun castle, El Morro, perched on the north-western headland, and further south the four-gun Santa Elena. To inhibit entry still further the Spaniards sank two ships, one the *Begona*, in the middle of the channel, and anchored the frigates in a defensive position in the harbour. The treasure, which had brought both Don Pedro and Drake to San Juan, was safely stowed ashore.

Since the English had sacrificed surprise, they needed sense and resolution to take San Juan, but displayed little of either. Sir Francis approached the eastern flank of the

[1] Maynarde, Andrews, 90.

island first, but made no serious attempt to challenge the defences there, anchoring instead in El Cabrón Bay, which the Spaniards had believed incapable of sheltering such a force. But it was unsuitable, for two of the eastern batteries began to direct the fire of five guns against the ships and scored some direct hits on Drake's *Defiance*. The admiral was nearly killed. As he sat at supper with some friends, drinking beer, a shot broke into the steerage, smacked the stool from beneath him and wounded four or five others at the table, two of them, Sir Nicholas Clifford, whose thigh was broken, and Brutus Brown, fatally. The fleet found it prudent to withdraw towards the western extremity of the island, where an attack was planned by way of the main entrance into the harbour.

Drake seems to have regarded the frigates as key elements in the defence of San Juan, and on the night of the 13-14 November made a bold attempt to destroy them. The attack was misconceived inasmuch as the assault force was instructed to burn the enemy ships rather than to cut them out. However, twenty-five boats and pinnaces stole quietly through the darkness, navigated the main channel beneath the guns of the El Morro castle and sped towards Don Pedro's anchored frigates. They were seen, and fell under fire, but they swarmed around the Spanish ships and set them alight with incendiaries. For an hour the contest raged. The Spaniards aboard the ships successfully extinguished all of the fires except one that enveloped the stern of the *Magdalena*, the largest frigate, and they had to watch her burn to the waterline, but the blaze threw a glare across the entire anchorage and enabled the Spanish shore batteries to find their mark. Drake's men were driven away after each side had suffered about forty killed and others injured.

Little more was done. The next day the Spaniards further secured the western channel by scuttling the damaged flag frigate and two other ships in the roadway, close to the vessels that already rested there, and after consulting his officers Drake eventually decided against another attack. He returned a few prisoners his men had taken during the attack on the frigates (each supplied with a new suit of clothes), asked for the good treatment of any English captives, watered his ships and left.

There was more that might have been attempted. The eastern approaches of the town had hardly been tested, but it seemed that Drake and his officers simply decided that San Juan's capture was not worth the losses likely to be incurred. Panama lay ahead, and success there might change the entire prospect, sinking the repulse at Puerto Rico into oblivion. Sir Francis evidently believed that risks were undesirable at this stage of the campaign, when the principal objective of the voyage remained untried. As he told Baskerville and the other senior subordinates, 'I will bring thee to twenty places far more wealthy and easier to be gotten.'[1]

Yet although the voyage was redeemable, the disappointment at Puerto Rico increased the pressure upon Drake to succeed elsewhere. Every failure, every delay made the job harder. News of his presence was passing feverishly through the Caribbean, reaching Cartagena on 25 November and Panama on 2 December, and the possibilities of disease and demoralization in the fleet increased. The men had seen Francis Drake rebuffed twice now, at Grand Canary and San Juan, and inevitably their concern was mounting, especially in those whose pay depended upon the plunder taken.

[1] *Ibid*, 93.

To mariners who had sailed under the admiral's flag in better times it was increasingly obvious that Sir Francis was at the bottom of his form. He was not the man he had once been.

After leaving San Juan, Drake should have sailed straight for the isthmus of Panama. Had he done so he could have attacked it before any appreciable additional defences had been arranged, but with almost irresponsible negligence he turned to a successful but overlong tour of those towns along the Main east of Cartagena. On 1 December he fell upon Rio de la Hacha, of ill-famed memory, and captured it without much opposition. The Spaniards had heard he was on the coast and abandoned the town with their valuables, and although the English occupied the deserted settlement and eventually opened negotiations for its ransom there was little profit in it. At one point some of the citizens of Rio de la Hacha agreed to a ransom in pearls, but delivered so few that Drake sent the goods back in disgust. Then, on the 16th,

> the governor [Francisco Manso de Contreras] came into the town about dinner, and upon conference with the General [Drake] told him plainly that he cared not for the town, neither would he ransom it, and that the pearl was brought in without his command or consent, and that his detracting of time so long was only to send the other towns word, that were not of force to withstand us, whereby they might convey all their goods, cattle and wealth into the woods out of danger. So the General gave the governor leave to depart, according to promise, having two hours to withdraw himself in safety.[1]

Drake had Rio de la Hacha burned to the ground, along with the neighbouring pearl-fishing town of La Rancheria and the settlements of Tapia and Sallamca, sparing only the churches and the house of a Spanish lady who had written directly to Sir Francis, begging him not to destroy her home. The English plundered a number of small vessels captured thereabouts, and foraged around the countryside to discover a little of the wealth hidden by the citizens, and left on the 19th. Sailing westwards, the next day they attacked Santa Marta, an attractive pearling town, expelling its small rearguard from buildings which had already been evacuated of anything valuable. Again word had preceded them. 'Nothing was left but the houses swept clean,' wrote one of Drake's men.[2]

It was 21 December when the fleet burned and quit Santa Marta, nearly a month after the repulse at Puerto Rico, a month in which the avowed destination of the expedition, Panama, received and acted upon the news of Drake's coming. Some plunder, principally in pearls, had been acquired, but nothing that would justify the diversion (although Drake sent a pinnace home with a sample of the loot for the queen), and it must be presumed that his primary purpose was to reprovision his force from what was certainly a well-stocked locality. Even so, the delay had been excessive, and possibly decisive. Despite several warnings that Drake was bound for the West Indies, the Audiencia and king's servants at Panama had done nothing material to defend Nombre de Dios, Puerto Bello or the city itself, except to call upon the Viceroy of Peru for help. At the beginning of December, as Drake was menacing Rio de la Hacha, Don Alonso de Sotomayor arrived in Panama from Peru, charged with

[1] Anonymous journal of the voyage printed in Hakluyt, ed., *Principal Navigations*, 10: 226-45, p. 235.
[2] *Ibid*, 236.

organizing its defences as captain-general. Two days afterwards the city learned that Drake was in the Caribbean, but even then it was not until the 10th that Don Alonso gained control of the situation and preparations to resist an attack began to be made. The new captain-general found the isthmus in an almost helpless condition, a condition that Drake would have encountered had he not lingered on the Main. Sotomayor had only a few hundred soldiers and armed militia at his disposal, but in the event of an assault planned to evacuate Nombre de Dios and Puerto Bello and concentrate his meagre forces at strategic locations on the route across the isthmus to Panama. Never before had Sir Francis approached an important target so clumsily.

He reached Nombre de Dios on 27 December. In a brutal irony he had come full circle, to the scenes of his first triumphs, and it was here, a place of such bitter-sweet memories, that his fiery career finally began to flicker out. He had taken this town once, with a handful of Devon men. Now he entered it again at the head of a strong force, its skeleton garrison retiring to the hinterland after only a nominal defence, as they had been instructed. The wide streets were found empty, the shops bare, the inhabitants gone, and search revealed little of value, although a watch-house yielded a bar of gold, twenty bars of silver, and some plate and coin. Even the fruit, which was plentiful, was considered dangerous to eat because of the unhealthy climate of the place.

There were two ways to reach Panama, one by the River Chagres which led to Venta Cruces, a few miles from the city, and the other by a mountainous path through Capirilla Pass. The obvious route was the former, for at that time of year the river was swollen and Drake had the launches to ascend it without too much difficulty. Furthermore, although the fortification of the Chagres had been ordered and there were troops upon the river, little progress had been made. On the other hand, the overland route was at its worst at this season, lacerated by cart-wheels, miry and extremely rugged. It proceeded up a steep, narrow and easily defended gorge at Capirilla, where a small force of soldiers was being stationed. Both routes were also covered by a reserve assembled at Venta Cruces. Rarely had Sir Francis needed his fabled good luck more than he did now, but it deserted him. Probably, he reasoned the river would have been the most powerfully defended approach, and that he might outsmart his opponents by using a route considered to be almost impracticable at that time. It was agreed that Sir Thomas Baskerville would lead eight hundred picked men across the isthmus by land, and that when Panama had fallen Drake would bring reinforcements by the Chagres. It was an entirely logical presumption that could have worked, but in this instance it was the wrong decision.

Sir Thomas marched from Nombre de Dios on 29 December, his men carrying several days' biscuit, cheese and bread on their backs, and the arquebusiers confined to forty rounds each. For two days the army scrabbled up hills, sloshed through mud and stumbled in hollows, 'such a way that I think never Englishman went the like. The way in divers places is cut out through rocks high and steep, with mountains that one man could but pass at once, and coming to ye valleys we waded to the girdles.'[1] After completing a march of some 30 miles, perhaps about half the distance to Panama, Baskerville reached Capirilla and found a small fort squatting defiantly upon a hill-top

[1] Account of the voyage in Fox, ed., *Adams's Chronicle of Bristol*, 144-9, p. 147.

across the narrow defile, barring further advance. The Spanish defences were not more than two days old, so belated had been their preparations, and consisted of no more than 120 soldiers under Captain Juan Enriquez Conabut, some of them the garrison recently turned out of Nombre de Dios, but they were strongly entrenched behind barricades of tree trunks. The English made a furious effort to break through, some along the main path and others scrambling up the hill through the scrub into the mouths of the Spanish arquebuses. For three hours Baskerville's men advanced and wilted before the enemy fire, leaving dead and wounded behind them, but they failed either to dislodge their enemies or to inflict serious damage upon them. The Spaniards admitted a loss of only seven men killed, compared with the sixty or seventy dead or injured Englishmen. Sir Thomas became discouraged:

> I grew to advise with the captains what course to hold, and having called our guides, and found by them there was no other way but only through the fort and to get that there rested no hope, we resolved to return, necessity calling us to use expedition for all our powder, victuals and means to relieve ourselves were wholly consumed, and many hurt men and those of our best lay upon us, and how to carry them we knew not . . .[1]

How far Baskerville's apology may be taken at face value is questionable, because it is difficult to believe that a handful of Spaniards, sheltering behind an abattis of felled trees, could resist so superior a force for long, but his irresolution was consistent with the English behaviour right through the voyage. He possibly feared that the immediate obstacle was only one of many before him. Anyway, he turned back and his force dribbled into Nombre de Dios on 2 January, 1596.

There seemed nothing that could now save the doomed expedition, but two days later Drake put a brave face upon it and laid the alternatives before his officers. He offered to lead them into Lake Nicaragua to attack Granada and other towns or into the Bay of Honduras in search of plunder. Baskerville declared manfully that they would take both, one after the other, and it was determined to make for Nicaragua first. Nombre de Dios was destroyed, along with a village of Negroes who had aided the Spaniards (another indication of the changing times), and the fleet withdrew to the island of Escudo.

Despite the optimism that was part of Drake's nature, he was falling into a deep depression, which found little relief in intelligence gained at Escudo that the towns on Lake Nicaragua were poor. The English remained off the island for thirteen days, with the winds for the most part contrary, building pinnaces and refitting and reprovisioning as best they could. Sir Francis feared that his resources were at an end, but continued to refuse to acknowledge that the failure lay primarily in bad management, much of it his own bad management. He insisted that the Caribbean had changed. Thomas Maynarde, who saw him often during these final days, remembered that 'since our return from Panama he never carried mirth nor joy in his face.' Maynarde tried to ascertain whether the admiral had any further plans, but

> he answered me with grief, protesting that he was as ignorant of the Indies as myself, and that he never thought any place could be so changed, as it were from a delicious

---

[1] Baskerville's narrative, Andrews, 121.

*and pleasant arbour into a waste and desert wilderness, besides the variableness of the wind and weather, so stormy and blusterous as he never saw it before. But he most wondered that since his coming out of England he never saw sail worthy the giving chase unto. Yet in the greatness of his mind, he would in the end conclude with these words: 'It matters not man, God hath many things in store for us, and I know many means to do Her Majesty good service and to make us rich, for we must have gold before we see England.'[1]*

That powerful spirit still struggled to assert itself, to cheer the men, to wrest victory from disaster, to save them from an ignominious return. But this time Sir Francis Drake would not return, for the island proved a sickly haven, and a number of men were buried there. The crew of the *Defiance* gradually became aware that the admiral no longer kept the deck, but remained in his cabin, attended only by his servants, friends and senior officers. On 23 January the fleet eventually weighed anchor, steering not for Nicaragua but back towards the isthmus of Panama, towards Puerto Bello and the ruins of Nombre de Dios.

What was on the dying admiral's mind? The wind, it was said, was unfavourable for advancing, but it is just possible that Drake contemplated another stroke at Panama, hoping that its vigilance had declined and the alarm subsided. He had employed exactly that tactic when he had ambushed the mule-trains way back in 1573. But there would be no more triumphs.

The fleet reached the island of Buena Ventura, near the entrance to Puerto Bello. Sickness had been claiming more victims, including Captain Josias of the *Delight* and James Wood, a surgeon of the fleet, and Drake had not quitted his cabin for days. He was suffering from dysentery, and on 27 January had become so ill that the human vultures began closing in. Drake's servant, Thomas Rattenbury, was said to have been approached by Jonas Bodenham (now captain of the *Adventure*) and offered £100 if he would leave Bodenham and his friend Thomas Webb alone with the admiral in the cabin. Rattenbury distrusted their motives, and refused to go, but an hour or two later Thomas Drake called upon his dying brother, who 'lay then languishing in manner speechless', and found Bodenham at his bedside, pressing him to sign and seal two documents. One was 'the form of a release or general acquittance of all accounts, debts and other actions', by which Bodenham perhaps hoped to forestall any attempts to recover monies Drake had left in his hands. The other appointed Bodenham an executor of the admiral's will. So testified Thomas Drake in later years; for his part, Bodenham accused the admiral's brother of rifling the possessions in the cabin 'before the breath was out of the body of the said Sir Francis Drake.'[2]

Ill he was, but Drake could see the difficulties ahead, and made a final effort to settle his controversial estate. He dictated a codicil to his will, declaring himself 'perfect of mind and memory (thanks be therefore unto God) although sick in body.' Yarcombe was willed to young Francis Drake of Esher, provided he paid £2,000 within two years, and Sampford Spiney went to Bodenham, while Thomas Drake was named as the sole executor of the will and (in a separate document) his heir, thus set-

---

[1] Maynarde, *Ibid*, 100-1.
[2] These details depend upon the answer of Thomas Drake (1597), Chancery proceedings, Public Record Office, C2/Eliz.I/B8/32; bill of Thomas Drake (1597), C2/Eliz.I/D1/41; and the answer of Jonas Bodenham (1597), C2/Eliz.I/D1/41.

ting up for his brother's family a claim to Buckland Abbey and other properties after the death of Elizabeth.

Even in these dying hours, Drake not only foresaw difficulties with Sir George Sydenham for breaching a marriage contract, but also between Thomas Drake and Bodenham, and he called the two to his bedside and had Bodenham 'plight his troth and give his hand to this defendant [Thomas] to deal faithfully with him and to assist him in his troubles.' He appointed Bodenham to succeed him as captain of the *Defiance*, his last duty to the young wife he had left buried in Plymouth, so far away, and he distributed some gifts to his servants.

Late that night the condition of the admiral deteriorated, and in the early hours of 28 January he became delirious. He rose from his cot and bade William Whitelocke, a servant, to help him dress and buckle on his armour, so that he might die as a soldier, but then he was persuaded to return to his bed. Within the hour, at four o'clock in the morning, he died quietly.

The fleet anchored at Puerto Bello, which had been evacuated by the Spaniards and would shortly be destroyed by the English in final tribute to the passing of a mighty captain. Mr Bride gave a sermon aboard the *Defiance*, before Baskerville and the captains and principal officers, and the body of the admiral, encased in a lead coffin, was gently lowered into the sea to the 'doleful' notes of trumpets and the thunder of guns as the ships pealed their last respects.

In the Bibliothèque Nationale in Paris are preserved some vivid paintings of coastlines made during the voyage, probably at Drake's direction, for he had himself executed similar works during his voyage around the world. They record the appearances of landforms and information on bearings, tides, depths and harbours, details significant for navigators like Drake. Beneath his impression of the entrance to Puerto Bello the artist wrote simply:

> *This morning, when the description noted or taken of this land, being the 28 of January, 1595 [1596], being Wednesday, in the morning, Sr Francis Drake died of the bloody flux, right off the island de Buena Ventura, some 6 leagues at sea, whom now resteth with the Lord.*[1]

Not merely a man but an age had passed.

[1] Paris profiles, Andrews, plate 7.

314

CHAPTER TWENTY-THREE

AFTERWORD


And you that live at home and cannot brook the flood,
Give praise to them that pass the waves to do their country good.

Contemporary ballad on Drake


BASKERVILLE BROUGHT THE FLEET HOME, BRUSHING ASIDE A SPANISH PURSUIT
force near Cuba as he did so. In England the news of Drake's death was received sorrowfully, nowhere more than among his own people in the west. Inspired by the Rouse family, the poet Charles FitzGeffrey devoted a full-length epic
to Drake, extolling him as the embodiment of the quintessential Protestant hero.
The English seamen had their own way of commemorating their most celebrated
leader. They followed the wake he had carved, attacking Spanish towns, cities
and ships. Puerto Rico fell, and Puerto de Caballos in Honduras, Campeachy in
Mexico, St Vincent in the West Indies, and yet again Puerto Bello. After capturing the last in 1601, Captain William Parker, himself a Plymouth man, drew up
his ships 'somewhat to the eastward of the castle of Saint Philip, under the rock
where Sir Francis Drake, his coffin, was thrown overboard', in a fitting salute to
the man who had shown them the way.[1]

The Spaniards, of course, saw it differently. Some, who had either known him
or served against him, were not without respect for a fellow warrior, a man who
had fought his war vigorously, but seldom with the outright barbarity of so many of
the contestants. Thus the soldier Juan de Castellanos had already honoured him
in his ambitious verse about the voyage of 1585-6. And so now did Don Alonso de
Sotomayor, Drake's last opponent, reflect somewhat ruefully upon the passing of
'one of the most famous men of his profession that have existed in the world, very
courteous and honourable with those who surrendered, of great humanity and
gentleness, virtues which must be praised even in an enemy.'[2] But in Spain many
merchants, who had suffered by Drake's raids, were less magnanimous. This was,
after all, the man who had ravaged more than a score of Spanish towns and cities,
overthrown Philip's fleets and taken over five hundred ships. They illuminated
Seville in exultation at his end. And the most devoted of Catholics spoke as if the
Devil himself had been slain. When Lope de Vega, whose reverence for the
Church eventually led him to holy orders, wrote his famous La Dragontea in 1596
and 1597, celebrating Drake's death, he had not a good word to say for his subject.
He was charged with cowardice, brutality and incompetence – no falsehood was
too monstrous if it served to denigrate his memory.

Sir Francis, however, might not have been displeased, for the jubilation of
enemies of his faith was testimony to what he had done. There was one epitaph in

---

[1] Gill, Plymouth, 194.
[2] Jameson, 'Some New Spanish Documents Dealing with Drake', 29. For Lope de Vega's treatment of Drake
see the same author's 'Lope de Vega's La Dragontea', and Ray, Drake dans la Poésie Espagnole.

particular that might have amused him. When word of Drake's death was brought to an exhausted, sick and failing old man hidden in his huge and lonely monastery at the Sierra de Guaderrama, the tired face flickered with a delight his servants had rarely seen. 'It is good news,' said Philip II, 'and now I will get well.' Thus did the ruler of the greatest empire the world had yet seen acknowledge for the final time that a sailor from a diminutive but insolent island had reached out and humbled him.

Neither Philip nor Elizabeth lived to end their war. The king revitalized his navy, and sent out two more armadas, but they were dispersed by storms before reaching England. More successfully, but no less indecisively, the English retaliated, and even sacked Cadiz in 1596. Still, when the conflict was wound up by the Treaty of London in 1604, there had been few such victories, and it was the profits of privateering, in terms of both plunder and experience, that constituted the principal English legacies of the later years of the war.

As Drake had anticipated there was an unseemly squabble over his will. He had appointed his brother Thomas as his executor, with the power to collect monies and discharge debts and to account to the investors in the last voyage, but although the will was proven in London as early as May 1596 its repercussions sounded for years. First there was Elizabeth, Lady Drake, furious that the codicil had deprived her of Yarcombe and Sampford Spiney, and asserting her right also to the profits from the mill rents, willed her by her husband. Supported by the previous executors, Strode, Harris and Rouse, she went to court to annul Drake's codicil. Thomas successfully defended his appointment as the sole executor of his brother, but in 1598 a county escheator upheld Elizabeth's claim to Sampford Spinney and Yarcombe on account of her marriage settlement.

Elizabeth was still young and attractive, and the death of her father the same year left her extremely rich. To Buckland Abbey, Sampford Spinney and Yarcombe she could now add Combe Sydenham, the manors of Sutton Bingham and Bossington, and other properties. With such assets she could have commanded a range of suitors, and it is surprising that she ended her widowhood about 1597 by marrying someone as unprepossessing as Sir William Courtenay. Nevertheless, it did not last. Elizabeth died suddenly in 1598, of what is not recorded, leaving no heirs by either of her marriages, and her first husband's properties reverted to the Drake family.[1]

With Elizabeth gone, Thomas Drake's opponents were Jonas Bodenham and the Drakes of Esher, and he had a wretched time with them, battling through one cause after another. A deep-rooted animosity between Bodenham and Thomas now cast off all restraint. Bodenham boasted that he would not leave Thomas 'worth the gloves on his hands ere he had done with him', and told a servant of the Duke of Lenox 'that he could and would (unless Mr Drake did otherwise satisfy him) discover against him such matters as his whole estate could hardly answer.' No doubt Bodenham was a vindictive spendthrift, as Thomas alleged, but perhaps the fault did not lie entirely with him, for the brother of Sir Francis Drake was far

---

[1] In addition to the account in Eliott-Drake, *Family and Heirs of Sir Francis Drake*, see Dasent, ed., *Acts of the Privy Council*, 26: 21-2, 49-50, 137-8.

from an innocent operator. The proceedings of the Court of Requests contain a complaint by Lucas Bourne and John Welch and their wives in which they charge Thomas Drake with trying to cheat them of an inheritance, some property in the ward of St Andrew in Plymouth. He had, they said, 'by sinister means gotten into his hands or possession the deeds, charters and evidences concerning the said premises', and was seeking to dispossess them.[1]

For years Jonas Bodenham and Thomas Drake did battle in the courts, with the latter unsuccessfully attempting to recover papers from Jonas that would help square Drake's accounts. After Elizabeth's death Bodenham secured Sampford Spiney, as Sir Francis had wished, but Thomas recovered it for the Drake line by purchase in 1601. He also got Yarcombe, when the Drakes of Esher failed to provide the price within the time stipulated in the admiral's will, and the leases of the corn mills. Not the wisest man in Christendom, someone once called Thomas, but assuredly not the simplest either, for although bitter litigation continued until his death in 1606 he preserved most of Sir Francis Drake's property for the family. The legal proceedings were vicious throughout, with Richard Drake of Esher even stooping to charge Sir Francis with having embezzled money from the 1585 voyage and the capture of the *Rosario*. Although some historians have avidly repeated these charges, the circumstances in which they were produced and the paucity of the evidence adduced in their favour entitles us to regard them with great suspicion. The 1585 voyage was thoroughly audited at the time, when the events were fresh, and the problems about the transfer of the plunder from the *Rosario* have been described. In neither case did contemporaries charge Drake with embezzlement, nor were those accusations convincingly raised by his detractors in later years.

Four centuries have now passed since the waters of the Caribbean closed over the body of Sir Francis Drake, but he has not been forgotten. The story of the Devonshire man driven by faith, patriotism, personal ambition and profit to challenge a huge empire embodied so much of the quality of legend that it was bound to be remembered. It still continues to exercise the imagination. Indeed, so powerful has been its appeal that English folklore, no less than the contemporary Spanish superstition, endowed Sir Francis with supernatural powers, but, whereas his enemies saw him as the reincarnation of the Devil, his admirers told of the miraculous super-hero, who could hurl a cannonball across the earth, whittle chips of wood into water and transform them into ships, and return from the dead to ride across Dartmoor with spectral hounds or defend his country whenever it was endangered. As John Knox Laughton remarked towards the end of the last century: 'From among all moderns Drake's name stands out as the one that has been associated with almost as many legends as that of Arthur or Charlemagne.'[2]

---

[1] Drake Papers, Devon County Record Office, Exeter, 346M/F552, ff. 9, 28; deposition of Francis Crane, 13 May, 1605, Public Record Office, London, E.133/47/3; procs. of Court of Requests, *Ibid*, Req. 2/87/14. The litigation between Bodenham and Thomas Drake can most conveniently be studied in the notes and transcripts of Lady E. F. Eliott-Drake, Drake Papers, 346M/F534, F551-68, F590, F710-11, E688, and in her *Family and Heirs*, 1: 137-48, 174-92.

[2] Dict.Nat.Biog., 5: 1346.

A number of interconnected but distinct traditions of Drake developed. One, embedded in children's literature, exploited the entertainment value of sensational derring-do; another, deeper and more sophisticated, emphasized Drake's role in the formation of England's naval and maritime tradition; and a third used Sir Francis to inspire endeavour and achievement, particularly in times of adversity. The first thread matured only in the last years of the nineteenth century, after a popular press had risen upon the expansion of public literacy. Beginning with G. A. Henty's *Under Drake's Flag* in 1882 the tales hit the bookstores, one after another, patriotic books for boys, fact and fiction, weak on analysis and uninterested in motives, but strong on action. Their titles tell it all: *With Hawkins and Drake, At Sea with Drake, Drake on the Spanish Main, For Drake and Merry England, Sea Dogs All, The Fighting Lads of Devon, The Boy's Drake*, and many more. This trend continued until the 1960s, in such books as Douglas Bell's *Drake Was My Captain* (1953) and Peter Dawlish's *Young Drake of Devon* (1954) and *He Went with Drake* (1955). There were relatively few mature treatments of Drake in fiction, and books aimed at adults (among them Julian Corbett's *For God and Gold*, F. Van Wyck Mason's *The Golden Admiral* and Margueritte Wilbur's *Immortal Pirate*) seldom precluded a juvenile audience.

It was this tradition that was transferred to film during the twentieth century, although Sir Francis's motion picture début was in a slushy silent called *Drake's Love Story* in 1913. Featuring Hay Plumb as Drake and Chrissie White as Elizabeth Sydenham, it was inspired by Louis Napoleon Parker's *Drake, A Pageant Play* (1912), in which corny expressions ('Child's Play', 'Odzookers!') mingled with action scenes and romantic dialogue between the hero and his betrothed ('in the burning tropics, in the whirlwind and the gale, the one thought in my brain was Bess!'). This book made Elizabeth Sir Francis's life-long romance, and deleted poor Mary Newman from the story completely. After the uncertain tilt at romance, the Drake films reverted to unpolluted action in *Drake of England* (1935); *The Sea Hawk* (1940), which fused a proposed film biography of Drake with Sabatini's novel of the same title and was consequently true to neither; and *Seven Seas to Calais* (1962), an Italian-American production. Television followed suit with twenty-six half-hours of *Sir Francis Drake*, made by the British ABC and ATV companies in 1961 and 1962. In this series Drake (played surprisingly convincingly by Terence Morgan) untangled the problems not only of Queen Elizabeth (Jean Kent), but also of a cast of sixteenth-century celebrities that ranged from Dr Dee and Thomas Stukeley to Miguel de Cervantes. Westward Television's *Drake's Quest* (1977), in celebration of the quadri-centennial of the circumnavigation, stuck more closely to history and was the screen's only attempt to offer a deeper insight into the man and his times.

If there was a pedagogical element in the derring-do tradition, it was the inculcation of patriotism. Thus, Richard Lovett's *Drake and the Dons* (1888) was proclaimed 'the best boys' book that has appeared for many a day, and we trust that parents and teachers will encourage the children who look to them for guidance to read it, and thus become acquainted with the secrets of England's present greatness.'[1] This comment was typical of its time, for it was then that the more academic interpretation of Drake's career matured, a tradition that sometimes exalted the seaman as the founder of England's naval and maritime ascendancy.

This second view echoed Britain's position at the close of the nineteenth century as the leading (if fading) mercantile power and the supreme naval and imperial nation. The empire, just completed by acquisitions in Africa, was at its height, and the map of the world was plastered in pink. The Royal Navy had ruled the waves for as long as anyone could remember, and theorists such as A. T. Mahan saw 'sea power' as an essential instrument of national greatness. Warmed by the stirring glow of empire, British historians such as Julian Corbett, John Knox Laughton and Michael Oppenheim turned towards the period that they believed had laid the foundation of their country's naval strength and towards the men who had set England upon the path to maritime supremacy and the tremendous prosperity, security and international influence that were predicated upon it.

For Julian Corbett, Drake's best biographer, Sir Francis was more than a man of action *par excellence*, a hero meet for tales of high adventure. If Henry VIII had created the modern navy, it was Drake who had transformed it into a major vehicle of policy. His large-scale expeditions against Spain and the West Indies and his battles in the Channel had made it a force in Europe, helped preserve the Reformation and rescued England from invasion. During his operations, according to Corbett, Drake displayed a strategical and tactical genius and developed ideas that would become hallmarks of naval power, including the importance of the offensive and sailing ship tactics using broadsides and a line-ahead formation. Corbett's *Drake and the Tudor Navy*, published in 1898, was a powerful presentation of the creator of England's naval tradition and the forerunner of Nelson.

The eagerness with which Britain embraced this re-evaluation was particularly evident in the tercio-centennial celebrations of the Armada's defeat, in 1888. Based on Plymouth, they inspired special numbers of such periodicals as *The Illustrated London News*, *The Western Antiquary* and *The Graphic*, and extensive pageantry, including re-enactments and banquets. An exhibition, organized by W. H. K. Wright, eventually moved from the West Country to the Theatre Royal in London's Drury Lane. Poems by Douglas Sladen, Edward Capern, John Tate and others; new dramas; paintings such as F. Baden-Powell's *The Last Shot at the Spanish Armada*, and various Drake relics (including a silk purse, a walking stick, a tankard, a silver spoon, a dagger, two swords, astrolabes, curtains, plate and a snuffbox) were paraded to honour the occasion. At no time since his death had the nation felt more indebted to the little Devonian. In 1883 the ships of the British North American and West Indian squadrons planned an attempt to recover Drake's leaden coffin from the depths of the sea, an enterprise revived with no greater success in the 1970s. And it was about then that two great statues were raised in Devon. They were not quite the first sculptures of the admiral. Herr Andreas Friederich had sculpted a 14-foot statue out of fine-grained red sandstone and given it to Offenburg in Germany, where it was erected in 1854. Drake's left hand contained a bundle of potato stalks, while his right held a map of America, and the statue credited him with introducing the potato to Europe when he returned to England in 1586. It was another German, Joseph Edgar Boehm, who

[1] *The Western Antiquary* 8 (1888-9): 29.

created the large bronze statue that was unveiled in 1883 and awarded to Tavistock, where it still stands. But a replica, made the following year, is now more
famous, prominently established on Plymouth Hoe and gazing out to sea.

There is truth, of course, in this image of Drake, but Corbett exaggerated his
case. Under Drake's leadership, naval operations certainly expanded and diversi-
fied, but as Kenneth Andrews has so cogently argued, they frequently failed to
meet their aspirations, and Elizabeth's navy remained immature. It depended
much upon private enterprise, and had to respond to the profit motive as well as to
national policy. Although admirals strove to meet the new challenges of order,
discipline, organization and supply, the sea-keeping qualities of the fleets were
severely limited by the lack of effective remedies for disease, and their offensive
capacity was blunted by inexperience in battle. While the Tudor navy certainly
improved in these respects, its relative inadequacy was illustrated by Elizabeth's
constant recourse to privateering, which remained the typical form of naval warfare throughout the period.

Not only that, but an objective biographer must set Drake's weaknesses as an
admiral against his obvious strengths. In his early years he displayed extraordinary
qualities – courage and audacity; energy, determination and speed; aggression and
brilliant seamanship; and the ability to detect the strategical weaknesses of his
enemies and to profit by them. By exposing these flaws – such as the isthmus of
Panama, the route into the Pacific, and the general vulnerability of the Caribbean
– he held the initiative in his war against the Spaniards for years. They ran after
him, plugging the gaps in their defences that he had so sensationally advertised.
But Drake's deficiencies must also be noted. Even if those final miserable campaigns depicted a man of declining powers, a man whose grasp of the bases of his
earlier successes had been loosened, he had throughout his career diluted his
genius with some inadequacies. His victualling left much to be desired, and his
leadership was not above criticism. Affable, cheerful and loyal, willing to labour
beside all men, great or humble, yes. But he was also full of promises he could not
always fulfil, and his self-assertion and instant decision-making left some subordinates feeling both uninformed and undervalued. Able to inspire immense
affection in many close associates, he nevertheless experienced difficulties in most
of the fleets he commanded. Drake and his navy had made a good beginning, but
they were still far removed from the 'band of brothers' that won the battles of the
Nile and Trafalgar.

Corbett's view of Drake was, in any case, excessively narrow, for his contribution was to Elizabethan maritime history generally, rather than to that of the navy
only. He was the most daring of corsairs before he became an admiral, and it was
in this wider context that his significance fully emerges. The age of Drake was one
of endeavour rather than success. The Elizabethans failed to find the North-east
Passage, or the North-west Passage; they failed to colonize America; they did not
establish a sustainable trade with the Americas, and it was not until the seventeenth century that they finally opened a firm trade with the East. Amid such disappointments Drake's earlier voyages were striking, and provided the one hero
who could inspire others. They aroused the greed and enterprise of the country,
and unleashed a tide of imitators bent upon honour and profit. By demonstrating

that Englishmen could sail anywhere and fight anyone – even Philip of Spain – Drake injected his countrymen with the national self-confidence and pride that not only fuelled maritime endeavour but also enabled England to meet the crisis of 1588. Drake neither created the English oceanic movement, nor represented its full diversity, any more than Shakespeare embodied every aspect of the flowering of literature or Queen Elizabeth could be credited with all the achievements of the body politic. But he, like them, was the symbol that lingered in the imagination. More than anyone else, Drake broadcast to the world England's coming of age as a great seafaring nation.

The tradition of Drake as a founder of British greatness, so beloved by the Victorians basking in world empire, seemed less important to the subjects of the second Queen Elizabeth in the 1960s and after. While Sir Francis remained one of the legendary figures of history, common knowledge of his career dipped, and, curiously, professional historians began to regard the maritime heritage that had diffused the language, culture and influence of an island race across the globe as unimportant, or at least unfashionable. There were many reasons for the trend. Intellectually, the concept of empire now engendered more shame than pride, and as Britain's role in the world visibly shrank after 1945 her historians became increasingly insular in their thinking. There are few scholars of naval and maritime history in British universities, and the themes are greatly undervalued in general histories. Drake, like the other great men in the seafaring tradition, suffered scholarly neglect. It is interesting to note that the study of Cook's voyages owes most to Antipodean historians, that the only recent professional scholar to write a book about Nelson is a Dane, and that – always admitting Kenneth Andrews, Helen Wallis and a few other very honoured exceptions – knowledge of Drake has relied heavily upon American scholarship. In schools, too, the decline of history as a subject of study contributed to a growing ignorance about Sir Francis. In the 1960s the stream of substantial juvenile biographies and novels that had once facilitated instruction began to dry up.[1]

The retreat of the Victorian tradition was also marked by reassessments of the sailor and his significance. At its best this revisionism was exemplified by Andrews's fine study of *Drake's Voyages* (1967), an impressive and judicious antidote to Corbett's adulation that placed the subject within the greater context of Elizabethan expansion. At its worst it degenerated into the cynical denigration of Drake's character and achievements to be found in some recent writing, which depicts Sir Francis as nothing more than an avaricious corsair, whose quest for plunder subordinated any sense of duty. This view has condemned Drake for abandoning the blockade of Portugal in 1587, uncritically revived the ill-supported charge that the admiral deliberately jeopardized Howard's fleet in 1588 to snap up the wealthy *Rosario*, and emphasized the commercial over the strategic differences of opinion in the expedition of 1589. Overall, such an interpretation shows little

---

[1] The last flurry of full-length titles included Will Holwood, *The True Book About Sir Francis Drake* (1958); Edith Hurd, *Golden Hind* (1960); Jean L. Latham, *Drake, The Man They Called a Pirate* (1961); Ronald Syme, *Drake, Sailor of Unknown Seas* (1961); Frank Knight, *The Young Drake* (1962); Louise Andrews Kent, *Music for Drake* (1964); and M. J. Foltz, *Awani* (1964). Then, suddenly, titles thinned out. In all more than one hundred original books, fact and fiction, have dealt at full length with Drake's career.

insight into Drake's motivation, particularly his sharp Puritanism, and seriously underestimates the extent of his thinking and activity. Worse still, it does violence to the facts. But however partial and prejudiced, the view suggests the extent to which the late Victorian image of Drake has been abandoned by generations more conscious of the tawdriness of empire.

Yet, as the Spaniards had learned, Drake was never an easy man to keep down, and there may already be signs of a revival, if the enthusiasm of various quadricentennial celebrations on both sides of the Atlantic are an indication. And irrespective of the fortunes of the first two traditions we have described – Drake the hero of adventure stories and Drake the pioneer of British maritime superiority – there was another one that always acknowledged the myth's capacity for resurrection. For Drake lives on as a continuing inspiration, a symbol about which the British nation rallies when endangered, and which it recalls in moments of high endeavour.

Arguably, this was the first function of Drake's memory. In 1626, when he finally ushered into print Philip Nichols's account of the voyage of 1572, Drake's nephew entitled the book *Sir Francis Drake Revived* and called 'upon this dull or effeminate age to follow his noble steps for gold and silver.' The theme recurred throughout seventeenth-century literature. A collection of Drake narratives published in 1653 also employed the title *Sir Francis Drake Revived*, as did the first book-length biography, Nathaniel Crouch's *The English Hero, or Sir Francis Drake Revived* (1692). Crouch trusted that Drake's career 'may be a pattern to stir up all heroic and active spirits in these days to benefit their prince and country.' In the following century Dr Samuel Johnson, who knew so little of Drake that he could inform his readers that 'no series of success could ever betray [him] to vanity', nevertheless offered another biography that considered the sailor 'a sufficient proof that no obscurity of birth or meanness of fortune is unsurmountable to bravery and diligence.' Thus did Sir Francis become the model of the self-made man. And the process continues today, as ships of enthusiastic adventurers retrace his voyages and measure their own manhood against his. When the lone yachtsman, Francis Chichester, completed his epic circumnavigation of the world in 1967, Elizabeth II used Drake's sword to perform the ceremony of knighthood.[1]

Within living memory the most notable examples of this use of the myth occurred during the two world wars, when Drake's spirit was invoked to prop up morale in a Britain battered by conflicts worse than Sir Francis could ever have imagined. One image conjured up in those times, by, among others, Sir Winston Churchill, was the famous story of the game of bowls. Drake's alleged remark, 'There is plenty of time to win the game and beat the Spaniards too', was exactly the note of confidence the country needed in the face of an enemy. But it is doubtful if even Churchill raised Drake's ghost as effectively as did Sir Henry Newbolt in his famous poem, 'Drake's Drum'.

The drum in question, preserved at Buckland Abbey, is a side- or snare drum,

---

[1] Crouch, *English Hero*, foreword; Johnson, *Lives of Sir Francis Drake . . .*, 271-2. An earlier biography, Samuel Clark's seventy-two page pamphlet, *Life and Death of . . . Sir Francis Drake* (1671), was in the same vein.

21 inches high, with a shell or barrel of walnut. It certainly belongs to Drake's period, and is said to have accompanied him on his voyage around the world. Drake's drum had long been the subject of strange stories. Robert Hunt, writing before 1865, tells us that 'old Betty Donithorne, formerly the housekeeper of Buckland Abbey,' had assured him that if Drake heard the drum beating 'he rises and has a revel.'[1]

Newbolt knew something of these old superstitions and turned them to patriotic account. His verses, written in December 1895, when threatening noises from the German Kaiser were sending the Royal Navy to sea, declared that the drum could indeed summon Drake from the dead, not for a revel, but in defence of England, whenever the country was in danger. According to Newbolt the dying admiral called:

> Take my drum to England, hang it by the shore;
> Strike it when your powder's running low.
> If the Dons sight Devon, I'll quit the port of Heaven,
> And drum them up the Channel as we drummed them long ago.

Published in the St James's Gazette in January 1896, the poem was an immediate success, and gained further currency at the beginning of the new century when Sir Charles Stanford set it to music. In passage the tale was embellished, so that the drum itself was said to beat a ghostly tattoo to call Sir Francis from his watery grave at moments of national crisis. The men of the Brixham trawlers thought they heard it the day the Battle of Jutland was fought. And on 21 November, 1918, it was heard throbbing loudly aboard the Royal Oak as the Kaiser's ships surrendered to the British grand fleet at Scapa Flow. The captain of the ship reportedly instituted a search for the phantom drummer, but nothing that could explain the phenomenon was found and the spectral roll continued at intervals until orders were given for the German colours to be hauled down.

The legend re-emerged during the Second World War. In August 1940, in the midst of the Battle of Britain, the BBC went on air with a programme entitled Drake's Drum. This was broadcast on the Overseas Transmission in the series This Land of Ours and, the following month, was printed in London Calling. That same September, as the Luftwaffe lost its fight for mastery of the daytime skies, two army officers swore they heard the drum again, beating on a Hampshire seashore.

It was Colonel E. T. Clifford who, in 1916, summed up the importance of the drum story:

> In the great war that is now being waged be assured that we shall triumphantly emerge, largely because of our navy, which has generously adopted Drake's principles of naval war, and also because the spirit of Drake is still with us, and still animates the people of this Empire. That is the true significance of Drake's Drum. Confidence, resolution, bravery and patriotism were Drake's characteristics. Let us follow so great an example.[2]

During the Second World War an anxious public was also being exhorted to forti-

---

[1] Hunt, Popular Romances of the West of England, 231.
[2] The material on the drum is based principally on Ditmas, The Legend of Drake's Drum.

tude by words that Drake had written more than three and a half centuries before. He had been addressing Walsingham as his ship, the *Elizabeth Bonaventure*, rode off Sagres on 17 May, 1587: 'There must be a beginning of any great matter, but the continuing unto the end until it be thoroughly finished yields the true glory.' Those words were re-called by the Vicar of Harrow in an article for the London *Times* of 20 November, 1939, and something in them struck the mood of an embattled people. Soon Drake's words had been converted into a prayer by Eric Milner-White and G. W. Briggs, a prayer that has become one of the most popular in the language:

> O Lord God, when thou givest to thy servants to endeavour any great matter, grant us also to know that it is not the beginning, but the continuing of the same unto the end, until it be thoroughly finished, which yieldeth the true glory.

Wartime Britain took the words to heart, and they were repeated time and again during the darkest years of the conflict, on London placards and in Christmas cards, on radio broadcasts (one by General Montgomery) and in church services. They were featured during the National Day of Prayer on 23 March, 1941, and when the war was over the prayer survived as a statement of resolution, and was a favourite of Prime Minister Margaret Thatcher, who most recently quoted it during a difficult financial crisis in October 1989.[1]

Determination, courage, verve, patriotism – above all faith. Drake would have approved of the qualities he had come to represent. No less would he have been pleased to learn that in death, as in life, he watched over his people.

---

[1] For this subject see Bonner-Smith, 'Drake's Prayer'. An example of Thatcher's use of the prayer is described in the *Daily Telegraph* for 28 October, 1989.

# GLOSSARY

ALCALDE A justice or official at the head of a Spanish or Portuguese town.

ARQUEBUS A muzzle-loading firearm, the forerunner of the musket, in which the trigger brought the end of a slow-burning match into contact with the powder that discharged the ball.

ARTILLERY Although definitions of artillery pieces were imprecise, the English widely recognized two types of larger battery guns, cast either in bronze ('brass pieces') or iron. 'Culverins' generally possessed a bore of four or five inches and fired shot of from 9 lbs (the 'demi-culverin') to 17 lbs. 'Cannons' had six- to eight-inch bores, and fired heavier shot of up to 66 lbs. It was then believed that the longer barrels, as well as the lighter shot, of the culverins conferred a greater range, but increased length made guns difficult to manage and did not, in fact, much alter the range, which was ineffective beyond a few hundred yards. Spanish terminology for artillery did not correspond with the English nomenclature.

ASTROLABE A nautical instrument used to measure the altitude of the sun or stars during the calculation of latitude.

AUTO-DA-FE The execution of a sentence of the Inquisition, possibly including the parade of penitents or the burning of heretics.

BARK A small ship of standard rig and build.

BOATSWAIN Ship's officer responsible for sails and rigging and the mustering of the men.

BRIGANTINE A small, manoeuvrable vessel, employing both sails and oars, often used as a tender to larger ships, for reconnoitring or prize-taking.

BUCKLER A round shield.

CAPSTAN A cylinder installed on the forecastle deck of larger ships and used to work anchors, weights and heavy sails.

CARAVEL A Mediterranean trading vessel, lateen-rigged with two masts, converted into a three-masted ship for oceanic exploration by the Spanish and Portuguese.

CARRACK Three-masted square-rigged trading ship, larger and stronger than the caravel, and carrying high fore and stern castles. They were a principal instrument of the Portuguese East Indies trade.

CORREGIDOR A Spanish justice.

CORSELET A piece of armour covering the trunk.

CROWN English coin worth five shillings.

DUCAT The relative values of currency varied considerably throughout the period, but in 1586 the Spanish silver ducat was worth about 5s 6d in English money. The exchange value of the Spanish gold ducat about that time was probably seven English shillings or more. See also peso, pistolet, and real.

FASTS (as in HEAD and STERN FASTS) Lines by which a ship is secured to a pier.

FLYBOAT A medium-sized vessel, commonly used by the Dutch as a carrier or transport.

FORECASTLE A raised deck at the front of a ship, used to dominate the decks of an enemy ship. The improved Elizabethan warships had reduced forecastles and a more streamlined appearance.

FORECOURSE The sail on the FOREYARD, the lowest yard on the foremast of a ship.

FORESTAY Stay from the head of the foremast to the bowsprit of a ship.

FRIGATE A swift, light sailing ship, sometimes employing oars.

GALLEASS Large three-masted fighting ships with oars, attempting to fuse the advantages of the oared galley and the war galleon.

GALLEON Principal three- or four-masted fighting ship. The Elizabethans developed a flush-decked galleon of about 300 to 500 tons, with a deep draught and a length to breadth ratio of a little under 3:1. Early Spanish galleons, built in 1568 to 1570, were small, but after 1578 Spain produced larger, three-decked, galleons with a beam to length ratio of about 1:3.3. These galleons lacked the sailing qualities of their English counterparts.

GALLEY Oared fighting ship, with one or two masts. Characteristic of the Mediterranean, they were unsuitable for oceanic voyages, and could not effectively be equipped with artillery.

HALYARDS Tackle for raising sails, spars or yards aboard ships.

HOURGLASS A sand-glass that ran for an hour.

HOY A Dutch ship, rigged fore and aft, and used as a freighter or transport.

LATEEN RIG Having a lateen or triangular sail set at an angle to the mast.

LAUNCH A ship's long-boat.

LORD ADMIRAL The chief executive officer of the Elizabethan navy, and a member of the Privy Council.

MASTS Principally fore (front), main, and mizzen (rear).

MUSKET A heavier form of the arquebus, usually fired upon a tripod, and employing the same matchlock firing principle. Muskets were introduced in the late sixteenth century.

NAO A strong, multipurpose vessel used on the northern coasts of Spain. The nao had fore and stern castles, two or three decks, three masts and a bowsprit, and its beam to length ratio was about 1:3. It was not unlike the Spanish galleon.

NAVY BOARD The body responsible for the maintenance of Elizabeth's ships and their ordnance. There were five offices: Clerk of the Ships, Comptroller, Surveyor of the Ships, Master of the Ordnance and Treasurer.

PESO Spanish coin. The value of the gold *peso de oro* increased over that of the silver *peso de plata* throughout the period. In 1573 the gold peso was worth about 8s 3d in English money.

PIKE A weapon with a pointed iron head at the end of a long wooden shaft.

PINNACE Small, shallow-draught vessel, usually having a single deck and two masts, and auxiliary oars. Generally employed as a tender, scout or a commerce-raider.

PISTOLET Spanish gold coin, worth about 5s 10d in English money in 1560.

POOP The short aftermost deck, commanding the quarterdeck of a ship.

PORT SIDE Left-hand side of a ship, looking forward. The right is termed STARBOARD.

PRIVY COUNCIL The principal instrument of Elizabethan government. It consisted of some twenty important dignitaries, including the ministers of state, and was appointed by and was responsible to the sovereign. Elizabeth did not attend the Council's meetings, but received the results of their deliberations through various of its members. She normally accepted the Council's advice, but was not bound to do so.

QUARTERMASTER Ship's officer, assistant to master.

QUINTAL A Spanish hundredweight.

REAL Small silver Spanish coin, valued at about six English pennies in 1586.

RUTTER A book of sailing directions, often illustrated with views of prominent landmarks, ports and the coastline.

SHALLOP The term was used to describe either a heavy, large boat with fore-and-aft sails (running lengthwise) or lug sails, and sometimes carrying guns, or a shallow-draught boat using oars or a sail.

SQUARE-RIG The placing of yards and sails across the masts, as opposed to lengthwise in the fore-and-aft rig.

TARGET A shield.

TOPGALLANT Additional sail raised above the topsail on a mast.

VIOL A musical instrument played by plucking at five to seven strings with a bow.

WHERRY A light rowing boat, principally used to ferry goods and passengers on rivers.

WINDWARD A ship is said to be to windward if it is in the direction from which the wind blows. A ship to leeward is on the sheltered side.

# BIBLIOGRAPHY

*Unpublished Sources*
Public Record Office (London):
  Port Books of Plymouth
  State Papers (Domestic)
  State Papers (Ireland)
  E.133/47/3-5. Barons' Depositions, Drake v. Drake.
  Req. 2/87/12 and Req. 2/87/14. Proceedings of the Court of Requests.
  C.2/Eliz.I/B8/32 and C.2/Eliz.I/D1/41. Chancery Proceedings, Drake v. Bodenham.
  C.33/93-98. Entry Books of Decrees and Orders kept by the Registrars of the Court of Chancery,
  Drake v. Bodenham.

Department of Manuscripts, British Library (London):
  Lansdowne Mss
  Additional Mss
  Cotton Mss
  Harleian Mss
  Sloane Mss
  Stowe Mss

West Devon Record Office (Plymouth):
  Parish Register of St Budeaux, Plymouth, 1538-1656 (542/1)
  Deeds, leases and indentures relating to Drake (277/6-14)
  Plymouth Black Book

Devon County Record Office (Exeter):
  Drake Papers, 346M. Part of the family papers, principally notes and transcripts of Lady E. F.
  Eliott-Drake.

Cambridge University Library:
  Conway Papers

*Published Primary Sources*
Andrews, Kenneth R., *The Last Voyage of Drake and Hawkins* (Cambridge, 1972).
Avis, Fernandez, *La Dragontea* by Lope de Vega (Madrid, 1935, 2 vols).
Batho, G. R., *A Calendar of the Shrewsbury and Talbot Papers* (London, 1966-71, 2 vols).
Beazley, C. Raymond, *An English Garner* (Westminster, 1903, 2 vols).
Brewer, J. S. and William Bullen, *Calendar of the Carew Manuscripts, 1575-88* (London, 1868).
Bridgeman, C. G. O. and J. C. Walker, *Supplementary Report on the Mss. of the Late Montagu Bertie, Twelfth Earl of Lindsey* (London, 1942).
Brown, Horatio F., *Calendar of State Papers and Manuscripts Relating to English Affairs Existing in the Archives and Collections of Venice and in Other Libraries of Northern Italy, 1581-91* (London, 1894).
Bruce, John, *Correspondence of Robert Dudley, Earl of Leycester* (London, 1844).
Brushfield, T. N., 'The Spanish Invasion of 1588', *The Western Antiquary* 7 (1887-8): 274-9.
Burnard, Robert, 'Petition by Sir Francis Drake and the Mayor of Plymouth', *The Western Antiquary* 7 (1887-8): 313-14.
Butler, A. J., et. al., *Calendar of State Papers, Foreign Series, in the Reign of Elizabeth* (London, 1863-1989, 27 vols).
Camden, William, *The Historie of the Most Renowned and Victorious Princesse Elizabeth . . . By Way of Annals* (London, 1630).
Castellanos, Juan de, *Discurso de el Capitán Francisco Draque* (Madrid, 1921).
Collins, Arthur, *Letters and Memorials of State . . . Written and Collected by Sir Henry Sidney* (London, 1746, 2 vols).
Conway, G. R. G., *An Englishman and the Mexican Inquisition, 1556-60* (Mexico City, 1927).
Cooley, W. D., *Sir Francis Drake, His Voyage, 1595* (London, 1849).

Corbett, Julian S., *Papers Relating to the Navy During the Spanish War, 1585-87* (London, 1898).

Dasent, John Roche, et. al., *Acts of the Privy Council of England*, new series (London, 1890-1964, 46 vols).

Devereux, Walter Bourchier, *Lives and Letters of the Devereux, Earls of Essex* (London, 1853, 2 vols).

D'Ewes, S., *The Journals of All the Parliaments During the Reign of Queen Elizabeth* (London, 1682).

Digges, Dudley, *The Compleat Ambassador* (London, 1655).

Donno, Elizabeth Story, *An Elizabethan in 1582* (London, 1976).

Duro, Cesáreo Fernandez, *La Armada Invencible* (Madrid, 1884, 2 vols).

Dyer, Florence E., 'Drake's Voyage of Circumnavigation', *Mariner's Mirror* 9 (1923): 194-201.

*Ephemeris Expeditionis Norreysii & Draki in Lusitaniam* (London, 1589).

FitzGeffrey, Charles, *Sir Francis Drake, His Honorable Life's Commendation, and His Tragical Death's Lamentation* (Oxford, 1596).

Greepe, Thomas, *The True and Perfecte Newes of the Woorthy and Valiaunt Exploytes Performed . . . by that Valiant Knight, Syr Frauncis Drake* (London, 1587).

Greville, Fulke, *Life of Sir Philip Sidney* (London, 1652).

Hakluyt, Richard, *Principal Navigations . . . of the English Nation* (1589; reprinted, Glasgow, 1903-5, 12 vols).

Hamilton, H. C., *Calendar of State Papers Relating to Ireland, 1574-85* (London, 1867).

Hampden, John, *Francis Drake, Privateer* (London, 1972).

Haslop, Henry, *Newes Out of the Coast of Spaine* (London, 1587).

Hindley, Charles, *The Roxburghe Ballads* (London, 1873-4, 2 vols).

Historical Manuscripts Commission, *Third Report* (London, 1872).

— *Calendar of the Manuscripts of the Marquis of Salisbury Preserved at Hatfield House* (London, 1883-1976, 24 vols).

— *Twelfth Report, Appendix, Part I: The Manuscripts of the Earl Cowper* (London, 1888-9, 3 vols).

— *Thirteenth Report, Appendix, Part VI: The Manuscripts of Sir William Fitzherbert and Others* (London, 1893).

— *Fifteenth Report, Appendix, Part V: The Manuscripts of the Rt. Hon. F. J. Savile Foljambe of Osberton* (London, 1897).

— *Report on the Manuscripts of Lord de L'Isle and Dudley* (London, 1925-66, 6 vols).

Hopper, Clarence, *Sir Francis Drake's Memorable Service Done Against the Spaniards in 1587* (London, 1863).

Hume, Martin A. S., *Calendar of Letters and State Papers Relating to English Affairs Preserved Principally in the Archives of Simancas* (London, 1892-9, 4 vols).

Keeler, Mary Frear, *Sir Francis Drake's West Indian Voyage, 1585-86* (London, 1981).

Kempe, William, *The Art of Arithmeticke* (London, 1592).

Klarwill, Victor von, *The Fugger News-Letters, 1568-1605* (London, 1924-6, 2 vols).

Laughton, John Knox, *State Papers Relating to the Defeat of the Spanish Armada* (London, 1894, 2 vols).

L'Ecluse, Charles de, *Caroli Clusii Atreb* (Antwerp, 1582).

Lemon, Robert, et. al., *Calendar of State Papers, Domestic Series* (London, 1856-72, 8 vols).

Littleton, T. D. and R. R. Rea, *The Spanish Armada* (Cincinnati, 1964).

Markham, Clements, *Early Spanish Voyages to the Strait of Magellan* (London, 1911).

Maura Gamazo, Gabriel, Duque de Maura, *El Designio de Felipe II* (Madrid, 1957).

Morton, Ann, *Calendar of the Patent Rolls, 1580-82* (London, 1986).

Murdin, William, *A Collection of State Papers Relating to Affairs in the Reign of Queen Elizabeth, 1571 to 1596* (London, 1759).

Naish, G. P. B., 'The Spanish Armada', in Christopher Lloyd, *The Naval Miscellany* (London, 1952).

Nichols, John Gough, and John Bruce, *Wills from Doctors' Commons* (London, 1863).

Nuttall, Zelia, *New Light on Drake* (London, 1914).

Oppenheim, Michael, *The Naval Tracts of Sir William Monson* (London, 1902-14, 5 vols).

Oria, Enrique Herrera, *La Armada Invencible* (Valladolid, 1929).

Owen, G. D., et. al., *Calendar of the Manuscripts of the Most Honourable the Marquess of Bath* (London, 1904-80, 5 vols).

Peele, George, *A Farewell Entituled to the Famous and Fortunate Generals of Our English Forces: Sir*

*John Norris and Sir Frauncis Drake* (London, 1589).

Purchas, Samuel, *Hakluytus Posthumus, or, Purchas, His Pilgrimes* (Glasgow, 1905-7, 20 vols).

Quinn, David B., *The Roanoke Voyages, 1584-90* (London, 1950, 2 vols).

— and Neil Cheshire: *The New Found Land of Stephen Parmenius* (Toronto, 1972).

*Relation was der Capitan Drackh unnd Colonel Noriz Welche Anno 1589* (Munchen, 1590).

Roberts, Henry, *A Most Friendly Farewell Given by a Wellwiller to the Right Worshipful Sir Francis Drake* (London, 1585).

— *The Trumpet of Fame, or Sir F. Drake's and Sir J. Hawkins' Farewell* (London, 1595).

Rodger, N. A. M., 'A Drake Indenture', *Mariner's Mirror* 64 (1978): 70.

Rowe, Margery M., *Tudor Exeter* (Torquay, 1977).

*Sir Francis Drake Revived, Being a Summary and True Relation of Four Several Voyages Made by Sir Francis Drake to the West Indies* (London, 1653).

Stow, John, *A Survey of London* (1603; reprinted, Oxford, 1908, 2 vols).

Sugden, John, 'A Diary of the Expedition of Drake and Norris, 1589' (in preparation).

Taylor, E. G. R. 'More Light on Drake', *Mariner's Mirror* 16 (1930): 134-51.

— *The Troublesome Voyage of Captain Edward Fenton, 1582-83* (Cambridge, 1959).

Temple, Sir Richard Carnac, and N. M. Penzer, *The World Encompassed and Analogous Contemporary Documents Concerning Sir Francis Drake's Circumnavigation of the World* (London, 1926).

Tilton, W. F., 'Lord Burghley on the Spanish Invasion, 1588', *American Historical Review* 2 (1896-7): 93-8.

*True Discourse of a Cruel and Inhuman Murder Committed Upon M. Padge of Plymouth, the 11 Day of February Last, 1591, by the Consent of His Own Wife and Sundry Other* (1591; reprinted in *The Shakespeare Society's Papers*, 2 (1845): 79-85).

Underwood, Stephen, *The Great Enterprise* (London, 1978).

Vaux, W. S. W., *The World Encompassed, by Sir Francis Drake* (London, 1854).

Wernham, Richard B., *The Expedition of Sir John Norris and Sir Francis Drake to Spain and Portugal* (London, 1988).

Worth, R. N., *Calendar of the Plymouth Municipal Records* (Plymouth, 1893).

Wright, Irene A., *Spanish Documents Concerning English Voyages to the Caribbean, 1527-68* (London, 1929).

— *Documents Concerning English Voyages to the Caribbean and the Spanish Main, 1569-80* (London, 1932).

— *Further English Voyages to Spanish America, 1583-94* (London, 1951).

*Secondary Sources*

Aker, Raymond, *Report of Findings Relating to Identification of Sir Francis Drake's Encampment at Point Reyes National Seashore* (Point Reyes, 1970).

Alexander, J. J., 'Crowndale', *Transactions of the Devonshire Association* 46 (1914): 278-83.

Anderson, R. C., 'The "Golden Hind" at Deptford', *Mariner's Mirror* 27 (1941): 77-8.

Andrew, C. K. Croft, 'Sir Francis Drake and Captain James Erisey', *Devon and Cornwall Notes and Queries* (1940-1): 255-7.

Andrews, Kenneth R., *Elizabethan Privateering* (London, 1964).

— *Drake's Voyages* (London, 1967).

— 'The Aims of Drake's Expedition of 1577-1580', *American Historical Review* 73 (1968): 724-41.

— *The Spanish Caribbean* (New Haven and London, 1978).

—, N. P. Canny and P. E. H. Hair (ed.), *The Westward Enterprise* (Liverpool, 1978).

— 'The Elizabethan Seaman', *Mariner's Mirror* 68 (1982): 245-62.

— *Trade, Plunder and Settlement* (Cambridge, 1984).

Bagwell, Richard, *Ireland Under the Tudors* (London, 1885-90, 3 vols).

Barber, James, 'Sir Francis Drake's Investment in Plymouth Property', *Transactions of the Devonshire Association* 113 (1981): 103-8.

Barrow, John, *The Life, Voyages and Exploits of Admiral Sir Francis Drake, Knight* (London, 1843).

Bell, Douglas, *Drake* (London, 1935).

Benson, E. F., 'Drake's Duty: New Light on Armada Incident. A Slur Removed', *The Times*, 17 September, 1926.

— *Sir Francis Drake* (London, 1927).

Bishop, R. P., 'Drake's Course in the North Pacific', *British Columbia Historical Quarterly* 3 (1939): 151-82.

Black, J. B., *The Reign of Elizabeth* (Oxford, 1936).

Boulind, Richard, 'Drake's Navigational Skills', *Mariner's Mirror* 54 (1968): 349-71.

— 'John Saracold or John Scaracold', *Mariner's Mirror* 71 (1985): 338-41.

Bovill, E. W., 'The "Madre de Dios"', *Mariner's Mirror* 54 (1968): 129-52.

Bracken, C. W., *A History of Plymouth* (Plymouth, 1931).

Bradford, Ernle, *Drake* (London, 1965).

Brereton, Robert Maitland, *Question: Did Sir Francis Drake Land on Any Part of the Oregon Coast?* (Portland, Oregon, 1907).

California Historical Society, *Plate of Brass* (San Francisco, 1953).

Callender, Geoffrey, 'Drake and his Detractors', *Mariner's Mirror* 7 (1921): 66-74, 98-105, 142-52.

— 'Fresh Light on Drake', *Mariner's Mirror* 9 (1923): 16-28.

— 'The Greenwich Portrait of Sir Francis Drake', *Mariner's Mirror* 18 (1932): 359-62.

Canny, Nicholas P., *The Elizabethan Conquest of Ireland* (Hassocks, Sussex, 1976).

Chaunu, Pierre, *Séville et L'Atlantique, 1504-1650* (Paris, 1955-9, 10 vols).

Cheyney, Edward P., *A History of England* (London, 1914-26, 2 vols).

Christy, Miller, *The Silver Map of the World* (London, 1900).

Clark, Peter, *English Provincial Society from the Reformation to the Revolution* (Hassocks, Sussex, 1977).

Clark, Wallace, *Rathlin – Disputed Island* (Portlaw, 1971).

Clarke, Samuel, *The Life and Death of the Valiant and Renowned Sir Francis Drake* (London, 1671).

Clifford, E. T., 'Drake's Treasure', *Transactions of the Devonshire Association* 44 (1912): 512-29.

Corbett, Julian Stafford, *Sir Francis Drake* (London, 1890).

— *Drake and the Tudor Navy* (London, 1898, 2 vols).

Cornwall, Julian, *Revolt of the Peasantry, 1549* (London, 1977).

Crouch, Nathaniel, *The English Hero, or Sir Francis Drake Revived* (London, 1692).

Cumming, Alex A., *Sir Francis Drake and The Golden Hind* (Norwich, 1975).

Damm, Hans, *Francis Drake als Freibeuter in Spanisch-Amerika* (Leipzig, 1924).

Davidson, George, *Identification of Sir Francis Drake's Anchorage on the Coast of California* (San Francisco, 1890).

— *Francis Drake on the Northwest Coast of America in 1579* (San Francisco, 1908).

Davidson, James B., 'On Some Points in Natural History First Made Known by Sir Francis Drake', *The Western Antiquary* 4 (1885): 134-7.

Dickens, A. G., *The English Reformation* (Glasgow, 1967).

Ditmas, E. M. R., *The Legend of Drake's Drum* (St Peter Port, 1973).

Dodd, A. H., *Life in Elizabethan England* (London, 1961).

Drake, Henry H., 'Drake – The Arms of His Surname and Family', *Transactions of the Devonshire Association* 15 (1883): 487-93.

— 'Facts Not Generally Known About Francis Drake and Francis Russell', *The Western Antiquary* 4 (1885): 25-9.

Dyer, Florence E., 'Spain and the Fortification of Magellan's Strait', *Mariner's Mirror* 35 (1949): 68-9.

Eliott-Drake, E. F., *The Family and Heirs of Sir Francis Drake* (London, 1911, 2 vols).

Elliott, John, 'The Decline of Spain', *Past and Present* 20 (1961): 52-75.

— *Europe Divided, 1559-98* (Glasgow, 1968).

— *Imperial Spain, 1469-1716* (Harmondsworth, Middlesex, 1970).

Elton, G. R., *England Under the Tudors* (London, 1955).

— *Reform and Reformation: England, 1509-58* (London, 1977).

Fernández-Armesto, Felipe, *The Spanish Armada* (Oxford, 1988).

Fox-Bourne, H. R., *English Seamen Under the Tudors* (London, 1868, 2 vols).

Froude, J. A., *History of England* (London, 1856-75, 13 vols).

Gibbs, Lewis, *The Silver Circle* (London, 1964).

Gill, Crispin, *Buckland Abbey* (Plymouth, 1956).

— *Plymouth, A New History* (Newton Abbot, 1966).

Glasgow, Tom, Jr, 'The Shape of the Ships That Defeated the Spanish Armada', *Mariner's Mirror* 50 (1964): 177-87.

— 'The "Revenge" Reviewed', *Mariner's Mirror* 53 (1967): 54.
— 'The Navy in Philip and Mary's War, 1557-58', *Mariner's Mirror* 53 (1967): 321-42.
— 'The Navy in the First Elizabethan Undeclared War, 1559-60', *Mariner's Mirror* 54 (1968): 23-37.
— 'The Navy in the Le Havre Expedition, 1562-64', *Mariner's Mirror* 54 (1968): 281-96.
— 'Maturing of Naval Administration, 1556-64', *Mariner's Mirror* 56 (1970): 3-26.
— 'List of Ships in the Royal Navy from 1539 to 1588', *Mariner's Mirror* 56 (1970): 299-307.
Graham, Winston, *The Spanish Armada* (London, 1972).
Green, V. H. H., *Renaissance and Reformation* (London, 1964).
Hadfield, A. M., *Time to Finish the Game* (London, 1964).
Hair, P. E. H., 'Protestants as Pirates, Slavers and Proto-Missionaries: Sierra Leone 1568 and 1582', *Journal of Ecclesiastical History* 21 (1970): 203-24.
Hale, J. R., *The Story of the Great Armada* (London, 1913).
Hamilton, A. H. A., 'The Justices of the Peace for the County of Devon in the Year 1592', *Transactions of the Devonshire Association* 8 (1876): 517-25.
Hanna, Warren L., *Lost Harbor: The Controversy over Drake's Californian Anchorage* (Berkeley, 1979).
Hardy, Evelyn, *Survivors of the Armada* (London, 1966).
Harry, Reginald George, *Tavistock's Sir Francis Drake Statue and Medal* (Bidworth, 1984).
Hart-Davis, Duff, *The Armada* (London, 1988).
Hasler, P. W. (ed.), *The Commons, 1558-1603* (London, 1981, 3 vols).
Heizer, Robert F., *Elizabethan California* (Ramona, California, 1974).
Hervey, Thomas, *Some Unpublished Papers Relating to the Family of Sir Francis Drake* (Colmer, 1887).
Hind, A. M., *Engraving in England in the Sixteenth and Seventeenth Centuries* (Cambridge, 1952-55, 2 vols).
Hoffman, Paul E., *The Spanish Crown and the Defense of the Caribbean, 1535-85* (Baton Rouge, 1980).
Hoskins, W. G. *Devon* (London, 1954).
Howarth, David, *The Voyage of the Armada* (London, 1981).
Hume, Martin A. S., *The Year After the Armada* (London, 1986).
Hunt, Robert, *Popular Romances of the West of England* (London, 1896).
Jameson, A. K., 'Some New Spanish Documents Dealing with Drake', *English Historical Review* 49 (1934): 14-31.
— 'Lope de Vega's "La Dragontea": Historical and Literary Sources', *Hispanic Review* 6 (1938): 104-19.
Jewers, Arthur J., 'The Arms of Sir Francis Drake', *The Western Antiquary* 1 (1881-2): 2-3, 9-10.
Johnson, A. H., *The History of the Worshipful Company of the Drapers of London* (Oxford, 1914-22, 5 vols).
Johnson, Samuel, *The Life of Mr Richard Savage . . . to which are Added the Lives of Sir Francis Drake and Admiral Blake* (London, 1777).
Johnstone, Christian Isobel, *Lives of Drake, Cavendish and Dampier* (Edinburgh, 1837).
Kemp, Peter, *The Oxford Companion to Ships & the Sea* (London, 1976).
— *The Campaign of the Spanish Armada* (London, 1988).
Kenny, Robert W., *Elizabeth's Admiral* (Baltimore, 1970).
Klinkenborg, Verlyn, *Sir Francis Drake and the Age of Discovery* (New York, 1988).
Knight, Frank, *That Rare Captain: Sir Francis Drake* (London, 1970).
Kraus, Hans P., *Sir Francis Drake, A Pictorial Biography* (Amsterdam, 1970).
Kretzschmar, Joannes, *Die Invasion Projekte der Katholischen Machte Gegen England* (Leipzig, 1892).
Lathbury, Thomas, *The Spanish Armada, A.D. 1588* (London, 1840).
Lee, Sidney, and Leslie Stephen (ed.), *Dictionary of National Biography* (London, 1885-1901; reprinted 1967-8, 22 vols).
Lemonnier, Léon, *Sir Francis Drake* (Paris, 1932).
Lessa, William A., *Drake's Island of Thieves* (Honolulu, 1975).
Lewis, Michael, 'The Guns of the "Jesus of Lubeck"', *Mariner's Mirror* 22 (1936): 324-45.
— 'Fresh Light on San Juan de Ulua', *Mariner's Mirror* 23 (1937): 295-315.
— *The Spanish Armada* (London, 1960).

— *Armada Guns* (London, 1961).

Lloyd, Christopher, 'Drake's Game of Bowls', *Mariner's Mirror* 39 (1953): 144-5.

— *Sir Francis Drake* (London, 1957).

Loades, D. M., *Two Tudor Conspiracies* (Cambridge, 1965).

Lynch, John, *Spain Under the Habsburgs, 1516-98* (London, 1964).

McBride, G. K., 'Elizabethan Foreign Policy in Microcosm', *Albion* 5 (1973): 193-210.

McKee, Alexander, *From Merciless Invaders* (London, 1963).

— *The Queen's Corsair: Drake's Journey of Circumnavigation, 1577-80* (London, 1978).

Maddocks, Margaret, *The Church of Our Lady St. Mary, Stogumber, Somerset* (Stogumber, n.d.).

Malakhovskii, Kim Vladimirovich, *Krugosvetnyï beg 'Zolotoïlani'* (Moskva, 1980).

Maltby, William S., *Alba* (Berkeley, 1983).

Martin, Colin, *Full Fathom Five: Wrecks of the Spanish Armada* (London, 1975).

— , and Geoffrey Parker, *The Spanish Armada* (London, 1988).

Martin, Paula, *Spanish Armada Prisoners. The Story of the Nuestra Senora del Rosario* . . . (Exeter, 1988).

Marx, Robert F., *Battle of the Spanish Armada* (New York and London, 1966).

Mason, A. E. W., *The Life of Francis Drake* (London, 1941).

Mattingly, Garrett, *The Defeat of the Spanish Armada* (London, 1959).

— *The Invincible Armada and Elizabethan England* (Ithaca, New York, 1963).

Merriman, Roger Bigelow, *The Rise of the Spanish Empire* (New York, 1918-34, 3 vols).

Motley, John L., *History of the United Netherlands* (London, 1875-6, 4 vols).

Neale, J. E., *Elizabeth I* (London, 1934).

— *The Elizabethan House of Commons* (London, 1949).

— *Elizabeth I and Her Parliaments* (London, 1953-7, 2 vols).

Oko, Francis A., *Francis Drake and Nova Albion* (Point Reyes, 1964).

Padfield, Peter, *Armada* (London, 1988).

Parfitt, E., 'Sir Francis Drake v. Sir Walter Raleigh and the Introduction of the Potato Plant', *The Western Antiquary* 2 (1882): 61-2.

Parker, John, *Books to Build an Empire* (Amsterdam, 1965).

Parry, J. H., *The Age of Reconnaissance* (New York, 1963).

Pierson, Peter O'Malley, 'A Commander for the Armada', *Mariner's Mirror* 55 (1969): 383-400.

Pollitt, Ronald, 'John Hawkins's Troublesome Voyages: Merchants, Bureaucrats, and the Origins of the Slave Trade', *The Journal of British Studies* 12 (1973): 26-40.

— 'Bureaucracy and the Armada: The Administrator's Battle', *Mariner's Mirror* 60 (1974): 119-32.

Power, R. H., 'Drake's Landing in California: A Case for San Francisco Bay', *California Historical Quarterly* 52 (1973): 100-28.

Preston, Richard Arthur, *Gorges of Plymouth Fort* (Toronto, 1953).

Prideaux-Naish, F. C., 'The Mystery of the Tonnage and Dimensions of the "Pelican-Golden Hind"', *Mariner's Mirror* 34 (1948): 42-5.

Quinn, David Beers, *England and the Discovery of America, 1481-1620* (London, 1974).

— (ed.), *The Hakluyt Handbook* (London, 1974, 2 vols).

— , and A. N. Ryan, *England's Sea Empire, 1550-1642* (London, 1983).

Ray, John Arthur, *Drake dans la Poésie Espagnole, 1570-1732* (Paris, 1906).

Rea, Lorna, *The Spanish Armada* (London, 1933).

Read, Conyers, *Mr. Secretary Walsingham and the Policy of Queen Elizabeth* (London, 1925, 3 vols).

— *Mr. Secretary Cecil and Queen Elizabeth* (London, 1955).

— *Lord Burghley and Queen Elizabeth* (London, 1960).

Real, Cristobal, *El Corsario y el Impero Espanol Drake* (Madrid, 1941).

Risk, J. Erskine, 'Some Recent Revisions of the Drake Chronology', *Transactions of the Devonshire Association* 15 (1883): 196-201.

— 'Some Recent Revisions of Plymouth History', *Transactions of the Devonshire Association* 16 (1884): 553-8.

— 'The Rise of Plymouth as a Naval Port', *Transactions of the Devonshire Association* 30 (1898): 350-61.

Robertson, John W., *The Harbor of St. Francis* (San Francisco, 1926).

— *Francis Drake and Other Early Explorers Along the Pacific Coast* (San Francisco, 1927).

Robinson, Gregory, 'A Forgotten Life of Sir Francis Drake', *Mariner's Mirror* 7 (1921): 10-18.

— 'The Trial and Death of Thomas Doughty', *Mariner's Mirror* 7 (1921): 271-82.

— 'The Evidence About the "Golden Hind"', *Mariner's Mirror* 35 (1949): 56-65.

Robjohns, Sydney, *Buckland Abbey and Sir Francis Drake* (Plymouth, 1877).

Roche, T. W. E., *The Golden Hind* (London, 1973).

Rodriguez-Salgado, M. J., et. al., *Armada, 1588-1988* (London, 1988).

Rose-Troup, Frances, *The Western Rebellion of 1549* (London, 1913).

Routh, C. R. N., *Who's Who in History. England, 1485 to 1603* (Oxford, 1964).

Rowse, A. L., 'The Dispute Concerning the Plymouth Pilchard Fishery, 1584-91', *Economic History (A Supplement to the Economic Journal)* 2 (1930-3): 461-72.

— *Sir Richard Grenville of the 'Revenge'* (London, 1937).

— *Exhibition of Historical Relics of Sir Francis Drake* (London, 1952).

— *The Expansion of Elizabethan England* (London, 1955).

St Clair Byrne, M., *Elizabethan Life in Town and Country* (London, 1925).

Scammell, G. V., 'Manning the English Merchant Service in the Sixteenth Century', *Mariner's Mirror* 56 (1970): 131-54.

— 'The English in the Atlantic Islands, c.1450-1650', *Mariner's Mirror* 72 (1986): 295-317.

Scott, William Robert, *The Constitution and Finance of English, Scottish and Irish Joint Stock Companies to 1720* (1912; reprinted, New York, 1951).

Senior, W., 'Drake at the Suit of John Doughty', *Mariner's Mirror* 7 (1921): 291-7.

Skelton, R. A., *Explorers' Maps* (London, 1958).

Skilliter, S. A., *William Harborne and the Trade with Turkey, 1578-82* (London, 1977).

Smith, D. B., 'Drake's Prayer', *Mariner's Mirror* 36 (1950): 86-7.

Strong, Roy, *Tudor and Jacobean Portraits* (London, 1969, 2 vols).

Swinburn, R. Neville, *All Saints Monksilver* (Taunton, 1975).

Sugden, John, 'Edmund Drake of Tavistock, Father of Sir Francis Drake', *Mariner's Mirror* 59 (1973): 436.

— 'Sir Francis Drake, a Note on Portraiture', *Mariner's Mirror* 70 (1984): 303-9.

Taylor, E. G. R., 'Master John Dee, Drake and the Straits of Anian', *Mariner's Mirror* 15 (1929): 125-30.

— 'The Missing Draft Project of Drake's Voyage of 1577-80', *Geographical Journal* 75 (1930): 46-7.

— *Tudor Geography, 1485-1583* (London, 1930).

Tenison, E. M., *Elizabethan England* (Leamington Spa, 1933-61, 13 vols).

Theed, W. A. C., *Combe Sydenham Hall* (Monksilver, Somerset, 197?).

Thomas, David A., *The Illustrated Armada Handbook* (London, 1988).

Thompson, I. A. A., 'Spanish Armada Guns', *Mariner's Mirror* 61 (1975): 355-71.

Thomson, George M., *Sir Francis Drake* (London, 1972).

Thrower, Norman J. W. (ed.), *Sir Francis Drake and the Famous Voyage, 1577-1580* (Berkeley and Los Angeles, 1984).

Tilton, F. W., *Die Katastrophie der Spanïschen Armada* (Freiburg, 1894).

Uden, Grant, *Drake at Cadiz* (London, 1969).

Unwin, Rayner, *The Defeat of John Hawkins* (London, 1960).

Upcott, J. D., *Drake and the Beginnings of English Sea Power* (London, 1927).

Vincent, John A. C., 'Sir Francis Drake', *Notes and Queries* 3rd ser., 4 (1863): 189, 502-3.

Wagner, Anthony, *Drake in England* (Hanover, New Hampshire, 1970).

Wagner, Henry R., *Sir Francis Drake's Voyage Around the World* (San Francisco, 1926).

Wallis, Helen, 'English Enterprise in the Region of the Strait of Magellan', in John Parker (ed.), *Merchants and Scholars* (Minneapolis, 1965), 193-220.

— Sarah Tyacke and Pat Higgins, *Sir Francis Drake* (London, 1977).

Waters, David W., 'The Elizabethan Navy and the Armada Campaign', *Mariner's Mirror* 35 (1949): 90-138.

— *The Art of Navigation in England in the Elizabethan and Early Stuart Times* (New Haven, 1958).

Wernham, Richard B., 'Queen Elizabeth and the Portugal Expedition of 1589', *English Historical Review* 66 (1951): 1-26, 194-218.

— *Before the Armada* (London, 1966).

Whiting, Roger, *The Enterprise of England* (London, 1988).

Williams, Jay, *The Spanish Armada* (London, 1968).

Williams, Neville, *Sir Francis Drake* (London, 1973).

Williams, Paul, 'The Ownership of Drake's *Golden Hind*', *Mariner's Mirror* 67 (1981): 185-6.

Williamson, James A., *Sir John Hawkins* (Oxford, 1927).

— *The Age of Drake* (1938; reprinted, London, 1960).

— *Hawkins of Plymouth* (London, 1949).

— *Sir Francis Drake* (London, 1951).

Wilson, Derek Alan, *The World Encompassed* (London, 1977).

Wood, William, *Elizabethan Sea Dogs: A Chronicle of Drake and His Companions* (New Haven, 1918).

Woodrooffe, Thomas, *The Enterprise of England* (London, 1958).

Worth, R. N., 'Sir Francis Drake: His Origins, Arms and Dealings with the Plymouth Corporation', *Transactions of the Devonshire Association* 16 (1884): 505-52.

— *The History of Plymouth* (Plymouth, 1890).

Wright, W. H. K., 'The Armada Tercentenary Exhibition', *The Western Antiquary* 8 (1888-9): 1-9, 33-41, 67-9.

'Wyvern Gules', 'Hele and Harris', *The Western Antiquary* 1 (1881-2): 183.

Youings, Joyce, 'Drake, Grenville and Buckland Abbey', *Transactions of the Devonshire Association* 112 (1980): 95-9.

— *Sixteenth Century England* (Harmondsworth, 1984).

Ziebarth, Marilyn (ed.), 'The Francis Drake Controversy: His California Anchorage, June 17-July 23, 1579', *California Historical Quarterly* 53 (1974): 197-292.

# INDEX

Rutland, Earl of, 178, 287
Rye, 245n

Sabatini, Rafael, 318
Sadler, Robert, 205
Sagres, 212–13, 324
Sagres Castle, 212
St. Andrew's church (Plymouth), 77, 164, 317
St. Augustine (Florida), 52, 198
St. Bartholomew's Day massacre, 71
St. Bartholomew's Island, 115
St. Budeaux church (Plymouth), 43–44, 164
St. George's Island, 115
St. Julian's (Portugal), 276–77, 279
St. Kitts, 186
St. Mary Bothaw church, 290
St. Mary's Port (Cadiz), 209–10
St. Nicholas Islands, 5, 292–93
St. Philip Castle, 315
Salada Bay, 124
Salcombe, 287
Salconstall, Richard, 301
Salisbury, Margaret, Countess of, 291
Sallamca, 310
Saltash, 23, 37, 43, 148, 286, 298
Salvatierra (ship owner), 51
Sampford Courtenay, 5
Sampford Spiney, 162, 175, 288, 306, 313, 316–17
Samu Sea, 143
San Bernardo Islands, 60
San Blas, Gulf of, 63n, 77
San Francisco, 133
San Francisco Bay, 134–35
San Francisco Bridge (Cartagena), 193–94
San Juan (Florida), 198
San Juan (Puerto Rico), 12, 308–10
San Juan d'Ulua, 32–34, 36–39, 41–42, 53, 55, 86, 121, 123, 182, 205, 233, 240
San Juan River, 71
San Lorenzo, 125
San Lorenzo de Escorial, 176
San Lucar, 182, 209–10, 229, 242n, 307
San Quentin Cove, 134
San Sebastian, 262, 265, 267, 281

Sanders, John, 43
Sandwich, 281
Santa Barbara Channel, 136
Santa Barbara Church (Santo Domingo), 188
Santa Cruz, Alvaro de Bazan, 1st Marquis of, 176, 181, 191, 201, 209–10, 213–14, 216, 218–19, 231, 265
Santa Cruz de Tenerife, 24–25
Santa Elena Castle, 308
Santá Fe de Bogotá, 13, 170, 191
Santa Marta, 31, 51, 59, 64, 177, 310
Santander, 262, 265, 267, 269, 271, 275, 280–81
Santiago (Cape Verdes), 20, 103, 182–86, 192
Santiago (Chile), 119, 123
Santo Domingo (Cape Verdes), 183
Santo Domingo (West Indies), 12–13, 18, 21, 28, 49, 51, 177, 181, 186–93, 195–96, 200, 211
São Miguel, 215
Sapi peoples, 27
Saracold, John, 100, 105
Savoy, Duke of, 200
Scarcies River, 27
Scheldt River, 255, 258
Schouten, Willem, 155
Scilly Islands, 222, 230–31, 234
Scotland, 17, 39–40, 82, 84–85, 96, 222, 262
Sea Beggars, 71
Segar (portrait painter), 290, 290n
Selsey Bill, 251
Selwood, Humphrey, 162
Selworthy, 174
Sergeant, Noah, 37
Setúbal, 164
Seven Sisters (Dover), 135
Seville, 12–13, 18, 32, 37, 57, 146, 148–49, 152, 177, 181, 191, 200, 209, 265, 315
Seymour, Edward, 297
Seymour, Sir Henry, 223, 227, 239–40, 242n, 251, 253–54, 256, 258, 261
Shakespeare, William, 321
Sheffield, Edmund, Lord, 228, 251

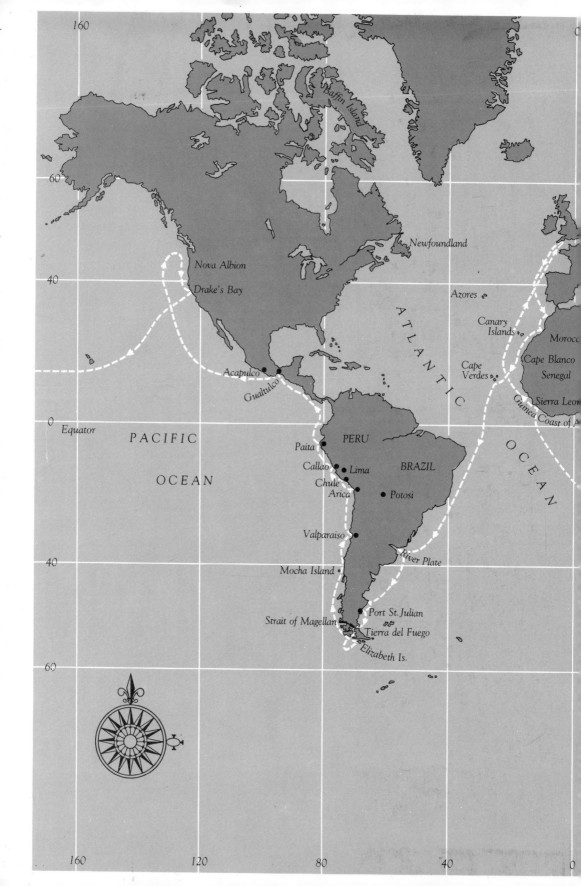

160

60

40

0   Equator

40

60

*Baffin Island*

*Newfoundland*

*Nova Albion*

*Drake's Bay*

*Azores*

*Canary Islands*

*Cape Verdes*

Moroc

*Cape Blanco*

Senegal

*Sierra Leo*

*Guinea Coast of A*

ATLANTIC

OCEAN

PACIFIC

OCEAN

*Acapulco*

*Gualtulco*

PERU

*Paita*

*Callao*     *Lima*

*Chule*

*Arica*

*Potosi*

BRAZIL

*Valparaiso*

*River Plate*

*Mocha Island*

*Strait of Magellan*

*Port St.Julian*

*Tierra del Fuego*

*Elizabeth Is.*

160

120

80

40

0